Mar

# Managing Risk

Alan E. Waring
Head of Risk Management Consulting
Aqumen Services Ltd, UK

and

A. Ian Glendon
Associate Professor
School of Applied Psychology
Griffith University, Queensland, Australia

INTERNATIONAL THOMSON BUSINESS PRESS
I(T)P® An International Thomson Publishing Company

London • Bonn • Boston • Johannesburg • Madrid • Melbourne • Mexico City • New York • Paris
Singapore • Tokyo • Toronto • Albany, NY • Belmont, CA • Cincinnati, OH • Detroit, MI

**Managing Risk**



First published by International Thomson Business Press

A division of International Thomson Publishing Inc.
The ITP logo is a trademark under licence



*British Library Cataloguing-in-Publication Data*
A Catalogue record for this book is available from the British Library

**First edition 1998**

Typeset by J&L Composition Ltd, Filey, North Yorkshire
Printed in Hong Kong

**ISBN 1-86152-167-7**

International Thomson Business Press
Berkshire House
168–173 High Holborn
London WC1V 7AA
UK

International Thomson Business Press
20 Park Plaza
13th Floor
Boston MA 02116
USA

http://www.itbp.com

The views expressed are the authors' own and do not necessarily represent those of their respective employers.

# Contents

# List of figures

# List of tables

# Foreword

Einstein's conclusion that $E=MC^2$ is perhaps one of the best-known mathematical equations. However, as anyone who has tried to explore its power will inform you, this elegant solution, known so well, conceals a web of mathematical and philosophical complexity. In a similar manner, the simple title of this book camouflages the complex nature of the subject matter that it contains. For, it is undoubtedly true that organizations and the environments in which they exist are highly complex, dynamic and non-linear in nature.

It is perhaps not surprising to find as we head towards the millennium that, with the growth of global organizations and rapid changes in technology, increasingly those who study organizations recognize that traditional management approaches are of limited value and that an integrated or holistic approach needs to be taken. This book, drawing on a variety of empirical and theoretical sources, bravely challenges many of the orthodox views surrounding risk, management and change.

Using what initially and superficially may appear to be unrelated case studies, the authors demonstrate, through the use of a thematic matrix, how theoretical aspects of risk can have wide empirical relevance. However, unlike many authors who write on the subject of organizations, they do not suggest that their findings should be utilized as a panacea or as a prescription for executive action. Rather, the reader should employ them as a framework to aid thinking when considering organizational issues relating to risk, management and change. The analysis contained within this volume is most thought provoking and, for those who believe as I do, that there is no substitute for original thinking, I commend it to you.

*Professor Brian Toft*
*Assistant Director*
*Sedgwick UK Risk Services Ltd*
*July 1997*

# Acknowledgements

The authors would like to thank the following for their assistance in preparing this book:

Professor Brian Toft, Assistant Director in Risk Consulting at Sedgwick Risk Services Ltd and a leading consultant, author and academic researcher in risk issues. Brian advised the authors from the book's conception through to completion.

Michael Collins who works at Lloyds of London for providing helpful information on fire safety and Alan Marsden of Alan Marsden & Associates for providing helpful information on financial risk.

Hassan Mehdizadeh, a corporate financial adviser and a special investment adviser trading on the Tehran Stock Exchange. He was formerly a corporate finance adviser to major pension funds in the UK.

Ja'far Mara'shi, Managing Director of the Industrial Management Institute in Tehran and special policy adviser to the Iranian Minister for Industry. He has had a major influence on the Iranian Five-Year Plans.

Dr Zachary Scheaffer for providing useful comments on chapter 11 based on his own detailed study of the Barings Bank collapse.

Professor Richard Taffler and Guenter Steinitz of Syspas Limited for providing copies of the Syspas reports on the Health of Corporate UK.

John Bowden, London Management Centre, University of Westminster, for years of stimulating debate on culture, power and change issues.

Staff of 'Australia Rail' for granting extensive access to their organization and for permission to use the case study material in chapter 12.

Julian Thomas and his colleagues at International Thomson Business Press for their professional input throughout the publishing process.

Mehri Waring, Sue, Oliver and Roland Glendon for their understanding and support over the two years it took to write and complete the book.

# Introduction

## Aims and style of this book

Typically, risk is treated (in both research and practice) as a vaguely connected set of quite disparate topics. For example, in the health and safety field, risk is usually considered in terms of hazards to personal safety and associated non-speculative (pure or absolute) risks. Focus on physical hazards and risks has led to a subject area dominated by engineering ideas about and approaches to risk. In the insurance world, however, while the concept of risk is concerned with dangerous settings and activities, it is also very much concerned with speculative risks of underwriting and brokerage. In the finance sector, risk typically refers to speculative risks associated with investment, whereas in government and public services risk often means political risks associated with decisions and actions. Risk specialists in these various sectors tend to regard their particular work as being separate from other kinds of risk work and, despite the common conceptual ground emphasized in this book, there is little methodological or theoretical dialogue between them. A particular aim of this book is to encourage an integrative perspective among those engaged in analysis, assessment and management of 'risk' in a wide sense of the term.

Few traditional approaches to risk deal with the contextual realities of organizations perceived to be affected by risks. Yet, the inner context of culture, power relations, human resources, finances, major changes, etc. is likely to be pivotal to decisions and actions which create, exacerbate, avoid or reduce risks. Furthermore, the outer context of influences from regulation, the economy, social expectations, competition, technological changes, political climate, etc. has profound effects on what organizations do – or fail to do. Risk (analysis, assessment, management) cannot be dealt with effectively in a narrowly defined, compartmentalized fashion – as if it were context-free.

There is, in short, a need to introduce a broader perspective to the subject of risk and to recognize that approaches towards risk and towards management and change are beginning to converge. Management processes implicitly involve perceptions and assessments of risk, both speculative and non-speculative. Management decisions and actions affect the degree of risk. Both pressures for change and change processes themselves (including legislation) demand risk analyses and assessments. This book seeks to address what is at present an early and somewhat fuzzy convergence of approaches to management, risk and change, whether in research, teaching or practice. A thematic matrix or reference utility (see Table A) is developed in chapter 9 and used to link a number of superficially unrelated case studies which demonstrate the wide-ranging application of theoretical ideas about a convergence of 'management, risk and change'.

*Table A* Thematic matrix linking theoretical aspects of risk with empirical case studies

| *Risk contexts* | | *Cases* | | | | | |
|---|---|---|---|---|---|---|---|
| | | *Offshore* | *Barings* | *Railways* | *Iran* | *IT* | *Health authorities* |
| | *Chapter* | *10* | *11* | *12* | *13* | *14* | *15* |
| Organizational environment | 6 | | | | | | |
| Economies and markets | 6 | H | H | H | H | H | H |
| Public policy, legislation and regulation | 6 | H | H | H | H | M | H |
| Social and political climate | 6 | M | M | H | H | M | H |
| Technology | 6 | H | M | M | L | H | H |
| History, operating territories and conditions | 6 | H | H | H | H | M | H |
| Human factors | | | | | | | |
| Culture | 4 | H | H | H | H | H | H |
| Power relations, political processes and decision-making | 5 | H | H | H | H | H | H |
| Perception, cognition and meanings of success | 8 | H | H | H | H | H | H |
| Formal coping arrangements | | | | | | | |
| Risk management | 1 | H | H | H | H | H | H |
| Risk assessment | 2 | H | H | H | H | H | H |
| Management systems | 3 | H | H | H | M | H | H |
| Approaches to change | 7 | H | H | H | H | H | H |

Code: H = High significance
M = Medium significance
L = Low significance

On the basis of empirical studies, the authors have identified a number of contextual factors which appear to exert a significant common influence on management, risk and change. Table A shows these factors, which are introduced and discussed in Part 1 of the book, and indicates their particular significance for the case studies in Part 2. This thematic matrix is a set of linked ideas which appear to be significant to understanding relationships between management, risk and change. Practical implications are almost bound to follow from these empirical observations, as discussed particularly in chapters 9, 17 and 18, although the matrix itself does not represent a formula for action. In other words, this book is essentially an aid to thinking about risk and related issues rather than a prescriptive guide on 'how to make your organization resilient to risk and change'. Practical risk management techniques are covered by a number of other books such as *Managing Risks and Decisions in Major Projects* (1994) and *Risk Handbook* (1996) both by Chicken; *Kluwer Handbook of Risk Management, Business Risk Management* by Ritchie and Marshall (1993), *Managing Industrial Risk* by Woodhouse (1993) and a number of American texts.

The background and practical experience of the authors in risk is broad, as indicated by the case studies, but is by no means comprehensive. For example, they do not claim expertise in financial risk management or medical risks. Indeed, the scope of risk management is so great that no individual is likely to be expert in more than a few areas and perhaps only in one. This fact does not detract from the book's message and strengthens the argument for an integrative framework of theory and practice in risk which caters for the broad spectrum of sectional interests, but whose overall content and structure are not determined by any one or a few of them. The authors believe that this book challenges many hallowed assumptions about risk, management and change and offers an integrative framework for critical discussion and further development.

The authors recognize that the scope of risk management is wide and that particular professions and disciplines frequently use risk terms in different ways. For example, the term 'risk' itself has a variety of meanings. There is also a problem of terms which may appear to represent discrete and independent categories of the subject but whose meanings overlap in various ways. For example, risk control has a variety of meanings which overlap with meanings of other options for risk strategy. Some risk topics may be regarded as either pure risks or speculative risks or both, depending on assumptions. Rather than seeking to choose a 'correct' set of risk definitions from one sector of risk experts and applying these throughout the book – a bold option, given the large number of professions and disciplines claiming risk expertise – the authors instead take an eclectic approach and use their own terminology and definitions where necessary. A glossary is provided at the end of the book.

## Who should read this book?

This book challenges traditional boundaries among professions which claim to have a predominant interest in risk and seeks to show that an integrative perspective has greater utility than do artificial barriers between professions. The book is primarily a text to be used by lecturers and students on a variety of undergraduate, post-graduate and short courses, either as a main text or as a support text, as listed below.

### *MSc courses in risk*

For example, in the UK:

- Risk Management and Safety Technology (e.g. Aston University).
- Risk and Reliability (e.g. Cranfield, Edinburgh Universities).
- Risk, Crisis and Disaster Management (e.g. Leicester University).
- Safety Management (e.g. Bournemouth University).
- Occupational Safety & Health (e.g. Greenwich University).
- Insurance and Risk Management (e.g. London, City Universities).

Similar courses at universities in other countries include Delft University of Technology (Holland), University of Arizona (USA), University of New South Wales (Australia).

### *Undergraduate and post-graduate courses in management*

Courses which necessarily include coverage of risk, either as specific modules on risk or within other modules, for example:

- MBA (Master of Business Administration) especially universities in Australia, New Zealand and Pacific Rim countries whose syllabuses include specific modules on risk. The MBA courses at Bradford University and Bolton Business School in the UK also include elective modules on risk management.
- MA in Human Resource Management (various).
- MA in Public Policy (various).
- MA in Organizational Studies (various).
- Open Business School courses (UK).

- BA in Management Studies (various).
- BA in Insurance Studies (e.g. City University).
- BA in Industrial Economics (e.g. Nottingham).
- Open University (UK) courses such as T301 Complexity, Management and Change.
- BSc in Risk Management (e.g. Glasgow Caledonian).
- BSc in Occupational Safety & Health (various).
- BSc in Environmental Studies (various).

## *Vocational and professional syllabuses*

For example, in the UK:

- CII (Chartered Insurance Institute), ACII Core Subjects 510 and 511, Menu Subject 655.
- Institute of Risk Management.
- NEBOSH (National Examinations Board in Occupational Safety & Health) Diploma Part 2.
- Post-graduate diploma for Health & Safety Executive professional staff.

## *Professional groups*

A number of professional groups, which are readily identifiable as being wholly or largely concerned with risk, will also form part of the intended readership. For example:

- technical and major hazards risk analysts;
- loss prevention managers and advisers;
- insurance risk managers in industry and commerce;
- insurance underwriters and brokers;
- health, safety, environment and quality advisers/managers;
- IT directors and managers;
- human resource directors and managers;
- policy advisers in large organizations;
- strategic planners;
- financial, investment and business risk analysts;
- operations directors and managers;
- organizational analysts;
- marketing directors and managers;
- consultants in management, risk and change.

## The book's content

The authors believe that a threshold has been reached beyond which increasing integration of management, risk and change issues (both study and practice) will be inevitable. The book's content reflects this view and provides some pointers to future development of approaches to risk.

The book is in three parts. Part 1, Risk Contexts, seeks to examine the spectrum of contexts in which risk is currently understood and key theoretical concepts and factors which appear to be significant to thinking and action in relation to management, risk and change.

Chapters 1 to 9 respectively cover:

- Risk Management;
- Risk Assessment;
- Management Systems and Risk;
- Culture and Risk;
- Power and Risk;
- Organizational Environment and Risk;
- Risk and Change;
- Risk Cognition;
- A Fuzzy Convergence.

**Chapter 1**, Risk Management, discusses the proposition that hazards and threats and their associated risks can be managed in order to reduce the probability and impact of serious damage or loss (in pure and speculative risk areas) and to increase the probability of relative gain in speculative risk areas. Risk management assumes that it is both feasible and desirable to manage hazards and threats in such a way that (a) pure risks are eliminated, reduced or controlled, and (b) speculative risks result in enhanced utility or benefit. Different meanings of risk management and their consequences are discussed. A framework for strategic risk management encompasses strategies for avoidance, deferment, reduction, retention, transfer, sharing, limiting and consequence mitigation. Current difficulties arising from a fragmented approach to risk management and the need for a more integrated and strategic approach are discussed.

**Chapter 2**, Risk Assessment, describes and discusses the nature and scope of risk assessment and different approaches to it, ranging from technical risk assessments concerned with prevention of accidents or engineering failure, to strategic risk assessments concerned with avoiding business or organizational failure. Although pure risks (in which complete success means avoidance of damage, loss or failure) and speculative risks (in which consequences may range from spectacular gains to spectacular losses) are distinguishable, their interaction is often overlooked. The general approach to risk assessment incorporates identification and analysis of hazards or threats and analysis, estimation and evaluation of their attendant risks. Variations in approach to different risk areas occur, such as safety and health, major hazards, environment, business and finance, politics, security and terrorism.

**Chapter 3**, Management Systems and Risk, describes underlying system concepts and different ideas about management systems and discusses not only their potential benefits to risk management but also the risks which attach to management systems themselves. The absence of a commonly agreed set of constructs and language regarding management systems and different assumptions about and expectations of management systems affects risk in organizations. The weaknesses of reduced 'salvation' models currently tied to national or international standards and certification schemes, or to organizational improvement schemes such as TQM and business process re-engineering, are discussed. Attractive concepts such as these and management systems integration may prove to be a significant risk for some organizations.

**Chapter 4**, Culture and Risk, describes and discusses various aspects of culture at different levels (national, inter- and intra-organizational and professional) which are likely to have a bearing on risk. Different world-views about culture and risk and their implications are discussed. It is noted that popular management strategies for 'culture change' are unlikely to result in a simple and straightforward shift from one major valuation to another. Culture change is much more likely to be a complex realignment of a pattern of different valuations, some of which may change more rapidly and more lastingly than others. The controversial topic of culture assessment is discussed and in particular the theoretical, practical and ethical problems which arise. Caveats are raised about the 'riscomancy culture' (see Glossary) of risk experts, particularly that associated with technical risk analysts who exert a powerful self-protective influence over what may be discussed and considered and the risk methodologies which may be adopted. The phenomena of 'hindsight failure' and 'organizational learning' in relation to risk are discussed. Labelling organizations, industries or nations as either risk-orientated or risk-averse is likely to mislead as it masks the multicultural assemblages and complex contexts involved.

**Chapter 5**, Power and Risk, examines the concept of power in relation to organizations and relationships between power and risk, in particular between political processes, strategy and meanings of success in the context of risk. The substance, bases and sources of power are discussed, together with manifestations and consequences of power concepts. Powerful interests inside and outside a particular organization, which may have a significant influence on risks for that organization, are examined. In addition to culture, risk cognition and management systems, four power-related topics are especially important to understanding organizational behaviour and therefore risk behaviour. These are: management of meanings, decision-making, key strategic figures, and organizational structures. Despite the power of key figures to manipulate visions of corporate or project success, such power is limited when it comes to personal dimensions of success which may be powerful motivators. Such matters are important risk factors in management of change.

**Chapter 6**, Organizational Environment and Risk, addresses the outer context or environment of an organization and how the various environmental factors influence attitudes and behaviours towards risk within the organization. The main headings examined are economies and markets; public policy, regulation and standards; social and political climate; technology; history, operating territories and conditions. It is noted that although the outer context has a significant effect on risk perception and action, it is not necessarily predominant. Risks for an organization are likely to be increased if it does not have an effective means to monitor the outer context for significant changes.

**Chapter 7**, Risk and Change, examines the inter-relationship between risk and change at an organizational level, in particular the role of risk as a contextual mediator in change processes in organizations. Although there may be risks attached to not seeking to manage change at all, there may also be risks attached to the particular change methodology used and the assumptions which underpin it. Sources and types of change are examined along with decision-making models and strategies for change. Caveats about programmatic change and the risks of failure are raised. Risk in general and crises in particular are discussed as contextual mediators in change processes. On the basis of a synthesis of previous theories and models, an alternative model of change processes links political processes, strategy and meanings of success as core components with organizational culture, structures, resources, risk perceptions and outer context as mediators. The chapter notes that the most risky aspects of an organization may lie not in physical hazards or in investment and other speculative decisions but in the self-reinforcing behaviour associated with power relations, culture, motivations and risk perceptions in the organization.

**Chapter 8**, Risk Cognition, introduces an individual level of analysis for risk and in particular emphasizes that, at an individual level, risk is a cognitive phenomenon which overlays more objective characteristics of hazards and threats. 'Objective' risk, 'subjective' risk and behaviour towards risk are rarely coincident. Risk cognition is influenced by a range of individual factors including motivation, individual differences and emotions, and group factors such as culture and power relations. Effects of risk cognition may be identifiable in phenomena such as human error and accidents, and also in activities such as ergonomic design, risk assessment and strategic planning for risk management.

**Chapter 9**, A Fuzzy Convergence, provides an argument for addressing risk, management and change as linked areas in research and practice. A thematic matrix (see Table A) for appreciating links between risk, management, and change in the case studies of Part 2 is developed and discussed.

Part 2 (Chapters 10 to 15) provides a range of case studies which exemplify the common ground developed in Part 1 and particularly the thematic matrix. Chapters 10 to 15 respectively cover:

- The Offshore Oil and Gas Industry after Piper Alpha;
- The Barings Bank Collapse;
- Safety in the Railway Industry;
- Iran – a Risk Profile;
- The Introduction of New Computer Systems;
- UK Health Authorities Struggle to Survive.

In concluding the book, Part 3 contains two chapters (16 and 17) which provide respectively

- A Management Agenda
- A Research Agenda

and which flow from theoretical considerations of Parts 1 and 2.

As an aid to the reader, the final sections of the book comprise a glossary, literature references, subject index and author index.

# Part I
# Risk contexts

Chapter 1

# Risk management

## Overview

Hazards and threats and their associated risks can be managed in order to reduce both the probability and impact of serious damage and loss (in both pure and speculative risk areas) and to increase the probability of relative gain in speculative risk areas. Most large and medium-sized organizations carry out risk management to varying degrees and risk management is implicitly or explicitly a strategic component of any organization's survival and development. This is reflected, for example, in organizations employing a director of risk management or subsuming a range of decisions under a risk management executive or function. This chapter examines risk management at both strategic and operational levels and discusses some current issues (Waring and Glendon 1997).

## Introduction

Risk management may be defined as a field of activity seeking to eliminate, reduce and generally control pure risks (such as from safety, fire, major hazards, security lapses, environmental hazards) and to enhance the benefits and avoid detriment from speculative risks (such as financial investment, marketing, human resources, IT strategy, commercial and business risks).

Hazards or threats may be physical entities, conditions, substances, activities or behaviours which are capable of causing harm. Hazards and threats to an organization come in many forms. An organization may be damaged by cumulative effects of many small incidents or by a spectacular but rare major incident. Resulting damage could be to the health and safety of employees, to plant, equipment or an entire installation, to the environment, to products, or to financial assets. Damage to intangible factors such as credibility, status and bargaining power may also result.

The consequences of such damage may involve business interruption, loss of markets, stock losses, loss of public and customer confidence, and loss of staff morale. Financial losses are nearly always incurred, directly or indirectly. In the worst case, an organization may be damaged severely (for example Occidental after the Piper Alpha disaster in 1988, Union Carbide after the Bhopal toxic release) or may collapse (for example, BCCI in 1991, Polly Peck in 1993, Barings Bank in 1995).

In popular speech, 'hazard' and 'risk' may be used interchangeably. However, 'risk' represents more than the mere existence of a hazard – it should take account of the likely scale of consequences, the frequency, duration and extent of hazard exposure, the probability that an unwanted/desired event will occur and the time-scale over which consequences might be manifested and probabilities assigned – for example, health hazards associated with tobacco and asbestos. There is also a need to distinguish between 'pure risks' and 'speculative risks' and to recognize the interaction and synergy between the two. Pure risks are associated with hazards such as health, safety, environment and security where success with risk control can never be better than removal of the hazard so that exposure is zero and no harm can result, e.g. no accidents, zero product defects, no crimes. Speculative risks, however, are associated with business, finance, investment, human resources, IT strategy and politics where success is always *relative* to that of the economy as a whole, the market sector, competitors, and the power attributes of others. Risk management assumes that it is both feasible and desirable to manage hazards and threats in such a way that (a) pure risks are eliminated, reduced or controlled, and (b) speculative risks result in enhanced overall utility or benefit.

## The scope of risk management

The scope of risk management is extensive. Selecting key dimensions depends on the standpoint of the individual which, *inter alia*, is likely to be influenced by his or her training, qualifications, experience and membership of professional groups. For example, the authors' categorization of political and social/cultural risks as speculative risks and quality as a pure risk may not align with other parties' views of these topics. One way of envisaging the scope of risk management is to consider four key dimensions:

1 hazards or threats i.e. the objects of risk management;
2 risk contexts;
3 risk management objectives;
4 risk management methods.

*Figure 1.1* The scope of risk management (simplified)

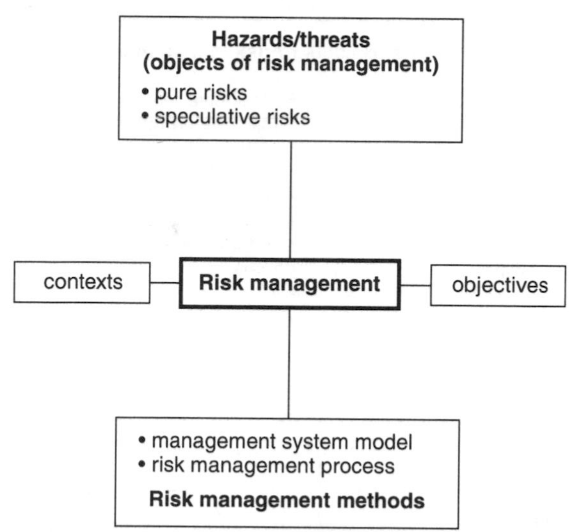


The relationship between these dimensions is depicted in Figure 1.1 and in an expanded version in Figure 1.2.

Figures 1.1 and 1.2 reflect the authors' search for a way of summarizing the scope of risk management. These scoping models are likely to be more comprehensive than orthodox models adopted by sectoral interests. For example, many risk specialists would consider that the box labelled 'Risk Management Process' in Figure 1.2 adequately expresses the full extent of risk management. However, such a process model and similar models (e.g. AS/NZ 4360 (1995)) could not cater for the range of relevant factors and integrative themes discussed in this book. Glendon and Waring (1997) and Waring and Glendon (1997) propose that the risk management model described in this chapter, which serves as a model for the contents of this book, could also provide senior management of organizations with a strategic and integrated approach to risk management. Elements of Figure 1.2 are discussed in the following sub-sections.

## *Hazards and threats*

Hazards and threats represent the objects of risk management (see chapter 2). Typically, 'hazard' is used in connection with health, safety and environment, whereas 'threat' is often used in connection with security and some speculative

*Figure 1.2* The scope of risk management (expanded)

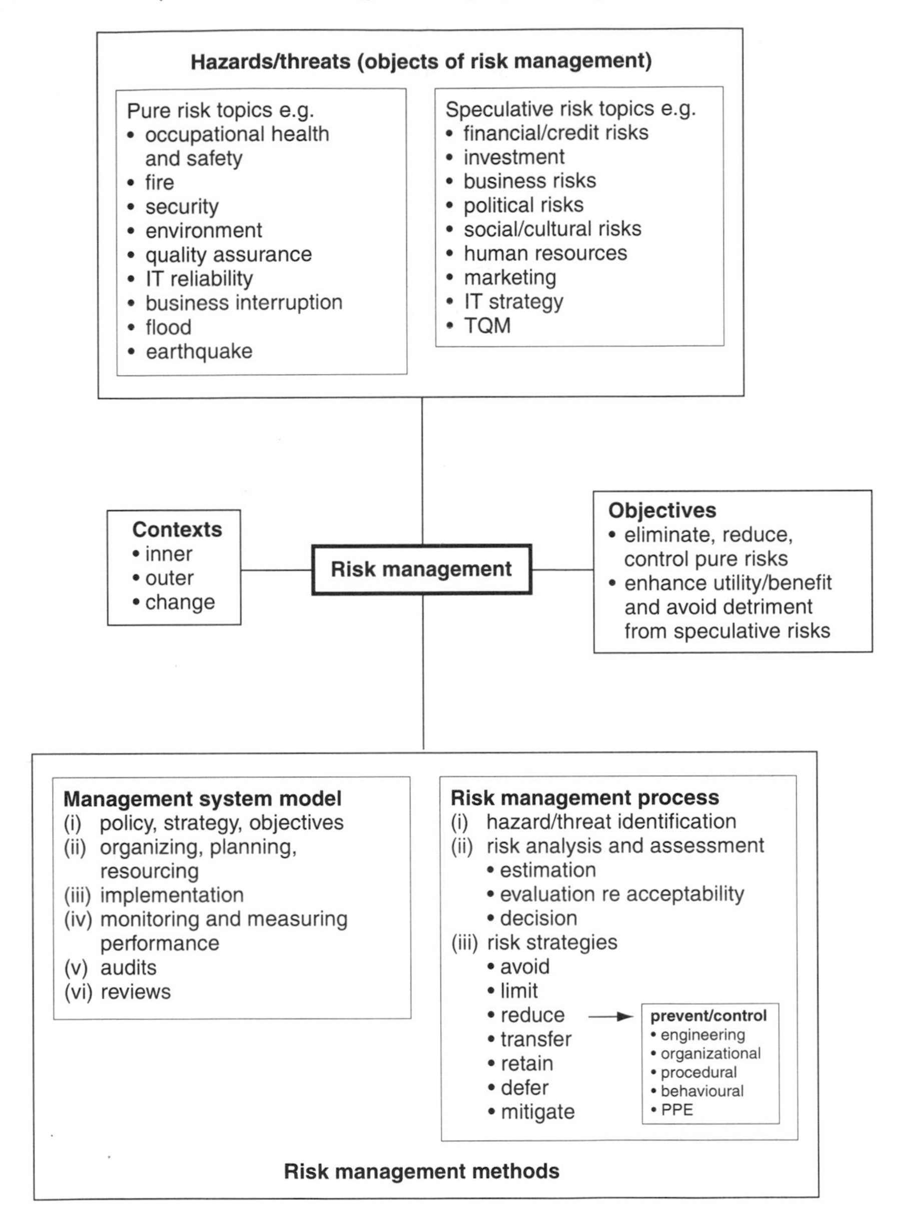

risk topics. However, there are no universally accepted rules on such terminology and there is likely to be continuing disagreement between professions and disciplines on such terms.

In a pure risk sense, hazards or threats are objects, substances, activities, behaviours or situations which are capable of causing harm. The best that can be achieved in managing pure risks is that no harm results from the particular hazard or threat. Examples of pure risk topics are included in Figure 1.2. For speculative risk topics, however, the risk management process is essentially a gamble in which success often means maximizing financial, political or other returns on speculative investments of various kinds and avoiding loss or disadvantage.

## *Risk management objectives*

Risk management helps to improve bottom line positions by cost reduction (loss prevention, reducing insurance costs etc.) and improving the likelihood of overall business success. Spectacular risk management failures such as Barings, Piper Alpha and the Sea Empress disaster grab headlines but many organizations suffer large cumulative losses from a myriad of lesser incidents.

The objectives of risk management may be summarized as:

- eliminating, reducing and controlling pure risks;
- gaining enhanced utility or benefit from speculative risks.

Because pure and speculative risks often interact, creating artificial boundaries between them may be inappropriate. For example, an organization's financial, investment and business risks are likely to be adversely affected by uncontrolled security risks (e.g. fraud – see chapter 11) or IT risks (e.g. unreliable hardware or software – see chapter 14). It is therefore advantageous that both sets of risk management objectives should be considered in a holistic way.

## *Risk contexts*

The context(s) in which risks are perceived to exist and to which risk management responds set the scene for identifying and understanding relevant hazards and threats and analysing the corresponding risks. One way of structuring context at an organizational level is by reference to the inner and outer contexts of the organization and to changes in those contexts (Pettigrew 1985, 1987, Waring 1993). For example:

*Inner context*

- Organizational structures – see chapters 5 and 7.
- Resources – see chapter 7.
- Culture – see chapter 4.
- Power relations – see chapter 5.
- Risk cognitions (perceptions) – see chapters 2 and 8.
- Strategy – see chapter 7.
- Motivations and meanings of success – see chapters 5 and 8.

*Outer context (organizational environment)* – see chapter 6

- Economies and markets.
- Public policy, regulation and standards.
- Social, historical and political climate.
- Physical conditions and climate.
- Technology.

## *Risk management methods*

### *Management system model*

A system model of management processes offers a logical meta-level framework to which the risk management process relates. The management system model outlined in Figure 1.2 and also described in chapter 3 provides a coherent framework for management in any organization.

### *Risk management process*

Hazard or threat identification and analysis and assessment of risk form an essential pre-requisite to risk actions and, for pure risks, seek to answer such questions as 'What could cause harm?'; 'What is the probability that harm will result?'; 'How severe would likely adverse effects be?' and 'Is the present level of risk acceptable?' For speculative risks, the analysis would also have to address positive or beneficial outcomes.

As a component of management systems, risk assessment is crucial to determining priorities for development of policy, strategy and objectives and in organizing, planning and resourcing. Regular operational risk assessments are also likely to be required during implementation.

As described in more detail in chapter 2, the risk management process begins by identifying hazards or threats and analysing them in terms of potential consequences, i.e. risk profiling. On the basis of the information and understanding gained, a risk assessment is then carried out with the following main steps:

- risk estimation (Measuring the risk);
- risk evaluation (How big in a scale of risks?);
- risk decisions (Is the risk acceptable against specified criteria?);
- risk action/strategy (What combination of strategies should be selected?).

Risk strategy relates to a particular approach, or combination of approaches, to one or more risks. Strategic risk management encompasses at least three meanings of 'strategic':

1 strategic risks – i.e. those which endanger the organization's corporate or business strategy, including survival, as described later in this chapter;
2 a strategic (i.e. overview) approach to risk and its management;
3 risk management activity at a high or corporate level in an organization.

One approach to undertaking a strategic approach to risk management is to select the most appropriate combination of the following strategic options:

| **Strategic Option** | **Illustrative Activities** |
|---|---|
| Avoidance: | Withdraw; do not enter market; cease activity. |
| Deferment: | Wait and see; defer decisions and actions. |
| Reduction: | Improve prevention and control measures; target risks and apply remedial programmes to reduce risks to as low as reasonably practicable. |
| Retention: | Captive (internal) insurance and/or bearing the risk (part of risk financing). |
| Transfer: | External insurance via premiums (part of risk financing). |
| Sharing: | Joint ventures with other organizations. |
| Limitation: | Limit scale or scope of presence or activities. |
| Mitigation: | Damage limitation. |

As these options are not mutually exclusive, they may be combined. Further, some of these terms may have different meanings among different professional groups. They are not truly independent categories, and some people may argue that, for example, strategies such as avoidance, deferment and limitation are sub-categories of reduction or particular examples of prevention.

Frequently, specialist knowledge and expertise is required to carry out hazard analysis and risk assessment and to identify risk control measures. At an operational level, managers usually only have local discretion within the overall strategy in respect of application of risk avoidance and risk reduction/loss control techniques. These are, of course, vitally important at operational level since it is by such means that hazards and threats are dealt with practically. Principles include cessation, substitution, reduction of scale, separation, segregation, automation, system design, information and training. Risk control measures which apply in particular to health, safety and security risks may also be categorized as follows (Waring 1996a):

- engineering;
- organizational;
- procedural;
- behavioural;
- personal protection.

Risk control is rooted in the control paradigm, i.e the notion that deviation from a desired standard or position may be prevented or corrected. Significant differences between control in engineered or designed technical systems and control in human activity systems are described in chapter 3.

## Meanings of 'risk management'

The term 'risk management' has multiple meanings and this may lead to confusion. For example, although 'risk management' may be used synonymously with 'risk control', risk control is an important component of risk management. Until relatively recently, in the insurance world risk management meant, in effect, securing the best liability cover for the lowest premiums. Although some parts of the insurance industry (notably some of the larger brokerages) now take a broader view of risk management, it is still true that many underwriters and company risk managers regard 'the risk' purely in terms of the entity being insured and the amount being underwritten. Underwriting decisions are still often based on limited information rather than adequate risk assessments although this attitude may change in the light of particularly disastrous claims experience during the late 1980s and early 1990s, e.g. asbestosis, Piper Alpha (ABI 1994).

In party politics, risk management is not a term used frequently. However, the concept is well exercised as a fundamental part of 'impression management' seeking to limit potential damage to credibility, gain public approval and ultimately win electoral fortunes. Every politician, political adviser and senior civil servant is implicitly his or her own 'risk manager', with varying degrees of success. It is likely that the popularity of the UK television comedy series *Yes, Minister* and *Yes, Prime Minister* arose in large part from an exaggerated display of political 'risk management'. In organizations, political processes at personal and professional levels represent a similar kind of risk management. Management of meanings is inextricably bound up in such actions (see for example Pettigrew 1973; Mangham 1979; Pfeffer 1981; Watson 1982; Vickers 1983; Pettigrew 1985 and 1987; Waring 1993a and b). Chapter 5 considers issues of power and risk in greater detail.

Public awareness of hazards and risks has increased owing, in particular, to media attention (Wilkins and Patterson 1990). For large organizations, whether industrial, commercial, public authority or governmental, risk management has come to mean managing a public which is increasingly sceptical about official and company statements on risk issues. Individuals may have become more assertive in challenging failures in duty of care and be more ready to sue for compensation than hitherto. Organizations can no longer realistically expect the public to be deferential towards them and their technical experts. In an analogous way, the relationship between doctors and their patients has become in recent years tacitly more 'contractual', more equitable in the two-way trade of information and respect (see for example Vincent *et al.* 1993).

Sir Alistair Morton, chairman of Eurotunnel, told a conference in London in November 1995 that many organizations might have to rethink their 'contract' with the public on matters of risk. Prevention and other risk control measures not only have to be adequate in themselves but must also be convincing and address risks which the customer has *not* contracted to buy, such as injuries, delays and consequential losses. 'There is no point in wishing you had thought about emergency planning when you are surrounded in Folkestone by 600 angry, frustrated and, possibly, frightened customers whose cars have gone to Calais following an evacuation' (Morton *et al.* 1995). In November 1996, a major fire emergency involving injuries, delays and consequential losses for many parties occurred in the Channel Tunnel.

The debacle in 1995 of water shortages in the area covered by Yorkshire Water is another example which bears testament to the need for companies to heed Morton's words. The rear-guard actions by Yorkshire Water to avoid rationing and standpipes were costly as they involved round-the-clock transport of water by hundreds of tankers into the area. In addition, a series of highly publicized PR blunders involving announcement of vast company profits and increases in senior executive pay and perks occurred which reduced the company's credibility and consumer

### Example 1.1: Defensive 'risk management' against consumers

The rise of consumerism and consumer power in the UK is reflected in the popularity of consumer protection organizations such as the Consumers' Association and television programmes such as *Watchdog* and *The Cook Report*. Some companies still adopt an arrogant, defensive stance towards customers and their complaints, despite the evidence that such behaviour is financially damaging, both directly and long-term through damaged reputation. As an example, The Consumers' Association survey of swimming pool safety at hotels in Spain and Portugal (*Which?* 1995) suggested that despite their official policies, leading tour operators had persistently failed to ensure adequate safety standards at hotels they use. The report indicates that the situation had remained essentially unchanged for a number of years despite repeated representations from the Consumers' Association and repeated assurances from tour operators that they undertook adequate safety inspections and took appropriate action where safety standards were not met.

Thus, some tour operators are apparently aware that they owe a legal duty of care not to place their customers in danger. Nevertheless, there is evidence that not all have undertaken suitable and sufficient risk assessments at resorts and customer complaints about specific hazards are frequently ignored. It may be inferred from this that some tour operators regard risk management cynically in relation to customer safety as a trade-off exercise between, on the one hand, doing little and (in their perception) the probability and likely consequences of accidents and, on the other hand, practising what they preach and the operational costs that may be involved. This approach to risk management is not what is meant by the legal principle of 'so far as is reasonably practicable' (Hendy and Ford 1993, 1995) or 'ALARP' (HSE 1988; Rimington 1993), nor does it take heed of Sir Alistair Morton's warnings cited above about the commercial consequences of 'waiting until the horse has bolted before closing the stable door'.

The consequences of a flawed approach to risk management in the consumer area are further exemplified by the damage to the reputation of high street banks in the UK resulting from persistent reports and legal cases regarding overcharging and denial of liability for such things as bad advice, incompetent administration of accounts, and 'phantom' withdrawals of cash via supposedly secure automatic teller machines. At one stage in the early 1990s, the political fall-out from the scandal threatened the poll ratings of the incumbent government who were seen by many as responsible for poor banking regulation.

satisfaction even further. The chief executive was widely reported in the media that he claimed to conserve water at home by strictly limiting his showers and baths (but neglected to reveal that he took those instead at a relative's home!).

The Royal Society Report (1992) uses the term 'risk management' to denote regulatory measures (both in public policy and corporate practice) intended to shape who can take what risks and how. Risk-benefit analysis is often used to identify an acceptable balance between overall risks and overall benefits of a proposed course of action and exenditure of resources. According to Chicken (1994), 'the decision maker with comprehensive responsibility for determining the acceptability of a project will require detailed information about the acceptability of the technical, economic and socio-political aspects of a project' – see also Chicken (1996). At the grand level of public policy decisions and major corporate projects, this requirement makes good sense but the level of resolution implied in such a reductionist model may unwittingly introduce hidden distortions. For example, in Chicken's model, socio-political assessment is at the grand level of societal and political acceptability. It is tempting, indeed commonplace, to assume that risk decisions made at such a high level reflect fairly an aggregation of views on the particular risk issue throughout society. This assumption ignores the fact that political acceptability refers to political processes at the level at which the decision is made. As Pettigrew (1994) has noted, political processes operate essentially at the micro level – i.e. the relatively small group of people engaged in influencing and making a particular decision. Such people may make quite erroneous assumptions about what is socially and politically acceptable at all the loci likely to be affected by the decision. As chapters 2 and 3 discuss, criteria for 'acceptability' as established and rationalized by risk experts and risk decision-makers may not match the views of those 'at risk'. Socio-political assessment therefore needs to embrace a realistic spectrum of interested parties, including those who are responsible for particular projects involving risk issues within organizations (see chapter 5 for further discussion).

*Table 1.1* Examples of strategic risks

| *Pure risk areas* | *Speculative risk areas* |
|---|---|
| Security/fraud | Investment/finance |
| Fire | Product development |
| Environment | Business strategy |
| Health and safety | Marketing |
| Quality assurance | Political risks |
| IT reliability | Social/cultural risks |
| Business interruption | Reorganization e.g. business process re-engineering |
| Earthquake | IT strategy |
| Flood | |

## Strategic risks

### *Strategic risk management*

Strategic risk management seeks a holistic approach to risks, both pure and speculative, which involve significant hazards or threats to an organization, enterprise or political entity (Waring and Mehdizadeh 1996). Strategic risk management addresses interactions between pure and speculative risks, as discussed in Table 1.1. Strategic risks may be seen as those which, if realized, could seriously threaten an organization's business or its viability. This definition covers pure as well as speculative risks.

It is important to recognize that pure and speculative risks interact. For example, poor security may damage investments and assets; under-resourced projects may increase all the pure risks. A major fire or explosion at an industrial installation may interrupt business and deter investors as well as lose a major asset. An investment decision to set up a new chemical processing plant carries with it not only the life-cycle financial risks but also inevitably risks concerning major hazards and pollution.

Many large employers and their recruiters fail to appreciate the nature and scope of strategic risks affecting their organization. For example, recruitment advertisements and job specifications may use language such as 'strategic role' and 'strategic management of risks' whereas the actual job may entail little more than ensuring compliance with health and safety legislation. A major corporation with global operations was willing to pay a salary of £60,000 per annum for a post styled as 'head of risk management', whose holder was restricted to acting as a 'troubleshooting' safety officer addressing local operational health and safety compliance topics in the UK. An internationally renowned scientific organization expected the corporate head of health and safety to act as the technical safety officer in hundreds of establishments and not to be developing policy and strategy. Failure to deploy risk management resources appropriately could result in only a small fraction of the full array of strategic risks affecting an organization being recognized and addressed.

Debatable assumptions about the scope and depth of strategic risk management may be encountered among risk management specialists, including consultants. For example, one international consultancy asserted that holistic strategic risk analysis encompasses the core functions of a business such as marketing, production and finance. Nevertheless, this consultancy included neither financial risk nor health, safety and environment among its areas of 'holistic' strategic risk expertise.

Hutchinson (1992) argues that environmental protection (traditionally considered to be a pure risk area) is now an essential component of corporate strategy seeking to improve an organization's competitive advantage (i.e. speculative risks): 'Industry needs to prove that it is capable of operating in ways that are sustainable . . . The environmental challenge must be seen as an important strategic decision. Achieving a sustainable future must become part of the agenda for each individual business. In the same way as legality is now an accepted part of business life, so, in the future it is likely that 'sustainability' will become an accepted condition of doing business' (see also Jose (1996)).

Another area which demonstrates links between pure and speculative risks is 'quality management'. Today's market for manufactured goods is essentially worldwide and the competition between suppliers is fierce. Each manufacturer is seeking to gain as much competitive edge as possible on a range of parameters including design, product reliability, price and availability. Demonstration of product quality has become an important means by which a manufacturer can gain a competitive edge, whether in the home market or in exports. If an organization can show that all its various functions and processes which contribute to product quality, such as design, marketing, production, safety, human resources, sales and finance are working at peak efficiency and effectiveness, then in principle it stands a better chance of commercial success.

One important contributor to product quality is having effective and efficient management systems, as discussed in chapter 3. An international standard ISO 9000 series specifies essential requirements for a 'quality management system' and many organizations apply to be audited and certified to this standard. Possession of such a certificate can make sales of products easier to customers who demand it. However, currently ISO 9000 only attests to compliance with minimal requirements for administrative procedures and does not address actual product quality

(Binney *et al.* 1992; Wilkinson *et al.* 1994). Supply of poor quality products is still a strategic speculative risk whose consequences may have to be faced by purchaser and suppliers who rely solely on ISO 9000.

## *Foreign business risks*

Strategic business risks include speculative risks associated with product development, marketing, sales and finance. For example, in order to manage adequately strategic risks relating to overseas markets, it is essential to have available up-to-date and reliable information about the target market. A variety of information sources may be tapped such as the DTI, ECGD, local embassies and industry and trade associations. However, experience suggests that much of the information from such sources becomes quickly out-of-date and is incomplete. There is no real substitute for first-hand information gathered by personal visits to the territory. Having gathered information (which is an on-going process), an organization should be in a better position to identify and analyse hazards and threats and assess corresponding risks. Risk assessment results could then contribute to a conventional SWOT analysis.

Strategic risks of doing business in 'difficult' territories are relevant to many organizations. Difficulties may arise in the processes of doing business whereby long delays and bureaucracy may add to costs and uncertainties about outcomes. Failure to understand local legal requirements, company law, language and the subtleties of foreign cultures and expectations may add to risks of failure and financial loss (see for example Lasserre and Probert 1994). Crime, whether general lawlessness or being targeted by organized criminal gangs, is an additional threat in some territories. Health hazards and transport hazards may also be encountered. Political instability may threaten armed conflict, a change of government and new trade policies. Russia, the Caucasian and Central Asian Republics and some African and South American states have become territories requiring particular caution. See also chapter 13. Table 1.2 summarizes such risks.

## *Foreign policy risks*

In international affairs, the strategic risks to governments which arise from their foreign policy, defence, trade policy and migrant policy are just some of those to be faced. Management of such risks comes in the form of diplomacy. The following are examples:

*Table 1.2 Risks of doing business in difficult overseas territories*

| *Pure risks* | *Examples* |
|---|---|
| Security: | Fraud, corruption, embezzlement, theft, terrorism, kidnap, extortion, armed conflict. |
| Environment: | Local laws, standards, public liability, major hazards. |
| Health & Safety: | Local laws, standards, product liability, employers liability, major hazards, health hazards, transport hazards. |
| Quality assurance: | Poor QC standards and methods, failure to recognise quality ethos and requirements. |
| *Speculative risks* | *Examples* |
| Investment/finance: | Local laws, profit repatriation, taxation, economic performance, nationalization. |
| Commercial: | Prices/controls, disposable incomes, fuel prices, inflation, fashion/taste, usance terms, payment. |
| Competition: | Foreign companies, local companies, product prices and profiles. |
| Political: | Instability, foreign trade policy, trade embargoes, diplomatic relations. |
| Cultural: | Attitudes, behaviours, social expectations. |

- Western Alliance and NATO relationship with Russia and the old Warsaw Pact states post-Cold War. If economic reforms fail and the populations continue to suffer hardship, Russia could come under control of hardline regimes (neo-fascist or neo-communist) which favour an anti-Western stance. Western Alliance and NATO seek to reassure Russia that economic support will continue and that defence alliances with neighbouring states are not threats to Russia.
- Global markets versus protectionism and the risks of trade wars, e.g. brinkmanship between the USA and Europe, USA and China, USA and Japan, Europe and Japan.
- Foreign policy of Western governments in the Bosnian crisis perceived in Muslim countries as duplicitous and anti-Muslim. Previously pro-Wester[illegible] Mus-lim states were incensed at what they saw as tacit complicity in g[illegible] Western-trained military officers sever psychological ties with the W[illegible] prochement between Iran and Iraq potentially a new focus for Musli[illegible]

Prospect of pan-Muslim 'cold war' against the West. Early 1995, UK Foreign Office sends envoy on crisis management mission to Middle East capitals seeking to prevent further and permanent diplomatic damage as far as UK is concerned.
- Nuclear tests in the Pacific by the French government cause riots in French Polynesia which widen into independence protests. Major diplomatic rift occurs between France and Pacific states. French goods boycotted in Australia and New Zealand. French diplomacy (based on assertion of rights to test, no apology and no change of policy) is received badly.

## An integrative strategy

The risks of management and of change are inseparable from managing risks and change. It is becoming increasingly necessary to adopt a coherent and integrated approach towards managing the full spectrum of risks. The success, if not viability, of an organization may be threatened by a variety of risks simultaneously or consecutively (pure, speculative or hybrid). An integrated approach is therefore needed within organizations in order to ensure a common understanding of and responses to hazards and risks. Nevertheless, whereas the rhetoric for holistic, integrated risk management is widespread, practice may not fully reflect this. One organization (Glendon *et al.* 1998) sought to integrate financial and occupational health and safety components of risk through decision-making processes within their senior executive team. While this process appeared to work effectively for these two components (finance, health and safety), the status of other risk issues was ambiguous.

An important reason for strong rhetoric and weak implementation of integrated strategic risk management lies in fragmentation of the various disciplines and professions which engage in risk management. It will remain difficult to integrate the various potential components until there is common understanding of the scope of the whole subject, a common technical language, communication between areas and motivation among parties to integrate their respective disciplines. Different risk professions value their separateness and may fear that integration of ideas will lead inevitably to calls for integration of risk functions in organizations and to inter-professional power struggles to control an integrated function. Such struggles may lead to priority attention being given to some risk areas and less to others – e.g. quality management at the expense of safety. Decisions and allocation of responsibilities on this matter at board level in organizations are required before integrated risk management can begin.

## Conclusions

Risk management is at present a collective term for a variety of activities concerned with avoiding, reducing and controlling pure risks and with improving the benefit side and avoiding/reducing the loss side of speculative risks. In the extensive field of risk management, four key dimensions may be identified: hazards or threats, risk contexts, risk management objectives, and risk management methods. Interaction and synergy between pure and speculative risks is not always appreciated and integration of different risk management functions, disciplines and activities remains weak or non-existent in most organizations. Senior management of organizations tends to have a poor understanding of the scope of risk management, implications for strategic risks and the organizational and resource requirements for addressing these adequately. However, increased awareness of strategic risk issues and implications is likely to see more organizations adopting an integrated approach to risk management. Chapter 2 examines risk analysis and assessment, which is a central component of risk management.

# Chapter 2
# Risk assessment

## Overview

Risk assessment is a central component of risk management. This chapter describes general approaches to risk assessment, which incorporate identification and analysis of hazards or threats, and the analysis, estimation and evaluation of their attendant risks. Different approaches to hazard identification and risk assessment are discussed in relation to safety and health, major hazards, environment, business and finance, politics, security and terrorism.

## Introduction

Chapter 8 emphasizes that risk is essentially a cognitive phenomenon (Glendon 1987; Glendon and McKenna 1995). Risk is therefore subjective and so-called 'objective' risk is merely a convenient way of expressing the fact that some people share a particular, normative view of risk which implies or seeks to suggest that risk can be disentangled from human biases (see for example HSE Discussion Document 1995a; Chicken 1996). In this book, 'objective' risk refers to a general agreement among risk analysts about the nature and degree of a particular perceived risk. However, social, cultural and professional biases may have a considerable effect on how a particular group of people perceive a particular risk (Douglas 1992; Royal Society 1992) and such biases affect approaches to risk assessment. For example, the 'objective' risk associated with offshore installation disasters such as Piper Alpha is likely to be viewed differently by safety engineers and by investment risk analysts (see for example Torhaug 1992 and Lovegrove 1990 respectively). As chapter 8 discusses in detail, various meanings of risk include:

- the popular conflation of 'hazard' and 'risk';
- the probability-and-consequences concept of failure to control hazards, as adopted by safety engineers;

- the potential monetary loss or insured entity as understood by insurance underwriters;
- the potential financial gain or loss from investment decisions;
- the potential gain or loss in standing and bargaining power associated with political decisions.

The sections comprising this chapter seek to demonstrate both the unique features of approaches to risk assessment used by different disciplines and any features which they share.

## The nature and scope of risk assessment

Risk assessment is the general term used to describe the process of gauging the most likely outcome(s) of a set of events, situations or options and the significant consequences of those outcomes. Risk assessment is inherent in human existence. Cognition, perception, motivation and attitude interplay with decision-making and prioritizing actions across the spectrum of individual interests, needs and concerns (Glendon and McKenna 1995). At an individual level, informal risk assessments are a more-or-less continuous cognitive process, whether crossing the road, purchasing goods, engaging in social interaction, gauging job prospects or whatever.

At a formal level, risk assessment adopts an analytical approach to uncertainty and a rationalistic methodology has arisen, examples of which are shown in Figures 2.1, 2.2 and 2.3. The aim of (formal) risk assessment is to provide information on which decisions may be made about proposed actions, the adequacy of risk controls and what improvements might be required. Typically, such risk assessments focus on so-called credible event or situation 'scenarios' – i.e. those deemed by risk 'experts' to be credible and significant. For example, for an offshore oil and gas installation, major hazards to the installation would include ship collision, riser blow-out and helicopter crash. For an investment bank, major threats would include multiple loss of key executives in an air crash, major bad debts and rogue trading.

Although a 'major hazards' rationale is often necessary, it is important to recognize that (formal) risk assessments carried out by technical risk analysts or other risk 'experts' often fail to include due allowance for other equally important factors. Toft (1996) and Toft and Reynolds (1994, 1997), quoting examples such as Three Mile Island, argues that a purely rationalistic approach to hazard identification cannot identify all pertinent routes to causes of disasters, which are theoretically infinite in number. Allied to this caveat is the failure in (formal) risk assessment to recognize the relevance of individual heuristic risk assessments, whether among those subject to risk, those engaged in risk decisions, or those used by individual 'experts'. It is instructive that the HSE Discussion Document on risk (HSE 1995a) defines *assessed* risks as those determined by experts whereas, apparently, non-experts are capable only of *perceiving* risks! Similarly, Chicken (1996) defines 'objective risks' as those determined by experts, whereas 'subjective risks' are determined by non-experts.

This book stresses the importance of subjectivity in risk assessment (whether by expert or non-expert) in view of risk cognition and the individual, cultural, political, social and economic factors which influence such perception (see also Douglas (1992) and Glendon and McKenna (1995)).

## Different approaches to risk assessment

Two broad approaches to risk assessment have arisen – the heuristic and scientific approaches. Although an heuristic or 'rule-of-thumb' approach may include some form of quantification, generally it is qualitative and 'subjective', relying on individuals' collective judgement. A 'scientific' approach, however, employs quantitative modelling and generally requires formal training in the mathematics used – see Chicken (1996) for example.

There is evidence that risk terminology is used variably within even a single area of application. For example, risk assessment, risk analysis, risk estimation and risk evaluation are frequently used loosely and interchangeably in the health and safety field. Figures 2.1 and 2.3 below show two similar models of risk assessment methodology in which risk analysis and risk estimation are transposed, as are identification of hazards and identification of outcomes. This is not to say that those using the terminology necessarily possess radically different mental models of risk and its assessment, although scientists and engineers tend to have a narrower view of risk than do social scientists (Douglas 1992, Royal Society 1992, Waring 1992a, Toft 1993). Rather, the recursive nature of terms such as 'hazard' and 'risk', and terms such as 'assessment', 'analysis', 'estimation' and 'evaluation' in everyday speech, creates fertile ground for ambiguity and confusion, especially in risk communication (Glendon and McKenna 1995).

Attempts have been made (for example Royal Society 1992; HSE 1995a) to produce standard definitions for risk but the problem of recursive language remains. The courts have not helped by imposing their own version of 'risk' which supports the popular conflation of 'hazard' and 'risk' – a view not widely held among those engaged professionally in risk work. In the Science Museum case in

*Figure 2.1* Risk assessment process – example 1

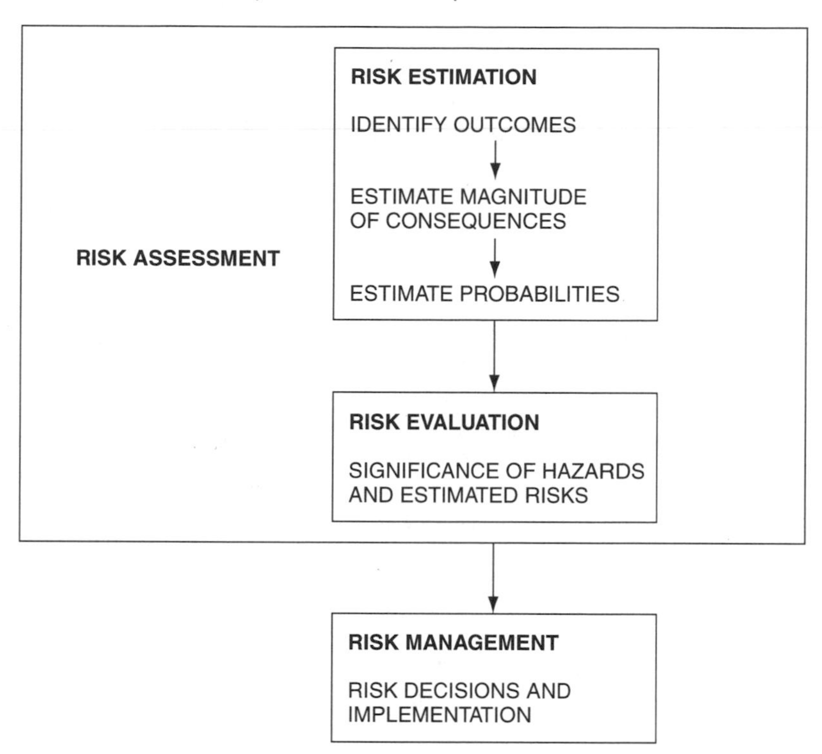


*Source*: compiled from Royal Society Report (1992: 3)

England, for example, the Court of Appeal in 1993 (AELR 1993) held that in the context of the Health & Safety at Work etc. Act 1974 'the word "risk" conveys the idea of the possibility of danger' – i.e. however small the probability of harm. Conflating the 'possibility of danger' with the 'probability of harm' appears not to be problematic for the courts and industrial tribunals (e.g. UK Industrial Tribunal case number 47174/94) whereas to risk analysts it is anathema.

There is a tendency to regard simple heuristic approaches to risk assessment as being inherently inferior to sophisticated scientific approaches. Both Toft (1993, 1996) and Waring (1996a) argue that such a view is unwarranted and is based on a failure to recognise that all risk assessment, however sophisticated the mathematics involved, is inherently value-laden. For example, the detailed but none the less narrow base of *technical* knowledge on which many quantified risk assessments (QRA) are made may create a false, reduced picture of real-world settings in which risk behaviour is actually much more complex. The most risky aspects of an

*Figure 2.2* Flow diagram of risk assessment – example 2

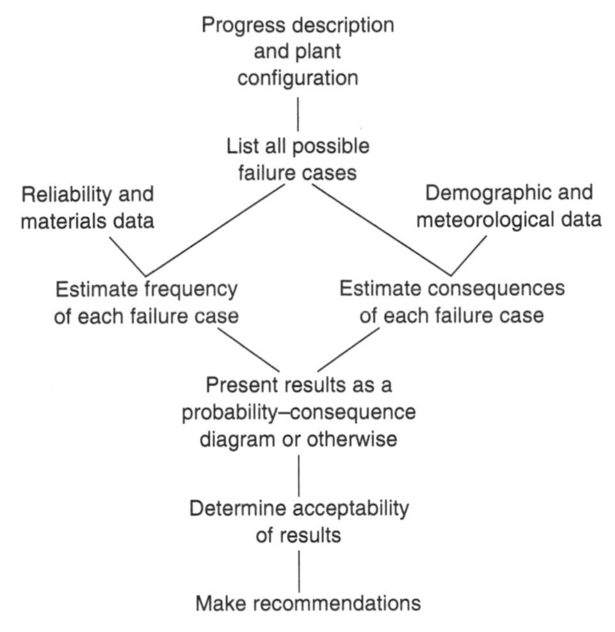


*Source*: Thomson (1987), reproduced by kind permission of Addison Wesley Longman Ltd. Also appears in Hazards Forum (1992)

organization may lie not in physical hazards but in the self-reinforcing behaviour associated with power relations and culture in the organization. Risk assessments are carried out by individuals who are neither culturally nor politically neutral. Current QRA methods are not capable of a complete and therefore convincing assessment of risks to safety arising from organizational culture, ideologies, power relations, motivations, attitudes or perceptions, a view supported by ACSNI (1991) and Douglas (1992, 1994). The same argument applies to other areas of risk – a theme developed throughout this book.

## Risk assessment procedures

Risk assessments inform decision-making about effective actions for 'managing' risks – i.e. avoiding, removing, reducing, improving and generally controlling risks. Risk assessments may be undertaken at different organizational levels, ranging from broad strategy at corporate level ('risk profiling') to detailed operational activities. An initial coarse risk assessment may be needed in order to identify risk priorities so

*Figure 2.3* Risk assessment methodology – example 3

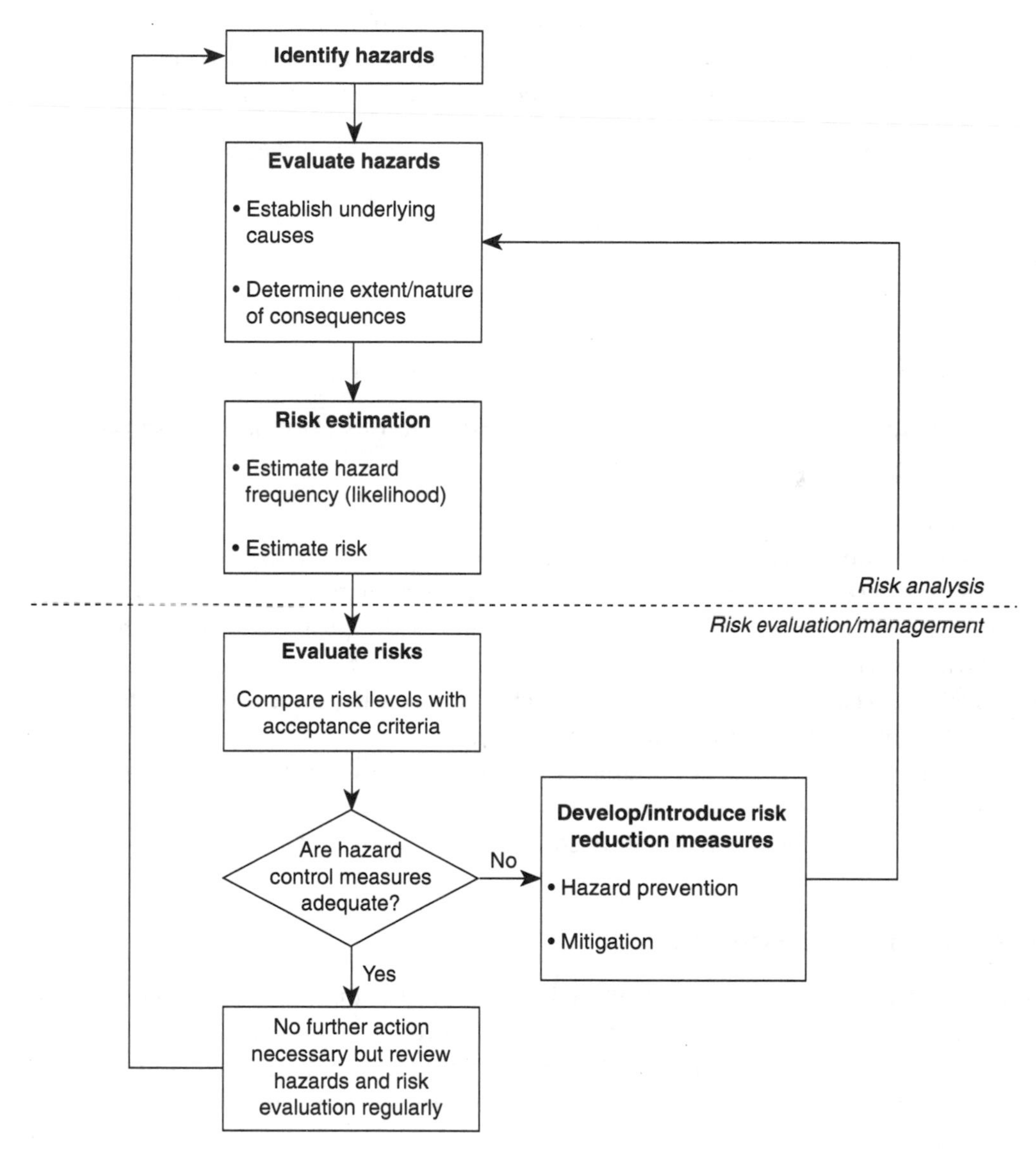


*Source*: Patel (1994)

that strategy development and planning can proceed on a rational basis. More detailed risk assessments may then follow as part of a broader decision-making process which includes selection and implementation of practical responses.

A risk assessment might seek to answer questions from among the following:

- What is the nature of the hazards and the severity and likelihood of unwanted consequences?
- Are our present risk control efforts effective?
- What is the degree of risk – i.e. how big is it?
- Is the risk acceptable?
- What, if anything, should be done about it?
- What could be done about it? What are the control options?

In order to answer these and related questions, risk assessment procedure is generally as follows:

- Define the boundaries of what is to be assessed.
- Identify and describe the hazards or threats.
- Analyse hazard effects and consequences and estimate the likelihoods of occurrence and of unwanted outcomes – i.e. what is the possibility of danger?
- Estimate risk values.
- Evaluate risk values by assigning them to risk categories - i.e. is the overall probability of harm high, medium or low?
- Decide whether risk is acceptable or unacceptable by comparing risk values with acceptance criteria.
- Decide if control action is required and, if so, what and how.

## Simple risk assessment

There continues to be considerable debate and confusion about the relative values of risk assessments undertaken by 'experts' and 'non-experts' (see chapter 8). There is evidence (HSE 1995a; Chicken 1996 for example) that some experts consider that whereas expert risk assessments are objective and superior, those of non-experts are subjective and inferior. Further, the use by some experts of sophisticated techniques involving complex mathematics helps to foster a false idea that simple methods which could be used by anyone (including non-experts) are inherently inferior. Toft (1993, 1996) points out that sophisticated quantitative risk assessments are overkill for most situations and that worse, because of methodological assumptions, unwarranted confidence in the results may be created. It is therefore important to emphasize that whether a particular risk relates to safety hazards and/or some other hazard capable of causing harm (e.g. security lapse, financial deal, political decision), simple rule-of-thumb risk assessment techniques will be appropriate for most applications, at least initially.

One simple approach to operational risk assessment used in occupational safety and health management is described in Waring (1996a). The first stage comprises hazard identification in relation to locations or areas and main activities, which involves a combination of techniques such as:

- hazard spotting;
- experience and prior knowledge, including accident data;
- job analysis;
- information, reports and guidance from such parties as insurers, safety audits, regulatory bodies;
- information and guidance from specialist advisers.

Having identified hazards associated with each location or activity, these are then analysed in terms of:

- potential consequences and harm;
- present control measures;
- likely numbers and types of person potentially exposed to the particular hazard;
- exposure characteristics such as frequency and duration.

The information gained from hazard analysis on the possibility of danger is then used to derive an estimate of the risk associated with each particular hazard, for which an estimate is made of:

- the potential consequences of the hazard as presently controlled (C);
- the typical frequency and duration of people's exposure to the hazard (E);
- the probability that the hazard will result in an accident (P).

The risk score (R), which relates to the overall probability of harm, is then obtained from the formula:

$R = C \times E \times P$
where:

C (consequences/severity)
1 = minor injury
2 = serious injury
3 = major injury

4 = multiple casualties
5 = at least one fatality

**E** (exposure)
1 = rare/never
2 = infrequent (1–3 months)
3 = frequent (weekly)
4 = high (daily)
5 = constant

**P** (probability of accident)
1 = very unlikely (once in next 10 years)
2 = unlikely (once in next 1–5 years)
3 = likely (once in next 12 months)
4 = very likely (once in next month)
5 = inevitable (imminent)

In the above scheme, variants of which are widely used, an assessed hazard would have a risk score in the range 1–125.

Risk scores obtained by this formula can be evaluated by reference to risk categories, for example:

| *Risk score* | *Urgency of action required* |
|---|---|
| High = 75 or over | Top priority; action now |
| Medium = 27–64 | Deal with over next few weeks/ months |
| Low = below 27 | Deal with if attention warranted |

An even simpler approach advocated by some risk experts is to multiply only consequences (C) and probability (P), since it is claimed that P automatically includes exposure frequency (E). However, although E and P are not truly independent variables there is a degree of independence which it is wiser to make explicit.

Schemes such as the above are open to criticism on a number of counts. First, the number of individuals exposed is not separately identified as a variable and, although partly subsumed within C (consequences) and E (exposure), leaves an assessment open to different interpretations. Second, the scales used for the C, E and P components are all ordinal and therefore the R scale is also ordinal. This means that the final score gives a rating indicating the relative position of different risks but not the extent to which one risk is greater or less than another. For example, a score of 80 for one risk and 40 for another indicates that the first is a greater risk than the second but to infer that the first risk is twice as big as the second is false. Third, the values of the ordinal scales may be too wide-ranging and also may not allow for zero exposure. A better and simpler approach may be to use qualitative ratings such as high, medium and low since these do not involve numerical scales, which may be potentially misleading.

It should be emphasized that risk scoring as in the examples above is an heuristic or rule-of-thumb technique and does not provide accurate measurements of risk. The values estimated for each factor are judgements of those doing the assessment and, as noted above, the variables are not truly independent. However, these caveats are of no great consequence because this simple technique is only a device for collapsing a great deal of information quickly in a rough and ready way to help identify or confirm risk priorities – i.e. to aid risk evaluation and guide action. There may be social, political or cultural reasons for prioritizing risks which are ranked as low by such a scheme.

Having evaluated a risk score and categorized it as either high, medium or low, a decision is needed as to whether the risk is acceptable. In the scheme described above, low category risks would be considered acceptable, whereas high category risks would not. Medium category risks become increasingly unacceptable as the risk scores increase. However, as the next section indicates, the whole topic of risk acceptability is controversial. A number of case studies which exemplify the application of simple risk assessment in health and safety at work are described in Waring (1996a).

As risk scoring is heuristic, risk assessors are likely to develop customized safety risk estimation formulae to meet their own particular requirements (see below). For example, property damage could be a consequence and different values could be assigned to the variables. Different risk evaluation categories could be used. Provided a consistent approach is used for similar applications within an organization, such variations may be acceptable.

Simple risk estimation schemes are also feasible for other risk areas such as security and environment. Security, health and safety, and environmental risks are traditionally classed as pure risks – i.e. the best that can happen is that the particular hazard does *not* produce an undesirable effect. Financial, business, investment and political risks, however, are usually classed as speculative risks – i.e. the consequences can be either good or bad and the degree of advancement of utility or benefit for one group 'at risk' is likely to be associated with a degree of detriment for one or more rival groups 'at risk'. For example, in political risk, 'consequence' is *relative* gain/loss resulting from a particular political situation or process, while 'probability' refers to the *relative* likelihood of a particular situation arising or process occurring.

Although the Barings Bank collapse highlighted a number of risk factors which

relate to the particular kind of banking involved (Board of Banking Supervision 1995), some were of a more general nature (see chapter 11). Examples of key factors that would need to be addressed during the identification and analysis of financial/business hazards include:

- exposure in the light of recent trading experience;
- market conditions and prospects;
- information from financial audits;
- competences and behaviour of key personnel;
- internal financial monitoring and control systems;
- adequacy of independent audit arrangements;
- client reactions;
- competitor positioning;
- policy and company ethics.

Speculative types of risk differ from pure risks in that both desirable and undesirable outcomes are possible, and this needs to be reflected in the assessment methodology. One simple risk estimation scheme for political risks (that could be adapted easily for use with financial, business and investment risks) is as follows:

| **P** (probability) | **C** (consequences) |
|---|---|
| 1 = low | *Good outcome* |
| 2 = medium | + 1 = minor enhancement |
| 3 = high | + 2 = significant enhancement |
| | + 3 = major enhancement of credibility, bargaining power, alliances, etc. |
| | *Bad outcome* |
| | − 1 = minor damage to credibility, bargaining power, alliances, etc. |
| | − 2 = significant damage |
| | − 3 = major damage to credibility, bargaining power, alliances, etc. |

Since the same process or situation being assessed could lead to either or both 'good' and/or 'bad' outcomes – even at the same time – arguably each needs to be calculated separately rather than on a single scale. Inclusion of a positive sign for a 'good' outcome and a negative sign for a 'bad' outcome helps to avoid confusion.

A negative risk score indicates that preventive or control action is required, analogous to actions against ranked risk scores for pure risks (see risk evaluation table above). A positive risk score indicates that actions should be taken to ensure that the desired outcome is attained or bettered.

Financial investment risks are frequently assessed by calculating indices such as Net Present Value (NPV) which seeks to compare the return on the proposed investment over a given period (typically the project life) with leaving the same sum in an interest-bearing bank account. A large positive NPV suggests that the investment risk is worthwhile, whereas a large negative NPV suggests that leaving the money in the bank will bring a better return. However, the NPV index alone is rarely used as the sole criterion for decision-making. The NPV approach is used typically to assess project investment risks such as new product development, property investments and major engineering projects. Waring (1989, 1996c) provides an NPV case study. Chicken (1994, 1996) describes risk ranking techniques in detail and with particular application to risks and decisions in major projects, including how financial institutions assess risks of loans and credit in relation to such projects.

## Risk acceptance and risk acceptability

If a particular risk is judged to be unacceptable, then appropriate action is assumed to be required to reduce the risk until it is acceptable. Medium risks are a 'grey' area in which acceptability of the risk needs to be judged in terms of both the practicability and the costs of each option for risk reduction. Under the ALARP (As Low As Reasonably Practicable) principle (HSE 1988, Rimington 1993), as much effort as is reasonably practicable needs to be made to reduce health and safety risks as far as possible towards the low (acceptable) region – see Figure 2.4. Nevertheless, this summary of the evaluation process (whether risk values are based on 'simple' or on 'scientific' methods of risk estimation) masks fundamental ethical, political and empirical problems concerning risk acceptance and risk acceptability (see below).

It is sometimes assumed that the process of risk acceptance necessarily denotes that a particular risk is acceptable. Three issues are especially important. First, a risk may be 'accepted' reluctantly even though the person making the decision does not find the risk acceptable. An obvious example is where other risks force a reluctant 'acceptance', for example risk trade-offs between the warring factions in Bosnia in accepting peace terms. Other examples of such 'revealed preferences' are provided by Glendon and McKenna (1995).

Second, 'expressed preferences' such as those gleaned from surveys are poor indicators of an individual's judgements about risk options because questions frequently force the respondent to make relatively simple judgements which may

*Figure 2.4* The ALARP principle

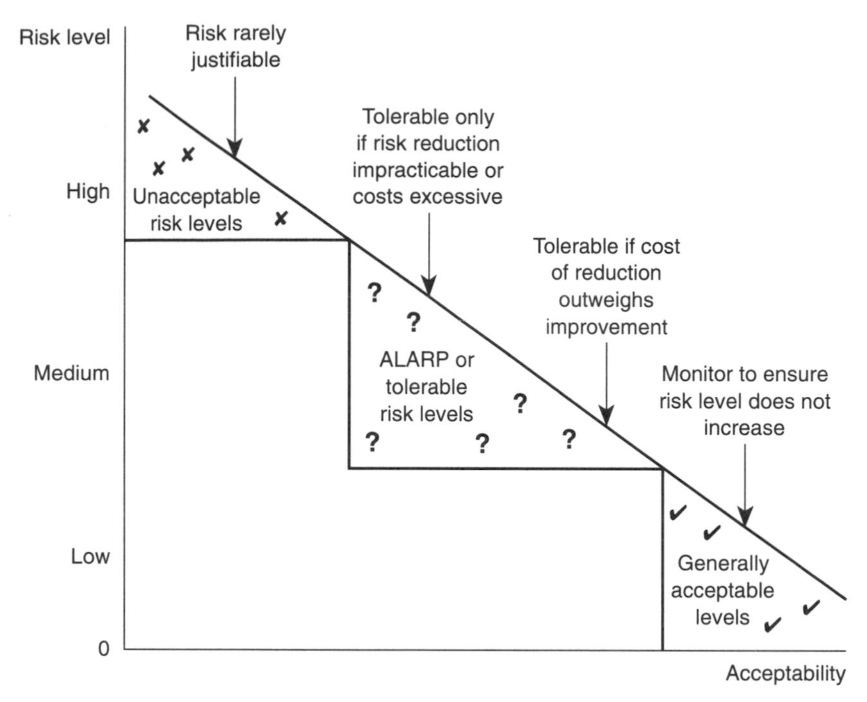


*Source*: based on ideas in HSE (1988)

not reflect his or her true feelings about complex matters or may not relate to the individual's risk exposure. Thus, an aggregation of individual risk preferences into a population or societal measure may be misleading. Such problems undermine concepts such as 'tolerable risk' (Chicken 1996; HSE 1988; Rimington 1993) or 'a risk that society is prepared to live with in order to have certain benefits and in the confidence that the risk is being properly controlled' because it is revealed preference which more accurately reflects tolerability.

Third, those who evaluate risks, who make decisions and accept risks as part of their official remit (whether implicitly or explicitly), frequently are not those who are exposed to the hazards. By their nature, risk assessments and risk decisions cannot be neutral or value-free. It cannot be safely assumed that risk assessors and decision-makers (whether risk expert or not) always take into account the well-being or interests of those exposed to the hazards. The risk perspective of a chemical plant manager who lives miles away from the plant is likely to be quite different from the housewife who lives next door to the factory – and who would be so arrogant as to suggest that somehow her perspective and valuation is any less valid, less significant or less of a priority than those of the factory manager or any number of risk experts? The fact that people may remain resident for years near to a site containing major hazards is not a sound indicator that they consider the risks acceptable. Such residence may simply indicate either habituation to surroundings or a revealed preference of individuals who, because of other risks such as financial constraints, lack of employment elsewhere, or inability to sell their home, feel compelled to remain.

Individual attitudes to risks are multi-dimensional and complex. Individual cognitions ('subjective' risks) may not be congruent either with an 'expert's' view ('objective' risks) or with their own expressions of concern or fear about such risks (Waring 1987, 1996a). Table 2.1 sets out eight possible nodes for the logical combinations of 'objective' risk, 'subjective' risk and expressions of concern. Two particular points emerge from this table. First, what people say about a risk may not match either what they believe or what they do in relation to the risk. Second, although variations among individuals occur, individuals themselves are frequently inconsistent about risks. For example, an individual may avoid eating beef because of BSE risks yet smoke many cigarettes per day or drink too many measures of alcohol before driving. An individual's attitude and behaviour towards a risk may vary over time, even though 'objective' conditions may not have changed – e.g. changes in emotional state, awareness (see chapter 8).

The measurement of risk and the units of measurement used and quoted in support of risk acceptance and acceptability are also not politically neutral or value-free. As Laszlo and Petrakis (1995) note, 'The units selected for presentation are not innocent and can affect the perceived riskiness of technologies. Today's coal mines are much less risky than those of 30 years ago in terms of accidental deaths per ton of coal, but marginally riskier in terms of accidental death per employee'. The process of risk acceptance itself attracts political risks, especially in cases where the public or various interest groups perceive that hazard and risk data and risk criteria quoted by decision-makers are flawed or misleading – e.g. controversy over safety of nuclear power stations.

Risks may be expressed in various ways. Glendon and McKenna (1995) give the following examples of expressions for pure risks concerning health, safety and mortality:

- frequency of deaths per year (absolute numbers);
- fatal accident rate (e.g. rate per 1000 exposed);
- probability of death per annum (e.g. 1 in 1000);
- loss of life expectancy (e.g. in years);
- dreadfulness of outcomes (e.g. injury severities).

*Table 2.1* Examples of the logical combinations of risk and expressed fears

| *Combination* | *Examples* |
|---|---|
| 1. H/H/H | Passengers of an aircraft during a crash dive<br>Someone driving a car in icy of foggy conditions and expressing concern to the passengers |
| 2. H/H/L | Experienced construction operatives working at heights with inadequate safety controls<br>Workers fearing redundancy more than the actual hazards of their work<br>Some cigarette smokers |
| 3. H/L/H | People raising safety issues in order to gain improvements in non-safety matters when in fact the actual risk is higher than they think |
| 4. H/L/L | Perceptual defence, e.g. low impact of gory accident posters<br>Some heavy cigarette smokers<br>Some heavy drinkers of alcohol<br>Habituation, e.g. exposure to high noise levels throughout the working day<br>Expectancy, e.g. development of an unannounced earth fault making the casing of electrical equipment live |
| 5. L/H/H | Complaints about the safety of nuclear power stations in general<br>Complaints about radiation hazards of VDUs<br>Complaints about the safety of high-density asbestos composites with sealed surfaces |
| 6. L/H/L | Workers fearing redundancy more than the perceived hazards of their work |
| 7. L/L/H | People raising safety issues in order to gain improvements in non-safety matters when in fact both the actual risk and the perceived risk are low |
| 8. L/L/L | Risks are adequately controlled and perceived to be controlled<br>Few expressions of concern |

Key: L = low, H = high
Sequence: 'objective' risk/'subjective' risk/expressed fears
*Source*: Waring (1987, 1996a)

Chapter 4 of the Royal Society report (1992) provides a large number of examples of these and other expressions of risk. One difficulty in using such expressions is the generally large numbers involved which may interfere not only with communications about risks but also with decisions about them. Different professional and other interest groups may have significantly different opinions about the relative importance of different risks (see Fischhoff (1975)). The caveats above taken together cast doubt on any statistic which is claimed to represent 'society's' view of a particular risk.

## Major hazards

The recognition that there are hazards which, because of their scale, pose special dangers to the health and safety of people has arisen relatively recently. The concept of 'major hazards' only became coherent and widely recognised during the 1970s, largely owing to a series of industrial disasters such as the cyclohexane explosion at the Nypro caprolactam plant at Flixborough in June 1974 (Parker 1975) and the massive release of dioxin from the Hoffmann la Roche plant at Seveso, Italy in 1976. Subsequent disasters such as Bhopal and Piper Alpha have reinforced the need for special attention to such hazards. The characteristics of major hazards are:

- large scale technology or technical activities;
- large scale storage or use of high energy sources and/or toxic materials;
- potentially large numbers of people 'at risk';
- special implications for hazard management, risk assessment and risk control concerning normal, abnormal and emergency conditions.

The main kinds of site or installation at which major hazards are likely to arise are:

- nuclear installations;
- chemical process factories handling large quantities of highly flammable and/or toxic materials;
- offshore oil and gas installations, oil refineries and petrochemical plants;
- water treatment plants using bulk chlorine;
- bulk storage of highly flammable materials.

In the light of major accidents in the railway industry such as King's Cross (see Fennell 1988) and Clapham (see Hidden 1989), the concept of major hazards has now been extended to incorporate railway activities, at least as far as UK legislation is concerned. Marine disasters such as the Herald of Free Enterprise and others have broadened the scope to include all forms of transport. Although the level of technical complexity and its scale are arguably less for transport hazards than those for the industrial activities cited above, large numbers of people could be injured or killed in a single credible transport accident. Major hazards are also now considered to include major environmental hazards, discussed in the next section.

Approaches to risk assessment of major hazards focus on Quantified Risk Assessment (QRA) (see for example Torhaug 1992) and the ALARP principle – i.e. that risk levels should be demonstrated to be As Low As Reasonably Practicable (HSE 1988; Rimington 1993). The ALARP principle is summarized in Figure 2.4.

As much effort as is reasonably practicable should be made so as to reduce risk levels as far as possible down the slope. The lower right region in Figure 2.4 represents an acceptable level of risk which demands no further action to improve the risk, whereas the upper left region represents an unacceptable level of risk which demands action. In between is a 'tolerable' region with risk tolerability decreasing towards the unacceptable region and demanding action commensurate with the risk.

With major hazards, hazard identification typically begins with credible event or failure scenarios, for example a major fire, explosion or toxic release at a petrochemical plant or a high-speed collision or derailment of a passenger train. Various techniques such as fault tree analysis, event tree analysis, FMEA (failure modes and effects analysis), HAZOPS (hazard and operability studies) and MORT (management oversight and risk tree) may be used to analyse the particular hazard. Quantitative results from the analysis are then used to carry out consequence modelling in which hazard-consequence behaviour is reduced to a relatively simple cause and effect relationship. For example, for a chlorine release the consequence model typically used is that for chlorine dispersion, which is based on input of data for variables such as hole size in the chlorine container, volume of container, leak rate, ambient temperature and wind speed. Dose-effect and population density data can then be used to estimate numbers affected and probable effects on humans at various radii from the release point.

Various expressions of risk are used in QRA as summarized in the Royal Society report (1992), HSE (1988, 1995a) and Laszlo and Petrakis (1995). Common risk expressions include:

- mortality rates (fraction of the population at risk which suffer death per unit time);
- activity mortality rates (number of deaths per unit measure of activity);
- loss of life expectancy due to specified hazard exposure;
- FN curves (cumulative frequency of fatalities versus number of fatalities);
- risk-cost benefit analysis (costs of avoidance of specified number of deaths per year).

It is clear that there are justifiable uses of QRA as a support for decision-making about major hazards. For example, in conjunction with ALARP and acceptance criteria, QRA provides a way of determining whether the hazards and associated risks from a particular operation, activity, process or installation as presently controlled are acceptable to 'technical risk experts'. QRA provides a design basis for risk improvement on the ALARP principle and is a cornerstone of 'safety case' legislation such as for offshore installations, nuclear installations and railways, and 'safety report' legislation such as that resulting from the EC Seveso Directive (CIMAH in the UK) and the forthcoming EU COMAH Directive. See chapters 10 and 12 for case examples.

Nevertheless, important as QRA undoubtedly is, its unbridled use without due consideration of its weaknesses must be challenged. Caveats raised by the Royal Society report (1992), Douglas (1992), Laszlo and Petrakis (1995), Toft (1993, 1996) and Waring (1994, 1996a) concern both issues of technique and of interpretation. Because of its essentially judgemental nature, risk assessment cannot be neutral or value-free, whoever carries it out and however impartial they seek to be. Unfortunately, the dominant position of QRA and the technical risk analysts required to carry it out leaves such experts in the dangerous position of potentially propagating the myth that the risk associated with a particular hazard is what risk experts say it is!

Moreover, technical risk experts are often in a position of recommending, or even making, decisions based on QRA which they have carried out or contributed to. The inherent biases in QRA technique and assumptions, fuelled by the training, work and culture of *technical* risk analysts, do not admit that there are other equally valid 'voices' which need to be heard (Douglas 1992). A common conclusion of major hazard inquiries such as Kings Cross (Fennell 1988), Piper Alpha (Cullen 1990) and Clapham (Hidden 1989) was that each particular organization's culture and management systems played a large part in determining the overall level of risk. Therefore, major hazard risk assessment should include appropriate input from those suitably qualified in management and social sciences, who should be able to contribute a more holistic and detailed view of organizational behaviour, in contrast with the narrow and unsatisfactory 'programmable robots' view of 'human factors' prevalent among some technical risk analysts. See also chapters 3, 4, 5 and 7.

Also difficult for QRA are the observations of Toft (1996) that, since any set of accident causes and routes can result in an infinite number of accident outcomes, the credible event scenarios of QRA are inadequate. This 'equifinality' principle of systems concepts (see for example Morgan 1986) means that it is never possible to identify all the possibilities or to predict those which are most likely. Moreover,

QRA, which claims to identify 'all possible failure cases' (see for example Hazards Forum 1992), may create a false sense of safety.

## Environmental risks

Environmental hazards may be categorized as:

- water contamination;
- soil contamination;
- air contamination;
- inappropriate land use;
- inappropriate activities

any of which may cause harm or detriment to humans and/or other natural systems by way of physical damage, health effects, economic damage, social damage, loss of amenity or undesirable ecological changes.

Typically, in seeking to identify environmental hazards and their effects (actual or potential), consideration will be given to:

- controlled and uncontrolled emissions to atmosphere;
- controlled and uncontrolled discharges to water;
- waste management;
- contamination of land;
- use of land, water, fuels, energy, and other natural resources;
- noise, odour, dust, vibration and visual impact;
- effects on specific aspects of a particular environment.

A 'life-cycle' view is often taken, such that environmental hazards are assessed in relation to:

- past, current, planned and potential activities;
- normal operating conditions;
- abnormal operating conditions;
- incidents, accidents and emergencies.

The oil pollution along the coast of Alaska caused by the Exxon Valdez spillage in 1989 is one of the more spectacular examples of an environmental hazard realized. Moreover, cases such as the Exxon Valdez in 1989, the Braer spillage in the Shetlands in 1993 and the Sea Empress at Milford Haven in 1996, highlight the knock-on financial and political risks associated with environmental risks. Governments have been forced to react to a growing number of environmental pollution cases by introducing stringent legislation. Many medium and large manufacturers now have to spend considerable sums of money on ensuring that their environmental control measures are adequate and meet regulatory requirements. As one example, water pollution and the quality of drinking and coastal bathing waters have become big political issues in the UK, and have become entangled with other political controversies surrounding privatization of the water industry, water shortages, increased consumer costs and increases in the remuneration of senior water company executives. Although some of these kinds of risk were foreseen (see for example Meredith 1992), by no means all were. By 1995, as a result of media attention, water companies in the UK had become synonymous in the public's eye with the 'unacceptable face of capitalism', a phrase coined some 20 or more years earlier by the then Prime Minister, Mr Edward Heath.

Shell was embarrassed internationally by two cases in 1995 involving environmental issues, one concerning the decommissioning of its Brent Spar offshore oil installation in the North Sea (see for example Hunt 1995) and the other concerning its oil extraction activities in the Ogoni region of Nigeria (which then became entangled in other issues about Shell's relationship with the Nigerian government and state repression). The objective 'rights' and 'wrongs' of disputes and controversies surrounding risk issues are of little value in determining the financial and political effects on large corporations and governments. Mostly, they will come off badly and be forced into defensive positions because the public are sceptical of big business and politicians and are more willing to believe environmental pressure groups (even when they get things wrong).

Although risk assessment is implicit to some degree in any assessment of environmental hazards and their effects, the term 'risk' is used infrequently in this context. The emphasis is far more on effects (i.e. direct consequences of environmental hazards) than on probabilities. Environmental impact assessments typically include sampling of air, water and soil and a range of physical, chemical and biological analyses together with observations by 'experts' at relevant impact locations and other information. A commonly used principle in environmental risk assessment and control is BATNEEC (Best Available Techniques Not Entailing Excessive Cost). In essence, BATNEEC is similar to the ALARP principle used in major hazards risk assessment. Another principle of environmental control is BPEO (Best Practicable Environmental Option).

## Security risks

Security risks concern the hazards of criminal activity against any or all of:

- persons;
- property;
- organizations;
- the state.

Security hazards which organizations might have to contend with include:

- Theft of goods, stock, money, credit cards, vehicles, etc.
- Theft of intellectual property (designs, patented ideas etc.), including copyright material (publications, computer software, videos, etc.).
- Theft of commercially valuable information (confidential files, memoranda of board decisions, tenders, bids, positions, etc whether original documents, photocopies, or disks or via computer hacking or electronic bugging).
- Illicit use of commercially valuable information (insider share dealing, rogue trading (e.g. Barings – see chapter 11), conspiracy to fix prices, etc.).
- Fraud (obtaining money, goods, services or other financial advantage by deception, including insurance fraud).
- Blackmail, extortion, protection rackets, kidnapping and other forms of terrorism for personal financial gain, e.g. poisoning foodstuffs in supermarkets.
- Piracy (attacks on ships or aircraft for personal financial gain).
- Political terrorism (any of the above may be employed by political terrorists as means to their ends; also armed assault and/or bombing of individuals, premises, installations, etc.).

Security risk assessment tends to be an art-and-judgement approach based on analysis of hazards and threats and actual experience of criminal activity. Assessment typically focusses on the following:

- **Opportunities** and the adequacy of current measures to deny criminals or opportunists access to valuable assets.
- **Criminal methods** and the adequacy of current counter-measures.
- **Criminal motivations** and the adequacy of current measures to deny criminals intelligence about potential targets.
- **Intelligence** and the adequacy of current information systems about criminal activity.

## Financial and investment risks

In the financial sector, risk is generally associated with decision-making about such topics as investments, credit and buying and selling shares. Increasingly, however, financial risk is being viewed on a broader basis as not simply the risk of the decisions themselves in any organization but also risks associated with the whole organizational structures, processes, management procedures, human resources and culture which affect decision-making processes.

In a special edition of *Business Week* (31 October 1994) which focused on managing risk, the lead article (Barrett and Zweig 1994) noted that 'Internal auditors, once regarded as moles who ferreted out waste and fraud, are enjoying expanded roles as monitors of such 'soft' items as ethical standards, which, if violated, can increase a company's vulnerability. Risk managers are also scrutinising compensation structures to make sure they do not reward behavior which allows employees to boost their short-term results while jeopardising their firm's long-term reputation'. Within four months of this article, the Baring's Bank scandal involving just such behaviour was revealed, which led to the collapse of the bank (see chapter 11).

Whereas a 'risk management' approach to financial risk is becoming more prominent, the efficacy of risk assessment methods used is less certain. Compared with major hazards and safety risks, for example, formal risk assessment within financial institutions appears to be very much an art-and-judgement approach based on audit results (see for example the Cadbury Report 1992 and the associated Code of Best Practice for the Financial Aspects of Corporate Governance). Although formal risk assessments would be necessary in order to comply with much of the Code, they are not mentioned either directly or obliquely in the Report or Code and there is no guidance on methodology or technique. Reference is made to a board's duty to maintain 'risk management policies' but there is no amplification on what such a policy should contain or how practically it would have to be implemented through a risk assessment-risk control logic. Similarly, methods for managing fraud risks (see for example Huntingdon and Davies 1994) emphasize threat identification and threat control measures and are thin on risk assessment. Even the special edition of *Business Week* referred to above, which was devoted to risk management, contained no indication of a formal risk assessment methodology. In short, in contrast to the increasingly extensive regulatory framework for industrial safety risks, the financial sector in most countries has no comparable history of legislation or development of broadly agreed methodology for formal risk assessment of fraud and corruption. This apparent weakness also contrasts with established methodology used by financial institutions in assessing risks of loan and investment applications, described in Chicken (1994, 1996).

As noted in previous sections of this chapter, financial risks are interdependent with other risks such as pure risks (safety, environment, security, etc.) and other speculative risks such as political risks. For example, a significant dip in turnover or loss of profits may deter expenditure on control of pure risks which in turn may increase those risks. Conversely, failure to reduce or control pure risks adequately may increase financial risks both for the organization and for other organizations (see Lovegrove (1990) on the knock-on effects to other oil and gas companies of Occidental's Piper Alpha disaster).

Another example of security risks affecting finance is provided by 'shrinkage' or employee theft. Retail organizations such as supermarkets typically experience annual losses of one per cent of stock turnover through shrinkage. Such losses can be significant for profitability, especially if margins are slim.

Uncontrolled safety risks may also affect financial positions. According to HSE (1993), BP's own estimate for the costs of its refinery fire at Grangemouth in 1987 (see HSE 1989) was £50m in property damage and a further £50m in business interruption costs. In the same report of accident costing studies, HSE stated that accidents (mainly many small ones rather than major ones) cost one organization as much as 37 per cent of its annualized profits, another the equivalent of 8.5 per cent of tender price, and a third organization five per cent of its running costs. Most of these costs are not recoverable. A case study of the interaction between safety and financial risks in the UK Pumped Storage Business of an electricity generating company is presented in Glendon, O'Loughlin and Booth (1998).

## Political risks

Political risks relate to the hazards of decisions, actions and membership of or association with a particular interest group. Political risks are speculative as they relate to the probability of attracting the support, or the indifference or the wrath of other interested parties as a result of how the latter perceive those decisions or actions or the group itself. Political risks are thus inextricably bound up with effects on political processes and power relations between different parties (see chapter 5).

Different levels of political risk may be involved. For many purposes, it is useful to separate the political risks of life within a particular organization (see chapter 5) from the wider political risks for the organization as a whole which relate to its outer context and its relationships with national and local governments, pressure groups, competitors, etc.

Powerful parties in an organization are likely to have a considerable impact on both external relations and political processes and power relations within the organization. The political hazards which they may create, exacerbate or reduce include employee dissatisfaction, inter-departmental wars, and disputes with trades unions, all of which can have knock-on effects such as high staff turnover, stress, low morale, absenteeism, poor product quality and poor overall performance. Periods of major reorganization and job losses are particularly hazardous in these respects. The period of stewardship of Bob Horton at BP in the early 1990s may be cited as one example. Another is the period of rule of a Vice-Chancellor at Aston University (see Glendon 1992).

Public perceptions of the attitudes, policies and actions of an organization or an industry or a government in relation to particular political issues are likely to affect investments, consumer confidence, consumer purchasing and voting intentions. Voters include not only the public who elect political representatives but also shareholders in company elections. For example, at the 1995 annual general meeting of British Gas shareholders, a significant number of small shareholders and institutions were reported to have subjected the Chief Executive to several hours of humiliating and, at times savage, criticism concerning his high remuneration in relation to consumer dissatisfaction, staff cuts and low staff pay awards. The government was then inevitably drawn into the furore on the defensive since it had privatized the gas industry. Such shareholder reaction is unusual but, in the context of wide public disquiet about perceived vast salaries and other rewards (e.g. share options) of senior executives in the privatized former public utilities, it may be seen as a warning of the political risks faced by such executives and politicians if they fail to act wisely in such matters.

Table 2.2 outlines examples of various political issues which have arisen in recent years and some of the risks attached to them for different parties.

Assessment of political risks is a prime concern of politicians, political commentators and political journalists. As with other speculative risks, political risk assessment is frequently an art-and-judgement technique seeking to speculate about possible and likely turns of events as contexts develop, relative trade-offs of risks and benefits, and the most judicious combinations of timing and actions. However, many large organizations, especially those engaged in investment or trade abroad, also undertake more formal assessment of political risks that are associated with their activities. For example, the political stability of the new Russia, CIS states and Central Asian Republics is a major concern for foreign investors and suppliers, as are security and financial risks which accompany

*Table 2.2* Examples of UK political issues and different risks to different individuals or groups

| *Political topic* | *Salient issues and events* | *Parties at risk* | *Risk type* |
|---|---|---|---|
| NHS reforms (1990s) | Adequacy of health care.<br>Morality of better care according to ability to pay.<br>Realism of health care performance measurements.<br>Budget holding and clinical decisions (see chapter 15). | Health Ministers and government<br>Directors of Health Authorities and Trusts.<br>Patients<br>NHS staff | P<br>P, F, B<br>H, Q<br>Em |
| Prison reforms (1995–) | Privatization of prison services.<br>Professionalism, training and integrity of private services.<br>Operational independence of Prison Service from Home Secretary. | Home Secretary and the government<br>Private security companies and prison operators<br>Prison governors and staff<br>Prisoners | P<br>P, B, F, Em<br>P, I, F, Em<br>HR |
| Contraceptive pills (1995) | Public panic caused by Dept of Health advice to cease using certain types.<br>Whose information and advice is to be believed? | Health Ministers and the government<br>Women of child-bearing age | P<br>H |
| Stiffer criminal sentencing (1995–) | Do stiffer prison terms deter criminal behaviour?<br>Who should decide sentences, judges or the Home Secretary?<br>Separation of the judiciary from the executive as a cornerstone of democracies. Law Lords accuse Home Secretary of 'despotic' behaviour and 'playing politics'. | Home Secretary and the government<br>Judges<br>The citizen<br>Prisoners<br>Prison staff | P<br>P, I<br>S<br>HR<br>P, S |
| State lottery (1995–) | Scale of prizes and bad effects on attitudes to effort-reward.<br>Distortion to the economy.<br>Encouraging low income groups to overspend.<br>Relative allocation of funds to charities and the arts. | Heritage Secretary and the government<br>Charities<br>Arts groups<br>The poor | P<br>P, F<br>P, F<br>F |
| Brent Spar decommission (1995–6) | Dispute over method of decommissioning and environmental effects.<br>Dispute over hazardous materials inventory.<br>Greenpeace takeover Brent Spar and force Shell into embarrassing response and climbdown. | Shell<br>Greenpeace<br>UK government<br>Marine life | P, F<br>P<br>P<br>E |

| | | | |
|---|---|---|---|
| Export of live animals (1994–) | Adequacy of humane methods and conditions for transport of live farm animals during export. How much latitude should be given to animal rights protestors when the rights of others are infringed? Costs of policing at ports besieged by protestors. | Agriculture Ministers and the government | P |
| | | Animal rights campaigners | P, S |
| | | Local authorities | P, F |
| | | Port operators | P, F, S |
| | | Livestock transporters | P, B, F, S |
| | | The police | P, F, S |
| Actions/attitudes of privatized utilities (Gas, Water, Power) (1990s) | Self-discipline of senior executives in relation to their own pay and perks. Ensuring proper balance between shareholder, customer and employee interests. | Chief and senior executives of utilities | F, P |
| | | Industry Ministers and the government | P |
| | | Customers | F, Q |
| | | Shareholdres | F, P |
| | | Employees | P, F, Em |
| BSE in meat (1995–) | Deaths from CJD attributed to BSE infected beef products eaten before 1989. Relevance of culling herds now. | UK and EU governments | P |
| | | Public | H |
| | | Farmers | P, B, F, Em |
| | Has EU over-reacted against British beef? | Cattle transporters | P, B, F, Em |
| | Does public understand issues? | Meat retailers | P, B, F, Em |

Code: B = business, E = environmental, Em = employment, F = financial, H = health, HR = human rights, I = independence, P = political, Q = quality, S = safety

political difficulties or instability. The case study in chapter 13 is especially relevant – see also chapters 5, 6, 7, 14 and 15.

## Conclusions

Because risk is a multi-dimensional concept, different approaches to risk assessment are required to cover the varieties of risk and their contexts. All share an essential common purpose, which is to estimate or assess a particular risk or set of risks on the basis of the best available information – which by its nature is always imperfect.

Risk assessment techniques can be objective to the extent that they use validated methodologies in a consistent way. However, the process of risk assessment is subjective because the decision about which particular methodology to employ is made on the basis of judgement, even if this is expert judgement. Similarly, most individual decisions about probabilities, projected outcomes and other components of risk assessment, while they may be based on best available evidence, are also judgemental.

Risk assessment methodologies have been developed as a means of dealing with uncertainty in a variety of situations. Basic human motivations of predicting and controlling our surroundings and other external factors, mediated by managerial and organizational imperatives for effectiveness and survival, have combined to produce formal risk assessment methodologies. The latter extend *ad hoc* cognitive processes, which define assessments of the many and varied risks confronting most individuals more or less constantly.

Risk assessment techniques are a valuable aid to decision-making, in this case on the acceptability or tolerability of a particular risk or risks, and on the desirability and nature of actions to help in managing risk. However, the broader (e.g. financial, cultural, political) context of decision-making needs to be acknowledged (as discussed, for example, in chapters 4 and 5). Therefore, whereas 'acceptability' may be defined in terms of a risk assessment model, such as ALARP, ultimately this term is problematic because it represents the outcome of a political decision-making process in which parties' interests inevitably conflict.

Risk assessment becomes overtly political when judgements are made by one or more parties (e.g. government, large organizations) in respect of one or more other parties such as individual citizens, population sub-groups or employee groups. The parties affected by the decision may have a direct voice in the decision-making process, as in the case of relatively powerful pressure groups such as trades unions with sufficient resources to make representations in relevant fora. It is more likely, however, that any influence by those most affected by the outcomes of risk decisions will be indirect and diffuse – for example via the media, letters, protest marches, consumer action and casting of votes in public elections.

Whereas the basic principles of risk assessment are common, and may be extended to any risk topic, a variety of risk assessment techniques may be used. These range from relatively 'simple' approaches, based upon judgements of people with knowledge about a situation on key risk components such as exposure and likelihood, to more complex quantified techniques. Thus, risk assessment techniques may be used to assess both pure risks (e.g. those associated with various forms of pollution of the physical environment) and speculative risks (e.g. those associated with financial investment and political decisions).

Although pure risks may be assessed on a uni-dimensional scale, speculative risks require two separate assessments – respectively for potentially 'good' and 'bad' outcomes for a particular party. For speculative risk assessments, the judgemental nature of the risk assessment process is likely to be even more evident than is the case for pure risks. The final judgement is made partly on the basis of a comparison of the two risk outcomes. In the case of major hazards viewed as pure risks, more complex quantified approaches to risk assessment are required. Whatever type of risk assessment is undertaken, the basis is knowledge and therefore the assessment (whether by 'expert' or 'non-expert') cannot be unbiased or value-free.

# Chapter 3
# Management systems and risk

## Overview

There is a variety of meanings of the term 'management system' but typically these relate to means by which pure and/or speculative risks may be controlled to some degree, directly or indirectly. This chapter describes underlying systems concepts and different ideas about management systems and discusses not only their potential benefits to understanding risk and change but also risks which are attendant upon management systems.

## Introduction

In official reports into disasters ranging from the Kings Cross fire (Fennell 1988), Piper Alpha offshore fire and explosion (Cullen 1990) and Clapham railway accident (Hidden 1989) to the collapse of Barings Bank (Board of Banking Supervision 1995; San & Kuang 1995), failures in management systems were cited as playing a significant role in the development of conditions leading to disaster. Development of adequate management systems has become a commonplace activity in many organizations as a response to such reports and related influences. It is perhaps therefore not surprising that with such a focus on 'management systems', there is a wide range of meanings for and approaches to the subject. Equally unsurprising is the weak theoretical basis of much practical 'management systems' thinking (Waring 1996a and 1996c). As Kennedy (1995) notes in relation to safety management systems, for best effect, approaches to management systems should be based on 'first principles' rather than blind acceptance of some stated dogma or orthodoxy (see also Vickers 1983).

This chapter addresses the subject of management systems and risk on the basis of fundamental systems concepts developed and tested through a long theoretical and empirical tradition. The validity and value of more recent normative approaches to management systems relating to health and safety, quality and environment (such as advocated by national and international standards organizations) are discussed in relation to fundamental system concepts.

## System concepts

Both the study and use of system ideas are hampered by a wide variety of meanings for the term 'system' both within and between different disciplines and professions. To varying degrees, different understandings of the term 'system' share a common theme, namely that of a whole consisting of components which are interconnected in an organized way. Some common examples are:

- a systematic method or procedure;
- characteristics of an organization, as in 'the system';
- particular arrangements of computer and information technology;
- a systematic framework of specific practical activities.

By regarding systems in such terms, there is a tendency to think of the particular system of interest as an objective entity which exists in the real world. However, such functionalist tendencies ignore the fact that *per se* 'system' is a *perceptual* construct and not a normative uncontestable truth. The normative stance of a functionalist approach to systems (e.g. quality management systems, integrated management systems, information technology systems) is itself risk-laden and explains why it often fails to deliver claimed outcomes.

Systems thinking is a way of examining the 'real' world for the purposes of understanding and/or improving aspects of it. The notion of a system is closely tied to an individual's world-view or characteristic way of seeing the world (see the subsection below on system ownership). A system is therefore a metaphor for a wide range of topics which may be labelled and described equally well and often more accurately by other terminology. Systems thinking and practice carry with them a set of assumptions which can affect outcomes. Since meaning and action are dialectically linked (Denzin 1978; Johnson 1987; Waring 1993, 1996c), different meanings attached to particular terms such as 'system' are likely to result in correspondingly different actions and outcomes. Naïve formulaic approaches to systems work are accompanied by a danger of unwarranted faith in the products of that work, and in communication failures with other interested persons. One way of avoiding reification (regarding a concept as being a real-world object) is to refer to 'perceived system' or 'notional system' rather than using the term 'system' in an unqualified way. The following sub-sections summarize the key elements of systemic or holistic thinking as it is understood in the systems tradition.

## *System characteristics*

Although there is no universally agreed definition of 'system', there are a number of defining characteristics (see for example Carter *et al.* 1984; Checkland 1981; Checkland and Scholes 1990; Morgan 1986; Open University 1984, 1993; Vickers 1983; Waring 1989, 1996a and 1996c). As a concept, a system is a recognizable whole which consists of a number of components or elements which are interconnected in an organized way. Interactions between components signify processes and system outputs. Further characteristics are:

- Components are perceived to be interrelated in hierarchical structures.
- Addition or removal of a component changes the system and its characteristics.
- A component is affected by its inclusion in the system.
- Means for control and communication which promote system survival are identifiable.
- The system has emergent properties, some of which are difficult to predict.
- The system has a boundary.
- A 'system environment' which affects the system exists outside the system boundary.
- Someone 'owns' or has an overriding interest in the system for the purposes of understanding and/or improving aspects of the real world.

Typically, the majority of these system characteristics are not recognised by many people in their perceived systems. The connection between such a narrow view and the adverse consequences of that view also goes unrecognised. For example, a view of management systems as being only control processes or systematic procedures is most inadequate since, at best, it only addresses efficiency and is very unreliable regarding effectiveness or success. There are obvious risk implications from this, since a management system whose model and design are naive is unlikely to be able to achieve what its owners claim and its beneficiaries expect. Both pure and speculative risks may be adversely affected as a result (see the sections on management systems and standards for management systems).

## *System categories*

A number of categories of perceived system are in common use (Checkland 1981), for example:

- natural systems (e.g. oceans, pathogens, forests);
- abstract systems (e.g. computer languages, signing systems);
- engineered or designed technical systems (e.g. chemical process plant, computer systems, aircraft, information systems);
- human activity systems (e.g. relating to work organizations – could include social systems and political systems);
- social systems (e.g. families, institutions, towns, societies);
- political systems (e.g. government, international diplomacy, corporate management).

Although there may be widespread agreement about which category a particular perceived system belongs to, categorisation is not pre-ordained and categories are not mutually exclusive. For example, how a particular system is perceived will influence how it is categorized. World-view and purpose are therefore highly relevant (see sub-section on world-view later in this chapter).

## *Structures and processes*

Two kinds of system component are usually recognised – structural and process components – which are interrelated. The structure of a perceived system comprises relatively stable and perseverant components which either carry out processes or are acted upon by processes. For example, in an organization perceived as a system, structural components might include functions such as finance, marketing, production and so on. Processes include action, change, growth, decline, influence, etc.

The dialectical link between structure and processes is inextricable. Without structure, there can be no processes and without processes the structure cannot be sustained or changed. Moreover, the character of system processes is heavily influenced by the character of the system structure. Where human activity systems are concerned, the system structure necessarily is *both* a product of functional requirements and of complex human factors such as power and culture (see later in this chapter and chapters 4 and 5) *and* a creator and sustainer of them. This essential mutuality is not admitted in what have now become conventional approaches to 'management systems', especially for safety, quality and environment (see sections below on management systems and standards for management

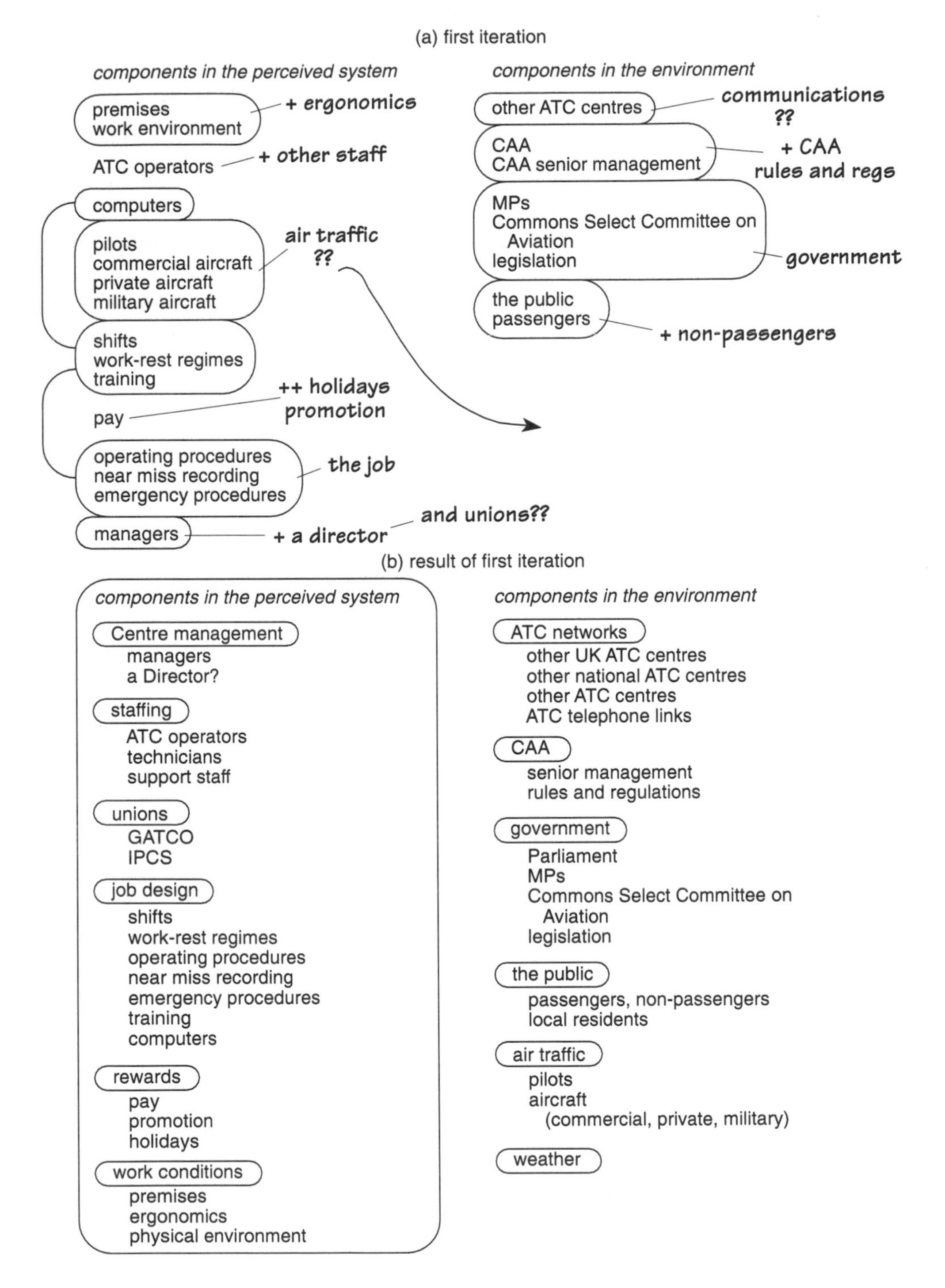
(a) first iteration
components in the perceived system
premises
work environment
+ ergonomics
ATC operators
+ other staff
computers
pilots
commercial aircraft
private aircraft
military aircraft
air traffic
??
shifts
work-rest regimes
training
++ holidays
promotion
pay
operating procedures
near miss recording
emergency procedures
the job
managers
+ a director
and unions??
components in the environment
other ATC centres
communications
??
CAA
CAA senior management
+ CAA
rules and regs
MPs
Commons Select Committee on
Aviation
legislation
government
the public
passengers
+ non-passengers
(b) result of first iteration
components in the perceived system
Centre management
managers
a Director?
staffing
ATC operators
technicians
support staff
unions
GATCO
IPCS
job design
shifts
work-rest regimes
operating procedures
near miss recording
emergency procedures
training
computers
rewards
pay
promotion
holidays
work conditions
premises
ergonomics
physical environment
components in the environment
ATC networks
other UK ATC centres
other national ATC centres
other ATC centres
ATC telephone links
CAA
senior management
rules and regulations
government
Parliament
MPs
Commons Select Committee on
Aviation
legislation
the public
passengers, non-passengers
local residents
air traffic
pilots
aircraft
(commercial, private, military)
weather

*Figure 3.1* (opposite) Iterative adjustment of component resolution of the notional CAA system for operating the air traffic control centre at West Drayton
*Source*: Waring (1989, 1996c)

---

systems), in which only an ill-defined 'management process' is recognised whose normative truth and adequacy are, apparently, obvious and uncontestable. The very naïveté of such 'management process' models used in isolation, therefore, brings increased risks of failures resulting from their application.

## *Hierarchy and resolution*

Focus, resolution and hierarchy concern the level of detail of system structure which is considered appropriate to a particular purpose. When a system boundary is set and boundaries of sub-systems identified, this is part of an organizing process of mentally 'bracketing off' components, putting closely connected components together (i.e. 'like with like') and seeking to ensure that identified components are at the appropriate level of detail or resolution. Typically, conceptual and other representational diagrams of systems are constructed and developed iteratively in order to clarify focus, resolution and hierarchy. The number of components contained within one system diagram should be limited to 7+/−2 (i.e. a minimum of five and a maximum of nine) for ease of comprehension (Miller 1956; Turner 1988). In practice, levels of resolution are adjusted up and down during systems work according to purpose and applying the 7+/−2 rule, as shown in the example in Figure 3.1.

Organizations may be viewed as systems and one assumption is that a relationship exists between their size and structural complexity on the one hand and operational efficiency and effectiveness on the other. Many people believe that making organizational hierarchies smaller and simpler makes an organization more efficient and effective. The late 1980s and early 1990s saw a vogue for smaller, leaner, flatter organizational structures having looser hierarchical reporting relationships. Many large organizations deliberately cut out most of their middle managers and reduced numbers of junior managers and supervisors on the premise that it should be possible to run a more cost-efficient and effective organization that way – a very attractive proposition in permanently competitive world markets and harsh economic climates. Although some successes have been claimed for business re-engineering (see for example, Talwar 1993), it has not proven to be either a prophylactic or a panacea for all organizational ills (see for example, Caulkin 1995; Davies 1993; Kennedy 1994). Indeed, in the UK at the end of its 1990–1995 recession, when manufacturing demand for exports increased sharply, some companies that had divested themselves of many functional managers experienced great difficulties in coping with the consequences of new expansion in operations and workforce without enough managers. Hiring of replacement managers became necessary. Nevertheless, whatever the shape of a particular organization and even if many aspects of management hierarchies are dismantled, there will always be discernible hierarchies in system terms.

## *System environment*

In everyday speech, the term 'environment' signifies the surroundings of an entity of interest. Such an environment may relate to one or more of the physical, social, political, economic or cultural environments. In systems terminology, 'system environment' may also include such topics but has a more particular meaning, namely components outside the system which affect it and which the system is unable to control directly and is unlikely to be able to affect to any significant extent. For example, the environment of an organization viewed as a system might include public policy, legislation, taxation, the economy, product markets, technology, operating terrain, etc. – as discussed in chapter 6. An organization's attempts to control and influence such matters through, for example, industry associations, public relations and lobbying may be successful to a degree but their effect will always be limited.

In conventional systems thinking a system boundary must be set, and so the concept of environment is important as it determines where the particular analyst or system viewer sets the boundary between components inside the perceived system and components outside it. Obviously, different boundaries will have different implications for system outcomes as will different perceptions of topics to be considered in the environment.

A further problem of meanings arises from the widespread use of the term 'environment' to mean the surroundings of people, whether at a local level or at more global levels, and the wise use of resources and technical processes to avoid damage to that environment. For example, protection of the environment might include such activities as purchasing goods whose manufacture seeks to reduce adverse effects on limited natural resources, altering factory processes to limit pollution, controlling waste and managing its disposal so as to avoid contamination of land and water. It is usual for 'environment' in this sense to be seen as a resource affected by 'processes' and unusual for it to be seen in systemic terms as described here. The wide variation in meanings of 'environment' is becoming problematic, as are different meanings of 'system'.

In order to avoid confusion over the use of the term 'environment', at least so far as organizations viewed as systems and management systems are concerned, an alternative term 'outer context' is advocated to substitute for 'system environment' and 'inner context' refers to the internal environment such as culture, power relations, motivations, etc. as discussed in chapters 4, 5 and 6.

## *Prediction and control*

Prediction and control are closely linked desirable attributes of systems. These attributes relate to a perceived system's ability to avoid dysfunction and to survive adverse conditions. Prediction and control therefore rely on certain assumptions and in particular that desired goals, objectives and criteria are identifiable and that monitoring and control functions are appropriate. Data based on control experience or analogy enable prediction of the particular perceived system's behaviour. Necessary conditions for control include:

- The process to be controlled must be understood.
- Inputs and outputs must be capable of being monitored reliably and at a suitable frequency, using appropriate means of measurement.
- There must be an adequate communication link between monitor and controller.
- Reference standards, goals and other performance criteria must be compatible with outputs being monitored.
- Time delays between monitoring, control action and control effect should be within tolerable limits.
- There should be no overshoot in terms of control effect.

Nevertheless, the more complex the perceived system and the factors which influence it, the less likely that control will be reliable and that predictions will always be accurate. Recognition of this caveat is especially important when considering management systems, organizations and other aspects of human activity which are inherently complex (Toft 1996). Many risks may be increased unnecessarily as a result of naïve simplification of complex issues relating to management systems. System promulgators often convince themselves and others that a systematic model and control procedures are sufficient in themselves to control all pertinent risks. As a result, only the parameters of the particular reduced model may be addressed and the need for additional vigilance may not be recognised. It must be stressed that the scope of control and process characteristics in human activity systems are qualitatively different from those in other kinds of system (e.g. engineered or designed technical system) which do not rely on variable, fallible, wilful and unpredictable human beings.

## *Emergence and holism*

A simple 'process control' view of systems is based on a cause-effect model whereby the outcomes (effects) are both predictable and controllable by close attention to system inputs and process (see above). In other words, with such a simple view, for a given system one should expect only the system outputs which are readily predictable from the system components, inputs, process and control characteristics. However, the very interactions which characterize a system also produce a synergy and emergent behaviour which could not readily be predicted merely from consideration of its disconnected components. For example, despite a general improvement in the UK economy and a return of the so-called 'feel good' factor in public perceptions of the economy in the second half of 1995, this did not readily translate into a corresponding willingness to vote for the incumbent government in the General Election of 1997. Effects on voting intentions as an emergent property of the national economic system are not predictable by sole reference to government policy and economic indicators. Vickers (1983, 1985) provides further examples.

A holistic view of systems is one which seeks to consider the widest set of components, systemic interactions, influences and emergent properties which may be relevant to a particular perceived system. Holism does not imply consideration of every possible aspect of the particular whole but a consideration of the essence of all the significant aspects. Holism is in contrast with reductionism whereby significant features may be lost deliberately (and often in ignorance of the adverse effects on understanding and outcomes) in the search for simplicity, elegance and convenience (see sections on management systems, standards for management systems and conclusions for further discussion). Both Toft (1992, 1996) and Waring (1996a) discuss holism in relation to examination of health and safety issues.

## *System ownership*

The term 'ownership' crept into management patois in the late 1980s and early 1990s as an expression seeking to describe development of an organizational culture in which employees recognise both a responsibility for and a stake in the benefits of various management concepts and systems. However, in conventional systems terminology, 'system owner' has a different meaning to that of a stakeholding beneficiary of the system. System owners are those who are interested in the particular perceived system for the purposes of system design, study, improvement, implementation, problem-solving, and so on. System ownership implies a perception that it is worthwhile regarding a particular entity as a 'system'. It is generally agreed (see for example Checkland 1981; Checkland and Scholes 1990; Open University 1984, 1993) that a system owner is someone who has the power to alter the perceived system significantly or, indeed, terminate it. In contrast, individuals who have an operational role in the perceived system (such as stakeholding employees in an organization) usually have no such power. There is thus a risk of false expectations for success of particular management systems in cases where system ownership is perceived by senior managers as being vested in the employees whereas the employees do not have the necessary authority.

## *World-view*

Chapter 8 discusses risk perception from a psychological perspective and the essential cognitive processes involved. In this section, the broader perceptual phenomenon called 'world-view' or *Weltanschauung* is outlined as it forms an essential part of systems thinking (Checkland 1981; Checkland and Scholes 1990; Davies 1988) and organizational analysis (Johnson 1987; Waring 1996c).

World-view may be regarded as a kind of 'perceptual window' or 'tinted spectacles' through which each person interprets the world and his or her relationship with it. Vickers (1983) refers to a broadly equivalent term called 'appreciative system' by which individuals and groups appreciate or make sense of the world and themselves. The mutual influence between the world-view of an individual and the collective world-views of groups to which the individual belongs is significant in examining the influences of culture and power in organizations including their effects on management systems and attitudes towards risks.

A particular world-view denotes a complex and dynamic set of beliefs, values, assumptions, opinions, attitudes and motivations. A world-view may therefore be regarded as a characteristic set of perceptual biases about how the world functions. A collective or shared world-view may also be regarded as a component of culture and equivalent to ideational culture (Johnson 1987; Waring 1993). Shared world-views are important for integration and stability in organizations. In some circumstances, different world-views may be so irreconcilable that clashes and conflicts occur, for example employer-trade union disputes such as in the UK coal industry in the 1980s and the French public service worker dispute with the government in 1995.

It is therefore important in many cases for risk assessment to include analysis of relevant world-views, although this requirement is rarely addressed by technical risk analysts because it falls outside their training, experience and generally their professional world-view. As Douglas (1992) notes, 'When he brackets off culture from his work, the well-intentioned risk analyst has tied his own hands. He wants to be free of bias, he would rather pretend that bias is not important than sully himself by trying to categorize kinds of bias'.

Burrell and Morgan (1979) identified four principal world-view types: structural/functionalist, interpretive, radical structuralist and radical humanist, each of which describes a particular emphasis on two dimensions, that is subjective-objective and regulation-radical change (see Figure 3.2). The functionalist world-view rests firmly in the objective/regulation area and is consistent with beliefs that the structures of society, politics, business and organizations have a pre-ordained timeless function. The status quo justifies itself and is necessary for social order. Functionalism is betrayed by a self-declared rationalism and claims to objectivity and a conviction that quantification is inherently better than qualitative data. Beliefs, underpinned by relatively simple cause-effect models, in such concepts as market forces, survival of the fittest, efficiency in the use of resources, organizational benchmarking and, ironically, business process re-engineering are all indicative of a functionalist world-view. Functionalist perspectives would be at home in banks and financial institutions. Other tell-tale characteristics include beliefs that organizational culture (i.e. collective world-view) is a commodity which exists to support and serve corporate and system interests and is firmly in the gift of senior management to manipulate, control and predetermine. Such assumptions have been challenged by various authors such as Smircich (1983).

*Figure 3.2* Burrell and Morgan's world-view framework (simplified)

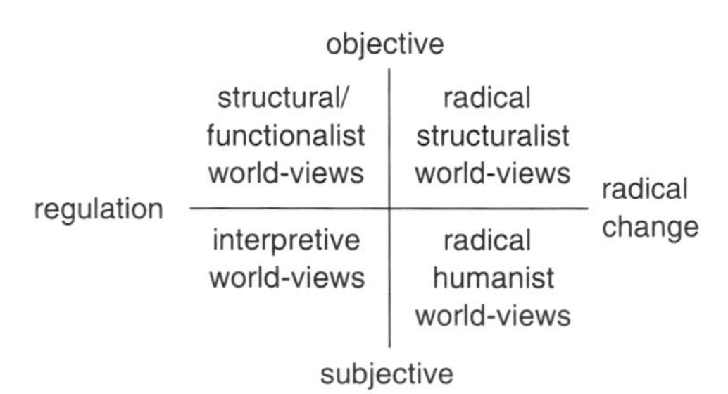


*Source*: Waring (1996c)

Interpretive world-views combine a desire for order with assumptions that characteristics of society, politics, business, organizations, etc. are not pre-determined but are socially constructed. An interpretive world-view is pluralistic in that multiple interests and rationalities are recognised as legitimate. For example, non-'expert' perceptions of risk, which might be marginalized as a nuisance or dismissed as insignificant in a functionalist world-view, would be regarded as highly relevant by an interpretive perspective.

Radical world-views value change of society and its institutions by revolutionary means – the 'righting' of 'wrongs'. The desired change is essentially a redistribution of power from those deemed to possess it to those deemed to deserve it. Radical structuralists see whole classes of person as being dominated and exploited by social, economic and political structures set up by wealthy and powerful classes to ensure the status quo. Such a world-view is consistent with authoritarian ideologies of various kinds. Any risk issues which are acknowledged are frequently seen as issues of blame to be laid at the door of the exploiting classes.

Radical humanists see the domination issue as essentially focused on the individual who is alienated and at the mercy of society itself. By failing to throw off the shackles imposed by social structures and norms, the individual acquiesces to his or her own domination. Individual anarchic action is advocated as the means of empowerment. Physical attacks, sabotage and intimidation against symbols of social order and power would be extreme examples of behaviour consistent with such a world-view.

Academic debate has tended to polarize differences between functionalist and interpretive world-views to the point where they have become regarded by some as mutually exclusive (see for example Burrell and Morgan 1979; Carter and Jackson 1991). However, a synthesis of different perspectives enables a more complete understanding of organizational phenomena and is in line with the 'new theory' (Reed 1991b) which in the longer term may enable organizations to be more effective and experience fewer failures (Turner 1992). Chapters 4 and 5 discuss the world-view issue further in relation to risk.

## Management systems

Although agreement commonly exists about the need for 'good management', there is an absence of a commonly agreed set of constructs and language regarding management systems. In practice, the approach is highly varied, even within a single organization. How people describe a management system reflects their world-view and the mental models they have about how the world functions. Different kinds of model have been described and compared (Waring 1996a) in relation to safety management systems. The same principle applies to management systems in general. These models include:

- sausage machine;
- clockworks/programmable robots;
- clockworks-plus-humans/socio-technical models;
- human activity systems.

In summary, both sausage machine and clockwork/robots views of effective management systems are mechanistic and based on a simple input-process-output model and simple cause-effect assumptions about how people think and act. Prediction and control are seen as straightforward reliable outcomes of decrees, instructions and company manuals which 'wind up' the organization to perform just like clockworks or a set of identikit programmable robots. Effectiveness is measured typically in quantitative terms only. Such a model is consistent with a highly functionalist world-view.

The clockworks-plus-humans or socio-technical approaches focus on technical efficiency of formal management systems backed up by formal attempts to manipulate and control the human contribution through staff selection, training and motivational techniques. Such an approach is essentially functionalist and consistent with Total Quality Management (TQM) (Waring 1992, 1996a) which expects rapid results to follow from the TQM process.

An approach based on human activity systems seeks a more holistic consideration of the inherent complexity of people as social actors and their organizations as social constructions. The baseline assumption is that any well-designed management system should possess the following *systematic* characteristics:

- A systematic framework which connects up all the components.
- Clear policy, strategy and objectives.
- Clear responsibilities, accountabilities and authority of individuals.
- Adequate means for organizing, planning, resourcing and decision-making.
- Adequate means for implementing plans and decisions.
- A coherent and adequate set of measures of performance.
- Adequate means for monitoring, assessing, auditing and reviewing both the quality of the system itself and how it functions.
- Adequate numbers and allocations of competent well-led people.
- Flow of adequate information to all those who need it.
- Adequate intelligence about the inner and outer contexts of the organization (see for example chapters 4–7).

- Compatibility, if not integration, with other management systems in the organization.

In addition, in order to function effectively as a human activity system, factors in the inner context such as organizational culture, power relations, motivations and meanings of success would be critical as, indeed, would be responsiveness to the outer context. It is all these *systemic* contextual factors which are so often overlooked or ignored. Figure 3.3 depicts an overview model of a management system as a systematic framework.

## Standards for management systems

If an organization can show that all its various functions and processes which contribute to product quality such as design, marketing, production, safety, human resources, sales, finance, etc. are working at peak efficiency and effectiveness, then in principle its chances of commercial success are improved significantly. Demonstration of product quality is therefore important strategically to most companies.

One important contributor to product quality is having effective and efficient management systems. A number of national and international standards have been drawn up to cover the functionally related management areas of safety, quality and environment (SQE).

ISO 9000 Specification for Quality Management Systems and ISO 14001 Specification for Environmental Management Systems are both specification standards which carry with them 'third party' certification schemes. The relevant standards body provides certificates of compliance to an organization provided that it has successfully passed an audit by an approved or accredited auditor (the third party). However, confusion has arisen about such standards and their status. There are also frequently unrealistic expectations of a 'clockworks' cause-effect relationship between applying such standards and achieving rapid success. The relationship between certification and *actual* quality or environmental performance in a particular organization is very debatable. The models and approaches incorporated are over-simplified and naive as paradigms for success in this subject area (the 'as if' problem). At this stage, ISO 9000 certificates only attest to compliance with minimal requirements for documentation and administrative procedures and do not address actual product quality. Therefore, although such certificates are passports to markets, they are no gaurantee of a company's products *per se*. Binney *et al.* (1992) and Wilkinson *et al.* (1994) are two relevant independent studies whose findings support a cautious approach to claims made for benefits relating to quality

*Figure 3.3* Overview model of a management system

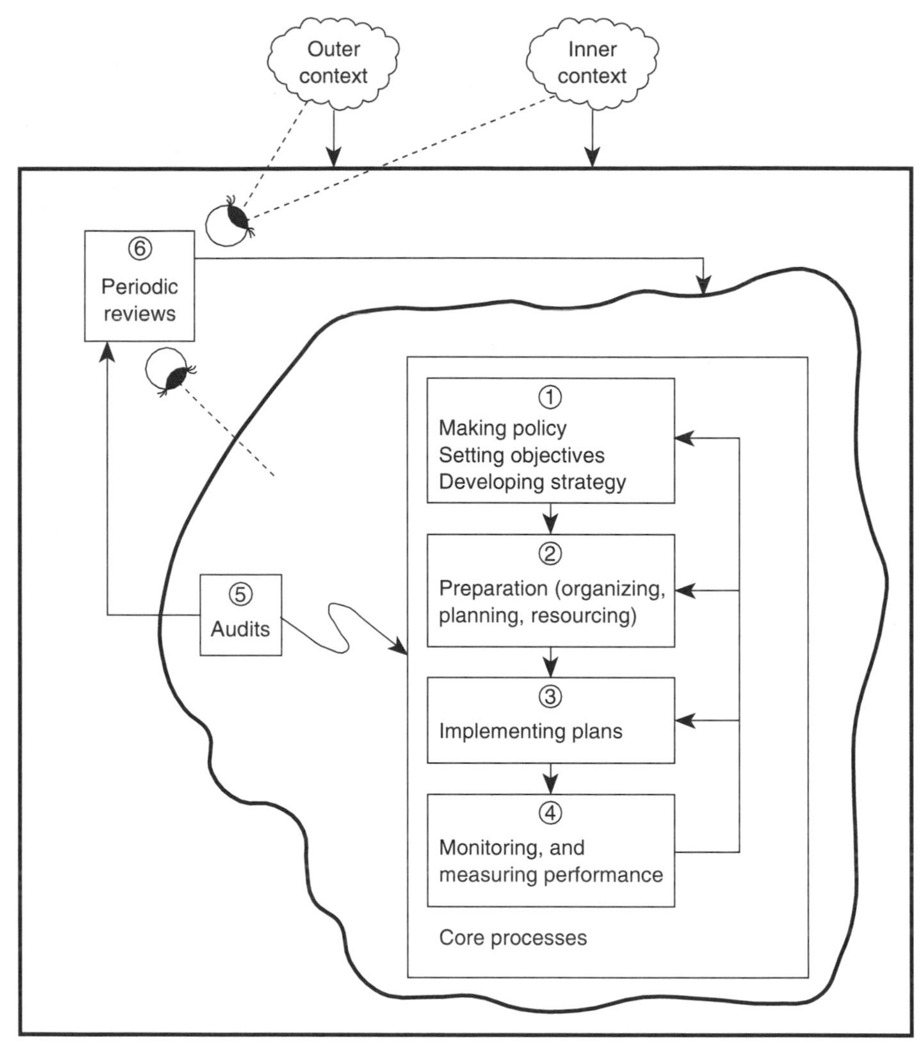


*Source*: Waring (1996c)

management systems and certification. Byrom (1996) adds further caution regarding inferences that quality management systems necessarily benefit health and safety.

In addition, proponents of certification often point to the large number of organizations which have become certified as evidence of the value of certification.

However, experience suggests that many certified organizations only demand that their suppliers be certified because the scheme requires it and not because they believe that certification necessarily brings added value. If becoming certified requires that only other certified suppliers are used, then so-called 'demand' is little more than a self-fulfilling prophecy. There is a danger of certification becoming not a measure of high quality but a measure of, at best, mediocrity among weak and average organizations seeking to bolster their image and self-confidence.

Widespread concerns about the weaknesses of certification standards for safety management have been raised, especially on grounds that compliance certificates may encourage false inferences about full compliance with government safety regulations and absence of hazards. Auditing in the health and safety field requires professionally qualified safety auditors, whereas no comparable requirement is specified by ISO 9000 and ISO 14000. The requirements specified in ISO 9000 and ISO 14000 series and auditor qualifications at present fall far short of what would be absolute minimum requirements in the health and safety and major hazards fields. The British Standard BS 8800 Guide to Occupational Health and Safety Management Systems, based loosely on Guidance Document HS(G) 65 (HSE 1991), was drafted deliberately as a guide and *not* as a specification. Its contents are much more detailed and wide-ranging than those of ISO 9000 and ISO 14000 series. The Australian and New Zealand joint standard on Risk Management (AS/NZ 4360: 1995) is also framed as a general guide.

In September 1996, ISO examined the possibility of preparing an international standard for health and safety management systems. In view of the kinds of problem cited above, there was less enthusiasm for a certification standard than had been the case for quality management and environmental management systems. It was decided that there was insufficient demand for the development of such a standard, although a number of countries have developed their own – e.g. BS 8800, AS 1470.

A number of proprietary approaches to safety management systems are promoted by a variety of organizations such as trade and industry associations, campaigning bodies and consultancy firms. For example, in the UK:

- Responsible Care, Chemical Industries Association;
- International Safety Rating System, DNV Technica;
- CBI health and safety 'benchmarking' scheme.

Most proprietary schemes are linked to relevant standards such as ISO 9000, ISO 14000 and BS 8800 and are operated as commercial schemes by their owners or sponsors.

## Integration of management systems

Integration of safety, environmental and quality management (SQE) systems is now high on the agendas of many large organizations. In principle, SQE integration sounds an attractive proposition in terms of greater efficiency and consistency. Certainly, integration of safety and environmental management systems would be an advantage for management of emergencies. For example, a toxic release is likely to have both safety and environmental impacts. However, although the goal is seductive and the rhetoric easy, in many organizations people are struggling to cope with what for them are often unfamiliar concepts in three technical specialisms – S, Q, E – all at the same time. There is also the risk of failing to appreciate the technical breadth, depth and legal requirements essential for adequate management of safety and environment compared with that of quality.

Waring (1996a) and IOSH (1997) identify a number of reasons why integration of management systems may be difficult. These are:

- In organizations there is often confusion about the scope and practical requirements of the various management systems to be integrated.
- There are often significant differences in the scope and depth of activities involved in different areas of management and hence significant differences in skill requirements, and these facts may not be appreciated by those involved.
- Because the consequences of failures in some areas such as safety and environmental management can be so serious, the latter require special diligence beyond that applied to other areas of management such as quality, a requirement which may not be appreciated.
- Health, safety and environment are covered by a great deal of detailed legislation requiring specific managerial and technical arrangements, whereas quality and many other areas of management are not. Adequate management systems for health, safety and environment are mandatory and must be coherent, but this does not necessarily warrant their full integration.
- Professional rivalries often exist between different management functions such that control of integration and of the newly integrated system becomes a power struggle which adversely affects the outcome.
- Other aspects of the inner context of the organization may not be receptive to integration of management systems.

Some people advocate a radical step-change approach to integration and other changes claimed to be system-enhancing, on the basis that incremental approaches merely seek to make present activities more efficient and effective rather than addressing the fundamental issue of 'being' (Talwar 1993). However, although administrative integration and other transformations may be relatively straightforward, it is well known from management research and experience (see for example Waring 1993b and chapter 7 in this book) that 'big bang' or radical approaches to major organizational change are more likely to fail than are incremental approaches. The Horton regime at BP (1989–3) is a classic example.

Integration as a 'big bang' process would require either the most favourable organizational conditions to exist or a crisis of such proportions that only a radical solution makes sense. The non-extreme 'grey area' in which most organizations exist provides treacherous ground for radical change of any kind. It is often wrongly assumed that like creating flatter, leaner and more flexible organizations, integration is a quick and automatic means to the end of improved organizational and cost efficiency. Integration should therefore be a long-term goal approached gradually through better coordination and coherence between different management functions.

## Management system risks

The success of an organization may depend on how narrow or how holistic a view is taken of its situation, goals, problems, opportunities etc. In human activity system terms, organizational success rests on two important conditions: (a) an adequately designed and operated systematic framework of management functions, and (b) adequate consideration of the contexts of the particular organization and especially complex human factors within the organization.

Management systems may be a necessary part of achieving success and avoiding failure. Risks associated with not having adequate management systems should be self-evident. However, having naïve management systems which are claimed to be adequate may be more dangerous as the social actors may be ignorant of the defects and their potential consequences. There is a need to remain aware of the 'as if' problem, namely that no system model reflects reality in a complete way but models are frequently used 'as if' they do. All system models are reductionist, some more so than others. Highly reduced models bring advantages of simplicity and ease of understanding but a potential risk lies in naïve expectations of success. Assumptions about prediction and control may be unrealistic, especially that objectives and criteria are appropriate and inclusive and that complex human factors are not significant.

Because current proprietary and management system standards models (such as ISO 9000, 14000 etc) are so highly reduced and address the lowest common denominator (e.g. the Deming wheel), they cannot guarantee success or anything like it. So much fine structure is lost that compliance with the model or standard is little more than showing the barest minimum of control. Radical integrationists fail to recognise that although a common basic model for management systems may be identifiable, there are significant differences in detail which demand plurality. Marginally more sophisticated 'system' approaches such as TQM, business process re-engineering (BPR) and organizational benchmarking offer the same seductive promise of finding the organizational 'holy grail' yet suffer from the same fundamental flaws (Beer *et al.* 1990; Crainer 1996; HSE 1996a).

Such management fads are dangerous because they are seductive and promise quick returns and never-ending success – which they cannot deliver; vast emotional, intellectual, financial and other resource commitments are made in their name with often little which is sustainable in return (see for example Binney *et al.* 1992; Wilkinson *et al.* 1994).

Caulkin (1995) and Crainer (1996) in articles in *Management Today* are particularly scathing in their criticisms of corporate managements who persistently fall for the latest formula for organizational success which then proves to be unsustainable or creates new problems. Caulkin refers to 'the obstinate failure of cost-cutting and restructuring exercises to galvanize companies into promised high performance'. Ruthless re-engineering has instead produced a growing army of highly skilled people whose only loyalty is to 'Me PLC'. Those former employees who were encouraged or forced to become contractors are now extracting what they regard as 'overdue payment' and selling their services to the highest bidder. Others waiting to go freelance remain only so long as the employer is prepared to increase rewards. Organizations are quoted as having to review their executive rewards policy on a weekly basis simply to keep staff at all. Among those who remain, 'presenteeism' is characteristic, i.e. present in body only. The drive towards a 'contract culture' which promised organizational nirvana has instead created an increasingly uncontrollable many-headed monster which is likely to have an overall adverse effect on risks unless re-engineering is managed well – see HSE (1996a) and Kennedy (1994).

## Conclusions

The systems concept, applied to organizations and management, has demonstrated both its robustness and its versatility in providing a conceptual framework for understanding how risk and change may be managed.

Systems may be conceived in concrete, functionalist terms as 'real' entities or, more realistically, as perceived entities within an interpretive framework. Seeing systems as real (reified) entities leads to the danger of believing that by 'programming' system elements (e.g. people, procedures) the system will operate in a predictable and controllable way according to some grand design. Such an approach reflects the world-view of the observer rather than the nature of systems as representations of reality. It is important to remember that system models are just that – reduced representations of reality and not the reality itself.

Systems are more than the sum of their parts. For organizations viewed as systems, their inner context contains a number of sub-systems. Systems are also not independent entities since they interact with other systems in their environment (or outer context of organizations viewed as systems). Thus, any given system is part of the environment of other systems and vice versa. Both types of interaction ensure that absolute control of a system, such as an organization, by management or any other party is not possible.

A systems approach allows for enquiry at different levels of complexity – which can be reflected in system representations. To overcome problems of comprehension of complexity, such representation should be limited ideally to a maximum of nine components. Beyond this number, it is desirable to break the system representation down into further hierarchical levels to ease comprehension of structures, component interactions and system processes.

In management of risk and/or of change, it is essential to be aware of and to take due account of differences in cognitions, or world-views. These are both individual – and therefore unique – and also shared, as in cultures of groups or organizational sub-systems. At a higher level, types of world-view have been identified which may, in various combinations, characterize particular types of organization. An appreciation of the collective world-view of an organization (or sub-system or individual) is important for understanding what motivates that (sub)system or person.

Systems designed to enhance the management of pure risk topics such as quality, the physical environment, security and occupational health and safety make certain assumptions about the nature of those systems. The high failure rate for full absorption of these add-on management systems at least partly reflects the different cultures or world-views respectively (a) required for their successful adoption, and (b) represented within organizations as collections of sub-systems with divergent cultures and interests. Motivations for seeking to adopt ISO and other management standards within organizations may be founded on a flawed understanding of the degree of prediction and control which is possible through such models. Naïve management systems intended to control particular risks may be therefore only partly effective while creating an illusion that they have been fully controlled. To be effective, risk management should ensure that management systems take full account of the inner context of the organization (including history, structures, cultures, resources, motivations and power relations) and its environment or outer context, both of which affect how risks are perceived and what is done about them.

Chapter 4

# Culture and risk

## Overview

This chapter describes and discusses various aspects of culture at different levels (professional, national, inter- and intra-organizational) which are likely to have a bearing on risk. Different world-views about culture and risk are outlined and implications discussed.

## Introduction

Culture, especially of an organization, is increasingly identified as a key factor in the success or failure of enterprises. Official inquiries into safety disasters such as Chernobyl, King's Cross and Piper Alpha specifically pinpointed cultural characteristics as important both to understanding why the disasters occurred and as indicators for other organizations in reducing the likelihood that they would experience similar events. However, stating that culture is vitally important in determining risk is relatively easy. It is much more difficult to establish a well-informed and realistic practical approach to this complex topic.

Along with concepts such as power, love and, indeed, risk, culture is yet another recursive, sensitizing concept which alerts us to a litany of other related concepts in an endless, circular pursuit of 'the truth' about the human condition. To a great extent in the West, 'culture' has become a managerial label for a rag-bag of ill-defined and poorly understood ideas about 'how we do things around here'. The 'we', of course, generally is expressed by senior managers in a particular organization on an assumption that 'we' means everyone in the organization. Such a normative stance tends to ignore the fact that most organizations are assemblages of multiple cultures (Turner 1988) of which managerial culture is only one. Indeed, there may be different identifiable cultures within an organization's management.

It is likely that a particular world-view (see chapter 3) will include closely allied perceptions of and attitudes towards culture, risk and many other issues. For example, those who regard risk as an objective phenomeneon which is best approached through a limited set of quantifiable parameters concerning prediction and control are likely to regard culture in a similar vein. It is therefore important to consider different perspectives of these topics and implications of the differences for managerial practice and outcomes. This chapter seeks to describe and discuss different perspectives on culture and risk, including some of the more controversial aspects such as cultural assessment and culture change.

## The nature of organizational culture

For the purposes of comparison and contrast, the literature on organizational culture may be assigned to one or other of two categories, functionalist and interpretive (Burrell and Morgan 1979; Smircich 1983), as discussed in chapter 3. These two categories are equivalent respectively to modernist and post-modernist sociological perspectives of organization and organizational analysis (Carter and Jackson 1991; Jeffcutt 1991; Reed 1991b). The two categories are also equivalent to the normative and descriptive categories discussed by Davies (1988) and ESRC (1993).

Although, as described below, the modernist and post-modernist approaches and discourses are different, there is much common ground among authors about the components of organizational culture – for example, inclusion of characteristic sets of values, beliefs, assumptions, symbols and so on in the essential concept of organizational culture. To an extent, such similarities emphasize the 'new theory' tendency of commensurability (Reed 1991b) which holds that world-view types are not mutually exclusive.

Lundberg (1990) states that organizational culture is 'a phenomenon of reality construction – allowing members to see and comprehend particular events, actions, objects, utterances and whole situations, including their own behaviours, in an acceptable way that is sensible and meaningful'. Quoting Deal and Kennedy (1986), Lundberg notes that organizational culture has three layers of meaning:

- Manifest level – symbolic artefacts
  – language
  – stories
  – rituals
  – normative conduct

- Strategic level – strategic beliefs
- Core level – ideologies
  – values
  – assumptions

Waring (1996a) provides examples from the health and safety area of risk for each of the above levels and components. These layers of meaning refer to the content of organizational culture. Gorman (1989) adds three further dimensions:

- Strength – extent to which organizational members embrace core level meanings.
- Pervasiveness – extent to which beliefs and values are shared across the organization.
- Direction – extent to which organizational culture embodies behaviour consistent with espoused strategy.

Localization could be added as a further dimension – i.e. the extent to which particular locations in the organizational structure have their own (sub)cultural identity within the overall organizational culture. Localization would also apply to different countries, regions, religions, professions, etc. Because individuals usually belong at one and the same time to a number of different groups, they may as individuals exhibit characteristics of several different cultures – e.g. Texan (i) engineers (ii) working in an offshore drilling (iii) company (iv) which has been based for many years in the Gulf of Mexico (v).

Smircich (1983) introduces the notion that organizational culture is yet another metaphor for organization along with (interpretive) metaphors such as theatres and political arenas, and (functionalist) metaphors such as organisms and machines. She suggests that organizational study and cultural study are analogous as they are both concerned with patterns and order. Organization and culture provide two intersecting sets of images.

## Functionalist views of organizational culture

Functionalist views of organizational culture are characterised by the following assumptions (Waring 1992a, 1993b, 1996a):

- Organizational culture has a pre-determined function.
- Organizational structures epitomize the particular organizational culture.
- The function of organizational culture is to support formal, rationally designed management systems and strategies.

- Organizational culture can be reduced to relatively simple cause-effect models – i.e. a large degree of determinism, predictability and control.
- Organizational culture can be and should be manipulated to serve corporate (i.e. managerial) interests.
- There exists an ideal type of organizational culture to which organizations should aspire.
- There exist ideal or appropriate ways in which to manipulate organizational culture for the purposes of (managerial) prediction and control.

For example, Kono (1990) in discussing the relationship between corporate culture, strategy and long-range planning, offers a very rationalistic cause-effect model for producing a revitalized culture based on corporate philosophy, product market strategy, organizational structure and the personnel management system, and top management attitudes. Dobson (1988), Green (1988) and Gorman (1989) offer similar prescriptions.

Strategic beliefs 'refer not to the long-range plans or strategic pronouncements of organizational spokespersons, but rather to the fundamental "oughts" in the minds of the influential organizational leaders' (Lundberg 1990). Leadership is seen by functionalists as a key determinant in both cultural change and organizational change that such culture change is thought to enable.

Westley (1990) reports a case study of cultural change involving an attempted socio-technical re-design of a large automobile assembly plant. He notes that culture is a crucial factor in determining the receptivity of an organization to change. However, he also notes that although some individuals underwent 'conversions', 'efforts to change core assumptions through structural and stylistic interventions met with resistance . . . Consensus decision-making became a new means for blocking initiatives and passing the buck' (see further examples in chapters 14 and 15). All-in-all, Westley observed that the 'transition was experienced as a kind of human relations nightmare'.

In six large organizations undergoing change, senior managers believed that 'promulgating companywide programs – mission statements, corporate culture programs, training courses, quality circles, and new pay-for-performance systems – will transform organizations' (Beer *et al.* 1990). However, such beliefs about such programs themselves may constitute the greatest obstacle to revitalization – 'the fallacy of programmatic change'.

The case studies of Westley and Beer *et al.* underline the difficulty of functionalist approaches to organizational change (through culture change) in that there is likely to be a difference between, on the one hand, managerially espoused values and change strategies and, on the other hand, enacted values and strategies in the organization as a whole. Gorman (1989), for example, assumes that company goals are the only set which operate within the organization and that they have been articulated clearly and are understood and agreed upon by the organization's members. His reference to the appropriate culture for an organization is discussed only in terms of the corporate leaders' view. There may be an assumption that problems (as defined by management) relating to an organization exist and that these can be solved by formal engineering of a cultural change by management.

The modernist or functionalist approach to organizational culture places the topic of culture very much in a supporting role to managerial ideology, goals, strategies etc. However, Smircich (1983) notes: 'Those of a more sceptical nature may also question the extent to which the term corporate culture refers to anything more than an ideology cultivated by management for the purpose of control and legitimation of activity.' In extreme cases, culture change programmes may lead to managerial use of 'culture' as a weapon of internal coercion and control.

For those aspects of risk which can be shown to follow a reliable cause-effect relationship or model (for example, readily quantifiable relationships), functionalist assumptions are well suited. However, culture needs to be regarded more as a mediating factor than as a causal one, and certainly not one that can be reduced satisfactorily to being part of a quantitative relationship. For example, it is not simply a matter of classifying a culture on a scale of, say, risk averseness and then trusting that the particular measurement will enable reliable prediction about what will happen in that organization in all matters to do with risk. An organization judged to have a highly risk averse culture may avoid spectacular failures in speculative risk areas but is also less likely to enjoy large financial successes. Risk averseness in speculative risk often goes hand-in-glove with risk-taking in areas of pure risk – e.g. reducing risk controls in the name of cost control.

## Interpretive views of organizational culture

Interpretive views of organizational culture are characterized by (Waring 1992a, 1993b, 1996a):

- Culture is regarded as an emergent phenomenon of social groupings.
- Organizational culture is regarded as complex and incapable of reduction to a (relatively) simple cause-effect model.
- Organizational culture is a means for the organization's members to interpret

their own existence, identity and actions and to institute, guide and moderate those actions.
- Organizations may be regarded as multicultural assemblages having characteristic discourses within and between them.
- Organizational structures, systems, strategies, processes and culture(s) reflect each other.
- Formal structures, systems, strategies and processes support the prevailing organizational culture.
- 'Ownership' of organizational culture is not the sole prerogative of senior management.
- Pursuit of an ideal type of organizational culture begs the question '*whose* ideal?'; each organization's culture is a unique creation of *all* of its members.
- Managerial attempts to manipulate organizational culture to achieve rapid organizational change are likely to fail.

Turner (1988) describes organizations as 'cultural assemblages' and contrasts the interpretive and functionalist approaches. Whereas the modernist or functionalist view is characterized by those who want to have things cleared up, sorted out and neatly stacked, interpretive analysts see the importance of seeking out, acquiring and interpreting data through a unique personal perspective in which the subjective and objective are in constant interplay. The cultural web model for understanding stability and change in organizations (Johnson 1987) is very much an interpretive approach (see chapter 7).

Whereas functionalism seeks to eradicate or deny ambiguity in organizations (whether in study and analysis or in managerial action), interpretive approaches recognise the multiplicity of sub-cultures and discourses which none the less are mutually translatable within the organizational culture as a whole. Parker and Dent (1991) explore this theme in relation to the National Health Service and specifically the 1989 White Papers and Resource Management (see chapter 15). They argue that the government of the day had been trying to change the prevailing NHS culture radically from the language of paternalism and medical responsibility to a language based on market rationality and business metaphor. In doing so, however, the government failed to recognise that the NHS is a multicultural assemblage whose various discourses are distinct and sometimes in disagreement.

Davies (1988) criticizes normative (functionalist) notions of successful organizational culture management: '. . . stating that an organization is successful and manages its culture is not evidence that such management causes success. Such causal links are very difficult to show within the complex scenarios found in organizational behaviour'. Davies further suggests that, for individuals, 'success' is *both* socially and culturally defined *and* functionally defined. For example, the 'organizational value which espouses that participation is the most morally acceptable form of decision making, may be in direct conflict with the departmental ones which recognise that in fact decision making is autocratic'. In other words, autocracy (as an example) may be a functional but culturally biased stance linked to survival in a particular organization. This argument is to some extent supported by empirical evidence (Waring 1993b) – i.e. political processes (largely opaque) having a functional overlay (manifest), both of which are mediated by context (e.g. cultural).

An interpretive view of culture change in organizations involves 'organizational learning' (Lyles and Schwenk 1992; Toft 1992, 1996; Turner 1992). This concept has been expressed (Toft 1996) as the results of a shared immersion in organizational life and exposure to change-related activities over a considerable period of time. This view is somewhat different to the cognitive psychological view of learning in organizations (Argyris and Schon 1977). See section later in chapter on a cultural dimension to risk.

An interpretive perspective of culture has an explicit inclusion of multiple rationalities, interests, etc. and, unlike a functionalist perspective, is not deliberately reductionist. Unlike the extremes of a functionalist perspective, culture is not seen as a euphemism for corporate or managerial policy and strategy to be hijacked and used as a cynical weapon of control against potential dissent or even constructive criticism within the organization. Culture is not seen as a commodity or resource which is there at the beck and call of particular groups to support their interests, decisions and actions. Rather, culture is seen as a dynamic collective property emerging from all the members of the particular organization or entity which reinforces behaviour and is therefore linked with psychological survival. An interpretive perspective enables better understanding of culture as a qualitative concept and its relationship with the highly subjective concept of risk.

## Culture, actions and meanings

From the previous sections of this chapter, it is clear that organizational culture is a complex, recursive concept which sensitizes observers to a range of related topics. This chapter argues from a largely interpretive standpoint that functionalist (modernist) and interpretive (post-modernist) approaches to organizational analysis are commensurable.

Johnson (1987), in his account and analysis of an organization undergoing substantive change, concludes that the action(s) of strategy formulation and enactment are dependent on the meaning systems of the social actors concerned, which in turn are dependent on the interactions between managerial cognition and ideology on the one hand and organizational culture on the other. He argues that organization is a paradigm made up of sub-paradigms and that the most fitting is that of ideational culture or the core beliefs and assumptions specific and relevant to the particular organization (see Glossary). Johnson argues that the ideational culture paradigm is at one and the same time a device for interpretation and a formula for action. Strategies evolve from this cultural device (see chapter 7).

Manifest organizational changes such as reorganization do not represent an immediate switch from one culture to another; rather, they represent a culture which is changing its structural manifestations – the people have changed hardly at all in their fundamental beliefs and values. Thus, in one case – see chapter 14 – the suggestion that the organization's culture changed from that of a charity to that of a business is crude. There were manifestations of both 'old guard' cultural components such as campaigning, team briefings, and values based on a human relations model, coexisting with 'new guard' components such as business plans, market research, and client targeting. This is not a case of one replacing the other overnight. During the long period of transition, their coexistence *was* the culture. Since 'old guard' values were enshrined in the organization's legal constitution, it is likely that they would remain as the bedrock indefinitely whereas 'new guard' components would become prominent for practical reasons. It would be a cultural realignment over some years, the major change strategy being a feature of the organizational learning process.

Perceptions of culture and of desired culture changes may reflect organizational structures, political processes and power relations. Whereas authority power of senior managers may impose some changes relevant to culture, it is unlikely to be able to enforce a lasting change on an inner context of conflicting sub-cultures, especially where local group values differ markedly from those of senior management. Countervailing effects of influence power from and among individuals and groups within the organization must also be taken into account. Culture change is unlikely to be a simple and relatively rapid shift from one major valuation to another. It is much more likely to be a complex realignment of a pattern of different valuations, some of which may change more quickly and more lastingly than others.

## Safety culture

The term 'safety culture' arose in British ministerial comments about the Chernobyl nuclear disaster in 1986 which attributed cause to a breakdown in the organization's 'safety culture' (Toft 1992). The concept has arisen as a substantive issue in official enquiry reports into subsequent disasters such as King's Cross (Fennell 1988) and Piper Alpha (Cullen 1990) and the term is now commonplace in the vocabulary of health and safety management. However, as with the general concept of culture, there is a wide range of meanings attached to 'safety culture', three of which are summarised in IOSH (1994):

- Those aspects of culture which affect safety (Waring 1992a).
- The characteristic shared attitudes, values, beliefs and practices concerning the importance of health and safety and the necessity for effective controls.
- The product of individual and group values, attitudes, competencies and patterns of behaviour that determine the commitment to, and the style and proficiency of, an organization's health and safety programmes. Organizations with a positive safety culture are characterised by communications founded on mutual trust, by shared perceptions of the importance of safety and by confidence in the efficacy of preventive measures (ACSNI 1993).

The latter two definitions indicate a functionalist or normative perspective. Others may be found in CBI (1990), Pidgeon *et al.* (1991) and Ryan (1991). Glendon and McKenna (1995) describe safety culture as 'the embodiment of a set of principles which loosely define what an organization is like in terms of health and safety'. The term 'safety culture' emerged from use of the term 'safety climate' (Zohar 1980; Brown and Holmes 1986; Cooper and Phillips 1994; Guest *et al* 1994; Glendon and McKenna 1995).

Carter and Jackson (1994) describe and discuss a broader concept than safety culture which they call 'riscomancy' – see sub-section on a cultural dimension to risk later in this chapter. Riscomancy refers to the 'risk culture' particularly prevalent in western societies and which, by inference, is manifest in different forms in different social institutions, professions, industries, etc. and in public attitudes towards risk issues.

## Assessment of culture

### *Assumptions*

One of the more controversial aspects of organizational culture concerns its assessment. In businesses and other employing organizations, particularly the larger ones, it has become increasingly fashionable to seek to assess a range of parameters thought to indicate how far the organization meets criteria such as 'total quality' or 'worldclass benchmarks'. Culture is typically a key parameter. The pressure to make such assessments is attributed by organizations to the need to know their performance characteristics in a fiercely competitive world market so that these can be portrayed to customers, employees, financiers and anyone else who makes critical judgements about the organization. On this basis, the principle appears reasonable and difficult to criticize. However, as soon as attempts are made to operationalize the principle, substantive theoretical, ethical and practical problems arise concerning the assessment of culture. Unfortunately, many organizations are unaware of such problems.

For any topic to be assessed, those involved require (a) a notion of cause-and-effect which relates to important and relevant aspects of the topic – i.e. what can cause those aspects to change (otherwise if they cannot be changed what is the point of assessing them?), and (b) some means of scaling, qualitatively or quantitatively, those aspects. Where culture is the topic of interest, unfortunately the underlying cause-effect models used in assessments are usually woefully inadequate, for example assumptions that a significant and rapid change in organizational culture is caused by:

- Beliefs espoused in boardroom edicts, mission statements and policy documents.
- Briefings and training courses about a desired culture change.
- Quality circles and TQM programmes.

Beer *et al.* (1990) and Waring (1993b, 1996a), while not decrying the possible value of such functionalist prescriptions to the good of the organization, point out that as cause-effect models of *culture* they are extremely naïve and almost certain to dissappoint those who rely on them, in the long if not the short term. Glendon and Bamber (1996) offer similar caution.

The problem of selecting appropriate cultural dimensions is also difficult as there is no widespread agreement about what those should be. The recursive nature of the subject and terminology does not help. Waring (1996a) suggests that rather than seeking to measure organizational culture in a comprehensive way, it is more defensible in the light of present limitations on definitive knowledge about the phenomenon to measure only selected dimensions which are better understood. If this suggestion is taken up, two caveats are necessary. First, the limited nature of the measurements must be emphasized; it is not culture which is being measured but only specific aspects of it. Second, the collection, analysis and interpretation of data about culture requires expert knowledge. In addition to dimensions proposed by Gross and Rayner (1985), dimensions of culture which would be suitable for measurement are those identified in an earlier section (the nature of organizational culture), namely:

- content or layers of meaning;
- strength, pervasiveness and direction;
- localization.

## *Measurement of safety culture*

According to Glendon and McKenna (1995), safety culture or climate is measured typically by surveying workforce attitudes and key elements are then extracted to establish which attitudes are important – i.e. which predict changes or differences in accident rates. The measurement of 'safety climate' proposed by Zohar (1980) is problematic in that the definition of 'safety climate' attached to his proposition is limited to a set of perceptions or beliefs held by an individual and/or group about a particular entity. It does not seek to measure other key dimensions such as those identified above. Brown and Holmes (1986) failed to validate Zohar's model and proposed a modified model whose validity and reliability they claim is supported by factor analysis. However, the fact remains that what is measured by such methods is only a very limited aspect of culture compared with the dimensions identified above. Factor analysis is inherently limited to those factors which are analysed and cannot take account of factors which are excluded or remain unrecognized, and these may account for a large portion of the variance.

Difficulties in measuring safety culture are noted in IOSH (1994). There may also be ethical issues surrounding not only the way in which 'safety culture' is measured but also how the results are presented and applied – see sub-section on ethical issues below.

## *Three methodologies*

Three particular methodologies for cultural assessment are worthy of note. These are the 'stream of cultural enquiry', used as part of Soft Systems Methodology (SSM) (Checkland and Scholes 1990), organizational climate surveys backed up by triangulation methods (Rousseau 1990; Glendon and Bamber 1996), and grid-group analysis (Gross and Rayner 1985; Douglas 1992; Royal Society 1992).

SSM is a systems methodology which seeks to enable social actors in the setting of interest to reach a level of understanding about themselves in terms of 'purposeful human activity systems' which then enables them to decide what, if anything, could and should be done about these notional systems (Waring 1996c). SSM has developed from an original seven-stage methodology (Checkland 1981) which focused on 'wicked', 'messy' and other intractible problems associated with human relations in organizations in which the system analyst acted as 'therapist', to a more advanced methodology (Checkland and Scholes 1990) which does not preclude the analyst, problem owners and other social actors collaborating closely. Although cultural analysis in a limited way was an implicit task in the original SSM, in the developed form it has been expanded into a 'stream of cultural enquiry' which incorporates analyses of roles, relevant 'social systems' of roles, norms and values, and relevant 'political systems' of power characteristics and power relations. One criticism of SSM is that the methodology tends to attract system specialists who are rarely knowledgeable about the breadth and depth of organizational behaviour and there is always the suspicion that the elaborate sounding 'stream of cultural enquiry' masks a superficial and possibly distorted analysis. Further discussion is raised in chapter 5.

Glendon and Bamber (1996) report a case study of attempted rapid culture change in a brewing organization in which a single measure of organizational climate was developed. Its application by means of a questionnaire was then supplemented (or triangulated) with other methods, such as focus group discussion, performance reviews, individual focused interviews, customer perceptions, absence rates, grievances, industrial disputes, accidents and ill-health records. Climate profile scores were then derived as a way of measuring changes over time. As Glendon and Bamber (1996) note, one drawback of this methodology is that trends can only be determined as real with any confidence over at least a five year – and preferably ten year – period. Senior management, however, are required to demonstrate performance improvements over much shorter time scales than this, and so correlation of performance change with culture change may rely on management beliefs that a correlation exists rather than on substantive evidence.

The grid-group approach of Gross and Rayner (1985), based on the work of Douglas, seeks to measure the consistency of patterns of ideas and behaviour in a social organization with its social structures. The grid component measures the overall strength of the system of categorical distinctions such as boss/worker, adult/adolescent/child. Multiple hierarchies of grid components may be applied such as role specialization, role entitlement, accountability etc. The group component measures the extent to which the behaviour of individual members depends on their membership of the social unit. Group components might include proximity (degree of involvement in the network of activities), transitivity (probability of interaction), frequency (proportion of available time allocated to interaction), etc.

In the grid-group approach, four sets of cultural biases are identified. These are:

- hierarchists (high grid-high group);
- fatalists (high grid-low group);
- sectarians/egalitarians (low grid-high group);
- individualists (low grid-low group).

Hierarchists view risks as being relative in a hierarchical way. They take for granted what they are told by risk experts and tend to believe offical views on risk acceptability. Fatalists seek to avoid risks as far as they are able within the extent of their knowledge but accept that their actual degree of control is limited. Sectarians and egalitarians regard industrialization, technology development, business interests and economic growth as posing linked threats to their particular lifestyle. They tend to exaggerate the risks in order to advance their case for protecting their world-view at the expense of others. Individualists are seen as opportunists whose attitude towards risks is likely to vary according to how big an opportunity is perceived. Their overriding focus is on speculative aspects of any particular risk setting.

The four major cultural biases emanating from grid-group are world-views by any other name, although not coincident with those paradigms posited by Burrell and Morgan (1979). A problem for this 'cultural theory' of risk is similar to that faced by Burrell and Morgan and supporters of the argument that world-view types are necessarily mutually exclusive (see Carter and Jackson 1991 for example, and also discussion in chapter 3 of this book). Indeed, the Royal Society report (1992) notes that 'there remains a basic problem in unambiguously classifying existing social units in terms of the grid and group dimensions, that the basic . . . . cultural types may oversimplify more complex shades of social difference'. Individuals frequently possess combinations of apparently contradictory beliefs, attitudes and motivations concerning different risks – i.e. a complex and dynamic interplay between different world-views, rather than having a single world-view which can be fitted by force into only one of the 'pigeonholes' created by incomplete analytical devices such as grid-group.

Gross and Rayner (1985) pose a number of hypotheses. Different organizations with the same grid-group scores will reflect similar cultural patterns of behaviour and attitudes, regardless of whether the organizations are as different as, say, the London Stock Exchange and a village in the Amazon rain forest. A further hypothesis is that risk cognitions in modern societies are subject to the same cultural biases as those in traditional societies. Such biases influence, for example, what evidence is selected on which to base assessment of risk. The idea that cultural types are independent of organizational context is intriguing, if not debatable, but none the less may lead to an unrewarding focus on comparison of types instead of actual characteristics of the particular organization in the particular context. Senior managers are more likely to be interested in the strategic implications of their organization or particular parts of it having a particular location in the grid-group matrix and, moreover, may seek to compare their organizations with others.

### *Ethical issues*

Gross and Rayner (1985) point up the ethical problems of cultural analysis and particularly the danger of making comparisons between organizations. They note that 'it is easier to substantiate a judgement that a particular organization has evolved to become, say, less competitive and more ritualistic, than to prove that one organization is more competitive or less ritualistic than another'. Waring (1996a) goes further: 'seeking to measure an organization's culture is rather like seeking to measure the culture of a nation or the quality of a religion – it can be described but against what standard can it be measured? Who would be so arrogant as to suggest a benchmark? Could one ever really establish that the culture of organization A is better than the culture of organization B, a logical and tempting extension of "measurement"'?

Thus, although it may be worthwhile to make qualitative judgements of particular cultural dimensions which could be used for internal comparisons over time, such measurements should not be used for competitive inter-organizational comparisons or 'benchmarking'. Descriptive comparisons may be enlightening and may lead to better understanding of the present state of the organization and indeed to possible change strategies but that is quite different to competitive benchmarking.

## The culture-risk axis

A central assumption of this book is that, at one level, risk is a largely socially constructed phenomenon whose cognition is culturally mediated. In this respect, the authors belong to the 'sociological camp' of risk analysts acknowledged to exist by the Royal Society Report (1992). The sociological argument for a broader and less technically biased basis for risk analysis and assessment proposed by Douglas (1992), Turner (1988, 1992), Toft (1992, 1993, 1996) and others is gaining increasing acceptance. This shift is inevitable given the inability of exclusively technical approaches to risk to answer satisfactorily increasingly important questions which the sociological camp may be more able to answer. Culture, a sociological concept, is one such aspect of risk for which technical risk analysis is inappropriate.

## *A cultural dimension to risk*

The 'riscomancy culture' (Carter and Jackson 1994) particularly prevalent in western society attributes special knowledge and authority to risk experts who nonetheless may not always know everything of significance. Such risk experts are rarely exposed personally to the risk scenarios which they assess and frequently are not involved in decisions about those risks. Because of their assumed knowledge, they enjoy a privileged, almost priest-like, status which absolves them from getting too involved with the messy realities of organizations and the consequences of their risk assessments for individuals who may be exposed. As Douglas (1992) notes, risk analysts detest anything 'sticky or messy' which might confound their clean, scientific formulae. Riscomancy is also embedded in the cultures of particular industries and organizations and one may cite the major hazards industries as prominent examples as far as pure risks are concerned. However, other industries and other organizations with different cultures may have no time for risk experts, preferring instead to practise their own unstructured risk assessment and risk management, focusing on areas of risk which they 'know' to be more important.

Such differences are associated with cultures which may be risk-orientated in some areas and risk averse in others and with inconsistent and even contradictory rationales for the different areas (as noted in the discussion above about grid-group). For example, some major management consultancies, law practices and financial institutions which are intimately engaged in speculative risks (on their own and their clients' account) may none the less send their top fee earners into high-risk territories and settings (e.g. civil strife, epidemics, lawlessness, unsafe aircraft, industrial hazards, etc.) with minimal efforts to protect them. In the cultures of such firms, such pure risks are to be played down and ignored as part of the macho image they wish to project in relation to their primary tasks. Unfortunately (or perhaps fortunately), a growing number of such professionals are women who are less willing to honour such traditional priorities. The grid-group theory of risk and culture offers a rationale for different risk orientations although, as noted above, it does not offer a complete explanation.

Another aspect of the riscomancy culture concerns the risk experts themselves – the subject of the discourse. They exert a powerful self-protective influence over what may be discussed and considered and the risk methodologies which may be adopted. In view of the fact that for mainly historical reasons pure risk areas have been dominated numerically by physical scientists and engineers for so long, it is unsurprising that social scientists and their knowledge are still largely excluded. The Royal Society report on risk (1992), which acknowledges that social science requirements are not met by conventional views on risk, has not been widely read, let alone accepted, by the technical risk fraternity. Chapter 5 considers further the unobtrusive power (Hardy 1985) of risk experts and the riscomancy culture.

## *Failures of hindsight*

Brian Toft's PhD thesis (Toft 1990), entitled 'The Failure of Hindsight' and later abridged as a management text (Toft and Reynolds 1994, 1997), has become a landmark in the development of understanding of risk behaviour in organizations. It had been assumed that organizations not only seek to learn from their own and other organization's accidents but also actively seek to implement changes which would help to avoid those kinds of accident. Toft showed that such an assumption is generally unwarranted. The general prevailing culture of industrial organizations tends towards denial of failure, and even disasters in which multiple organizational and human failings have been demonstrated as causes are explained away as 'freak accidents'. For example, when the authors were engaged in examining aspects of the King's Cross disaster they discovered, despite the findings of Fennell (1988), a general reluctance among employees of the organization to acknowledge and accept that there had been serious shortcomings which required change. If an organization experiences difficulty in learning from its own mistakes and accidents, is it surprising that organizations may also find it difficult to learn from the mistakes of others? The failure of hindsight is a general phenomenon (see also Fischhoff 1975).

The concept of hindsight failure has led to a search for better understanding of how organizations 'learn' and for improved learning methodologies. The concept of 'organizational learning' is itself problematic in that its meaning varies according to how functionalist or how interpretive a world-view is being expressed. For example, Toft (1992) states that since culture is both a product and a moulder of people, organizational learning has to recognise a much longer term, holistic approach than simply policy, framework, procedures and rules – i.e. 'a cumulative, reflective, saturating process through which all the personnel learn to understand and continually reinterpret the world in which they work by means of all the formal and informal organizational experiences to which they are exposed'.

Organizations may be regarded as multicultural assemblages and have a corresponding number of different reference frames for thinking and learning (Turner 1992). 'New' organizational learning focuses not only on 'learning within frame' or enhancing what a particular group already know but also on 'out of frame learning' which means taking on board other world-views and changes in world-views. Turner stresses that 'new' organizational learning may also involve 'liminal learning' or learning on the threshold of more than one framework of understanding.

'Old' organizational learning is associated with cognitive psychological and cybernetic models at the level of the individual, i.e. logic driven information processing. The double-loop learning concept (Argyris and Schon 1977) is a well-known example. Such instrumental approaches are 'within frame' and encourage a 'training' or 'encounter group' view of facilitating the process whereas Turner's suggestion is to regard organizational learning as a *cultural* activity – i.e. continuous.

## *Some risk cultures*

It is sometimes said that certain cultures are risk orientated and others risk averse. To what extent is this true and what are the implications? One can identify kinds of industry, organization and even nations whose characteristics may appear at first glance to be either more risk orientated or averse than others. For example, public sector organizations tend to be cautious in all areas of decision making and to be averse to political risks. Public accountability in theory also makes them risk averse in matters of finance, yet they are not immune to financial failures and scandals such as those which befell the London Borough of Lambeth in the early 1990s and Liverpool City Council in the 1980s. The threat of individual surcharging of councillors by the District Auditor was apparently considered an acceptable risk by some councillors in the 'homes for votes' scandal at Westminster City Council in the late 1980s and early 1990s (see High Court ruling 19 December 1997).

These varied cases reveal a common feature of public sector organizations, namely a risk-averse sub-culture of professional staff informing elected councillors of what could and should be done and what may be done legally, countered by a risk-orientated sub-culture of elected councillors who do not always wish to be so constrained. The overall culture of such organizations is therefore neither purely risk-orientated nor risk-averse. A dynamic tension exists between two major sub-cultures with different attitudes towards risks. Their meanings of success may share some common components but are nevertheless significantly different.

Such relativism may be identified in many kinds of culture which is not surprising since total cultural homogeneity is rare. Cultures are often said to be risk-orientated on the basis of prominent examples of behaviour of particular individuals or groups but, of course, this may mask quite different characteristics of other people. The new Russia, the Middle East and Far East are thought of as being especially risk-orientated in matters of business and many examples of entrepreneurial risk-taking are evident. However, it is important to consider the particular context in which such a risk-taking sub-culture flourishes. If the country's economy is in serious trouble, individuals may feel that there is little to lose and a lot to gain from adopting a high-risk entrepreneurial strategy. Pride, assertiveness and avoiding loss of face are also influential on risk behaviour in some cultures. For example, in many Middle Eastern countries driver behaviour is very risk-orientated by Western standards. Individual drivers feel compelled to assert their control over the territory of the highway in competition with other drivers. Giving way to another driver is taboo until the last possible moment to avoid an accident. This appears not to be 'road rage' or aggressiveness in the Western sense but more a game of skill, and accidents are surprisingly rare.

Context is all-important. In the West, large sections of the population seek to at least hang on to and hopefully improve the material possessions they gain relatively early in life. Home, mortgage, car(s), video(s), computer(s), satellite TV, foreign holidays, etc. are all part of a growing me-centred consumerist culture change catalysed by UK government policy since the early 1980s. Fear of losing such possessions, particularly through unemployment, has made many people risk-averse in their attitudes towards work and consumer expenditure – the very antithesis of the entrepreneurial model of risk-taking which the government of the day sought to encourage. In many countries, where consumer affluence is not widespread and people are used to a less materially sophisticated existence, fear of losing possessions they do not have is not a demotivator and hence individuals may feel they have a lot to gain by entrepreneurial risk-taking.

From the above, it may be seen that labelling organizations, industries, or nations as either risk-orientated or risk-averse is likely to be misleading as it masks the multicultural assemblages and the complex contexts involved.

## Conclusions

Organizational culture may be regarded as two kinds of paradigm. One paradigm is a means for an organization's members to interpret their own existence, identity and actions and to institute, guide and moderate those actions. It is their world-view. The other kind is culture applied as an analytical paradigm by external observers. The latter is as problematic as the former since, as Jeffcutt (1991) notes, the 'understanding of organization is inseparable from the organising of understanding'.

Since culture both influences and is influenced by the values and meaning systems of the social actors in an organization, the latter's understanding and actions in relation to particular processes are assumed to be culturally linked.

Cultural aspects of organizations are therefore important factors to be addressed in relation to risk.

Like risk, culture is a problematic concept, with even more possible dimensions. Although many attempts have been made to reify, evaluate or even to manage culture, they depend on numerous debatable assumptions which are often not recognised by those who make such attempts. Different levels and manifestations of culture in organizations are identifiable. Lack of cultural homogeneity in most organizations may confound attempts to measure organizational culture, including particular aspects such as safety culture and risk culture.

Organizational culture is linked inextricably with organizational change. Thus, if the culture of an organization changes, then by definition that organization also changes. What is less definitive is whether, if an organization changes (for example in terms of numbers of employees, kinds of activity or achievement of 'success'), its culture necessarily changes.

From a functionalist perspective, some managements have sought to change organizations by manipulating their culture in the form of beliefs or behaviours of employees, with the aim of exercising control. As with systems, however, while certain aspects of an organization's culture may be within the power of management to influence, other elements exist and persist beyond such control. From an interpretive standpoint, culture is regarded more as a metaphor for understanding how organizations function and why they respond in characteristic ways towards a wide range of topics and issues, such as those relating to management, to risk and to change. Given the complexity of human behaviour, and culture as a particular component of it, an interpretive perspective on culture and risk may be a more appropriate precursor to actions seeking to modify culture to achieve risk benefits.

Culture is also linked closely with those risks (pure and speculative) which characterize an organization. A rapprochement is developing between the divergent perspectives of technical (functionalist) and cultural (interpretive) approaches to management and organization, in both study and practice. Nevertheless, controversy still remains about the relationship between culture and risk and the relative merits of functionalist and interpretive perspectives on both.

# Chapter 5
# Power and risk

## Overview

This chapter examines the concept of power in organizations and relationships between power and risk. In particular, the relationship between political processes (as a key manifestation of power relations), strategy and meanings of success in the context of risk is discussed.

## Introduction

Power within and between organizations as a topic of study has often been subsumed within the topic of culture (see for example Checkland and Scholes 1990; Douglas 1992). In this book, however, power is accorded a distinct status on the grounds that whereas cultural analyses focus on shared characteristics, typologies and comparisons, power analyses focus on differentials and the power relations and political processes which result – and, more important, their effects on strategy and approaches to risk. In this respect, this chapter may be aligned with the work of organizational specialists such as Pettigrew (1973, 1987) and Pettigrew *et al.* (1992).

Although there is a considerable literature on power, particularly throughout the 1980s, literature which connects power and risk is relatively rare. Bensman and Gerver (1963) cite power as a source of variance in relation to risk behaviour. The Royal Society report of 1992, however, makes no specific or even general reference to the subject, although it has been recognised in several publications in the 1990s – for example, Douglas (1992) and Waring (1992a, 1994, 1996a). This chapter seeks to help to redress this shortcoming. The following three sections describe the characteristics and dimensions of organizational power, while the fourth considers risk issues within a power framework.

## Substance of power

The very question 'what *is* power?' attracts responses having reified overtones, as if power has physical substance and can be quantified. Typical is the definition proposed by Weber (1947) as reported by Bacharach and Lawler (1980): 'power is the probability that a person can carry out his or her own will despite resistance'. This definition is analagous to that of risk in that power may be conceived as being the product of probability and outcome despite resistance, whereas risk may be conceived as the product of probability and consequences despite existing control measures.

Cognitions and perceptions of power are informed by an individual's world-view (see chapter 3). Thus, for example an individual whose world-view is predominantly functionalist is likely to interpret power in a way that accords with his or her interpretations of organizations.

In order to overcome difficulties in proposing a universal definition of power which is capable of withstanding substantive criticism, Bacharach and Lawler (1980) suggest that power is best understood as a sensitizing device – i.e. a primitive term that may be used in a loose way to sensitize us to other phenomena which contribute to power and which are perhaps less elusive. They propose two categories for characterizing the substance of power: (a) form, or the basic pattern or configuration present in all power situations; these comprise relational aspects, dependence and sanctions; (b) content, or the dimensions specific to a situation and, in particular, authority and influence.

### *Forms of power*

The choice of level of resolution or unit of analysis influences power interpretations. For example, functionalist views tend to regard individuals as if they were simple, inanimate components embedded within a wider structure which determines power – i.e. wholly purposive marionettes existing within a sub-unit instead of complex beings whose behaviour is partly purposive and partly consciously self-willed. Such reductionist views lead to the fallacy of aggregation by which power is attributed to organizations on the assumption that it accurately represents power spread evenly throughout the organization. Micro-level analyses of interaction, however, enable the inextricable link between power and politics in an organization to become visible.

## *Dependence*

Bacharach and Lawler (1980) summarize power-dependence thus: power is based on the availability of alternative sources of the valued attribute and the degree of value attached to the outcome at stake. Thus, there appears to be a close analogy with psychological theories of motivation such as expectancy theory.

## *Sanctioning*

Sanctioning refers to the power of actors materially to affect the outcome of interaction in so far as each other is concerned - e.g. the manipulation of rewards and punishments. Thus, sanctioning refers to the more overt and observable aspects of power such as coercive potential. Power potential and power use are distinct. For example, outcomes may be manipulated merely by creating the impression (i.e. management of meanings) that sanctions are available and will be used. Sanctioning power is therefore dependent on both objective conditions (i.e. actual capacity) and subjective interpretation of other actors (i.e. anticipation of action).

Sanctioning power, unlike formal authority, is not necessarily associated with legitimated structure or hierarchy. To varying degrees, all individuals in an organization possess some sanctioning power. For example, a production worker may choose to increase production or work overtime when requested (i.e. to reward management) or to work to rule or withdraw labour (i.e. punishment).

## *Authority and influence*

Formal authority may be regarded as the right to make unilateral decisions which affect the outcomes of the activities of others in the organization. This implies an hierarchical structural model in which power 'flows' downwards to affect targets of control who are assumed to accept, voluntarily or involuntarily, that authority. Authority is associated with formally legitimated locations of power, typically managerial positions, and roles embodying certain underlying rules recognised by other actors.

Influence, however, is concerned with information provision or exchange and is not confined to legitimated locations of authority power. On the contrary, individuals in lower echelons frequently seek to influence decisions made by others in positions of authority. Influence, therefore, may 'flow' in any direction within a hierarchy. Further, whereas authority is a static phenomenon associated with a right to make decisions (i.e. it either exists or it does not), influence is dynamic and constrained only by the cognitive and perceptual limits, motivations, information and presentation skills of the social actors. Thus, formal authority tends to serve as a social control mechanism whereas influence may serve as a source of potential change, either adaptive or radical.

Authority and influence are not distributed evenly throughout an organization. Whether assessing organizational change or risks, it will be important to identify sources of particular influences and the interactions of such sources, especially with sources of authority. Influence may be a particularly salient feature if, for example, its source is expertise residing within a particular functional group – e.g. health and safety specialists, IT department.

## *Decision-making and participation*

The complementary nature of authority and influence is evident in decision-making mechanisms. Much decision-making is carried out by those with legitimated authority to do so. Nevertheless, decisions are frequently influenced by contributions from individuals and groups having little or no formal authority. In recent years, the advantages of participation and empowerment schemes in decision-making have been promoted widely.

A central difficulty with such propositions is the uncertainty about what is meant by participation and empowerment. Being enabled formally to try to *influence* decisions is quite different from being given a share of authority to *make* decisions. Expectations of authority-sharing are unlikely to be met and this may lead to poorer rather than enhanced industrial relations (see for example Morley and Hosking 1984). Even formal schemes of influence may not be welcomed by those in authority. For example, Storey (1987) reports that Mumford's proposals on participation within ICI met an unenthusiastic response from managers. Similar difficulties posed by conflicting values, interests and goals in 'participative' IT introduction are discussed in chapters 14 and 15).

Participation schemes are frequently proposed either as panaceas for organizational difficulties or as prophylactics for untroubled introduction of changes. Usually, they are based on idealized consensus models of organization. Since realistically they can only cope with variables associated with influence, their effectiveness is bound to be limited.

Despite such difficulties, health and safety is one area of risk in which participation to varying degrees has become a widspread feature among work organizations (see chapters 10 and 12). In some countries, such as the UK and other EU states, worker participation in the furtherance of health and safety improvements is enshrined in law. Safety committees and safety representatives, for example, were identified by Lord Robens (1972) as a vital component in ensuring health and safety at work. Their role is primarily advisory and as such they seek to influence managerial decisions on health and safety matters.

## Bases and sources of power

### *Power bases*

A base of power refers to an attribute that is being controlled. French and Raven (1960) identify five bases of power which relate to power form and content thus:

| Base | Definition | Form/content |
|---|---|---|
| Coercion | threat of decreasing another's outcomes | sanctioning |
| Reward | promise of increasing another's outcomes | sanctioning |
| Expertise | formal or specialised knowledge | influence |
| Legitimacy | rights of control/obligation to obey | authority |
| Referent | personal affect – e.g. charisma | influence |

Control of information and management of meanings are crucial factors in both management of risks and management of change (see chapter 7 and the case study chapters in Part 2). Outcomes of such management processes are likely to be affected significantly by what information is known and considered relevant, what knowledge is brought to bear and how problems, issues, solutions, criteria, practical requirements, etc. are defined – i.e. which group(s) or individual(s) controls or manages meanings.

### *Power sources*

Four sources of power are salient:

1. office or structural location (legitimacy);
2. personal characteristics (e.g. leadership, charisma);
3. expertise (specialized knowledge);
4. opportunity (information access embedded in informal structures).

Expertise is an important source of control over power bases. An individual's skills comprise personal skills (i.e. referent power sourced in personal characteristics) and expertise or technical competence (i.e. sourced in education and training and in cognitive abilities). One difficulty is that individuals in positions of authority and having formal responsibility for managing risks and change may not always possess adequate skills.

### *Ideological power*

Power as a concept often reflects the approach of analysts whose commitments and world-views are grounded in managerial ideology. This suggestion of theorizing power fits with the argument that particular groups exercise power through the management of meanings (i.e. which are grounded in theories). Chapter 4 discussed in detail the ideological power of risk professions in general and technical risk analysts in particular to assert that 'risk' is what risk 'experts' determine it to be (Douglas 1992, 1994; Carter and Jackson 1994). Power struggles which involve competing ideologies inherently affect risk issues, whether the particular struggle is within an organization or within a nation or between nations.

In many countries, the clergy exert considerable ideological power. Notable examples are the power of the Catholic church in Italy and Latin America to dissuade the largely Catholic populations from practising modern forms of birth control. Through absolute control of the state and the media, the Muslim clergy in Iran are able to reinforce Islamic ideology among those who have already embraced it.

The rise of Islamic fundamentalism since the 1970s is focusing attention on the power of Islamic ideology to exert significant influence on people and events both within the Muslim world and beyond. In its strict form, Islamic fundamentalism demands a literal interpretation of the Qur'an and a return to a complete embrace of traditional Islamic beliefs and practices by every professing Muslim in their daily life. A central tenet of this religious philosophy is that there can be no division between a secular state and religion – i.e. the values and principles of Islam are indivisible from those required of government. A salient example of Islamic fundamentalism in practice is the Islamic Republic of Iran (see chapter 13 for detailed case study).

### *Unobtrusive power*

Ideological hegemony takes on a more subtle meaning in the shape of unobtrusive power (Hardy 1985). Unobtrusive power means the ability to secure preferred outcomes by preventing conflict from arising. In other words, social actors possess cultural and normative expectations which make them unaware that they are in effect acquiescing to their own domination. These cultural and normative assumptions stem from the ability of those possessing ideological power to define the reality and legitimacy of the status quo (i.e. to manage situational meanings). In particular, symbolic aspects of power may be used unobtrusively not only to manipulate and secure attitudes but also substantive outcomes such as the distribution of valued resources.

Both the obtrusive and unobtrusive power of cultural expectations and taboos must be considered. Every nation, society and organization has its own unobtrusive ideological backdrop which underpins its culture. There is a tendency to judge other cultures against one's own as a standard or benchmark for what is 'good', 'correct', and 'acceptable' but of course such ethnocentrism often ignores the very taken-for-granted unobtrusive features of one's own culture which in the eyes of other cultures may be seen as pretty appalling. Some examples follow. The globe fish is a popular delicacy in Japan, despite the risk of fatal poisoning if the fish is prepared incorrectly. Competitive driver behaviour that would be considered dangerous in the West is a cultural imperative in many countries in the Middle East. In northern Europe, excessive drinking of alcohol and participation in violent disorder at football matches (with attendant risks to self and others) is a rite of passage within some sections of the population. Until relatively recently, the wearing of personal protective equipment and obeying safety regulations were largely taboo in the construction industry.

## Powerful interests and risk

The following sub-sections examine and discuss risk issues and their connections with some powerful interest groups. The groups have been selected to indicate some of the complexities and different kinds of risk which may be involved and include examples of powerful interests residing in both the inner and outer contexts of organizations. A large number of other powerful groups which could also have been cited such as the pharmaceutical industry, the automobile industry, newspaper publishers, oil companies and so on have been omitted for reasons of space.

### *The professions*

Douglas (1992) emphasizes the unobtrusive ideological power of technical risk analysts. Carter and Jackson (1994) concur in their critique of 'riscomancy'. Such risk analysts are in a powerful position which enables them not only to determine what risk topics and key questions about them are deemed important but also the criteria for acceptability and the response options which should be considered.

The recipients of risk analysts' wisdom (whether employers, clients, regulators or the public) are therefore generally in a position where they feel forced to accept and place on trust the validity of the risk analysts' pronouncements. However, professional opinions may differ. This has been demonstrated starkly in the 1996 public health crisis concerning BSE (bovine spongiform encephalopy) prevalent in beef cattle and the risks of transfer of the disease to humans. Different microbiologists entered into public debate in the media giving widely different estimates of the risk in terms of numbers of humans in the UK who might contract the disease. The government, politicians and interest groups then used particular pronouncements from particular scientists to support their respective arguments about what should be done to reduce the risk – and who was to blame for the health scare, the loss of public confidence in beef and the economic damage to the beef industry.

A feeling of powerlessness to check and test the validity of pronouncements from professionals is not just reserved for professions normally associated with risk such as engineers, safety experts, medical professions, etc. The problem is wide ranging, including for example car mechanics, bank managers, electricians, lawyers and computer specialists. Rowe (1985), in a study of failure in computerized stock control, quotes a manager referring to the computer experts:

> I remember we were presented with this big orange folder, all about the computer we were going to get. I must confess it didn't mean much to me – it was all in computer jargon. But I didn't want to look daft so I didn't say anything. They explained it and it seemed reasonable, but I didn't really understand it. Of course it was decided by then that we were going ahead with it.

In another case study, Waring (1993b) noted similar characteristics (see also chapter 14 in this book):

> Some senior figures saw their own lack of IT knowledge as creating a powerlessness to resist the arguments for IT plans of 'those closest to it'. As one senior figure put it: 'Old decisions tie you into new decisions. There's a level of unsophistication about IT in most people. The ability to make real judgements is limited. Each stage is linked. It's an inherent problem for all lay senior managers'. Another said 'On the IT system, having a plan unfold at a meeting sounds OK so we endorsed it. But later we felt we would have criticized it if we had had more information'.

Nevertheless, despite a continuing cultural expectation that risk experts and other professionals are infallible (even when they disagree!), in some sectors there has been a slow but discernible loss of deference towards professionals and others in positions of authority whose decisions and actions affect risk. For example, in the West both the doctor–patient relationship and the bank manager–customer relationship are much less deferential than once was the case. One reason for greater equity in such power relations is a greater assertiveness among patients and customers engendered by consumerism and increased awareness of consumer rights. There is a greater readiness among individuals who believe that they have suffered loss at the hands of professionals to press for compensation and to sue if necessary. Allied to consumerism, particularly in health care, has been the determination by the government in the UK from 1979 to 1997 to curb the traditional power of the medical professions to dictate patient care and expenditure on it. The introduction of general management, resource management, budget holding, purchasing authorities and internal markets are all part of that process but there are risks attached (see case study in chapter 15).

## *Industry and employer groups*

Like professionals, industry and employer groups are frequently involved in taking policy positions and making pronouncements on risk issues. However, even though they may employ professionally qualified people to advise them, it is not always the case that such bodies take a position which coincides with the professional views obtained or with the wider body of professional opinion on the particular subject. Industry and employer associations frequently take positions which reflect the perceived commercial and/or political interests of their member organizations. However, the committee structures of such associations, coupled with the interests of full-time officials means that positions and policies sometimes may reflect narrow sectional views and interests rather than the broad views of the overall membership.

Vested interests often seek to influence approaches by employers towards risk issues. For example, committees may be established by employers' bodies and standards organizations to develop model policies, standards, procedures and guidance in such areas as occupational health and safety management and security management. Many organizations may be represented on such committees. One section of representatives may accuse another section of representing vested commercial interests in a particular outcome of a committee's work, as a way of preventing that party influencing the outcome. However, while adopting a lofty moral tone, the accusers may fail to declare their own vested commercial interests in the outcomes – i.e. influencing outcomes so as to protect their own jobs as employees of the bodies they represent rather than serving the best interests of their members or other people who may be affected.

## *Trades unions*

Trades unions, particularly in the West, have long established themselves as powerful organizations acting on behalf of workers seeking to gain improved working conditions and greater equity in deals struck with employers. Historically part of the socialist labour movement, British trades unions have always had constitutional affiliations to the Labour Party (although this may change as 'New Labour' has made a distinct shift to the right under Party Leader and Prime Minister Tony Blair). Indeed, by the late 1970s, trades unions in the UK had gained a reputation for being effectively in control of Labour Party policy. Media coverage of the infamous 'winter of discontent' in late 1978 and early 1979, which saw massive strikes by public sector employees and the streets and public places stacked with uncollected refuse, created an indelible image among voters that the trades union 'tail' was wagging the Labour government 'dog' at their expense. At the 1979 general election, the Conservative Party under Mrs Thatcher swept to power on a promise of, among other things, trades union reform. Since then, successive Tory (Conservative) governments through legislation systematically curbed trade unions' powers and employee rights. The incoming Labour government in 1997 stated that it would not seek to return to the situation of the 1970s although it is likely that some relaxation of Conservative anti-union legislation may occur.

Periods of economic recession since 1979 resulted in large scale unemployment, particularly in the period 1989–94. Employers took the opportunity to restructure and to use labour-efficient technology and contract labour on an increasing scale under euphemisms such as 'downsizing', 'outsourcing', 're-engineering' and plain old cost-cutting. With unemployment still officially running at over 2.5 million in 1996, trades unions had lost a significant number of members and therefore membership revenue. With employment law increasingly favouring employers and with the ever-present fear of unemployment, trade union members still in work and their local officials were reluctant to enter into major disputes with their employers.

Faced with a real reduction in the power relationship with employers and with the government, trades unions tended to negotiate as best they could using argument and persuasion and increasingly a 'common interest' theme *vis-à-vis* employers. The old 'Them-and-Us' perpetual struggle with employers is much less evident but that is not to say that it is dead. The old 'might is right' approach of traditional grass roots 'cloth cap' trades unionism may have given way to articulate university graduates with mobile telephones and capable of sophisticated and subtle discourse, but there is still a prevalent 'two sides of industry' world-view. This is not simply unthinking obduracy on the part of trades union officials. They are well aware of what they are doing. Moreover, such a view is also expressed by employers and their representative bodies. The 'two sides' appear to find it convenient to perpetuate the notion that there are only two positions worthy of consideration and that all other voices must be silenced.

An example of this hegemonic stance is provided by the Trades Union Congress's (TUC) and Confederation of British Industry's (CBI) respective attitude towards health and safety at work. Albeit from different standpoints, both the TUC and the CBI regard health and safety risks as a bargaining issue, just one of a number of important negotiating chips in a struggle for supremacy between the 'two sides'. This is not to belittle the very real improvements in health and safety achieved over 150 years or so, especially through trades union efforts, but the fact remains that the struggle between the 'two sides' has always been more important to them than the intrinsic and economic benefits of safety improvements or indeed whether their policies and actions are likely to succeed.

However, those engaged professionally in health and safety work, typically as advisers to employers or as independent consultants, tend to see the main issue as one of 'duty of care' – i.e. those who create risks and who work with them owe a duty of care to ensure the health and safety of persons who might be affected. The duty of professionals is to ensure that the best professional advice and guidance is given and to seek to ensure that the duty of care principle does not become diluted or subverted by other interests. In this regard, their advice should be impartial in disputes, negotiations or power struggles between employers and trades unions. It is therefore crucial that their 'voice' be heard. An independent view may be no bad thing and it is sophistry to argue (Tudor 1996) that government Health & Safety Executive officials, despite their dependent position, are the sole authoritative voice on professional health and safety matters. Some comfort may be drawn from the tripartite TUC, CBI, IOSH study of health and safety issues set up in 1997.

## *Government departments*

In the modern world, government departments find it difficult to deal adequately with the many risks which they face or which they seek to regulate, if only because they are often under intense public scrutiny via the media. Risk assessment is not an exact science and risk management involves making compromises and trade-offs.

The public, on the other hand, may expect categorical assurances that something is absolutely safe and demand risk control measures which offer a 100 per cent gaurantee. Examples include:

- nuclear power (perennial);
- BSE scare concerning beef cattle (1996–);
- listeria in cheese (early 1990s);
- contraceptive pills (1996);
- E. coli food poisoning (1996–7).

In all of this, there is sometimes an assumption that representative politics (such as via councillors, MPs, industry associations, professional bodies, lobby groups and government committees) meet all conditions needed to ensure that at government level the concerns and interests of people at local level and the 'wider public interest' are addressed. Indeed, Rimington (1993) referred to the power and politics of risk in precisely such terms. Such an assumption is flawed since it is based on the fallacy of aggregation of political views and processes – i.e. that political activity at high level equals the sum of political activities at lower levels (see sub-section on forms of power earlier in this chapter). As Pettigrew (1985, 1987, 1994) and Pettigrew *et al.* (1992) emphasize, political processes operate mainly at the micro level between individuals and within and between small groups, whether they are at local level where issues have a direct impact, at higher representational levels or at high level in government.

This representational 'drift' suggests that interests being protected when issues are addressed at high level in government departments are unlikely to equate to those at local level, although such a discrepancy may never become overt or be admitted or perhaps even recognized. One of the consequences of failing to recognize the fallacy of political aggregation and the salience of local power relations is the naïve expectation that requirements of safety legislation will be implemented by all employers because the requirements are 'commonsense' and have been debated and approved by a wide range of interests including bodies representing employers. Such democratic processes are necessary, but resulting legislation is a blunt instrument when it comes to pre-determining actual behaviour – the 'fallacy of predetermination' (Mintzberg 1994; Waring 1996a).

The work of government departments is fraught with political risks, both in their relations with ministers, Parliament and with external interest groups. In the UK, a high profile example is provided by the mounting difficulties faced by the Department of the Environment, Department of Transport and the Highways Agency over road building through rural areas. Since mid-1995, major road developments have been severely disrupted by determined pro-environment protestors. Initially led by a variety of environmental and civil rights groups with a campaign of civil disobedience at development sites, they were joined by some local residents and businesspeople who disputed that the developments were warranted or that the decisions to go ahead were arrived at democratically. The dramas were heightened by television news coverage such as that which showed outraged local people berating their MP for supporting the development. The costs of extra daily policing to prevent public disorder at these sites have been high as have the costs of road-building programme delays. The extra costs have added to the public humiliation and general political fallout affecting the government. One lesson which may have to be learned from such episodes is that it is too risk-laden to proceed with major developments such as these without long and careful public inquiries which are seen to listen to public concerns rather than appear (however inaccurately) to be swayed or even steamrollered by the wider interests of government and big business.

## *Financial institutions*

In financial institutions, risk is seen almost exclusively in terms of investment and security issues. The Cadbury Reports and code of practice (1992) on corporate governance and financial risk emphasize this view, the Barings Bank collapse providing an example (see case study in chapter 11). However, there is also a growing realization in such institutions that staff and customers may also be at risk from a health and safety point of view, whether they relate to bank premises and activities or elsewhere. For example, investment banks may send staff to hazardous industrial sites in territories such as parts of the former Soviet Union where travel may be unsafe, health hazards may be endemic, robbery may be commonplace and armed conflict may threaten. Kidnapping and hostage-taking are also risks in some parts of the world. Some banks now routinely conduct health and safety risk assessments and audits and issue codes of practice and procedures backed up by training and other support facilities.

There is also the issue of public confidence in banks regarding a number of topics. The Barings collapse tended to overshadow a long-running simmering resentment at alleged high street bank practices, notably:

- hidden and excessive bank charges;
- creative charging;
- precipitate debt foreclosure;
- bad advice leading to financial loss;
- high interest rates and poor terms of loans.

Until the late 1980s, high street banks in the UK had traditionally fostered a personal relationship with customers. With deregulation of financial services, however, the banks found themselves in competition with building societies for banking services. Moreover, both building societies and numerous financial services advisers were also selling a wide range of financial products including insurance policies, pensions and mortgages. The banks had to follow suit in order to survive. However, a consequence of the new strategy was a focus on 'bottom lines' and meeting sales targets and on cost-efficient staffing.

Redundancies and job losses in banking from 1990 onwards were unprecedented and this led inevitably to fewer staff doing more work and carrying more responsibilities, to faster promotions for less experienced staff, and to more frequent job changes within banks. In short, the personal continuity in bank-customer relations greatly diminished and this is unlikely to help in cases where disputes arise and may even make them worse. Creative and illicit charging are particularly sensitive issues. In 1996, the government's Office of Fair Trading began an investigation following press revelations that banks and building societies were making up to £160m per year in additional profits by secretly charging mortgagees interest on monies already repaid.

Banks in the UK are risk-averse towards loans, whether they are personal or business loans. Risk aversion may well be prudent in many cases but where innovation is concerned there is a dilemma. Successful product innovation represents future long-term wealth creation and warrants adequate investment. However, front-end R&D and manufacturing may require several years of costly investment before sales revenue flows, yet the product's very novelty defies accurate prediction of sales. The Sinclair C5 covered tricycle is an example of an innovative product which flopped, despite its inventor having a very good record of other successful innovations. Banks are therefore wary of making such loans. Alan Sugar, one of the most successful British product innovators of the 1980s and 1990s, who pioneered the Amstrad range of computers and hi-fi products, is reported to have been so angered by the reluctance of financiers in the City of London to help him in his early days with Amstrad that he still takes delight in insulting their timidity whenever he can.

## *Insurance industry*

The insurance industry has the most mature experience of risk management dating back to the Industrial Revolution. Traditionally, the insurance market has been in the business of risk transfer – i.e. by paying a premium, an insured party seeks to defray the financial loss associated with specified perils being visited upon him or her. Premiums are calculated on a range of factors but particularly data relating to risk classifications to which the insured is assigned and historical data concerning the insured. The overall logic of this approach is reasonable but increasingly there is evidence that it can be a rather blunt instrument which places too much emphasis on classifications and not enough on the individual risk characteristics of the insured party. For example, job classification is a key variable in motor insurance and a person classed as, say, a management consultant would probably be required to pay a higher premium than, say, an industrial scientist. These discriminations are based purely on actuarial data of claims for these classifications and bear no relation to the individual. This can lead to a situation where an individual who practises as both a management consultant and an industrial scientist can be quoted very different motor insurance premiums depending on which profession he or she cites on the application. As these crude classifications are rarely revealed by insurers and brokers, an applicant may be quite unaware that he or she may be paying more than is necessary.

The unchecked power of underwriters to determine the risk and the premium is mitigated solely by aggregate market forces and the option of insurance applicants to 'shop around' for the best quotation. Indeed, it has become essential to do so as experience shows that several insurers presented with the same information from an applicant may present very different premium quotations and cover restrictions. In one instance, one of the authors obtained travel insurance from his usual insurer to travel to Iran. The premium for ten days was quoted as including a 10 per cent territory loading on the basic premium. Two weeks later when the author was back in England and planning a further imminent trip to the same territory, the same insurer quoted a 90 per cent loading on the basis that the country was subject to a 'hot spot' warning. To the author's knowledge as someone who knows the territory and up-to-date developments well, such an assertion was unjustified. A number of possible threats, such as epidemic, insurrection and earthquake, could have made it a 'hot spot'. However, if the insurers were aware of much higher risks to be faced by the insured, it was surely their professional and ethical duty to disclose the relevant information about the 'hot spot' warning to the insured. This proved not to be the case. The author's suspicions that the underwriters were either misinformed, incompetent or simply hoping that a gullible applicant would pay an extortionate premium were strengthened by him obtaining reasonable quotations from other insurers and without any 'hot spot' warning. The trip went without incident.

Other examples of the roulette wheel of insurance quotations across the spectrum of personal insurances (life, health, house, travel, etc.) are legion. Save for *caveat emptor*, the power in the relationship between insurer and insured is unevenly distributed in favour of the insurer. As discussed above, it is unwise to assume that a quoted insurance premium accurately reflects the risk, in so far as this can be ascertained. It is also unwise to assume that an insurance claim will be met in full or at all. Insurers have a duty to ensure not only that a claim is valid but also that the terms and conditions of the policy have been met by the insured. Sometimes resisting claims on a tough interpretation of the 'small print' has led to complaints that insurers are not just seeking legitimately to avoid liability but also seeking to evade their contractual obligations to meet valid claims. There are frequent complaints about such matters from insured parties to consumer protection organizations and consumer protection columns in the media.

A fundamental assumption of insurance is that the value of claims of the few are far exceeded by the total premiums of the many, thereby spreading the financial risk. However, in some areas of insurance this assumption is no longer born out. In employers' liability (EL) insurance, for example, since the 1970s total claims paid out have risen steadily in relation to total premiums. From 1987 to 1992, UK insurers made an EL underwriting loss of £588m and this has led to indemnity capping which sets a limit of £10m for claims arising from any one occurrence (ABI 1994). In addition to indemnity capping, other insurer responses include general increases in premiums, scrutiny of individual claims history and, increasingly, making insurance cover and premium quotations conditional upon prevention by the insured. In other words, other options of risk management such as risk avoidance and risk reduction and control (see chapter 1) are becoming more salient. Nevertheless, after more than 20 years of calls for a more pro-active, preventive involvement from insurers, the current position in the insurance market is still largely one in which risk is both viewed and managed in a reactive, fragmented way involving underwriting decisions made on the basis of little objective evidence about the actual risk.

The gradual move by the insurance market towards a more preventive strategy also emphasizes the fact that insurance as a passive strategy within risk management can only soften the blow of damage or loss. Risk transfer cannot cover all losses and cannot restore irreparable damage such as many kinds of personal injury, whereas other risk management strategies actively seek to avoid, prevent or reduce such effects. It is therefore naïve to expect insurance to be able to offer a complete approach to managing risks.

## *Intra-organizational factors*

The last six sub-sections have discussed powerful interests which reside largely in the outer context of organizations (see also chapter 6). This chapter would be incomplete without some discussion on power factors within organizations, which may be at least as important in relation to risk as those in the outer context. Some of these inner context factors have been discussed in preceding chapters, notably organizational culture, risk cognition and management systems, and in preceding sections of this chapter (substance of power; bases and sources of power). Four power-related topics are especially important to understanding organizational behaviour and therefore risk behaviour:

1 management of meanings;
2 decision-making;
3 key strategic figures;
4 organizational structures.

Management of meanings and mobilization of bias are central to understanding organizational behaviour. The management of meanings is inextricably bound up in the concepts and uses of power. Key figures, and particularly strategic orchestrators, seek to achieve ends by ensuring that their definitions of organizational reality and goals are espoused by other key figures.

Case studies (Waring 1993b) have shown that fantasy manipulation appears to be important in deciding the content of IT strategies. Whereas in these cases there was evidence that IT strategies had been only partly successful according to 'objective' criteria, frequent redefinition of IT success by key figures made assessment of success difficult from the point of view of other actors within the organization. Over a period of time during which unobtrusive redefinition occurred, all the actors, including the orchestrator, underwent a learning process to varying degrees but the orchestrator appeared to be able to maintain an edge sufficient to sustain his role as fantasy manipulator. Lyles and Schwenk (1992) refer to the role of key figures and decision makers in such a process of organizational learning.

Manipulation of fantasies about past, present and future is an important part of the process of negotiated order (Vickers 1983). Perceptions of risk and of actual or potential crises are also manipulated by orchestrators as a means of securing among doubters acceptance of the benefits of proposed changes as a means of risk reduction. For example, in Waring's (1993b) cases, the ready acceptance of the particular changes was projected as being much more preferable in its effects (organizational, customers, job security) than either rejection or reluctant acceptance. Indeed, ready acceptance was promoted as the only means of preventing or mitigating the effects of the particular feared crisis. In one case, the cost-cutting benefits of the new IT system in a financial crisis were promoted. In another case, the argument for getting the IT system operational was to strengthen negotiating positions in a recently announced merger and to offer hope of survival after statutory restructuring of the health service market (see case studies in chapters 14 and 15).

Organization structures, including reporting relationships, accountabilities and delegated authority, may facilitate or curb risk-taking by individuals in positions of power. For example, the organizational structure encompassing the London headquarters of Barings Bank and Barings Singapore undoubtedly had an effect on the trading activities of Nick Leeson and the unwarranted financial risks he was able to take for so long (see case study in chapter 11).

## Towards a potential model of power and risk behaviour

Meanings need to be recognized in context. For example, people in different locations in an organizational structure and who belong to different sub-cultures tend to ascribe their own particular meanings to concepts. In particular, meanings of 'success' are likely to vary according to the location and the individual. Corporate pronouncements on goals, missions, strategies, etc. which express implicit visions of 'success' often fail to recognise the fact that the organization does not comprise a set of identikit programmable robots or clones of the senior managers. Despite the power of key figures to manipulate visions of corporate or project success, such power is limited when it comes to personal dimensions of success which may be powerful motivators. Such matters are important risk factors in management of change (see chapter 7).

A potential model for understanding managerial processes in relation to change and risk has been developed (Glendon and Waring 1996; Waring 1993b, 1994). The proposed model comprises eight components including risk. Of these components, the three most salient and which form the core of the model as depicted in Figure 5.1 are:

1 power/political processes;
2 strategy;
3 meanings of success.

The core components are influenced in an interdependent relationship by contextual mediators, namely organizational structures, organizational culture, resources,

*Figure 5.1* A potential model of power and risk behaviour

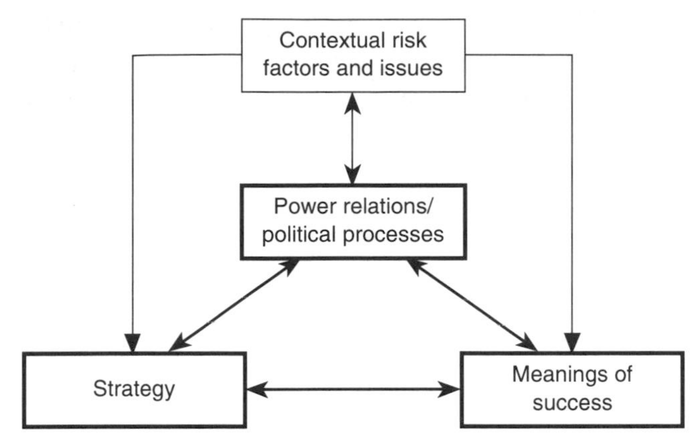


*Source*: Waring (1993b, 1994); Glendon and Waring (1996)

risk/crisis perceptions and the organization's outer context. The proposed model is described and discussed in more detail in chapter 7.

## Conclusions

Power in organizations is a complex phenomenon having multiple dimensions, although it is frequently treated as if it were a unitary concept. In developing understanding of risk in relation to organizations, their management and change, it will be important to examine power relations and to identify sources of particular influences and the interactions of such sources. Influence may be a particularly salient feature if, for example, its source is expertise residing within a particular functional group (e.g. IT, finance, risk specialists). Power relations and political processes involving management of meanings are particularly relevant to understanding risk behaviour in organizations, for example relations between those who do have and those who would like to have powers to decide the nature of risks and what, if anything, should be done about them. In other words, strategy (both explicit and implicit) is closely linked with political processes and meanings of success. Similar relations are also influential on risk issues in the wider public arena.

Power, and its derivatives such as influence and legitimated authority, is one of a number of factors external to individuals which affect their risk cognition and the expression of risk concepts by parties generally. Perception and understanding of a risk may be as much to do with the extent to which individuals and groups trust and believe the reported pronouncements of experts about the risk in question, as it is to do with their own direct experiences. Given the relative paucity of most people's first-hand experience with many risks, 'expert power' may in particular influence people's acceptance of a given risk - particularly those which relate to technology or those arising from 'invisible' hazards (e.g. nuclear waste, environmental pollution, food contamination, HIV infection).

The power of experts and politicians, usually translated through the media, is often an important determinant of individuals' cognitions of a particular risk. Collective response to that risk may be exercised subsequently as 'consumer power' through purchasing decisions (e.g. in the case of food), or through some form of democratic process, including forms of protest, at least in states where this is a realistic option.

Thus, in many cases (e.g. nuclear power, national food scares as with eggs or beef), people respond not so much to the 'objective' risk – as in any case this cannot be established for them as individuals – but to the nature of the power relations between themselves, politicians, other interested parties and experts, with media also playing a potentially powerful role.

An interesting reversal of the 'NIMBY' (Not In My Back Yard) protests of an earlier era is being observed in the 1990s. The focus of protest has changed. For example, in the case of road-building programmes, protests once focused on local interests not wishing to be overridden by national ones. Now long-term 'global' interests (e.g. in respect of the environment) are being invoked as being threatened by predominantly local issues (e.g. building a bypass).

# Chapter 6
# Organizational environment and risk

## Overview

This chapter examines the effects of an organization's environment or outer context on risk cognition and behaviour in relation to risk within the organization.

## Introduction

As explained in chapter 3, in order to avoid confusion with the physical environment, there is a growing tendency to refer to the outer context of an organization rather than to its operating 'environment' (Pettigrew 1985). However, in this chapter we stick with tradition since the meaning here is self-evident.

Whether one takes a strictly systems view of an organization and its environment or a conventional management view, there is common agreement that the organization is in a largely dependent and reactive role and that attempts by the organization to influence and control its environment can only have limited success. However, this recognition differs from the claims of some management consultants that an organization is totally reactive to external events. For example, some argue that all change in organizations is externally rooted and driven. This absolute view is based on an over-zealous application of a biological model to organizations. Organizations not only seek to influence their environments and control environmental conditions perceived to be detrimental but also may achieve modest success on some occasions. They may undergo change processes which are only partly influenced by external factors.

There is also a need to recognise that factors perceived to be in an organization's environment are not a loose collection of independent components. Many, if not most, will interact with each other in a systemic fashion – i.e. the environment may be regarded as a set of interacting systems. For example, public policy and legislation are not completely independent of public opinion. The courts and judiciary are not independent of public policy. Product markets are not independent of technology. The systemic nature of the environment partly explains why it is difficult for an organization to control it.

The following sections categorize environmental components, factors and conditions which are likely to have an effect on risk and on its cognition and behaviour towards it in organizations.

## Economies and markets

Under this heading, the following components (not in any order of importance) are salient:

- financial climate and general trading conditions;
- product markets and competition;
- labour market and skill base;
- industry sector culture;
- shareholders and investment;
- trades unions;
- insurance market.

### *Financial climate and trading conditions*

Generally, economic recession and a difficult financial climate produce perceptions of increased business risk within organizations because cash-flow tends to become more vulnerable, both to creditors and to debtors who are also likely to be under pressure. Manufacturers, constructors, distributors and suppliers of services are all likely to 'feel the pinch' and many may go into liquidation as occurred during the 1989–1995 UK recession. However, many speculators regard such conditions as ideal for making speculative gains on the basis that assets, stocks and shares or even companies may be purchased at low price with an expectation of significant gains when the share price index improves. Perception of risks associated with the financial climate and trading conditions therefore depends on the individual and their position and role in these matters, as discussed in chapter 8. The politician, stockbroker, asset stripper, shareholder, insurer, factory worker, public sector worker and company risk manager are all likely to have different perceptions of such risks.

The interaction between pure risk areas and speculative risk areas is often overlooked when considering the financial climate. For example, a decision to invest in capital projects such as new factories or new products will almost certainly have implications for safety, quality, environment and security. However, even in robust financial and trading conditions there may be perceptions that such implications are minor but high cost which then harden into cost-control justifications for doing little about them. Alternatively, if the implications are seen as low cost, this may provoke a justification for marginalizing them.

Increasingly, organizations wish to create a capacity to anticipate and respond to rapidly changing economic conditions. A key argument for strategic use of IT, for example, has been its potential for placing less reliance on permanently employed costly staff. Remote terminals enable contract staff to work away from the business premises thus reducing the need for costly office space. In some cases, the lure of an IT-driven organization, with its potential for competitive advantage as opposed to merely an IT-using organization, has provoked attempts to introduce radical change using IT as a vehicle. However, risks of not introducing IT also need to be considered in tandem with risks associated with its introduction (see case study in chapter 14) – i.e. through a speculative risk assessment comprising two components, as outlined in chapter 2.

## *Product markets*

Fashion, taste, image and market trends are all speculative risk factors in the outer context of organizations. If a company's products are mismatched with such factors, sales are likely to be affected adversely – e.g. the Sinclair C5. Equally, a company needs to detect any significant changes in such factors early and to respond appropriately. Such a reactive style may not apply to the small number of companies recognised as trend setters in their particular sphere but, as exemplified by Sinclair, such companies are sometimes very successful in product innovation and sometimes very unsuccessful.

Nevertheless, when pure risk issues in the product market arise they often do so unpredictably and their effects on markets may be considerable. Examples include:

- listeria in cheese;
- BSE in beef;
- salmonella in eggs;
- plasticizers in baby milk powder;
- growth hormones in meats;
- fire retardents in baby mattresses;
- silicone breast implants.

The position of risk consultants of various kinds also needs to be considered. This service market is largely uncontrolled, save for professional registration schemes operated by some professional bodies (see sub-section on standards later in this chapter). In recent years, especially since 1992, a large number of self-styled consultants have entered the UK health and safety consultancy market, for example providing services such as risk assessments, training and advice on relevant management and technical matters. At best, many of these consultants are competent technicians who are unable to meet the two additional criteria essential for consultants, namely advanced knowledge (e.g. a relevant higher degree or published research) and enhanced skills (e.g. substantial experience in dealing satisfactorily with complex issues). The problem is compounded by client organizations who lack the knowledge or motivation to discriminate between consultants other than on cost. Such ignorance is likely to be aggravated by loss of staff (e.g. 'downsizing', contracting out - see sub-section on trade unions in chapter 5 and section on labour markets below) having the required knowledge and expertise to decide who are appropriate consultants and how to use them. Low-cost technician skills may well be appropriate to some client needs but many situations require genuine consultants who will almost certainly charge fee rates commensurate with their standing. Clients who opt for low-cost technicians may well not appreciate that, as a result, their risk position may not improve or may get worse.

## *Labour markets*

Since the late 1980s, labour contracting in various forms has become a pervasive characteristic of labour markets in the West. The main justification has been cost control, since the employer is responsible for less overhead costs associated with people hired on a 'contract for services' basis as opposed to a 'contract of service'. Contracting out may also be attractive to particular kinds of employee such as highly skilled professionals whose skills are in demand or individuals seeking part-time work or those who prefer to work at or from home. To some extent, the advantages to such people and to employers have been over-played by suggestions that *all* current employees would benefit from contracting out and that there is no downside to the employer (Kennedy 1994).

Chapter 4 referred to the growing problem of 'Me PLC' which has resulted from ruthless and sustained cost-cutting, restructuring and staff being either seduced or forced into contracted-out status. Employers are no longer able to rely on staff loyalty and increasingly are being held to ransom by skilled employees (Caulkin 1995). Expectations that staff will continue to be generally cooperative and do unpaid overtime, for example, are not being met as ordinary employees who remain see their wages pegged while directors receive relatively large increases in rewards. Even opportunities for paid overtime may be declined if employees dislike the general work arrangements and what they perceive as poor employer attitudes towards them.

Contracting out and the contract culture have brought problems in the pure risk area. In particular, intuitively it would be much harder to ensure effective communication and integration among all the independent parties in a contractor environment and this has been the case in practice. The development of a safety culture or desirable behavioural characteristics is also more difficult in such a context of fragmentation and interface discontinuities. For example, the potential safety implications of such fragmentation resulting from privatization of the railway industry in the UK have received increased attention in recent years (see chapter 12).

Skill shortages are now prevalent in many sectors. For example, in the UK National Health Service, hospitals regularly seek to recruit nurses from abroad because UK supplies are inadequate. Student nurse numbers are failing to meet demand, partly as a result of perceived bad effects of NHS reforms and previous government policy towards the health care sector in general and the nursing profession in particular (see chapter 15). Many qualified nurses have switched from the NHS to private hospitals and nursing agencies for overseas contracts, thus reducing further the pool of nurses in the home market.

The long-term failure of British industry and commerce to invest in adequate training and re-training of its personnel has added to the current 'Me PLC' problem for employers. Training is still regarded by many employers as representing time away from productive work – i.e. an unwanted overhead. However, it is also generally true that 'blue chip' and 'world-class' companies invest heavily in training. For example, the human resource management case study of New Zealand Breweries by Glendon and Bamber (1996) suggests that the company regarded training as a major focus in its strategy for a culture change.

## *Industry sector*

Particular industries tend to have specific or special risks associated with them and these are likely to have an effect on individual organizations in that sector. In the safety area, for example, the activities and technologies of the railway industry, nuclear industry and offshore oil and gas present hazards and risks peculiar to these industries. Organizations in these industries are required to comply with safety legislation and regulatory control regimes which apply only to the particular industry. Some examples of sectoral risks are:

| **Industry** | **Risk issues** |
|---|---|
| Offshore oil and gas | Major hazards; prospecting; oil prices |
| Banking | Futures trading; fraud; security |
| Health care | Patient care vs. market economics; medical accidents |
| Railways | Privatization; major accidents |
| Construction | Public policy on housing |
| Financial services | Probity and ethics; fraud |
| Food | Public health |

Industry sectors often have their own characteristic culture which both influences and is influenced by how organizations within the sector approach hazard and risk issues and the responses which are expected. The unobtrusive and self-protective nature of culture often results in 'blind spots' and inertia towards recognition and acceptance of the size of particular risks, even when there is ample evidence of such risks. There is a tendency for industry associations (reflecting input from individual members) to play down risks by suggesting that a particular disaster was an aberration and that similar conditions are not prevalent in the industry as a whole. This 'failure of hindsight' (Toft 1990) may partly explain why whole sectors of industry are slow to learn from disasters (see chapters 4 and 5 – in particular sub-sections on unobtrusive power, and industry and employer groups – and chapters 10, 11 and 12).

## *Shareholders*

Until relatively recently, it was accepted wisdom that shareholders were only interested in dividends and other direct returns on their investments. Increasingly, however, ethical investors (individual and institutional) feature in the lists of shareholders of public limited companies. Such investors seek to invest only in companies which meet and maintain certain criteria regarding their activities. For example, prior to the fall of apartheid in South Africa, some ethical investors refused to invest in UK companies perceived to be supporting apartheid through discriminatory and exploitative employment practices in South Africa. Since then, the Co-op Bank has run television advertisements which specifically invite investors who wish to be assured that their bank will not invest in regimes which are manifestly corrupt, or which ignore human rights or which damage the environment. A number of 'blue chip' companies now employ special agencies to monitor the activities of companies listed on the stock market in respect of a range of ethical parameters such as environmental protection, health and safety of employees, public liability, product liability, customer care, remuneration and rewards policies for top executives, and so on.

There are investment risks attached to companies whose conduct falls below acceptable standards. Disinvestment and 'black listing', while not a major threat to such companies at present, may nonetheless affect share prices and adverse publicity is unwelcome in a climate of growing public disapproval of corporate wrong-doing. Increasingly, alliances against abuse of boardroom power are being struck between small shareholders and investment groups representing substantial interests such as public sector pension funds which have policies on ethical investment. Prominent examples include dumping of Shell shares in 1996 following the execution in Nigeria of eight pro-democracy campaigners who had been challenging Shell's record on environmental pollution in Nigeria. Shell's corporate reputation had not long been sullied by its plan in 1995 to sink its Brent Spar oil installation in the North Sea.

Turner & Newall, once one of the largest producers of asbestos products, saw its shares fall 8 per cent in value in one day in May 1996 as a result of failing to limit personal injury claims for asbestosis in the United States. By November 1996, the company is reported to have paid out over £300m to meet such claims with further claims outstanding. T&N then negotiated a capping deal for future payouts which improved its share price but left it vulnerable to hostile takeover bids.

The 1995 annual general meeting of British Gas shareholders was unprecedented in the reported sustained ferocity with which the chief executive was vilified by shareholders over the increases in already large pay and benefits which he and fellow board members were awarding themselves. The quality and scrupulousness of corporate governance has become a risk issue in that shareholders are increasingly intolerant of a range of senior wrongdoings.

It was widely reported in the media that at the British Aerospace annual general meeting of shareholders in May 1996 the board was berated by anti-arms campaigners, including several MPs, for its record on selling arms to repressive regimes. A direct accusation was reportedly made against the company's chief executive that he personally had been involved in a plot to kidnap or murder a prominent Saudi dissident Dr Mohammed al-Mas'ari whose presence and activities in Britain might jeopardize an arms deal with Saudi Arabia worth £20bn. Memoranda of conversations between the chief executive and other industry and defence figures, in which plans to 'stifle personally' Dr al-Mas'ari were allegedly discussed, were apparently quoted. The board's apparent failure to provide a satisfactory rebuttal to this accusation is one of the odder aspects of a bizarre story and undoubtedly tarnished the company's reputation.

Such cases as BAe, Shell and British Gas highlight the risks which boards face if increasingly assertive shareholders and the public feel aggrieved by what they perceive as boardroom wrongdoing. Managed ethical funds have increased rapidly since 1985 and now stand at over £1bn. From 1990–95, ethical funds typically outperformed unit trusts by 10 per cent.

## *Trades unions*

The traditional aim of the trade union movement has been the improvement of employee rights and their terms and conditions of labour (see section on trades unions in chapter 5). Winning compensation for employees injured at work or for those who have suffered discrimination or unfair dismissal is also an important activity. These aims and activities remain but since the early 1980s there has been a steady decline of trade union power to obtain results through strikes and other forms of industrial action. This change, particularly in the UK, has arisen through a combination of factors such as anti-union employment legislation, economic recession and world competition.

Legislation in particular has curbed the custom-and-practice rights of trades unions to call strikes without ballots and to spread industrial action from a dispute with a single employer to a whole industry or to other industries. Recession led to high unemployment and to stuctural changes in employment practices, such as contracting. Foreign competition from low cost labour markets has added to the pressure. Job security has been an inevitable casualty. Union membership has fallen significantly and members are more reluctant than in earlier decades to take industrial action.

In such a climate, employers may store up problems for the future by dismissing trades unions as a spent force and not granting them due respect. Some employers may be encouraged to assume that unions are never better than a troublesome nuisance. In labour market politics, it is not inevitable that trades unions will either remain in a relatively weak position or will not develop a major role in industrial development. There is a danger of underestimating the staying power of unions and ignoring the quiet revolution which has forced many of them to adopt a 'business thinking' approach to their role and relationship with employers (Caulkin 1996). Many UK employers have responded positively to EU Directives concerning worker participation under the Social Chapter and now have improved collaborative arrangements with transformed trades unions – even though the previous government in 1996 opted out of the EU 'Social Chapter' which would have made such participation schemes compulsory.

In a more specific area of risk, employers often fail to heed early warnings about health and safety issues raised by trades unions. Prominent examples have included:

- work-related upper limb disorders (WRULD) in a range of occupations;
- asbestosis;
- occupational deafness;
- occupational stress;
- management hostility towards their statutory health and safety responsibilities in particular industries and companies.

## *The insurance market*

In the pure risk area, a range of insurance policy types is available to provide recompense in the event of specified perils being visited upon the insured. Policies include:

- business interruption;
- fire, theft and damage;
- employer's liability (EL);
- public liability (PL);
- product liability;
- professional indemnity (PI);
- motor and vehicles;
- shipping and aircraft.

In principle, insurers could exert a powerful influence on companies to prevent losses, for example via premium penalties and discounts. However, historically there has been little activity of this kind. More recently, however, in the face of underwriting losses, insurers and brokers have begun to adopt a more proactive loss prevention role in client risk management. The shift is not unequivocal and in general risk assessments are rudimentary but, in the longer term, insurance cover and premium calculations are likely to be based as much on current risk exposure of the insured as on data about the class of the insured or claims history.

The problem of the insurance market is exemplified by employer's liability (EL). In the 1970s, the EL account was a very small part of most insurers' general business but since then claims and pay-outs have risen rapidly. From 1987 to

1992, UK insurers made an underwriting loss of £588m in EL (ABI 1994). Factors include:

- sharp increases in injury awards;
- long-term disease claims such as for asbestos-related diseases, noise-induced hearing loss and work-related upper limb disorders;
- a greater willingness for plaintiffs to take legal action;
- improved diagnosis of work-related injuries and diseases.

In addition to diseases which are well-established as being of occupational origin, other newer categories of claim such as for occupational stress have already been successful in the United States and the UK. Changes in employment practices such as contracting out have also had an effect. A single incident could result in muliple claims against several policies. The trend for increasing claims and awards appears to continue.

In the past, insurers have usually provided EL cover without specifiying a monetary limit of indemnity. In the light of heavy EL losses, however, indemnity capping has now been introduced in the UK with a limit of £10m for claims arising from one occurrence. Conditions in the insurance market are now such that some insurers have withdrawn from the EL market. Premiums are beginning to reflect more closely the claims history of the insured and, for those with a poor claims record, cover is often hard to place. Underwriters and brokers are placing policy-holders and proposers under greater scrutiny and are assessing the adequacy of both technical safety measures and management systems in underwriting decisions and premium calculations. For some companies, the difference between a good and bad assessment can result in several £m difference in their EL premiums.

Nevertheless, the approach by underwriters to such insurance business depends on whether the market conditions are 'hard' or 'soft'. Scrutiny of an insured party's risk status may be greater when policy business is buoyant than when it is slack. Insurers may be making more money on investments than on premiums.

## Public policy, regulation and standards

Components which are significant in this area include:

- government policy and legislation;
- regulatory enforcement;
- the courts;

- professional regulation;
- standards.

## *Government policy and legislation*

A common theme of public policy in western countries since about 1980 has been a philosophy of individual-centred self-sufficiency and reduced state control in matters which could be handled by the private sector. The burgeoning cost of social welfare, health, education and policing has strengthened the arguments of those who are opposed ideologically to what they see as a 'dependence culture'. Privatization of state services and state-controlled companies gathered momentum throughout the 1980s and 1990s. Speculative risk taking at all levels in all spheres of activity and life has been given a tacit, if not declared, seal of government approval – e.g. shares in privatized public utilities, the National Lottery, etc. Hand-in-glove with the concept of a share-owning democracy, a climate of short-term work contracts and a 'Me PLC' culture (Caulkin 1996), has been a redistribution of personal financial risks based on survival of the fittest or, perhaps more accurately, luckiest.

Apart from political risks to incumbent administrations which engage in any kind of radical change programme, perceptions of risk and risk acceptability within organizations undoubtedly are coloured by government policy and actions. Examples include:

- monopolies and mergers;
- health care (see chapters 14 and 15);
- health and safety at work (see chapters 10 and 12);
- investment and insider trading (see chapter 11);
- policing and prison policy;
- privatization of state services, public utilities and nationalized industries (see chapters 12 and 15);
- education;
- foreign policy (see chapter 13).

The previous UK government sought to increase the efficiency and effectiveness of its policy by streamlining delivery services in many of these areas. A number of services previously operated as government departments were redesignated as agencies so that, in principle, ministers are responsible only for broad policy and strategy and not for executive implementation – e.g. the Prison Service, although in practice there has been speculation about ministerial interference in operational management of prisons. Ideas from market economics were introduced such as separation of purchasing and delivery functions – e.g. the National Health Service. Business planning, resource management and performance measurement are now key elements of all delivery functions of government policy, an approach which so far has been also followed by the new Labour government.

Within delivery services and among intended beneficiaries, whether individuals or organizations, some of the prominent risk issues which have arisen concern whether government legislation and drives for increased efficiency and effectiveness have produced significant improvements. For example:

- Are specified performance measures accurate and reliable? Are they focused on important qualitative measures of effectiveness rather than biased towards cost efficiency?
- Does legislation work?
- Do government policies and measures enjoy the confidence of the professions engaged in implementation?
- Does the public benefit sufficiently?

Most policy areas identified above address significant hazards or threats which affect both pure and speculative risks to a range of individuals, groups and organizations. If the answers to such questions are 'no', then it suggests that such risks are increased. Examples which have been the subject of public debate include:

- Validity of patient throughput and waiting lists as key measures of health care performance.
- Hospital funds for operations running out in the middle of the financial year, resulting in ward closures and cancelled operations.
- Effects of tougher prison sentencing policy on overcrowding and prison officer safety in a climate of prison staff cuts and limited capital programmes.
- Do longer prison sentences deter criminality significantly?
- Does privatization of public utilities and state industries benefit the public significantly in the long term in terms of lower prices and improved services?
- Does privatization and the fragmentation which accompanies it introduce significant safety risks through problems of management control and communication and cost pressures to cut corners?

## *Regulatory enforcement*

Two different approaches to regulatory enforcement are prevalent. One is to draw up prescriptive legislation and standards which set out precisely what organizations and individuals should do and how they should do it, and then to use enforcement mechanisms and penalties to catch and punish offenders. This approach is typical of policing but in many countries is also used in other spheres of regulatory control. An alternative, less prescriptive approach sets broad requirements and requires organizations to set their own goals and establish their own practical systems to achieve them. In this approach, regulatory enforcement seeks to educate and persuade people to manage their own affairs competently within the law, with punishments as a last resort. This self-regulatory preventive framework has found favour in the UK since the 1970s in such areas as health and safety at work and financial services.

One difficulty in deciding on the 'best' approach to enforcement arises from the fact that organizations are all different. Some well-run organizations will always keep their house in order without legislation whereas others will always ignore regulatory control of any kind. In principle, current self-regulatory approaches which require organizations to carry out risk assessments and to manage risks competently (such as in the areas of health and safety at work, environment, food hygiene, medicine, banking and investments) are likely to be more effective than prescriptive approaches because they require active involvement of managers and others. However, as chapters 1 and 2 note, much depends on how assiduously and competently organizations approach risk management and risk assessment. Statutory regulation and levels of penalties alone cannot pre-determine a desired outcome (see for example Mintzberg 1994 on the fallacy of pre-determination).

National cultures and general approaches to regulation are also relevant. For example, self-regulation may be appropriate to mature industrial societies in Europe which have a long history of prescriptive regulation prior to self-regulation. Many developing countries, however, have no such background and may have reactive cultures which respond only to 'policing'.

## *The courts*

Organizations need to follow development of case law as judgements may have a bearing on current policies, activities and procedures. New precedents may be set whether in an interpretation of law, or of employer duties, or in the scale of penalties or compensation. Typical areas of concern for employers are:

- employment discrimination on the grounds of sex, race, religion or disability;
- sexual or racial harassment at work;
- unfair dismissal;

- accidents, employer's liability and health and safety cases;
- environmental pollution;
- medical negligence;
- intellectual property;
- libel;
- fraud;
- product liability.

Examples of cases in the UK which have caused many employers to review their own policies and systems include:

- Multiple cases of compensation claims against the Ministry of Defence brought by female officers claiming discrimination over pregnancy.
- Racial and sexual discrimination cases brought against the Police by serving officers.
- The case against Northumberland County Council in 1994 (first successful employer's liability claim in the UK for occupational stress; £175,000 compensation awarded).
- Successful compensation claims by employees against a number of employers for the effects of WRULD (work-related upper limb disorders) caused or aggravated by keyboard work.
- The 1993 Lyme Bay canoeing tragedy (managing director of OLL company convicted on four counts of corporate manslaughter and jailed for 3 years, later reduced to 2 years on appeal; OLL also convicted of corporate manslaughter and fined £60,000).
- Major disasters such as the King's Cross fire 1987 and Piper Alpha 1988 raising numerous issues about safety management systems throughout employment.
- Criminal prosecution of companies for health and safety offences resulting in large fines (e.g. BP Grangemouth 1987, fined £750,000; ICI Nobels Explosives 1990, fined £250,000; Hickson International 1993, fined £250,000 plus £150,000 costs).

## *Professional regulation*

Professional regulation is intended to protect the public against the activities of unqualified persons which may be dangerous or damaging. Professional bodies therefore ought to be able to exert a powerful influence on risks arising from incompetence or negligence by ensuring that only competent persons are entitled to practise in the particular profession. More and more professions (such as medicine and pharmacy) are required to operate a statutory registration scheme of practising members. It is illegal to practise unless properly qualified and registered. However, not all professions are required to operate such schemes and in some cases people with dubious formal qualifications and weak experience are free to operate. Such shortcomings may be found in areas such as psychotherapy, diet management, 'alternative medicine', and health and safety at work where individuals may set themselves up as self-styled consultants. If such individuals do not belong to professional bodies having codes of professional conduct backed up by disciplinary procedures, they are beyond professional control.

In the health and safety area, UK professional bodies (notably the Institution of Occupational Safety & Health and jointly the Royal Society of Chemistry and Institution of Chemical Engineers) have set up registration schemes seeking to ensure that only pre-existing members who are fully qualified by examination and professional experience and who maintain a prescribed standard of continuing professional development which is subject to regular audit are entitled to use the designation 'registered professional'. However, while such schemes are laudable, they are weakened by a general level of ignorance among employers and clients about registration and possible risks entailed in using inadequately qualified persons.

## *Standards*

Both national and international standards influence organizations on a range of matters to do with risk. For example:

- management systems standards (safety, quality, environment, etc.);
- product standards;
- design standards.

However, as noted in chapter 3, both the content and assumptions of the particular standard and the knowledge and attitudes of the particular organization will affect the degree to which the standard is adopted. There is no *a priori* relationship between adoption of a standard and outcome(s). The assumption that adoption of a standard automatically brings intended improvements is dangerously flawed. Naïve organizations, for example, may become convinced that having adopted or become certified to a particular safety or environmental standard they are complying fully with all relevant legislation and that risks are low. As a result of 'creeping complacency' (Toft and Reynolds 1994, 1997), they may become less vigilant and risks increase.

## Social climate

To a large extent, social climate in a country is intertwined with history, politics and culture which can all affect attitudes and expectations of the population generally. For example, people in countries with repressive regimes where life expectancy is relatively short and wars and revolutions are relatively frequent, may take a significantly different stance towards risks compared with people in societies with more stable characteristics. World-views at national and regional level therefore need to be taken into account, especially in cases where an organization operates in a number of countries. Attitudes frequently differ on such matters as:

- personal safety and risk;
- time and timetables;
- female emancipation;
- child labour;
- monetary interest, debt and bribery.

Foreign-based organizations that are unaware of such cultural differences or, worse, that try to change the local characteristics into a version of the foreign parent's, may well increase their risk exposure from disgruntled employees and offended governments. Ethnocentrism can be a precursor to accusations of cultural aggression, as currently proclaimed against the West by politicians in Turkey, Russia and Iran, for example (see chapter 13). Organizations operating in foreign countries therefore need culturally-sensitive local policies.

Social diseases and the vectors involved may also be viewed differently in different societies. For example, in some societies it is much more socially acceptable than in others for men to visit prostitutes. Use of condoms is more accepted in some societies than in others. Such social patterns of behaviour are likely to affect the spread of diseases such as HIV infection and other sexually transmitted diseases (STD). Organizations which operate in or send staff to territories where STD risks are high, such as former Soviet territories and South East Asia, need to consider their approach to informing staff of the risks and precautions required. For example, according to official figures (WHO 1996), over the period 1990 to 1995 the incidence of syphilis in the Russian Federation, CIS and Central Asian Republics approximately doubled each year, and other forms of STD also increased significantly year-on-year. This epidemic arose largely through the rundown of health services in these territories following the collapse of the Soviet Union. Many foreign companies are either unaware of this epidemic and the risks to their employees and families or choose to ignore the facts in their possession.

## Physical conditions and climate

The geographical locations of an organization's operations will affect its risk exposure. For example, if operations are conducted in difficult or hostile physical environments, adequate arrangements are required to provide management systems, procedures and technical precautions to ensure people's health and safety. Examples include:

- Offshore exploration and production for oil and gas, especially in the North and South Atlantics and the North Sea where high winds and extreme cold are prevalent, and tropical regions where typhoons and tropical storms may occur.
- Work in Siberia and northern Russia where daylight is short and temperatures are very low for months at a time.
- Work in former USSR and Soviet bloc territories where industrial pollution and radioactive contamination are prevalent.
- Work in areas where communicable health risks are prevalent such as hepatitis, plague and tropical diseases.

## Technology

Developments and changes in technology pose obvious risks to an organization in that failing to introduce more efficient and effective technology may make it more vulnerable to competitors who are able to deliver better quality products faster and more cheaply. Of particular significance are:

- computer technology in manufacturing processes;
- information technology to aid decision-making, shape strategy and assist administration and communication (see chapter 14);
- information technology to deliver products e.g. Internet, cable and satellite links.

However, whereas there are risks attached to not investing in new technology fast enough or at all, there are also risks attached to technological change itself. The world is replete with examples of disasters which have befallen organizations whose decisions and implementation programmes concerning new technology proved to be faulty. Typically, problems arise in the following general areas:

- Strategic decisions about technology change made by poorly informed and ill-prepared managements.
- Optimistic assumptions about the technical complexity involved.
- Unrealistic assumptions about implementation timetables.
- Naïve assumptions about complex human factors such as culture, identity, power relations and motivations – all of which are likely to be affected by major change and which determine how well such a change progresses.
- Under-resourcing of implementation and maintenance programmes.
- Inadequate skills applied to the change programme.

Chapters 14 and 15 provide case examples of some of the risk issues connected with introduction of information technology (IT).

## Conclusions

The interrelationship between an organization and its outer context or environment has a significant impact on risk cognitions and actions within the organization. Although this fact is generally recognised, what is often not appreciated is the number and variety of factors in the environment which can influence organizational decision-making and behaviour. In some instances, different external factors or threats may be inter-dependent and in other instances may even suggest contradictory responses. The need for an integrated approach to risk (see chapter 1) is therefore highlighted.

Five key areas of organizational environment (economies and markets; public policy, regulation and standards; social climate; technology; history, operating territory and conditions) are likely to have a major impact on risk cognition and behaviour. However, although organizations recognise these areas to varying degrees, typically the many dimensions to these areas are only partly appreciated and they are rarely addressed systematically or coherently. As a result, an organization's personnel may be unaware that risks are increasing.

Factors in the external environment, such as market forces, economic climate and regulation, also influence perceptions in an organization of the need for change. However, few organizations in reality need to be in a purely reactive mode to external factors. Whereas strategic changes may focus on external competition as a means of reducing risks of business failure, assumptions which underpin particular organizational changes may be unwarranted and some risks may actually increase as a result of strategic change. For example, an over-zealous drive to create a highly cost-efficient, low staffed and therefore cost-competitive organization (i.e. reducing external risks) may, if handled badly, inadvertently damage staff motivation, morale and retention (i.e. increasing internal risks to product and service quality and ultimately to competitiveness) – see Caulkin (1995). Chapter 7 expands on the complex relationships between risk and change.

Chapter 7

# Risk and change

## Overview

This chapter examines interrelationships between risk and change at an organizational level. In particular, risk is discussed both in terms of a contextual mediator in change processes in organizations and how changes may modify risks.

## Introduction

'The management of change' has become in the 1990s a core component of management rhetoric. Change agents attempt to engineer substantive change in organizations so that they are more cost-efficient, less burdened with costly staff and outmoded practices and more adaptable and responsive to changes in the outer context. Few would argue with these aims. However, it is not at all clear that relatively straightforward prescriptions for achieving these ends such as Business Process Re-engineering (BPR) and Total Quality Management (TQM) are reliable. Thus, although there are risks attached to not seeking to manage change at all, there are also risks attached to the particular change methodology used and the assumptions which underpin it. Pettigrew *et al.* (1992) note that change should be seen as a consequence not only of problem-solving processes, nor of the weight of technical evidence and analysis, nor of managerial drives for efficiency and effectiveness but also of processes which recognise historical and ongoing struggles of power and status as motivators. This chapter examines the relationship between organizational change and risk and distinguishes between strategies which are espoused and those which are enacted. A potential model of risk-mediated change processes is proposed which focuses on power relations/political processes, strategy and meanings of success.

## Organizational change

Where do changes in organizations come from? Some people see the stimulus for change coming from the extra-organizational environment in terms of such forces as technology change, economic and market factors, and changes in social patterns and structures – as discussed in chapter 6. This stimulus-response approach is consistent with biological paradigms and a functionalist world-view. However, such external factors *per se* are not the sole stimuli for change in organizations. Rather, their perceived implications for and effects on the product market, labour market, costs, etc. may stimulate change. Not all stimulus for change originates in an organization's environment. Purposeful and even radical decisions for change may arise within an organization when no substantive pressure from without is perceived. Indeed, discoveries and inventions of new product types may occur which have a dramatic effect on the product market in the organization's environment. Such an observation is consistent with strategic choice views which assume that the environment is not a set of intractable constraints and can be 'changed and manipulated through political negotiation to fit the objectives of top management' (Astley and Van de Ven 1983).

It is argued that for organizational change to begin, at least one person possessing power of some kind (see chapter 5) has to perceive a need for change in the context of his or her definition of the situation – i.e. to enhance current benefits and/or avoid or reduce detriment for the organization. Implicitly, if not explicitly, such cognition will be risk-related. That person may also perceive some personal benefit to be gained in terms of, for example, career, reward, job security or status. Beyond the initial perception of the need for change, all else is contingent upon social interaction and political processes. These processes are in turn influenced by the values and relative powers of individuals and the groups to which they belong (especially interest groups). They also depend on the skills of those who engage in the political processes and their definitions of self and situation. See chapters 5 and 6 for more detailed discussion of, respectively, power and culture in organizations and their implications for risk.

A change history may be described in terms of a sequence of phases in the change process which is matched by a sequence of resistant phases (e.g. so-called 'storming, forming, norming'). However, such a plausible model only holds in some cases. Homeostatic or self-maintaining behaviour may be a feature of all organizations but homeostasis and resistance to change are not synonymous (see chapter 3). Organizational homeostasis involves an element of choice (i.e. purposefulness) and it is not a necessary feature of change (i.e. is not purposive as in the biological stimulus-response sense). As Blackler and Brown (1987) put it in relation to IT changes, there is no *a priori* cause-and-effect relationship between IT adoption and any structural and behavioural consequences. Prescriptive approaches (cf. Model 1 in Blackler and Brown 1987) assume that the organizational aspects (i.e. the network of social interactions and processes) are of little consequence to the outcome.

The relative powers of actors and the nature of decision-making processes are important features in determining the character of a particular change within an organization. Pfeffer's (1981) analysis offers four model-types for the analysis of decision-making processes, namely:

1 **rational choice models** which assume
  - behaviour reflects purpose or intent;
  - purpose pre-exists;
  - purposive choices of consistent actors;
  - goals and objectives are pre-ordained;
  - search process produces a set of decision-making alternatives;
  - search only continues until necessary and sufficient conditions have been met.

2 **bureaucratic models** which assume
  - procedural rationality substituted for search and rational choice;
  - rules determine choice;
  - feed-forward or even open-loop control.

3 **decision-process models (e.g. 'garbage can' model, Legge 1984)** which assume
  - choice determines preferences;
  - goals loosely defined, if at all;
  - retrospective rationalization.

4 **political models** which assume
  - action is the result of political process;
  - when preferences conflict, relative power of social actors determines outcome;
  - important factors are:
    Who are the actors?
    What determines each actor's stand?
    What determines each actor's relative power?
    How does decision process work?
    How do various preferences become combined?

Mangham (1979) argues that organizational change occurs as a result of changes in membership, definitions (by individuals or by groups), goals (or low attainment of goals) and roles. These changes require adjustments – i.e. a series of revisions by the process of negotiated order. However, change depends on the location and strength of power. In contrast to conflictual models, this view does not hold that all members possess equal powers (however defined) or have shared values or motives.

As Pettigrew (1973) notes, change has no terminal state even though terms such as 'introduction' and 'implementation' suggest some clearly defined time markers. Pettigrew (1987) proposes a context-content-process model of organizational change in which change processes are usually slow and incremental until and unless a crisis is perceived (usually emanating from the outer context). When this happens, substantive change occurs rapidly. The strength of this model lies in its emphasis on inner and outer contexts and political processes. However, empirical research suggests that strategic change is not contingent upon crisis perception (Waring 1993b).

Johnson (1987, 1992) proposes a cultural web model for analysis of change processes in organizations. This symmetrical model has a core component, the ideational culture paradigm or prevalent world-view in the organization. The core paradigm is enveloped by seven intersecting components, namely: stories and myths, symbols, power structures, organizational structures, control systems, rituals and routines. This model may be criticized for ambiguity in such terms as 'control systems' and 'power structures'. For example, control is only one aspect of management. Is this model using the term 'control' widely, narrowly or, indeed, appropriately? Similarly, does the model intend to limit consideration of power to 'power structures', or does it acknowledge the importance of the processual aspects of power - i.e. political processes?

Based on work within ICI, the National Health Service, and other sectors Pettigrew *et al.* (1992) have developed the content-context-process model of change (Pettigrew 1987) into a model of five critical success factors, namely:

1 coherence;
2 leading change;
3 linking strategic and operational change;
4 human resources as assets and liabilities;
5 environmental (outer context) assessment.

Although these factors are identified as critical, Pettigrew *et al.* assert that contexts are unlikely to be receptive to change unless a further eight factors are addressed appropriately. These are:

1 quality and coherence of policy;
2 environmental (outer context) pressure;

3 supportive organizational culture;
4 change agenda and its locale;
5 simplicity and clarity of goals and priorities;
6 co-operative inter- and intra-organizational networks;
7 managerial-professional relations;
8 key people leading change.

## Strategies for change in organizations

Implicitly, all strategies for change are risk-strategies as they are intended to enhance or radically improve existing situations and avoid unwanted consequences. Chin and Benne (1985) describe three strategy types for change: empirical/rational, normative/re-educative and power/coercive. Empirical/rational strategies rely on the benefits of change becoming perceived as 'obvious'. However, the setting, the culture, the nature of the change and many other factors have to be conducive to a 'change agent' working effectively. An example of such change in a TV company is furnished by McLoughlin *et al.* (1985) and, as Pettigrew *et al.* (1992) point out in relation to a number of cases, appreciation of the unique context of the particular organization is crucial to successful change.

Normative/re-educative strategies assume that individuals are essentially rational, will co-operate for group benefit, and will identify their self-interest with the need for change. Individuals are regarded as amenable to consultation or participation.

Power/coercive strategies, on the other hand, assume that individuals will recognise and accept the legitimate authority of managers to make unilateral decisions. Individuals have little to contribute to decisions about change and should accept the decisions of those in authority. The term 'power' is used here in the sense of legitimated authority to make decisions unilaterally and take actions that may materially affect the interests of other members of the organization. However, there are other kinds of power such as reward power, expert power and referent power that also affect social interactions.

The strategies proposed by Chin and Benne (1985) may be criticized on the grounds of rationalistic assumptions about the relationship between cause and effect. The location of an individual or group in a particular setting partly determines the individual's or group's set of attitudes towards the change. These attitudes both inform and are informed by world-views (see chapters 3 and 8). Similarly, attitudes and world views interplay with heuristic cost-benefit calculations about the likely consequences of a planned change. The distribution of attitudes and their expressions ranges from strong favour and advocacy of the change to strong disapproval of and opposition to it.

Among many factors influencing the distribution and strength of attitudes of staff towards a planned change, the attitudes and behaviour of key figures in the change process will be of prime importance. For example some, perhaps many, individuals value being consulted about proposed changes that may affect them. If they perceive that their concerns and interests are being ignored by managers or other key figures, they may develop an adverse attitude towards the change. In some cases, an adverse attitude focusing initially on a particular change to a particular aspect of their job may generalize into an adverse attitude to the job as a whole.

Various 'risk' strategies have been proposed for avoiding adverse effects of change in work. New technology agreements, participation and empowerment schemes have enjoyed considerable advocacy. However, the rationale of participation is based on a set of assumptions about organization that are rarely met in practice. True participation requires an equal sharing of decision-making power at all levels of an organization. In reality, participation is often a euphemism for consultation or having views taken into account by those who hold real decision-making power (see the section on decision-making and participation in chapter 5). Mangham (1979) refers to such strategies as pseudo-agreement and pseudo-participation. He also notes that, paradoxically, true participation is *less* likely to facilitate change. Barriers to change are represented by the interests of other people and therefore the more power that is shared the more difficult it is to effect change. Hartley (1984) also notes that where true participation is attempted it cannot ensure a balance of expert and referent power and frequently managers and key figures possess more knowledge and information than workers with whom they are supposed to share power. The implication is that participation is an illusory concept and the application of participation strategies in some circumstances may arouse levels of expectations for power sharing that are not met. Adverse attitudes and dissatisfaction may then ensue which may have risk implications – e.g. staff unrest, industrial relations disputes.

A degree of planning for change features in all models of strategy. However, in the authors' experience both in research and consultancy, not all managements enact the strategies which they espouse. They may *say* that they do and may produce policy documents in evidence (the 'official' history) but in practice it may be 'muddle all the way' with short-term contingencies and expedience dictating decision-making.

Although some authors, notably Mangham (1979), Watson (1982) and Pettigrew (1985) acknowledge that information and skill are required for effective negotiation in social interaction, they do not mention that technical knowledge may be a pivotal factor. The assumption that managers responsible for introducing new technology, for example, have an accurate and detailed knowledge and understanding of what it can and cannot do may not be justified. Although it may not be necessary for each manager to have expert knowledge of the technical aspects of computers and computing, it is argued that they do need sufficient knowledge in order to manage associated risks – i.e. to frame realistic objectives, to ensure that appropriate specialists and other resources are made available if necessary, and to assess the relative worth of different proposals.

Beer *et al.* (1990) conclude from extensive studies that programmatic change does not work. They claim that senior managers understand the necessity for change to cope with new competitive realities but often misunderstand what it takes to bring it about. Senior managers tend to share two false assumptions, namely (a) that promulgating companywide programmes such as mission statements, corporate culture programmes, training courses, quality circles and new pay-for-performance systems will transform the organization, and (b) that employee behaviour is changed by altering a company's formal structure and systems. Westley (1990) draws similar conclusions and Pettigrew *et al.* (1992) state bluntly that 'in terms of competitive success, the management of strategic change is the result of an uncertain, emergent and iterative process. There are no grand blueprints for long-term success or quick fixes for immediate salvation'.

According to Mintzberg (1989), strategy takes two forms, namely a deliberate plan and emergent action over time. These forms are at the opposite ends of a continuum. His three models of strategy formation are as follows:

- planning – a deliberate process which tends to impede strategy making;
- visionary – there is a dominant orchestrator as keeper of the corporate culture;
- learning – an emergent, bottom-up process characterized by incrementalism and occasional spontaneity.

He concludes that organizations change either as a result of external pressure or crisis, or the arrival of a new CEO, or the internal capacity to revitalize. However, whereas Mintzberg describes how strategy occurs, his model does not offer reasons why it occurs other than reference to functional context. It has been argued (Waring 1993b) that the underlying role of strategy is to protect as far as possible the organization's ideational culture.

Corporate strategy may also be regarded as a discourse linked to power relations and the exercise of power (Knights and Morgan 1990, 1991). It could therefore be argued that strategy as an emergent set of practices is power-in-action. Analyses of strategy may not be reducible either to rationalist accounts of markets and environments or to interpretive understandings of actors' frames of reference, thus suggesting that neither modernist nor post-modernist analyses are adequate. Strategy as a discourse constitutes the problems for which it claims to be a solution. The notion of strategy which is typically bound up in contemporary managerial thinking and action is limited by managerial ideology, power relations and political processes such as the management of meanings (see chapter 5).

## Risk as a contextual mediator in change

Change in organizations tends to be slow. For long periods, slow incremental changes occur through a process of political learning. Crisis, as a particular risk issue, provides legitimacy for rapid discontinuous change. However, a crisis does not actually have to occur before a strategic change process begins. What is important is the perception of a likely *future* crisis in the context of the organization and a proactive decision to either avoid or cope with such a crisis. Preemptive coping or avoidance strategies are in essence both strategic changes and risk strategies.

Crises occur in different forms. Some occur in the form of accidents having serious and immediate adverse consequences, e.g. a fire may cause considerable material damage and loss of business information, as a result of which the organization's business is disrupted for several months. Other crises are identified as possible future events but on an heuristic scale of probabilities social actors judge them to be unlikely. For example, in two cases in the National Health Service (Glendon and Waring 1996; Waring 1993b) the potential disaggregation of the Health Authority was known to be on the Department of Health's (DoH) agenda for some time. Similarly, the ending of DoH funds for a particular project was always a known factor. The DoH requirements for quarterly returns of Körner data were known for several years but the likelihood that DoH initial deadlines would not be met or that the computerized Körner system would still not be operational two years later was not recognized (see chapter 15).

Although crisis perception is likely to mediate change processes, this is only a special case of the more general effects of risk cognition (see chapter 8). For example, in industries which have experienced disasters such as offshore oil and gas, railways and chemicals, companies have altered their whole approach to risk management as a means to prevent incidents, to control incidents which do occur and to mitigate the effects of such incidents – i.e. to limit death, injury and disastrous damage which could create a crisis for the particular company or entire industry. In such a context, crisis avoidance is an ultimate goal of a more general risk reduction strategy which is (or should be) front-end loaded – i.e. emphasis on prevention. Risk assessment is therefore (or should be) focused not only on the more obvious major hazard/threat scenarios but also on the more mundane precursors and the behavioural characteristics of the people in the organization such as awareness, motivations, politics and cultures.

Risk cognition is central to change processes in organizations and to change-related strategy, both formal and implicit. At senior level, formal strategy flows directly from risk cognitions and at least some strategies are likely to represent a significant change compared with the organization's current approaches. Table 7.1 lists some examples of risks and appropriate strategies, which for a particular organization may include strategic changes.

Risk cognition and behaviour are not confined to physical hazards nor to risks to the particular organization. Within individuals, 'meanings of success' conflate many risk-bearing issues, both pure and speculative. Thus, for example, success can relate to a wide range of informal/valuational risk motivations concerning job security, career, rewards, professional identity, status, etc as well as more 'objective' organizational goals which may include avoiding and controlling risks to the enterprise. If power holders and power wielders are perceived to take a certain stance towards particular risks, others are likely to fashion their own responses in relation to that stance so as to avoid risks to their own personal success strategy. Similarly, if 'group-think' or a socially constructed mind-set dictates an expected set of responses to risk issues, then individuals are likely to behave accordingly, regardless of official policies, strategies, procedures and information.

Reactions to other organization's disasters demonstrate that risk cognitions and heuristic risk calculations which suggest a remote risk are more influential than those which suggest a significant risk of a similar disaster befalling their own organization. The official inquiries to the King's Cross disaster and the Piper Alpha disaster both emphasized the need for a substantive change in the culture of the respective companies involved and also within their respective industries. However, the response of other companies has been largely one of compliance with regulatory and legislative requirements emanating from the inquiries which in effect is still a 'prescriptive compliance culture', despite widely expressed beliefs that there now exists a self-regulatory 'goal setting culture' – see chapters 10 and 12. The prevalent attitude is 'what is the minimum we have to do to keep the regulators at bay?' rather than 'what does our strategic risk assessment tell us we need to do minimize avoidable loss in the pure risks area and to minimize losses and maximize gains in the speculative risks area?' The warnings of Beer *et al.* (1990), Westley (1990) and

*Table 7.1* Examples of risks and potential strategic changes

| *Risks* | *Overall objectives* | *Strategic options e.g.* |
|---|---|---|
| Competition (see chapters 14 and 15) | Long-term survival | Market re-focus<br>Product innovation<br>Acquisitions<br>Divestments<br>New technology<br>Structural change<br>Culture change<br>HR change |
| Major hazards (see chapters 10 and 12) | Disaster avoidance, prevention and mitigation | Risk-assessment (ALARP)<br>Process modification<br>Management systems<br>Loss prevention<br>Culture change |
| Fraud (see chapter 11) | Deter, prevent and mitigate | Management systems<br>Purchase authorizations<br>Separation of functions e.g. sales and accounts<br>Staff selection procedures<br>External audit<br>Culture change |
| Seizure of overseas assets or investments (see chapter 13) | Deter, avoid and mitigate | Withdraw<br>Limit scale<br>High levels contacts<br>Intelligence system<br>Long-term strategy<br>Risk contingency plans |

Pettigrew *et al.* (1992), that substantive organizational change in general and culture change in particular are not amenable to quick fixes or simplistic programmes, continue to go unheeded.

## Change as a risk modifier

It is evident from the previous section that risk cognitions are likely to result in substantive changes in the form of strategies to avoid, reduce, improve or otherwise control those risks. The risk-change model is therefore not uni-directional, as change strategies will have some impact on the risks whose cognition originated them. Risk monitoring and (re)assessment are therefore required to establish that strategies have been effective (see chapter 2).

The bi-directional nature of the risk-change model also suggests that changes, both those planned by an organization and those occurring in its external environment, are likely to modify risks to the organization. It is rarely the case that a change strategy intended to modify a particular risk does not have consequences for other risks. For example, a business process re-engineering (BPR) strategy intended to boost competitiveness and ensure long-term survival may achieve competitive gains in the short term through staff cuts and improved cost-efficiency. However, such a strategy may also have an adverse effect on human resource risks, such as staff morale, staff retention and industrial relations which may, in the long term, damage both organizational and product quality, thus reducing competitiveness and confounding the strategic objective of survival (Caulkin 1995; Kennedy 1994). Such a strategy may also increase security, fire and health and safety risks if BPR leads to poorly managed contracting out of functions and to a dereliction of internal responsibilities (HSE 1996a). Proposed strategic changes seeking to improve a particular risk therefore need to be carefully examined in order to assess not only their likely efficacy but also their implications for other risks.

## Previous theories and models of change

A number of analytical frameworks have been proposed for analysis and understanding of change-related processes in organizations. Tables 7.2 and 7.3 (Glendon and Waring 1996; Waring 1993b) differentiate between analytical models which are essentially functionalist and those which are essentially interpretive. The concept of world-view as a paradigm is discussed in chapters 3 and 4.

Tables 7.2 and 7.3 summarize what previous theories and models predict would occur as far as strategy is concerned. The models and theories have been used in a variety of ways by various authors either as analytical/descriptive devices or as normative/imperative devices or as both. Tables 7.2 and 7.3 treat all the models and theories listed *as if* they were analytical/descriptive and summarise what the assumptions built in to them would predict for strategy.

There is a problem of overlapping meanings concerning the use of the terms 'theories' and 'models' in that the models listed are expressions of particular theories and a theory may be regarded as a set of constructs – i.e. a theory implicitly incorporates a model. The theories listed in the left hand column of tables 7.2 and 7.3 are intended as a shorthand for the higher order theories which lie behind the

*Table 7.2* Summary of functionalist/modernist approaches to change processes

| *Organizational theory linked to strategy* | *Predicted strategy characteristics* | *Illustrative models of change processes* |
|---|---|---|
| Evolving strategy | Reactive, muddling through, emergence of strategy, post-hoc rationalization | Decision-Process (Pfeffer 1981); (Disjointed) Incrementalism (Mintzberg 1978, Johnson 1987, Legge 1984); Garbage Can (Legge 1984); Model 0 (Blackler & Brown 1987) |
| Scientific management | Rationalistic design, planning and development by managers and specialists | General Systems (Checkland 1981, Morgan 1986); Bureaucracy (Pfeffer 1981); Rational Choice (Pfeffer 1981); Rational Comprehensive Model (Legge 1984); Logical Incrementalism (Quinn 1980, Johnson 1987); Model 1 (Blackler & Brown 1987) |
| Scientific management and human relations | Rationalistic design, planning and development by managers, specialists plus staff participation | Model 2 (Blackler & Brown 1987); Socio-Technical Systems (Mumford 1981, 1983, Morgan 1986, Westley 1990) |
| Scientific management plus organizational homeostasis | Key figure responses to outer context plus rationalistic design, planning and development by managers and specialists | Population Ecology/Sector Dynamics (Astley & Van de Ven 1983, Child & Smith 1987) |
| Scientific management plus human relations | Rationalistic design, planning and development by managers and specialists plus staff participation plus attempts to manipulate culture | Cultural Learning (Dyer & Dyer 1986, Mintzberg 1989, Westley 1990) |

(theoretical) models listed in the column headed 'models of change processes'. The degree of regression applied has been a matter of judgement. It is possible to cite even higher order theories which lie behind the theories listed. For example, scientific management and human relations theories rely to varying degrees on theories of motivation and reward.

*Table 7.3* Summary of interpretive/post-modernist approaches

| *Organizational theory linked to strategy* | *Predicted strategy characteristics* | *Illustrative models of change processes* |
| --- | --- | --- |
| Social action | Enacted strategy may not match espoused strategy; strategy is dynamic and reflects power relations and world-views of social actors | Power and Political Processes (Pettigrew 1973, 1985, 1987, Pfeffer 1981, Morgan 1986); Context-Context-Process (Pettigrew 1987); Ideational Culture (Schein 1985, Johnson 1987); Strategic Discourse (Knights & Morgan 1990) |

In view of the recursive complexity surrounding even a relatively small number of models and theories, it has been found necessary to construct Tables 7.2 and 7.3 so that relational sense may be drawn from them. Without such utilities, it would be difficult to appreciate such relationships.

## *Accuracy of predictions*

Empirical studies (Glendon and Waring 1996; Waring 1993b) suggest that none of the theories and models cited above is, on its own, accurate in predicting everything that occurs in particular cases. Particular functionalist/modernist models which are grounded in theories categorised broadly as scientific management and/or human relations were predictive in relation to some of the formal objectives of the organizations' members. However, such predictions only obtained at certain stages of the particular change processes, each of which spanned several years. For example, in one case the early years of the project were characterized by slow incremental changes in strategy, as directors learned by trial and error. Model 0 ('muddling through') characteristics were also in evidence in two other cases in the early phases. The Model 2 characteristic of participation also featured in one case throughout, although full representational participation was reduced after the failure of the project to make headway.

In essence, to varying degrees all models could be discerned at all times throughout all three cases. However, although a particular model was prominent at a particular time in a particular case, the situation was dynamic, and other functionalist models became more relevant at other times. Nevertheless, interpretive models were in evidence as a continuous feature throughout all three cases.

## *A synthesis of previous theories and models*

The empirical research cited above showed that in practice strategies as enacted comprise elements of all the models in Table 7.2. At different times, particular process types predominated as contexts changed. However, at all times the underlying bedrock was political processes. This conclusion has received support from other empirical research (Coombs 1992). This bedrock relates to the 'informal and valuational' criteria for success which individuals possess, for example personal or professional advancement, job security, competitive advantage between work or professional groups. These risk criteria are largely hidden and rarely become articulated in official meetings or documents, yet exert a powerful influence on decision and action.

A hypothesis (Waring 1993b) is that strategy formulation and enactment in an organization is in part a purposive and perhaps *preconscious* embodiment of ideational culture or world-view retention by political process. The risk that is being 'managed' is that of potential loss of existing cultural characteristics which organizational members value highly. Attempts, often unobtrusive and passive rather than open and active, to retain these characteristics may operate at one and the same time as major programmes to change them.

Some people may be aware of some of these protective responses. For example, in two cases in the NHS (see chapter 15) respondents privately stated that no matter how much they adopted the language and methods of Resource Management they would always believe that all patients were entitled to proper health care which would be their first priority. Some respondents were consciously seeking to retain the cultural characteristics of the organization or their part of it while at the same time 'going through the motions' of culture change at an overt level. However, given the extent and complexity of political processes in which individuals in any organization engage, it is likely that much of this defensive risk management activity is purposive and perhaps preconscious (Dixon 1981; Diamond 1986). The very taken-for-grantedness of organizational culture means that most of its characteristic structures and processes, including the propensity for defence against change, remain unobtrusive to the social actors engaged in it.

Functionalist models, however, relate to *espoused* strategy – the overt rationalistic processes which are observable during projects in the language of 'official' decision-making, and in related documents. These are rationalistic *overlays* to political processes. Even though participants may be conscious of 'politics', there is little evidence that they regard this as anything more than 'horse trading' and rivalry. Much of the political processes evident may not be made overt in formal settings and their covert nature may only be revealed in private conversation with trusted parties.

As Coombs (1992) has noted about the NHS, a large part of IT investment is not being applied to areas requiring improved operational efficiency (as a functionalist rationale would imply) but to IT systems which draw doctors into accepting responsibility for the costs of medical treatment – i.e. political processes. At the strategic level of political processes described by Coombs, it is self-evident that those engaged in such processes are conscious of this 'hidden agenda'. The latter activity is apparently concerned deliberately with changing key aspects of organizational culture i.e. changing attitudes, values, behaviour etc.

As Douglas (1992) notes, risk is always political. Deliberate use of political processes may seek to change aspects of organizational culture – e.g. as a strategy for dealing with particular risks. However, at a more fundamental level, it is argued that political processes have a hidden function in sustaining the integrity of underlying cultural characteristics or world-view of organizations or groups within them. This hidden function appears to be largely preconscious. Those involved do not appear to be conscious of the wider outcome of political processes in retaining core values and other cultural characteristics. Indeed, it could be argued that the character of political processes themselves in a particular organization represents a feature of that organization's culture. The full role of political processes and the full extent of cultural influences remain unobtrusive and pass unnoticed by the social actors concerned. Johnson (1987) refers to strategy as 'culture in action'. This book argues that the vehicle for such unobtrusive action is the interrelationship between political processes and meanings of success. It is therefore inappropriate for political processes to be accorded consistency with any particular formal strategy type since political processes apply to them all and are not usually formally recognized in strategy formulation or recorded in strategy documents.

Whereas political processes as a whole may appear to act towards retaining cultural integration in both a purposeful and purposive way, it does not follow that either cultural characteristics or political processes are necessarily integrative. There are likely to be instances of organizations which encounter crises which are not survivable if the overall 'culture-protective' behaviour of the social actor members ignores pertinent threats. For example, the potential for dis-integration in the event of unsustainable financial crisis is self-evident (e.g. Barings).

Change-related strategy formulation and enactment may be in part a rationalistic process of protecting and enhancing the particular organization as contexts change, in part a conscious process by individuals and groups to protect and advance personal and professional interests, and in part a purposive, preconscious way of retaining ideational culture (Waring 1993b). The four 'risk management' purposes are:

1. Protection of personal and professional interests.
2. Protection of organizational integration.
3. Fulfilment of one or more key strategic figures' commitment to susbtantive change in how the organization functions.
4. Retention of cultural characteristics of the organization or parts of it.

Both strategy formulation and enactment are influenced by other aspects of the inner context of the organization (e.g. risk cognitions, pre-existing structures, resource availability, personnel characteristics, historical development) and by outer context (e.g. public policy, legislation, product market conditions, perceived threats). Political processes provide the principal means by which strategies in general and risk strategies in particular are formulated.

The four purposes listed above inform meanings of success for a particular strategy. Meanings of success held by individual social actors comprise a mixture of formal, factual and largely overt criteria and informal, valuational and largely covert criteria, relating to the four purposes. Meanings of success are inherently risk-related (i.e. achieve desired outcomes, avoid unwanted outcomes) but it should not be assumed that officially stated goals, risks and criteria will pre-determine behaviour – the 'fallacy of pre-determination' (Mintzberg 1994).

## A potential model of risk and change processes

An improved model for understanding change processes and the role of risk would have to take into account inferences from the above discussion, namely that no single model which has been proposed so far appears to possess high predictive power in respect of all major aspects of lengthy change processes. An improved model would have to try to capture the essence of the complex phenomena being addressed.

The proposed model (Glendon and Waring 1996; Waring 1993b, 1994), which acknowledges the work of Johnson (1987), Pettigrew (1987) and Pettigrew *et al.* (1992), comprises eight components:

- outer context;
- organizational culture;
- organizational structures;

- resources;
- risk cognitions;
- political processes/power relations;
- strategy;
- meanings of success.

Of these eight components, three are salient – namely political processes/power relations, strategy and meanings of success. The latter two are influenced by political processes/power relations in an interdependent relationship. The remaining five components are contextual mediators. The model is depicted as influence diagrams in Figures 7.1 and 7.2.

*Figure 7.1* A potential model of risk and change processes in organizations

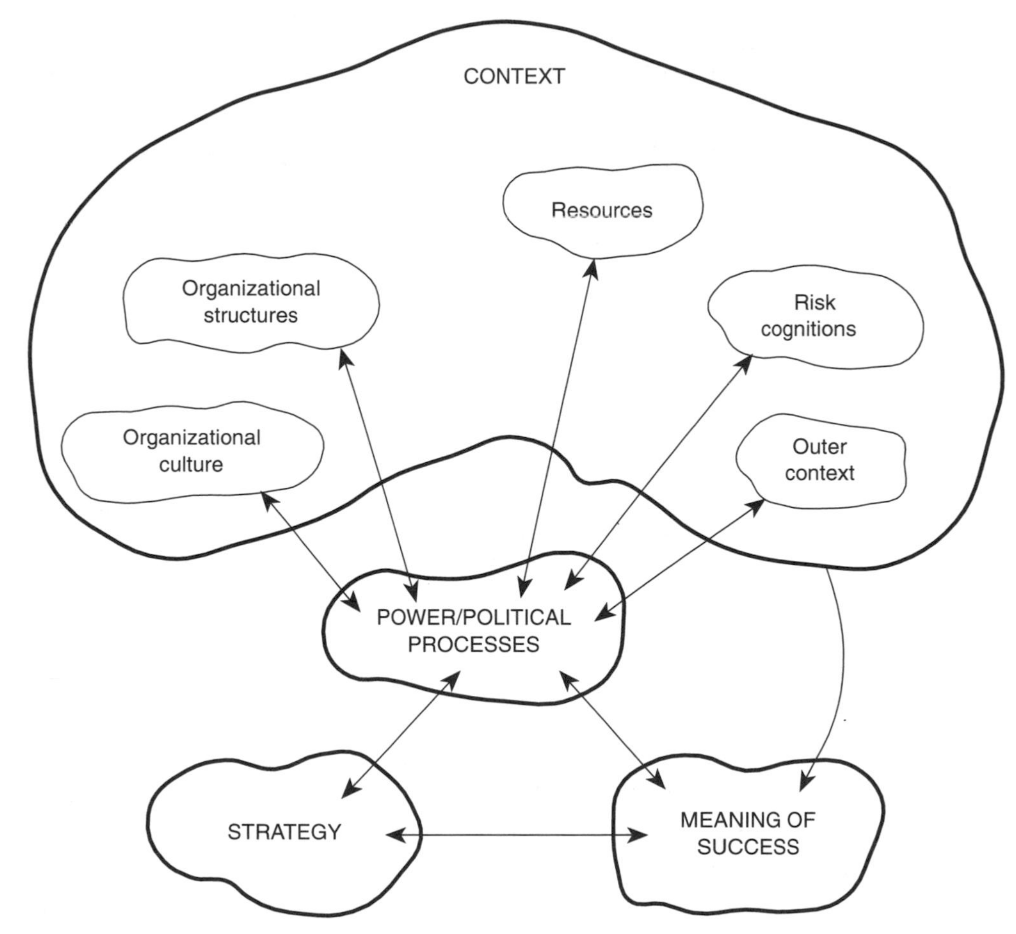


*Source*: Waring (1993a and b)

*Figure 7.2* Relationship between strategy, meanings of success and power/political processes

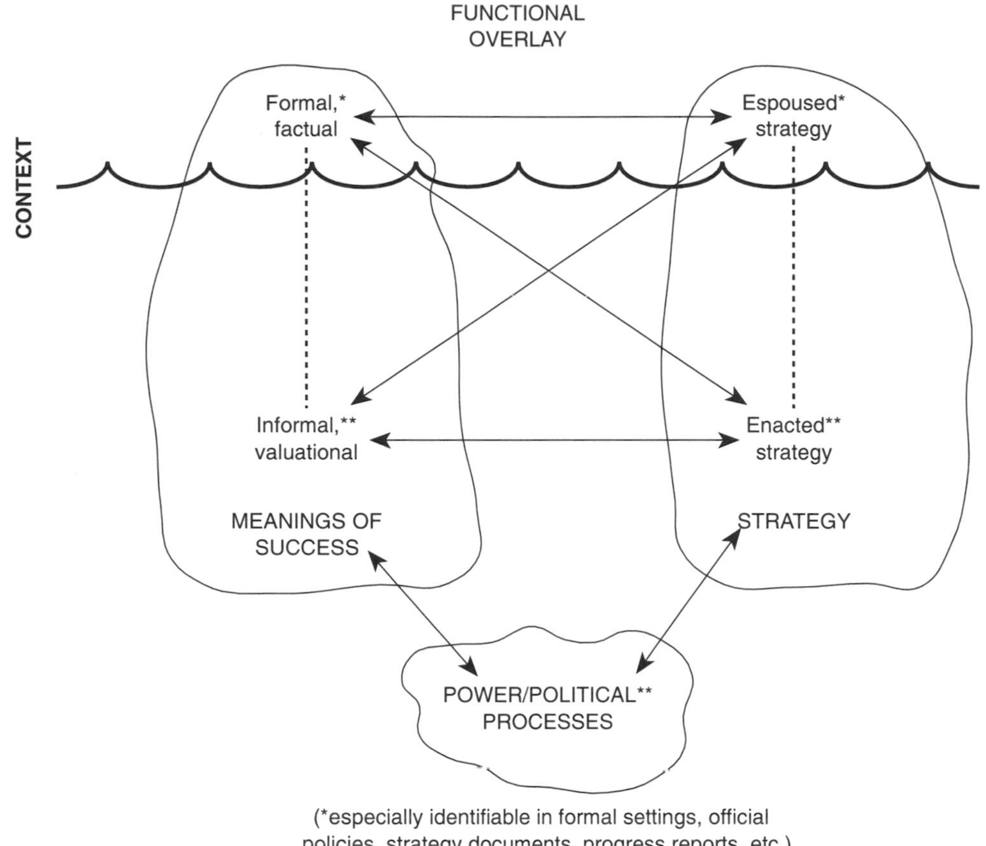


*Source*: Waring (1993a and b)

## Conclusions

Change processes in organizations are complex and an adequate model for understanding such change processes and their relationship with risk would need to capture the essence of the complex phenomena involved. The issues surrounding both understanding by external analytical observers and the action-meaning processes within an organization are debatable. It is clear that the perspectives of many disciplines would be required in order to furnish a relatively complete mode such change processes.

Despite the inference that change processes are fluid rather than deterministic, it is clear that in organizations undergoing change, order is usually maintained, crises are frequently survived and formal objectives are achieved (at least in part). Therefore, it would appear that interpretive concepts such as power, political processes, and ideational culture operate in the real world primarily to ensure social stability within the organization so that formal structures and processes can function, which in turn help to sustain the integration of the organization. During non-crisis phases, i.e. most of the time, the relatively slow process of organizational learning is mediated by risk cognitions as well as by other factors indicated in the model. Programmatic and prescriptive approaches to change often fail to recognize both the contribution of risk cognitions to change processes and effects that change processes are likely to have on risks. Equally, programmatic and prescriptive approaches which are often very seductive in their elegance and promise of early results may nonetheless unwittingly increase risks (such as failure to meet objectives, and the consequences of such failure) because of their very naïveté.

The most risky aspects of an organization, therefore, may lie not in physical hazards or in investment and other speculative decisions but in the self-reinforcing behaviour associated with power relations, culture and motivations in the organization. Despite all the efforts to produce fully harmonized, culture-sensitive 'learning organizations' (e.g. through TQM, business process re-engineering and culture change programmes), there remains in many organizations a significant gap between espousal and enactment. Such a gap is maintained by power and cultural factors which often go unnoticed in the organization concerned. The effects of such factors on thinking and action lie behind the 'failure of hindsight' (Toft 1990) which continues to create 'disasters waiting to happen'.

# ition

## Overview

Individual risk cognition can be considered to be the basis for risk appraisal at all levels – including organizational assessments and even international political dramas. As humans are involved in every risk appraisal scenario, it is vital to understand something of the elements and processes which shape individuals' risk assessments. By developing a series of models, this chapter considers individual-level processes which may account for risk appraisal, and where appropriate, draws parallels with risk assessment processes at collective (organizational) levels described in earlier chapters.

## Introduction

In this book, the term 'risk cognition' is preferred over the more commonly used 'risk perception' as representing a more inclusive indication of processes involved when individuals appraise risk – analogous with risk assessments undertaken by organizations (see chapter 2).

From an evolutionary perspective, individuals have been appraising risk for far longer than have organizations in their contemporary forms. Because of this head-start of many millennia it is unsurprising that there are parallels between procedures adopted by organizations in pursuit of this task and psychological processes which characterize individual risk cognition. If individual risk cognition is an appropriate model for organizations' risk assessments and monitoring strategies, then individual behaviour in relation to risk is analogous with organizational measures for addressing pure risk. Individuals also appraise speculative risks, in which there are potential costs and benefit outcomes. Individual speculative risk appraisal also parallels that undertaken by organizations – for example in the financial domain.

This chapter considers individual risk appraisal and risk management – in the form of cognitions, emotions and behaviour. Where appropriate, this will be compared with risk assessments and the risk management process within organizations. Potentially these represent components of parallel models or even elements on a continuum. Another theme of the chapter is that, in a qualitatively different way from those who assess risks as 'experts', individuals appraise risks in their own lives and have learnt from experience how to assess and manage these risks. 'Objectively' people might be considered to be poor at appraising risks, but this ignores powerful and important emotional components of human risk appraisals.

Risk cognition, as well as encompassing our experiences of occasional mishaps, incidents, and even rare accidents involving injury, also relates to personal strategic risk planning (e.g. avoiding unemployment, making a will, selecting pension plans, life insurance) and design of our personal environment (e.g. making your house safe for you and your dependants). Thus, there are various parallels between individual risk management and overall risk management processes practised by organizations.

## Risk cognition and the organizational environment

Risk cognition and its derivatives, including risk perception, can be considered as part of the inner context of organizational functioning. Possible links between broad categories of inner context components are shown in Figure 8.1.

Organizational, process and mediating factors are dealt with in other chapters. Individual risk cognitions depend partly upon an individual's world-view – or at least those aspects of it which impinge upon risk appraisal and behaviours in relation to risk. They are also strongly influenced by each individual's unique experiences, as represented by the pattern of memories, emotions and other cognitive components (considered in the next section and illustrated in Figure 8.2) and by their current circumstances – e.g. relative poverty or affluence, and their scope for decision-making.

Risk cognitions will also be determined to some degree by immediate stimuli impinging upon an individual. These may be salient events in the outside world (for example, crossing a busy road with a child; being obliged to choose between alternative insurance policies) or they may reflect internally derived thoughts (such as deciding which numbers to fill in on a National Lottery ticket and imagining what one could do with a large win). The origin of these stimuli respectively is analogous both with external pressures on an organization that

*Figure 8.1* Possible links between inner context components

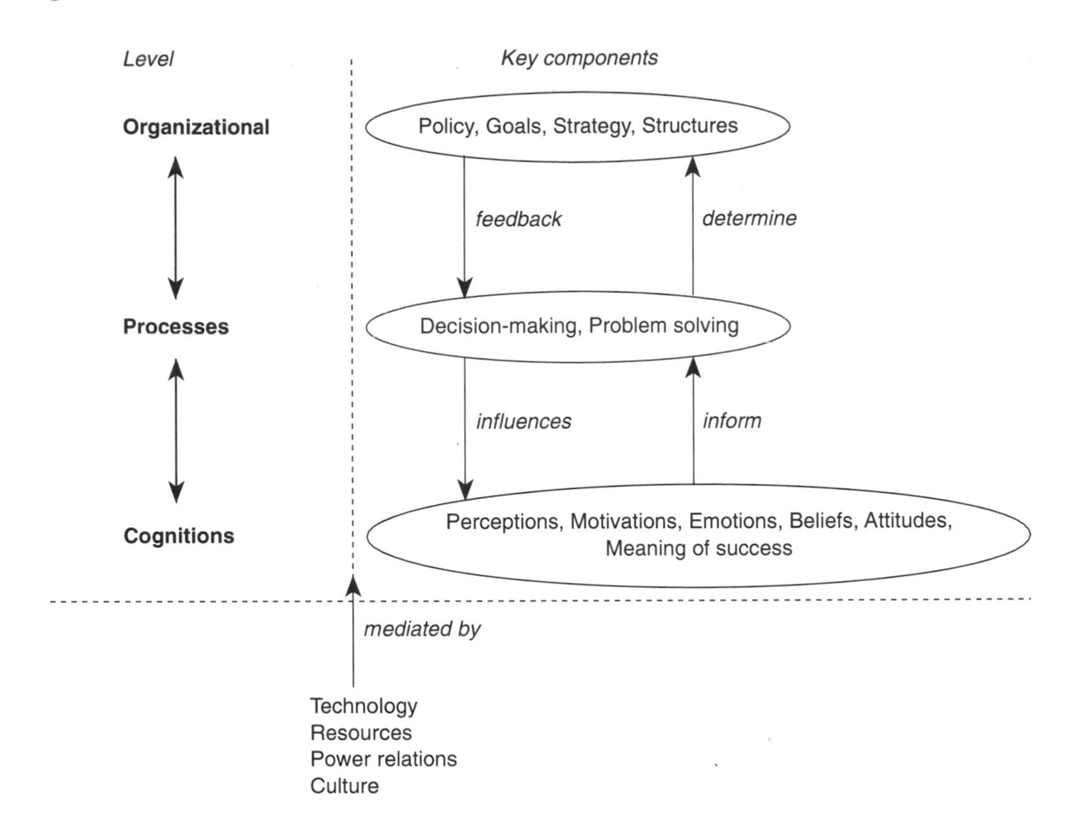


demand a response – such as a significant move by a competitor, and internally derived policies – for example an executive decision to reorganize staff and departments.

At group level, risk appraisal depends partly upon the salience of individual risk relevant cognitions, as described above, and the particular combination of these which characterize group members. Also important are the preferred team working styles of individuals comprising a group (Belbin 1981, 1993) and the ability and desire of each member to seek to influence or impose their cognitive deliberations upon other group members. There will also be parameters within which the group is obliged to operate as well as group processes at work when decisions involving risk are being made, such as groupthink (Janis 1972), shared responsibility (Kogan and Wallach 1967) and possible polarization effects (Semin and Glendon 1973).

When decisions involving risk are being made at a strategic level within an organization the salience of individual cognitions pertinent to risk of those in influential or powerful roles will again be a key component of the decision-making process. These will be mediated – either supported or influenced in some other way – by the type of factors outlined in Figure 8.1, and considered elsewhere in this book. They include: technology, resources, power relations and organizational culture. At national level, decisions involving risk depend considerably upon the balance of political judgements, such as described in chapter 1, particularly the section on strategic risks. The cultural and social environment for risk cognition is considered in chapter 4.

## Towards a model of risk cognition

Risk assessment, as typically carried out by organizations, is increasingly part of a formal exercise using standard frameworks (see chapter 2), and there is an implicit assumption that such risk assessments are objective and unbiased. However, risk appraisal as undertaken almost continuously as part of individual human cognitive functioning, is frequently identified as being *ad hoc* and subject to a variety of biases and contemporaneous influences (see for example, Kahneman *et al.* 1982; Glendon and McKenna 1995). People are generally portrayed as being poor at making risk-related judgements because of the continuous influence of such biases and the difficulty of making judgements involving large numbers or probabilities (Fischhoff 1975; Lichtenstein *et al.* 1978).

While it is true that, as measured by results from laboratory or otherwise controlled conditions, humans can readily be presented as poor or irrational decision makers, the heuristics that they have developed to aid decision-making have, of necessity, been devised to make decisions over a far wider range of situations than could ever be replicated in a laboratory. Therefore, it could be argued that 'testing' human decision-making on risk over a very restricted range of topics or areas is inviting 'failure' of a system which evolved to address a complex and fast moving set of issues and perhaps to satisfice outcomes over a range of decisions rather than attempting to maximize the outcome of every decision. An analogy might be a financial dealer who accepts that they cannot hope to clear the maximum possible profit with every deal, but rather seeks to maximize outcomes in the longer term by a combination of strategies. These might include realizing when the time costs of continuing with a particular negotiation are likely to be greater than the costs of accepting a less than perfect deal in order to pursue the next option. The dealer adopts an optimization strategy by satisficing outcomes across their complete portfolio of deals over a given time period. Individuals behaving rationally in situations involving speculative risk are likely to invoke the 'law of diminishing returns' in respect of their efforts in relation to a given choice and to be aware of opportunity costs involved in any decision.

Through personal experience, the risk taker in any field – which includes all of us – will learn to balance the costs and benefits of various strategies and courses of action through their personal risk appraisal process. Thus, if we are to progress beyond the truism of merely stating that 'people are poor at making risk judgements' or 'individuals simplify the risk appraisal process by using heuristics' or 'you cannot significantly improve humans' ability to appraise risks because of fundamental attributional biases', then it is necessary to understand more about possible components of risk cognition.

Figure 8.2 represents a first attempt to model key components of risk cognition – the process by which individuals appraise risks in their lives. It is implicit in the model that, in appraising risk in their own lives, individuals are expert to the extent that they have survived and prospered on the basis of their numerous past risk judgements and consequent behaviour. This individual expertise is intuitive rather than formal. Certainly chance factors and a capricious environment (e.g. 'luck') will have played a part. However, in aggregate it is postulated that those whose risk judgements and behaviours are most appropriate are most likely to survive and prosper. The model is proposed as a basis for seeking to discover more about a process, which has hitherto been subsumed under a more restricted label of 'risk perception' – which, as seen from Figure 8.2, is only one of the components involved.

The model in Figure 8.2 illustrates some of the main components and processes involved in risk cognition. A range of both internal and external stimuli – some of which imply or explicitly involve risk – are input on a more or less continuous basis and are perceived by the individual. Thus, the risk cognition process first requires some triggering stimulus, for example seeing a media item on a risk topic of interest, having a sudden thought spring to mind, being asked a question about something or helping a young child across a busy stream of traffic.

However, (risk) perception is not merely a process of receiving data or information but also involves interpretation of that input. Thus, we observe relevant stimuli from the outside world and interpret them on the basis of previous knowledge and experience. For example, when driving, in appraising the risk involved in overtaking a vehicle in front, as well as taking into account the stimuli immediately available – relative speeds and distances of the vehicles, other traffic which is visible or which might be masked, etc. – we would also, usually unconsciously, draw upon our pooled previous overtaking experiences, our general knowledge about local road

*Figure 8.2* Towards a model of risk cognition

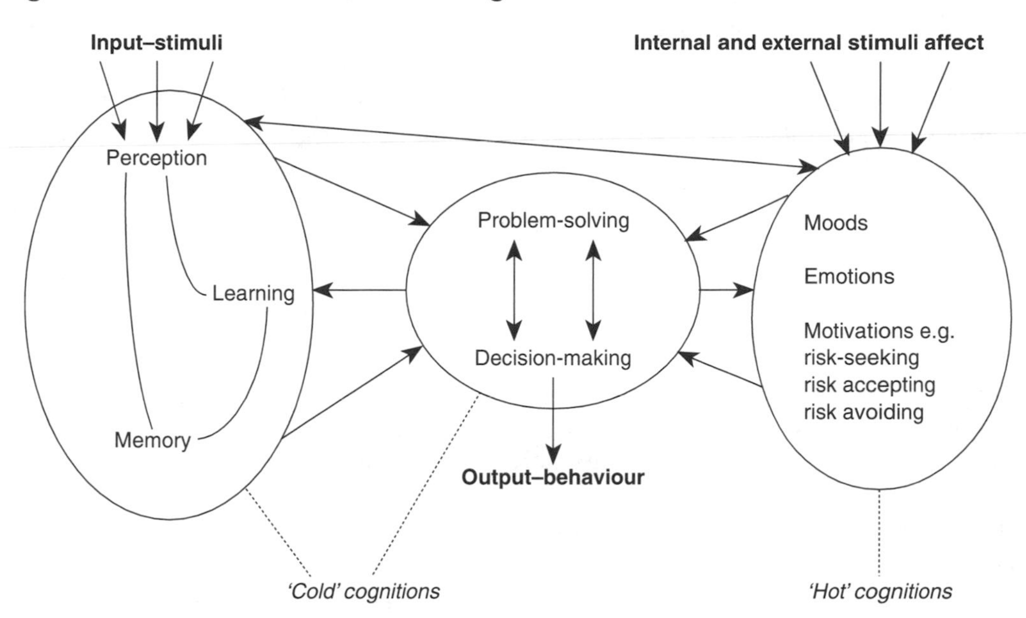


conditions and perhaps geography of the area. This information would be combined to make a fairly rapid (risk) assessment of possible outcomes, and the likelihood of success of the overtaking manoeuvre would be judged qualitatively. Thus, in describing the expertise involved in making what for many people are everyday decisions, humans' alleged poor judgement in respect of making decisions involving risk can be held to be largely irrelevant, as our subsequent actions, based upon our experience, nearly always leads to a behavioural response which brings a successful outcome – i.e. in this case overtake without accident. In such situations, 'meanings of success' are much less problematic than is the case for many organizational decisions – see chapter 7 for a discussion.

Previous experiences of risk events or occasions which can inform the interpretation process because they are similar to – or different from – the current situation, are accessed (almost inevitably imperfectly) from memory. While there is no known limit to the amount of information which may be stored in the human memory, there can be severe limitations in respect of what and how much information may be accessed when needed for problem-solving or decision-making, particularly when required urgently by a situation.

Through many experiences with risk situations, individuals learn about dealing with external stimuli which involve risk. Learning about risk results from repeated exposure to different types of risk, making decisions about them and experiencing a range of outcomes based upon those decisions. Learning may be reactive or proactive. The latter involves actively seeking out occasions and opportunities to experience risk and related outcomes, for example by playing the stock market, through involvement in competitive sports or by participating in seemingly hazardous leisure pursuits such as bungy jumping or hang gliding. More mundane reactive learning is represented by reflecting upon relatively passive day-to-day experiences involving risk, such as purchasing and consuming a wide range of products, selecting modes of transport (see also section on risk homeostasis and risk compensation below) and making new acquaintances. At a knowledge-based level, risk-related experiences can enhance learning. Once an activity, such as driving, becomes routinized (rules-based) then learning opportunities diminish, the perceived level of risk inherent in the activity may reduce and habituation to risk stimuli (e.g. overtaking manoeuvres, tailgating) result.

Some situations involving risk require the individual's problem-solving mechanism to operate in order to deal with complex information, for example that dealing with a mixture of qualitative and quantitative data, involving various potential costs and benefits associated with different possible outcomes. Examples of such risk-related problems might include: buying a house, assessing a possible career move, making financial investments, designing a control room, considering a radical change in a personal relationship, wondering what to do when faced with an armed potential assailant.

While it is often satisfying for a person to exercise their brain in problem-solving activity, sooner or later a decision is usually required – or if no decision is made, then by default the individual opts to let events take their course. Therefore after a number of possible iterations, the decision-making process comes into play so that at some point a decision is made about what action to take and this is translated into externally observable behaviour. The need for a decision may be urgent – as in the case of what to do when faced with an armed assailant; or it may be possible for the person to leave a decision almost indefinitely – for example, house purchase; or for more information to be obtained over a long period – as required in control room design. Whatever the circumstances, the decision made – which is held by the model immediately to precede the action then taken – is based upon previous experience as well as the internal knowledge and external information available. Choices available to individuals making decisions on risk issues are likely to be analogous with strategic options available to organizations identified in chapter 1 – i.e. avoid, defer, reduce, retain, transfer, share or limit the risk.

The components described briefly so far in this section comprise those traditionally ascribed by psychologists to the cognitive process. Because of the ostensibly rational nature of the process described, apparently involving logical receipt of information from the outside world, processing this according to previous experience, and then producing a sensible decision which is based upon all the available information, the features involved have been described as 'cold' cognitions. This implies that we make decisions entirely rationally.

However, while it is certainly possible for humans to act according to rational criteria, we are also driven by different types of processes. It is well recognised that we are subject to influences which are neither rational in their form, nor logical in their impact upon decisions that we make. 'Crimes of passion' is a recurrent theme in both literature and the law, and reflects the often overwhelming influence of what have been termed 'hot' cognitions. In Figure 8.2 these are described as our varying moods – which can swing between different positions within relatively short periods of time (a few minutes for example). There are also considerable individual differences in emotions, both as a relatively enduring personality difference (see for example, Briggs Myers and Briggs Myers 1980) and as reflecting current preoccupations (such as the current state of our personal relationships or our present bank balance) and our immediate environment (compare for example, city driving with resting under a tree in a quiet park). Goleman (1995) argues that at least as important as traditional views of intellect is 'emotional intelligence', – involving self-awareness, impulse control, empathy, self-motivation and social abilities. Basic emotions such as sadness, happiness, surprise, fear, anger and disgust are universal. Goleman's approach to managing risks which arise through emotional incompetence is illustrated in chapter 17.

Other individual differences which affect decision-making in respect of risk, include motivations. These also operate either as long-term personal characteristics or as more temporary states, depending upon our current objectives. Thus, individuals may be characterised by one or more personality traits which predispose them either to seek out certain types of risk (risk, or thrill seekers) or merely to accept risk as being part of daily life and deal with it as required. Alternatively, some individuals may go out of their way to avoid risks because of the discomfort and stress which they have experienced from risk in the past and which they wish to avoid as far as possible in the future.

Not only will our moods, emotions and motives affect the decision-making process, they can also have a direct impact upon the way in which memories are stored and retrieved (consider the way in which a particular piece of music or a specific aroma might trigger a memory of the way you felt at a certain time in the past). This means that emotions are also very much involved in the learning process and in the way in which risks are perceived. One way in which this influence is likely to operate is through the selective filter which is known to be important in the perception process.

Because it is impossible for us to focus upon all of the many stimuli which impinge on us throughout our lives, we manage the perception process by attending selectively to external stimuli. Our selection of which stimuli to attend to is governed very much by our motives and emotions – that is our needs of the moment and our feelings at the time. Thus, hot cognitions represent an essential part of the perceptual filter through which stimuli from the external world must pass. It might be said that our emotions and motives form part of our world-view as they help to determine how we see the world.

## Individual decision-making on risk

In this section and the next, the decision-making element of the risk cognition process described in the previous section is unpacked and extended. Here the various types of risk about which individual decisions may be made are considered, while in the following section a model of individual behaviour in the face of risk (or potential danger) is reviewed.

Figure 8.3 describes the various types of risk which have been identified as being within the sphere of human decision-making (see for example, Dowie and Lefrere 1980).

For individuals, the focus of their decision-making in respect of risk is psychological. This can be divided into risks relating to the ego or self, and risks which can impinge upon a person's social position. Risks relating to an individual's social position might for example involve personal relationships or social gatherings at which they are required to perform in some way – for example to make a public presentation. Such a public performance might serve either to enhance or to reduce (or possibly leave unaffected) that person's standing in the view of their audience. Generally social facilitation effects operate in social contexts involving individual performance (e.g. Zajonc 1980). Thus, if a person is already competent in respect of a particular activity then having an audience will generally enhance their performance. However, being obliged to perform publicly in an activity in which you are not skilled will tend to diminish performance. Competent risk takers will be aware (possibly unconsciously) of such effects. Other risks which might be included in the social category include those associated with certain types of sexual encounters.

As well as being concerned about risks to one's social standing or status – i.e. how

*Figure 8.3* Individual decision-making and different types of risk

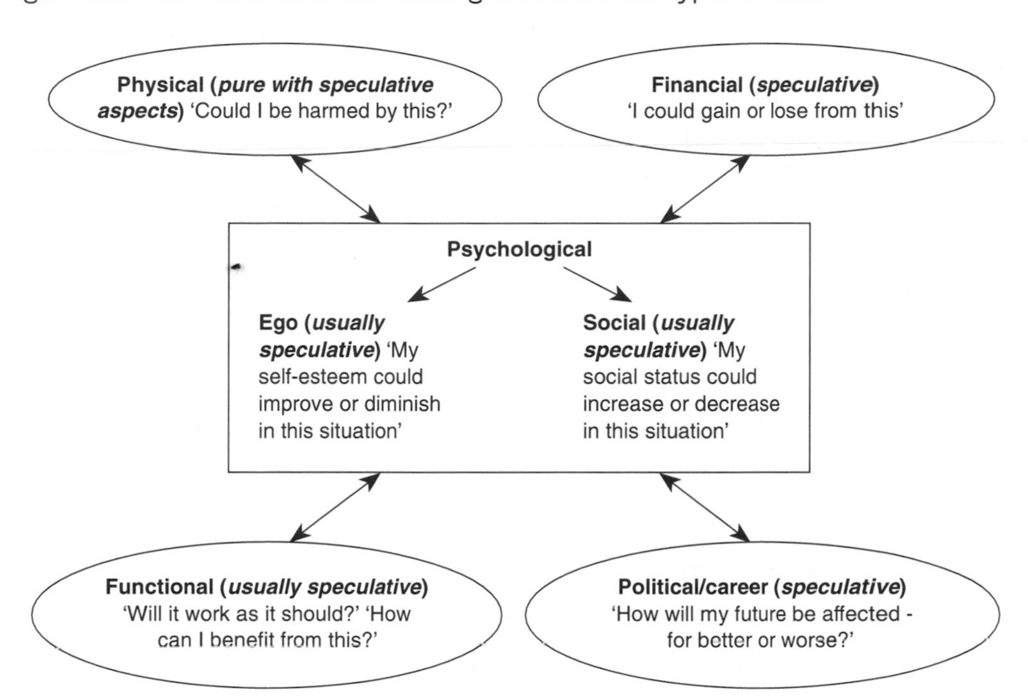


we are perceived by others – individuals are also very aware of the way in which they perceive themselves, reflected in their self-image and level of self-esteem. Thus, by engaging in different activities, many involving risk, we test out and develop the way in which we perceive ourselves. We may set ourselves challenges, physical, mental or spiritual, in order to find out what sort of person we are as part of our personal development throughout life. Individuals differ considerably in the extent to which they desire to test themselves, for example in respect of need for achievement (McClelland *et al.* 1953). Almost any encounter with risk – e.g. hazardous novel leisure pursuits, making new friends, moving to another region or country, driving – provides a potential opportunity either to enhance or to diminish our self-image.

Risks associated with our core psychological being are almost inevitably speculative in nature, as they can either lead to an improvement or to a diminution of key areas of our psychological functioning – however minuscule any such changes might be.

Another type of risk which has been identified as operating upon individuals is in the financial area – e.g. making an investment on the stock exchange or purchasing an item of value in the hope/expectation that its value will increase and can be realized in the future. These will always be speculative risks, involving the type of risk cognition process described in Figure 8.2, although these particular examples will only be available to people who have resources with which to speculate – many people are excluded from this type of risk taking.

Individuals also make decisions about their futures based upon job and career choices. Such speculative decisions again involve risk cognition processes. When those in positions of power make decisions affecting others – for example, political leaders or representatives, bosses of large corporations, influential financiers – then one of their prime concerns is likely to be the extent to which different outcomes are likely to affect their political or business futures. Their risk cognition process may involve many iterations and might incorporate advice from a variety of sources before a decision about some key political, business or financial issue is made.

As consumers, we are involved in appraising functional risks relating to a wide range of goods and services, often on a daily basis. Essentially we are concerned about whether the products that we purchase will function as we wish them to. Scientific knowledge, translated by the media, serves to inform consumers about a variety of products, for example food, which can strongly influence consumer choice. In order to reduce risks associated with product purchase, both consumers and marketers have devised strategies to reduce such risks. These include: brand loyalty (to ensure predictable outcomes), store loyalty, purchasing well-known brands, seeking/offering product warranties/guarantees, trial before purchase (e.g. sampling a new food/drink, test driving a car), information seeking/provision, rendering abstract services more concrete (e.g. emphasizing benefits to be derived), using high price as a proxy for quality, or alternatively purchasing a low price brand – thereby trading off functional with financial risk.

There is also a possible element of pure risk involved in product purchase as it is always possible that certain types of product could harm the consumer and every year consumers are killed or injured through interaction with a variety of products (Consumer Safety Unit 1995). These might include electrical goods, step ladders, hazardous toys and chemical-based products. There is also evidence that consumers are increasingly using safety and security criteria when purchasing cars (Lex Service 1994, 1995, 1996). See also product liability in chapter 16.

Finally, there is a category of physical risks to humans, which most people in western societies face rarely, which while they are generally considered to be pure risks, may frequently be found to have speculative elements – as evidenced by associated risk/benefit trade-offs. Examples include the potential harm faced in cases of personal assault by other people or animals or in the course of natural events such as floods or hurricanes. There is also the important category of occupationally related risks which in the UK still result in hundreds of traumatic deaths through accidents every year (Health and Safety Executive 1996) as well as over 2000 deaths from occupationally related diseases. Even in the case of such risks, there may be a trade-off aspect as it is frequently found that individuals who are killed in occupationally related incidents, have been seeking more predictable benefits, including 'keeping the work flowing' (Nichols and Armstrong 1973) and other rewards such as pay or merely keeping a job (Stellman and Daum 1973).

Thus, in only a relatively small proportion of instances of individual exposure to risk is the risk pure in nature. Either speculative aspects – involving possible gains and/or losses – will be very obvious, or else they will be implied in the risk cognition or decision-making process. The speculative nature of most individual risk taking is often not addressed in psychological work on risk perception or risk cognition – a theme which will be considered in the particular context of risk homeostasis and risk compensation in later sections.

Each of the different types of risk described can be independently rated on an ordinal scale in respect of the type of risk appraisal criteria described in chapter 2. The likelihood scale would translate into probability of success – although this is to simplify a complex and multi-dimensional concept. In the case of speculative risks both costs and benefits need to be assessed and compared, again using a methodology analogous with that described in chapter 2 and considered in more detail in the section on the theory of individual cognitions and behaviour in relation to speculative risk. Other dimensions which might be of relevance are those which are typically described in the literature on risk perception (see for example, Royal Society 1983; Cox and Cox 1996), and include long-term versus short-term considerations.

## Individual behaviour in the face of pure risk

In this section, we move from the cognitive decision-making process to individual action in the face of pure risk. In addressing this topic, we explore a version of a model first proposed by Hale and Glendon (1987) and revised by Thomas, Booth and Glendon (1996). The model was used by Thomas (1996) to analyse 230 fatal accidents in UK agriculture.

Figure 8.4 comprises a series of decision points for an individual who is faced – knowingly or unknowingly – with a number of decisions when confronting various types of risk. The model is limited to the extent that it relates to instances of pure

*Figure 8.4* Matrix developed from Hale and Glendon (1987), individual behaviour in the face of danger model

| | A SKILLS (Identification) | B RULES (Identification) | C KNOWLEDGE (Identification/assessment) | D RULES (control) | E SKILLS (control) |
|---|---|---|---|---|---|
| Programmed or insistent danger signals Y N | Correct response in programme Y N Danger uncontrolled 1 | | | | Response correctly executed N Danger– unaffected increased decreased Y Danger under control |
| | 2 | Obvious warning Y N | | Correct procedure known Y N Danger uncontrolled | |
| | 3 | | Responsibility for implementing procedure accepted Y N Danger uncontrolled | Correct procedure chosen Y N Danger uncontrolled | Procedure correctly executed N Danger– unaffected increased decreased Y Danger under control |
| | 4 | | Need to test for danger known/recognised Y N Danger uncontrolled | | |
| IDENTIFICATION | 5 | | Responsibility for testing accepted Y N Danger uncontrolled | | |
| ASSESSMENT | 6 | Correct test chosen and correctly executed Y N Danger uncontrolled | Need for action recognized Y N Danger uncontrolled | | |
| CONTROL | 7 | | Responsibility for action accepted/allocated Y N Danger uncontrolled | Procedure plan/procedure chosen N Danger– unaffected increased decreased Y | Plan/procedure correctly executed N Danger– unaffected increased decreased Y Danger under control |

risk and a series of 'yes' answers is required if the risk is to be successfully avoided or dealt with. The axes of the model are represented by different levels of individual functioning – skills-, rules- and knowledge-based behaviours which are shown as A–E across the top of Figure 8.4. The nature of these individual levels of functioning, derived from the work of Rasmussen and others (see for example, Rasmussen, Duncan and Leplat 1987), are explained in terms of examples below.

The letters, combined with the numbers down the left-hand side serve to identify a particular cell within the matrix in which an error might occur. Blank cells are void for the purpose of locating errors. The other dimension of the model is that concerned with personal risk appraisal – indicated by the degree of shading of the 14 'active' cells within the matrix. Thus, all activities are coded as being either identification of a hazard (cells A1, B2, C3, C4, C5, B6) or by assessment of the risk represented by that hazard (cells C6, C7) or are control measures taken by the individual (cells E1, D2, D3, E3, D7, E7). This classification is analogous with that used by organizations which undertake risk assessments (see chapter 2) as part of their risk management process (see chapter 1). In the model, a 'no' answer to any question in the sequence leaves the danger uncontrolled by the individual. Depending upon the nature of the danger, this might either represent a situation of increasing danger, decreasing danger, or 'steady state'.

The most straightforward situation is one in which an individual is confronted with some danger signal which is so obvious that the correct response is chosen almost immediately and then executed (represented by moving from the start point in the top left-hand cell of Figure 8.4 through cell A1 and then directly to cell E1). An example would be a person seeing a vehicle coming towards them and moving rapidly out of the way to avoid contact. This happens entirely at the skills-based level of behaviour and occurs when an incoming stimulus is appraised and acted upon immediately, with minimal access to decision-making but often with rapid access to a repertoire of stored learned responses. Other examples of insistent danger signals which would normally trigger a response of immediately departing the danger would be being close to fire/smoke and powerful noxious smells.

However, if the danger itself is not immediately confrontational, then if the individual is to avoid being harmed, they need to receive some other warning. For example, while the approaching vehicle might not have been seen, a horn warning might alert the pedestrian to the possibility of danger from this quarter and the person moves from cell B2 to cell D2 (knowing that a check for an approaching vehicle is required). Successfully implementing this stage moves the individual to cell C3 – accepting personal responsibility for implementing some appropriate control procedure and thence to cell D3 (choosing the correct procedure) and finally to cell E3 – as before, moving out of the way of the approaching vehicle. The difference between this and the skill-based sequence described above lies in the requirement for the person to 'plug in' to their (cognitive) risk appraisal process to confirm the hazard identification before taking appropriate action. Thus, the individual implements a rule for action whenever a horn is heard in the street – particularly when crossing a road. The behaviour therefore occurs at the rule-based level. Other examples of warnings which could invoke rule-based behaviours include control room enunciator panel lights and fire alarms. Once habituation occurs, a rule may be invoked at a preconscious level – there is no hard and fast line between behaviours at skills- and rules-based levels.

Much human behaviour, particularly when well practised, is at either the skills-based ('automatic') or rules-based (selecting from a number of pre-programmed action choices). However, at some stage all our behaviour has to be learned and thus when we lack knowledge about a situation we are operating at the knowledge-based level. In this case, we might have to work things out from first principles and more cognitively complex problem-solving processes come into operation (see Figure 8.2). In terms of decision processes represented in Figure 8.4, if there is no obvious warning then there is no clear way that we can be alerted to the presence of danger. Thus, if we are to avoid the danger successfully we need to know how to test for its presence (cell C4) and then to accept responsibility for doing so (cell C5). If this is done, then we must choose the correct test and execute it (cell B6).

Having successfully identified the hazard, we then need to assess the risk, first by recognising the need for taking action (cell C6) and then by either accepting that we should take action ourselves or ensure that another party accepts responsibility (cell C7). If this is achieved, then we move back to the rules-based level. The correct plan or procedure must be chosen (cell D7) and finally this must then be executed adequately (cell E7) at the skills-based level. An example of such a sequence might be an emergency which has not been encountered previously by staff at a process plant. The operatives would need to be aware of the need to test for danger, perhaps through continuous monitoring of the plant's operation, and accept responsibility for doing so. If they discovered a suspicious circumstance then they would need to choose the correct test and execute it, recognise that action was required, deal with the emergency, and then devise and execute an appropriate plan – hopefully to render the plant safe.

As well as describing the decision process in respect of risks faced by an individual, the model can be used to assess the adequacy of the decision-making process when made by others in respect of risks encountered by a target party. At one level, making decisions – explicitly or implicitly – on behalf of another party (for example, a designer or manufacturer in effect requires the end user to accept the risks associated with using the product as designed and manufactured), is political. Governments make decisions about the distribution of resources in respect of health, social welfare, education, defence, etc. thereby affecting risks in the lives of millions of people. Thus, individuals' preferences on risks and the decisions which they are able to make, are subsumed within a complex broad picture in which motives and interests of powerful others provide bounded parameters for individual decision making on risk.

To counter external controlling influences, individuals can perceive situations to be more under their control. This can be represented on the one hand as a generalized personality trait (compared with 'externals', those individuals who have an internal locus of control consider that events generally are more under their control). Alternatively, people may perceive that while events in general are outside their control, by engaging in specified (superstitious) behaviour, for example always using the same series of numbers (e.g. based on family birthdays) when completing a weekly National Lottery ticket, they can 'control' events within a limited domain. Thus, although Government and National Lottery organizers have ensured that the chances of any individual being rewarded by a substantial win is many millions to one against, the probability (i.e. extremely low) side of the risk appraisal process may be considered by each individual player to be secondary compared with the possible winnings (potentially vast). Intermittent small winnings serve to reinforce individuals' Lottery ticket purchases. In such specific circumstances people's generally adequate *ad hoc* risk appraisal processes are of very little use – marketeers understand how to manipulate stimuli presented to consumers – emphasizing past winners and the size of the current jackpot, never the minuscule chance of winning for any given player.

## Risk homeostasis and risk compensation

It is the controversial assertion of Risk Homeostasis Theory (RHT) (Wilde 1982, 1994) that the unique determinant of accident loss (all costs associated with accidents) is not the level of risk within an environment, but rather the target level of risk desired by individuals within that environment. Determinants of individuals' target levels of risk are indicated by the optimization of utilities (benefits) presented in box (a) in Figure 8.5. If one or more of the utilities in box (a) change, then the target level of risk will change, and ultimately this will affect accident loss. RHT was originally proposed as a population-level, closed loop description of driver behaviour. Information entering the closed loop would include that about vehicle

*Figure 8.5* Wilde's closed-loop model of risk homeostasis

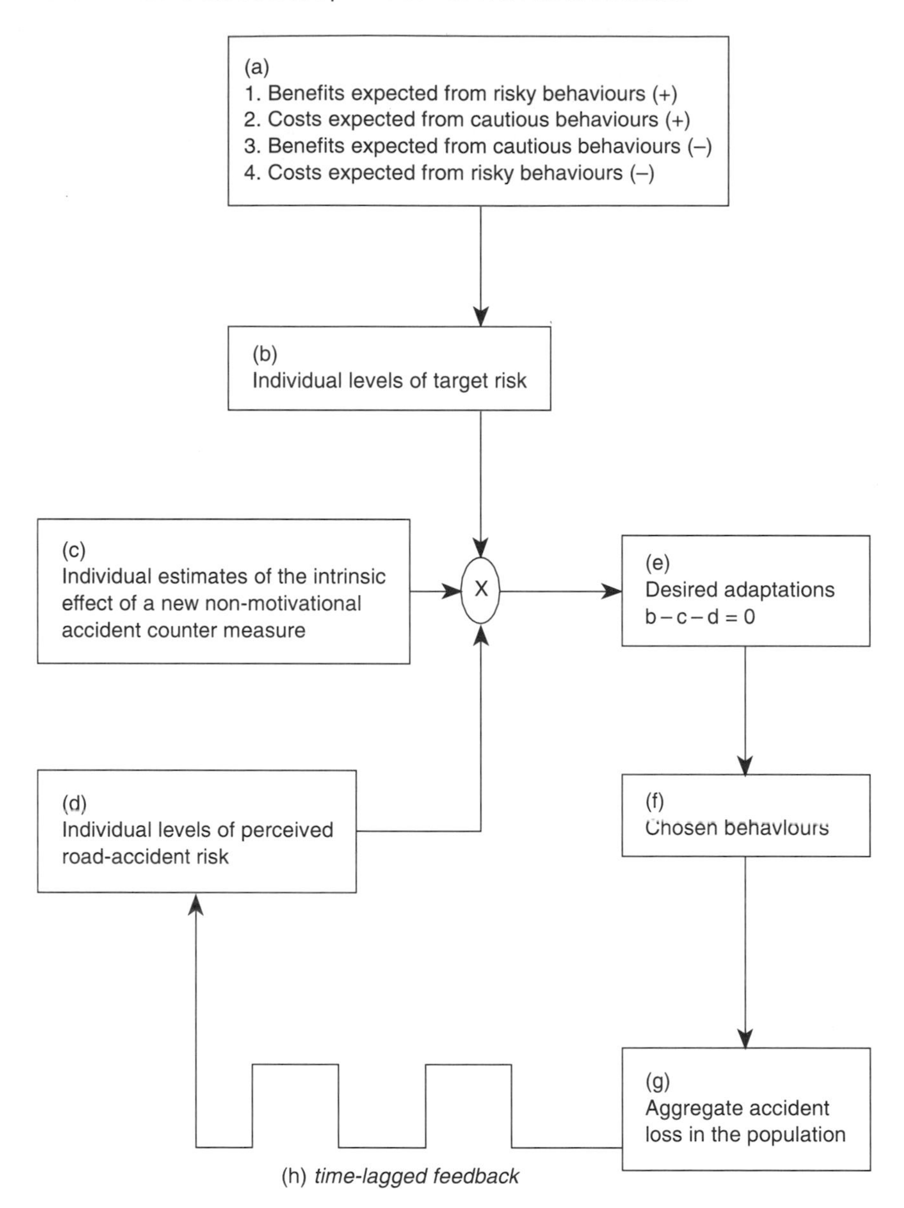


*Source*: reproduced with permission from Wilde (1994)

accidents (e.g. reading about accidents, being involved in an accident or near miss). This information would warn the population about actual levels of risk in the environment. If target risk and actual risk are not aligned, then RHT asserts that individuals will change their behaviour to bring the two into line.

RHT posits three main pathways that individuals can use to compensate for changes in target risk:

1 **Behavioural adjustments within the environment** – there may be numerous ways that individuals can change their level of risk in driving, e.g. more or less overtakes, drive faster or slower, increase or decrease attention, more or less frequent mirror checks.
2 **Mode migration** – if individuals cannot reduce the level of risk by behavioural adjustments, they could use a safer form of transport, e.g. train, bus, walking.
3 **Avoidance** – if the situation is perceived to be too risky then it can be avoided altogether, e.g. a particular journey may not be made because of adverse weather conditions.

Proponents of RHT would predict that behavioural changes (in terms of accident loss) are most likely to be produced by manipulating the four sets of utilities directly – for example, increasing the costs and decreasing the benefits associated with risky behaviours, and decreasing the costs and increasing the benefits associated with more cautious behaviours, rather than attempting to adjust risk levels within the environment – which will tend to be compensated for in any case. A major problem with RHT is that proponents and detractors have tended to adopt entrenched positions from which it becomes difficult to find common ground and either to move the theory forward or to abandon it. In a review of some of the problems of RHT, Hoyes and Glendon (1993) suggest that the proposition that behavioural compensation can occur is one that could be agreed upon by all contributors to the RHT debate.

RHT is a theory which embraces speculative risk because it acknowledges that risks are taken for some purpose or benefit – generally referred to as utility, including the thrill or challenge which may be derived from certain forms of risk-taking activity. A possible basis for this type of utility comes from reversal theory (Apter 1989, 1992, 1997; Svebak and Apter 1997), a general theory of the structure of mental life which deals with culturally universal motivational, emotional and personality aspects of subjective meaning and behaviour. Interestingly, reversal theory maintains that homeostatic models of motivation are inadequate and should be replaced by the more sophisticated concept of multi-stability. Reversal theory postulates that all individuals move through qualitatively different experiential (or meta-motivational) states, each deriving from a basic psychological desire or value and having an associated range of emotions. A second basic idea is that these fundamental states go in pairs of opposites so that change consists of movement between members of a pair with only one of them being operative at any given time – with switches between a pair of states being the 'reversal' which gives the theory its name. Thus people not only change over time but can be self-contradictory.

An example of an oppositional pair is the telic and paratelic states. The telic state is serious-minded, in which individuals see themselves as engaged in a purposeful activity which is important beyond itself (e.g. work). In contrast, the paratelic state is playful, so that the immediate activity is engaged in for its own sake – e.g. enjoyment of socializing, sexual or sporting activity. The contrasting utilities are for achievement and for fun. In the telic (serious) state, the range of emotions is from relaxation to anxiety, while in the paratelic state (fun) emotions range from boredom to excitement. Apter (1992) uses this oppositional state idea to explain a range of behaviours, including why people engage in dangerous sports or commit recreational violence, why military combat is attractive and the nature of PTSD. This theory provides a possible route to greater understanding of emotional aspects of risk taking. Apter (1997: 219) considers that: '. . . people gratuitously confront themselves with risk in dangerous sports like parachuting and rock-climbing, in order to achieve high (not moderate) arousal. This high arousal may be experienced as anxiety, but if the danger is overcome (and thereby a protective frame set up), then there will be a switch to the paratelic curve, and this will result in excitement as intense as the anxiety had been . . .'.

There are known to be individual differences in risk taking and there have been attempts to relate these to personality dimensions. For example, compared with sensation-avoiders, sensation-seekers have been found to choose closer following distances when driving, reinforcing the likelihood that this represents a motivational difference in risk-taking behaviour (Heino, van der Molen and Wilde 1996). Individuals also differ in their level of target (preferred) risk, possibly as a result of future time orientation (Björgvinsson and Wilde 1996). These authors propose that individuals who think about and plan for future events (high future time orientation) have a lower level of target risk than do those who take one day at a time (low future time orientation).

The RHT approach to risk contrasts with an implied assumption of formal risk assessment and risk management within organizations, which maintains that by systematically and thoroughly assessing and managing risks, accidents and other losses will be reduced. Within organizations, as discussed in chapters 1 and 2, the regulated setting for managing risk operates at a collective level where individual choices are subservient to the methodology of risk assessment and the risk management process. As with RHT, the system is characterized by a closed-loop process. However, operation of the feedback mechanism in the case of risk assessment (e.g. as in Figure 2.3) is controlled by those managing the system rather than by individuals, who are generally unable to operate as autonomous elements within it.

It is an implicit belief of those operating within a risk management framework that environmental risk can be reduced by applying appropriate controls or by other risk management applications (see chapter 1 for a consideration of these). A basic assumption of the UK Management of Health and Safety at Work Regulations 1992 and other legislation requiring organizations to conduct risk assessments, is that occupational risks can be effectively controlled by applying externally-driven control measures. The idea that behavioural compensation by individuals might occur in response to changes in risk levels is generally not considered in organizational risk assessments.

Stanton and Glendon (1996) review some key issues in the potential debate between advocates of risk assessment and associated risk management measures, and those who might urge caution with respect to possible risk compensation effects (e.g. allowing automatic functions rather than operators to check system states). They ask: could risk compensation reduce or even negate certain risk control (i.e. safety) measures? Evidence to date is scanty and is mainly restricted to the road environment. By comparison, in work locations, individuals are more likely to have:

- reduced opportunities, if any, for mode migration;
- fewer opportunities, if any, for risk avoidance;
- limited opportunities for behavioural changes – e.g. reduced attention (to monitoring devices, etc.) or greater risk of exposure if wearing personal protective equipment or if an operator thinks that their health and safety is being looked after in some other way.

An immediate impact of a newly introduced occupational safety (e.g. risk control) measure may be seen. However, given the timescale over which homeostatic or compensatory effects are said to operate – up to eighteen months – it may require evidence over several years to establish whether a change has occurred which is robust enough to resist behavioural compensation. The issue of whether a safety measure is sustained in the longer term may be rendered problematic by the absence or impracticability of adequate measurement techniques and only partial control over extraneous variables, for example organizational culture. While it may be possible to block behavioural, mode migration and other risk compensation strategies effectively (it could be argued that one task of risk management is to achieve this) there are bound to be costs involved in meeting this objective. Application of effective controls is designed, at least in part, to block possible risk compensation effects by individuals, in tacit recognition of their importance.

RHT and traditional risk assessment/risk management essentially operate in different domains. Although a few researchers have sought to bridge the gap (e.g. Hoyes 1994), RHT has concentrated almost exclusively on the road transport environment and has been virtually silent with respect to non-transportational issues. Risk assessment has largely been concentrated in the more intensively regulated domain of organizational functioning. This division is well illustrated by Glendon and Stanton (1996) through a series of papers in a special issue of *Safety Science*. They point out that while there is no *a priori* reason why risk assessment could not be applied within other domains, including road transport, the nature of road transport systems in terms of generalized feedback to individual system users ensures that attempts to control the risks identified will be problematic. RHT proponents would argue that addressing individual motivations by seeking to change the relative utilities associated with costs and benefits of relatively safe and unsafe behaviours is likely to be the best way forward. This may be seen for example in campaigns seeking to change drivers' motivations in respect of the potential costs of drinking and driving.

In contrast, in an increasingly regulated occupational sector, it becomes more and more difficult to find examples of individual workers or operators exercising significant degrees of choice with respect to risk-taking at work. Risks in work environments are likely to be determined by the nature of the activity which individuals are contracted to undertake, moderated by managerial and legislative frameworks which are beyond an individual worker's control. In such a highly regulated domain, individual choices with respect to risk are bounded by imposed costs and benefits of operating in the work environment. By comparison, the relatively open system of the road transport domain continues to provide almost limitless opportunities for each individual within it to behave in more or less safe ways, depending upon their individual matrix of utilities, which interact to produce their target level of risk (see Figure 8.5).

This analysis implies that risk management methodologies in different domains need to take account of critical dimensions of those domains. RHT may only apply in situations in which individuals who have access to the required resources, are reasonably free to exercise a fairly high degree of choice over their risk-taking behaviours (e.g. actions on the road, sexual practices, dietary preferences, drug use, leisure pursuits, social contacts, financial/career planning). Addressing individuals' risk perceptions through motivational channels – via people's personal utilities for relatively safe and unsafe behaviours – may be the most appropriate method for influencing risk cognitions in such domains. Traditional risk assessment, as described in chapter 2, has been developed as a network of tools and techniques resting on the assumption that, within already highly regulated occupational environments, risks can be assessed and managed by a variety of techniques – described in chapter 1. A fundamental tenet of such an approach is that individuals within the system are essentially not authors of their own destiny, but are elements operating within a bounded system.

## Towards a theory of individual cognitions and behaviour in relation to speculative risk

The rather cumbersome title of this section reflects the early developmental stage of a theoretical perspective on this topic. Figure 8.4, described in an earlier section, is concerned with individual decision-making and behaviour in respect of pure risks, most of which are likely to be immediate, but which could equally well be long term in nature. Development of a parallel model, describing how speculative risks are dealt with by individuals, would be a useful first step in improving our understanding of how individuals appraise and behave in respect of such risks. Compared with pure risks faced by individuals in their everyday lives, speculative risks are more likely to be long term in nature – although by no means all of them will be. For example, while purchase of insurance policies and other financial products are long-term behaviours, purchases of many consumer goods (some involving risk) are mostly short-term.

Speculative risk-taking affects so much of our lives that any model seeking to describe the processes involved must at one and the same time be multi-faceted so that a number of key elements can be represented and, like all models, be a simplification of these processes so that the general picture can be appreciated without being swamped by detail. Like any venture, presenting a model – as with writing a book – represents a speculative risk in which the authors' personal motivations (e.g. to increase their perceptions of self-worth and desire for enhanced external recognition) are set against the possibility that they or others may subsequently consider the effort to have been a waste of time. We are prepared to accept that risk!

The model shown as Figure 8.6 incorporates features of a number of other models or theories. Its basic format reflects the standard stimulus-organism-response (S-O-R) model used for many decades by psychologists and others to

*Figure 8.6* Individual behaviour in relation to speculative risk: possible links between elements

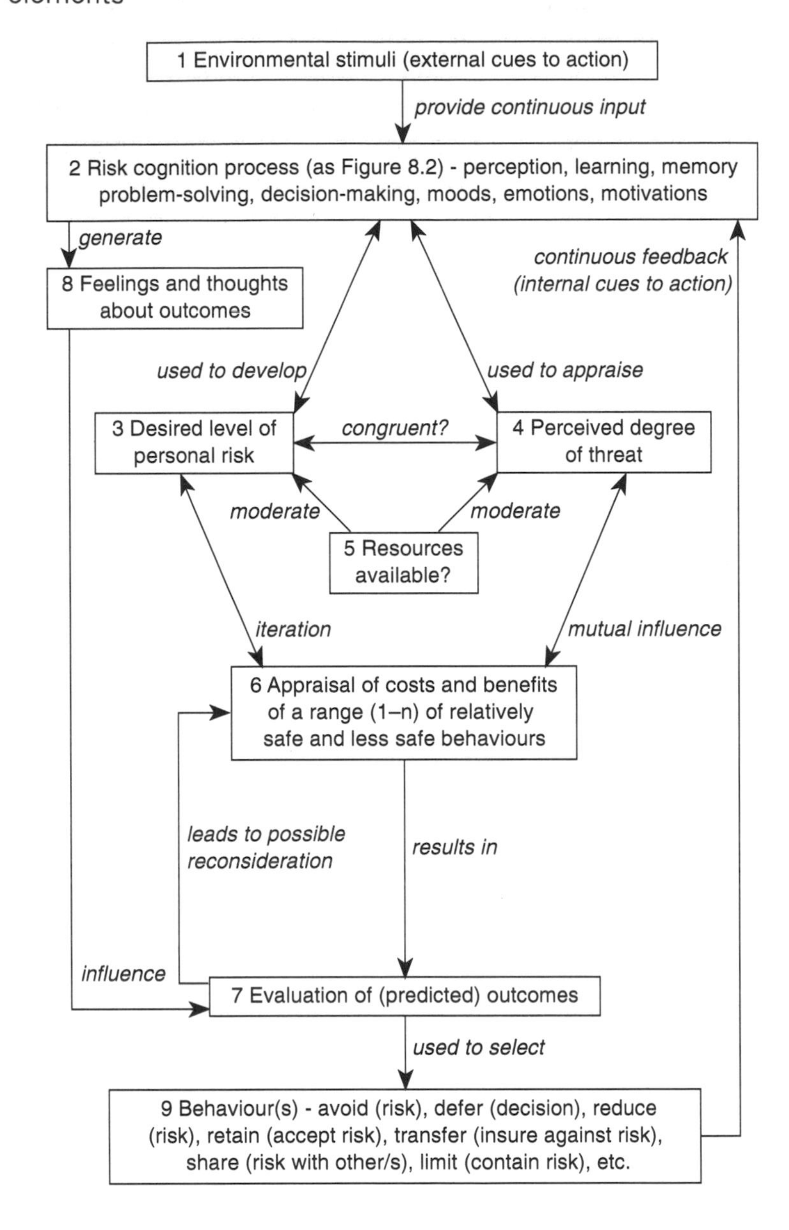

describe input-output aspects of human behaviour. It also incorporates the risk cognition process described in Figure 8.2 within a single box and thus extends that model. Also incorporated are the seven behavioural elements of the risk management model described in chapter 1 and referred to earlier in this chapter. Two elements from Wilde's RHT model – see Figure 8.5 – are also included. The influence of two models not described elsewhere in this book are also reflected in the speculative risk model in Figure 8.6. The first of these is the health belief model, first devised by Becker (1974) and elaborated by Becker and Janz (1987), while the other is the transactional model of stress, associated with Lazarus and Folkman (1984) – see also Folkman and Lazarus (1988).

Like the transactional model of stress, the individual model of speculative risk taking described in Figure 8.6 incorporates different levels of appraisal, and as does the RHT model (along with many other models of human behaviour) it involves feedback – in this case in a number of instances nested within the model. The model itself is speculative at this early stage and requires rigorous testing by empirical research and critique. In the following description, reference to elements of the model in Figure 8.6 is identified by the numbered boxes and italicized text.

In the speculative risk model, *external cues to action* (1) are provided in the form of continuous input stimuli from the outside environment. These will reflect the various types of risk outlined in Figure 8.3 – physical, financial, functional, etc. This potential external input is selectively perceived, interpreted and dealt with by the individual's *risk cognition process* (2), along the lines described in the earlier section – towards a model of risk cognition – and Figure 8.2. The risk cognition process is also instrumental in developing the individual's *desired level of personal risk* (3) (target risk in RHT) and is also involved in appraising the *degree of threat* (4) represented by an external stimulus. This element is analogous with primary appraisal in the transactional model of stress. Both these personal assessments are integrated within the risk cognition process, and continuously updated. They are also subject to a type of appraisal in which the individual considers whether they are congruent. They are represented by separate boxes within the model to reflect their importance at the next stage of appraisal. They are also moderated by the extent to which *resources are available* (5) for meeting the desired level of risk and also dealing with the threat. Resources might be financial, emotional (personal efficacy), social (support), etc.

This next stage is also a characteristic of other models, including RHT and the health belief model and is the *appraisal of costs and benefits* (6) perceived to be associated with a range of outcomes likely to follow from alternative behaviours. Key aspects of the risk cognition process – the desired level of personal risk and the degree of threat posed by the risk(s), as perceived by the individual, moderated by available resources, inform this appraisal process. There may be only a single risk to consider, although even in this simplest case there will be alternative possible outcomes as the individual must decide from a range of possible behaviours in respect of the risk. However, there may be a complex variety of risks to be appraised and in this case the appraisal process is likely to involve the use of heuristics in order to simplify the task. *Outcomes* predicted by the appraisal process will then be *evaluated* (7). Evaluation about various predicted outcomes will also be influenced by the risk cognition process in the form of the individual's *feelings and thoughts* (8) – themselves the product of complex processes. In turn, the evaluation may lead to a re-appraisal of expected costs and benefits of different courses of action before the final evaluation leads to the selection of one or more *behaviours* (9) in respect of the risk.

The behaviour(s) selected by the individual in response to the risk are also part of the feedback loop – analogous with the monitoring function in traditional risk management as practised by organizations (see for example, Figure 2.3). They constitute internal cues for potential further appraisal by the risk cognition process – for example in the case of risks which require a staged or series of responses, each of which depends upon feedback from the previous action. Examples might include dealing with a control room emergency, conducting a delicate negotiation between parties in conflict or any series of actions at the knowledge-based level of functioning.

## Conclusions

Risk cognition, as an attempted comprehensive description of the processes involved when individuals appraise risk, particularly speculative risk, as a basis for behaviour, is still in its infancy. To some extent its development has been attenuated by previous emphasis upon more dramatic pure risk appraisals through attempts to define the processes involved too narrowly (e.g. as 'risk perception'), and by efforts to reveal what human beings are apparently **not** 'good' at (e.g. perceiving risks 'accurately'). These attempts have usually taken as a starting point the particular perspectives of the researchers involved and have failed to address the full gamut of risks faced by individuals in the context of their daily lives. This chapter has sought to present a top down theoretical approach, developed through a series of models, to elucidate the main processes involved when individuals are confronted by a variety of risks.

Appreciating the nature of individual risk cognition processes should help us to understand better the requirements at organizational level, for example when risk assessments are carried out as part of risk management processes. The possibility that risk assessments may need to be broadened to incorporate possible compensation effects by individual operators and others in certain environments may need to be further investigated.

From a psychological perspective, compensation effects observed in many RHT studies may be interpreted as reflecting individuals' attempts to maximize the degree of mastery or control over their environment. One cost of such motivated behaviour is a toll of death, injury and disease which shows at least some resistance to various attempts to reduce it. In contrast, the work environment is increasingly characterized by external control over risks, in which individuals have relatively much lower levels of individual control – either to increase or to reduce the level of risk to which they are exposed.

The model of speculative risk, describing individual risk cognition and behavioural elements, is proposed as a starting point to improve understanding of how people appraise risk in their daily lives. How such a model might be examined and tested by further work is among the topics considered in chapter 17.

# Chapter 9
# A fuzzy convergence

## Overview

This chapter summarizes the first eight chapters and identifies recurrent themes which permeate the overlapping and increasingly convergent areas of management, risk and change. The argument for addressing risk, management and change as linked areas in research and practice is developed. A thematic matrix or utility for appreciating links between management, risk and change in the case studies of Part 2 is outlined.

## Introduction

A central argument of this book is that both theoretical and practical approaches to the three subject areas – management, risk and change – are not only linked but are also convergent. For example, to assert that the management of risks and of change are inseparable from the risks of management and change may seem obvious and rather trite. However, what is striking is the way in which these 'obvious' overlaps and interactions are not yet treated generally in a holistic way. In business schools and in organizations, even though some interactions are recognized, fragments are addressed in discrete packages.

This chapter seeks to highlight recurrent themes arising from the first eight chapters and to propose a thematic reference matrix or utility to aid understanding of the common features of the case studies in Part 2 of the book.

## Summary of previous chapters

### *Risk management*

Risk management is at present a collective term for a variety of different activities concerned with avoiding, reducing and controlling pure risks and with improving gains and avoiding detriment in the speculative risk area. The field of risk management is extensive but four key dimensions may be identified: hazards or threats, the context, risk management objectives, and risk management methods. The interaction and synergy between pure and speculative risks is not always appreciated and integration of different risk management functions, disciplines and activities remains weak or non-existent in most organizations. However, increased awareness of strategic risk issues and implications is likely to see more organizations adopting an integrated approach to risk management.

## *Risk assessment*

Because risk is a multi-dimensional concept, different approaches to risk assessment are required to cover the varieties of risk and their contexts. All share an essential common purpose, which is to estimate or assess a particular risk or set of risks on the basis of the best available information – which by its nature is always imperfect.

Risk assessment techniques can be objective to the extent that they use validated methodologies in a consistent way. However, the process of risk assessment is subjective because the decision about which particular methodology to employ is made on the basis of judgement, even if this is expert judgement. Similarly, most individual decisions about probabilities, projected outcomes and other components of risk assessment, while they may be based on best available evidence, are also judgemental.

Risk assessment methodologies have been developed as a means of dealing with uncertainty in a variety of situations. Basic human motivations of predicting and controlling our surroundings and other external factors, mediated by managerial and organizational imperatives for effectiveness and survival, have combined to produce formal risk assessment methodologies. The latter extend *ad hoc* cognitive processes which define assessments of the many and varied risks confronting most individuals more or less constantly.

Risk assessment techniques are a valuable aid to decision-making, in this case on the acceptability or tolerability of a particular risk or risks, and on the desirability and nature of actions to help in managing risk. However, the broader (e.g. financial, cultural, political) context of decision-making needs to be acknowledged. Therefore, whereas 'acceptability' may be defined in terms of a risk assessment model, such as ALARP, ultimately this term is problematic because it represents the outcome of a political decision-making process in which parties' interests inevitably conflict.

Risk assessment becomes overtly political when judgements are made by one or more parties (e.g. government, large organizations) in respect of one or more other parties such as individual citizens, population sub-groups or employee groups. The parties affected by the decision may have a direct voice in the decision-making process, as in the case of relatively powerful pressure groups, such as trades unions, with sufficient resources to make representations in relevant fora. It is more likely, however, that any influence by those most affected by the outcomes of risk decisions will be indirect and diffuse – for example via the media, letters, protest marches, consumer action and casting of votes in public elections.

Whereas the basic principles of risk assessment are common, and may be extended to any risk topic, a variety of risk assessment techniques may be used. These range from relatively 'simple' approaches, based upon judgements of people with knowledge about a situation on key risk components such as exposure and likelihood, to more complex quantified techniques. Thus, risk assessment techniques may be used to assess both pure risks (e.g. those associated with various forms of pollution of the physical environment) and speculative risks (e.g. those associated with financial investment and political decisions).

Although pure risks may be assessed on a uni-dimensional scale, speculative risks require two separate assessments – respectively for potentially 'good' and 'bad' outcomes for a particular party. For speculative risk assessments, the judgemental nature of the risk assessment process is likely to be even more evident than is the case for pure risks. The final judgement is made partly on the basis of a comparison of the two risk outcomes. In the case of major hazards viewed as pure risks, more complex quantified approaches to risk assessment are required. Whatever type of risk assessment is undertaken, the basis is knowledge and therefore the assessment (whether by 'expert' or 'non-expert') cannot be unbiased or value-free.

## *Management systems and risk*

The systems concept, applied to organizations and management, has demonstrated both its robustness and versatility in providing a conceptual framework for understanding how risk and change may be managed. Systems may be conceived in concrete, functionalist terms as 'real' entities or, more realistically, as perceived entities within an interpretive framework. Seeing systems as real (reified) entities leads to the danger of believing that by 'programming' system elements (e.g. people, procedures) the system will operate in a predictable and controllable way according to some grand design. Such an approach reflects the world-view of the observer rather than the nature of systems as representations of reality. It is important to remember that system models are just that – reduced representations of reality and not the reality itself.

Systems are more than the sum of their parts. For organizations viewed as systems, their inner context contains a number of sub-systems. Systems are also not independent entities since they interact with other systems in their environment (or outer context of organizations viewed as systems). Thus, any given system is part of the environment of other systems and vice versa. Both types of interaction ensure that absolute control of a system, such as an organization, by management or any other party is not possible.

A systems approach allows for enquiry at different levels of complexity – which can be reflected in system representations. To overcome problems of comprehension of complexity, such representation should be limited ideally to a maximum of nine components. Beyond this number, it is desirable to break the system representation down into further hierarchical levels to ease comprehension of structures, component interactions and system processes.

In managing risk and/or change, it is essential to be aware of, and to take due account of differences in cognitions, or world-views. These are both individual – and therefore unique – and also shared, as in cultures of groups or organizational sub-systems. At a higher level, types of world-view have been identified which may, in various combinations, characterize particular types of organization. An appreciation of the collective world-view of an organization (or sub-system or individual) is important for understanding what motivates that (sub)system or person.

Systems designed to enhance the management of pure risk topics such as quality, the physical environment, security and occupational health and safety make certain assumptions about the nature of those systems. The high failure rate for full absorption of these add-on management systems at least partly reflects the different cultures or world-views respectively (a) required for their successful adoption, and (b) represented within organizations as collections of sub-systems with divergent cultures and interests. Motivations for seeking to adopt ISO and other management standards within organizations may be founded on a flawed understanding of the degree of prediction and control which is possible through such models. Naïve management systems intended to control particular risks may be therefore only partly effective while creating an illusion that the risks have been fully controlled. To be effective, risk management should ensure that management systems take full account of the inner context of the organization (including history, structures, cultures, resources, motivations and power relations) and its environment or outer context, both of which affect how risks are perceived and what is done about them.

## *Culture and risk*

Organizational culture may be regarded as two kinds of paradigm. One paradigm is a means for an organization's members to interpret their own existence, identity and actions and to institute, guide and moderate those actions. It is their world-view. The other kind is culture applied as an analytical paradigm by external observers. The latter is as problematic as the former since the understanding of organization is inseparable from the organizing of understanding.

Since culture both influences and is influenced by the values and meaning systems of the social actors in an organization, the latter's understanding and actions in relation to particular processes are assumed to be culturally linked. Cultural aspects of organizations are therefore important factors to be addressed in relation to risk.

Like risk, culture is a problematic concept, with even more possible dimensions. Although many attempts have been made to reify, evaluate or even to manage culture, they depend on numerous debatable assumptions which are often not recognized by those who make such attempts. Different levels and manifestations of culture in organizations are identifiable. Lack of cultural homogeneity in most organizations may confound attempts to measure organizational culture, including particular aspects such as safety culture and risk culture.

Organizational culture is linked inextricably with organizational change. Thus, if the culture of an organization changes, then by definition that organization also changes. What is less definitive is whether if an organization changes, for example in terms of numbers of employees, kinds of activity or achievement of 'success', its culture necessarily changes.

From a functionalist perspective, some managements have sought to change organizations by manipulating their culture in the form of beliefs or behaviours of employees, with the aim of exercising control. As with systems, however, while certain aspects of an organization's culture may be within the power of management to influence, other elements exist and persist beyond such control. From an interpretive standpoint, culture is regarded more as a metaphor for understanding how organizations function and why they respond in characteristic ways towards a wide range of topics and issues, such as those relating to management, to risk and to change. Given the complexity of human behaviour, and culture as a particular component of it, an interpretive perspective on culture and risk may be a more appropriate precursor to actions seeking to modify culture to achieve risk benefits.

Culture is also linked closely with those risks (pure and speculative) which characterize an organization. A rapprochement is developing between the divergent perspectives of technical (functionalist) and cultural (interpretive) approaches to management and organization, in both study and practice. Nevertheless, controversy still remains about the relationship between culture and risk and the relative merits of functionalist and interpretive perspectives on both.

## *Power and risk*

Power in organizations is a complex phenomenon having multiple dimensions, although it is frequently treated as if it were a unitary concept. In developing understanding of risk in relation to organizations, their management and change, it will be important to examine power relations and to identify sources of particular influences and the interactions of such sources. Influence may be a particularly salient feature if, for example, its source is expertise residing within a particular functional group (e.g. IT, finance, risk specialists). Power relations and political processes involving management of meanings are particularly relevant to understanding risk behaviour in organizations, for example relations between those who do have and those who would like to have powers to decide the nature of risks and what, if anything, should be done about them – i.e. strategy (both explicit and implicit) is closely linked with political processes and meanings of success. Similar relations are also influential on risk issues in the wider public arena.

Power and its derivatives, such as influence and legitimated authority, are among a number of factors external to individuals which affect their risk cognition and the expression of risk concepts by parties generally. Perception and understanding of a risk may be as much to do with the extent to which individuals and groups trust and believe the reported pronouncements of experts about the risk in question, as it is to do with their own direct experiences. Given the relative paucity of most people's first-hand experience with many risks, 'expert power' may in particular influence people's acceptance of a given risk - particularly those which relate to technology or those arising from 'invisible' hazards (e.g. nuclear waste, environmental pollution, food contamination, HIV infection).

The power of experts and politicians, usually translated through the media, is often an important determinant of individuals' cognitions of a particular risk. Collective response to that risk may be exercised subsequently as 'consumer power' through purchasing decisions (e.g. in the case of food), or through some form of democratic process, including forms of protest, at least in states where this is a realistic option.

Thus, in many cases (e.g. nuclear power, national food scares as with eggs or beef), people respond not so much to the 'objective' risk – as in any case this cannot be established for them as individuals – but to the nature of the power relations between themselves, politicians, other interested parties and experts, with media also playing a potentially powerful role.

## *Organizational environment and risk*

The interrelationship between an organization and its outer context or environment has a significant impact on risk cognitions and actions within the organization. Although this fact is generally recognized, what is often not appreciated is the number and variety of factors in the environment which can influence organizational decision-making and behaviour. In some instances, different external factors or threats may be interdependent and in other instances may even suggest contradictory responses. The need for an integrated approach to risk is therefore highlighted.

Five key areas of organizational environment (economies and markets; public policy, regulation and standards; social climate; technology; history, operating territory and conditions) are likely to have a major impact on risk cognition and behaviour. However, although organizations recognise these areas to varying degrees, typically the many dimensions to these areas are only partly appreciated and they are rarely addressed systematically or coherently. As a result, an organization's personnel may be unaware that risks are increasing.

Factors in the external environment, such as market forces, economic climate and regulation, also influence perceptions in an organization of the need for change. However, few organizations in reality need to be in a purely reactive mode to external factors. Whereas strategic changes may focus on external competition as a means of reducing risks of business failure, for example, assumptions which underpin particular organizational changes may be unwarranted and some risks may actually increase. For example, an over-zealous drive to create a highly cost-efficient, low-staffed and therefore cost-competitive organization (i.e. reducing external risks) may, if handled badly, inadvertently damage staff motivation, morale and retention (i.e. increasing internal risks to product and service quality and ultimately to competitiveness).

## *Risk and change*

Change processes in organizations are complex and an adequate model for understanding such change processes and their relationship with risk would need to capture the essence of the complex phenomena involved. The issues surrounding both understanding by external analytical observers and the action-meaning dialectical processes within an organization are debatable (see for example the modernist/

post-modernist/'new theory' debates and the debates about individual and group behaviours). It is clear that the perspectives of many disciplines would be required in order to furnish a relatively complete model of such change processes.

Despite the inference that change processes are fluid rather than deterministic, it is clear that in organizations undergoing change, order is usually maintained, crises are frequently survived and formal objectives are achieved (at least in part). Therefore, it would appear that interpretive concepts such as power, political processes, and culture operate in the real world primarily to ensure social stability within the organization so that formal structures and processes can function which in turn help to sustain the integration of the organization. During non-crisis phases (i.e. most of the time), the relatively slow process of organizational learning is mediated by risk cognitions as well as by other factors such as culture, power relations, resources and external influences. Programmatic and prescriptive approaches to change often fail to recognise both the contribution of risk cognitions to change processes and the effects change processes are likely to have on risks. Equally, programmatic and prescriptive approaches which are often very seductive in their elegance and promise of early results may none the less inadvertently increase risks because of their very naïveté.

## *Risk cognition*

Risk cognition, as an attempted comprehensive description of the processes involved when individuals appraise risks, particularly speculative risks, as a basis for behaviour, is still in its infancy. To some extent, its development has been hampered by previous emphasis on the more dramatic pure risks and through attempts to define the processes involved too narrowly (e.g. as 'risk perception'), and by efforts to reveal what humans are apparently not 'good' at (e.g. perceiving risks 'accurately', in so far as it is possible to make a value-free judgement of such accuracy). These attempts have usually taken as a starting point the particular perspectives of the researchers involved and have failed to address the full gamut of risks faced by individuals in the context of their daily lives.

Appreciating the nature of individual risk cognition processes should provide a better understanding of the requirements at organizational level, for example when risk assessments are carried out as part of the risk management process. The possibility that risk assessments may need to be broadened to incorporate possible homeostatic or compensation effects by individuals needs to be further tested and investigated.

From a psychological perspective, compensation effects observed in many risk homeostasis studies may be interpreted as reflecting individuals' attempts to maximize the degree of mastery or control over their environment. One cost of such motivated behaviour is a toll, of death, injury and disease which shows at least some resistance to various attempts to reduce it. In contrast, the work environment is increasingly characterized by external control over risks, in which individuals have relatively much lower levels of individual control – either to increase or to reduce the level of risk to which they are exposed. Further development of a potential model of individual speculative risk is required to improve understanding of how people appraise risk in their daily lives.

## Convergent themes

Previous chapters have identified a number of topic categories which are highly relevant to the theme of the book. These are:

- **Management** of risks and strategic options.
- **Assessment** of risks, risk bearing and risk acceptance.
- **Systems** thinking and systematic arrangements for managing risks.
- **Culture**, actions, meanings, organizational learning and a cultural dimension to risk.
- **Power** relations, organizational structures, decision-making and political processes and their effects on strategy and risk.
- **Environment** of the organization and its risk implications.
- **Change**, strategies, contextual mediators and risk.
- **Cognition** of risks and control over events.

It should be apparent from the preceding chapters that these categories are useful labels and do not signify exclusive or independent categories. Nevertheless, the frequency with which these themes recur in the literature on management, on risk and on change as well as in management practice suggests that they are significant. Such themes occur not only across the relevant literature but are also well represented in practice, thus suggesting a potential convergence of ideas.

Of particular significance is the often overlooked interdependent and systemic relationship between all these factors. For example, it is a false assumption that management strategies such as those to reduce, improve or control risks or to change an organization's culture or to improve organizational effectiveness through structural and programmatic change, will always have the desired effect. Expectations of quick and permanent salvation through such activities are unlikely to be met in such a simple cause-effect way and, moreover, because of their naïveté may actually increase risks.

## Convergence in research and practice

Since the late 1980s, researchers from a range of disciplines and backgrounds have moved into the risk area, as evidenced in the UK by developments such as the ESRC-sponsored series of risk seminars at the London School of Economics, the ESRC Risk and Human Behaviour Research Programme and the many university departments now engaged in risk research. Numerous academic conferences and seminars on risk topics have accompanied this upsurge of interest – e.g. sessions at the British Academy of Management Conferences, the annual risk and culture conference sponsored by a number of northern universities since 1993, etc. These activities in the UK have been paralleled by similar activities in other countries and internationally.

Many of the themes identified above appear on research agendas and conference programmes, although still in a relatively fragmented way. Risk management, risk assessment, management systems, culture and change are also frequent topics on management agendas although still in a relatively fragmented and deterministic form. For example, the Commission on Management Research (ESRC 1993) found that there remains an emphasis on normative assumptions and biases in management research generally. Nevertheless, a slow and rather fuzzy convergence of themes about and approaches to management, risk and change is detectable.

## A thematic utility

It is possible to reorganize the common themes identified above into a number of risk contexts which, it is suggested, would need to be addressed in any serious examination of how a particular organization seeks to cope with management, risk and change issues. These risk contexts are:

1 **Outer context/organizational environment**
- economies and markets;
- public policy, regulation, standards;
- social and political climate;
- technology;
- history, operating territories and conditions.

2 **Inner context**
*Human Factors*
- perception, cognition and meanings of success;
- organizational culture;
- power relations, political processes, decision-making.

3 **Formal coping arrangements**
- risk management;
- risk analysis and assessment;
- management systems;
- approaches to change.

Table 9.1 presents a matrix in which the left-hand column displays these risk contexts and the chapters in Part 1 which discuss their theoretical contribution to understanding management, risk and change. Columns across the table denote the case study chapters in Part 2. The codes H (High), M (Medium) and L (Low) indicate the degree to which the case studies demonstrate that particular risk

*Table 9.1* Thematic matrix linking theoretical aspects of risk with empirical case studies

| *Risk contexts* | | *Cases* | | | | | |
|---|---|---|---|---|---|---|---|
| | | *Offshore* | *Barings* | *Railways* | *Iran* | *IT* | *Health authorities* |
| | *Chapter* | *10* | *11* | *12* | *13* | *14* | *15* |
| Organizational environment | 6 | | | | | | |
| Economies and markets | 6 | H | H | H | H | H | H |
| Public policy, legislation and regulation | 6 | H | H | H | H | M | H |
| Social and political climate | 6 | M | M | H | H | M | H |
| Technology | 6 | H | M | M | L | H | H |
| History, operating territories and conditions | 6 | H | H | H | H | M | H |
| Human factors | | | | | | | |
| Culture | 4 | H | H | H | H | H | H |
| Power relations, political processes and decision-making | 5 | H | H | H | H | H | H |
| Perception, cognition and meanings of success | 8 | H | H | H | H | H | H |
| Formal coping arrangements | | | | | | | |
| Risk management | 1 | H | H | H | H | H | H |
| Risk assessment | 2 | H | H | H | H | H | H |
| Management systems | 3 | H | H | H | M | H | H |
| Approaches to change | 7 | H | H | H | H | H | H |

Code: H = High significance
M = Medium significance
L = Low significance

contexts are significant. At the end of each chapter in Part 2, the signifance of these risk contexts for each particular case is summarized.

## Conclusion to Part 1

The chapters in Part 1 have raised a number of common factors or risk contexts which have become salient in the study of and practice concerning respectively management, risk and change. The following chapters 10 to 15 of Part 2 seek to demonstrate the diverse range of cases in which the common themes apply.

# Part II
# Case studies

# Chapter 10

# The offshore oil and gas industry after Piper Alpha

## Overview

This chapter provides a case study of the impact of the Piper Alpha offshore installation disaster in 1988, not only on the main owner and operator (Occidental Petroleum) but also on the offshore oil and gas industry in the North Sea and worldwide and on other industries, including the insurance market.

## Introduction

On 6 July 1988, an explosion occurred on the Piper Alpha offshore installation in the North Sea which led to the loss of 167 lives and destruction of the installation. What set this disaster apart from other accidents in the offshore industry was the spectacular nature of the explosions and fire, the scale of human and asset losses, the knock-on losses to the industry, government and insurance market, and the long-term impact on risk cognition, risk management and regulation of major hazards. In addition to the loss of life, the direct and consequential financial losses for a number of parties (insurers, Piper Alpha owners, other operators, UK economy) were high. According to Lovegrove (1990), the UK government is estimated to have lost over £2,000 million in revenues and a further £2,800 million in balance of payments. The estimated net impact on Occidental's cash flow was a loss of over £200 million, with other operators losing nearly £600 million. It has been reported that these losses contributed to the major financial crisis in the Lloyds insurance organization in the early 1990s.

Immediately after the Piper Alpha disaster, the UK government set up an inquiry chaired by Lord Cullen to examine the circumstances and causes of the accident and to make recommendations designed to prevent such offshore disasters recurring. The Cullen Inquiry lasted two years and the inquiry report (Cullen 1990) and its recommendations, which were accepted by the government, demanded a new approach to management of safety risks by companies in the industry and to safety regulation by government. Enormous effort and expense were injected to implement the Cullen recommendations and to create a new 'safety culture' in the industry, but the process of culture change is necessarily slow (see chapter 4) and is likely to continue into the 21st century and onward.

The remainder of this chapter outlines the development of the Piper Alpha disaster and summarizes the findings and recommendations of the Cullen Inquiry. An assessment is also given of the industry's efforts to respond to the disaster and to implement the Cullen recommendations. This analysis is based on the work of one of the authors over several years as a consultant to a number of offshore companies, both operators and drilling contractors, in development of improved safety management systems and in statutory 'safety case' preparation – see chapter 3 and Waring (1996a and 1996b).

## The Piper Alpha disaster, 1988

### *Background*

#### *The Piper Alpha installation*

The installation was designed as an all-in-one platform combining production and drilling areas and accommodation areas for the crew and had been in operation since 1976. The topsides structure (i.e. above sea level) included four production modules A to D on the Production Deck, a number of other modules on the deck above, Accommodation Units above these, and finally the Helideck at the top (see Figure 10.1). At the time of the disaster, 226 men were on board, including employees of contractors, and the great majority were off duty in the accommodation area. A number of divers were also at work underwater.

#### *Occidental Petroleum*

Occidental Petroleum (Caledonia) Ltd (OPCL) was the major partner in a consortium of owners and also operated the Piper Alpha installation. The company was part of the giant American Occidental Group, a long-established oil company with considerable resources. OPCL had a written safety policy and had established safety procedures, including permits-to-work (PTW) systems which had become a standard approach to hazardous operations not only in the offshore oil and gas industry but also many others. However, as the Cullen Inquiry found, 'the safety policies and procedures were in place: the practice was deficient'.

*Figure 10.1* The Piper Alpha platform: east elevation (simplified)

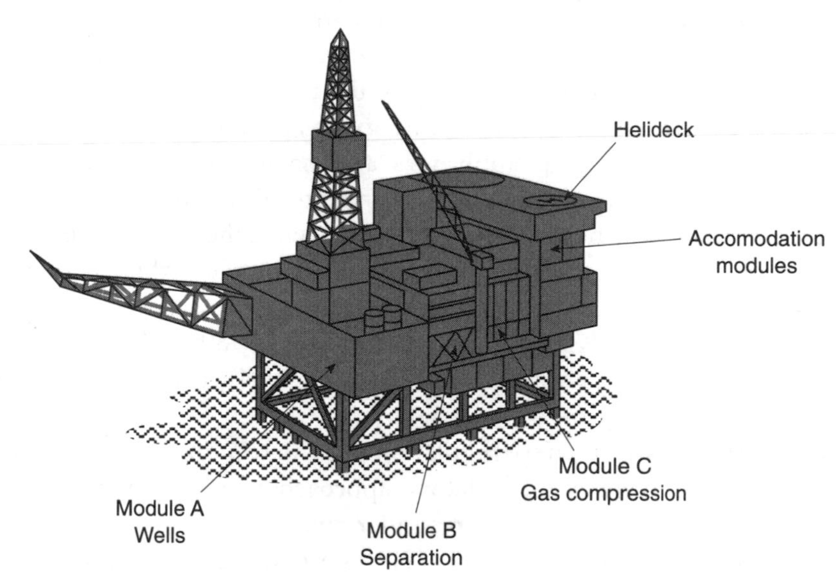


## *Safety regulatory regime in the 1980s*

Offshore installations such as Piper Alpha were subject to regular government inspections by the Department of Energy. Typically, such inspections were carried out on a sampling basis with a view to assessing the adequacy of safety of the installation as a whole. Inspections of Piper Alpha had been carried out in June 1987 and in June 1988, shortly before the disaster.

The Cullen Report noted:

> The findings of those inspections were in striking contrast to what was revealed in evidence at the Inquiry. Even after making allowance for the fact that the inspections were based on sampling it was clear to me that they were superficial to the point of being of little use as a test of safety on the platform. They did not reveal a number of clear cut and readily ascertainable deficiencies . . . the evidence led me to question, in a fundamental sense, whether the type of inspection practised by the Department of Energy could be an effective means of assessing or monitoring the management of safety by operators.

Before Piper Alpha, both offshore safety legislation and the regulatory approach of the Department of Energy were prescriptive with a technical 'nuts-and-bolts' focus rather than a holistic view of what would be needed to achieve safety. In relation to installations, Department of Energy inspectors, who were relatively few, acted the role of policemen on a flying visit and were treated as such by operators (see Woolfson *et al.* 1996). The Cullen Report stated: 'Persistent under-manning has affected not only the frequency but also the depth of their inspections'.

In addition to the Department of Energy inspections, the adequacy of fire-fighting equipment, life-saving appliances and navigational aids on installations were subject to biannual inspection by Department of Transport inspectors acting for the Department of Energy. Operators also relied heavily on certification by marine insurance engineers as a measure of safety. However, whereas such certification of installations was necessary, it did not cover many key aspects of safety and, in the light of the Alexander Kielland disaster in March 1980 in the North Sea which revealed similar deficiencies (Bignell and Fortune 1984), it could not be relied on implicitly as an overriding measure of safety.

In short, neither offshore safety regulation nor the responses of operators were in step with the goal-setting self-regulatory approach to safety which had been in operation across UK industry onshore under the Health and Safety at Work Act 1974, following the Robens Report (1972). The essence of self-regulation is that legislation should state the goals to be achieved by employers but employers themselves are required to decide how to achieve them. The effective management of safety, including risk assessment, planning, organizing, resourcing, risk control, monitoring and auditing, is therefore a continuing responsibility of each employer. Discharging that responsibility requires a broad and proactive approach rather than a narrow approach which reacts to government prescription only when pressure is brought to bear (see chapter 6).

### *North Sea environment*

The North Sea is recognised as being a relatively hazardous physical environment for offshore activities. High winds and storms are frequent and the weather can change rapidly and unpredictably. Seawater temperatures are always cold and without a survival suit a person entering the water is unlikely to survive for more than a few minutes. It is now considered essential for anyone travelling or working offshore for more than a short 'one-off' trip to successfully complete an approved practical training course in offshore survival. Such a course, which typically lasts five days and must be repeated every three years, includes not only escape and evacuation from an installation and survival and rescue from the sea, but also fire fighting, use of respirators, smoke survival and first aid. This kind of approved course run for the industry is in addition to any specific emergency training provided on installations by owners or operators.

Fortunately, the weather and sea state at the time of the Piper Alpha disaster were good. A number of individuals wearing survival suits climbed or jumped from the installation into the sea and were rescued. Of the 61 survivors, 28 escaped in this way.

## *The disaster unfolds*

In order to appreciate the multiple causes of the disaster, it is necessary to consider a fatal accident which occurred some ten months earlier on Piper Alpha on 7 September 1987. On that occasion, it was found by a Department of Energy investigation that the permit-to-work (PTW) procedures for lifting heavy gear were not followed, which resulted in a maintenance worker falling and sustaining fatal injuries. A PTW system is a formal written system of safety checks and controls which have to be signed off as satisfactory by an authorized person before the work starts and at various stages of the work. A permit is issued as valid for a stated period of time. For jobs which extend across shifts, permits are required to be renewed at shift handovers and this demands effective communication.

The investigation found that work handovers between shifts were uncoordinated and communication was poor. Further, a new permit had not been raised to cover a change in the maintenance task which involved lifting a heavy motor. OPCL were prosecuted on these matters under the Health and Safety at Work Act and pleaded guilty on 17 March 1988. Among OPCL responses to this fatality, management issued instructions that permit tasks and instructions were to be worded unambiguously and with the detail necessary to ensure that safety requirements would be met. However, the Cullen Report found evidence that this management instruction was not followed. In evidence to the Cullen Inquiry, it also appears that OPCL production and maintenance managers were unaware that the company had pleaded guilty on matters concerning communication at shift handovers and no action on this aspect occurred. This is an example of a 'failure of hindsight' and a lack of organizational learning (Toft 1990, 1992, 1996; Turner 1992).

On the evening of 6 July 1988 at 21.45, one of two condensate injection pumps on Piper Alpha tripped out. Night-shift personnel sought to restart the other pump which had been shut down for maintenance and this caused a leak of condensate which built up into a low-lying vapour cloud. At 22.00 hours, this vapour cloud was ignited in Module C, the gas compression module, causing the initial explosion of the disaster. In his report, Lord Cullen states:

> I conclude that the leak resulted from steps taken by night-shift personnel with a view to restarting the other pump which had been shut down for

> maintenance. Unbeknown to them, a pressure safety valve had been removed from the relief line of that pump. A blank flange assembly which had been fitted at the site of the valve was not leak-tight. The lack of awareness of the removal of the valve resulted from failures in the communication of information at shift handover earlier in the evening and failure in the operation of the permit to work system in connection with the work which had entailed its removal.

The initial explosion caused extensive damage and was followed immediately by a large crude oil fire in the oil separation module (Module B) which engulfed part of the installation in dense black smoke. The fire spread through breaches in the firewall into C Module and was fed by oil from the installation and from a leak in the main oil pipeline to shore. At about 22.20, a second major explosion intensfied the fire massively. This resulted from a rupture of the riser on the gas pipeline from the neighbouring Tartan installation. Further intensification of the fire occurred at about 22.50 and 23.20 as the risers on the gas pipelines connected to the Frigg and Claymore installations respectively ruptured.

The main power supplies and the installation Control Room were put out of action by the initial explosion. Although the emergency shutdown system was activated and appeared to function, the other emergency systems failed immediately or shortly after the initial explosion. The fire water system was rendered inoperative but in any event the pumps were set on manual mode.

In the words of the Cullen Report, 'The system of control in the event of a major emergency was rendered almost entirely inoperative . . . and little command or control was exercised over the movements of personnel'. Smoke and flames outside the accommodation made evacuation by helicopter or lifeboat impossible. Diving personnel, who were on duty, escaped to the sea along with other personnel on duty at the northern end and the lower levels of the platform. Other survivors who were on duty made their way to the accommodation; and a large number of men (estimated by one eye witness to be about 100) congregated near the galley on the top level of the accommodation. 'There was no evidence that this was the result of any positive actions on the part of anyone in a position of authority'. Conditions there were tolerable at first but deteriorated greatly owing to the entry of smoke. The Offshore Installation Manager (OIM) in overall executive charge of the Piper Alpha was described by witnesses as unable to take command and reach a decision for them to evacuate the galley. A number of personnel in the accommodation unit took individual initiatives to escape and many of these survived. 'If leadership occurred in these escapes, it arose by individuals joining those who seemed to know their way around'. However, at least 81 persons did not leave the accommodation unit and perished. 'Some waited in the hope of a helicopter coming. Some stayed because they had been told to wait there and had received no other instruction. Some would not have remained there if they had known the full gravity of the situation which threatened the platform. Others remained because they simply did not know what else to do. There was no systematic attempt to lead men to a means of escape from the accommodation'.

A picture emerges from the Cullen Report which suggests strongly that mutiple weaknesses and failings in the safety management system (see chapter 3) of OPCL and Piper Alpha, of which failure of the PTW system was a symptomatic example, combined with failings in the fire safety design of the installation to cause the initial explosion and the subsequent development of the conflagration. Failings in other aspects of the SMS, especially emergency command and control, led to fewer survivors than otherwise might have been expected.

## The Cullen Inquiry

### *The 'forthwith' studies*

It was recognised that, as the inquiry would be lengthy, any early provisional findings which could be translated into practical requirements should be made known to the industry as soon as possible and in advance of any statutory regulations which might ensue. A number of such early issues included the need for a formal risk assessment of major hazards to each installation, and EER (escape, evacuation and rescue) and TSR (temporary safe refuge) evaluations. The EER analysis was considered especially important and recommendation 76 of Lord Cullen's report asked for offshore operators and drilling contractors to undertake EER studies 'forthwith' and in advance of legislation. These studies became known as the 'forthwith studies'.

### *Key findings*

The Cullen Inquiry report is in two volumes totalling 488 pages and covers a vast array of relevant issues which are too numerous to relate in detail in this chapter. The following summarizes key findings in the report.

- The overall safety management system (SMS) of both Occidental's onshore activities and the Piper Alpha installation was inadequate. Safety of such installations depends critically on the existence of an effective SMS, including robust procedures such as permits-to-work (PTW).

- The culture of the most commercially successful companies in the industry was built on a belief that systematic safety management is an integral part of achieving commercial success. The industry as a whole should develop such a culture.
- Offshore safety legislation was too narrow and prescriptive and regulatory enforcement by the Department of Energy was too oriented towards technical safety compliance with inadequate attention to safety management.
- Major hazards associated with offshore oil and gas activities were not being assessed systematically by operators and contractors for risk acceptability.
- Approaches to installation design and construction needed to pay far greater attention to the location and integrity under fire conditions of accommodation, temporary safe refuges (TSR), escape routes and embarcation points.
- Escape, evacuation and rescue (EER) arrangements for each installation needed to be better planned, organised and tested.

## Cullen recommendations

The Cullen Inquiry report made a total of 106 recommendations which are condensed and summarized in the following sub-sections.

### Key requirements

New goal-setting safety regulations, backed up by guidance notes, should be drawn up. Offshore safety should be regulated by a single body, more particularly a discrete division of the Health and Safety Executive devoted exclusively to offshore safety.

Each operator should be required by regulation to submit to the regulatory body a 'Safety Case' in respect of each of its installations. The Safety Case should demonstrate that certain objectives have been met, including:

- That the SMS of both the company and the installation are adequate to ensure that the design and the operation of the installation are safe.
- That potential major hazards of the installation and the risks to personnel on it have been identified and appropriate controls provided.
- That adequate provision is made for ensuring, in the event of a major emergency affecting the installation, a temporary safe refuge (TSR) for personnel and their safe and full evacuation, escape and rescue.

The SMS should set out the safety objectives, the system by which these objectives are to be achieved, the performance standards which are to be met and the means by which adherence to these standards is to be monitored. It should draw on quality assurance principles similar to those stated in BS 5750 (now ISO 9000).

Risk analyses should include a quantified risk assessment (QRA) of major hazards, a fire risk analysis and an analysis of EER. The acceptance standards for risk should be set (for the time being by the regulator) by reference to the ALARP principle (see chapter 2). The operator should demonstrate through risk analysis and safety cases how those standards would be met.

### *Other recommendations*

Other recommendations concern more detailed aspects of safety management and process safety:

- permits-to-work;
- safety committees and safety representatives;
- incident reporting;
- control of the process;
- hydrocarbon inventory, risers and pipelines;
- fire and gas detection and emergency shutdown;
- fire and explosion protection;
- accommodation, TSR, escape routes and embarcation points;
- emergency centres and systems;
- pipeline emergency procedures;
- evacuation, escape and rescue – general;
- helicopters;
- totally enclosed motor propelled survival craft (TEMPSC);
- means of escape to the sea;
- personal survival and escape equipment;
- standby vessels;
- command in emergencies;
- drills, exercises and precautionary musters and evacuations;
- training for emergencies.

## Discussion of the offshore industry's responses

The Cullen Inquiry took evidence from a wide range of witnesses, including senior representatives from a number of offshore operators. The findings and recommendations faithfully reflect much of their evidence which focused on the need for adequate safety management systems and a culture change. However, although a consensus on these matters clearly existed, in the authors' opinion the Inquiry failed to identify some subtle but important characteristics of the industry and its approach to safety which were to slow down attempts to introduce significant changes demanded by Cullen. Woolfson *et al.* (1996) suggest that there 'are real grounds for concern that there will be an actual worsening of offshore safety' as the effects of Cullen wear off.

## *Approaches to risk assessment*

During the 'forthwith' period (see above), the industry re-evaluated its approach to major hazards risks, as directed by Lord Cullen. Both operators and drilling contractors embarked on formal safety assessments (FSAs) which eventually became the basis of their safety cases. Although such assessments were recognised as requiring close attention to safety management and other qualitative aspects of risk (see for example Spouge 1990), most attention was directed in practice at quantified risk assessments (QRA) of major hazards, TSR and EER. Such studies, typically undertaken by external consultants, became the main focus during 1989–91.

Risk studies of major hazards relied then, and still do, on systematic identification and analysis of major hazard scenarios. For an offshore installation, such scenarios typically included events such as fire, explosion, ship collision, dropped heavy object, riser failure, blow out, toxic release and helicopter crash. Torhaug (1992) emphasizes two particular assumptions of QRA, namely that it 'should consider all hazards relevant to the problem studied' and that assessment of causes and consequences should be 'complete and realistic'. Further, certain theoretically possible events are excluded 'because there is a 'general' agreement that either the probability of occurrence or the possible consequences are negligible'.

These core assumptions of QRA are open to challenge both on theoretical grounds and from empirical observation. For example, Toft (1992, 1996) suggests that there are inherent limitations in quantified risk assessment methodologies, which render problematic any predictions which might arise from their use. He questions the following assumptions (see chapter 2):

- Risks and their assessment are value-free and neutral.
- Modelling of risks is a neutral, objective activity resulting in a final quantitative assessment which is unbiased and independent of the analyst.
- An exhaustive set of failure modes for the risk activity can be identified.

- Reliable historical data are available for past events, which can be used to calculate risk probabilities.
- The complexity of human behaviour in general, and human errors in particular, can be pre-specified and reduced to a simple numeric.
- The future trajectory of an organization will be similar to that of the past.

Toft (1992, 1996) quotes examples of disasters which involved major hazard events, either which had not been identified (e.g. Three Mile Island), or which had been dismissed as an acceptably low probability. For example, a major fire occurred in the Channel Tunnel railway in November 1996, within its first year of operation, a highly unlikely event in QRA terms. The inherent limitations of QRA, which demand great caution in its use in decision-making about risks (Cassidy 1994), have not always been recognised and accepted. The original position of the HSE Offshore Division on overall risk acceptability was to set an acceptance criterion of a specified event not occurring more frequently than once in 10,000 years. The Cullen Report recommendations stated that 'For the time being it should be the regulatory body which sets these standards'. It soon became apparent that such an approach was too prescriptive and was encouraging companies to adopt an external 'numerical target' approach to offshore safety instead of setting their own risk goals within their own QRA and ALARP framework.

One has to consider who carries out such risk assessments and why there continues to be such a narrow emphasis on QRA. The overriding enthusiasm for QRA is a hallmark of technology-based industries such as the offshore industry and the railway industry (see chapter 12). To an extent, this is understandable in the offshore industry in the light of the Cullen Report. However, as discussed in chapters 2, 4 and 5, it has been argued that such a bias to handling risk is not a methodological necessity but rather a cultural artefact which has arisen from the dominant position of the engineering professions in the industry. There were no social scientists among the assessors appointed by Lord Cullen to his inquiry and this bias is likely to have affected the outcome. Both Douglas (1994) and Waring (1995, 1996a) have suggested a need for broadening the skill base for risk assessment to incorporate social scientists, but generally this call has been ignored in the offshore industry.

## *Approaches to safety management systems*

The overwhelming response of the industry to the requirement for effective SMS was to accept Cullen's suggestion that an SMS 'should draw on quality assurance principles similar to those stated in BS 5750 and ISO 9000'. Since these standards are undemanding and not directly suited to meeting the 'duty of care' requirements of safety, it is unlikely that Cullen intended that his recommendation to follow their principles should be interpreted as meaning that companies should slavishly tie their SMS to BS 5750/ISO 9000 certification (see sections on standards for management systems and management system risks in chapter 3). Indeed, the Cullen Report makes clear that to impose such an approach would be 'going too far'. However, many companies sought to do this and were encouraged to do so by the self-perpetuating requirement of the certification process to ensure that suppliers were also certified. Whereas there may be benefits in connecting quality and safety management ideas and procedures, many organizations failed to recognise the inherent differences in statutory, technical and 'duty of care' demands between the two and were content to follow the lesser demands of quality management systems.

Approaches to management and to safety management systems in the offshore industry remain mechanistic or functionalist, as described in chapter 3 (see for example Barrington 1993; Lawrenson 1990; Owen 1992; Guy 1992; Weyndling and Sandham 1992). The models for SMS have been derived from those of BS 5750/ISO 9000 which in turn are derived from the engineering control paradigm as discussed critically in chapter 3. Such an approach fits well with the dominant culture of engineering in the industry – i.e. reductionism, but not with the complexities of human cognition, behaviour, culture and power relations. The engineering control paradigm on which the offshore industry's approach to SMS has been based necessarily **counteracts** change, whereas the SMS envisaged by Cullen should not only be able to achieve control of hazards and risks when contexts are relatively stable, but should also itself be adaptable to significant changes in context (see chapter 7).

Commenting on offshore safety, Kennedy (1995) a respected quality and safety manager in the offshore industry, stated that 'consideration of the need for a management systems approach should always be at a first principles level, and the use of various quality assurance and other similar standards should not be considered until the principles and targets are clearly worked out by the parties involved, thereby creating ownership on their part. The blind application of standards or 'ready-made' systems will inevitably create problems and will not be helpful in answering the inevitable questions of the 'why are we doing this?' variety.

Examples of consequences of the mechanistic approach to SMS in the industry have been noted in Waring (1992a and 1996a). For example, it is commonplace for the SMS to be written up as a procedures manual very much in the style of engineering procedures. Whereas procedures clearly form part of an SMS, there are many other crucial components which cannot be captured satisfactorily in such a prescriptive way. The approach of SMS manuals also encourages a false expectation that all significant risks will be controlled simply by following the manual or, worse, that the very existence of the manual will ensure that people will follow it assiduously at all times.

Apart from individual cases of offshore companies treating their SMS in a more human-orientated and holistic way, the majority have continued a mechanistic approach. The Exploration & Production Forum (E&P Forum 1994) issued guidelines on health, safety and environmental management systems, which presented considerable detail systematically, based on ISO 9000. However, the content and assumptions are still in the mechanistic tradition of the industry.

The Cullen Report found that the escape and evacuation system on Piper Alpha failed in large part because the OIM failed to take command and exercise control. Recommendation 98 stated: 'The operator's criteria for selection of OIM's, and in particular their command ability, should form part of its SMS'. Lord Cullen heard from a number of witnesses that selection of OIMs was based on a combination of technical qualifications, offshore operational experience, command experience and understanding of the offshore physical environment gained by experience. Witnesses were adamant that psychometric testing was not a valid method for selection and would be resisted by the industry. However, the Cullen Report noted that the disaster:

> clearly demonstrates that conventional selection and training of OIMs is no guarantee of ability to cope if the man himself is not able in the end to take critical decisions and lead those under his command in a time of extreme stress. While psychological tests may not appeal to some companies, the process used and proven successful by the armed forces or Merchant Navy, who have to rely on their officers to lead under stress, should be seriously considered by operating companies.

It should be noted that the armed forces use tests of suitability in addition to psychological tests.

In practice, the industry largely rejected Lord Cullen's conclusion and advice. In the experience of one of the authors, companies were not persuaded to use objective selection techniques for key posts such as OIMs, Superintendents, Drillers and Barge Engineers, even as an adjunct to their traditional methods. The arguments expressed against psychometric testing appeared to be largely emotional and lacked substance and were indicative of a conservative culture which is fearful and resentful of significant changes of an 'alien' nature. Engineering and technical changes could be absorbed, whereas psychometric tests were perceived to require an influx of psychologists who were not of the engineering faith and who might contaminate companies with 'dangerous' ideas, which might undermine selection practices deemed by offshore companies to be time-honoured and time-tested. It could be argued that, by ignoring Cullen's views, the risks to company culture attached to introducing new selection procedures were seen by some as greater than the risks of appointing unsuitable key personnel whose adequacy during an emergency would be paramount.

## *Approaches to human factors*

The term 'human factors' is used widely in relation to offshore safety and has a variety of meanings. Sometimes the term is used in a loose way to cover a vaguely defined set of factors attributed to human beings and which are perceived as 'getting in the way' of neatly designed systems. The term is also used as an alternative to individual human reliability. In the latter, the emphasis is on **individuals**. With such an approach, it is often assumed that group behaviour can be readily predicted simply by aggregating individual behaviours. For example, there may be an assumption that by exposing a set of individuals to the same training programme, information, EER exercises, etc. it may be safely assumed that they will all behave in the same way in relation to these topics (see for example Fitzgerald *et al.* 1990; Kirwan 1987; Pedersen 1986).

Treating aspects of human behaviour in isolation is problematic. For example, emergency response behaviour does not exist in a vacuum. How people behave during emergencies is not totally different from their behaviour at other times. Yet, traditional approaches to EER, which have continued since Piper Alpha, appear to regard people as if they become like programmable robots during an emergency – whatever they have been taught or instructed to do they will do without fail on each and every occasion once the right signal has been given, and then revert to being 'normal' once the emergency is over.

In seeking to predict and control human behaviour, it is certainly necessary to address individual characteristsics. However, it needs to be recognized that individuals also belong to groups and that group characteristics affect how individual members think and act. Prediction of behaviour in any particular setting therefore becomes more complex than a simple collection of individuals would suggest. Two sets of human factors which are important in understanding this complexity are culture and power (see chapters 4 and 5).

Approaches to escape, evacuation and rescue offshore have continued to focus on human behaviour *during* the emergency. There has been considerable research in this area. However, it is at least as important to understand human behaviour under the *non*-emergency conditions which prevail most of the time. Prevalent behaviour (i.e. the effects of the unobtrusive cultural backdrop) is likely to be more predictive of behaviour under relatively rare emergency conditions than are the idealised assumptions of what people will do in emergencies. A relevant example is the Ocean Odyssey blow-out (Ireland 1991; Woolfson *et al.* 1996).

The engineering bias towards safety in the industry is exemplified by the narrow approach to human factors in EER. Although attempts have been made to recognise that during emergency evacuations 'people do not behave like ball-bearings' (Fitzgerald *et al.* 1990), the overwhelming emphasis in offshore human factors studies has been on use of reduced models (often computer-based) which seek to enable prediction of personnel movements on board for EER purposes (see for example Stephens and Lucas 1993; Drager and Wiklund 1993; Flin and Mearns 1993). Wise use of such models may bring benefits, but to imagine that people will behave in reality like identikit programmable robots under any kind of circumstance or that reliable predictions can be made is to show a lack of understanding of human behaviour.

## *Approaches to safety culture*

Culture and power relations in the offshore industry materially affect safety through motivations, attitudes, decision-making, allocation of resources, and beliefs about cause-and-effect. Mistrust of and lack of enthusiasm for outside influences, especially those associated with non-engineering approaches to safety issues, is observable in the industry. This was clearly evident in the general approach to safety culture and the expectation of quick results, although not all companies took such a deterministic view.

Whereas there remains considerable academic debate about the concept of safety culture (see chapter 4), there is general agreement that it is complex and takes many years to develop or change. However, the offshore industry appears to have had few qualms about defining it and taking action on it. The overwhelming response of companies was to regard safety culture as a simple behaviour set which could be manipulated and fixed readily according to company specification. There was an evident desire to keep the concept of safety culture remote from the messy reality of human behaviour, and treat it as if it were an engineering entity which could be captured readily in manuals and manipulated simply by managerial decree or prescription (see for example Barrington 1993; Owen 1992; Guy 1992).

In the offshore industry there is a traditional rivalry between Corporate, Projects and Operations groups although, with slimming down and merging of projects and operations in some companies in the mid-1990s, the characteristic became less noticeable. Essential as good communication is in any organization, it is not enough on its own to overcome the strong 'nation states' cultural characteristic of the industry. Indeed, the rival power groups often communicate very effectively with each other – they just do not always agree about what should be done, how and by whom, with all the attendant arguments about allocation of resources, control of work, job gradings, etc. Nation states behaviour is self-reinforcing – the more it continues the more embedded and 'natural' it becomes. Whichever divisions, departments, functions, or disciplines exercise a dominant role may decide the approach to safety in general and SMS and safety cases in particular. Sometimes this may have no adverse effects but there is always a need to distinguish between decisions and actions that reflect a synthesis of the most powerful arguments and those that reflect the arguments of the most powerful.

Attitudes towards safety responsibilities, risk taking and risk acceptability are moulded by cultural and power characteristics. A particularly important set of power relations is that between safety representatives and management. In addition to the Cullen Report recommendations on safety committees and safety representatives and specific regulations, the Offshore Installations (Safety Case) Regulations guidance requires safety cases to make explicit the arrangements for workforce involvement in activities such as risk analysis, audits, PTW development, etc. However, 'workforce involvement' is interpreted variably. In some companies, particularly drilling contractors, 'them and us' divisions are relatively weak and involvement is part of their culture. Drilling crews are often like 'families', the dangers are great and management-workforce teamwork is often taken for granted.

In other companies, however, management has only grudgingly involved the workforce and offered only token compliance with the pertinent regulations on involvement. Although in such companies there is an overt compliance (e.g. there are safety reps, safety committees), the latter are not invited to assist in risk assessments, accident investigations, training reviews, safety case reviews, etc. Indeed, in one company audited by one of the authors, the management themselves were not even aware of their own legal obligations to do such things.

The reluctance in some offshore companies to allow adequate involvement of the workforce in safety matters does not apparently stem from a desire to injure people or from a belief that they have little to contribute or that they would encourage loss of production time. It has much to do with managerial beliefs about their own status and a fear that they will lose both **symbolic** and actual power on a more general basis if they were to engage in constructive dialogue in which the workforce could influence safety matters.

## *Approaches to safety cases*

A safety case is a statement, usually a set of documents, which seeks to justify on safety grounds, both to the operator and to the regulatory authority, why the particular installation or operation should be allowed to operate or continue to operate (Waring 1996a). It must therefore not only contain relevant facts and description, but also show how the organization arrived systematically at the conclusion that both particular risks and the overall risk from major hazards are as low as reasonably practicable (ALARP), as discussed in chapter 2. A safety case has three main uses:

1 to provide an internal focus for co-ordinating safety effort and action plans;
2 to provide an entry point and 'route map' for audits, whether internal or external;
3 to provide the necessary documents for submission to statutory authorities.

A safety case needs to set out and develop a coherent argument based on clear objectives which reflect the safety goals set by the organization for itself and for the installation. Many offshore companies initially failed to grasp that a safety case is not just a list of relevant headings under which is described what the organization believes ought to be done about them, as this would make the safety case little more than a prescriptive safety manual. Safety manuals are reference documents which support the safety case, but the safety case itself requires a very different approach. For example, each topic addressed should contain a summary of the strengths and weaknesses of the current approach to it, what is currently being done about weaknesses (if any) and a timetable of improvement activities. Without such honesty, it is difficult to see how either the operator or the regulatory authority could make a sound judgement about whether the overall document had made a convincing case.

Different phases in the life cycle of an offshore installation are likely to require their own safety cases, e.g. design, project, operations, combined operations, decommissioning. In an offshore company, the overall safety management system (SMS) may comprise several SMSs which reflect the organizational structure, e.g. projects, operations. Following the Cullen Report and subsequent regulations regarding safety cases, there were often tussles within such companies for control of the definition, substance and preparation of safety cases. For example, in a number of companies the US corporate headquarters felt that they should be in charge of these topics whereas their UK operations felt that knowledge and experience of local requirements and expectations justified their own claim to it. In some companies, Projects and Operations groups each struggled to wrest control of safety case activity. Some groups felt that their safety case should contain honest statements about identified shortcomings and what was being done to improve them whereas the 'rival' group regarded this as unacceptable 'washing of dirty linen' in public. Some groups regarded the safety case as a set of statements on their approach to risk assessment and risk acceptance with token coverage of their SMS whereas other groups demanded a more balanced approach.

Although the Cullen Report and subsequent regulations required that a wide range of topics including the SMS should be covered in every offshore safety case, analysis of the organization's safety culture was not included. There was no reason why companies should not include such an analysis and indeed some companies did so. Since safety culture has such an impact on safety, it is difficult to see how a safety case could be regarded as complete and convincing without this topic being adequately addressed. It is evident that many companies regarded the Offshore Installations (Safety Case) Regulations 1992 and the official HSE Guidance to them as a prescriptive list of topics to be complied with rather than as minimum content to be developed. In this sense, the culture changed little after Piper Alpha. Indeed, Kennedy (1995) highlighted the contrast between the growth of technical regulations and the paucity of attention given to cultural conditions in organizations, which may predispose them to accidents.

## Costs of Piper Alpha

It is unlikely that the total financial and economic costs of the Piper Alpha disaster will ever be known as there is no agreed costing model which could be used and, so far as the authors are aware, no one has been engaged in a systematic and comprehensive costing study over a sufficiently long period of time after the event. Woolfson *et al.* (1996) provide only three pages on the general and typical costs of day-to-day offshore accidents. However, some attempts have been made to make estimates of the Piper Alpha costs based on a variety of data sources. Notable is the work of Lovegrove (1990) as reported to the Institute of Petroleum who identified the following potential economic cost elements:

1 **For Occidental**
   - compensation claims for death and personal injury;
   - environmental restitution;

- replacement of installation and equipment;
- loss of production and potentially loss of access to crude for refinery feed-stock;
- loss of cash flow and profits;
- impact on project NPV;
- damage to company image.

2 **For the UK offshore industry**
- need to install new safety equipment on all installations;
- loss of production while new equipment is installed;
- loss of cash flow and profits;
- damage to the industry's image;
- cost of responses to new safety legislation.

3 **For the UK national economy**
- adverse effect on balance of payments;
- loss of royalties and tax revenues;
- costs of a government inquiry and subsequent legislation.

According to Lovegrove's estimates, the Piper Alpha disaster cost the Occidental group approximately £2,020 million by the end of 1992, expressed in 1988 prices and before tax reliefs. However, because of various savings in petroleum revenue tax and corporation tax, this loss was reduced to an estimated £210 million at the end of 1992. The aggregate cost of the disaster to the whole UK industry is estimated by Lovegrove to be approximately £3,640 million by the end of 1992. Of this figure, only some £800 million was paid by the industry because of taxation arrangements. The aggregate cost of the Piper Alpha disaster to the UK government over the five-year period to the end of 1992 was estimated to have been a loss of £2,060 million in balance of payments plus £2,840 million in loss of royalty and tax revenues.

Lovegrove's cost headings do not directly include costs to companies associated with preparation and maintenance of safety cases. In the early stages of response to the Cullen Report, companies typically spent large amounts of money using external consultants to help them prepare their safety cases. Kennedy (1995) estimates that the cost of preparing an offshore safety case for a new installation is about £1 million. However, he also points out that an early benefit may come from reduced insurance premiums as a result of identification and reduction of risks on the ALARP principle. The cost of safety case preparation for a typical North Sea installation could be recouped within two or three years from reduced insurance premiums, and with subsequent years producing a net saving.

Another cost outcome of Piper Alpha for the industry as a whole needs to be added to Lovegrove's list. The offshore industry is a global one and typically companies operate wherever oil and gas has been found in exploitable amounts. Moreover, companies continually seek new prospects and so at any one time exploration may be underway in many territories, including countries not traditionally recognised as oil and gas producers. For example, the traditional major offshore oil and gas regions of the Gulf of Mexico, Middle East and the North Sea have been joined by countries such as Indonesia, Canada and Mozambique and, more recently, by Vietnam, Malaysia, Turkmenistan, Russian Far East and the Falkland Islands. Although the Piper Alpha disaster occurred in UK waters, the knock-on effect globally was inevitable. Oil and gas producing countries bordering the North Sea such as Holland, Norway, Germany and Denmark were quick to introduce statutory requirements on operators in their sectors which were comparable to those recommended by the Cullen Report. Other countries such as Canada and Indonesia followed suit. At one stage, a number of US-based operators considered withdrawing from the North Sea because of the new safety costs. However, because of the global effect of Piper Alpha, it became clear that it would be difficult for an operator based in the United States, for example, to undertake major hazard risk assessments and prepare safety cases only for those of its installations in the UK sector of the North Sea. In any event, drilling installations were frequently moving in and out of different territorial waters around the globe. Major offshore companies who operate globally have therefore been forced to act comprehensively regarding their installations, with all the cost implications of this. As far as the North Sea is concerned, from 1993 onwards operators tended to adopt an approach called CRINE – i.e. cost reduction in the new era – which seeks to avoid unnecessary Cullen-related costs as the North Sea oil and gas fields decline. Woolfson *et al.* (1996) suggest that CRINE has had a negative effect on safety by legitimizing cost reduction as a priority.

Lovegrove's analysis focuses on costs to companies and the government. However, it is also pertinent to consider the cost to those who were killed or injured in the disaster and their families. The authors have no data on financial costs to individuals but one aggregated estimate may be obtained from Lovegrove's data which quotes insurance liabilities of £116 million for the dead and injured.

Lovegrove suggests that damage to image and reputation is an economic cost factor to consider. Certainly, the name of Occidental became synonymous with the Piper Alpha Disaster. By 1990, Occidental Petroleum (Caledonia) Ltd had transferred its

North Sea interests to Elf under the name EE Caledonia. The new company continued the construction of the Piper Bravo installation intended to replace Piper Alpha and remained a successful operator in the North Sea.

## Major hazards risks to offshore oil and gas companies

### *Hazards and threats*

Based on the foregoing description and discussion, the main safety hazards and threats to companies engaged in offshore oil and gas exploration and production are as listed below.

#### *Investment and strategy*

Positive aspects include:

- Major hazards risk reduction and safety case programmes funded by individual companies as part of a strategy to remain in key territories in the face of Cullen-based local legislation.

Key threats are:

- Success of risk control (i.e. infrequent incidents without major consequences) may lead to complacency and lower safety investment beyond a prudent level.
- Emphasis on cost reduction (i.e CRINE) may result in unforeseen reduction in safety in some cases.
- Periodic falls in oil prices may deter safety investment when margins are tight.
- Periodic falls in demand for exploration and increased competition may deter safety investment by drilling companies.

#### *Fire and explosion*

Positive aspects include:

- Increased attention to systematic fire risk analysis including EER as part of major hazards risk control programmes.

Key threats are:

- Excessive engineering focus and methods may encourage unreliable predictions about human behaviour in fire emergencies.

### *Safety management*

Positive aspects include:

- Increased focus on SMS as a necessary component of safety cases and remaining in the offshore exploration and production industry.

Key threats are:

- Mechanistic, prescriptive and incomplete approach to SMS in many companies degrades potential benefits and may lull companies into believing that their safety management is adequate.
- Complacency about degree of implementation.
- Inadequate auditing of SMS.

### *Culture*

Positive aspects include:

- Increased awareness of importance of organizational culture in determining levels of safety and risk.

Key threats are:

- Engineering domination of beliefs about hazards and attitudes to risk control which is beneficial in some contexts may be detrimental in others.
- Mechanistic, prescriptive and incomplete approach to safety culture in many companies may lull them into falsely believing that they are able to effect a significant culture change quickly.

### *Power relations*

Positive aspects include:

- Stable, mature industry tends to produce a dynamic equilibrium between major functions in offshore companies.
- Increasing realization that offshore safety cannot remain immune to industrial relations arrangements long considered standard in onshore major hazards industries.

Key threats are:

- Some companies may retain a macho approach to management which may adversely affect workforce involvement in safety.

- Contractors may be unwilling to raise health and safety issues with operators for fear of losing future contracts.

*Change*
Positive aspects include:

- Awareness of changes in the outer context which are likely to affect the oil and gas industry significantly.
- Adequate resources available to most companies to respond to demands from external changes.

Key threats are:

- Excessive focus on internal changes, such as company re- engineering, as a panacea for reducing business risks.
- Assumption that changes affecting the offshore oil and gas industry are so special that little could be learned from other industries.

### *Risk assessment*

The following table summarizes potential risk levels for the threats discussed above. The attributed risk levels are based on the authors' judgements. Both positive and negative outcomes for any given threat may co-exist.

| **Threat** | **Potential risk levels** | |
|---|---|---|
| | **Negative outcomes** | **Positive outcomes** |
| Investment and strategy | Low–Medium | Medium |
| Fire and explosion | Medium–High | Medium |
| Safety management | Medium–High | Medium |
| Culture | Medium–High | Low–Medium |
| Power relations | Medium–High | Low–Medium |
| Change | Medium | Medium |

## Comparision with thematic matrix

Table 10.1 indicates the relative salience of each of the risk contexts identified in Part 1, and particularly chapter 9, in relation to this case study. In the table, H = high, M = medium, L = low.

*Table 10.1* Thematic matrix applied to the offshore major safety hazards case study

| *Risk context* | *Salience in case study* |
|---|---|
| *Organizational environment* | |
| Economies and markets | H |
| Public policy, legislation and regulation | H |
| Social and political climate | M |
| Technology | H |
| History, operating territories and conditions | H |
| *Human factors* | |
| Culture | H |
| Power relations, political processes and decision-making | H |
| Perception and cognition | H |
| *Formal coping arrangements* | |
| Risk management | H |
| Risk assessment | H |
| Management systems | H |
| Approaches to change | H |

## Conclusions

The Piper Alpha disaster caused the largest loss of life in a single offshore intallation accident. The ramifications in terms of costs to Occidental and the other consortia members, to the offshore oil and gas industry globally, to the insurance market and to the UK government have been extensive. So too have been the ramifications for the offshore industry worldwide in terms of how companies are now expected to address major hazards and their attendant risks. Companies undoubtedly have injected large amounts of resources since Piper Alpha in seeking to improve their whole approach to risk reduction and risk control on the ALARP principle and to such key factors as SMS. However, many safety specialists believe that the noble intention of replacing old prescriptive legislation with new goal-setting self-regulatory requirements has been only partly successful in its implementation. Despite praiseworthy efforts in many companies, there remains a fundamentally mechanistic, prescriptive and incomplete approach to SMS, safety culture and an array of related safety topics. This approach, which is linked to a 'failure of hind-sight' (Toft 1990), is embedded in the culture of safety engineering which traditionally has dominated all aspects of safety in the industry. Although some aspects of the industry's culture may have changed since Piper Alpha, there has yet to occur a significant shift in the engineering culture which might bring about the safety culture envisaged by Lord Cullen. Barely two years after the Piper Alpha disaster, Lovegrove (1990) 'having regard to simple statistics' predicted another installation disaster in the North Sea before the fields run dry in the early 21st century. Safety specialists have also made similar predictions in the North Sea context and, on a global basis, such a disaster somewhere regrettably appears probable.

## Chapter 11
# The collapse of Barings Bank

## Overview

'The bankruptcy of Barings was the biggest cock-up in the history of British banking . . .' (Fay 1996: 266). This chapter provides a case study to review factors associated with corporate failure, from which several lessons may be learned. It is included in this book as a prime example of what can go wrong when financial and human risks are not properly managed. Using a framework broadly premised on chapters in part 1, it seeks to identify features of risk management which are common to many organizational failures.

## Introduction

Barings Bank may be the best documented of all corporate failures, having been the subject of a number of reports and considerable media coverage into the circumstances surrounding its collapse. Comprehensive reports were produced by the Bank of England's Board of Banking Supervision (BoBS 1995) and the Singaporean Ministry of Finance (San and Kuang 1995) while a report was also produced by a UK Parliamentary Commons Committee (House of Commons 1996). The trader at the centre of the affair ghosted a book (Leeson 1996) and at least three other books on the case have been published (Rawnsley 1995; Fay 1996; Gapper and Denton 1996).

The potential to learn from Barings' story is considerable – a prime reason for its appearance here. A summary of the case should be required reading for all senior executives of finance companies. Managers of many other organizations might also usefully learn from the case. As Fay (1996: 296) notes: 'For Eddie George, governor of the Bank of England, the one bonus of the affair was Barings' role as a dreadful example to the industry at large. In the ensuing days and nights, City banks worked overtime checking their risk-management and control systems. "I think that the collapse has done more durable good than all the efforts of the world's regulators laid end to end", says George'. However, while some 1800 pages have already been published as books and reports alone on the Barings collapse, preparation of a text devised specifically for management to learn from is still awaited.

Given the problems of evidence, we do not claim that our interpretation of the Barings case is more valid than any of the others that have been produced. However, while our account can only be second-hand, we have the benefit of being able to evaluate those other accounts and from them to express a perspective which has not been developed elsewhere. As has been pointed out many times (e.g. Fischhoff 1975; Hidden 1989) hindsight confers advantages not available to those parties who find themselves players in what may subsequently be variously labelled as a 'crisis' or 'fiasco' (Sheaffer, Richardson and Rosenblatt 1998). Specialist terms and details of the case are kept to a minimum, as these are well described in other publications (e.g. BoBS 1995; San and Kuang 1995). Definitions of specialist terms in this chapter are taken from these reports.

As probably the first scholarly paper on the Barings case, Sheaffer *et al.* (1998) provide a useful analytical framework for analysing the case based upon non-detection of early warning signals by Barings management and staff. Sheaffer *et al.*'s broad framework is crisis management, which provides a valuable perspective when considering decision making and associated perceptions during crises. Their analysis includes reference to:

- the 'success-breeds-failure' syndrome;
- management failure to adopt basic financial control systems;
- deficiencies in organizational culture, structure and functioning;
- external regulatory failures;
- malevolent environments ('colliding with ill-prepared organizations');
- wider societal influences – particularly the 'free market', as a major source of organizationally induced crises.

Sheaffer *et al.* (1998) note the nine early warning indicators identified by the BoBS (1995: 13) inquiry report and consider the Barings crisis in the light of these key indicators.

Theoretical models can be extremely useful in analysing and assisting understanding of crises resulting from complex forces. However, often such models do not provide clear guidelines for organizations in respect of action to avoid similar crises. While acknowledging the value and insights derived from a crisis or disaster management perspective, within the context of this book our approach is to consider the

Barings case from a broad risk management viewpoint. In this chapter, Barings' failures to manage various forms of risk are identified so that it should be possible to derive lessons for avoiding similar disasters. One focus will be upon an aspect of risk management which is often considered to be of secondary importance – people management.

Accounts of Barings' collapse each present evidence from particular perspectives. For example the House of Commons (1996) report reviews the role of regulatory bodies and arrangements in Barings' collapse and makes recommendations for future regulation, focusing upon a lead regulator. This report points to the 'regulatory culture' not being conducive to communication between regulators in different countries – reflecting competition between different countries' financial exchanges. The UK Commons report also notes a proliferation of regulators, tensions between them and confusion over responsibilities. This situation may be contrasted with the occupational health and safety (OHS) sphere in which a single body (HSE) has, over a nearly 25-year period, absorbed most of the previously separate OHS regulatory bodies.

To self-regulate effectively, a system needs to be able to detect risk from within. Although not the focus of our orientation upon the Barings case, it has been pointed out (e.g. House of Commons 1996: xviii) that if information available to the financial exchanges in Singapore, Tokyo and Osaka had been pooled, for example by some regulatory body, then Barings' net position would have been revealed earlier. However, because information between exchanges is limited, no single body has the full picture regarding a company's dealings.

The various accounts of Barings' collapse agree that there were critical failures in Barings' management – in one case these failings were attributed to named individuals (San and Kuang 1995), while in others organizational systems (BoBS 1995) or culture – for example 'panic, ignorance and greed' (Fay 1996) were blamed. Analyses may make attributions which leave the reader incredulous in respect of what various players must have known at the time events unfolded. However, such attributions are subject to a range of biases (see for example Glendon and McKenna 1995), including those that observers usually make in respect of actors – seeing individual players as primarily responsible for events – the fundamental attributional error. Actors in the drama are much more likely to be aware of the magnitude of the circumstances surrounding them and of their relative lack of power or controlling ability. Another attributional bias which might be discerned in the Barings case is that because the ramifications were so extensive then they 'must' have been foreseen by the parties who were identified as the major players in the subsequently labelled crisis.

However, as crises are generally one-off events for an organization – for which no previous experience may exist, at least among those closely involved – then a self-protecting reluctance to recognize warning signs (Sheaffer *et al.* 1998) can be readily accommodated within a model which recognizes individuals' needs to persist with a belief that they continue to control their environment. It may be that only once evidence becomes overwhelming do they acknowledge the extent of the crisis of which they are a part. Subsequent efforts to understand the crisis, for example as a basis for future learning, are liable to be hampered by a socially learned reaction to avoid personal blame – part of people's motivation to protect their self-esteem. However, restricting analysis of the Barings case to an individual psychological level would be inappropriate. More comprehensive analysis requires invoking a broader risk perspective – in this case involving organizational and system level variables operating within an international framework.

The Barings case might be considered to be a classic instance of a failure of an organization to manage risk, to the extent that it collapsed because of this failure. Although the focus of the blame for the collapse of the Bank was laid squarely with Mr Nick Leeson, the 'rogue trader' who carried out the deals, underlying the collapse were totally inadequate systems for monitoring trading – the essence of the bank's business. There is some irony that an organization whose core business involved risk management was unable to manage the risks it faced adequately. However, within a capitalist system, if any single organization should fail then this allows others, who may perform better, to take its place. Thus, others gained from Barings' losses.

## Critical events in the collapse

Some key events in the development of the Barings case are shown in Box 11.1.

An important step in Barings' collapse was the purchase in 1984 for £6m, of a 15-strong team of expert dealers in Far Eastern stocks, described in detail by Gapper and Denton (1996). This relatively autonomous group became Barings Far East Securities (later Barings Securities) and made massive profits on the growing Japanese stockmarket. Its energetic chief, Christopher Heath, achieved celebrity status as the most highly-paid man in Britain – reputedly earning in excess of £2.5m in 1986 – rising to a peak of £8m in 1989 as the Nikkei reached a high point (Gapper and Denton 1996). Fay (1996) describes the high morale, 'loyalty and affection' engendered among staff at all levels within this company, boosted by large bonuses which enabled them to have a lavish lifestyle characterized by conspicuous consumption. The organizational culture was characterised by strong leadership,

### Box 11.1: Key events in the Barings case

| | |
|---|---|
| July 1989 | Mr Nick Leeson joins BSL as a settlements clerk |
| February 1992 | BSL applies to SFA for recognition for Leeson to be recognized as a registered representative; Leeson maintains that there is no unsatisfied judgement debt against him – later found to be untrue |
| April 1992 | Leeson appointed Derivatives Operations Manager of BSS |
| June 1992 | Leeson passes Institute of Banking & Finance, Futures Trading Test |
| July 1992 | BFS begins trading on SIMEX; Leeson one of two BFS traders |
| July 1992 | Leeson opens error account 88888 |
| July 1992 | Leeson applies for SIMEX registration as an Associated Person; again makes false statement regarding civil judgements entered against him; BFS confirms that information supplied is correct |
| August 1992 | Leeson's application for Associated Person to SIMEX approved |
| Oct–Nov 1992 | Leeson forges confirmation to resolve external auditors' point |
| June 1993 | Leeson appointed Assistant Director and General Manager of BFS |
| 11 January 1995 | SIMEX queries margin requirements for BFS account 88888 |
| 14 January | C&L Singapore identifies a discrepancy in their audit; C&L try to obtain an explanation from Leeson |
| 16 January | BFS informed that SIMEX auditors have noted that BFS has violated SIMEX rules and legislation |
| 17 January | Kobe earthquake |
| 24 January | Barings' Asset and Liability Committee (ALCO) are concerned about lack of accuracy of margin calls from Singapore and decide to ask Leeson to reduce Barings positions because of funding pressure |
| 27 January | C&L Singapore raise a discrepancy between balances in individual trading accounts and those shown on Leeson's SIMEX transactions |
| 27 January | SIMEX questions BFS ability to meet potential losses/margin calls |

| | |
|---|---|
| 30 January | BSL ask Leeson for a corrected statement of house positions for submitting returns to Bank of England |
| 2 February | Leeson presents various forged documents to C&L Singapore to support his explanation on a bogus transaction |
| 2 February | Barings staff aware that Leeson had performed an unauthorized trade; staff member going to Singapore told not to confront Leeson with this as it was being handled 'at the highest levels' |
| 8 February | Bogus transaction discussed at ALCO and reported as an operational error; meeting told that a report would be prepared |
| 8 February | Barings verbally assures SIMEX of ability to meet its obligations |
| 10 February | ALCO confirms BFS obligations to SIMEX in writing |
| 16 February | ALCO decides that Leeson should not increase his positions further |
| 17 February | Barings employee finds 14bn yen fund account discrepancy |
| 19 February | Baker orders Leeson to reduce his positions |
| 20 February | Norris informs ALCO that after talking with Leeson, he has decided that the positions in Singapore are not to be reduced |
| 23 February | Leeson and his wife leave Singapore for Kuala Lumpur |
| 24 February | Leeson faxes Jones and Bax apologizing and offering his resignation |
| 26 February | Barings goes into administration |

firm discipline and rewards for loyalty (Fay 1996). Barings Far East Securities business underwent massive growth so that by 1989 it was returning more than half the entire Baring Group's profits. It had entered the new options and futures markets in 1988 as a hedge against the falling Nikkei 225 index.

Fay (1996: 68) notes that:

> Baring Securities made so much money that the bonuses became a bonanza. Although the biggest bonuses were reserved for the bosses of Baring Securities,

> everyone got one, from the latest Baring to become chairman of the board to the most junior settlements clerk. This may appear admirably democratic, but it was, in fact, divisive, setting brokers and salesmen against bankers and corporate financiers, newly hired hands against veterans, and energetic young men against the experienced old guard. Money had become the main, perhaps the sole, standard of judgement of a person's value . . . The culture clash almost tore Barings apart.

The booming Barings Securities business spawned 21 offices in 19 countries. The resulting overheads – described (by Fay 1996: 68) as 'any aspect that did not make money' – and bonuses, required increasing profits to sustain. Infighting began in the early 1990s, focused upon Barings' future direction – described as 'savage office politics' by Fay (1996: 52), who comments that '. . . the management of a broking business is driven by the fear that, if it does not pay the bonuses, its best staff will be poached by firms that can' (1996: 53). Profits began to fall and by 1992 Barings Securities was reporting a loss. A Barings Securities director of that time is quoted by Fay (1996: 60) as the business having '. . . fingers in too many pies. . .'. In February 1993 the Bank of England told Barings that the '. . . parlous state of Barings Securities might topple the . . . bank' (Fay 1996: 64). Following Heath's dismissal in March 1993, Barings Securities and Baring Brothers merged (solo-consolidation) to form Baring Investment Bank (BIB).

Peter Norris (BIB Chief Executive) describes solo-consolidation as the 'engine room that created the collapse' (Fay 1996: 104). During 1993, Barings effectively created the structure that would allow Nick Leeson to get away with illicit dealing until the company went bust. Disagreements about the type of business to be carried out continued. The post-Heath regime wanted a return to Barings' previous risk-averse culture – essentially involving agency business on clients' behalf. However, its Far East traders continued to combine this with proprietary trading, on the banks' own behalf, insisting that it was risk averse. While Tokyo might have been preferred other things being equal, because its margin requirements were much lower than those in Tokyo, Singapore was the better location for this business, and in this role Leeson was given increasing amounts of freedom and promotion.

Whereas in 1992 Barings had had to seek Bank of England approval to make loans to Barings Securities Osaka, solo-consolidation in 1993 enabled Barings to make larger loans to its constituent parts without reference to the Bank of England. The basic principle of supervision is that no bank should ever risk more money than it can afford to lose. Large exposures (more than 10 per cent of a bank's capital) need to be reported in writing. While the Bank of England was concerned about Barings' situation, 'informal concessions' were allowed and Barings' exposure by the end of 1993 was nearly 45 per cent of its capital – without any large-exposure returns to the Bank of England being made. As this figure exceeded the 25 per cent permitted limit, without the controversial 'informal concessions' stipulation, Barings directors would have been liable to prosecution. The Bank of England supervisor making this concession resigned after Barings' collapse, admitting ignorance of Barings' securities business. These 'informal concessions' and the supervisor's resignation let Barings' directors off the hook, for as Fay (1996: 246) notes: 'They could hardly be prosecuted for an action that had been condoned by the banking regulator'.

The contrasting cultures of Baring Brothers & Co (the London-based group) and Baring Securities, based in the Far East, may be summarized along the following dimensions:

| **Baring Brothers & Co** | **Baring Securities** |
|---|---|
| Bankers | Brokers |
| Long-term view | Short-term view |
| Naturally conservative | 'Gung-ho' |
| Traditional controls | Opposed to traditional controls |
| Passive | Active |

Solo-consolidation merged two conflicting cultures. Experienced traders left the company, leaving bankers in charge of proprietary trading. The new system was more complex and therefore harder to understand. Solo-consolidation meant that controls on credit lines to Far East traders were applied less stringently and large losses in the 88888 account became harder to spot. Leeson's loss position almost doubled in January 1994, although he did not become recognized as a proprietary trader until March 1994, which lent greater authenticity to the profits he reported to London. Without solo-consolidation, Leeson's position would have been spotted earlier because pressure on Barings' capital would have appeared sooner.

## Official reports on Barings

The Barings case can be analysed in a number of ways. While there was no fully independent report, the main official reports, commissioned respectively by agents of the UK and Singaporean governments, in their own ways each present meticulous chronological accounts of many of the details of the case and reach broadly similar conclusions on the basis of their findings. There was some co-operation between the parties conducting the two inquiries, although, as noted in both reports, neither had access to the complete facts or to all the witnesses and documentation that they would ideally have required for a full account of events. The Board of Banking Supervision (BoBS 1995) makes mention of this point on several occasions during its 337 pages.

Legal issues seemed to intervene to prevent complete access to documents by those carrying out the inquiries. Here is a clear case of the legal process for establishing culpability taking precedence over the full establishment of what actually happened. It reflects the position that assigning guilt and apportioning blame in the case of corporate failures is superordinate to other considerations – including deriving lessons for other organizations. Despite access problems, both reports are detailed and comprehensive in their own ways. The House of Commons (1996: xix) report maintains that: '. . . comments in the reports . . . suggest that the two investigations . . . considered themselves to be in competition'.

The two reports differ markedly in their style as well as in the material that they choose to present and their conclusions. Given the substantial resources that were devoted to these exercises, this also suggests that in such cases, it is not merely the collation and presentation of 'facts' that is central to arriving at a given conclusion, but also the interpretation that is made of a set of facts via a specific combination of experiences gained within economic, cultural and socio-legal frameworks.

Whereas the BoBS report goes into considerable detail into many matters, it does not address the issue of culpability of the parties involved. Neither does it deal with the issue of points at which actions might have been taken to prevent the disaster from being played through to the end. In contrast, the Singapore report makes great play of the culpability of many parties, pointing to the details of inconsistencies and improbabilities in their evidence. The authors of this report have no hesitation in apportioning blame in many directions, reserving most of this for three of the Barings directors deemed to be most culpable in respect of covering up the nature of Leeson's activities – even though at the time they did not appreciate the full extent of these. The Singapore report lays bare many of the human weaknesses – including guilt, shame, greed and self-seeking, which are attributable with the benefit of hindsight. Perhaps it is unsurprising that Leeson (1996: ix) maintains that 'The Bank of England's report is a waste of paper and is shamed by the Singaporean version'.

It is as though the Singaporean investigators could not believe from the start that such a collapse could not have occurred without some party or parties being seriously culpable. However, while acknowledging evidence of some cover-up, Fay (1996) considers that there is no basis for a conspiracy, and challenges the Singapore report in respect of their conclusions on Norris and other Barings' managers. The BoBS team on the other hand may have taken the view that the matter was one which stemmed from systems level problems, and has been criticised for a lack of independence on the grounds that the Bank of England was a party to the Barings case, or of being 'judge and jury' in its own case (Fay 1996: 244). Unsurprisingly, the BoBS report absolves the Bank of England of any blame, although questions regarding its role remain. As Fay (1996: 221) notes: '. . . with the collapse of Barings, the other merchant banks knew . . . that they could no longer rely on the Bank of England to look after their interests. For two centuries the Bank had been like a mother hen protecting her chicks. A long historical relationship had now ended. The disaster would alter the way the City of London saw the Bank in the future'.

It is evident that each inquiry report was premised upon seeking explanations at different levels and that these relate to cultural differences within the respective societies in which each was conducted. In the management of organizations, as in other aspects of community life, where Asian society may place considerable reliance upon individual integrity, western society affords greater emphasis to system integrity. Specific cultural differences between the UK and Singapore which are relevant to the Barings case are the blame-oriented safety rules often found within Singapore organizations and the highly prescriptive safety legislation typical of that country. UK safety legislation by comparison, is more oriented towards the adequacy of safety management systems within a framework of enforcement with vestiges of self-regulation from an earlier era.

## Risks faced by Barings

Risks attributable to Barings are summarized in Figure 11.1, which shows that the Bank faced four major categories of risk in relation to its business. One of these was a generic category of pure risks such as business interruption or computer system failure. A 'good' outcome in respect of pure risks is that nothing bad happens. The case raises the important issue of the likelihood of a potential collapse of financial systems as a result of one such failure. The UK Government and the Bank of England would only have considered intervening in the rescue attempts on Barings if there had been a threat to the whole British banking system or beyond. However, Fay (1996: 296) notes '. . . the danger . . . some day, wild gyrations in prices will bankrupt a major derivatives-dealer, and that spreading contagion will plunge the banking system into chaos . . .'.

Like all similar institutions, to survive and be successful Barings would have had to manage these categories of risk at least adequately. While the market might be

*Figure 11.1* Summary of risks attributable to Barings Bank

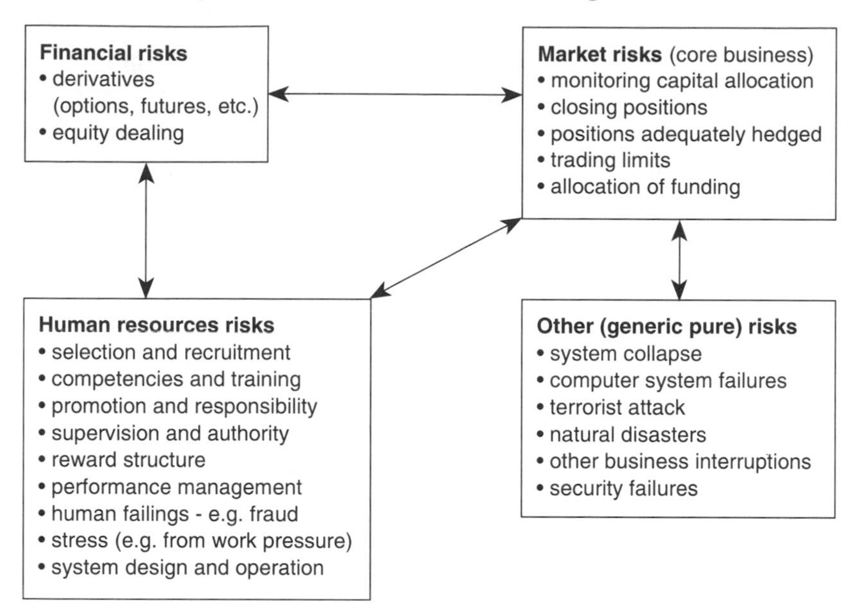


NB While 'human failings' such as fraud and human error may more accurately be categorized as pure risks, from the perspective of the salience of this type of risk to the Barings case, they are considered under the human resource heading here. Similarly, 'system design and operation' should be under a fifth heading of 'operational risks'. How risks are categorized is less important than that they are adequately managed.

forgiving of lapses in respect of managing one or more of them in the short term, significant failures in any of them would in the medium term put the institution at a disadvantage with respect to its competitors, and if uncorrected, put the long-term survival of the institution in jeopardy. It was Barings' failure to manage adequately its total portfolio of risks that led to its collapse.

Strategically, Barings had a relatively straightforward combination of major types of risk to manage. However, effective management of those risks, and especially of interactions between them, was crucial to its survival and success. It is the integration between these risk categories that makes risk management in such a business particularly critical. Aspects of three of these risk categories are considered in the sections below. In the typology used in this book, e.g. as described in chapter 1, financial risks and market risks are examples of speculative risks because both benefits and losses are possible outcomes of managing them.

Human resources risks are also speculative risks because outcomes relating to them can be either good or bad. For example, organizations speculate in the labour market in selecting competent staff and the quality of an organization's outputs reflect the diligence of this process. Similarly in training staff appropriately, an organization is in effect speculating upon the outcomes of such a process. Performance management, for example through appraisal interviews and supervisory assessments, is a speculative risk because there are many alternative ways of organizing performance management systems and for any given organization some approaches lead to improved staff performance while others have detrimental effects on performance. There follows a brief review of the risks faced by Barings and their management of these risks, as may be ascertained by evidence presented in the various reports and accounts available.

## Financial risks

Abolition of restrictive practices in the City of London in 1985 ('Big Bang') had a powerful influence upon financial dealings and their associated risks in all financial markets. A contributor to the House of Commons (1996: xxii) inquiry pointed to the large opportunities and risks created by opening up the global financial system, noting specifically that 'it's the new areas of activity that really give rise to risk'. Derivatives are among the new areas of activity referred to.

San and Kuang (1995) define derivatives as 'An asset or security whose value is related to or derived from the value of some underlying base product'. These assets can be commodities, shares, bonds or any asset which has a value and a fluctuating price. Traditionally, banks acted either as advisers to clients or as sellers of assets. Derivatives trading falls between these two positions. One problem for a bank or other financial institution is how to control or manage the risks associated with buying and selling these powerful financial instruments. By their nature, derivatives allow traders to take up large and potentially very profitable positions at only a fraction of the cost of buying in the cash market. Thus, because of the leverage (gearing) involved, the risks of dealing in derivatives are greater than with most other securities. Derivatives add to volatility and have the potential to create losses on a larger scale than equities do. Like most securities, derivatives are subject to a number of risks, which Duhs (1995) identifies as:

- **market risk** – i.e. sudden price movements in the value of the underlying asset;
- **personnel risk** – misjudgement or fraud by trading staff;
- **counter-party risk** – substantial in the case of over-the-counter contracts (transactions concluded privately between two parties and which are unregulated

by an exchange), but minimal in the case of exchange-traded contracts where the clearing house bears the risk;

- **systemic risk** – e.g. total failure of computer system – usually negligible.

## Market risks

### *Closing positions*

A long position is held by a net holder or buyer of an instrument. It appreciates in value when the market price increases. A holder of a put position is long in respect of the contract but profits when the underlying market declines. Conversely a short position is held by a net seller of an instrument. It appreciates in value when the underlying market price declines. The seller of a put option benefits from an increase in the price of the underlying market or instrument. An open position refers to a position in futures and options, either long or short, which is not matched by offsetting transactions or satisfied by delivery. Generally, all positions would be balanced at the end of each trading day. Where long and short positions are equal and offsetting, they are said to be matched.

A straddle refers to an option position achieved by combining a put and call option on the same underlying instrument and with the same strike price (the price at which an option begins to have a settlement value – usually set at the time the option contract originates). Sellers of straddles anticipate that the underlying price will stay close to the level of the strike price of the options they have sold, or that the volatility of the price will be less than implied in the option process. Leeson's (1996: 63) own account of his use of these financial trading instruments provides one of the clearest expositions. In his case he was using the premiums from the straddles to cover his losses in the 88888 account, but his positions were unhedged (i.e. remained open).

### *Adequacy of hedging of market positions*

Hedging is a generic term for use of derivatives where the primary purpose is to reduce risk exposure. San and Kuang (1995) report that in 1992, it had been envisaged that Leeson's trading role would be limited to executing orders placed by Baring Group companies elsewhere on behalf of external clients (agency business). However, his role changed so that by the end of 1993, Leeson was trading on behalf of the Baring Group itself (proprietary trading). By the end of 1994, it was considered that Leeson had become a major contributor to Baring Group profits. As a proprietary trader, Leeson's main activity was to arbitrage between prices quoted for identical contracts on the SIMEX (Singapore) and Japanese stock exchanges (Tokyo and Osaka). Typically this was done by entering into matching (hedged) purchase and sale contracts on two exchanges almost simultaneously so as to take advantage of favourable price differences.

In written evidence to the House of Commons (1996: vii) inquiry a specialist adviser noted that: 'Leeson was authorized only to take large fully hedged positions. . . This strategy should have been very cheap and absolutely riskless', adding in oral evidence, 'his [Leeson's] official trading activities were . . . about the simplest trading strategy it is possible to have. It is much easier than trading in equities or bonds or index arbitrage in which Barings were also involved'. The report points out that '. . . the particular products traded [by Leeson] may have risk attached to them but . . . the authorised strategy of BFS was virtually risk free' (1996: vii).

## *Trading limits*

Refers to the cash value limit set upon a particular trader's transactions in a given period – usually one trading day. Leeson was given certain intra-day risk limits by BSL, within which he was allowed to maintain unhedged positions. There were no gross limits on the volume of arbitrage transactions that could be entered into by Leeson. Baring Securities risk committee in London set out Nick Leeson's trading limits. In June 1994 his daily unhedged limits were set at 200 Nikkei 225 futures contracts, 100 Japanese Government Bond (JGB) futures and 500 Euroyen futures. No overnight positions were authorized. Clearly these limits were vastly exceeded and yet, while Barings management sought to get him to reduce his positions, no effective action was actually taken. Of his trading position at the beginning of September 1993, Leeson (1996: 94) records his positions as: 5,000 Nikkei futures, 2,000 JGB futures, 1,000 Euroyen futures and '. . . a trunkful of options totalling 20,000'.

## *Allocation of funding and monitoring capital allocation*

Funding for positions in the form of cash or securities deposited with an exchange both as a form of collateral and a way of settling realized and unrealized profit and loss on positions, is known as margin. Margin also attempts to ensure that resources are sufficient to support open positions. A margin call is a demand from an exchange or from a broker or dealer carrying a customer's position, for additional cash or collateral to cover that position.

As soon as BFS began trading on SIMEX early in July 1992, Leeson opened trading account 88888 as an error account. Leeson (1996) describes how he initially used account 88888 to hide colleagues' trading errors. Some transactions booked through this account had been transacted through other Baring Group accounts while others were booked directly into account 88888. An error account is usually used to record sales pending their investigation and clearance. The volume of such trades are small and would normally be quickly cleared from the account. However, account 88888 was characterized by the following:

- The size of the positions was large from the outset and grew quickly – by the time of the collapse the size of the positions booked in this account was so large that when market prices moved unfavourably, it caused the collapse of the Baring Group.
- Transactions in this account were not hedged by matching positions so that Barings was exposed to enormous potential losses even from small market movements.
- Transactions consistently reflected losses from the time the account was opened – where transactions were transferred from other Baring group accounts this was done to generate an artificial profit for these other accounts to the detriment of account 88888.

To finance the losses and margin deposits that had to be placed with SIMEX for account 88888 transactions, Leeson needed funds from other Baring companies. However, Barings management maintained that account 88888 was unauthorized and that they had no knowledge of it. San and Kuang (1995) ask how it is possible that Leeson obtained S$1.7bn from the Baring Group without accounting for it.

Barings' high level Asset and Liability Committee (ALCO) monitored the Group's risk positions, its trading limits and performance and funding allocation daily. San and Kuang (1995) note that:

> The vast sums of money remitted to BFS, which exceeded the total value of the Baring Group's assets, should have attracted close scrutiny by ALCO. ALCO discussed the issue of funding BFS on at least six occasions in January and February 1995. By this time Mr Leeson's reported trading activities had assumed very large proportions, causing the Baring group to almost miss a SIMEX margin call on 24 January 1995. However, the preoccupation of these meetings was to arrange adequate funding lines to meet Mr Leeson's large requirements, rather than to investigate the causes underlying these requirements. At some stage, ALCO did decide that Mr Leeson should be asked to reduce his positions, but this decision was never effectively implemented.

The Singaporean report also points out that while Barings' Financial Controls Department might have been expected to discover account 88888's existence, it failed to do so. San and Kuang (1995) report that Barings management proffered many explanations as to how account 88888 escaped detection, but maintain that Barings management either knew or should have known about this account and detail a number of reasons for this. One of these reasons relates to an internal audit late in 1994 in which Leeson's powerful position controlling both the front (where business is initiated) and back (where trade processing and settlement occurs) offices of BFS is noted. This meant that Leeson was both chief trader and head of settlements and was thus in a position to record the trades that he himself had executed in any way he wished. The internal audit report highlights this fact as creating a significant risk – that normal internal controls could be overridden. No reconciliation controls existed for Leeson's trades for other Baring Group companies – which was most of his business.

Of the above situation San and Kuang (1995) note: 'BSL's claim that it was unaware that account 88888 existed, and also that the sum of S$1.7 billion which the Baring Group had remitted to BFS, was to meet the margins required for trades transacted through this account, if true, gives rise to a strong inference that key individuals of the Baring's Group management were grossly negligent, or wilfully blind and reckless to the truth'. Leeson (1996: 6) himself notes that: 'Barings management could have found out in half an hour if they'd done the most obvious check: looking at the positions I reported to SIMEX (which included the 88888 account) compared with the positions I reported back to London (which made no mention of it)'.

## Human resources risks

Neither of the main reports advises as to whether Barings had an identifiable human resource management (HRM) function. However, in neither the organization structure diagrams prepared by Peter Norris for the BoBS report nor in the lists of over 100 Barings personnel identified as having been interviewed by those producing the various accounts, is there any mention of anyone who might remotely be considered to be from an HRM or personnel-type function. There is no reference to any person concerned with training for example nor with selection and recruitment or other activities traditionally subsumed under HRM or personnel. Fay (1996: 67) notes that under Barings' 'new regime' (after Heath and others had been sacked) from 1993, 'Internal audit and risk-management systems would be put in: they would even have a personnel department'. It must be concluded that, despite this stated intent, Barings had no such function and that the aspects of HRM which are subject to careful management in many well-run companies, were carried out in an ad hoc fashion within Barings. The sections which follow seek to extract such information as is available from the various accounts in respect of HRM functions to ascertain the extent to which these failed to meet criteria which might be considered to be HRM 'good practice'.

## *Selection and deselection*

Neither of the inquiry reports considers Barings' general policies or practices in respect of selecting and recruiting personnel. However, the Singaporean report in respect of Leeson's appointment to Singapore, does note that 'Mr Leeson had no prior trading experience at all . . .' (San and Kuang 1995: 7). The report further explains that prior to his posting to Singapore, Leeson had applied to be registered with the SFA in the UK. However, BSL had withdrawn this application after the SFA discovered that Leeson had falsely informed them that there was no unsatisfied judgement debt against him. 'Neither the outstanding judgement, nor the SFA's discovery and the subsequent withdrawal of Mr Leeson's application by BSL was disclosed by Mr Leeson or BFS or BSL to SIMEX (Singapore International Monetary Exchange Ltd). . . . Mr Leeson made a similar false statement in his application to SIMEX, for registration as an Associated Person' (San and Kuang 1995: 7). The report goes on to observe that Leeson was effectively entrusted with responsibility for BFS's front and back offices without adequate checks on his activities or integrity.

During the time that Christopher Heath ran the securities side of Barings, Fay (1996) notes that over a period of 5–6 years, Heath conducted every job interview himself – until the task became too great, conceding only one mistake in that time (Heath did not personally appoint Leeson). 'I gave everybody lots of responsibility, but everyone was accountable . . . no one was allowed to exceed their limits. People who did were watched like hawks [sic] . . .' (Fay 1996: 29). This quote also indicates a 'hands on' approach to supervision and monitoring activities at that time. Baring Securities grew from 20 to 1400 employees in seven years (Gapper and Denton 1996).

When the time came for deselection as Barings hit a loss-making patch in 1992, Fay (1996: 59) notes that 'Heath is a man who prefers hiring people to firing them. . .' and was reluctant to grasp the nettle of soaring overheads and reduced revenues. During this period of reorganization, difficult decisions had to be made on staff cutbacks, although there is no indication in any of the accounts of how these decisions were made. Fay (1996) refers to '. . . a mass blood-letting . . .' (1996: 61) when firings were done on the third floor of Barings offices, so that 'The third floor quickly became known as the gas chamber' (1996: 61) and 200 staff were made redundant in September 1992. A slightly different version is provided by Gapper and Denton (1996: 150) who report that the sackings were effected on the second floor and that the lift became known as the 'Auschwitz lift'. The already poor personal relations between Norris (Chief Executive) and Heath subsequently worsened and Heath himself was fired in March 1993 along with Baylis and Martin.

The precise mechanism of Leeson's appointment to Baring Securities is not well documented. One account is that he approached Mr Tony Dickle of BSL, who was initially in charge of establishing BFS's operations. Tony Dickle was not interviewed by the authors of either of the inquiry reports and does not appear on Peter Norris's organization charts in the BoBS report. Gapper and Denton (1996: 196) identify him as Baring Securities' Development Officer and he appears in Leeson's (1996) own account. The circumstances indicate that for a person who was to have responsibility for large amounts of money – both the bank's own and that of clients – the procedure by which Leeson came to hold his position, particularly given the extent of his false declarations, was inadequate. The seeds for a disaster were already sown by the appointment of someone who was neither trustworthy nor capable of fulfilling the duties he was to perform. A fundamental fault lay with the inadequate procedures that Barings had for the selection and appointment of personnel to highly responsible positions.

Of the philosophy which underlay the appointment and dismissal of staff in Singapore, there are hints from Leeson's (1996: 44) account, when he observes of Simon Jones (Chief Operating Officer, Barings South East Asia and a BFS director) that: 'He couldn't care less. He'd lost about half a dozen secretaries in the last year'. This referred to the dismissal of the clerk who had made the initial error which allegedly provided the rationale for account 88888. Leeson (1996: 40) blames Barings' poor recruiting policy and the inexperience of his staff for the initial trading error on 17th July 1992.

Fay (1996) reports that Leeson was initially appointed to Barings through John Guy, who ran the Settlements Department until 1990. The person who Fay (1996) states appointed Leeson to the Singapore position in 1992 was Ian Martin, at that time Barings' Finance Director, whom Fay reports as considering Leeson to have excelled within his peer group, adding that 'Excellence is a matter of putting in hours, and he worked hard; he also had intellectual ability and good lateral thinking. He was a cut above the rest. He had no experience as a trader, but it was a matter of learning on the job' (Fay 1996: 77). This quote reveals a considerable amount not only about the qualities deemed to be desirable in a candidate for such a post, but also about the typical approach to learning about the job. Gapper and Denton (1996) describe Leeson's earlier career with Barings and how he made a good impression when carrying out various tasks. Leeson (1996: 29) provides further details of these tasks, including his success in sorting out a £100m hole in Barings' accounts in Jakarta, which was instrumental in getting him the Singapore post.

## *Competencies and training*

Baring's Financial Products Group, part of the matrix which Leeson worked for, was developing new and complex financial products. In this context, San and Kuang (1995: 36) note that 'the severe shortage of qualified personnel to perform good quality back office function became increasingly evident'. These authors point out that traders had insufficient information about their individual profit and loss positions because of incomplete information on costs of funding proprietary trading activities. Leeson's product managers at the end of 1994 (Baker and Walz), the report notes, 'had limited experience in equity derivatives. Hence there was a limit to which they could effectively function as product managers of a trader who did not candidly report his activities'. Fay (1996) also notes that Baker admitted his lack of expertise in an area in which the tradition is to 'learn as you go'. At the time Baker did not realize that he was not getting good information and therefore couldn't learn about risk management. This account is confirmed by Gapper and Denton (1996). Leeson (1996: 5) expresses surprise that for over a month immediately before the collapse, he was able to fool Tony Railton (BSL's Senior Futures and Options Settlements Clerk), who was detailed to find out what was going on in Barings' Singapore office.

San and Kuang (1995: 36) note that 'As a result of this lack of experience, Mr Leeson's reports of very high profits were not met with scepticism or inquiry'. Fay (1996: 123) considers that 'Good managers in the securities business ought to be as suspicious of startling profits as they are of heavy losses', noting that a problem for the internal auditing function at Barings was to find someone who understood the business well enough. The delay to the 1994 audit could have been crucial. Barings' London staff continuing to oblige requests for money from Singapore resulted from their lack of understanding of the margin calls system used by SIMEX. Evidently no one at Barings had given any thought to training these staff or ensuring that they were competent to release money from Barings until it went bust! The same comment might be made in respect of Leeson's staff in the Singapore office, who are absolved from responsibility in the Singapore report, in which blame is firmly attributed to Barings London-based managers.

If such levels of insufficient experience were to be typical of Barings operations, then the picture would be one of inadequate training and/or experience throughout the organization. Gapper and Denton (1996: 172) note that 'The tradition at Baring Brothers was for management to be done by corporate financiers like Tukey [Barings Chairman] in their spare time, or full-time by those who did not make the grade as revenue earners'. While it is true that for many jobs, 'on-the-job learning' is important, where high risk activities are involved, it is surely crucial that the personnel involved and their managers are competent to perform the functions that they are (very well) paid to perform. One might imagine the public opprobrium that would rightly follow a discovery that a high risk process plant or nuclear facility which had failed had been found to have carried inexperienced staff in some of its key functions. In Barings case, while many of its own staff were heavily contaminated from the shock waves which continued to reverberate through the organization, the worst of the fall out landed on Barings bond-holders.

Leeson's lack of appreciation of risk calculations and its consequences is documented thus by Gapper and Denton (1996: 241):

> . . . Leeson was an amateur in the world of options. He lacked an option pricing model on a computer that would show him the correct price for volatility. By borrowing blindly and in desperation Leeson was underpricing volatility. By January 1994 hedge funds and investment banks were trawling the world, seeking mispriced volatility. This was an adults' game and somebody like Leeson was way out of his depth. Every time he walked to the options pit to sell straddles he was shouting his ignorance of the market. The options traders assumed he was selling on behalf of a rather ill-informed or naïve customer and piled in to take advantage of whoever it was.

Of his final day at SIMEX, Leeson (1996: 3) acknowledged 'The rest of the market had smelled what Barings back in London were completely ignoring: that I was in so deep there was no way out'.

## *Promotion and responsibility*

Allied with issues of selection and competence, there is the issue of how Leeson achieved the position that he did. The authors of the Singapore report identify the process in a succinct paragraph thus:

> Mr Leeson executed trades on the SIMEX floor almost immediately after BFS was granted clearing membership. Some time after this, Mr Killian recommended to Mr Norris, who was then Chief Executive Officer of BSL, that Mr Leeson be promoted to General Manager. In our view, Mr Killian's judgment

> in recommending Mr Leeson's promotion notwithstanding the latter's scant experience, is questionable. Mr Leeson was promoted to the post of Assistant Director and General Manager of BFS on 28 June 1993. This was a rapid climb for Mr Leeson who had started his career not long before this as a settlements clerk and who had no trading experience prior to joining BFS. Mr Killian justified his recommendation on the basis that it was helpful for Mr Leeson to have a 'senior title' in order to facilitate his access to senior managers outside the Baring Group. It was not clear to us what the nature of such access was (San & Kuang 1995: 8).

The promotion process by which Leeson reached his position might charitably be described as *ad hoc*. If such arbitrary and weakly supported promotion procedures were common throughout Barings, then it might reasonably be supposed that it was only a matter of time before someone was promoted well beyond the level of his or her competence and without the support or ability to achieve the required competence for their position.

## *Supervision and authority*

A matrix structure for an organization, while it has strengths (for example in respect of co-ordinating separate functions across different departments or regions), also has potential weaknesses – which need to be addressed, particularly at the monitoring stage of managing risks. For example, there can be ambiguities in respect of who has primary responsibility for monitoring the activities of an individual employee. This can offer an opportunity for an individual to conceal the nature of their activities from a superior with a legitimate right to monitor them on the grounds that reports are being made to a superior in another limb of the matrix. This problem is likely to be compounded within an organization that is undergoing frequent changes of either or both structure and personnel. This allows for ambiguity, which is liable to be endemic to matrix organizations, to become a source of confusion and potential conflict.

San and Kuang (1995: 7) note that there was confusion from the start of his appointment over whom Leeson should report to. Fay (1996) records that he was initially required to report to Barings' London office but that there was a memo from the Singapore office urging that Leeson should report there. However, in the light of events, in an attributional context of reducing the blame attaching to oneself, it is likely that those identified as people to whom Leeson allegedly reported would seek to repudiate or to diminish their links with him so as to increase the distance between themselves and the source of the collapse. This is a familiar feature of disasters and the authors of the report draw their own conclusions in respect of reporting lines.

In the BoBS (1995) report, Peter Norris the Chief Executive of Baring Investment Bank Group (BIB), had prepared three separate structures for the Baring Group, which had existed within a period of just over three years. Throughout his time with Barings, Leeson always had at least two reporting routes and even though there was some stability in respect of the personnel involved, the structure within which these reporting links existed represented a changing, and potentially confusing environment. Even as Barings was moving towards its collapse, Gapper and Denton (1996: 246) report that different arms of the matrix (Killian vs. Baker) wanted to 'capture' Leeson once the 'profits' from his trading became evident.

Of the matrix structure, Leeson (1996: 61) himself records the comment that: '. . . my lines of communication with London were so vague that nobody knew who I reported to'; ' [I was] . . . supposed to report to four different people . . . It was a bizarre structure, and one which allowed me to run my own show without anyone interfering' (Leeson 1996: 65). Leeson's product managers are reported (San and Kuang 1995) as accepting reports of his very profitable activities with admiration rather than scepticism, perceiving no irregularity in his trading despite the inherent limit to the profit potential of Leeson's arbitrage activities.

The Singaporean report points out that while the matrix structure appears to combine the best of two management systems – location and function, it can give rise to situations where there is insufficient accountability because each reporting line abdicates responsibility to the other (San and Kuang 1995: 37). They proceed to point out that this situation is compounded if managers in the matrix fail in their respective responsibilities – as happened in this case. They accuse Leeson's local managers of not having adequate knowledge of details of the products that Leeson was trading in, while his product managers lacked sufficient detailed knowledge to discharge their role effectively. While the implied blame in this report is cast upon individual managers in the organization's matrix, a lack of corporate responsibility can be identified as an underlying reason for:

- a lack of care in selecting managers with sufficient experience;
- ensuring that they had the aptitude and opportunity to acquire the requisite competencies;
- providing such training as would be necessary for them to become competent to perform their responsibilities effectively.

The shared and uncertain responsibilities which prevailed within Baring's management, like the infamous trading accounts, were never adequately reconciled.

## *Reward structure*

Barings' remuneration policy gave directors and senior employees a significant direct interest in the Group's annual results. Group policy was that around 50 per cent of profits before tax went into a bonus pool, which was allocated according to the performance of each product group and the individuals within it. Bonuses were a high proportion of total remuneration – at director level bonus was typically three times base salary. A benchmarking study showed that Barings remuneration levels were among the highest among comparable institutions in the UK and USA. Fay (1996: 59) records that '. . . bonuses were sacrosanct' and even though the '. . . best brokers . . . reported that they were getting job offers every hour . . .' that '. . . good bonuses bound them to Barings with golden handcuffs . . .' (Fay 1996: 60).

Of the unreality which accompanied the high salaries and bonuses paid to the traders, Leeson (1996: 99) remarks: 'We were a motley crowd. Nobody would have thought that these were some of the fastest brains and most highly-paid people in the world. They all looked down-at-heel and hungover, as if they'd stumbled out of some homeless shelter. . . . And so we filed into SIMEX, each of us earning perhaps £200,000 a year, wealthy beyond the dreams of most of the rest of the world, and we started buying and selling numbers'.

When Norris is presenting Barings' case at the rescue meeting and makes reference to the 1994 balance sheet, which revealed that bonuses for the year would amount to more than £100m, Fay (1996: 214) records that: 'These were hardened bankers, not easily shocked, but most were genuinely staggered when they learned the size of Barings' bonuses'. This is confirmed by Gapper and Denton (1996: 50) who comment on Norris's presentation at the would-be rescue meeting to the assembled bankers who

> . . . listened in icy silence. But this irritated mood turned to outrage as they looked at the figures on the first chart. They showed that after taking out Leeson's profits, Barings intended to declare a pre-tax profit of £83 million for 1994 while paying bonuses to its staff of £84 million. This seemed utterly unbelievable to the heads of clearing banks. Their suspicions of merchant bankers had been confirmed more strongly than they could have imagined. The directors of Barings were paying themselves and their staff more than

> they declared in profits. Even the heads of other merchant banks were taken aback. They were used to handing out between a quarter and a third of profits in bonuses.

However, contrasting the old with the new approach to employment, as the would-be consortium of bankers considered the possibility of a rescue package, Fay (1996: 218) notes: 'The new breed of clever bankers and traders were more like mercenaries, hiring out their labour to the highest bidder. If Barings did not pay the 1995 bonus, the best of their staff would be clearing their desks and moving on. This would reduce the value of the company into which the other banks were proposing to invest £650 million'.

Bonus expectations continued after the eventual takeover by ING, which paid out between £90 and £95 million in bonuses to Barings' managers not directly implicated in the collapse. However, Barings' bond-holders fared far worse, with ING offering them five pence in the pound with a vague future promise. Legal action of behalf of this group continued for some considerable time. Fay (1996: 232) ruefully notes: 'Had there been any real gentlemen left at Barings, they would have donated their bonuses to the bond-holders; but there weren't', adding 'it is hard to find any heroes in this story' (p. 270). Fay (1996: 269) is unequivocal on the role played by bonuses in the collapse of Barings, observing that: 'No one wanted to upset the goose that was laying so many golden eggs'.

Allocation of bonuses to individuals for 1994 had been determined by the date of the collapse. Three of Barings directors were to receive £1m or more in bonuses. Sections of the financial press were aghast at the initial insistence of certain Barings directors who approached the Bank of England to discuss a rescue package that they should be paid their bonuses for the previous year. The BoBS (1995) report concludes that there is no evidence that Barings managers' judgements were inhibited by the possibility that their bonuses might be prejudiced.

The extent to which individual Barings employees were motivated by their remuneration package must remain a matter for speculation. However, there is sufficient evidence in the BoBS report to justify concluding that it is possible that some Barings employees considered the remuneration system to be arbitrary in the allocation of bonuses. As a general point, it may be noted that in the absence of intrinsic work motivation, where 'performance' is judged exclusively on outcomes then it is the achievement of that measure of performance – whatever it may be, which is likely to be a primary driver of individual employees' work behaviours. The means by which those performance measures are attained may become secondary to the achieving of them.

As neither of the authors has any experience of working in the finance sector, we can only speculate on the possible range of motivations held by those that choose such work. From various accounts, a number of key drivers seem to emerge. One relates to the 'buzz' or 'high' which is obtained from operating at peak capacity under conditions which many people would find too stressful to bear. Another factor appears to be the image which an individual likes to have of themselves and which they would like others to have of them – Fay (1966) refers to the 'big swinging dicks' label. Another factor would be the lifestyle which is typically associated with such a job, frequently characterized by conspicuous consumption of goods. Making money could be related to all of these factors, and could also be a factor in its own right – valued as a commodity to be acquired rather than as a medium of exchange or even as a store of value. Other motives might include an opportunity to display particular types of skills, such as those associated with trading – including an ability to do rapid and accurate mental calculations or managing complexity and uncertainty under pressure, or even managing a successful business. However, people working in the financial sector produce no products nor anything of direct intrinsic value to anyone so that no one's life is immediately enriched or enlightened by what they do. Certainly wealth may be created for other parties but it is hard to envisage this as a prime motivator. One is left with a heavy emphasis upon prime motivators being the external ones of money, image and lifestyle and internal motivators being self-image creation or aggrandisement and experiences associated with high blood levels of adrenaline.

## *Performance management*

No reference to any commonly recognised form of performance management system within Barings can be found in any of the accounts published to date. Practices such as: performance appraisal, coaching, mentoring, development – personal, management professional and career – or related terms seem to have been alien to Barings' culture. It must be concluded that the evidence available indicates that Barings had neither knowledge, nor policy nor intention to implement any systematic form of performance management. One can only surmise that individuals' performance was judged largely or exclusively upon the amount of money which they brought into the company or upon intuitive impressions made upon more senior staff. The risks of relying upon a combination of a single outcome performance indicator and the strong possibility of people untrained in appraising others' performance being prey to personal biases, are considerable. When a financial company is operating in favourable times, a market may well forgive such severe lapses. However, when competition increases, the environment is less benign. As Peter Norris (BIB's Chief Executive) is reported as saying, 'In investment banking, the sad truth is that in a bull market you can run a poorly organized business at a profit' (Fay 1996: 57).

## *Human failings – e.g. errors and fraud*

Leeson (1996: 38) notes that many errors occurred in trading, estimating in the order of 50 per day in the case of Barings' trading in Singapore. Given the frantic nature and high pressure under which much trading is carried out, this is hardly surprising. It was a larger than usual trading error which, according to Leeson (1996: 39), led to the use of the 88888 account. He records that it was common practice to cover mistakes by making fictitious deals (Leeson 1996: 44) and that account 88888 was initially used to hide the losses which resulted from his colleagues' trading errors (Leeson 1996: 78). However, while trading errors may have been everyday occurrences, the nature of Leeson's main use of the 88888 account was not much to do with them.

In April 1994, a Wall Street trader who declared false profits was exposed by his employer. Barings then ordered an immediate review of its own risk controls and concluded that they were inadequate. However, 'Fortress Singapore' remained unaffected (Fay 1996: 131). Clearly, Barings had no system for detecting fraud of the type or scale perpetrated by Nick Leeson. Baring Securities' permissive culture enabled Leeson's relatively minor previous financial misdemeanors to be passed over. Leeson had earlier gained relevant knowledge through playing a key role in uncovering the mechanism by which '. . . an unscrupulous investor could manipulate his clients' funds to finance his own trading activities and how the company's reporting system could be bypassed' (Fay 1996: 77). Fay (1996: 78) describes two sides to Leeson, the 'Boy Scout, anxious to please and to be liked . . .' and the other '. . . wilder, more lawless, a rule-breaker'. Leeson's (1996) own account also describes his 'double life' in graphic detail.

Leeson's deception began in August 1992. Soon after this a £2–3m deficit (most of which could be accounted for by Leeson's 88888 account losses) was found by Barings staff in London, but account reconciliation was not rigorous and seemingly no action was taken. Leeson managed to get cash to fund his dealings and by not hedging his Nikkei 225 options, ignored the rules from the start. Profits were remitted to London by raiding account 88888. Settlements staff in Singapore made paper transfers of money to account 88888 at the end of each month so that it appeared in credit and then transferred funds back again at the start of the following month. Thus, Leeson's fraud required collaboration of the senior clerks in Baring Securities' Singapore office. Of one clerk, Leeson (1996: 176) records, 'Like all the girls in the back office, she was unswervingly loyal to me. I had fought for their bonuses, treated them well, and they would do anything in return'.

Leeson (1996: 60ff) provides the most comprehensive explanation of how his delicate balancing act was performed. Gapper and Denton, who also describe details of Leeson's trading, (1996: 220) note that account 88888 had been designated as a customer account as early as mid-July and that on 31st July 1992 Leeson found that by not declaring a loss of £50,000 he could hide the loss by adjusting the accounts. Because the market continued to demand attention, largely because of the volatility of the Nikkei 225, there was no opportunity to sort out the error account. A trading error by a clerk on 21st August 1992 resulted in a large loss, which Leeson opted to bury in account 88888 rather than to admit. Leeson gained popularity with customers and other traders by exchanging 'favours' and apparently doing 'good deals' – again using account 88888 to hide all the losses resulting from these favourable but illicit deals.

At the end of 1992, Leeson forged a letter which successfully fooled Barings' Far East auditors – at that time Deloitte & Touche. Gapper and Denton (1996: 228) note:

> By now he was at the heart of an almost surreal web of deception. Leeson had told himself in the past few weeks that he could resolve his problems and take up the life of an honest trader. But he could not hope for such an outcome any more. He was deceiving an array of people in different ways . . . Even if he could wipe the slate clean, it would not stop him needing the five eights account. Only with its support could he supply fills and rolls at the prices that brought him admiration and attention. Thus it was ironical that his growing reputation in early 1993 gave him even more business and even fewer opportunities to sort out account 88888. Leeson needed to gamble to get money to cover his losses and chose to gamble on the stability of the Nikkei 225 index, for which there were plenty of takers. Amazingly, by the end of June 1993, Leeson had retrieved all the money he had lost. His gamble had paid off and he had rescued himself.

The problem now was that he would lose his 'star' status if he didn't continue in the same way as before. The accounts might have been reconciled at this point, but he still had his image to sustain and the roller coaster began again. Leeson was considered to be a 'hero' within SIMEX because he had played a large part in this exchange gaining ground over the rival Osaka exchange. He was also lauded by

Barings and admired by his companions and his wife. He had so much to lose that he was obliged to take more and more risk to cover his activities and then worry about the losses later. None of this could have happened unless the environment had been conducive to such activity. As Gapper and Denton (1996: 249) record: 'He had found a perfect environment in which to commit a fraud: one in which few outsiders knew enough to grasp that something was wrong'.

There was nobody to check with because Leeson controlled the back office as well as trading. Leeson (1996: 64) records that: 'I was in a bizarre situation, in that I had one foot on the dealing floor and could authorize the sale of options to bring in the yen; but I was also in charge of the girls in the back office, who would carry out any of my requests. I could see the whole picture, and it was so easy. I was probably the only person in the world to be able to operate on both sides of the balance sheet. It became an addiction'.

There were numerous warnings that things were not as they should have been in the Singapore office (e.g. BoBS 1995). Of a scheduled audit early in 1994, Fay (1996: 124) notes:

> . . . before he arrived in Singapore, Baker was briefed by Tony Hawes, who not only harboured doubts about Leeson, but appreciated how difficult it might prove to expose him. Baker wrote: 'If something was amiss in Singapore (e.g. fraud, error, backlog) Tony is not confident that any of the senior clerks would speak up.' . . . Hawes' particular concern, however, was the amount of cash being sent to Singapore at short notice . . . A second warning came from . . . Norris's assistant, who thought that, by mixing agency and proprietary trading, Leeson was probably breaking SIMEX rules. . . . All the right questions were drafted.

However, Leeson managed to argue Baker out of reconciling his accounts and various parties faced the problem of breaking through alliances to get at what Nick Leeson was up to. Concern in London continued over Leeson's position with respect to both trading and running the settlements office. However, Fay (1996: 127) notes: 'All Barings senior managers in London appreciated that there was some kind of problem in Singapore, but none of them thought it was Leeson'. Leeson records his amazement at how various people swallowed his stories about the hole in the Barings account. Of Baker and Walz, he reports: '. . . they wanted to believe that it was all true. There was a howling discrepancy which would have been obvious to a child – the money they sent to Singapore was unaccounted for – but they wanted to believe otherwise because it made them feel richer. I must be doing more business, therefore we would *all* be richer.' (Leeson 1996: 161 – emphasis in original).

Given the number of illicit activities that Leeson was engaged in on a daily basis, in retrospect it seems amazing that his trading was not uncovered sooner. According to Fay (1996: 289) Leeson told his lawyer that '. . . if he had tried the same game at his previous employers, Morgan Stanley, he would have been exposed within two months' (or sooner). At Barings he had '. . . kept the ball in play for thirty-two months' (Fay 1996: 289). People constructed 'stories' about what he might be up to. Although increasing information about Leeson's position was coming to light, the full extent of his deception was not uncovered until it was too late. Fraud was not suspected by Barings' staff who investigated his dealings and who continued to trust him. It is as though Barings management and other traders were testing a number of hypotheses, for example that he was buying large numbers of options for a large and very rich client, without considering all the possible alternatives. Leeson obliged by inventing identities for these imaginary clients – thereby reinforcing others' preferred versions of events. After all throughout, people **wanted** to be satisfied. Who would have **preferred** the reality when Barings' management were so impressed by the 'profits' which continued to pour in?

After the Kobe earthquake introduced further volatility to the Nikkei index, Leeson was obliged to continue with wilder and wilder bets so that he painted himself into a corner. Towards the end he was obliged to gamble heavily, finally entering a cycle that couldn't be sustained. Leeson continued to mislead Barings' new auditors – Coopers & Lybrand – with forged letters, which should have been spotted.

## *Stress*

Despite the widely acknowledged high levels of stress experienced by trading staff and the well-known phenomenon of reduced decision-making capability under stress, stress management within merchant banks is probably underdeveloped. The various accounts mostly refer only tangentially to the pressures and stress upon staff working in different cultures or rapidly traversing the world or communicating across time zones. Barings' staff were required to undertake these activities as part of their normal duties and many were likely to have been under particular pressure as events unfolded in early 1995. Gapper and Denton (1996) describe Leeson's high alcohol and junk food consumption as he progressed through his time in Singapore – and Leeson (1996) makes a number of references to his changing shape. From the start of taking over Barings' SIMEX trading floor position Leeson was under pressure – trying to please everyone and having both the trading and back office to manage. He chose not to tell even his wife of his difficulties, and it seems that even if others perceived these and other symptoms they were unaware of what to do.

Of his own state, Leeson (1996: 148) records that: 'My 88888 account was hanging around my neck like a string of rotten fish-heads . . .' and, of his hopeless position at the end of 1994, 'I was drowning like an insect stuck in resin, clawing hopelessly but unable to pull myself out. I knew that the auditors were inching closer and closer . . .'. (Leeson 1996: 145). Of his brief 'holiday' in Malaysia after escaping from Singapore immediately prior to the collapse, of his own condition, Leeson (1996: 11) notes: 'For the first time in God knows how long I was feeling relaxed. I could feel some muscles loosening down my back which had been clenched tight for months'. Despite the intense stress that Leeson was under, no one was trained to recognise the symptoms, and there was no place in such a macho culture for remedial or palliative measures such as stress counselling. With no mentoring system there was no one that Leeson could turn to for help. Like the generals in the First World War, the best treatment for 'shell shock' was considered to be a return to battle, while deserters were shot as cowards.

## *System design and operation*

It is a well-established principle that front office trading should be kept separate from back office accounting, or settlements. Fay (1996: 68) notes:

> Settlements had never had a high priority in Baring Securities. Resources were not committed to developing global computer systems which would enable management in London to know the firm's position anywhere in the world; nor was information technology applied to risk management. 'It was all done on the back of an envelope', says John Guy . . . Working in the back office requires a different kind of temperament from a job on the trading-floor. It is painstaking work which demands patience and resignation, for good settlements clerks are like the enemy, always on the look-out for traders who make mistakes, whether by accident or design. One of Baring Securities' problems was that promising youngsters lacking such a temperament were recruited into the settlements department. All they wanted was a chance to switch to the trading-floor, for the glamour and the bigger bonuses.

However, the Singapore office of Barings Securities was organized contrary to the established principle, so that: 'besides running the back office, the person who ran it would also execute clients' orders on the floor of the exchange . . . ' (Fay 1996: 77).

The devolvement of responsibility for settlements from Leeson was suggested far too late in the day.

Gapper and Denton (1996) observe that derivatives trading is expensive because to take the large bets involved, large investment in technology is required as well as the capital to finance that form of trading. The company seemed to have no coherent investment strategy – in either people or technology. Substantial amounts of profit had been used to pay bonuses and its previous form of capitalization – in which bank loans were directed through other Barings subsidiaries and used as capital – was to be prohibited through a new European directive. Barings management were divided in respect of how the bank's capital should be used, and the purchase of a Wall Street company and financing growth in new countries left precious little capital for the necessary investment.

It may be counted among the ironies of automation (Bainbridge 1987) that while adequate investment in state-of-the-art technology could well have saved Barings, the technology which existed made hiding the fraud easier because no paper was involved and no money actually changed hands.

### *Conclusions on human resources risks*

Because Barings failed to manage its human resources effectively, it was unable to manage the financial and market risks that were its core business. Fay (1996: 124) notes 'The permissive style of management that was cultivated at Barings Bank: business first, control second'. There was confusion of authority and effectively no responsibility for crucial decisions that were taken. Clearly Barings had little notion of personnel risk and was effectively ignorant about good HRM practices. It was therefore unable even to identify any risks associated with inadequate HRM, let alone make effective improvements.

Something akin to groupthink (Janis 1972) prevailed. It might be termed 'orgthink' – a situation in which prevailing conditions reinforced by a dominant culture, provides fertile ground for organization members to hope that their worst fears will not be realized and to hold in check their suspicions about what might be happening.

## A risk management perspective

The House of Commons (1996: vii – emphasis in original) report notes that:

> . . . *it is not the case that the demise of Barings illustrates an inherent riskiness of derivative trading.* The main economic function of derivatives is to allow the

> trading of risks arising from changing economic variables such as interest rates, foreign exchange rates, equity and commodity prices. . . . derivatives do not create new risks, but redistribute existing risks among different market participants.

Gapper and Denton (1996: 166) describe Barings' definition of 'risk management' as '. . . going to companies and offering them complex futures and options'. If this was indeed Barings' definition of risk management, then it was by any standards inadequate. A risk management committee (ALCO) was formed in October 1993 from the Baring Securities Risk Committee and Baring Brothers Treasury Committee, and met daily to discuss trading positions and credit risks. No one on that committee had hands-on experience of the areas they were discussing and they harboured serious critical misperceptions such as believing that there were no proprietary positions and therefore no risk. Gapper and Denton (1996: 287) note that ALCO '. . . attendance was patchy. It was an uneasy combination given the past rivalries and present tensions'.

Various of the accounts record the numerous personal animosities and rivalries between Barings' staff, which contributed to poor communication. One such was between Broadhurst (BIB Group Finance Director) and Hopkins (BIB Group Treasury and Risk Director). Gapper and Denton (1996: 262) record that 'The isolation of Hopkins created a serious flaw in the management structure of the investment bank. Although there was a head of treasury and risk, Norris was not inclined to take anything he said seriously'.

Of Barings' situation in 1992, Fay (1996: 267) notes that the bank had first made losses after years of fat profits. 'They could have been the pretext for a management re-organization, the dropping of some surplus staff, and the tying up of some . . . loose ends . . .'. To this might be added, the development of an effective risk management system. Fay (1996: 267) records that 'Tukey and the bankers dreamed of a securities business that was risk-averse', but that '. . . there was no effective risk management in Baring Securities' operation . . . because the senior executives foolishly believed that they were not taking any risks in Singapore and Tokyo, they did not impose a risk management system' (Fay 1996: 268). Barings' London operation believed that Leeson's activities were risk-free because it suited them to believe that.

## *Threat identification*

Evidence indicates that Barings failed to identify all the threats which it faced. This is a critical stage because a threat that is not identified, or at least not identified before it can damage the organization, cannot be processed or monitored at later stages. Early in 1993, BIB's treasurer, Tony Hawes, found a £15m account deficit. However, Barings seemed to have had no effective internal system for checking its own accounts and trading as nothing really happened to try and locate this deficit. The Finance Director (Lynn Henderson) pursuing the case was made redundant – perhaps representing one in a long line of lost opportunities. Another possible missed opportunity occurred in April 1993 when Leeson was in trouble with SIMEX, which resulted in a fine. However, his boss in Singapore, Simon Jones, did not ask for an explanation. Fay (1996: 273) points out that SIMEX had not enforced its own trading rules on Leeson. SIMEX, like Barings, had a position to protect – increasing sales volume was its prime motivation, and was unwilling seriously to question, let alone kill the goose that was laying golden eggs. Thus, it required complicity from several parties for Leeson to pursue his trading as far as he did. Fay (1996: 273) points to the mild criticism of SIMEX in the Singapore report and remarks on that country's 'obsession with secrecy'.

Among the numerous occasions when Leeson's activities might have been picked up was a Barings internal audit report in 1993, of which Leeson (1996: 93) comments: 'The Audit made a number of sensible suggestions, which could have stopped me in my tracks if they'd been implemented . . .' – but of course they weren't. Of Simon Jones's response to the audit report's recommendation for the appointment of a Risk and Compliance Officer, Leeson (1996: 93) remarks: '. . . good old tight-fisted Simon Jones! He was obsessed with keeping staff costs down to a minimum, which was why he wouldn't allow me to hire the best people for decent salaries. And his refusal to pay for a Risk and Compliance Officer meant that I would continue to go unsupervised'.

Late in the crisis in January 1995, Coopers & Lybrand's annual audit of Barings' Singapore office account picked up a discrepancy in the accounts. However, Leeson managed to evade the auditors' questions. Around the same time, SIMEX auditors identified a problem with the 88888 account so that, with suspicions also mounting at BIB the net was beginning to close in. However, communications were hindered by personal dislike between Barings' staff, particularly between London and the Far East, and 'Fortress Singapore' tended to close ranks when attacked from London.

Barings' management 'knew' that there was a problem, but not exactly where it lay or the size of it. Questions continued after a story invented by Leeson about a £50m receivable to cover a year-end loss position. By February 1995, Barings Securities staff were severely worried by events. Leeson continued to enter false trades to cover his tracks and to keep various parties happy – the auditors, Barings in London and SIMEX in particular. Up until 6 February 1995, the position might have been recoverable, but thereafter the market fell persistently and losses in account 88888 mounted almost exponentially. Barings' '. . . fate was sealed by the absence of either the people or the systems needed to stop the flow of funds to Singapore' (Fay 1996: 183). By that time the bank was '. . . like a colander, leaking funds to Leeson through a variety of orifices . . .' (Fay 1996: 183). No checks were carried out when money was transferred from one part of Barings to another – because no apparent risk was involved, the job was allocated to junior clerks. Because no **systems** existed for detecting fraudulent activities, it was left up to individuals to pick up and interpret clues.

## *Risk assessment and evaluation*

Even for those threats which were identified the associated risks were inadequately analysed and assessed. The essential problem was not a failure to identify that something was wrong but a failure to act on the information that was available. Even a week from the collapse when many questions were being asked by many parties, when Norris met with Leeson in Singapore (16th February 1995), Gapper and Denton (1996: 313) note that: 'He [Norris] wanted to get this meeting over as fast as possible . . . Leeson stammered an explanation of his switching book . . . it was largely incomprehensible to Norris. He had never been a trader, and the floor of a futures exchange was an alien world'. Norris failed to raise critical issues at this meeting, such as the missing £50m and the strain of funding Leeson's trading from Barings' London office. Gapper and Denton (1996: 313) remark that 'It was his last chance to save his bank, but he did not pause long enough to see what a mess the young man sitting in front of him was in'. Of his first meeting with Norris, Leeson (1996: 141) notes: 'The only good thing about hiding losses from these people was that it was so easy. They were always too busy and too self-important, and were always on the telephone. They had the attention span of a gnat. They could not make the time to work through a sheet of numbers and spot that it didn't add up'. Of this particular meeting, Leeson (1996: 202) wrote: 'I wondered about telling him that I'd thrown up in the Gents before coming to see him, that I could still taste the bile in my mouth . . .'.

Because of inadequacies at earlier stages, evaluation of risk was bound to be inadequate. An example of this is solo-consolidation which the reports from both BoBS (1995: 247) and the House of Commons (1996: xxiii) note was not itself the cause of Barings' collapse, but which was inadequately evaluated as representing a greatly increased risk because of the potentially much larger exposure of the bank's funds.

### *Development and implementation of adequate controls*

As new parts of the business developed, controls were lax or non-existent. In what must be one of the greatest understatements made in connection with Barings, Andrew Baylis, managing director of Barings Securities regarded it as '. . . fair criticism that our management control and structure had probably not evolved at the same rate as the business' (Fay 1996: 60). Of the lack of knowledge among Barings' directors, Gapper and Denton (1996: 143) quote one of them as saying at a Board meeting during a discussion of whether Baring Securities was making profits, that: '90 per cent of us don't know what is going on 90 per cent of the time'.

The inquiry reports (BoBS 1995: 250, House of Commons 1996: viii, xvii) rehearse lessons spelled out in legislation and international guidelines for management in respect of developing and implementing appropriate controls, involving:

- management understanding their business;
- establishing clear duties and responsibilities;
- particular emphasis on top management's responsibilities;
- independent risk management and other internal controls;
- rapid resolution of significant weaknesses identified.

At the would-be rescue meeting during the weekend after the collapse, Gapper and Denton (1996: 51) describe the reactions of the fellow bankers to Barings' inadequate controls when the suggestion is made to let only the Barings company which held Leeson's losses collapse, set it adrift and refuse to pay – thereby escaping further losses. However:

> . . . Norris explained that it was impossible because Barings had already met margin calls on Leeson's trading of more than £700 million. The bankers were amazed. They had been told that Leeson had hidden all his futures and options in a secret account but here was the man in charge of investment banking saying that they had paid £700 million to cover trading they did not even know had existed. What sort of outfit was he running? By this time, most of the bankers' previous goodwill towards Barings had evaporated. They were being asked to risk their shareholders' money to rescue a bank which had paid inflated bonuses to directors who were so ignorant of what was going on under their noses that they had handed £700 million over to a crooked trader to help him defraud them. Some of the clearing bankers reflected that if this was how the City's merchant banks ran their affairs, perhaps it would be better to let them collapse.

## *Monitoring*

Once it had begun its roller-coaster ride to oblivion, it seemed that Barings had no effective mechanism for bringing the company back from the brink of that disaster. Thus, it was only very late in the day that a serious attempt was made to rescue the company – by which time it was too late. Had Leeson's transgressions been discovered prior to 1995, in all likelihood he would have been dismissed and the matter covered up by Barings staff. Perhaps other heads would have rolled as well, but the issue would probably never have become public to the extent that it did. It required the complicity – active or passive – of many parties to carry the disaster through to its final conclusion.

Barings staff had never encountered a similar situation before – and had certainly not undergone any 'disaster planning' type exercises and were therefore totally unprepared for it. Attempts to find explanations from sources other than the real one – the thought that a Barings employee could act in such a way – is unlikely to have crossed their minds. Many were aware that something was wrong but were genuinely puzzled by what it might have been. The scale of the misuse of funds was likely to be beyond their bounded rationality. The group that assembled to consider the situation after Nick Leeson had disappeared went through possible alternative scenarios. Eventually staff working from Singapore found the 88888 account and uncovered the size of the fraud. As the night wore on, the terrible truth about Barings' position became evident.

The series of events which led to Barings collapse bear some similarity to a near disaster in March 1979 at Three Mile Island (TMI) – a nuclear power plant in the USA (see for example Bignell and Fortune 1984). Although the respective time-scales, industries and outcomes of the two cases are quite different, there are interesting parallels. At TMI the operators were confused by a multiplicity of signals from their work environment and were attempting to make sense of the information which was before them, which represented a situation that they had never before encountered. Their mental picture of events was bounded by the state in which they thought the system was in rather than its actual state and it required insights from new shift operators who reappraised the situation to suggest new possibilities which led to a very late appreciation of the state of the system and possible remedies. At Barings, parties equivalent to 'new shift operators' effected a correct diagnosis but were on the scene too late to devise a remedy. The picture of events was as shown in Figure 11.2 and Table 11.1.

San and Kuang (1995) note that:

> . . . whether the Baring Group management in fact knew of account 88888 is hardly crucial. If they did not know of it at the outset, they would have learnt of it

*Figure 11.2* Barings case – management perception and actual situation

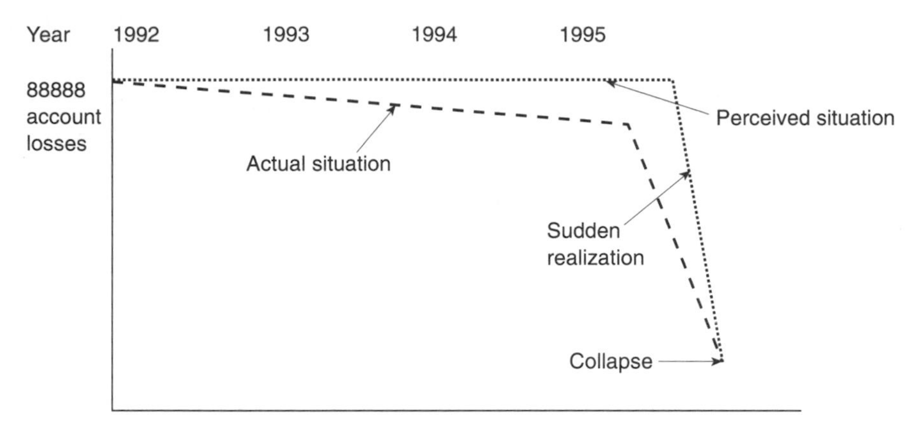


*Source*: BoBS (1995); Leeson (1996)

> once they undertook any of these steps to investigate the position [eight steps that Barings management could have taken are given in the report]. They could have remained ignorant of the account up to the time of the collapse only if they had persistently shut themselves from the truth. Mr Norris's explanation after the collapse, namely that the senior management of the Baring Group believed that Mr Leeson's trading activities posed little (or no) risk to the Baring group, but yielded very good returns, is implausible and in our view, demonstrates a degree of ignorance of market reality that totally lacks credibility.

There is evidence from the Singaporean report that the issue was seen as a rule-based issue rather than one requiring a problem-solving approach at a knowledge-based level. The authors of this report note that a recommendation from Barings internal audit report was that BFS's trading be subject to scrutiny by an external independent risk and compliance officer. The audit report maintained that over time, such a person would be able to detect trading activities which potentially broke the rules as well as significant changes in risks that were being taken. The internal auditors thought that such monitoring would act as a deterrent against trading malpractices.

After attempted rescue efforts over a full weekend had failed to avert the collapse, Barings' managers were keen to distance themselves from critical events at an early stage. Blame avoidance became the order of the day. Internationally, ramifications continued for some time between major players in London, Singapore, Japan and the US. Leeson was eventually extradited from Germany to Singapore where he received

*Table 11.1* Chronological losses from Leeson's account 88888

| *Date* | *Deficit in account 88888 (£)* |
|---|---|
| March 1992 | 20,000 |
| March 1992 | 60,000 |
| September 1992 | 150,000 |
| March 1993 | 220,000 |
| March 1993 | 3m |
| July 1993 | 0 |
| August 1993 | 80,000 |
| September 1993 | 1.3m |
| February 1994 | 2.3m |
| July 1994 | 50m |
| August 1994 | 80m |
| November 1994 | 90m |
| December 1994 | 160m |
| January 1995 | 200m |
| January 18 (Kobe) | 250m |
| January 31 | 300m |
| early February 1995 | 200m |
| mid-February 1995 | 300m |
| late February 1995 | 350m |

*Source*: Leeson (1996)

a six-and-a-half year jail sentence. In 1997, the UK Securities and Futures Authority (SFA) released details of the suspension or removal of various Barings directors and managers from their respective registers and awards of costs ranging from £5,000 to £10,000. During 1997, Barings managers continued to appeal, in some cases successfully, against SFA and DTI actions, while Barings bond-holders pursued their legal action to recover at least a portion of their losses from Barings ex-directors. A number of Barings ex-directors were also subject to third-party proceedings from Coopers & Lybrand – who were sued by Barings' administrators, Ernst & Young.

## *Systemic risk*

An issue which arose in the minds of a number of people after Barings' collapse was whether the potential for wilder market swings was a situation that could 'plunge the banking system itself into crisis' (Fay 1996: 50). The BoBS report considers that systemic risk from Barings' collapse was minimal, justifying the Bank of England's decision not to bail out Barings. The House of Commons (1996: x) argue that the Bank of England requires some authority to evaluate the internal workings of companies in the financial market, including the quality of their management. This is a tall order for any regulator and probably unnecessary as long as the market determines that others gain from the loss of one institution. However, complete systemic risk protection is bound to be beyond the capability of any single organization in the market.

## Risks to investment banks

### *Hazards and threats (see chapter 2)*

Based on the foregoing description and discussion, the main hazards and threats to companies engaged in investment banking are listed in the sub-sections below.

#### *Investment and strategy*

Positive aspects include:

- Constant attention to strategy facilitates positive and proactive direction for the organization.
- Long-term investment in the business improves its chances of survival and success over a period of time.

Key threats are:

- Inadequate investment in technology reduces competitiveness and effectiveness of controls.
- Inadequate investment in human resources undermines managerial effectiveness.

#### *Major accidents (systemic failure)*

Positive aspects include:

- Possibility of learning from lapses and collapses in similar organizations.
- Security and confidence from knowing that there is some protection from system failures.

Key threats are:

- Collapse or serious damage from events outside management control.

*Risk management*

Positive aspects include:

- Opportunity to integrate all aspects of management within a broader risk management function.
- Opportunity to involve staff at all levels in the risk management function and responsibilities.

Key threats are:

- Danger of viewing risk management as being solely or primarily the role of specialists rather than a line management responsibility.
- Absence of a policy on risk or a policy which is not formalized or communicated to employees.
- Inadequate procedures for management of dealing and dealing limits.
- Lack of internal controls, including segregation of duties.
- Lack of reporting systems to identify risks and exposure each day.
- Computer systems incapable of providing adequate reports and calculating exposure for all product trades.
- Lack of adequate involvement by directors.

*Culture*

Positive aspects include:

- Awareness of the importance of organizational culture to all aspects of the business.
- Influence organizational culture positively and empower employees.
- Acknowledge the relevance and importance of different organizational cultures in different parts of the organization as a strength.

Key threats are:

- Using culture differences as occasions for rejecting the contributions of others, devaluing others' perspectives.
- Lack of respect or understanding of the need for diversity in organizations that have multiple interfaces, particularly in different countries.

*Power relations*

Positive aspects include:

- Empowering staff to take decisions and action as necessary – for example, individual traders.

- Large degree of autonomy given to diverse groups enhances work performance and job satisfaction.

Key threats are:

- Using out-of-date structures to build empires rather than run an effective business.
- Individuals using power to enhance their own status or personal aggrandisement at the expense of the wider collective.

### *Change*

Positive aspects include:

- Opportunities to expand and become a more successful business.
- Occasions of learning and development for individuals and groups.

Key threats are:

- Tendency to be left behind, for example in updating technology.
- Unwillingness or inability of managers to understand the need for and the consequences of change – e.g. need for comprehensive risk management.

## *Risk assessment (see chapter 2)*

The following table summarizes potential risk levels for the threats discussed above. Attributed risk levels are based on the authors' judgements. Both positive and negative outcomes for any given threat may co-exist.

| **Threat** | **Potential risk levels** (as probabilities) | |
|---|---|---|
| | **Negative outcomes** | **Positive outcomes** |
| Investment and strategy | High | High |
| Major accidents | Low | Low |
| Risk management | High | Low–Medium |
| Culture | High | High |
| Power relations | Medium | Medium |
| Change | High | High |

*Table 11.2* Thematic matrix applied to Barings case study

| *Risk context* | *Salience in case study* |
|---|---|
| *Organizational environment* | |
| Economies and markets | H |
| Public policy, legislation and regulation | H |
| Social and political climate | M |
| Technology | M |
| History, operating territories and conditions | H |
| *Human factors* | |
| Culture | H |
| Power relations, political processes and decision-making | H |
| Perception and cognition | H |
| *Formal coping arrangements* | |
| Risk management | H |
| Risk assessment | H |
| Management systems | H |
| Approaches to change | H |

## Comparison with thematic matrix

Table 11.2 indicates the relative salience of each of the risk contexts identified in Part 1, and particularly chapter 9, in relation to Barings' case study. In the table, H = high, M = medium, L = low.

## Conclusions

Because of the size of the eventual losses and the knock-on effect upon other institutions, the collapse of Barings Bank has been the most spectacular failure to date in the financial sector. The volume of reports and accounts on the case are testimony to the impact that it has had on many parties. Like the pilot who is at the controls when a plane crashes, blame is often apportioned to this party (e.g. Department of Transport 1990). However, in order for a crash to occur, the system must not only allow a series of errors to occur without recovery, but also for worst case consequences to follow. Leeson may have been the pilot who crashed the bank, but Barings had to be inherently unstable for this event to occur, and also be inadequately supported by its regulatory and audit-based environment.

Barings collapsed because it did not manage risk effectively. This chapter has detailed the numerous ways in which this occurred. It is worth recording that Barings is by no means a 'one-off'. As Gapper and Denton (1996: 340) report:

> By the time Leeson went to jail, it was fast becoming the decade of the 'rogue trader' in financial markets. In June 1994 a trader called Joseph Jett was dismissed by Kidder Peabody, the US investment bank, for apparently conjuring up $350 million of fake profits by false accounting. . . . In October 1995 Toshihide Iguchi, a bond trader, was accused by his employer, Daiwa Bank, of concealing trading losses of $1.1 billion for eleven years. . . . in June 1996, Yasuo Hamanaka the head copper trader of Sumitomo Corporation, was accused by his employer of trying to manipulate the world copper market . . . He finally lost his battle, and Sumitomo faced a loss of up to $4 billion. In none of these cases did a 'rogue trader' seem to have gained personally through the deceptions, except in inflated bonuses. They instead seemed to have drifted into deception in an effort to be seen as star traders.

Table 11.4 shows that Barings is one of a dozen or so organizations in as many years known to have incurred major losses from financial dealing or trading which resulted from fraudulent or unauthorized dealing. However, most of these institutions could absorb the losses incurred, while because of its relatively small size, Barings could not. It would be surprising if these cases were the only ones to have existed or that the list is now closed.

While psychologists and others are developing a specialism in 'rogue trader' spotting (e.g. *Sunday Times* 9th March 1997), the numbers of such individuals available to study to date remains relatively small. They supposedly share common characteristics such as 'not in control of their careers . . . liable to much more stress . . . at the mercy of other forces, such as the markets, or the whims of their superiors . . . they want status, prestige and recognition just as much if not more [than money] . . . rose through the ranks quickly and established reputations as profit-earners that made them almost "untouchable" . . . don't take holidays . . . work long hours on their own . . . unable to delegate . . .'. How many of these characteristics might be shared by many employees in the financial sector? Identifying individuals who might be inclined to 'break the bank' from the inside might be one worthwhile component of a risk management strategy. However, by supposing that the problem lies at an individual level – the very term 'rogue trader' suggests as much – the danger is that more systemic risk controls will not be developed and

*Table 11.3* International financial 'fiascos'

| *Date made public* | *Organization & country* | *Case outline* | *Loss ($US)* |
|---|---|---|---|
| 1985 | AWA – Australia | Principal dealer of electronics company, initially successful, caught by moves against currency | 30m |
| 1987 | Merrill Lynch & Co – USA | Unauthorized transactions by top mortgage trader, Howard Rubin | 377m |
| Jan 1994 | Codelco – Chile state-owned copper company | Years of fraudulent trades by futures trader, Juan Pablo Davila | 200m |
| Jan 1994 | Metallgesellschaft AG – Germany | Oil futures contracts, entered into by US refining and marketing operation | 1.5bn |
| April 1994 | Kidder, Peabody & Co; parent – General Electric Co – USA | Charge against earnings to cover 'phantom deals' said to be made by head government bond trader, Joseph Jett | 210m |
| Dec 1994 | Orange Country, Ca – USA | Interest-rate derivatives contracts entered into by treasurer, Robert Citron | 1.7bn |
| Feb 1995 | Barings Bank Plc – UK | Japanese equity index futures trades by trader, Nick Leeson | 1.4bn |
| Sept 1995 | Daiwa Bank Ltd – Japan | 30,000 US treasury bond transactions over an 11–year period involving trader, Toshihide Iguchi | 1.1bn |
| June 1996 | Sumitomo Corp – Japan | Suspect copper trades involving trader Yasuo Hamanaka | 2.6bn |
| March & Aug 1996 | Jardine-Fleming – UK/Hong Kong | Senior fund manager, Colin Armstrong, booked successful deals to his personal account and dud deals to his clients | 30m |
| Sept 1996 | Deutche Bank AG/ Morgan Grenfell – Germany | Purchase of unregistered securities by leading fund manager, Peter Young | 710m |
| Feb 1997 | NatWest Markets – UK | Mispriced European interest-rate options contracts by trader, Papouis Kyriacos | 144m |

implemented. Only by addressing the full range of risk management issues are organizations in this sector likely to escape Barings' fate.

Political failure to learn by seeing the Barings case as a one-off or attributing the collapse to a single 'rogue trader' means that lessons for other organizations or for the system as a whole are less likely to be learned than if the regulatory environment is addressed. Issues include: How 'free' can a free market be allowed to be? The nature of financial dealing means that a demand for higher returns requires higher levels of risk to be taken. Pressure thereby incurred transfers down to individuals who have to take those risks to satisfy not only their own career ambitions, but also demands of clients and bosses for greater margins and higher profits.

Larger-scale issues concern governments and the nature of control and management of risks that have the potential to affect large numbers of people. The role of external regulatory bodies remains on the agenda as a result of Barings' collapse. Organizations such as the Basle-based Bank for International Settlements and the International Organisation of Securities Committees are aware that there could be a financial catastrophe unless all the information and knowledge relating to globalized markets is networked. One effect of globalized markets is to render irrelevant old divisions between traditional and investment banking. Hitherto, the two types of activity have been regulated through different bodies – in Barings' case by the Bank of England and the Singapore Monetary Authority on the one hand, and the Securities and Futures Authority and SIMEX on the other. While requisite knowledge and expertise exists, the ability of intelligence and control mechanisms to deal with a systems breakdown is problematic. There are also risks (e.g. stagnation) to an over-regulated system. From the point of view of growth, efficiency and investment, the G7 countries, global investment banks and monetary authorities are agreed that free capital movement brings substantial benefits throughout the world. However, at present the free market global system has left the institutional control framework lagging behind. It is unknown whether a global regulatory body might have saved Barings – or indeed any financial organization in similar circumstances.

In the UK, the blurring of boundaries between traditionally separate financial institutions – banks, building societies, insurance companies and asset managers, led to pressure for an overhaul of existing structures. In May 1997, one of the first acts of the newly-elected Labour Government in the financial services regulation area, was to create an enlarged Securities and Investment Board (SIB) to take over banking supervision from the Bank of England and all other existing regulatory bodies in the financial services sector. The new unified SIB – heralding the end of an era of self-regulation in this sector – is due to become a statutory body by 1999.

Chapter 12

# Safety in the railway industry

## Overview

This chapter reviews major safety issues relating to the railway industry and a variety of factors which may affect safety and risk management, including privatization and commercial fragmentation as well as organizational culture, power relations and approaches to management systems. These are dealt with through consideration of disasters in the industry as well as major changes and illustrative cases. A case study of an Australian rail company ('Australia Rail' – AR) demonstrates the global nature of such issues as well as providing an opportunity to consider less publicly salient but nevertheless important safety issues.

## Introduction

Rail travel continues to be an important means of transport for both people and goods. In many countries, large numbers of people commute daily by rail to and from their places of work. In developing countries in particular, rail provides a relatively cheap means of transport over long distances. Safety of both passengers and employees is therefore an important risk issue for railway companies anywhere in the world. Rail travel has traditionally been perceived to be among the safest forms of transport – justifiably so if considered on a per kilometre travelled basis, for example compared with most modes of road travel.

The railway industry is not generally high-tech. Although sophisticated computer and signalling systems are used increasingly for line control and on-board journey monitoring, the basic technology of railways remains unchanged. Many operational safety rules developed over decades remain in place, as they have been found to be as valid today as when first introduced – e.g. procedures relating to trackside working, rules relating to signals. However, although railway hazards are different in nature, technical complexity and scale to many of those classed as 'major hazards' in process industries such as the nuclear, chemical, petrochemical and oil and gas industries, a single railway accident can result in a large number of deaths and injuries. A cluster of such railway accidents in the UK since the late 1980s – King's Cross, Clapham, Cannon Street – prompted the UK government to introduce specific 'safety case' regulations for the industry, similar in principle to those introduced for the offshore oil and gas industry (see chapter 10). In the light of impending privatization of the state-run UK railway industry in the mid-1990s, a 'safety case' regime was also felt crucial to ensure availability of some objective evidence of safety management and risk levels regarding companies being bought and sold. Other safety regulations recently introduced within the UK cover: level crossings, safety critical work, approval of railway works and carriage of dangerous substances by rail.

This chapter first reviews some of the key risk topics and issues which are the focus of attention in railway safety. This review is based on the authors' work since 1987 as safety management consultants to railway companies, including work connected with the Fennell Inquiry (1988). A case study of Australia Rail (which has not experienced a disaster) serves to broaden the discussion of safety and risk management issues in the industry.

## Non-major accident hazards

Classification of railway accidents into major and non-major is not straightforward and such a distinction is merely a convenient way of summarising information. In the UK, for example, annual reports of the Health and Safety Executive's Chief Inspecting Officer for Railways do not use such a classification.

For those who are seriously injured or killed, any accident may be regarded by them and their families as 'major'. However, in the railway industry most accident hazards which lead to incidents are likely to result in injuries to a small number of people. Such hazards are not necessarily less important or significant to safety management but may be classified as non-major, to distinguish them from major accident hazards discussed in the next section. Non-major accident hazards include those associated with trackside maintenance work and a wide range of other activities.

Non-major accidents on railways typically result from deficiencies at the interface between rail vehicles and the rail infrastructure. Key safety aspects of these two main components of railway systems are described in detail in DoT/HSC (1993), and include such infrastructure features as permanent way, electrification, structures (bridges, tunnels, etc.), signalling, stations and level crossings. Rail vehicle features include: braking, gauging, speed and loading restrictions, conspicuity, cab ergonomics, doors and emergency equipment. Operational requirements also need to be adequate, including safe systems for train operation (e.g. shunting, coupling arrangements), requirements for loading and hazardous goods and emergency procedures. Besides such technical aspects of safety, human factors and management/organizational requirements, as outlined in Tables 12.1 and 12.2, are also very important.

*Table 12.1* Key safety and risk issues relating to human factors

- Employee selection and recruitment
- Training and relevant competencies – including authorization and re-examination
- Adequacy of procedures for operations, maintenance, modifications and emergencies
- Performance influencing factors – e.g. physical and other environmental stressors
- Task analysis and human error analysis for safety critical tasks
- Adequacy of supervision
- Motivation, reward and morale
- Safety culture and climate factors

*Sources:* Department of Transport/HSC (1993); Glendon and McKenna (1995)

*Table 12.2* Key safety and risk issues relating to management and organization

- Realistic safety policy, strategies and objectives
- Appropriate organizational structures and processes
- Adequate risk assessment methods and applications
- Adequate planning and resourcing
- Realistic selection of risk strategies, emphasizing risk reduction
- Adequate safety procedures for design and design modifications
- Adequate selection and control of contractors regarding safety
- Comprehensive accident/incident reporting and investigation systems
- Effective internal monitoring and verification audits
- Realistic attention to safety culture, including employee involvement and participation in safety improvements

*Source:* Adapted from Waring (1996a)

## Major accident scenarios

A major railway accident may be defined as one in which a large number of people are likely to be injured and/or killed in a single incident. Examples from the UK include those shown in Table 12.3.

Major accident hazard scenarios include the main types and causes shown in Table 12.4.

Proximate causes are those immediately preceding an incident. However, official inquiry reports into such incidents as the King's Cross fire (1987), Clapham

*Table 12.3* Major railway accidents in the UK

| *Year* | *Incident* | *Fatalities* |
|---|---|---|
| 1966 | Hither Green | 49 |
| 1975 | Moorgate | 43 |
| 1987 | King's Cross | 31 |
| 1988 | Clapham | 35 |
| 1991 | Cannon Street | 2 (542 injured) |
| 1996 | Watford | 1 (70 injured) |
| 1997 | Southall | 6 (160 injured) |

*Table 12.4* Main incident types and illustrative proximate causes in the railway industry

| *Incident type* | *Typical proximate causes* |
|---|---|
| Derailment | Dynamic wheel unloading; broken wheel; points failure or misalignment; track disturbance |
| Train collision (e.g. Watford 1996; Clapham 1988) | Two trains on same track section; out-of-gauge load or open door; on level crossing; conflicting movements; signals passed at danger |
| Buffer-stop crash (e.g. Moorgate 1975; Cannon Street 1991) | Speed restrictions not followed |
| Fire (e.g. Kings Cross 1987; Eurotunnel 1996) | Ignition of waste, detritus or other material |
| Hazardous cargoes | Rupture/leak of rail tanker; detonation of explosives |

*Source:* Department of Transport/HSC (1993); HSE (1992, 1996b)

Junction (1988) and others, emphasize the importance of underlying causes which typically involve complex combinations of management failures, human error and technical failure.

As with major accidents in any sector, major railway accidents serve to highlight financial and political dimensions of risk. For example, the parliamentary debate which took place five days after the 1991 Cannon Street accident, raised a number of issues, including:

- expenditure on safety – e.g. on new rolling stock with improved impact survivability design;
- adequacy of passenger service provision – e.g. passenger crowding and numbers of standing passengers in trains;
- technical back-up features to slow/stop trains approaching buffers (the Cannon Street train was travelling at only 8 kph on impact);
- previous similar accidents involving less serious outcomes;
- expenditure on safety provision in recent years and extent to which Clapham inquiry recommendations had been implemented;
- rail safety in general, compared with road travel.

While each of the items from the above list might merit a separate section, as an illustration of the complexity of such issues, a UK case study described by Williams (1992) involving a risk assessment exercise undertaken by HSE (1991) of the transport of dangerous substances will be outlined. From a list of nine categories of dangerous substances, three were selected on the basis of their potential to cause large numbers of casualties in the event of a major accident. These were:

- bulk toxic substances (chlorine and ammonia were used as exemplars);
- bulk flammable substances (LPG and motor spirit were used as exemplars);
- explosives.

The risk assessment undertaken comprised the following steps:

- review current movements of dangerous substances and past accident experience;
- identify main causes of incidents leading to loss of containment or explosive initiation;
- estimate frequency of such incidents;
- estimate nature and scale of release or explosion resulting from such incidents;
- quantify consequences for exposed populations;
- estimate individual and societal risks;
- consider any risk reduction or mitigating measures.

The assessment used QRA methods and the risk tolerability criteria described in HSE (1988), i.e. the ALARP model (see chapter 2, Figure 2.4). In a comparison of road and rail transport, it was found that:

- motor spirit transport was safer by rail, but that choice was only likely to be available for long haul routes;
- LPG risks were broadly comparable, but that groups at risk differed – rail passengers were less at risk than were road users in the respective scenarios;
- road transport was safer than rail for chlorine and ammonia because in the UK, unlike major road routes, rail routes pass through urban centres.

The study indicated that, when estimating relative risks of different forms of transport, it is important to consider the type of hazardous substance transported, its potential for harm, the particular routes travelled and also that situations may vary considerably between different countries. This study highlights the importance of applying a consistent approach to risk assessment as part of the risk management process, while acknowledging that individual assessments for specific sets of circumstances are required.

A further example is provided by Joing (1992), who describes the introduction of a new safety feature on the French railway system (SNCF) and its implicit cost-benefit aspects. SNCF records indicated that SPADs had remained at a constant level for around 20 years, implying that the number would be hard to reduce further by relying on the human operator alone – most of them being attributed to 'driver error'. Joing (1992) describes the introduction of an electronic system of track signalling beacons and automatic on-board speed monitoring equipment which can trigger braking independently of the driver's behaviour. Such systems are becoming common in rail networks throughout the world. Designed to reduce considerably – though not completely eliminate – the risk of accident through collision or derailment through a driver failing to comply with a 'slow' or 'stop' signal, the six-year programme is to equip 11,000 signals and 5000 engines with the new equipment. The cost benefit calculation undertaken deemed that the 5 billion francs expenditure would save five lives – and the value decision was that this was cost effective.

## Lessons from UK major rail accidents

### *King's Cross*

A number of recurrent themes have emerged from inquiry reports into major rail accidents in the UK. Two overriding themes are the need for adequate safety management systems (SMS) and an appropriate safety culture. For example the King's Cross fire, described in outline in Box 12.1, highlighted the ease with which a large well-resourced organization such as London Underground Ltd had formed an unchallengeable and unchallenged belief that a manual of safety procedures (the

### Box 12.1: Kings Cross underground station fire

On 18 November 1987 at 19.25, a discarded match or cigarette end (most probable cause) set fire to grease and rubbish on the Piccadilly line ascending escalator running track. Running tracks were not regularly cleaned because of ambiguous responsibilities. Smoke detectors were not installed on cost grounds and water fog equipment was infrequently used due to rust problems.

A booking clerk was alerted to the fire by a passenger (at 19.30), although only four of the 21 station staff on duty at the time had received any training in evacuation or fire drills. At 19.34, railway police evacuated passengers via an alternative escalator, although no evacuation plan existed for the station and no joint exercises had been conducted between London Underground staff and the emergency services.

A relief inspector, not regularly based at King's Cross and without any fire training, entered the upper machine room at 19.38 but could not get close enough to the fire to use a fire extinguisher and did not activate the water fog equipment.

At 19.39, police in ticket hall begun evacuation of area and requested that trains on Piccadilly and Victoria lines do not stop at King's Cross, although trains continued to stop there. At 19.41, metal gates to ticket hall are closed by police and soon after, first fire engines arrive. At 19.45, flashover occurred and the whole ticket hall was engulfed in intense heat and flame: 31 people were killed and many others were seriously injured.

The tragedy was aggravated by the lack of an evacuation plan, escape routes blocked by locked doors and metal barriers, outdated communication equipment, no access to station public address system by headquarters controller, non-functioning of cameras and TV monitors, lack of public address system on trains and absence of public telephones at the station.

A combination of factors resulted in a disaster made worse by a variety of behaviours and circumstances.

*Sources*: Department of Transport (1988); Reason (1990)

Rule Book) and limited induction training together formed an adequate operational SMS. The weak safety culture within the organization was further betrayed by such examples from Fennell (1988) as:

- a commonly held view that small fires in operational areas were inevitable and not preventable (pp. 32, 118);
- a belief that small fires in operational areas were not precursors to large fires – e.g. use of the term 'smouldering' to describe such small fires (p. 18);
- a belief that fire safety should emphasize fire emergency procedures rather than fire prevention (p. 18);
- a belief emanating from Board members that passenger safety was a secondary issue and not part of the company's statutory duties under the Health & Safety at Work Act 1974 (p. 116);
- failure to learn lessons from earlier fires and warnings directly relating to London Underground (p. 117);
- demarcation of safety responsibilities between Directorates and functions leading to key requirements not being met (pp. 115–16);
- close attention to financial audits but none to safety audits (p. 17).

The Fennell Inquiry report summarized the drastic changes required, namely from a reactive to a proactive preventive culture (p. 117) which established and maintained a substantial safety management programme, including vastly improved training, emergency planning and procedures and safety auditing.

Like other disasters involving crowd behaviour, particularly in fires, for example at Bradford City Football Ground (1985), the King's Cross fire highlighted the importance of considering relevant aspects of human behaviour when managing this particular type of risk. Studies (e.g. Canter 1990) reveal that, contrary to popular media reporting, in such situations people do not generally panic but behave more or less normally in the face of impending disasters, despite such behaviour being totally inappropriate. For example, it has been demonstrated many times that people will almost always leave the site of an emergency by the same route they entered or by a route that they are already familiar with. Sime (1980) found that if people are given sufficient prior information about emergency situations then they behave appropriately and do not panic in respect of aspects where information has been provided – although they may do so in respect of other aspects of a fire emergency (as in the Summerland fire in 1973). Proulx and Sime (1991: 851) found that a publicly broadcast message giving precise information about a 'fire' in an underground station exercise ' ... did *not* encourage irrational agitated behaviour ... The precise message identifying the incident and its location provoked sufficient stress to initiate an evacuation, while keeping passengers sufficiently calm to evacuate in a prompt and orderly fashion'. They also discovered that an alarm bell only was least effective of five evacuation signals as measured by appropriateness of passengers' behaviour and evacuation time. Promptness of giving a warning is also critical because, as Proulx and Sime (1991: 843) argue, ' . . . rather than avoiding "panic", a delay in warning the public is self-fulfilling. When an incident such as a fire gets out of hand, the delay is paradoxically a major determinant of flight behaviour, crushing and deaths in major crowd disasters'.

In an emergency people have a desire to get to ground level – from either a higher, or in the case of King's Cross Underground Station, from a lower level, where whatever the circumstances, they feel greater security – probably due to the greater number of options then available for escape and because we are essentially ground-dwelling creatures. Logic may not be applied by people under the severe stress of an emergency evacuation, where in any case options available are likely to be severely reduced. The larger the crowd involved the greater is likely to be the reduction in the number of alternative courses of action available for escape. Increasing crowd size can also be generally expected to increase the probability of a dangerous incident, the potential number of victims and communication difficulties. However, use of appropriate techniques which take account of relevant parameters of human behaviour in such emergencies (e.g. Sime 1993), can considerably improve the survivability of fires and other crowd-related emergencies.

While there are likely to be cultural differences between crowd behaviour in different cultures, for example collectivist as opposed to individualist (Hofstede) and those which are more expressive compared with those which are more affectively neutral and thus less likely to seek close proximity to unknown others, during emergencies, consistencies in people's behaviour are likely to be of much greater importance. This should aid essential planning and design features for emergencies, in which a range of parties with relevant inputs should ideally be involved. For example, people in crowds normally assume – often incorrectly, that there is someone who has responsibility for their safety or who is controlling their immediate environment. While this may be true to an extent, there are also likely to be authority conflicts because potentially controlling parties have different interests and objectives. For example, in the case of a mass transport incident, the transport operator will want to move people away from the danger zone while the police may seek to maintain public order – for example in the Hillsborough Stadium tragedy (1989) the police were first concerned that what they were witnessing was a pitch invasion. Other emergency services have a more explicit brief to save lives – introducing a further set of objectives into the arena.

The party whose actions are likely to be most critical at the time of an emergency are operating staff closest to the scene. Planning for emergencies must involve such staff. This is well demonstrated by the finding from the King's Cross fire that four different groups of people investigated the fire in its early stages before giving instructions or taking actions to deal with the threat. These investigations were mainly by junior people making an initial examination, then calling on more senior people to investigate. Fennell (1988) notes that time thereby lost contributed to the eventual loss of life. Prevarication can turn a problem into a disaster. Technological requirements include the need for warnings to be timely – because urgent action may be required, directed specifically at those who need to act and be explicit in telling them exactly what to do. As far as staff are concerned, there needs to be role clarity so that they know their responsibilities clearly, and empowerment so that they have authority to act when necessary. Appropriate training and refreshers should ensure that staff have the necessary competence to carry out their responsibilities.

## *Clapham*

Like the Fennell Inquiry, the Hidden Inquiry (1989) into the Clapham Junction disaster of 1988, described in outline in Box 12.2, found that, among other things British Rail had fostered a culture in which inadequate safety management systems were implicitly considered to be satisfactory. Evidence to the inquiry identified numerous background factors in respect of the accident, including: poor communication, out of date culture, inadequate selection procedures, unsettled industrial relations, slack work practices, insufficient training, work pressure, ineffective supervision and organizational change. The immediate cause of the accident was traced to unsatisfactory maintenance work on signalling equipment not being checked and two full passenger trains travelling in the same direction on the same track collided – a third empty train going in the opposite direction, also being involved. Key recommendations of the Hidden Inquiry report were the need for adequate SMS and safety auditing.

At the time of the Clapham accident, BR was in the process of implementing total quality management procedures (Reid 1992). The Hidden Inquiry's recommendations, supplemented by considerable governmental funds earmarked for safety provision, accelerated the organization's drive to instigate safety and risk management programmes. By 1990, BR had developed risk assessment procedures to measure benefits, initially of six pilot schemes and ultimately of hundreds of proposals, to improve safety in terms of reducing fatalities and injuries. This greater

## Box 12.2: Clapham rail crash

A collision occurred between the 07.18 Basingstoke to Waterloo train, the 06.14 Poole to Waterloo train and a train of empty coaches south west of Clapham Junction Station at about 08.10 on 12 December 1988. Thirty-five people were killed and many others injured.

A new signal had malfunctioned, so that the second the train was not prevented from occupying the same track as the earlier one and failing to stop the front of the second from running into the back of the first. The driver of the first train had seen the signal change from green to red as he passed it, and was obliged to stop and report the SPAD. He could not have known that the signal was faulty and that following trains had not also been stopped.

The immediate cause of the faulty signal was false feed of current from the old wire in the Clapham Junction relay room. This situation was the result of electrical work done on two separate occasions within the previous two weeks. On the first occasion, the senior technician responsible for the work made basic errors in not cutting back the old wire but merely bending it away. His work was not inspected by the supervisor, who was involved in other work. The second job, undertaken coincidentally by the same senior technician, compounded the initial error as the old wire reverted to its original position when a new relay was being installed.

However, the inquiry also identified responsibility among other parties who had allowed a situation in which such errors could be made and remain undetected when such work was inspected, tested and commissioned back into service. The supervision and monitoring of poor working practices was criticized for its inadequacy. Malpractice was found to be widespread, indicating a lack of adequate staff training. Management were criticized for 'incompetence, ineptitude, inefficiency and failure' (p. 73). Lessons from previous incidents had not been learned and it was concluded that 'concern for safety was permitted to co-exist with working practices which . . . were positively dangerous'. This unhappy coexistence was never detected by management and so the bad practices were never eradicated' (p. 163). Ninety-three separate recommendations were made.

*Source*: Department of Transport (1989)

integration of risk criteria into business decision-making involved other parties – for example in an assessor role, including HSE, Department of Transport and consultants. Key criteria in this proactive process included:

- transparency of decision-making;
- demonstrable safety benefit per pound spent;
- prioritizing of schemes using a risk-related ranking system;
- taking account of public perceptions as well as quantitative risk assessments.

In respect of this last mentioned criterion, it was acknowledged that events which had potential for major accident outcomes ('catastrophes') could be weighted more heavily than otherwise equivalent projects in the ranking exercise because of the public visibility of such events. Other moderating criteria affecting final decisions on the ordering of projects for action included: legal requirements (for example on fire prevention following King's Cross) and the degree to which risk might be voluntarily accepted by parties such as trespassers and 'vandals', for whom lower priorities might be accorded.

## *Eurotunnel*

At the time of writing, the first official inquiry report into the Eurotunnel fire of November 1996 – by the CTSA – had been published (DoT 1997). Echoing findings from those relating to the King's Cross and Clapham disasters, the CTSA report maintains that the fire exposed 'fundamental weaknesses in Eurotunnel's management of safety'. The chair of CTSA observed that while the accident resulted in no fatalities, emergency procedures were found to be too complex and demanding and that duty staff were inadequately trained in the procedures. Experience of the fire resulted in radical changes to safety procedures and the focus of the CTSA's report was on staff training. It is instructive to note that once basic design and principal operational aspects of such a major project as the Channel Tunnel have been established, then options remaining for improved safety are likely to be limited primarily to 'software' features such as operator training and emergency procedures.

With billions of pounds of debt, the Channel Tunnel was regarded by many potential investors as a poor financial investment from its early days. Construction costs soared as the predicted construction time lengthened. Safety versus competitive requirements was a continuous issue during construction of the Channel Tunnel. Rather than all safety features being designed in from the start, changes to the original concept were mandated by safety authorities and other public bodies who had no direct involvement in the design process. Risk reduction in the resultant structure was based on the 'fail to safety' principle rather than being a system which had safety as an inherent design feature.

The Canterbury Treaty, signed in February 1986, stipulated that the Channel Tunnel would be built by a private consortium with no state financial intervention. However, the states reserved the right of control over the project in respect of safety, security and environmental protection. An Intergovernmental Commission was established to take on behalf of France and the UK, any necessary decisions related to these risk-related criteria. The CTSA was set up within the terms of the Treaty to assist and advise the Commission, and to supervise prevention and protection aspects of the system through five working groups:

- civil engineering and general equipment;
- health and safety at work;
- dangerous goods;
- rescue and public safety;
- safety and railway technology.

The global risk study undertaken had five main stages:

1 Identify normal, transition and emergency (from preliminary risk analysis) situations.
2 Identify undesirable events as consequences of system failures.
3 Determine safety parameters to guarantee safety levels.
4 Evaluate risk distributions in classes based on probabilities and outcomes.
5 Qualitative and quantitative synthesis.

The final stage involved components of the ALARP methodology (see chapter 2, Figure 2.4) – widely adopted within the UK (e.g. HSE 1988), and more qualitative approaches preferred in France. Principles involved here include maintaining safety throughout the system life cycle and ensuring efficient management of emergencies in case of accident.

A general guideline operational safety objective for the Channel Tunnel was that a passenger journey should be no more dangerous than a notional conventional train journey between Calais and Folkstone (Perrod 1992). However, the risk assessments involved in such a major engineering venture were never going to be readily compared with more conventional rail travel. The Tunnel's ventilation system and passenger evacuation procedures were among the more complex issues to be addressed through discussions between the CTSA and Eurotunnel Consortium representatives. The CTSA disagreed with Eurotunnel's open wagon design for transporting heavy lorries (Perrod 1992). The compromise resolution was smoke detectors at the end of the shuttle trains and other provisions, although such provisions are not the same as built-in system safety. While including passenger safety within its remit, unlike the CTSA, Eurotunnel had a different risk orientation, in particular being obliged to consider the economic feasibility of the project as well as potential material damage and the possible effect upon future operating costs and profits, for example resulting from fire or major accident.

It is therefore perhaps ironic that although no lives were lost as a result of the November 1996 Channel Tunnel fire, there was extensive damage and considerable revenue loss. Inadequacies in many of the warning and protection systems were identified. Once these are corrected, system safety can be expected to improve. Commercial versus safety interests were also to the forefront during the debate about reopening the Channel Tunnel following the fire. Once such an incident has occurred – particularly as in this case, within three years of the Channel Tunnel opening – then *a priori* estimates about the frequency of major incidents may need to be revised. This happened belatedly in the case of the nuclear industry worldwide following the well-publicized incidents at Three Mile Island and Chernobyl as well as less well-publicized incidents elsewhere.

Those claiming that, because there was no loss of life, the Channel Tunnel fire demonstrated the effectiveness of safety and evacuation procedures, are missing some essential points. Aside from the fact that in this case not all detection, isolation and other safety features operated satisfactorily, the vulnerability of the entire system was highlighted as well as design shortcomings, at least some of which resulted from compromises with commercial considerations. Furthermore, there are numbers of documented cases of major incidents resulting in considerable loss of life, which have been foreshadowed by incidents with many of the same features, which through good fortune, have resulted in much less serious outcomes (see e.g. Toft and Reynolds 1997). Thorough risk assessments should take account of potential worst case consequences as well as use best possible data to arrive at respective likelihoods for these scenarios.

This case illustrates the close links between safety and cost in many large engineering projects. When private investment is the basis for such projects there is likely to be greater potential for conflict between return on investment risk over a given time scale on the one hand and public and employee safety on the other. In deregulated sectors, it is possible that at the margin the balance of decision-making could tip in favour of investment return rather than designed-in system safety – which is liable to delay and reduce payments to shareholders. This could be further exacerbated where projects have significant political prestige because of the 'invisible hand' of major stakeholders, such as national governments or broader communities, whose prime motivation could be the demonstrated successful operation of a project. In the case of the Channel Tunnel, while neither government made any financial investment in the enterprise, arguably both had a substantial political investment to recoup from the project's successful completion.

As with most accidents, there are warning signs of what can go wrong from experience with previous incidents. For example, an accident involving two trains in the eight-kilometre Severn Tunnel under the Bristol Channel in December 1991 resulted in 186 people being injured, although again no fatalities occurred. The HSE report into the accident maintained that the accident could have been avoided with better management practices and that BR management had failed to learn lessons from previous accident investigations, particularly Clapham (Toft and Reynolds 1997). This accident also highlighted the importance of adequate communication in respect of ensuring effective emergency rescue operations.

## Safety implications of railway privatization

Government proposals to privatize the UK rail monopoly British Rail were announced formally in 1992. The plan involved selling off discrete services such as freight, and to franchise passenger services. British Rail was to be reorganized into a smaller company (Railtrack) to own and operate the national railway infrastructure and a series of train service providers which would be in competition with private franchise operators. Stations and depots would be either sold, leased or retained with a substantial contracting out of functions.

With such a major change affecting the entire industry, the need to maintain and ensure safety standards was regarded by the government as paramount. On 12 January 1993, the Department of Transport and the Health & Safety Commission published a special report entitled *Ensuring Safety on Britain's Railways* (HSC 1993a). The report states that 'statutory control shall be the minimum consistent with ... control of risk . . .' (HSC 1993a) and notes:

> Companies with little or no previous experience of railway safety issues will enter the railway industry . . . Control of railway operations will be divided between many different organizations and this will generate a need to define the extent of the responsibilities of each party and to ensure effective management of safety (including emergency planning) particularly at the numerous interfaces between parties . . . Unless considerable care is taken to set up systems to ensure that new operators are properly equipped and organized, there can be no confidence that risk will be effectively controlled right from

> the start and that important matters do not fall between the safety arrangements of the various parties. The consequences of failing to achieve adequate systems of control will be seen in increased risk on the railway system and the likelihood of an increase in the numbers, and possibly also the severity of, accidents.

Each train service operator, station operator and the infrastructure controller (Railtrack) would be required by legislation to prepare a safety guarantee in the form of a 'safety case' or detailed justification, similar to those already in effect in the offshore oil and gas industry (see chapter 10). Before access to the network would be granted to an operator, its railway safety case would have to be validated by Railtrack. In turn, Railtrack's safety case and its validation arrangements for operators' safety cases would be approved by the government's Health & Safety Executive.

The report's recommendations were implemented through legislation and, in particular, the Railway (Safety Case) Regulations 1994. The content of railway safety cases is required to cover the following key topics:

- basic information about the entity covered by the case;
- safety policy;
- assessment of risks;
- management of health and safety
  - – safety management systems (SMS);
  - – performance monitoring;
  - – quality of SMS;
  - – organization;
  - – competence and training;
  - – information flow;
  - – consultation arrangements;
  - – accident investigation;
  - – contractors;
  - – emergency response;
  - – procurement of premises and plant;
  - – audit.

Many of the shortcomings and criticisms of offshore safety cases raised in chapter 10 and elsewhere (e.g. Waring 1996c) apply equally to railway safety cases. For example, there is no requirement to comment on safety culture, yet the government report on which the regulations are based (HSC 1993a) states (p. 21) '. . . however well safety standards are being maintained at present there is a need to continue the effort to improve and this is often a matter of improving safety culture and procedures rather than large scale capital investment'.

The railway industry has often adopted a mechanistic approach to safety management systems, safety culture and safety cases – which stems from the industry's strong engineering basis, traditions and personnel. There is often a naïve expectation that delivery of such vital outcomes as effective SMS and an appropriate safety culture can be contracted out to external consultants as if these outcomes were merely technical matters independent of the railway company's management. Unlike offshore, however, the railway industry has taken a proactive stance towards 'human factors', particularly at the human-task interface level of ergonomics and work-gang subcultures (see, for example, Guest, Peccei and Thomas 1994).

The break-up of the UK railway industry has led to boundary problems of safety responsibility and communication between different entities – a potential problem foreshadowed by the government's pre-privatization report (HSC 1993a). The new safety case regime was intended to prevent such problems but the large number of contractors now working within the industry has highlighted difficulties of ensuring that their selection and control are effective from a safety viewpoint. Commercial pressures may also influence management decisions unduly when evaluating risks. On 7 August 1996 (reported in *The Guardian*), following a 'near miss' incident with a train, five track workers sub-contracted by the Southern Track Renewal Unit were found to have bogus personal track safety certificates. Such certificates are required by regulations for anyone engaged in 'safety critical work' to ensure that only persons whose safety competence has been assessed are allowed to work in places of danger.

The rail privatization process, resulting in more than 80 separate companies which compete rather than co-operate, has been criticized from a cost perspective as well as raising safety questions. While the HSE (1996b) announced that accidental deaths to railway employees and passengers were at 'unprecedently low levels', several years of comparable data are required to confirm or challenge this view. Given the amount that was invested in many aspects of safety during the latter days of British rail, improved early safety experience of the new structure may not be surprising. The real test will be whether the record is sustained in the long term. While it may be too early to make a full safety assessment, the privatized UK rail network requires newly developed systems for ensuring future safety. Such radical changes in management and operating systems as were presaged by the advent of rail privatization mean that continuous review and improvement are required as key components of the risk management process.

Wherever more than one party is involved in rail operations, for example as in a privatized network, primary responsibility for safety lies with the party in control. However, ambiguity may exist in respect of which parties have responsibilities and all significant parties are likely to have some liability. Unless a particular issue is highlighted a problem may not be noticed and the larger is the number of parties involved, the greater will be the scope for potential confusion of responsibilities.

## Safety management in Australia Rail

As with many railway companies throughout the world, a considerable amount of awareness and attention is paid within Australia Rail (AR) to lessons from King's Cross, Clapham and other railway accidents elsewhere. While remaining aware, and partly because of this, to date, AR have experienced no major accidents on their system. AR is developing a new safety management system as part of forthcoming legal requirements for safety accreditation – analogous with the preparation of a 'safety case'. AR has a sophisticated system for monitoring and reporting on safety and risk issues.

While there are unique features both between and within safety cultures in rail companies, because of many common operational requirements, most rail companies' culture has features which would be recognizable between rail organizations. Thus AR is both similar to and has unique features when compared with, say, the UK national rail network or London Underground Ltd in its safety culture approach to safety management systems and other features of risk management. While it has some inter-State rail links, Australia's rail network is essentially State-based. AR is corporatized, meaning that it has some features of a privatized service, while retaining features in common with a nationally owned rail system.

In considering this case study, the intention is to emphasize the general nature of many problems relating to risk management within railway organizations. Emphasis is upon workplace risk management, i.e. of everyday or what we refer to in this chapter as non-major accident hazards, rather than major accident hazards.

The AR network is characterized by large distances between work locations, many of them in relatively isolated areas, and a legacy of geographically-based divisions. In most other respects, risk management issues within AR are comparable with those experienced by any railway company. This case study outlines some of the issues affecting safety on AR's system, particularly safety of personnel working trackside – the main risk to be managed.

## *The safety and risk management function within Australia Rail*

An important principle is integrating risk management within all AR operations. Risk management is driven from the top of the organization and becomes a line management function with specialist safety staff acting in an advisory capacity. Since 1994, AR has produced an annual safety plan – signed by the chief executive – which identifies safety as the highest priority for the CEO, the AR Board and for senior AR managers, as well as defining AR's risk-management based safety objectives and actions required by AR managers to deliver them. For production of the most recent safety plan, key risks were identified and priority ranked at a risk management seminar and objectives identified from this process as well as from results of a safety audit undertaken by the State Department of Transport.

AR's current safety plan objectives, some of which have specific number or percentage targets (not shown here) include:

- reduce number of signals passed at danger (SPADs);
- evaluate automatic train protection and alternative protection systems;
- reduce passenger injuries and security violations;
- reduce numbers of derailments;
- reduce public fatalities at level crossings and as a result of trespass;
- evaluate track safety and operational activities to reduce employee fatalities;
- ensure that all employees have 'position descriptions' detailing individual safety responsibilities, training and accreditation requirements and other relevant matters.

AR sees its strategic framework as being based around requirements to maintain the safety of passengers, public and employees. Its passenger fatality rate of one per 84.6 million passenger journeys compares well against other railways around the world, for example being half that for the UK rail system. However, being a relatively small railway in terms of track kilometres, a single passenger train derailment or collision could have dramatic effect upon such performance figures. Largely because of the large geographical area covered by the AR rail system, the public fatality rate (excluding suicides) is around three times higher than that associated with rail systems of many comparable countries. Fatality rates for AR exposed employees are around one per 4,500 employees. Such rates provide very general indicators of safety performance and this case study considers aspects of risk management at operational level, particularly as it affects AR employees.

AR has separate business units – Citytrain (suburban passengers), Traveltrain (long distance passengers), Freight, Coal & Minerals, Business Services, etc. with an integrated risk management structure operating across the whole organization – analogous with a matrix approach. Figure 12.1 illustrates links between the main components.

The Safety Division is located within Strategic Issues and has 18 full-time staff. There are six Group Safety Advisers, who meet monthly, and 25 OHS Officers operating from AR depots as well as Protection Officers and Control Liaison Officers. Other staff involved in safety include safety representatives and line managers such as Track Section Supervisors. The CEO, together with managers reporting directly to this position, plus a union representative, comprise the AR Safety Council. AR has around 50 safety committees.

A major challenge for AR's safety and risk management function is to maintain and establish forums in which staff generate practicable cost-effective ideas on safety and risk management and to identify and address problems in this field. Where this has been initiated, for example through AR health and safety committee members assessing risk exposure, managers appreciate that their time is usefully spent on important risk issues.

## *Trackside safety*

While for many AR staff, their regular work involves them being trackside for much of the time, one estimate was that around 75 per cent of AR employees could be

*Figure 12.1* Simplified view of AR's risk management function

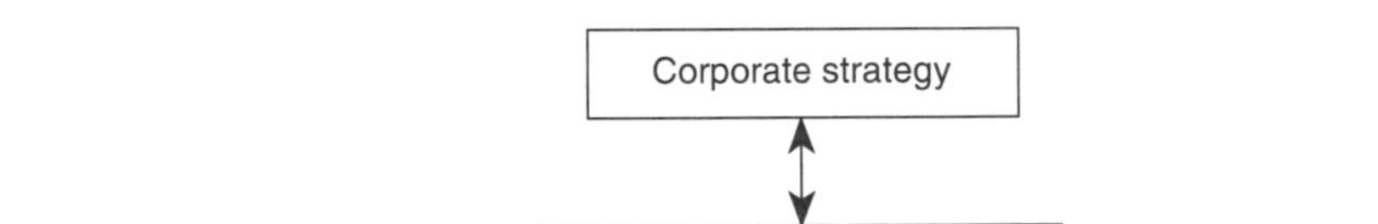


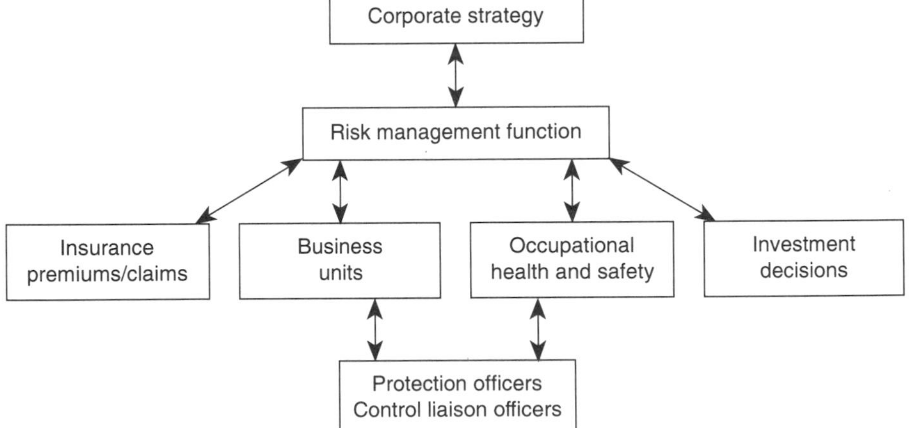

trackside at some time or another. AR staff whose work involves them being trackside include:

- construction workers – bridges, track, overhead work;
- maintenance workers – bridges, track, overhead work;
- fettling gangs;
- welders;
- train crews;
- signals and telecommunications staff – electrical and mechanical;
- electricians;
- cable workers;
- surveyors;
- engineer's office staff;
- track section supervisors and other supervisory staff;
- inspection staff (road/rail vehicles);
- safety division staff;
- depot safety officers;
- group safety advisers;
- protection officers;
- control liaison officers.

In addition to AR staff, numerous contractors are required to work trackside and members of the public are frequently exposed, including:

- passengers;
- pedestrians at crossings and elsewhere;
- motorists at crossings;
- farmers and others whose property is adjacent to AR tracks;
- trespassers – with and without intent to cause damage or injury;
- potential/actual suicide cases.

Given the range and variety of those who have access to AR tracks, the extensive and varied nature of the AR rail network, and the worst consequences of interactions between people and trains, the potential problem for AR in managing the total risk involved is considerable. Considering the variety of parties who have access to AR track, among the dimensions which need to be considered when managing risk are:

- legitimate/non-legitimate;
- experienced/naïve;

- good/poor risk perception;
- extensive/transitory exposure.

The nature of the risk will vary between parties with different characteristics. For example, those whose exposure is legitimate, who are experienced in trackside knowledge, whose perception of the relevant risks is good and whose exposure is extensive, might be expected to be ‘ safer’ than those with contrary characteristics. However, even experienced people have accidents, sometimes resulting partly from ‘over-familiarity’ with the hazards, and therefore risk assessment which includes reference to the variety of characteristics of those who could be exposed is required. Employees and others who do not venture trackside regularly or frequently are liable to be particularly ‘at risk’ on those occasions when they are trackside because of their under-developed perception of the risks.

Ideally separate risk assessments should be carried out by appropriately qualified persons for each trackside operation. In the case of complex work over a period of several days or longer, this is likely to be fairly extensive and formal. For smaller jobs, risk assessments may be relatively straightforward and informal, but should still be recorded in some way. Each time work moves to a new location, a new risk assessment should be carried out.

### *Protection officers*

AR has a system whereby locally based protection officers – operating predominantly in Citytrain environments – have responsibility for safety at each site. This system illustrates the importance attached by AR to trackside safety for its own employees and for contractors’ staff. Protection officers are experienced and knowledgeable AR staff who are well motivated to guard the safety of trackside workers. Their training enables them to operate in a wide variety of situations and they have excellent perception of risks involved in trackside work. For example, they need to be able to consider ‘what if’ scenarios when in charge of the safety of a group of workers. They also need to adopt the optimum position when responsible for the safety of a trackside gang, particularly when the gang is well spread out. Among other duties, protection officers are responsible for the condition of a section of track from a housekeeping point of view when this is handed back following completed work. At least one protection officer reported that he walked the relevant section of track after contractors had left because he ‘didn’t trust them’.

### *Trackside safety provision*

A variety of measures and tools is available to protect AR staff and contractors working trackside. These include:

- track closure;
- electrical isolation (electric trains only);
- local control of signals ('signal block' – protection officer has signal keys);
- clipping points ('points block');
- 'caution' and 'speed restriction' ('slow') boards;
- 'stop' boards;
- red flags;
- detonators;
- 'yellow ticket' system – for track vehicles;
- official lookouts;
- individual vigilance;
- mobile phones;
- radio communication (for train times, etc.).

These are used in appropriate combinations depending upon local conditions and the nature of the work being undertaken. Personnel should be clear of the track ten minutes prior to a train arriving. In most instances, it is essential to have at least two levels of warning operating – for example an early warning when a train is ten minutes distance from the work being carried out and again when its arrival at the worksite is imminent. Such early warning is not only required for protection of those at worksites, but also to ensure efficient running of trains.

### *Hazard communication*

It is important that there is no ambiguity in the system of lookouts, particularly in respect of who is responsible for giving warnings and communicating relevant information on hazards, particularly train movements; for example, identifying the person primarily responsible for lookout duties with some distinctive apparel. Because of the distance required to stop a train, the onus must be on trackside staff to look out for, or otherwise to protect themselves, from trains. Train drivers need to be constantly vigilant, use horn warnings as appropriate and communicate with control as required. Train controllers also play a vital role.

There is often the possibility for ambiguity in respect of who is responsible for trackside safety at an operational level as numerous parties are potentially involved – including the general public, line management, train controllers, drivers, track section supervisors, fellow workers and each individual worker. Adequate communication between these and other involved parties is critical to trackside safety.

### *Training and supervision*

AR has strengths in training – as evidenced for example by the award of a 1996 State Training Award for Best Training Initiative for its Rollingstock Maintenance Training Program. Training and supervision should be mutually complementary. Thus, while classroom training is essential for trackside workers, this should always be consistent with and supported by trackside supervisory practices. Supervision of inexperienced workers in effect constitutes 'on-the-job training'. Protection officers and supervisors in particular have a critical role to play here as do more experienced trackside workers. Because of the 'unforgiving' nature of the main hazard associated with trackside work, there may be limited scope for human error during such work. It should be emphasized by those involved in induction training that practical experience, including safety knowledge, can only be gained during actual work activity. For example, a recently trained worker placed detonators at exactly 100m (the required distance as laid down in the rules) from the worksite – which happened to be on a level crossing. A road vehicle, driven by an AR employee, set off one of the detonators. This illustrates the scope for individuals using their common sense and initiative rather than following rules slavishly to the letter, particularly when safety is thereby compromised.

Thus, while classroom training is evidently required, for trackside workers this is in many respects secondary to the training and education received from supervisors and peers. Compared with most classroom training, behaviours learnt during work activity are likely to exert a stronger pressure on patterns of behaviour. This puts considerable onus on supervisors in particular to reinforce proper (i.e. safe) methods of working and to correct unsafe work practices. Supervisors are encouraged to see themselves as having primary responsibility for the safety of their gangs. Safety officers and others in the full-time safety function provide support and guidance, while higher management support is also critical.

### *Visibility*

Given the range of circumstances under which trackside work may be encountered by train drivers, visibility is an important issue. Sunlight streaming through a cab window, possibly for long periods, is a frequent problem. Protection boards and trackside workers may be obscured by long grass and other vegetation. A minority of workers may not be wearing high visibility clothing or, if worn, it may be too dirty to be effectively visible. Confusing features for drivers could include any red coloured objects which are close to the track, for example a red oil drum. Drivers report that they 'automatically' go for the brake if they see anything red at the trackside. Confusion for drivers can also arise if a roadwork sign is displayed and yet no trackside work is observed. Possibilities include that the workers are taking a break, that they are working elsewhere or that they have forgotten to remove a board.

### *Potential work/safety conflicts*

The requirement for communication to be via train controllers means that train drivers and trackside staff do not have direct voice contact, for example via radio, although technically this is possible and in an emergency might be used. The generally accepted safety margin of ten minutes prior to the arrival of a train, while it might provide a welcome opportunity for a break during particularly hot weather, could also be considered to be a long time for a gang not to be working.

Train drivers, who can only communicate with a trackside gang using a horn warning, frequently encounter the problem of not knowing when trackside personnel who are foul of the track during their approach will move to a position of safety. This situation may cause a driver to apply the brake when approaching trackside workers, even though there is no possibility of stopping the train before reaching the gang. This is a costly and inefficient practice. Drivers report that trackside workers frequently seem to 'want to remain foul of the track until the last second', or report such staff returning from a position of safety to retrieve hand tools or equipment from close to the track. It is important for trackside personnel to be aware of train crews' perspective on trackside safety.

Train drivers can also experience uncertainty in knowing whether a horn warning has been heard, for example when noisy equipment, such as a jackhammer or hand drill, is being used. Acknowledgement by trackside staff of a horn warning may be absent, indistinct or ambiguous. A trackside gang using noisy equipment, particularly with hearing protection, might also not hear a phone call from control in respect of train movements. In such cases the lookout needs to be close enough to all gang members to be able to use touch to warn them of the approach of a train.

### *Risk perception*

This topic is central to many aspects of trackside safety. For drivers on long sections of track characterized by very little variation or punctuated by occasional noteworthy events or situations, there is the problem of 'expecting the unexpected' – something that humans are not well designed for. Typically people adopt a variety of coping strategies when faced with long boring tasks, for example breaking them up into smaller units with defined reference points – as is done by at least some AR drivers.

A comparable problem for trackside workers acting as lookouts is maintaining attention levels when the number of trains encountered is low. The issue of judging accurately the arrival time of a train, travelling at say 80 kph, could also be a problem for inexperienced workers particularly on straight sections of track. Distances and arrival times tend to be underestimated. In situations where vigilance is required, typically a combination of human and technological components (e.g. early warning system) provides optimum protection.

A more general issue is that of maintaining employee awareness when there has not been a recent fatal accident. The dilemma is that to maximize their self-protective capacity, each trackside worker needs to feel personally vulnerable but not so much as to reduce their work effectiveness. This is partly a matter of safety culture within the group (see Guest, Peccei and Thomas 1994) and also HR issues such as selection, training and supervision of individual workers.

### *Safety of the public*

Protection officers looking after the safety of gangs working near station platforms have no authority over members of the public in the vicinity. Members of the public might use 'illegal' routes, for example across tracks as shortcuts. Enforcing trespass restrictions against members of the public is a problematic issue for AR. Drivers may report a trespass incident to control, but even if this is followed up – for which there may be no more than an *ad hoc* system – the transgressor may not be there when an AR staff member or police officer goes to look for them.

Road vehicle drivers are frequently encountered by AR train drivers at level crossings, typically trying to cross just before a train reaches the crossing. Train drivers may experience the dilemma of needing to warn a road vehicle driver in a potentially dangerous situation, e.g. on a crossing just in front of an oncoming train, while being aware that a horn warning might confuse the driver so that the vehicle is stopped foul of the track.

A general risk management problem for AR is educating the public in risk perception at crossings. The HSE (1996c) found that three categories of driver were likely to be involved in accidents at level crossings:

- those who are unwilling to stop because they believe they have plenty of time to cross before a train arrives;
- those who are unable to stop because they are too close to the stop line at the onset of amber, or because someone is driving too close behind;

- those who are unaware of the signals because they are inattentive or are distracted.

Other issues relating to trackside safety include:

- Knowledge of trackside workers, in practical terms, about stopping distances of trains. This involves accurate perception of the risk involved, estimation of train speeds and distances, and knowing the distances required to pull up trains of different types travelling at various speeds under various circumstances, some of which might be evident (e.g. wet weather, darkness) and others much less evident to trackside staff (e.g. trainee/inexperienced drivers, different types of rollingstock, poor driver visibility).
- Literacy problem, estimated to affect around 10 per cent of AR staff and perhaps an unknown number of contractors. Basic education needs to be considered here – an issue which is being addressed by AR.
- An indication that some contractors are not very conscientious at checking the location of underground pipes and cables. Contractors need to be educated in respect of best practice as proclaimed by AR and their competencies audited.

## *Communication*

AR has an excellent trackside communications system which uses a combination of radio and mobile phones for protection officers and others requiring it. However, different groups may follow slightly different procedures based upon previously learned practices. For example train controllers may imagine the risks taken by trackside workers and add the standard accepted safety margin of ten minutes onto the train times given to track section supervisors. Trackside workers soon learn that they have a ten-minute 'safety margin' and add the ten minutes back on to the times given – thereby negating the safety feature. A ten-minute break being perceived by trackside staff as a long absence from work is likely to be particularly lengthy when trackside work is being undertaken during breaks in say, a 30–minute train service – typical of city suburban services. In such cases, with the 'ten-minute safety margin' it could be expected that only about 18 minutes of work in every half hour could be carried out – representing a fairly modest level of productivity.

One potential problem is train controllers using different criteria when reporting train times to trackside workers. For example, when giving train times one controller may add on a ten-minute margin, another may add another couple of minutes (for example knowing that the trackside gang will take the first ten minutes off the time given) while a third may give exact train times – and a gang may then add ten minutes to this time! Recently appointed controllers might be more 'cautious' in respect of giving train times to supervisors, whereas more experienced controllers might give accurate train times and rely on trackside supervisors to clear the track in good time. Thus, communicating about this crucial aspect of safety might differ between train controllers. However, while it is important to support worksite safety by maintaining on-time running where possible, whatever train times are given there remains the possibility of unexpected delays. An overall risk issue involves balancing the cost of safety, represented by the amount of work which is lost during train movements, and production or maintenance requirements.

Train drivers receive information about trackside work on a weekly basis and, as the track situation changes daily, up to one third of the information thus provided may be incorrect by the time a driver receives it or needs to use it. Train controllers do not always know about track section restrictions and rely upon track section supervisors contacting them. The system depends upon each of the central parties involved – train controllers, drivers and track section supervisors – having accurate perceptions of the current state of the system at any given time.

## *Safety culture*

As in most of industry, work pressure within AR is continually increasing and changes such as large staff reductions might contribute to a changing organizational culture, including safety culture. At one level, safety culture is reflected in attitudes and perceptions among AR staff in the shared use of language. One example of the way in which shared language helps AR staff to cope with the worst consequences of accidents, fatal injuries, is to refer to those involved as having been 'cleaned up'. Use of such euphemistic phrases is common among groups who are regularly required to face the gruesome effects of violent death, such as staff in the emergency services.

The dedication and professionalism of many AR staff in respect of safety is impressive. However, there is evidence of considerable variation across the AR network and between areas. This is to be expected in an organization the size of, and with the geographical spread of AR. Guest, Peccei and Thomas (1994) found differences in safety culture between groups of trackside workers within the much smaller area of the UK rail network, which at the time of their study was owned and operated as a single company.

In a few areas it might be necessary to overcome 'cultural lag' in certain forms of work behaviour in respect of safety, such as wearing high visibility clothing when trackside. Another example might be improving manual handling safety by changing the 'macho' approach to work, perhaps involving two people to lift a sleeper. Human resource management issues relevant to this problem include recruitment and selection of staff as well as training, management discipline and personal responsibility. A related issue is perceptions of workers in respect of their treatment by the organization – for example, provision of adequate hygiene facilities for trackside workers, who are frequently required to work in physically unpleasant and occasionally unhealthy conditions.

Many safety culture concerns are intimately bound up with human resource management issues. For example a difficult safety problem to address could relate to AR's labour turnover – between 10 per cent and 15 per cent per annum across the whole organization and very much higher in some areas. This creates potential problems in developing a strong safety culture. Different categories of workers – permanent, temporary and contractors – are likely to have different work and safety motivation, and may also be treated differently by management, supervisors and work colleagues. Temporary workers may well be unfamiliar with AR work practices, and rely mainly upon existing staff to transmit these. There may also be ambiguities in respect of safety responsibilities which are not clarified. Formalizing documented induction programmes which include safety issues goes some way to alleviating these problems, although trackside culture is likely to have a far greater impact upon individuals' behaviour because it is experienced every working day.

A useful aim for AR would be to achieve a more unified safety culture and to develop appropriate strategies for achieving a stronger safety culture across the whole organization, at least to the standard of the best levels currently displayed. Part of AR's changing organizational culture is from control by direction to personal responsibility through acquisition of individual competencies. This represents a shift in the location of the onus of responsibility, for safety as for all aspects of work. Human resource systems (for example involving: performance management, personnel appraisal, selection and recruitment, training, employee involvement, supervision, reward and motivation) should be congruent with and support the changes involved.

## *Accident and incident data collection and analysis*

A strategic approach to data gathering involves having a definite view of what is to be achieved, including:

- clear goals from the top of the organization;
- specific, measurable objectives for a given time period;

- a valid means of measuring them – for example safety audits as well as reactive data;
- criteria for improvement – for example, for reactive data such as accidents or incidents, a statistical process control approach using control limits.

Safety objectives should be driven by a coherent corporate risk management strategy incorporated within AR's Corporate Safety Plan. Safety objectives should be in such a form that they can be measured – otherwise it cannot be known whether any improvement has occurred. Quantification is desirable when the data allow this. The strategy should include case examples of how reductions in accidents and incidents – such as derailments – will be made. Arrangements for ensuring accountability by allocating responsibilities among appropriate parties should also be detailed to demonstrate senior management commitment. The plan should also indicate what will happen if the objectives are not achieved.

Data enter the system in various forms, including memos, written accounts, completed proformas, official reports or telephone conversations. There is an unknown amount of under reporting. Clarke (1996) found that certain categories of incidents or hazards tended not to be reported by UK train drivers.

AR's present 'data warehouse' approach for all 'safety' (i.e. accident or incident) systems is 'bottom up' and reactive. Key questions about any accident or incident data collection system include:

- Why are these data being collected?
- Why are they collected in this way?
- What use are they (e.g. in prevention or strategic planning)?
- Can they be validly analysed and interpreted?
- Are they part of an integrated risk management system?

In general, an essential purpose behind a data warehouse is to scan large quantities of information to look for patterns that would be almost impossible to find manually – i.e. it is a potentially powerful statistical tool. Data warehouses are also used to deal with *ad hoc* queries and to identify hitherto unknown correspondences. One problem is knowing in advance how a system might be used, as usage of a data warehouse may be more extensive than originally envisaged. However, data warehouses can be expensive and may be subject to over-ambitious claims by suppliers. Set up costs tend to be high if duplication of databases held on other systems is involved. As with any complex technical system, humans will always be required to interpret and act upon information generated. Thus, there may be considerable costs involved in training staff to use the system effectively.

Among other issues relating to the data warehouse approach are that accident injuries and other incidents involving members of the public and AR plant and premises should be part of an integrated risk management approach. There are specific problems – for example in AR's case the problem of developing a definitive comprehensive listing of all level crossings on the network, given an unknown number of 'unofficial' crossings.

AR's present emphasis is upon data categorization and coding, particularly of 'hard' issues, rather than a system designed on the basis of a strategic approach to data to produce information which can lead to greater understanding as a basis for effective control and preventive action. Data categorization is on the basis of outcomes, including level crossing accidents, derailments, suicides, trackside incidents, passenger injuries, etc., rather than seeking to determine relevant underlying features of the organization which could influence such outcomes – for example, management style, decision-making processes, communication channels or risk levels.

In any organization it is desirable to collect data that will facilitate underlying accident mechanisms being revealed – 'latent errors' or 'resident pathogens' (Reason 1990), possibly related to human resource management issues, design of the work environment, socio-technical issues (e.g. Cox and Cox 1996; Toft and Reynolds 1997) or organizational changes. A coherent set of proactive data should help in the management of risk, for example an audit and inspection programme, supported by various monitoring measures. Both reactive and proactive measures are outlined in BS 8800 (BSI 1996). At the time of writing, Standards Australia is developing an Australian OHS Management Systems Standard.

While it is axiomatic that any accident and incident recording system for a large organization should be computerized, it is also important to ask certain key basic questions about any such system. These might include:

- What are data being collected for?
- Who can enter data?
- Who needs to access data?
- Are people adequately motivated to report accidents and incidents?
- If not, why not? And what is to be done about it?
- What analyses are to be carried out?
- What particular aspects of accidents or incidents is information required about?
- What happens to the data in the long term?

The present AR system classifies reported operational accidents/incidents into 11 modes, or outcomes, and 203 'causes'. These causes actually constitute proximate causes, that is events or situations immediately preceding an accident or incident (a potential or near accident). One problem with such a classification is that, in the absence of further investigation, there is no mechanism for evaluating possible underlying features.

If an accident or incident has more than one cause, as most if not all would do, then a reporting/recording system should allow these to be recorded – otherwise a large amount of useful information is being permanently lost. This makes the use of this source of data much less useful than it could or should be for improving safety and managing risk.

Where categories of accidents and causes mostly describe outcomes, they provide little or no opportunity for considering the accident process as an unfolding set of events. A 'mode-cause-reason' classification is unlikely to be very helpful in managing accident risks because different types of events may be included under the same heading. Frequently, emphasis is on carelessness of other parties (victims, road motor vehicle drivers, etc). A problem-solving approach to investigation may be supplanted by an adversarial approach if the prime objective is to claim from a road vehicle driver's insurance.

One way of overcoming at least some of these problems is to develop a system which incorporated thorough investigation of all accidents and incidents, according to a systematic model or set of criteria, explicitly designed to determine root causes – not merely proximate ones. A systematic model for recording root causes – for example Toft and Reynolds' (1994: 124) socio-technical failure minimization system – provides an opportunity for more in-depth analyses. Such a system could reasonably be expected to contribute significantly to a proactive approach to managing risk.

Design of accident and incident report forms needs to reflect answers to some of the basic questions considered above. The main purpose of any such system needs to be clear and consistent with other risk management objectives. Purposes of an accident reporting system might include:

- a basis for making insurance claims;
- apportioning blame between parties involved;
- understanding proximate and underlying causes;
- calculating costs associated with accidents and incidents;
- a basis for problem-solving investigation.

As some of these possible objectives may be conflicting, it needs to be clear to all parties which of them the system is designed to meet.

An accident reporting and recording system needs to relate to other risk management systems. Adopting a risk management approach involves developing continuous proactive measures, which in the long term should reduce reliance upon exclusively reactive measures of risk. In the short term it is important to develop a system for learning more from accidents and incidents. However, accidents should not be used as a performance measure.

### *Near miss reporting*

Even when a reporting and recording system is intended to capture incidents as well as accidents, the issue of when some event constitutes an incident might be problematic. For example if there is no personal injury then an event might not be reported as an incident even if there was the potential for injury to have occurred. Some train drivers might consider that they have a 'near miss' almost every day, many of these involving the public rather than AR staff. AR staff working trackside would usually know when to move out of the way of an oncoming train, and thus what from a driver's perspective might appear to be a 'near miss' might not in fact be considered as such by trackside staff. However, a comparable and apparently similar situation involving members of the public near to the tracks might well justifiably constitute a near miss.

Many other AR staff working trackside might – perhaps even unwittingly – have experienced near misses. An important issue is the extent to which such experiences may be collated and transmitted throughout an organization so as to become useful data and add to the stock of knowledge that can be used to reduce risk. A train judged to be speeding in a restricted section may be reported to a train controller but the total number of such incidents is unknown. Drivers should report situations in which trackside working is taking place without the required protection. However, it is known from a UK study of British Rail drivers (Clarke 1996) that such 'incidents' may not be reported.

Information about near misses which is transmitted via the 'grapevine', dissipates wider learning opportunities. Supervisors might hear of a near miss event and warn their own staff but such an incident may not go beyond the district. Large numbers of near misses may well occur with only the parties involved knowing about them.

Near misses may be considered to represent a layer near the base of the 'pyramid' of events which has fatal injury accidents at its apex. Within a strategic approach to managing risk, it is important to be able to tap into near miss events – which are at the margin between reactive and proactive measures of safety and risk. A near miss reporting system, examples of which are described in van der Schaaf *et al.* (1991) – see particularly the chapter by Taylor and Lucas on railways – could be a useful tool within the armoury of safety measures used within all railway organizations.

## Safety risks to railway operating companies

### *Hazards and threats (see chapter 2)*

Based on the foregoing description and discussion, the main safety hazards and threats to companies engaged in operating railways are:

*Investment and strategy*
Positive aspects include:

- Compatibility between long-term efficient and safe operations.
- Opportunity to integrate financial and safety aspects of risk at strategic level.
- Good return in respect of long-term safe operation compared with other modes of transport.

Key threats are:

- Typical large-scale expenditure involved – therefore important to make good decisions, for example by involving many parties with different expertise.
- Potential for major investment decisions to be subject to short-term influence, for example by political posturing or salience of particular incidents.

*Major accidents*
Positive aspects include:

- Possibility of learning from these, not just your own but from those experienced by other rail companies or networks.
- Opportunity for fundamental overhaul of safety provision and assessment of balance between operational, maintenance and safety issues.

Key threats are:

- Only addressing those elements of the system which relate to proximate causes of a major accident.
- Seeking to 'plug gaps' (e.g. revising procedures so that a particular accident does not recur) rather than using opportunities for fundamental appraisals of safety management systems.

*Safety management*
Positive aspects include:

- Opportunity to integrate safety management within a broader risk management function.

- Opportunity to involve staff at all levels in the safety management function and responsibilities.

Key threats are:

- Danger of viewing safety management as being solely or primarily the role of specialist safety staff rather than a line management responsibility first and foremost.
- Incomplete and fragmented SMS model.

### *Culture*

Positive aspects include:

- Opportunity to make incremental improvements to safety culture – unable to change this radically, at least in the short term.
- Seek to influence safety culture positively and involve employees at all levels.
- Seek positive-sum outcomes, for example use the best aspects of different safety cultures represented in different parts of the organization.

Key threats are:

- Using an inappropriate model of culture, for example one that only addresses attitudes rather than behaviour, or trying to change the whole organization at once rather than reinforcing groups that are already changing culture.

### *Power relations*

Positive aspects include:

- Use of autonomous work groups – for example, rail construction or maintenance gangs; empowering staff to take decisions and action as necessary – for example, station staff or train drivers.

Key threats are:

- Assuming that a unitary perspective prevails throughout the organization.
- Seeking to improve rules and procedures by diktat rather than by involvement and empowerment of staff.

### *Change*

Positive aspects include:

- Opportunities to be proactive in making changes.

Key threats are:

- Overall tendency to be slow to change as the industry is not fast-moving in respect of basic operations or technology.
- Inertia culture within particular rail companies.

### *Risk assessment (see chapter 2)*

The following table summarizes potential risk levels for the threats discussed above. Attributed risk levels are based on the authors' judgements. Both positive and negative outcomes for any given threat may co-exist.

| **Threat** | **Potential risk levels** (as probabilities) | |
|---|---|---|
| | **Positive outcomes** | **Negative outcomes** |
| Investment strategy | Medium-High | Medium-High |
| Major accidents | Low | Medium-High |
| Safety management | Medium | Medium-High |
| Culture | Medium | Medium-High |
| Power relations | Medium | Medium-High |
| Change | Medium-High | Medium-High |

## Comparison with thematic matrix

Table 12.5 indicates the relative salience of each of the risk contexts identified in Part 1, and particularly chapter 9, in relation to the case study of railway safety. In the table, H = high, M = medium, L = low.

## Conclusions

Given the numbers of people simultaneously exposed, mass public transport is likely to continue to be the site of future disasters and major accidents. However, railway accident inquiries, traditionally oriented towards ensuring that a repetition of a particular accident is avoided, have made an important radical departure in the shape of the Fennell and Hidden inquiries. These reports herald a new era of identifying underlying factors in rail accidents with a view to managing risk more broadly and seeking to prevent not only a repetition of a particular type of accident but also to reduce the occurrence of all accidents. The approach is proactive rather than purely reactive.

*Table 12.5* Thematic matrix applied to railway safety case study

| *Risk context* | *Salience in case study* |
|---|---|
| *Organizational environment* | |
| Economies and markets | H |
| Public policy, legislation and regulation | H |
| Social and political climate | H |
| Technology | M |
| History, operating territories and conditions | H |
| *Human factors* | |
| Culture | H |
| Power relations, political processes and decision-making | H |
| Perception and cognition | H |
| *Formal coping arrangements* | |
| Risk management | H |
| Risk assessment | H |
| Management systems | H |
| Approaches to change | H |

While a considerable amount of learning already occurs between rail companies, there will continue to be scope for learning from more extensive analysis of accident data both in breadth and in depth. This includes alertness to 'precursor' accidents from the industry globally. An element of learning relates to safety culture within a rail company. While difficult to define, safety culture may be viewed as the organizational mirror in which safety and risk strategy is reflected.

While a risk management approach, and risk assessments and safety cases in particular, have become part of managing the risks of rail transport within the past ten years, a number of broader political issues have also become manifest. One of these is the issue of conflicting priorities for resources. Here public visibility can have a powerful role. For example, large numbers of lives lost or people injured in a single incident tend to have a much higher public visibility than do the same numbers killed or injured in many different incidents. Rail passenger deaths and injuries have higher public visibility than do the same number of rail company employee deaths and injuries.

Partly because of the large-scale nature of investment in the rail industry and because of the potentially conflicting interests of several parties with interests in operational and safety aspects of rail transport, rail safety is a political issue. For example, when a major and dramatic accident occurs, as at King's Cross, there is understandable public demand for rapid response from politicians. However, given that resources are limited there can be resultant conflicts in respect of safety improvements which are legislation-driven compared with those that are indicated by risk assessment processes. Calculating costs incurred to save each notional life is one measure which may be applied to determine the relative merit of potentially competing safety interventions. However, one hope is that with signs of continuous improvement across all aspects of risk management within the rail industry, more long term safety projects will be possible.

# Chapter 13
# Iran: a risk profile

## Overview

This chapter presents as a risk profiling case study the opportunities and difficulties faced by the Islamic Republic of Iran as an emergent industrial nation and by western trading nations and organizations seeking to do business with Iran. The perspective of the text naturally is that of the authors who are from a western culture. However, it is hoped that with the benefit of first-hand experience in Iran over the past 25 years sufficient insight into the all-important Iranian perspective is offered which offsets the authors' own biases. Description and discussion are developed which focus on risk contexts leading to analysis in terms of the thematic matrix (see chapter 9).

## Introduction

Why is this chapter significant to this book and its aims? The Islamic Republic of Iran is an important example of an emerging industrial economy which potentially represents one of the largest markets for foreign goods in the Middle East. The UK World Trade Review (Export Times 1997) ranked Iran forty-fourth out of 200 countries with a 23% increase in UK exports to Iran in the first half of 1997 compared with 1996. Iran also offers a relatively stable and safe gateway to other markets in Central Asia which South East Asian economies in particular are keen to use. Yet, difficulties have arisen because the Iranian government has embarked on an assertive policy based on the fundamental precepts of Islam which western governments and companies have generally not understood or have reacted against. For example, Iran has been portrayed in the media in the USA and the UK as a renegade state having malevolent intentions towards the West and having few redeeming features. Effectiveness of trade in world markets depends on understanding of history and geo-politics and particular regional and national contexts which affect a range of risk issues. However, we shall argue that ethno-centrism and 'cultural aggression' (Mara'shi 1995) are inappropriate stances for companies to take towards what, for them, may appear to be difficult and risk-laden foreign markets.

Iran was selected for a case study chapter because it has strategic significance (politically, economically, theologically and militarily) lying as it does between Iraq, Turkey and Saudi Arabia in the West and Afghanistan and Pakistan in the east, and between Russia and CIS states in the north and the Indian Ocean in the south (see Fig. 13.1). Iran presents many of the risk issues which foreign companies are likely to face in doing business with economies which do not share western culture or political ideologies. On a more practical and mundane level, one of the authors has longstanding personal and professional interests in Iran and its people and is a regular visitor to that country. Iran and its current development therefore provided an ideal case study.

The Islamic Republic of Iran has embarked on a major programme of industrial and economic development and in 1996 began to implement its second five-year

*Fig 13.1* Iran and neighbouring countries

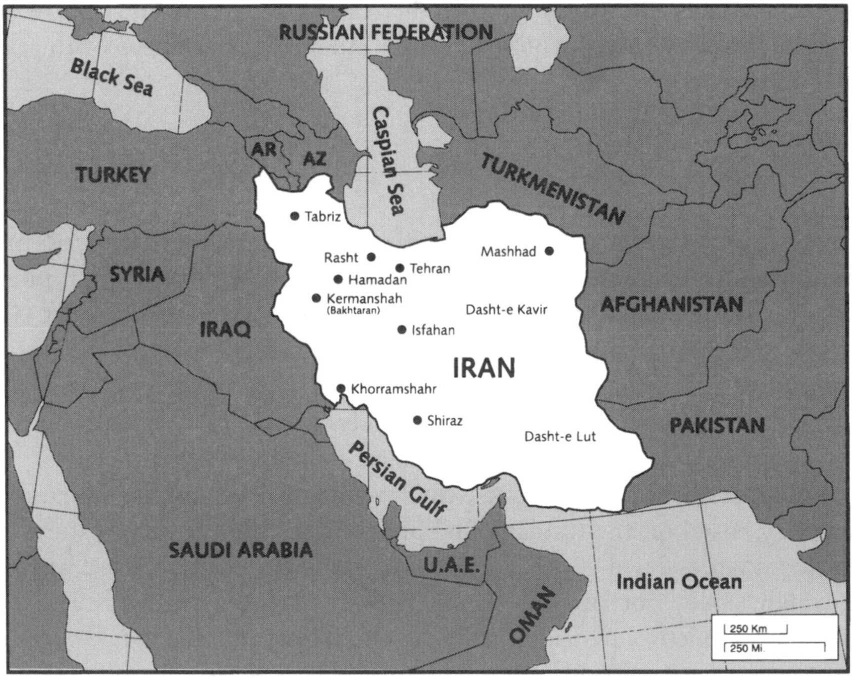

Plan (IRI-PBO 1996). The 'economy without oil' policy seeks to ensure that an economy almost totally dependent on oil and gas revenues will gradually become more self-sufficient and balanced, with the development of an array of downstream industries and manufactured products for export. Privatization of state-controlled industries is also underway and such companies must now survive and thrive within the private sector. The need to reduce avoidable loss and make sound speculative decisions (political, economic, business, financial, social, etc) suggests that strategic risk management will have an important role to play in the management of change within the Islamic Republic (Waring and Mehdizadeh 1996) – see chapters 1 and 7.

The remainder of this chapter seeks to discuss the present situation in Iran both from an Iranian risk perspective and from that of foreign companies doing business with Iran. A summary of the historical and cultural contexts of Iran follows which seeks to enable a better understanding of the present-day risk situation. General lessons to be learned about managing risks of trade with emergent economies are also outlined.

## Historical and cultural background

### *Cultural characteristics*

Over the past 3,000 years, Persia (now known as Iran) created two great empires and was itself fought over and conquered by a succession of invaders – Greeks, Mongols, Arabs. Each phase has left its mark on Iranian culture and language. The ethnic mix in Iran today includes, as minorities, Turks and Kurds in the north west, Caucasians and Azeris in the Azerbaizhan region, Armenians throughout the country, and Arabs in the south west. Armenians form the main Christian minority but there are also the Christian *ashouri*, descendants of the ancient Assyrians from Babylon.

Eight characteristics of Iranian culture are prominent:

- valuation of time;
- sociability;
- attitudes towards women;
- modernism;
- religious faith;
- risk taking;
- bargaining;
- emotionality.

Of these eight characteristics, the last five are especially important to an understanding of risk in relation to Iran, and are outlined below.

### *Modernism*

Westerners tend to think of Iran as epitomizing the residues of antiquity. Ancient Persia rivalled ancient Greece both in the strength and extent of its empire and in its contribution to art, science, philosophy and many other aspects of culture. Although this ancient heritage is certainly recognized by present day Iranians, an overwhelming modernist materialism pervades their society. There is a thirst for every latest technological gadget, consumer product and fashionable item, all of which are usually sourced in the West and hard to acquire. This materialism is a cultural trait which arose during the Shah's regime in the 1960s and which the present fundamentalist regime seeks to curb (IRI-PBO 1996). On the one hand, the 'hardline' faction (see later) would like to see a return to simple spiritual values in which western materialism is excised from the national psyche. On the other hand, the 'pragmatists' led from 1989 to 1997 by the then President Rafsanjani would like to develop a new Islamic consumerism in which consumer demand is partly satisfied by imports but increasingly by Iranian products. In the new consumerist culture, goods such as fast moving consumer goods, foodstuffs, cars and home entertainment products would become more widely available in a controlled way. Products deemed by the present regime to be un-Islamic and tawdry such as $200 'Barbie' dolls, American fast-food outlets and music and videos with any level of sexual content would continue to be banned.

### *Religion*

Iran is a predominantly Shi'ite Muslim country with significant numbers belonging to minority religions such as Christian (Armenian, Assyrian, and Catholic) and Zardosht (Zoroastrian). Religious faith forms an important part of the culture. The fundamentalist government rejects all forms of secularism. The underlying religious conservatism of the majority population, which values its Muslim identity and an implicit rejection of foreign secular philosophies, seems to contradict the modernist materialism so evident in everyday life. Yet although the fundamentalists claim that the two positions are mutually exclusive, the population at large does not appear to recognize any ambiguity. The population generally appears to be seeking a tolerable mid-point between two extremes: it has had enough of fundamentalist dogma and its adverse consequences on the economy and social freedoms but does not want to return to the abandonment and anti-social excesses which accompanied the Shah's regime. In particular, even those professed Muslims who reject the fundamentalist ideology tend to be very patriotic and equally reject any suggestion of a return to a state serving American interests (as was clearly the case with the Shah's regime).

### *Risk taking*

As noted in chapters 4 and 8, risk perception, cognition and behaviour towards risks are not context-free. The historical and present day contexts of Iran have created a populace having a complex but overall more risk-oriented attitude than in western countries. With economic instability, high price inflation and a limited and ineffective social security system, making significant financial gain is a high priority for most people in Iran. In such conditions, investment in property and stockpiling of consumer goods became the most popular hedge against inflation. In the period 1993–96, for example, property prices in Tehran trebled and became similar to those in London. Speculative and entrepreneurial risk-taking are culturally ingrained in Iran to the extent that it is common practice for individuals, including company employees, to have interests in several different business ventures. The fledgling Tehran Stock Exchange is an example of one of the world's emerging markets (Ehteshami 1995; Mehdizadeh 1995), with 250 companies registered by 1997.

Crimes of physical violence are rare in Iran. However, seeking to gain financial advantage by fraud or embezzlement has become much more prevalent and represents the main security risk for foreign companies doing business there. Corruption of officials on low wages is always a temptation. A prominent case was the multi-million dollar fraud against Bank-e Saderat for which one of the perpetrators was found guilty and executed early in 1996. Another concerned the owner of the Dolatkhah Company who swindled 7,000 investors out of approximately £175m for which he was sentenced to death in 1997. Attitudes towards personal safety are also generally more risk-oriented than in the West. Evidence which may be cited for this includes:

- Widespread bad driving (e.g. competitive driving and driving without lights).
- Consumer products with unsafe designs (e.g. electrical hazards and sharp edges ignored in deference to aesthetic appeal).
- Large scale personal sacrifice during the Iran-Iraq War (see below).

### *Deal seeking*

Making deals and driving hard bargains is characteristic of the *bazari* (wholesaler) and *bazargani* (commercial) sub-culture which extends way beyond the bazaars and into every facet of life and almost every family. In the Iranian context, the term *bazargani* needs to be interpreted more as a systematic 'dealer' or 'agent' than a shopkeeper. Iranian entrepreneurship focuses mainly on dealing – i.e. buying and selling in the product distribution chain, and traditionally the *bazaris* and *bazarganis* have dominated product markets and prices. Increasing concern about the stranglehold of the distribution system on the economy and the imbalance *vis-à-vis* the production system has been raised in relation to effectiveness of the five-year plans (Mara'shi 1995, 1997). However, the *bazari* culture is pervasive and extends into the upper echelons of government. Former President Rafsanjani, for example, heads a family import-export firm. It is therefore difficult to see how a significant shift in favour of manufacturing industry might occur with such powerful interests involved.

### *Emotionality*

In general, Iranian culture is non-violent in contrast to some of the more sensationalist portrayals by western media. For example, crimes of violence such as armed robbery, muggings and sexual assault are uncommon. In the experience of one of the authors, it is safe to walk unaccompanied in the street at any time of the day or night in Tehran. Foreigners are also treated with courtesy and traditional Iranian hospitality.

There are two topics, however, which are likely to inflame passions among Iranians: sovereignty and identity. It is these very same topics about which the 'man-in-the-street' feels particularly aggrieved in relation to western attitudes and actions and this affects a range of risk issues. There is a widespread feeling that the West respects neither Iranian sovereignty nor the religious tenor of Iranian cultural identity.

## *Sovereignty*

Since the mid-1700s up to the fall of the last Shah in 1979, foreign influence in Iran was predominantly British, although during the Pahlavi era American influence grew to rival that of Britain. However, in modern times, Iran has never been part of a foreign empire and therefore has no independence day. British influence can be traced back to expansion of the British Empire. The East India Company based in India became a *de facto* front for British political and territorial expansion which included territories in and around the Persian Gulf. For example, a British Political Agent operating through the East India Company was resident in Bandar Abbas by the 1750s (Mojtahed-Zadeh 1995).

The issue of Iranian sovereignty over its southern offshore islands in the Gulf was assumed by Iran to have been settled in the mid-1800s. According to Mojtahed-Zadeh (1995), the British were in no doubt about Iran's undisputed sovereignty over Bandar Lengeh and its dependent ports and islands, as demonstrated by a map produced by the acting British Political Resident in the Persian Gulf, Captain S. Hennell, as part of a maritime truce signed on 21 August 1835. His map specified the ports of Lengeh, Laft, Charak, as well as the islands of Qeshm, Tunb and Abu Musa as possessions of Iran. Further official British maps, including an Admiralty map of 1881, continued to show Iranian sovereignty over these territories. Around 1902, Great and Little Tunb and Abu Musa were annexed by Sharjah, then a British territory. Iranian protests over the islands continued until 1971 when Britain withdrew from the Gulf and the United Arab Emirates were established. The 1971 Memorandum of Understanding granted joint management of Abu Musa to Iran and Sharjah and subsequently joint management of Abu Musa and the two Tunbs to Iran and the UAE. Iran occupied the Tunbs in 1971 and has held de facto control of them ever since.

Despite Iran's historical claims to sovereignty over the islands of Abu Musa and the two Tunbs, in 1992 the Persian Gulf Cooperation Council (created after 1979 partly for containment of Iran) issued a statement claiming that the Tunb islands belonged to the UAE. This dispute remains unresolved and has upset Iran considerably. Not only have Iran-UAE tensions been raised but so also has Iran's mistrust of western nations who, from an Iranian perception, now appear to be taking sides on this issue. As McLachlan (1994) notes, there has been a large measure of US, European and Arab insensitivity to a valid Iranian desire for self-defence regarding its offshore islands. The present British position, however, is that it has no locus standi in this dispute and wishes for a peaceful settlement acceptable to both sides.

The strategic significance of these offshore islands has not been lost on Iran or the other countries involved in or influencing the territorial dispute. Significant sub-sea gas fields have been located in the area quite apart from the islands' military significance, lying as they do in a commanding position midway across the Gulf as it narrows into the Strait of Hormuz. As Mojtahed-Zadeh (1995) notes

> Given the location of Abu Musa and the two Tunbs in the strategically sensitive Strait of Hormuz, and given that both the regional countries of the Persian Gulf and the oil-consuming countries of the industrial world depend heavily on peace and security in the Strait of Hormuz, outside support for either side in this argument against the other could easily lead to a conflict potentially as explosive as the Kuwait crisis of 1990–91. The Iranians have

> warned the political leaders of the United States and Europe of the danger of hinting support for one side in this issue.

The official Iranian view is that security in the Gulf should be for all, otherwise all will be insecure.

From an Iranian perspective, the current territorial disputes over Abu Musa and the Tunbs epitomise perpetual foreign threats against Iranian territorial integrity stirred up by western powers seeking to serve their own interests. Hardline elements in the government point to treachery by western powers reneging on long-standing positions and treaties concerning Iranian sovereignty. Annexation of the Iranian mainland by Russia and Britain during the First World War and by the Allies during World War II (the Russians in the north and the British in the south) is also a reminder that Iranian sovereignty is vulnerable to military threat by foreign powers who believe that their strategic interests are critically threatened. These issues are examined further in the sections on the Iran-Iraq War and external relations.

## *The Pahlavi era 1926–1979*

### *Reza Khan Pahlavi*

Throughout the nineteenth century, Iran had been in steady decline as a regional power. British influence increased unabated. The opening up of the oil fields, the establishment of Iran's first oil refinery at Abadan and the formation of the Anglo-Iranian Oil Company in 1909 (see Bamberg 1994) sealed Iran's economic dependence on and political domination by Britain. Out of this humiliation stepped Reza Khan Pahlavi, an army officer who in 1921 headed a coup and then in 1926 ousted the Qajar monarchy.

Pronouncing himself Shah (king), Reza Pahlavi embarked on a western-inspired modernization programme founded on a military style, almost fascist, discipline. Roads, railways, hospitals, schools and universities were to be built as infrastructure. Aspects of religious culture which he regarded as symbols of Muslim feudalism, such as the *chador* covering for females and beards on men, were outlawed. Opponents were treated ruthlessly.

Reza Shah wanted to remain neutral in the Second World War but the Allies were suspicious of his fascist leanings and the potential for Iran as a strategic territory in the Middle East to fall under German control. On 25 August 1941, Iran was annexed by the Allies, Russia taking control of the northern part and Britain the south. Reza Shah abdicated and was sent into exile in South Africa where he died in 1944.

### *Mohammed Reza Pahlavi*

Reza Shah's son, Mohammed Reza Pahlavi, born in 1919 was western educated. On his father's abdication, Mohammed Reza, although still in his twenties, became Crown Prince and constitutional monarch of Iran under Allied occupation.

Mohammed Reza Shah saw himself as a visionary and agent of change. Iran was still a rurally-focused feudalistic country in which peasant farmers and villagers traditionally worked land owned by large landowners and paid religious taxes and tithes to the muslim clergy, many of whom were also landowners. Some had become both wealthy and powerful as a result, a situation which they wanted to maintain. He recognized that land reform was a high priority in creating a modern western-style economy. Early in his reign, for example, he gave away crown lands to peasant farmers in order to set an example. However, such actions and attitudes made enemies and he narrowly survived an assassination attempt in 1949.

### *Rise of nationalism*

In the turbulent post-War politics of Iran, nationalism was on the ascendant. Growing public resentment about foreign domination became focused on the question of ownership of Iranian oil and the large imbalance of revenues to the Anglo-Iranian Oil Company compared with royalties to Iran. In the early 1950s, a leading nationalist politician, Dr Mohammed Moussadegh, led a popular campaign for oil nationalization which eventually threatened to turn into an anti-Shah campaign as public pressure for nationalization was stalled. To appease the Iranian public, the Shah appointed Moussadegh as Prime Minister but in retaliation Anglo-Iranian withdrew from the Abadan refinery and organized a world-wide ban on purchases of Iranian oil (see Bamberg 1994).

### *Anglo-American plot 1953*

The US government regarded Moussadegh as a communist agent and therefore likely to turn Iran into a pro-Russian state. The American CIA and British MI6 were heavily implicated in a plot in 1953 to remove Moussadegh (*Janes Sentinel* 1995) but the plot backfired as Moussadegh's supporters were victorious and the Shah fled to Rome. However, within two days pro-monarchists backed by loyal army units took to the streets and routed the nationalists. Moussadegh was arrested and put on trial.

The legacies of the 1953 plot and counter-coup are of particular importance to understanding Iran today. In particular, in Iranian eyes, the affront of open CIA involvement was then compounded by the US government pouring in millions of dollars in aid and military advisers to prop up the Shah. Whatever economic or other benefits might have arisen from American involvement, a grumbling resentment remained about American interference and domination of the Shah which was to fester and later solidify as a component in the 1979 revolution.

### *The White Revolution*

In 1961, the Shah, backed by the US government, embarked on a programme of modernization called '*enghelab-e sefid*' or White Revolution. This programme included many of the elements from his earlier years and those of his father, namely land reform, female emancipation, public health, literacy and education, and a western-style economy. Throughout the 1960s and early 1970s, the White Revolution gathered momentum. Whenever he felt necessary, the Shah rode roughshod over opposition and criticism with decrees, arrests and press censorship. The wealthy classes, encouraged by the Shah's policy, adopted all the trappings of western liberalism. General prosperity increased as oil prices rose and the economy grew but the families of entrepreneurs, industrialists and western-educated professionals benefited most while the masses were kept in their place – economically and politically. Ostentatious wealth, consumption and western life styles became almost competitive among the wealthy. The relatively poor masses with traditionally conservative Muslim views looked on aghast and with increasing resentment at the proliferation of western materialism and associated life style such as night clubs, discos, alcohol and mini-skirted women.

The Shi'ite Muslim clergy who offerred a traditional source of comfort and support to the masses were themselves increasingly resistant to the Shah's programme. This was not only on ideological grounds but also because, in some cases, land reforms threatened the traditional wealth and feudal authority in the villages enjoyed by some of the clergy. Opposition to the Shah became focused on the holy city of Qom where a mullah named Ruhollah Moussavi al-Khomeini accused the Shah of acting against Islamic law. In 1963, Ayatollah Khomeini was arrested – an event which sparked off large-scale riots. Hundreds died when the army was called in to restore order. Khomeini was exiled to Najaf in Iraq where he became the rallying point for opposition to the Shah on an argument that the only salvation for Iran from cultural, political and economic anihilation by the West was a return to fundamental Islamic values and governance.

By the early 1970s, the gulf between the Shah and his retinue and supporters on the one hand and the masses on the other had widened, even though Iran was enjoying increasing prosperity. Unable to achieve rapid change through democratic means and popular co-operation, increasingly he ruled by decree and by 1974 had created a one-party state. The pace of cultural change being forced by the Shah was too fast and the growing disparity between rich and poor was becoming too apparent. The masses and, increasingly, western-educated professionals saw the Shah's White Revolution not only as hollow but also as a device which would expunge Iranian culture and replace it with a copy of western culture. This fear of loss of cultural identity became known in Iran as 'Westoxification' and this fear is as relevant today under the Islamic government as it was then (see for example tribute to Ayatollah Motahhari, *Tehran Times* 2 May 1996 and Ayatollah Seyed Ali Khameini's address on the 6th anniversary of the Islamic Propagation Organisation, *Tehran Times* 21 June 1997). Whereas under the Shah 'Westoxification' was seen as the consequence of simply believing and accepting that western values were superior, today there is additional concern that western values are being forced on Iran by the West as a form of 'cultural aggression' (Mara'shi 1995; Zarif 1996).

### *Popular anti-Shah revolution*

By the mid-seventies, the economic boom had stopped and in 1977 Khomeini felt bold enough to call for the monarchy to be overthrown. Anti-Shah demonstrations in Qom were put down by the army with a number of deaths. Further demonstrations by pro-Khomeini religious groups then followed with secular groups joining in. Within weeks, opposition to the Shah had surfaced in the form of strikes and unrest throughout the country and martial law was declared. On one day early in January 1979, an estimated 1.5 million people demonstrating against the Shah marched through the streets of Tehran. The Shah was forced into exile while an interim government awaited the arrival of Ayatollah Khomeini from his own exile in Paris. The Shah died of cancer in Egypt on 27 July 1980.

The fall of the Shah developed over years and, with such a long build up, it may seem surprising that the West did not anticipate it. Although western countries, particularly the United States and Britain, knew that the Shah had opponents, they believed that with western support the Shah could retain control. However, the West did not appreciate the depth of feeling among the population about their cultural identity and underestimated the power of the mullahs through championing the cause of identity to marshal the national will. The popular view in the West that the 1979 revolution was all about religion is misguided.

## The Islamic Republic

### *The Republic's formation*

Following the 1979 revolution, the interim coalition government of nationalists, fundamentalists and mujaheddin lasted only a short time before the Revolutionary Council took outright control. By 1981, an Islamic Republic had been declared and fundamentalist policies were enacted which included the closing of night clubs and casinos, the banning of alcohol, and the banning of books and films portraying sexual licence. Women were required to cover their body with a *chador* or equivalent and to ensure that their hair was not showing. Wearing of lipstick, nail varnish and sunglasses in public was banned, although this restriction is now rarely enforced. Women were forbidden to be alone with men to whom they were not married or closely related. Boys and girls were segregated in schools and men and women were separated on public transport and in other public places.

All the life-style restrictions and requirements exemplified above, plus nationalization of businesses and loss of political freedoms, came as a shock to the wealthy, western-educated professionals, businessmen and liberals, many of whom had supported the overthrow of the Shah with the expectation that a secular Muslim state based on parliamentary democracy would follow. Thousands went into self-imposed exile in the West. To a large extent, members of that same class who stayed in Iran have retained their values intact ever since and keep a low profile while waiting for change. Without the expertise of such people, the Islamic Republic would have experienced even greater economic difficulties than it has. They kept the country running throughout the Iran-Iraq War and after, and enabled the five-year plans to operate, albeit falteringly. As a result they have been left alone provided that they make no political challenge to the government. A kind of uneasy truce reigns between the fundamentalist government and the wealthy, pragmatic elite whose existence acts as a constant reminder of the failings of religious ideologues in running the country. Nevertheless, hardline fundamentalists such as Major General Mohsen Reza-i, commander of the Islamic Revolutionary Guard Corps, blamed (11 April 1996) such 'liberals' and their culture for failures in national reconstruction and indentified them as revolutionary targets because they were a 'cancerous tumour' which had never been 'seriously grappled with by the authorities' (reported in *Kayhan International* 13 April 1996).

## *The fundamentalist philosophy*

In seeking to understand the Islamic Republic, western attention, particularly by the media, has focused critically on life-style requirements and restrictions. These manifestations are easy to judge by western standards but they reveal little of the essence of the republic's philosophy and the challenge it represents to western assumptions about such topics as individual freedoms, economic development, production and distribution, national and international security, and a new 'world order'. As the section on the principles of Islamic governance below discusses further, the Islamic Republic is founded on lofty ideals of fundamental Islamic faith and the conviction that everyone's beliefs, life style and behaviour are inseparable from religion and God (Khameini 1996; Mara'shi 1995). The corollary is that government policy and actions must also be based closely on religious philosophy. In the fundamentalists' view, there can be no such thing as a secular government in a Muslim country such as Iran. To fundamentalists, a 'secular Islamic state' is an oxymoron just as much as to them a professed Muslim who drinks alcohol, even occasionally, is not a true Muslim.

The cornerstone of the government's philosophy is the principle of *velayat-e faghih* or the right of the supreme religious jurisprudent as head of the Guardian Council to 'guide' the Majlis (parliament) on the religious and Qur'anic basis of temporal policy. Ayatollah (now Imam) Khomeini held this supreme role until his death in 1989 which is now enacted by Ayatollah Ali Husseini Khameini. In 1994, Ayatollah Khameini also became spiritual leader of all Shi'ite Muslims in the world, thus increasing his personal political power in determining government policy and 'clipping the wings' of the more moderate incumbent President Ali Akbar Hashemi Rafsanjani. Constitutionally, President Rafsanjani could not stand for re-election in 1997 although he was the most popular choice. Moderate fundamentalists and ordinary Muslims in Iran feared that if a hardline president replaced him it would lead to Iran becoming isolated, politically and economically, and end in economic ruin. At the time of writing, the outcome of this election had just been announced (see following section).

Hardliners share an immutable belief that the fundamentals of Islam are divinely ordained and therefore cannot be debated let alone changed. This assertion makes the entire religious framework of government, based on the fundamentalists' belief in the indivisibility of religion and politics, self-justifying and self-sustaining (see chapter 5, the section on powerful interests and risk). Ordinary mortal base motivations such as power and greed in political life can easily be denied by reference to such standards as the spiritual leadership of *velayat-e faghih* and the

Qur'an. The fundamentalists claim that they constantly strive for a spiritually-based perfection in their temporal life. Cynics and critics argue that whereas some clearly do, others may use fundamentalism simply to acquire and maintain power, wealth and privilege.

## *The Majlis*

Iran is governed by a parliament (the Majlis) but it is not a parliamentary democracy as understood in the West. Members of the Majlis are elected by popular vote but only political groups and candidates approved by the Guardian Council of the Majlis can stand for election. For example, the Liberation Movement of Iran continues to be ineligible. The two largest approved groups are:

- Jaame-e Rohaniyat-e Mobarez (JRM, Society of Spiritual Fighters).
- Kargozaran-e Sazandegi (G6 Group, Servants of Iran's Construction headed by Rafsanjani).

In the 1996 elections for the 5th Majlis, 25 million out of 32 million eligible voted, representing a 78 per cent turnout (*Tehran Times*). Foreign independent observers reported that the elections were administered fairly. The results of the two-stage elections left G6 and JRM with roughly equal numbers of seats totalling approximately 75 per cent, the rest spread among other groups. Iranian official media described the balance in the Majlis as demonstrating a healthy diversity of views whereas others might argue that, with the exclusion of non-approved candidates and groups, it merely represents shades of fundamentalist opinion.

The 5th Majlis has continued the same foreign policies as before but has reviewed its internal policies, primarily economic development and social policy. The success of the new G6 group effectively meant that Rafsanjani pragmatists increased their power in relation to the conservatives and hardliners. However, 'pragmatists' and 'hardliners' are not labels recognized or accepted within the regime, but one used in the West for ease of explanation to a public audience who might otherwise find the nuances of Iranian politics impenetrable – see Ehteshami (1995) for detailed discussion.

At the time of writing, the 1997 presidential elections had just taken place and former President Rafsanjani had become chairman of the Expediency Council, the supreme assembly for the protection of the Islamic Republic. Majlis Speaker Ayatollah Nategh-Noori, a relative hardliner compared to Rafsanjani and representing JRM, was originally considered to be the likely winning candidate. However, Ayatollah Mohammed Khatami, a relatively liberal candidate and close associate of Rafsanjani, caught the public mood for change and swept to office on a popular vote, including women voters and many voters who had refused to vote since 1979. However, it should be noted that real power still rests with more conservative elements such as Ayatollah Khameini and the prospect of significant liberalization remains fragile.

## *Factions and influence (see chapter 5)*

Like governments the world over, the Iranian government is not a monolithic entity having no shades of opinion. Ideological power factions exist within ministries and often interpret policy differently. However, 'moderate/pragmatist' and 'hardline/purist' divisions are not clear-cut and may vary from issue to issue. There are also inter-ministerial rivalries (Ehteshami 1995). Such factionalism can make foreign trade deals difficult as most imports require government approval. For example, one ministry may wish to buy personal computer equipment from abroad. In the final stages of approving the importation, the Telecommunications Ministry could quash the deal on the grounds that the PCs contain modem chips and are therefore subject to their Ministry's prior approval.

In addition to ideological factionalism and rivalries, family connections are at least as important a factor in understanding how the government's administration works and the risk issues which may be involved. Iran is a family-centred culture in which families tend to be large and a family's traditional social status carries great weight. Many families regarded traditionally as powerful have names indicating their regional origins, for example Rafsanjani, Golpeygani, Ardebili, Shirazi. This long-standing social, political and economic power often arose as a result of family members becoming mullahs. What is different today is the fact that mullahs and their families have risen from being local power figures to become all-powerful from top to bottom of the administration which not only controls government contracts but also approves most import deals. It is traditional for people to use family connections to gain advantage and no less so under the present regime. Anecdotes abound of tenders for lucrative government contracts worked on assiduously for months and years by qualified bidders being handed at the last minute to someone who happens to be connected to a minister or senior official. Factionalism, rivalries and vested interests represent major business risks for foreign companies bidding for contracts, as they will often be required to work through Iranian partners or agents and it is difficult to assess the latter's status in relation to the bidding process and powerful interests which may intervene.

## The Iran-Iraq War 1980–88

### *Blitz on Khuzestan*

In many ways, the Iran-Iraq War provided a catalyst which ensured completion of the Islamic revolution. National survival became coincident with survival of the revolution. The initial attack by Iraqi forces took place in September 1980 on the twin ports of Khorramshahr/Abadan in Khuzestan, the province at the head of the Persian Gulf. The Iraqi leader Saddam Hussein predicted that the war would be over in four days. Instead, it lasted eight years – much longer than World War II. In the Khorramshahr attack, Iraqi forces were soon bogged down by ferocious hand-to-hand and house-to-house resistance from local townspeople and *pasdaran* (revolutionary guards) often armed with little more than pistols, RPGs and molotov cocktails, according to personal accounts of survivors given to the authors. The defence of Khorramshahr held out for 40 days before falling to the Iraqis and the city was dubbed 'Khuninshahr' or 'the city of blood' because of the high civilian casualties. A mass evacuation of the civilian population of Khuzestan to Tehran and other cities took place. The battle for Khorramshahr lasted over two years and was the bloodiest since Stalingrad. Iranian strategy was to block, exhaust and tie down the Iraqi forces using tactics such as waves of suicide squads of *baseeji* (volunteer mobilized forces). It was finally recaptured in 1982. On the day of recapture alone, 18,000 Iraqi prisoners were reported taken in the Khorramshahr enclave. Little of the bloody struggle for 'Khuninshahr' and the indelible impact it has had on the Iranian people is known in the West, which may partly explain western misunderstandings of the Iranian world-view in relation to foreign aggression.

### *Reasons for the Iraqi attack*

A number of explanations for the Iraqi attack on Iran are possible. The general view in the West has been that Saddam Hussein's political and military strength had increased compared with his position in 1975 when he signed a pact in Algiers with the Shah (Ehteshami 1995). His attack is therefore widely regarded in the West as opportunistic adventurism seeking to secure Iraq's access to the Gulf.

The view of the Iranian anti-revolutionary movement (the *mujaheddin khalq* based in Iraq) is reported to be that the tirade of the mullahs in Tehran against the Iraqi leader provoked him to attack.

The Iranian fundamentalist view is that the Iraqi attack was part of a western plot to overthrow the Khomeini regime under the cloak of Saddam Hussein's adventurism. The evidence cited by the fundamentalists includes the fact that the US government did not discourage him from making the attack and Iranian counter-revolutionary *mujaheddin* forces based in Iraq joined in the attack (a parallel they draw with the US-backed Contras entering Nicaragua from Honduras).

These three positions are not mutually exclusive. It is probable that each of these views is valid to some extent and that, together, they form a more complete explanation for the Iraqi attack. Nevertheless, a widespread perception in Iran is that the western powers (USA, France and UK) were not just neutral observers of a 'useless' war but were seeking to weaken both Iraq and Iran. The stance of the Soviet Union at that time towards Iran was also not neutral as it too had an interest in curbing the influence of a fundamentalist state on the largely Muslim populations of its southern republics.

### *Attitudes to war*

In the Iran-Iraq War overall, various estimates put Iranian dead at 450,000 upwards with a similar number wounded. A UN-brokered ceasefire took effect on 20 July 1988. In a western world-view, such death and suffering is something to avoid if at all possible. Fighting tends to occur only out of necessity and individuals do so reluctantly. In an Islamic world-view, however, national defence cannot be separated from spiritual duty and a martyr's death in battle (if it should occur) is to be welcomed as the pathway to *behesht* (divine paradise). Thus, whereas western values regard large scale death as obscene, Islamic values place no particular importance on numbers. This difference, of course, does not mean that individual families do not mourn or experience the natural emotions connected with death. It is important to appreciate that western and Islamic values on this matter represent two different perspectives and there is no value-free way of comparing them.

## Principles of Islamic governance and management

As noted in the section on the Islamic Republic above, the IRI government operates under fundamentalist Islamic principles – i.e. guardianship, evolutionary social system of choice, moral rectitude, work ethic, and protecting the 'oppressed' (Mara'shi 1995). It is not a socialist state in the sense either of western socialism or Marxist ideology but it does seek to regulate social welfare and social behaviour to a considerable degree. However, centralized control of industry and commerce is giving way under privatization to a large degree of free market enterprise.

Jafar Mara'shi, Director of the government's Industrial Management Institute (IMI) in Tehran, in a series of papers discussing conceptual challenges in the

Islamic System (1995, 1997), described his team's vision of an evolutionary system of social choice based on a dialectically linked jurisprudence system and spiritual/ religious system with intended outcomes of justice, power of choice and social agreement which is visualised by the authors in Figure 13.2.

The essence of this paradigm is the establishment of a 'new order' capable of challenging what fundamentalists regard as materialistic and hedonistic barbarism resulting from western 'cultural aggression' (Mara'shi 1995, Zarif 1996). There is the further potential of the model being used to eradicate a sense of deprivation among the 'powerless' in secular societies emanating from unequal power distribution fostered by capitalist economics – i.e. a potentially exportable philosophy to the Third World. Given that the IMI is the foremost management school in Iran and advises government on a wide range of policy matters, such models demand attention. The second five-year plan has undoubtedly been influenced by IMI's work.

The putative Islamic world-view system is based on 'objective materialism' – i.e. objective reality is not only socially constructed but constructed according to a unified common set of values seeking to protect the family, society and the world. For example, whereas the 'duty of care' is seen in the West as largely a legal and professional issue, in Iran 'guardianship' or protection of family, employees,

*Fig 13.2* Evolutionary social system of choice as conceived from an Islamic fundamentalist perspective

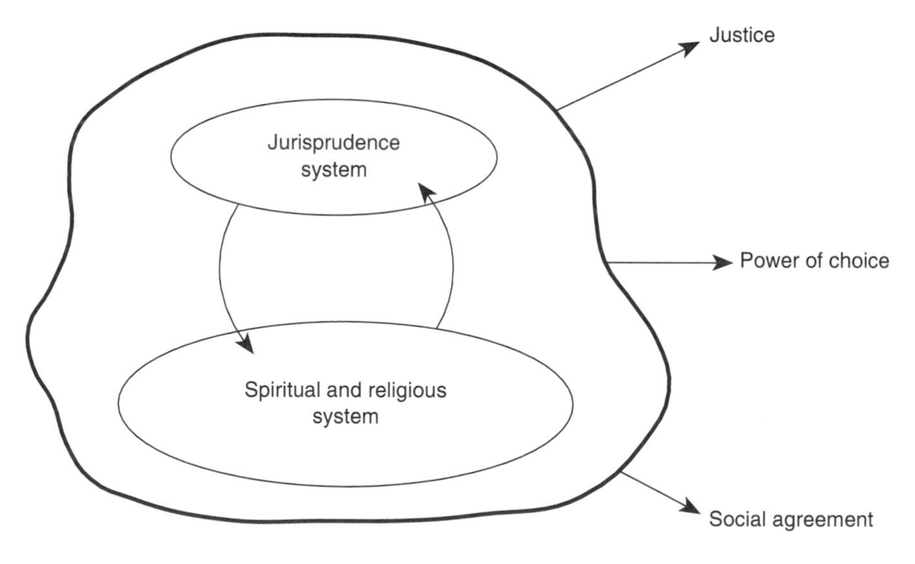


*Source*: developed from concepts in Mara'shi (1995)

colleagues, the country, Islamic identity, and the environment is seen as a universal spiritual obligation on all. Managers in organizations should therefore shoulder the moral responsibility to consider such matters actively and purposefully in the pursuit of material gain and profit. This principle of selflessness or piety is termed *taghva* (Mara'shi 1996).

## The five-year plans 1990–94, 1995–99

The first five-year plan 1990–1994 sought recovery from the damage resulting from the Iran-Iraq War. The focus was on infrastructure such as roads, bridges, hydro-electric dams, power, railways, buildings, etc. and transition from an oil economy to an industrial economy – i.e. to reduce dependence on oil exports by developing downstream and other industries producing goods for export. The latter goal was only partly achieved and the second five-year plan continues the drive towards self-sufficiency (IRI-PBO 1996). In order to achieve overall goals of economic stability and social justice, the second plan recognizes that the vast bureaucracy of government will need to be reduced and its systems streamlined. A corollary is that privatization of large swathes of industry will have to continue and one of the plan's 'qualitative macro goals' is to bring about 'a balance between the three economic sectors (cooperative, private and public)'.

### *Sources of investment and supply*

Iranian manufacturing industry is strong in manufacture of industrial goods and the fmcg sector (e.g. foodstuffs) and personal goods (e.g. leather goods, clothing), but weak in consumer durables. Although some white goods such as cookers and refrigerators are manufactured for sale in Iran and some are exported to neighbouring countries, most mass market electrical and electronic goods are imported. Apart from oil and gas and industrial chemicals, the main export products still lie in agricultural produce, e.g. nuts and textiles – although Iran is developing exports in such areas as technical and project management consultancy to the Caucasus and Central Asian Republics and computer software development sub-contracted by western companies for quality and cost advantages. An Islamic Common Market has also been proposed (Mara'shi 1995).

Car and vehicle manufacturing and assembly companies, which were nationalized in 1979, were privatized in 1992. However, assembly deals with foreign manufacturers such as Renault and Rover have tended to run into difficulties and either have never been sealed or have ceased. It was reported that Iran Khodrow planned to launch its first Iranian designed and manufactured car in 1997.

Foreign suppliers and investors see Iran as a huge potential market but remain cautious about the weak and unstable economy. Lack of foreign exchange, expectations of extended credit, LOC problems and government crackdowns on non-essential imports (e.g. a 1995 stop on car imports including goods already landed at Iranian ports) have all contributed to that caution.

The Rafsanjani and Khatami pragmatists seek open trade and other links with the West as an essential means for the IRI to survive. Hardline fundamentalists, however, see this as anathema. The success of the G6 candidates in the fifth Majlis elections in 1996 strengthened Rafsanjani's hand in fostering trade and diplomatic ties with western countries with the better prospect both of economic development and of isolating and neutralizing the United States' hostile policy towards Iran. The impact of a new Iranian President in 1997 remains uncertain but there is evidence that Khatami will accelerate liberalizing if he can neutralize hardline opponents.

The second five-year plan includes encouragement of foreign investment. Joint ventures are preferred and it is a requirement that foreign suppliers include after-sales support, training and technology transfer as part of their tender. France is particularly active in projects ranging from airport management and highways construction to offshore oil and gas exploration and production. However, the plan specifically seeks to reduce Iran's reliance on external suppliers, primarily on cost grounds, but also strategically to minimize external influences and dependencies. For example, former President Rafsanjani commented publicly that much of the new Tehran Metro had been built by Iran's own engineering firms at a cost of $750m compared with foreign bids of $4billion.

Major current or planned projects include:

- Phase 1 of the Tehran Metro due to open in 1997 with phased extension from Karaj to Mehrshahr.
- Iranian link in the Beijing-Istanbul trans-Asian railway 1997.
- Imam Khomeini International Airport, Tehran, due to open 1999.
- Tehran-Qom-Isfahan Expressway.
- Sarakhs-Mashad-Bandar Abbas railway linking Turkmenistan and CIS across Iran to the Gulf, completed in 1996.
- Reconstruction of Khuzestan Province (post Iran-Iraq War).
- New 'state-of-the-art' oil refinery at Bandar Abbas.
- Major expansion of offshore oil and gas drilling in the Caspian Sea.

*Table 13.1* Profile of Iran's imports and exports 1991–1999

| *Trade (US$m)* | *1991* | *1992* | *1993* | *1994* | *(exp) 1999* | *Total 1995–99* | *Annual growth % 1995–99* |
|---|---|---|---|---|---|---|---|
| Imports | 27450 | 23500 | 15820 | 16508 | 20419 | 91979 | 4.3 |
| Oil exports | 15802 | 16343 | 13020 | 13460 | 15896 | 72658 | 3.4 |
| Non-oil exports | 2610 | 2940 | 3801 | 4120 | 6165 | 27527 | 8.4 |

*Source*: IRI-PBO (1996)

- Export of technology and expertise to Caucasus, CIS and Central Asian Republics in oil and gas exploration and production, water technology, etc.

Table 13.1 summarizes the breakdown of imports and exports over the first five-year plan and those projected for the second five-year plan.

Key policy threats to foreign suppliers remain in the second five-year plan. These are:

- All major imports of good and services in the public sector are subject to justification tests on the basis of inability to source within Iran.
- Particular imports may be viewed as non-strategic luxury items and therefore subject to controls or embargoes at any time (Item 8, General Policy 2). For example, there is currently (1997) a ban on car imports.
- Inter-ministerial rivalries and factional interests within ministries result in variations in policy interpretation and attitudes towards particular companies over time.

## *Economic dangers ahead*

According to Peyvandi (1996), the first five-year plan saw a phenomenal growth in the Iranian oil industry's refinery production, from approximately 800,000 tonnes per annum in 1990 to a projected 9 million tonnes in 1996. The 1996 refinery processing capacity rose to more than 1 million barrels per day. There was a corresponding increase in the diversity of products, and the temperature and pressure ranges employed in refining and processing, as summarised in Table 13.2.

The reported production growth rate, product diversity and increased processing parameters are typical of the conditions which had arisen in the West by the 1970s and which had created major hazards which led to disasters such as Seveso, Flixborough, Milford Haven and so on (Waring 1996b) – see chapters 1 to 3.

*Table 13.2* Iranian oil refining industry statistics, first five–year plan

| | *1990* | *1995* |
|---|---|---|
| Refinery production (tonnes per annum) | 800,000 | 9 million (1996 est) |
| No. of flammable liquid products | 40,000 | 140,000 |
| Temperature range (deg C) | −35 to 1,200 | −200 to 1,300 |
| Max pressures (psi) | 1,700 | 30,000 |

*Source*: Peyvandi (1996)

Indeed, the explosion and fire at Arak refinery in September 1997 exemplifies the lack of major hazards risk control. At this point, it might have been assumed, reasonably from a western perspective, that the second five-year plan would continue with an inexorable growth rate. However, the precepts of Islamic governance intervened and required a re-examination of proposals in terms of the moral philosophy underpinning an imminent 'new world', based on truth seeking, justice, knowledge, guardianship and spiritual values (Mara'shi 1995). For example, the plan contains a basic policy of 'encouraging a life of virtue on the basis of Islamic morals and elevating the society's culture' and at least five sub-policies are aimed specifically at countering 'cultural invasion'. Inevitable growth based on taken-for-granted deterministic assumptions of secular materialism (i.e the capitalist West) is being rejected in favour of a more circumspect approach to sustainable growth using Islamic precepts.

Nevertheless, despite the Iranian government's expectation that religious principles will save the day, there exist very real economic difficulties and dangers for Iran which in turn entail social and political dangers. The current problems centre on:

- reform of chaotic monetary system;
- currency value;
- shortage of foreign exchange;
- removal of state subsidies from retail prices;
- price inflation at estimated 60 per cent per annum (1996);
- wage inflation at 22 per cent per annum (1996);
- privatization, decentralization and their consequences.

At one stage, there were five official exchange rates, plus the black market rate. Largely at the insistence of the World Bank, these have now been rationalized. Stiff penalties have been introduced for black market currency exchanges. Since the Revolution, the value of the Iranian rial and touman (10 rials) has fallen dramatically from approximately 120 rials to the pound. By 1992, the exchange rate was approximately 2,500 rials to the pound and by 1994 the value had fallen to 4,500 then 5,500, 6,500 and for one short period in 1994 the black market rate rose to 9,000 to the pound. Through most of 1995 and 1996, the rate remained fairly stable at around 4,750 to the pound (6,500 black market rate) before rising again. Late in 1996, the black market rate had risen to 8,500 to the pound.

Bank-e Markazi (Central Bank) sets exchange rates and approves all imports which are subject to credit arrangements. Owing to foreign exchange shortages, it has not been generally possible for foreign companies to obtain short and irrevocable letters of credit. Typically, LOCs are of twelve months duration. Import controls on non-strategic or luxury items are imposed periodically when state funds run low, as happened with cars in 1995. Late in 1997, it was reported that the usance system was to be scrapped in favour of cash payments.

Retail prices of utilities, foodstuffs and other consumer items have been heavily state-subsidized throughout the period of the Islamic Republic. A rationing system based on state coupons has buffered the mass of the population from abject poverty. However, by seeking to reduce state subsidies on retail prices as a necessary step in reducing the burden on the state, the impact of price inflation has been magnified, which in turn has made people even more dependent on the coupon system. Wage inflation is government regulated. For example, for 1996–7 it was set at 22 per cent. Price inflation, however, has not been tackled in any serious way and there is no policy for price controls. The net effect is that families see prices increasing at 60 per cent per annum while their incomes dwindle in comparison. For example, a state employee working in an office might typically earn £50 per month but inflation in the property market has seen his or her monthly rent rise to £50 per month. A kind of collective state of anxiety-and-depression about the economy pervades society. As the state is the biggest employer, plans for dismantling and privatizing the vast state bureaucracy would result in mass unemployment, thus adding to the burden of state dependency.

The government is caught by a dilemma about change (see chapter 7). If it proceeds with economic reform in a short timeframe there is likely to be social unrest on a calamitous scale, perhaps even provoking a popular uprising against the regime. If, however, in order to assuage the people the reforms are enacted too slowly or not at all, the economic situation will undoubtedly worsen which could antagonize the population still further.

Former President Rafsanjani, supported by the Free Zones Council and a team of economic advisers, devised a set of 'new consumerism' schemes which seek to offer the people hints of growing economic prosperity and hope for the future. For example, large western-style supermarkets (e.g. Refar chain) stocking wide ranges of goods have been opened throughout Tehran. A limited amount of product advertising appears on some Iranian television channels. Special free trade zones such as Kish Island and Queshm have been set up where Iranians are allowed to spend a limited amount to buy imported consumer goods. However, unless the uncontrolled price inflation which continues to hit hard the meagre disposable incomes of the majority of the population is tackled seriously, such schemes are cosmetic.

The 'new consumerism' advanced by Rafsanjani is endangered by a potential boom-bust 'snowball' effect in which increased demand for utilities and consumer goods, enhanced by rapid population growth, is hampered by lack of consumer confidence and decreasing disposable income. The success of the second five-year plan is vulnerable to many factors, as indicated in Figures 13.3 and 13.4. It is widely felt in Iran that the government's goods distribution policies since 1979 have been feeble (Mara'shi 1997). Deciding how to moderate and control such factors effectively will be an exacting task for the government.

## External relations

### *The West*

The geographical location and oil and mineral wealth of Iran make it of great strategic importance. To the north, Russia has long seen Iran as its route to warm water ports and, although today the threat of Russian invasion has subsided, Russian nationalist leaders such as Vladimir Zhirinovsky maintain the rhetoric about annexation of Iran. Long before oil was discovered, Britain's interest in Iran was very much concerned with curbing Russian influence and adventurism. During the Cold War, Iran was a critical strategic location in the West's containment of Russian communism. Today, however, Iran is regarded by the West as a threat, ostensibly because of the association of Iran's fundamentalist Islamic government with international terrorism, in the past if not the present. However, more cogent reasons for some western countries' displeasure with Iran may be cited. There are, for example, anxieties about the following:

- The spread of Iranian-style fundamentalist ideology to neighbouring states which could threaten political stability and western oil interests – e.g. in Saudi Arabia, UAE, Turkey, Pakistan.
- Iran becoming a dominant political and military power in the Middle East, which could enable it to draw or force neighbouring states into its orbit.

*Fig 13.3* Simple causal loop diagram of some key variables in the Iranian economy

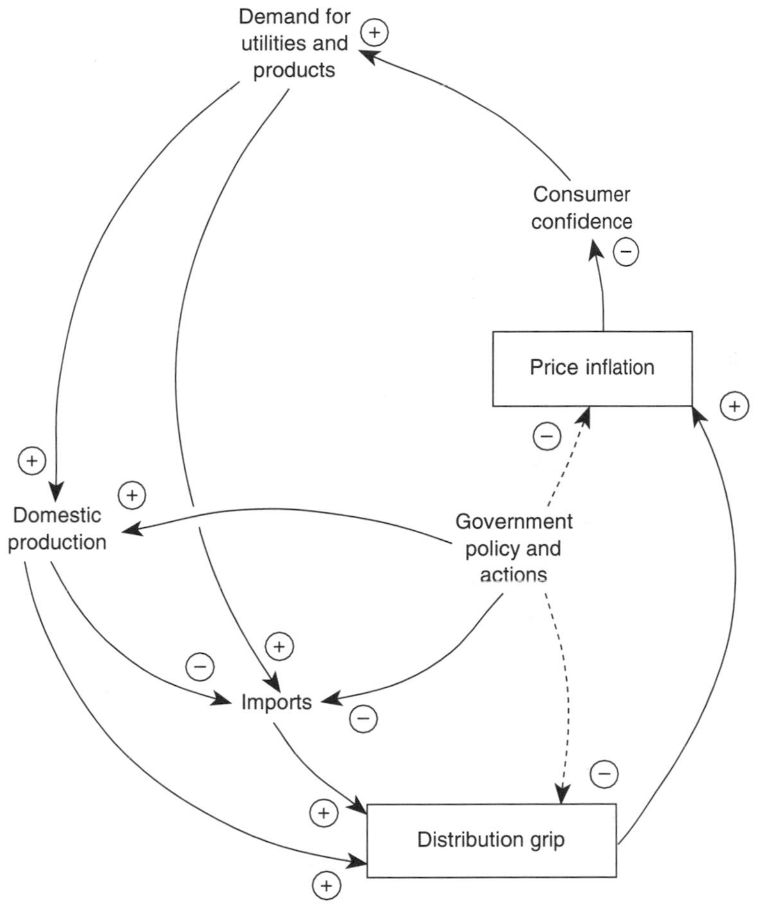

*Source*: see Waring (1996d) for causal loop diagramming technique

- Previously pro-western Muslim states shifting allegiance to Tehran on a pan-Muslim basis (e.g. after-effects of the Bosnian civil war; effects of creeping fundamentalism in Turkey).
- Rapprochement between Iran and Iraq enabling them to form a powerful anti-western axis.

The *fatwa* (religious edict) issued by Ayatollah Khomeini in 1989 against British author Salman Rushdie, for alleged blasphemy in his book *The Satanic Verses*, badly damaged relations with Britain and the EU. The *fatwa*, calling for the death of the

*Fig 13.4* Causal loop diagram of Iranian economy (greatly simplified) indicating vulnerability to uncontrolled variables

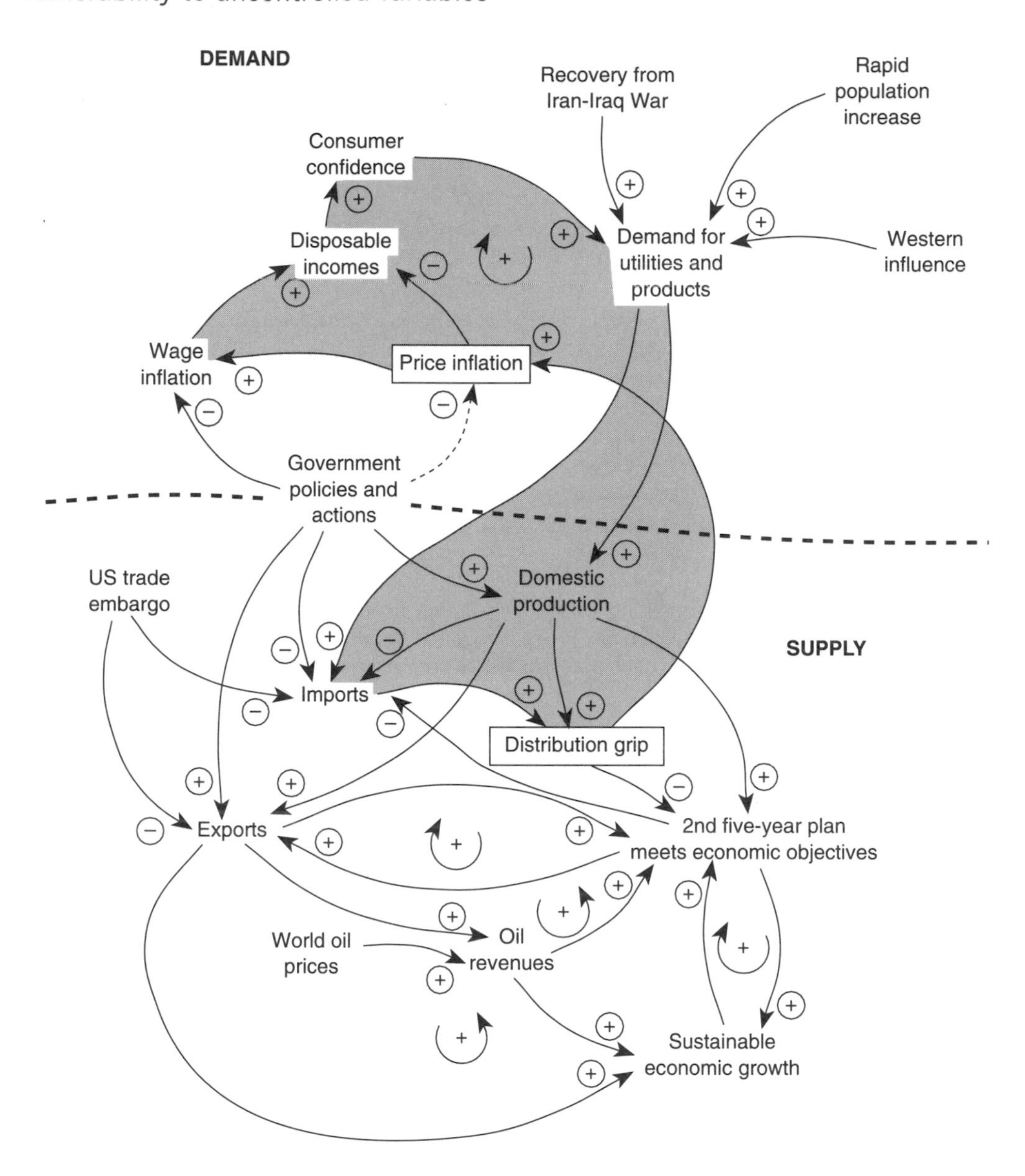

apostate, was interpreted by hardliners in Iran and by millions of ordinary Muslims worldwide as a literal death sentence which it was the duty of every Muslim to execute should the opportunity present itself. Mr Rushdie, the British government and other governments also took the *fatwa* seriously and Rushdie has been given special police protection ever since. Indeed, they were wise to do so given the hardline rhetoric surrounding the case and intelligence information indicating that attempts would be made on his life. Nevertheless, there is another side to this affair which reveals something deeper about the Iranian psyche and about power struggles in Tehran. Ehteshami (1995), for example, refers to the Rushdie affair as an after-shock in the wake of a rapid shift in the balance of power away from the hardliners.

A *fatwa* is essentially an instrument of religious law and not one within the judicial system *per se* of the Iranian government. However, the *fatwa* was exploited, both by hardline fundamentalist leaders in Iran and elsewhere who wanted to bash western secularism and by western politicians and media who wanted to bash Iran. The issue became a cause celebre on both sides, which has made its resolution much more difficult. The fact that former President Rafsanjani reiterated the *velayat-e faghi* as the basis of the fifth Majlis makes it difficult for him (19 April 1995) and other relative moderates such as Ayatollah Yazdi (May 1995) and Ali Akbar Velayati (5 June 1995) to proclaim convincingly that this *fatwa* is a symbolic instrument of religious jurisprudence which has no foundation in the state's judicial system and cannot be lawfully executed. Equally, for them to be forced to make such distinctions emphasizes that the hardline faction still enjoys influence and a degree of independence beyond the control of the official government. In February 1997, the Iranian fundamentalist non-governmental organization which had offerred a £2m reward for the assassination of Rushdie, announced a £0.5m increase to the reward, thus adding to the western view that the Iranian government neither wishes to nor is able to control such groups.

Iran feels misunderstood by the West and frustrated by what it regards as misrepresentation. Reference to western 'cultural aggression' (Mara'shi 1995) has been echoed by Iran's Deputy Foreign Minister, Dr M. Javad Zarif (1996), in addressing an international conference in Switzerland. He argued that Muslim countries were in danger of cultural anihilation by the West by a combination of assimilation, convenience and confrontation. The confrontational strategy of some western countries 'tries to impose all norms and values of the West on Islamic countries, brushing aside diversity of cultures, and depicting western values as the "universal" cherished values of humanity'. Thus, Muslim countries which seek self-determination through a non-western paradigm are automatically classed by some western countries as enemies simply because of that assertive difference. He proposed mutual respect and enrichment of western and Muslim cultures rather than confrontation and attempts of one to dominate the other.

## *USA*

In generalizing about the West, it is important to distinguish between the American position and attitude and those of the European Union, individual European governments, Canada, and other western or pro-western states such as Pakistan, UAE and Japan. Although there is a general western concern about Iranian fundamentalism, up to 1997 the majority of western governments adopted a 'business as usual' approach, summed up by the European Union's policy of 'critical dialogue' with Iran. This policy sought to explore differences where these were thought to pose significant risks to one or both parties, and to seek understandings and agreements where possible. The American position, however, is that it cannot and will not seek any kind of rapprochement with Iran's current leadership. A 'Mexican stand-off' has existed between the USA and the Islamic Republic since US embassy staff, taken hostage in October 1979 and accused of espionage and subversion, were released following the Algiers Agreement. The intense frustration felt in Washington at the continued failure of its policies to bring the Iranian government 'to heel' has led to increasing US threats and actions against Iran, including in 1994 a trade blockade and, in July 1996, laws against foreign investment in Iran and threats of pre-emptive military action. A steady stream of information about the threat posed to the West by alleged Iranian terrorist groups has been fed to the world's press, together with suggestions about possible US retaliation. However, until April 1997 when a German court convicted two Iranians of political assassination and directly implicated government ministers, most western countries declined to support the US view. The EU's critical dialogue policy was then suspended for a few months but US demands for a total diplomatic and trade ban continued to be rejected.

From an Iranian perspective, the USA after the collapse of the Soviet Union is seen as the sole super-power pretending to act as a reluctant world policeman while using this role as a cover to achieve world domination by a mixture of guile, economic and political subversion, and military threat. western media are seen as either gullible or willing purveyors of US propaganda against Iran.

Other US government actions against Iran include:

- In 1995 blocking collaboration on oil/gas production between Conoco and NIOC. Conoco's position was quickly taken up by the French company Total in a $600m investment to develop the Sirri offshore oil field in the Persian Gulf.

- In 1995 seeking and failing to block Iran's nuclear R&D programme. Russia has provided significant support for this programme. US allegations about Iran's nuclear weapons capability unproven (*Janes Sentinel* 1995).
- US decision in January 1996 to allocate $20m to destabilize the Iranian government.

The battle of hostile rhetorics between the USA and Iran (e.g. USA calls Iran 'terrorist pariah' and Iran calls USA 'the Great Satan') has created a mutually assured paranoia in which fact and fiction about the other side become blurred and imaginations run riot in seeking to justify their own hostility. One western diplomat commenting on the US-Iran spat is reported as saying (*Tehran Times* 10 March 1996) that policies and actions should be based on facts rather than emotion – a sign of increasing irritation among America's allies about US foreign policy towards Iran and some other countries. The EU and other countries are offended as a matter of principle by the extra-territorial jurisdiction sought by the US in relation not only to Iran but also in respect of Libya and Cuba.

## *The Middle East and Asia*

Iran is increasingly looking eastward. Iran is also re-emerging as a pivotal regional power, politically and militarily (Ehteshami 1995; *Janes Sentinel* 1995). Pakistan, CIS, China and other Asian countries increasingly see Iran as a bulwark against US domination. Russia too is seeing Iran as a moderating influence on regional disputes and Islamic nationalism in the Caucasus and Central Asian Republics. For example, Iran is credited with successfully brokering a cease-fire and peace talks between Armenia and the Republic of Azerbaizhan and for similar efforts between the two sides in the civil war in Tajikistan. Iran was careful to avoid taking sides in the war between Chechen Muslim separatists and Russian forces. Daily official announcements from Tehran regarding trade, economic co-operation and diplomatic ties with Muslim Central Asian Republics of the former Soviet Union indicate Iran's growing influence throughout central Asia. This ascendance, of course, invites counter efforts from rivals such as Turkey and the USA who feel their own interests threatened (Ehteshami 1995).

Diplomatic relations and limited trade have been re-established with Iraq. It should not be assumed that, because of the Iran-Iraq War, great animosity exists between these two peoples. They have a long tradition of good relations and Iranians make a distinction between Saddam Hussein and the Iraqi people. In response to the US policy of 'dual containment' of Iran and Iraq, both countries now see mutual benefit in non-aggression. During the Iraqi invasion of Kuwait,

Iran condemned Iraq but did not intervene militarily, thus deriving political benefits internationally while its regional rival became weakened by defeat (Ehteshami 1995). By agreeing not to intervene, Iran also got Iraq to agree to all its reparation demands remaining from the Iran-Iraq War (*Janes Sentinel* 1995).

Relations with states such as UAE, Qatar and Bahrein remain correct, if not cordial, at both popular and diplomatic levels, despite suspicions and suggestions in the West that Iran has been behind civil unrest in Bahrein, for example. The anxieties about potential Iranian expansionism and export of Iranian fundamentalism felt keenly throughout the 1980s (Ehteshami 1995) still exist but are less intense following diplomatic initiatives and rapprochement between Iran, the Gulf Cooperation Council and its individual members – notwithstanding the dispute over Abu Musa and the Tunbs. *Janes Sentinel* (1995) dismisses perceptions of Iranian expansionism as being without evidence. A relatively moderate Iran is now seen as a counterweight against Iraqi expansionism. Such problems which exist are seen as local matters for local resolution without western interference. Relations with Saudi Arabia, however, have been much more difficult. Iran has made no secret of its view that the Saudi Arabian leadership is corrupt and in the pocket of the USA. Until 1997, Iran barred its citizens from travel to Saudi with the exception of special travel documents for the annual Hajj religious festival at Mecca. Initiatives by President Khatami have removed travel restrictions between Iran and Egypt and Saudi Arabia.

The Iranian government views the rise of the Taleban Muslim fundamentalists in Afghanistan with alarm and distaste for two main reasons. First, Iran believes that the Taleban's ruthless treatment of females such as banishing them from schools and jobs and returning them to a medieval servitude is un-Islamic. Second, the Taleban is regarded as a tool of US attempts to secure a route for Central Asian products, particularly oil and gas, through Afghanistan and Pakistan to the Indian Ocean and so bypassing Iran. The conspiracy theory sees the US funding and supporting Pakistan which in turn supplies the Taleban. However, given the perpetually turbulent politics, coups and civil wars in Afghanistan, even if a trade route via Afghanistan could be opened up the risks would be unacceptable to Central Asian and other governments compared to the stability offered by an Iranian trade route.

## Risks for Iran and foreign countries (see chapter 2)

This section seeks to provide a summary risk analysis based on the foregoing description and discussion. The analysis is divided into two parts: socio-political, economic, change and war risks for Iran, and business risks for foreign companies trading with or operating in Iran.

## *Risks for Iran – hazards and threats*

### *Economy*

Positive aspects include:

- Gradual clearance of foreign debt.
- Oil, gas, petrochemicals and chemicals production and exports rising.
- Five-year plans provide focus.

Key threats to the economy are:

- High price inflation.
- Unproductive, overmanned and inefficient public sector.
- Stranglehold of the distribution system at the expense of the production system.
- High state subsidies of utilities, consumer goods and low paid may increase if inflation forces more people into poverty.
- Lack of foreign exchange hampering overseas purchases.
- Over-reliance on oil and gas as main industrial exports.
- Multiple hurdles for exporters.
- Second five-year plan may prove to be as overly optimistic as the first.

### *Social and political*

Positive aspects include:

- High degree of national pride, identity and social cohesion.
- Low rates of violent crime, drug abuse, alcohol abuse.
- Government actively encourages population to become involved in social development programmes.

Key social and political threats are:

- Continued failure to control price inflation may lose the government not only the tolerance of the middle classes but also its traditional support among the working class.
- Continued reduction in disposable incomes may provoke civil unrest.
- Continued banning of non-approved political parties and restrictions on freedom of expression and life-style will add to popular discontent about the economy.
- Factionalism and power struggles within and between ministries and government offices may lead to incoherent policy and action and the risk of misinterpretation and adverse reaction abroad.

### *Change*

Positive aspects include:

- The five-year plans seek to address strategic change in the economy and social system.
- Arrival of a relatively liberal President Khatami.

Key threats are:

- Economic changes introduced by government may be too little, of the wrong kind and too late to assuage an exasperated populace.
- Unwillingness to entertain political liberalization may store up public resentment.
- If Khatami is unable to deliver significant change for which he was elected, popular discontent against the regime may boil over into social unrest.

### *Military*

Positive aspects include:

- Military equipment in service roughly matches that of Saudi Arabia and numbers of military personnel roughly matches that of Iraq (*Janes Sentinel* 1995).
- Iran's defence expenditure ranks bottom out of nine Gulf states as a percentage of GDP and sixth in amount. It fell for three consecutive years 1991–93, thereby running counter to allegations of military expansionism (*Janes Sentinel* 1995).

Key military threats are:

- Attack by Iraq, although unlikely given Iraq's weakened state and mutual interest against a hostile USA, cannot be ruled out in view of Saddam Hussein's track record.
- Pre-emptive attack by US on nuclear and other strategic targets cannot be ruled out in view of US government statements but political damage to US would be high.
- Invasion by US and western powers to secure Middle Eastern oil supplies if seriously threatened by Iran in the future.

## *Risk assessment: risks for Iran*

The following table summarizes potential risk levels for the threats to Iran discussed above. The attributed risk levels are based on the authors' judgements. Both positive and negative outcomes for any given threat may co-exist.

| Threat | Potential risk levels (as probabilities) | |
|---|---|---|
| | **Negative outcomes** | **Positive outcomes** |
| Economy | Medium–High | Low |
| Social and political | Medium–High | Low–Medium |
| Change | Medium–High | Low–Medium |
| Military | Low–Medium | Medium |

## *Business risks for foreign companies – hazards and threats*

### *Demand*

Positive factors include:

- Population growth, currently 65 million at 1.7 per cent pa (50 per cent under 18 years of age).
- Young, educated and sophisticated population.
- Highly sociable, mobile culture.
- Economically active female population.
- Ageing technology and products requiring replacement.
- Requirements to fulfil second five-year plan.
- New consumerism (Rafsanjani effect).
- Always a market for high price consumer products – e.g. high end hi-fi systems.

Threats include:

- High price inflation.
- Falling state subsidies.
- Generally low wages.

} affecting disposable incomes and consumer confidence

- Lack of foreign exchange.

### *Supply and investment*

Positive factors include:

- Demands of second five-year plan.
- Modernist consumer demand.
- Improved terms for foreign investors.
- Increased port facilities with reduced demurrage.
- Stabilization of foreign exchange rates 1995–97.
- Tehran Stock Exchange an emerging market.

Key threats to foreign suppliers and investors are:

- Effects of being effectively absent from Iran market for many years.
- Entrenched foreign competitors.
- Import taxes and controls.
- Iranian competitors offering cheaper products.
- Product positioning.
- Unreliable local assembly deals.
- Unreliable/unscrupulous agents.
- Undue influence in award of contracts.
- Extended payments/LOC problems.
- US trade embargo and US threat to prosecute foreign investors.
- High risk-high return status of Tehran Stock Exchange as emerging market.

*Government policy*
Positive factors include:

- Foreign investment encouraged.

Key policy threats to foreign suppliers are:

- Government policy to give priority to Iranian products and suppliers wherever reasonably practicable.
- Priority import categories and controls may vary according to policy changes as well as state of economy.
- Government policy may be variably interpreted both within and between different ministries and departments.
- Government rules and regulations change too frequently.
- Foreign companies which heed US trade and investment embargo may be penalized in future trading relations with Iran.

*Security and safety*
Positive factors include:

- Low crime rate.
- Personal attacks are rare.
- Highways free of banditry.

Key security and safety threats to foreign companies are:

- Fraud and embezzlement.

- Falling victim to unscrupulous middlemen and agents.
- Very poor standards of driver behaviour and road safety.

*Culture*
Positive factors include:

- Enthusiastic, friendly and irrepressible.
- Ingenuity in coping with problems and determination in the face of adversity.
- Foreigners treated with great courtesy.

Key cultural threats to foreign companies are:

- Personal risk-taking of Iranians as evidenced by general evasion of rules, regulations and restrictions.
- Failure to understand Iranian caution and attitudes towards time.
- Failure to understand Iranian *bazari* attitudes towards business which makes foreigners vulnerable to unscrupulous or unreliable middlemen and agents.
- Lack of respect for Iranian codes of behaviour.
- Failure to appreciate Iranian sensitivities over sovereignty and identity issues.

### *Risk assessment: risks for foreign companies*

The following table summarizes potential risk levels for the threats to foreign companies discussed above. The attributed risk levels are based on the authors' judgements. NB Both positive and negative outcomes for any given threat may co-exist.

| **Threat** | **Potential risk levels** (as probabilities) | |
|---|---|---|
| | **Negative outcomes** | **Positive outcomes** |
| Demand | Medium–High | Medium |
| Supply and investment | Medium–High | Low–Medium |
| Government policy | Medium–High | Low–Medium |
| Security and safety | Low–Medium | High |
| Culture | Low–Medium | Medium |

## Comparison with thematic matrix (see chapter 9)

Table 13.3 indicates the relative salience of each of the risk contexts identified in Part 1, and particularly chapter 9, in relation to this case study. In the table, H = high, M = medium, L = low.

*Table 13.3* Thematic matrix applied to Iran case study

| *Risk context* | *Salience in case study* |
|---|---|
| *Organizational environment* | |
| Economies and markets | H |
| Public policy, legislation and regulation | H |
| Social and political climate | H |
| Technology | L |
| History, operating territories and conditions | H |
| *Human factors* | |
| Culture | H |
| Power relations, political processes and decision-making | H |
| Perception and cognition | H |
| *Formal coping arrangements* | |
| Risk management | H |
| Risk assessment | H |
| Management systems | M |
| Approaches to change | H |

## Conclusions

Iran's potential economic development has been compared with that of South Korea, in view of its natural resources, skill base and industries. However, for Iran to become the 'South Korea of the Middle East' would require, at the very least, a radical change from the present fundamentalist state to a secular government. Even with a new relatively liberal President and Past-President with the potential to create an Iranian perestroika, such a transformation to a western-style economic and political system is unlikely in the foreseeable future and the grand Islamic experiment may well continue. Mutual hostility between Iran and the United States shows no sign of abating.

Although considerable success has been achieved in reducing its foreign debt, Iran has so far failed to grapple with high price inflation and the domination of the domestic economy by the distribution system. Political will to act and a cultural transformation will be required to kill this particular problem. Cheap fuel, with 1997 pump prices at about 2.5 pence (£0.025) per litre, and a popular illusion that Iran has an endless oil and gas supply, are not incentives to create non-oil based industries and products for export – which will be essential both in the short and long terms.

Iran is potentially a huge market for foreign goods and services. However, there are many risks for the unwary or ill-prepared foreign company seeking to do business there. It is, of course, possible to carry out business with minimal information about and understanding of the market. Some succeed but many fail, become disillusioned and drop Iran from their list of priorities. Japanese, German and French companies have been particularly successful in Iran because of their long-term approach and understanding of the market. For example, these countries dominate the foreign exhibitor halls at the annual International Trade Fair in Tehran and many of their executives in Iran speak fluent Farsi.

There are also general lessons which may be drawn from this particular study about doing business with or in difficult territories.

Foreign companies need a risk profile of the target country and this would need to identify and analyse hazards and threats in the following broad categories:

- General state of the economy.
- General and product-specific demand factors.
- Sources of investment and product supply.
- Government economic and trade policies.
- Government legislation.
- Cultural, social and political factors.
- Foreign policy and foreign relations.
- Security and safety.

In order to manage strategic risks associated with such a foreign market, there is a need to:

- Obtain comprehensive, reliable information on a continuing basis.
- Select and maintain reliable contacts and agents.
- Make efforts to meet and understand the people.
- Have a culturally sensitive attitude.
- Carry out adequate risk assessment(s).
- Develop a long-term strategy regarding the territory.
- Draw up a risk contingency plan.

Although some common characteristics may be evident, each territory needs to be regarded as unique. For example, each country in the Middle East has unique variables and risk factors. Factors which may be significant and prominent in one territory may be relatively unimportant in another. For example, the risk of kidnap and extortion is high in some South American countries but low in other parts of the world. Armed robbery and assault is a significant hazard to western businessmen in the larger Russian cities but not in most countries in the Middle East and South East Asia.

# Chapter 14
# The introduction of new computer systems

## Overview

This chapter emphasizes that there are strategic risks attached not only to failing to invest in information technology (IT), but also to inadequate, inappropriate, untimely and poorly managed investment in and implementation of IT. A case study of IT implementation in the form of introduction of new computer systems in an organization is included, which demonstrates linked issues of management, risk and change.

## Introduction

The importance of information technology to the nation and to organizations was underscored by UK government initiatives throughout the 1980s and early 1990s to get the general public and schoolchildren in particular to embrace the use of IT at work and at home. Fear of IT-enhanced competition, whether from UK or foreign companies, has acted as a spur to using IT to obtain significant advantages in cost-efficiency and effectiveness. Also, many innovative companies have used IT to develop new kinds of product or service. The downsides of speculative risks – i.e. not embracing or investing in IT – are accepted by most people as self-evident.

The most pervasive examples of information technology are desk-top and lap-top computer and associated terminals (visual and non-visual display units of various kinds) and telecommunications systems. The convergence of computing and telecommunications is evident in that many office computer terminals incorporate data communications facilities. Full implementation of the ISO seven-layer model of a totally integrated communications network worldwide, in which any device such as a telephone, personal computer or fax may be attached, is rapidly nearing fruition. The current VDU arrangement of CRT display, central processing unit and keyboard is likely to remain for the foreseeable future. Flat screen technology, even as it becomes more commonplace, is unlikely to change the overall user-interface arrangement. However, the relative maturity and stability of basic IT arrangements and the widespread use of IT systems belies the fact that introducing IT, whether from scratch or to replace or upgrade an existing IT system, entails an array of risks. For example, as the case study of the Employment & Training Association (see section later in this chapter) shows, poor implementation of an IT strategy designed to reduce an organization's cash-flow risks may add to or even create the very types of problem it is designed to solve.

In short:

- IT is pervasive.
- IT is likely to continue to be introduced in varying forms for the foreseeable future.
- The consequences of IT introduced badly or well are likely to have profound effects on individuals, organizations and society.
- Thus there are risks attached not only in respect of failing to invest in IT at all but also to inadequate, inappropriate, untimely and poorly managed investment in IT and to poorly managed IT implementation projects.

This chapter examines and discusses an array of risks which any organization may face in relation to its approach to IT.

## Strategic risks relating to IT

### *Failure to invest in IT*

Most organizations have invested in IT to some degree and a complete absence of IT in organizations is now very much the exception. A principal threat now is that of failing to replace outmoded IT systems and misjudging the timing and speed of replacement or choosing an inappropriate system for an organization's changing needs. For example, it may be wiser not to install the latest concept system as soon as it becomes available but rather to wait to ascertain that the system is establishing a track record for reliability among other users. For example in 1995, Microsoft Windows '95 was heralded as a significant departure from its predecessors and many companies and invididuals switched to it as soon as it came on the market, only to find unforeseen technical difficulties in many cases. In essence, the main risks lie not in complete absence of IT investment but in ill-considered investment decisions and their subsequent implementation, as discussed below.

## *Poorly managed investment in and implementation of IT*

Segars and Grover (1996) point to a paradox faced increasingly by those responsible for IT strategy in organizations. On the one hand, boards are seeking competitive advantages in product markets and significant financial returns from IT investment. On the other hand, such results are demanded in shorter and shorter timeframes and with reduced financial investment. 'In such an environment there is little tolerance of error' and 'risks of cost overruns, ill-conceived prioritization schemes and technological incompatibilities' become critical. For example, the UK National Audit Office reported in 1996 that in the National Health Service (NHS) – see chapter 15 – a number of major computerization projects being run nationally for implementation in local hospitals had failed to meet key objectives such as being available to deliver intended information reliably, and being implemented on time and to budget. As one example, an integrated patient record system intended to link laboratory results to patient records and ensure that different departments use a single record per patient instead of each generating their own, had only been fully implemented in 13 hospitals with schemes in only a further 89 out of 400 hospitals in progress. Even five of the six pilot sites, where piloting cost the NHS Executive £56m and the six hospitals a total of £50m, were judged by the National Audit Office to be unsuitable. Other high profile examples of IT failures in the UK include:

- Computerization of Conservative Party Central Office in the 1980s.
- Computerized scheduling and control of the London Ambulance Service in the early 1990s.
- Introduction of SEAQ on-line information system at London Stock Exchange in 1986.

A systematic, if not systemic, approach to IT strategy and implementation is required which may involve a range of methodologies such as Soft Systems Methodology (SSM) – see chapter 4 – and Structured Systems Analysis and Design Methodology (SSADM). A management system framework will be required to link the key processes described in chapters 1 to 3, that is:

- Policy, strategy and objectives.
- Planning, organizing, resourcing including risk assessment and risk management

of project, technology, human resources and behaviour, culture, security, benefits, costs, etc.
- Project management of implementation: before, during and after.
- Monitoring and measuring performance.
- Audit and review.

Nevertheless, as Segars and Grover (1996) suggest, the effectiveness of an IT system once installed and implemented is only as good as the assumptions of the strategy which spawned it. A key difficulty for major IT projects is that business and organizational contexts and predicted changes in them often develop differently to what was anticipated when a strategy was drawn up. The longer the period of the IT project, the more likely it will be that either practical requirements will develop differently from original strategy or that strategy-in-action will subtly migrate and drift away from official strategy (Quinn 1980; Mintzberg 1992; Waring 1993b). Making sure that all those involved clearly know and understand the strategy and any changes to it is therefore necessary to reduce the risk of incoherent and contradictory implementation activities (Segars and Grover 1996). The Employment & Training Association case study below and the NHS case study in chapter 15 provide two specific examples of IT strategy migration and detrimental effects of poorly communicated strategy. Organizations need to be aware of the risks of strategy migration in long-haul IT projects just as much as they need to appreciate that rapid implementation of major innovative IT projects carries risks of narrow margins for error or unforeseen problems (for example, the implementation of SEAQ in the London Stock Exchange and the London Ambulance Service scheduling computer).

## Project management risks

Once IT strategy has been fixed formally, how the project is managed will determine the risks of implementation (see Chicken 1994, 1996 and Webb 1994). Project management risks occur throughout the entire process of planning, selection and purchase of hardware and software, installation and implementation of new systems, human resource management, training, etc. Feasibility studies and piloting are usually essential components in reducing implementation risks and avoiding failure. Segars and Grover (1996) emphasize the need for planning the architecture of information systems in a top-down way from the conceptual level, through the logical and into the physical level, an approach consistent with SSADM (see Cutts 1987). Such an approach includes:

| Conceptual Level Analysis | | |
|---|---|---|
| • Business/enterprise analysis | ⟶ | • Business model |
| **Logical Level Analysis** | | |
| • Logical systems design | ⟶ | • Communication<br>• Applications<br>• Technology<br>• Data |
| **Physical Level Design** | | |
| • Systems implementation | ⟶ | • Applications<br>• Databases<br>• Networks |

Poorly designed and worded 'help' screens and support documentation such as user manuals may result in mistakes and lost time by users as well as aggravating user resistance. Incomprehensible documentation has long been a source of complaint among computer users and an IT project therefore needs to plan for adequate resources to be applied in preparing such documents.

Overall, project management techniques such as job scheduling and Gantt charts will be needed to ensure that the implementation timetable is adhered to. Project reviews at major milestones should help to ensure that objectives and performance standards are met.

## Operational risks

Once implemented, operational threats in the use of IT systems are many and varied. For example:

- unreliable or faulty hardware;
- major computer failures or 'crashes';
- software errors or 'bugs';
- human error.

In many cases, operational risks are contained and remedied without undue consequences. However, such risks may involve business interruption or may cause adverse public and media reactions, for example grossly excessive bills or unwarranted disconnection threats received from the billing computers of utilities companies. In the worst case, operational risks can become strategic risks – i.e. they threaten business strategy or even the survival of the organization. Back-up and contingency arrangements are therefore essential to minimize business interruption and other harmful effects of specific operational risks.

It has been estimated that as the year 2000 approaches up to 80 per cent of computers could stop functioning properly because year dates have been encoded traditionally as only the last two digits instead of the full four. For example, 1900 is encoded as 00 and 1999 as 99. The year 2000 cannot be encoded as 00 as this is already reserved for the year 1900.

However, one mitigation will be the fact that, owing to rapid increases in price-performance ratios, most personal computers have an expected useful life of only 2–3 years before being replaced by a more advanced machine. Since the 'Millennium Bomb' problem has been widely publicized since early 1996, it may be anticipated that the fault has been corrected in subsequent machines and that the number in use which retain the fault will have reduced. However, the threat of chaos remains substantial and significant according to the UK government's Central Computing and Telecommunications Agency. For some organizations, the Millennium Bomb may prove to be a strategic risk which threatens their survival.

## Health, safety and security risks

Fire, flooding, security and safety hazards are particular operational risks which may become strategic if they threaten the business or organization. As with operational risks generally, adequate preventive, back-up and contingency arrangements are therefore essential.

### *Fire and flood*

Fire and flood can lead to considerable damage not only to computer equipment and premises but also to data files. For example, in the Employment & Training Association case study later in this chapter, a fire caused extensive damage resulting in several months' interruption of business and loss of accounts files, as a result of which £1m in revenues could not be traced.

### *Security*

Security threats may be classified under the main headings of:

- Fraud – use of computer systems to obtain money by deception.
- Theft – hardware, software, commercially valuable or sensitive information.
- Criminal damage – viruses, sabotage – e.g. logic time bombs, arson.

The 1996 UK national survey of information security breaches (NCC 1996) showed that approximately 90 per cent of 661 responding organizations reported at least one significant information security breach in the previous two years. There had been a marked increase in the incidence and cost of computer-related theft. One in five breaches had a significant or serious impact on the organization and in many cases it took over a week to restore operation of affected systems. Although the average cost of an incident was about £16,000, one reported theft cost £750,000, another over £500,000 and a case of fraud cost £650,000.

Organizations which have been victims of IT security failures are often reluctant to publicize the fact in case it damages their image or credibility. However, from time to time cases do enter the public domain, for example the spectacular Barings Bank collapse which involved use of computers at its Singapore offices (see case study in chapter 11). Reducing IT security risks entails using appropriate combinations of methods such as:

- Physical access control – restricted physical access, number coded door locks, classified areas.
- Terminal access control – multi-level passwords, data encryption.
- Remote access control – multi-level passwords, data encryption, 'fire wall' systems to block hackers.
- Personnel screening and selection procedures and monitoring of staff grievances and risk behaviour (e.g. alcohol or drug abuse, excessive gambling debts).
- IT security audits and cross-checks with financial audits.
- Anti-virus policy and procedures.

## *Health and safety*

Health and safety hazards associated with IT are generally low risk and comparable with general office activities (NRC 1983). Following extensive government and other studies in a number of countries during the 1980s, it was concluded that any risks to users from radiation which may be posed by VDUs are negligible (House of Lords 1988; WHO 1987). However, ergonomic requirements for use of display screen equipment are frequently not met in workplaces; in some instances, particular individuals may suffer maladies ranging from mild musculo-skeletal discomfort and visual fatigue to chronic irreversible conditions such as work-related upper limb disorders (WRULD). In addition to the personal health risks to such individuals, employers are at risk from prosecution by statutory authorities for failing to ensure their employees' health and safety and from liability claims by those individuals. A number of high profile cases of successful employer's liability claims for WRULD by computer users in the UK in the early-1990s caused employers to focus greater attention on such matters as job design, control and pace of data entry and ergonomics of VDU workstations. These health and safety requirements were further emphasized by a European Directive and statutory regulations in 1992 in member states covering the use of VDUs.

## Cultural risks

Cultural risks here refer to attitudes, motivations and behaviours of individuals and groups towards the organization and IT in both general and specific cases, which may have adverse effects in the organization. Market research reports on IT products and services often take for granted a technological imperative interworking with a business imperative. Product market competitiveness between computer manufacturers is so intense that price-performance ratios are improving dramatically year-by-year. Such competition has led to products becoming over-engineered for the majority of users and to obsolesecence within 2–3 years. Problems of introduction of IT products (such as new computers) are often regarded in terms of user resistance (e.g. products lack user-friendliness, hardware and software unreliable, new users doubt their own capabilities, etc.). However, various studies (Coombs 1992; Parker and Dent 1991; Waring 1993b) suggest that human behavioural factors, which are at least as important, include problems associated with IT such as:

- Fear of job loss.
- Actual or potential loss of control over work.
- Actual or potential marginalisation or devaluation of work.
- Loss of professional or personal identity.
- Power relations and inter-departmental rivalries to gain the lion's share of IT resources and symbolic rewards.
- Symbolic change of organization's culture and values.
- Fear of being 'left behind' or out-of-step with colleagues and peers in using the latest IT products.
- Cynicism about the IT industry and IT specialists being the main beneficiaries of an obsessional drive to install the latest IT products.

For those involved in or affected by introduction of IT in an organization, 'success' is therefore likely to mean far more than simply getting the physical system installed and operating properly, on time and to budget (Glendon and Waring 1996; Waring 1993b). Success for individuals will also mean not experiencing a range of adverse outcomes which may affect them on a very personal basis. The personal and often covert nature of many of these 'world view' concerns ensures that they are unlikely to be articulated to superiors or in public fora such as project meetings or among colleagues or be recorded in project reports. Nevertheless, there is evidence that such factors act as powerful motivators which affect the behaviour of people in organizations towards IT and the organization which may interfere with board expectations of rapid trouble-free 'success' such as culture change and re-engineering.

Rationalistic prescriptions for the introduction of IT in organizations focus on such common-sense topics as system design, hardware and software selection, staff training, staff participation and culture change programmes. Such activities may be necessary but may not be enough to ensure complete 'success' with new IT systems (cf Beer *et al.* 1990; Westley 1990). SSM (soft systems methodology) studies – see chapter 4 – provide one means of addressing the complex issues involved, but SSM should not be regarded as a panacea for reduction of human behaviour risks.

The following case study of the introduction of new computer systems in one large organization during the 1980s and early 1990s exemplifies the benefits, problems and risk issues which many organizations face when introducing IT.

## The Employment & Training Association

### *Significant developments*

#### *Background*

The Employment & Training Association (ETA) is a registered charity which aims to increase the effectiveness of work organizations through the best use of their human resources. ETA has always had a regional structure. Over the period 1988–91, ETA underwent a number of reorganizations based on regional development. In 1991, an emergency reorganization occurred in order to avoid insolvency.

Until the 1991 crisis, the day-to-day management of the ETA was headed by a Chief Executive and several Divisional Directors. The Divisions incorporated policy implementation departments whose function was to run promotional, sales and marketing campaigns.

During the late 1980s, staffing increased until at the end of 1989 there were about 500 staff in total. In 1990, centralization of various services resulted in a staff reduction to 450. The survival package introduced in 1991 reduced this number to under 300, primarily at the expense of central staff and the closing of a number of regional offices.

### *The 'Future Vision' project*

Until early 1991, the Operations Support Division incorporated ETA's Computer Department and was responsible for computer services within the Association. Before 1988, this Division held various titles and had been engaged in a series of computer development initiatives since 1982, as summarized in Figure 14.1.

In September 1988, it was revealed that a decision had been made to move the Computer Department to Manchester in 1989. The Operations Support Director, Eddie, announced his new long-term IT programme called 'Future Vision'. He stated that the strategy was changing from one of data processing to one of an IT-driven organization that reflected an integrated view of the Association. He said 'This next phase is my grand vision. I'm several paces in front of the others, I suppose. They need to understand that it is not a technical problem but a cultural one within the Association'.

### *Implementation of Future Vision*

Early in 1989, a major fire at ETA's headquarters caused disruption for many months and hampered progress of Future Vision. Accounts data were lost in the fire and staff were unable to reconcile a cash loss of £1m on the books. In addition, a business downturn was affecting cash flow and ETA was at its borrowing limits. In October 1989, Eddie reported:

> We recently took stock and decided that we had too many senior people, too many small teams and too many products. A decision will have to be made to save £0.5m. This financial crisis will work to the advantage of those of us who have been seeking more centralization. I've now also been able to persuade the other Directors to have a totally centralized Membership Records, thus saving £150,000 in salaries. We could not have done this without IT . . . All this is helping a cultural change.

By the summer of 1990, the second of the three phases of Future Vision had been implemented and the staff cuts and restructuring announced previously had taken place. General optimism for Future Vision was expressed in terms of expectations for greater efficiency but some senior staff stated their concern about the effects on the organization's culture. For example, one respondent said 'There is an issue

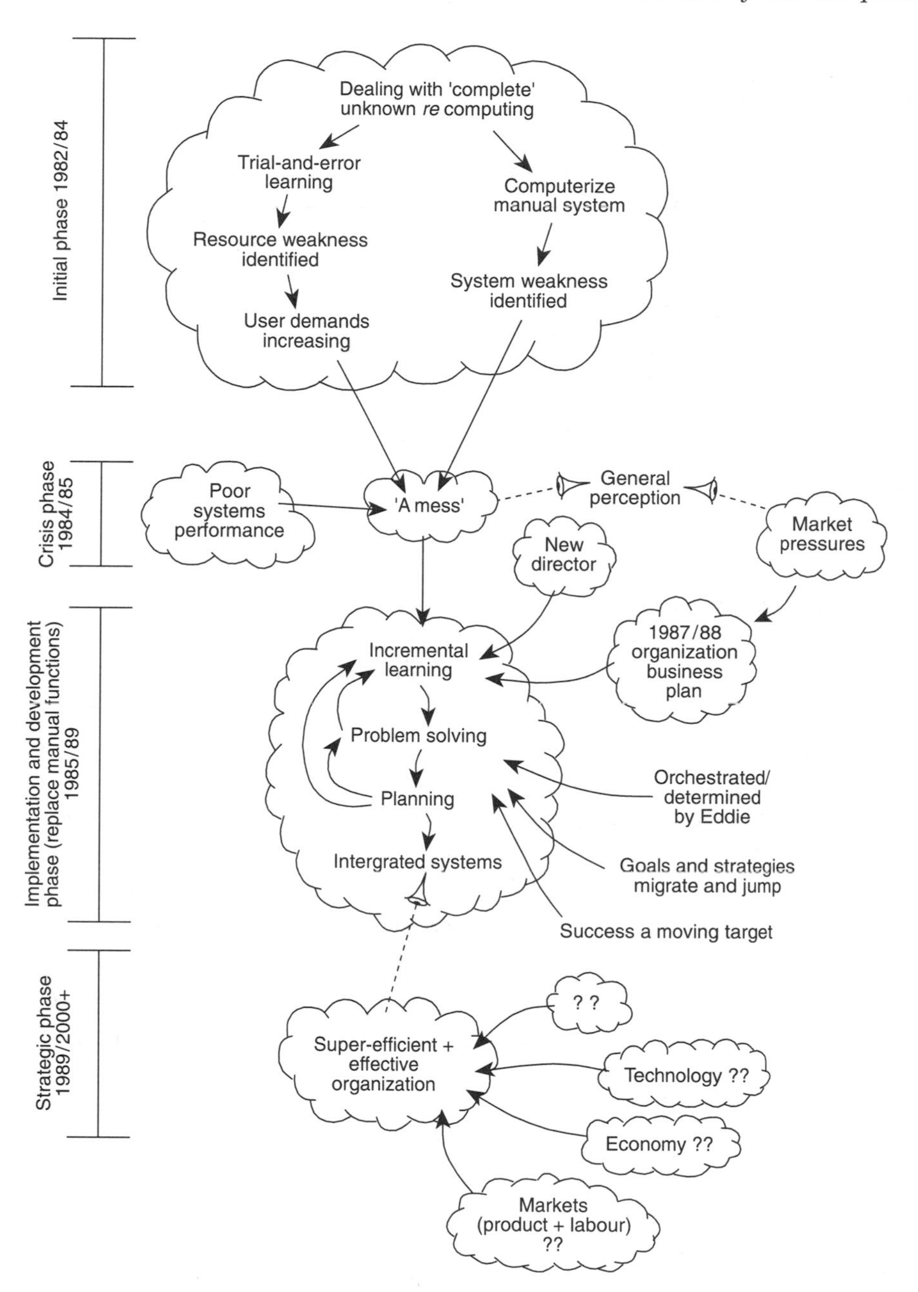


*Figure 14.1* (opposite) Event flow diagram of the ETA's early computerization process 1982–June 1989
*Source*: Waring (1993b, 1996c)

between the reactive short-term culture and the planning, strategic culture of the Future Vision.' Another said 'The team culture . . . is strongly embedded. . . . In the restructuring of units, how far can we go before destroying team integrity? We don't want the NHS situation. There is a sense of ownership which must not be destroyed. It's still unresolved.'

By the end of 1990, the final phase of the Future Vision implementation should have been complete (see Figure 14.2). The hardware system and the integrated applications software were apparently set up more or less on schedule. However, additional items to the original specification which had been identified as necessary by the Computer Department could not be purchased owing to financial restrictions. Also, it was reported that training of staff to use the new and relatively sophisticated computer system had not been adequate and funding for additional training was no longer available.

### *Major crisis*

Early in 1991, the Association was in serious financial difficulties – 'close to a crash' as one senior person described the situation. The Finance Director and several Divisional Directors, including Operations Support, resigned or were made redundant. ETA's Director also resigned. A new Finance Director was seconded from another organization to put together a rescue plan and a new Managing Director was appointed. The existing divisional structure was reorganized under the Finance Director into two groups of operations, each with a Group Operations Director, plus a Development Group.

In August 1991, one of the Group Operations Directors described Future Vision as badly conceived and implemented. 'The system suppliers had been in control with little involvement by operations people. So two-thirds don't know how to use it. The Computer Department kept creating more facilities on screen but gave very little help to users. The IT system was not fully usable so we could not cut staff significantly through its use as intended.' The new plan was to put simple operations applications on the IT system, e.g. simple management accounting spreadsheets and to train staff on each one gradually. Attempts to change the Association's culture through awareness and preparatory training had been abandoned in favour of modest skill training in computer applications related to tasks of individuals or groups of employees. The Group Operations Director said 'It will be a fait accompli. Directors will be told . . . IT will be locked in.'

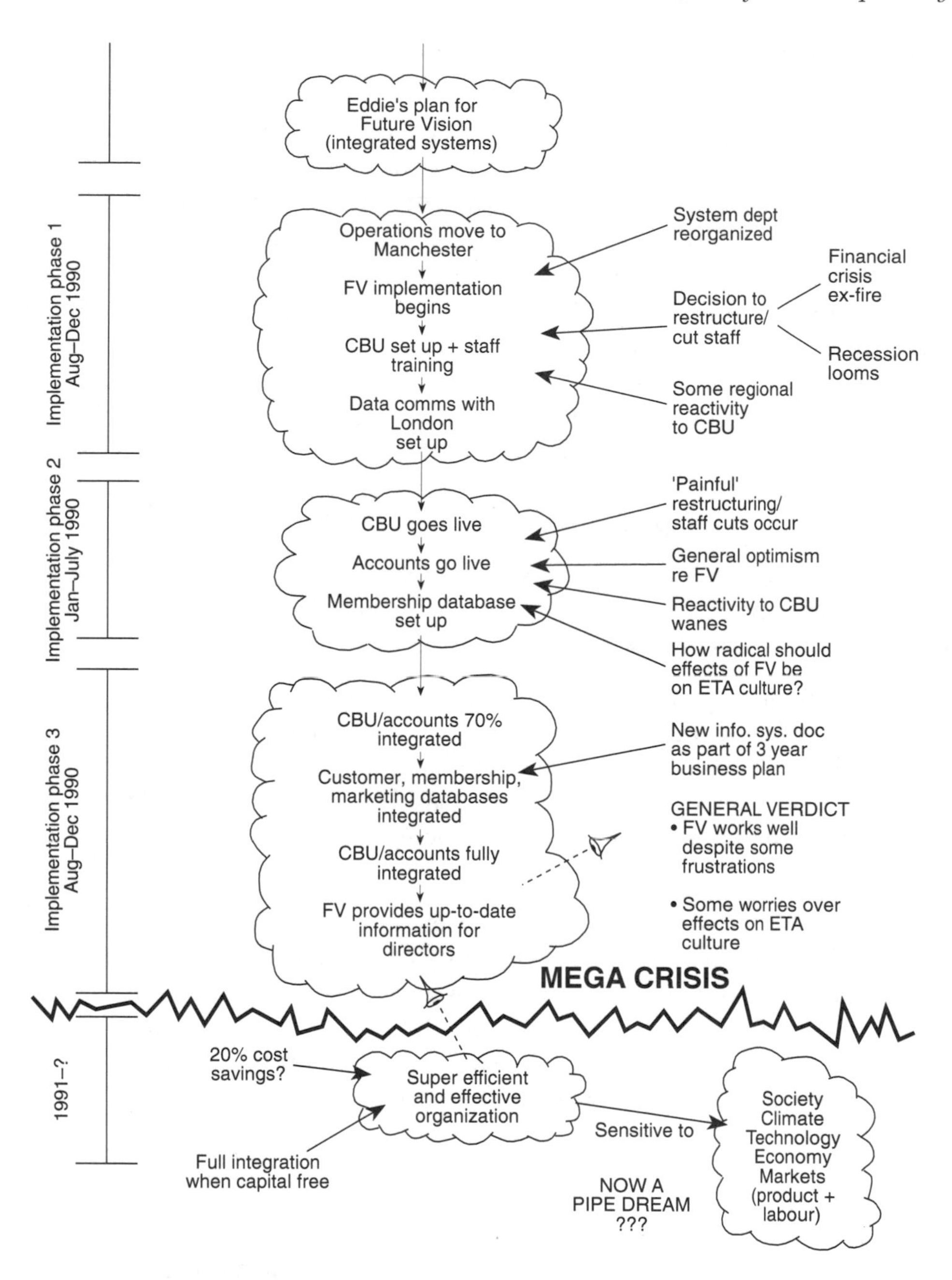


*Figure 14.2* (opposite) Event flow diagram of 'Future Vision' introduction, August 1989–December 1990, in the Employment Training Association

## *Analysis and discussion*

### *Strategy*

At the most senior level – where Association strategies might be expected to be formulated – radical changes were not evident during 1988. The Divisional Directors had made a so-called 'megadecision' about the Association's future computer development but to an outsider it seemed rather unremarkable. The existing system was obviously defective and would have required replacement in any event. However, recognition of the need for a business strategy for the organization (whether prompted by the external consultants or coincidental with their advice) became the unarguable reason for a new computer system.

Eddie saw the organization's formal structure having to change to fit the new information dominated business strategy of the next ten years. His espoused objectives were, in the light of organizational growth, increasing competition and improvements in the price/performance ratio of technology, to:

| | |
|---|---|
| • cut costs;<br>• increase efficiency;<br>• increase effectiveness. | } by integration of information systems and centralization of data entry |

Informal, unannounced objectives may have increased his power by domination of what would become the most vital of the Association's valued resources – information. For example, 'The database is a strategic asset – the most vital . . . We must have discipline, procedures and standards for accessing and using it.' The accrual of such power became evident later in the study. In 1990, for example, Eddie said

> As a result of the new system, we have been able to invest in *central* costs. Therefore Eddie's Operations Support Division got bigger in order to save elsewhere. Emotionally, there has been resistance to reducing the numbers of staff. They see my Division as not sharing the pain. A debate is bubbling. I may have to do some cuts to calm the waters. It's not right but . . . I may have to trade off small cuts in my Division to unlock the gains.

The centralization–decentralization tension highlighted by the introduction of the new IT system is evidenced by comments made by various individuals during 1988 and 1989. For example:

> Information in the organization was cellular. There was internal competition over who should keep and control it. That will have to change. We are too many small teams with large overheads and small benefits. Is it a 'nation

> states' situation? Yes, it is and we encourage it but we need treaties – hence the need for information exchange. Better communications could be achieved as a result of this project . . . There is still a feeling of there being Regional barons . . . IT implies a degree of centralization but it must not get out of control.

The underlying view of the 'new guard' appeared to be that IT use is a process which enables greater structural flexibility, responsiveness to changes in the outer context, and more efficiency with minimal staff increases (cf Blackler 1988). The advent of this utility was seen as an opportunity to enforce structural and attitudinal changes. However, if such a shift in attitudes towards the control of information did occur, how fundamental was it really? It would certainly have represented a change in the *formal* structures and mechanisms of the Association, but would the consensual hegemony which pervaded the organization from top to bottom have changed?

Although one person, i.e. Eddie, appeared to be clearly leading the IT strategy, reservations were expressed throughout the period up to the end of 1990 about whether the forecast beneficial outcome would in fact be achieved and at what costs. One senior person said 'I'm not convinced we've actually taken a leap forward – but we've moved a long way . . . We've not yet had the delivery. . . . There's concern over central expenditure on IT etc and the transfer to the new system makes the figures look worse.' Some senior figures saw their own lack of IT knowledge as creating a powerlessness to resist the arguments for IT plans of 'those closest to it'. As one senior figure put it: 'Eddie proposes. Old decisions tie you into new decisions. There's a level of unsophistication about IT in most people. The ability to make real judgements is limited. Each stage is linked. It's an inherent problem for all lay senior managers.' Another said 'On the IT system, having a plan unfold at a meeting *sounds* OK so we endorsed it. But later we felt we would have criticized it if we had had more information.' It is evident that work schedules and priorities at senior level limit the time available to acquire sufficient expertise needed to probe cogently assertions made by those having formal authority in computing matters (see Rowe 1985 for similar comment).

A number of uncertainties about IT strategy arise. For example:

- What do key figures and others mean by 'strategy'?
- What are the IT strategies?
- What forms the basis for the IT strategies?
- How formal are the strategies?
- What objectives do the strategies have?

- Are objectives formally defined in a measurable way?
- What meanings of success are applied?
- What measures of performance are used?
- Are measures used consistently over time within the organization by key figures?
- Are there hidden agendas?
- Who formulates the strategies?
- How prescriptive are the strategies?
- What are the physical manifestations of strategies?
- Is IT seen as a strategic issue in its own right, i.e. does corporate strategy depend on IT, or does IT follow from corporate strategy?
- How are strategies perceived by others within the organization?

### *Decision-making*

The 'megadecision' meeting referred to above provided an insight into how decisions were arrived at. There was an unannounced coalition between, on the one hand, the two Directors having acknowledged business skills (the Association's Chief Executive and the Finance Director) and, on the other hand, the one person having expert power in computer matters (Eddie, the Operations Support Director). It was evident that it was difficult for other Directors to argue with Eddie on technical grounds, especially when he was supported by outside consultants.

The Chief Executive and Finance Director added their quiet support which gave the impression that the three had already decided collectively in advance what was required. Their task was to steer the rest towards that same conclusion, i.e. mobilize bias to a consensus (Watson 1982). There is a parallel with the case study findings of Pettigrew (1973). Eddie held the key to who received valued resouces and rewards in the IT stakes. He was enabled to exercise such control because he had formed a coalition with other power figures.

### *Ideology and culture*

A Regional Manager noted that the ETA lived by its own gospel as preached to other employers, namely communication, consultation and involvement of staff. However, regional staff reported that they were denied these opportunities when it came to developing the computer system. Some went so far as to describe the London headquarters as 'power mad' in their apparent attempts to control all computer applications. Concern was expressed in various meetings about communication problems within the Association and with clients and the dangers of projecting 'an idiosyncratic image to customers'. Cynicism was expressed widely about the reliability of the computer system in improving such matters.

Eddie alluded to a culture change which he suggested must accompany Future Vision. 'The ETA is different now. It is no longer the small, friendly Association of 10–15 years ago. Informal networks will no longer do. . . . The Directors decided as policy to cut the external print budget and only allow the Print Dept to use it, but it never became practice. Now with the financial crisis we force it under pain of death. All this is helping a cultural change.' The need for 'Regional barons' to relax their grip on local files became to be seen as part of an imminent culture change.

One senior figure referred to a forced culture change being needed to ensure the ascendancy of the 'new guard' over the 'old' and so enable the organization to use the new IT system to best advantage in survival against competition. 'The old guard members will resist change and some will drop out, but we will be much *stronger*.' In 1990, another said 'There is a cultural transition required from the cellular to the centralist handling of information throughout. There is a danger of "tails wagging dogs".'

Nevertheless, whereas many senior figures expressed views similar to those of Eddie, an actual culture change of this kind did not really materialise. In August 1991, for example, one of the new Group Operations Directors expressed the opinion that a major reason for the organization's recent crisis had been the continuing influence of the 'old guard' culture aided by lack of leadership from the previous Chief Executive. As the Group Operations Director put it, 'powerful 'robber barons' had been left in position as Divisional Directors', thus indicating that the power structure and cultural characteristics associated with the earlier 'Regional barons' of mid-late 1980s had only undergone a cosmetic change.

Some senior figures rejected the assertion that the Association was by nature consensual on the basis that consensus to them meant a group view or decision. They claimed that the Association encouraged participation (really 'involvement', see Mangham 1979) but conflicts did arise and managers listened but made their own decisions. However, as one person put it, 'The question is often asked 'will there be a vote', and the answer is 'most definitely not'.' Another commented 'My image of how decisions have been made is one of a caucus of middle-aged men in a smoke-filled room. There is supposed to have been consultation but how much notice was taken? Was consultation to find out where the opposition was or just to confirm things?'

### *Power and political processes*

Because so much could hinge on the IT changes (e.g. business strategy, future developments, personal rewards), those who gained more than others from computerization itself also stood to gain more power than others did. At the same time, the new computer strategy would result in a shift in the Association's power structure. Perceptions of such shifts varied according to the location of individuals in the organization. Divisional Directors were looking forward to 'regional barons' no longer being able to keep key customer information to themselves. Staff in the regions, however, saw the centralization of data input as power madness sullied by a decrease in efficiency and an increase in costs. The devolution of key policy implementation and the centralization of computing seemed to conflict. The power shift could be argued to be both a consequence of the strategy for change and a reason for it.

The use of language and management of meanings (Pettigrew 1987; Knights and Morgan 1991) occurred frequently. Typically, the term 'strategy' was used to convey images of goals but virtually nothing about how they were going to be achieved. For example, one senior figure stated: 'I don't know the full scope of the project. I am not aware of any strategy document. I have seen bits and pieces but no real stuff.' Another said: 'Most of the people are clear about the project objectives. It's how we do it that's the problem.'

Numerous references were made which suggested that views of the IT strategy were supplied by the Operations Support Director. As one senior figure put it, 'The project is very much Eddie led. The Directors make the decisions based on Eddie's recommendations. He knows if the Director supports it or not before he comes to us . . . Consultation has been inherently limited. Eddie consulted us and got us to decide on the stages but we *knew* we were locked in at the time . . . If Eddie can deliver we will support it . . . IT implies a degree of centralization but it must not get out of control.' Generally, it appeared to be taken for granted up to the end of 1990 that Eddie was the rightful orchestrator, thus supporting the contention that fantasy manipulation by such a key strategic figure represents not simply formal authority but also unobtrusive power (Hardy 1985).

### *Meanings of success*

A variety of meanings of success for the IT project were attributed by respondents. These included formal and factual components such as getting the new FX system operational and on schedule, achieving more efficient course bookings, making significant cost savings through reductions in administrative staff, and in the longer term a better responsiveness to changing commercial conditions. By implication, success also meant not experiencing potential adverse effects which respondents mentioned, such as:

- Poor reliability of hardware, software, and technical support.
- Staff cynicism and paranoid feelings about managerial intentions.
- Unanticipated costs in outlay, upheaval, training, etc.
- Drain on service time, increased work, or nuisance resulting from the new system.
- Too much centralization leading to loss of efficiency or loss of personal contact.

Higher order goals over and above the formal objectives of the project were also evident. For example, improving communication between people in the organization and breaking down the 'nation states' isolationism that had developed in some parts of such a geographically dispersed organization. The Future Vision project itself carried with it a loosely articulated longer term goal of an IT-driven organization in a 5–10 year time frame ('Eddie's vision') as opposed to the more formal shorter term goal of an efficient IT-using organization.

The Operations Support Director had created a vision of success for the grand project. However, in practice, the implementation of this project concentrated on the technology aspects. Given the technical complexity of the task, this approach may have been justifiable if Eddie's assumption was realistic, namely that a change in culture to a technology-using and ultimately technology-driven Association would occur in tandem. Not everyone shared his vision in its entirety. Some saw Future Vision as a vehicle enabling the Operations Support Division to become dominant through expansion in its staff, its budget and its control of a strategic resource. For example, reflecting in August 1991 on the debacle, one of the Group Operations Directors expressed the opinion that the project's concept as implemented was a root cause of both its own failure and the near-crash of the Association. He said 'The project was about the growth of the IT system and departments, *not* about the growth of people and users. There was a leadership and direction issue. Powerful Divisional Directors were protecting their empires.'

It would appear, therefore, that although there was general agreement about the overall formal and factual meanings of success in principle, there were conflicting meanings of success for particular aspects of Future Vision itself and for its likely effects on power structures. Respondents implied that success for the IT project encompassed components which are much more informal and driven by personal or partisan values. For example, the issue of information ownership underscored perceived threats to control of work. Not losing present control of work as a result of the new IT system represented success to some people in the organization. The centralization–decentralization issue is closely related to the issue of control. Those who had previously enjoyed a large degree of local autonomy in the control and use of information for local decision-making regarded the retention of that autonomy as success. Those who perceived that their jobs would radically alter (for example, job content or relocation to Manchester) or might be lost altogether saw success in terms of the avoidance of such threats. As one person put it: 'The Departments moving to Manchester are not too thrilled. It's causing upset in their work, their lives and they think twice how loved they really are by the organization for all their hard work . . . '. Others frequently mentioned that their use of IT would improve the organization's image among clients and so by implication the enhancement of professional identity was seen by these respondents as part of what success for the IT project would mean for them (see chapter 7).

Throughout the study, informal and interest-related factors featured strongly in concerns and issues expressed by ETA staff. These factors relate to the working context in which they perceived themselves and their fellow employees and the symbolic role of the new computing system. These factors are summarized in Box 14.1.

## IT risks for organizations

### *Hazards and threats (see chapter 2)*

#### *Demand for IT*

Positive factors include:

- Wide recognition in organizations that unless IT is used to best effect the organization may become uncompetitive.
- Greater awareness of competitive threat posed by IT-enhanced cost-efficiency, service provision and product innovation.
- School-leavers and new graduates entering the employment market are generally computer-literate, confident in using computers and expect to use computers.
- Continuing improvements in price-performance ratios of IT products.

Key threats include:

- Failure to match own IT investment and strategy to competitive threat.
- Bad experiences with unreliable hardware and software.
- Cynicism about computer suppliers.
- 'Technofear' on the part of staff, especially older employees.

## Box 14.1: Concerns and Issues expressed by ETA staff

***Effects of general economic downturn and internal financial constraints on professional identity and ETA culture***

- To what extent should the Association be run as a business?
- Conflict between perceived economic imperative of reducing number of admin staff for business survival and the Association's 'caring' culture
- Conflict between perceived economic imperative of rationalising small semi-autonomous teams for business survival and the Association's 'caring' culture

***Ambiguous role of Future Vision (FV) in relation to protection of professional identity and ETA culture***

- FV intended to achieve significant reduction in ratio of admin staff to fee-earning staff
- FV intended to help achieve flexibility of response to rapid changes in economy or markets
- FV intended to enable revival of better campaigning – i.e. retention of Association's cultural characteristics
- Conflict between intention that FV would provide integrated, centrally-driven information system and desire for local control of information
- Conflict between cost control and the Association's campaigning priorities, but FV seen as essential to ensure both
- Conflict between, on the one hand, intentions that FV would enable restructuring and staff reductions and, on the other hand, maintenance of team values
- FV intended to highlight bad debts; how far can benign, charitable attitudes towards customers be sustained in a harsh economic climate?

***Decision-making processes in the Association***

- Who had and who ought to have had decision-making power concerning FV?
- How much leadership from the Chief Executive should have been manifest as crisis loomed, e.g. decisions to radically restructure the ETA against the vested interests of Divisional Directors?
- How much consultation can be allowed in times of crisis?
- Were the consultation mechanisms satisfactory?
- What did consultation and participation mean to ETA staff at different levels?

### *IT strategy*

Positive factors include:

- Growing recognition in organizations at senior level that IT investment is very important and cannot simply be delegated as a function of computer or user departments.

Key threats include:

- Poor understanding of the meaning of strategy.
- Failure to recognise that IT strategy and business strategy are inextricably linked.
- IT investment decisions may be driven by a small number of individuals with career interests in IT without other key people fully understanding the issues.
- Enthusiasm for computers may be based on market hype or unevaluated beliefs rather than a clear demonstration of cost-benefits.
- IT strategy and its implications may be poorly communicated to an organization's workforce.
- Strategy implementation may be badly managed.

### *Fire and flood*

Positive factors include:

- Insurers and statutory fire authorities generally specify precautions.
- Insurance may offset some, but not all, losses in the event of fire or flood.

Key threats include:

- Specified fire and flood precautions not implemented.
- Inadequate insurance cover.
- Inadequate or non-existent protected back-up data.
- Inadequate or non-existent contingency arrangements for business continuity.
- Inadequate or non-existent audits.

### *Security*

Positive factors include:

- Insurers generally specify IT security precautions.
- Standard guidance on IT security – e.g. BS 7799.

Key threats include:

- Specified security precautions not implemented.
- Inadequate insurance cover.

- Inadequate or non-existent protected back-up data.
- Inadequate or non-existent contingency arrangements for business continuity.
- Inadequate or non-existent audits.

*Health and safety*
Positive factors include:

- Health and safety requirements specified by statutory regulations and generally backed up by insurers.
- Health and safety hazards generally low risk.

Key threats include:

- Failure to adequately address ergonomic requirements such as IT job design, control and pace of data entry and workstation ergonomics.
- Potential action by statutory enforcement agencies.
- Employer's liability claims by employees whose health may have suffered as a result of IT use.
- Industrial relations disputes.

*Culture*
Positive factors include:

- General acceptance by employees that IT is an important part of modern work life.

Key threats include:

- Over-reliance by employees on IT systems and data makes organizations more vulnerable and less resilient to computer failure.
- Over-engineered and over-complicated IT products may engender user-resistance.
- Poor quality IT documentation may cause frustration and user resistance.
- Fear of job loss, loss of control over work, marginalization or diminution of work value, or loss of personal or professional identity as a result of IT may cause negative attitudes and behaviour towards the organization.
- Anti-change culture in particular organizations may interfere with smooth progress of IT introduction.

*Power relations*
Positive factors include:

- Growing recognition that IT users in organizations should have a more equitable stake in decisions about IT resources.

Key threats include:

- Professional IT departments determining IT strategy and distribution of IT resources without reference to actual business and organizational needs.
- IT resources allocated to powerful departments rather than to departments having powerful arguments for such resources.
- Industrial relations disputes and industrial action by computer staff, e.g. strikes.

*Change*
Positive factors include:

- IT may make possible significant beneficial changes in an organization's approach to strategy which otherwise could only be achieved with great difficulty or at great cost.

Key threats are:

- Frequency and pace of IT changes in an organiztaion may be more rapid than is necessary, thereby incurring extra direct and indirect costs.
- Some consequences of IT changes in an organization may be detrimental to that organization – e.g. more costly than estimated, poor system reliability, benefits less than anticipated.
- IT-related changes may be too slow or too late in relation to changes in an organization's context, thereby failing to deal with relevant risks.

## *Risk assessment (see chapter 2)*

The following table summarizes potential risk levels for the threats discussed above. The attributed risk levels are based on the authors' judgements. Both positive and negative outcomes for any given threat may co-exist.

| Threat | Potential risk levels (as probabilities) | |
|---|---|---|
| | Negative outcomes | Positive outcomes |
| Demand for IT | Medium–High | Medium–High |
| IT strategy | Medium–High | Medium |
| Fire and flood | Low–Medium | Medium |
| Security | Medium–High | Medium |
| Health and safety | Low–Medium | Medium–High |
| Culture | Medium–High | Medium |
| Power relations | Medium–High | Medium |
| Change | Medium–High | Medium |

## Comparison with thematic matrix

Table 14.1 indicates the relative salience of each of the risk contexts identified in Part 1, and particularly chapter 9, in relation to this case study. In the table, H = high, M = medium, L = low.

*Table 14.1* Thematic matrix applied to the IT case study

| *Risk context* | *Salience in case study* |
|---|---|
| *Organizational environment* | |
| Economies and markets | H |
| Public policy, legislation and regulation | M |
| Social and political climate | M |
| Technology | H |
| History, operating territories and conditions | M |
| *Human factors* | |
| Culture | H |
| Power relations, political processes and decision-making | H |
| Perception and cognition | H |
| *Formal coping arrangements* | |
| Risk management | H |
| Risk assessment | H |
| Management systems | H |
| Approaches to change | H |

## Conclusions

The risks associated with IT introduction relate to cognitions of 'success', not just for the process itself and whether the IT system functions adequately but also for the organization's business objectives and for personal and professional objectives of numerous individuals and interest groups. However, some people argue that 'success' for IT introduction is largely predictable by close attention to and manipulation of such things as:

- IT strategy and its relationship with business objectives;
- systematic approach to strategy implementation;
- technical requirements (right equipment, software, etc.);
- resource requirements (staffing, specialist support, etc.);
- staff training;
- staff participation in whys, whats, hows, etc.;
- leadership by a key strategic figure;
- organizational structures and processes (reporting relationships, more devolved decision-making, etc.);
- organizational culture (attitude changes, new outlook, etc.);
- neutralizing fire, security and safety hazards.

Few people would argue with the common-sense approach of at least some aspects of this prescription. However, are these factors necessary and sufficient in themselves to ensure a large measure of agreement about whether 'success' has been achieved? Success for a project may be judged by those involved on many factors which are not concerned with the project *per se*. The particular project may be regarded by those involved or affected as an ambiguous symbol. On the one hand, the project may be seen as helping to raise operational efficiency and business effectiveness, both in the long term and during short-term difficulties. On the other hand, it is also symbolic of what some people in an organization may see as substantive changes in the traditional priority values of the organization or their own professional group. Criteria for success and how those criteria are decided upon and by whom (i.e. power and political processes) appear to be critical issues (see chapter 7). How narrowly or how broadly those criteria are defined is likely to affect an organization's approach to managing the risks of IT introduction.

# Chapter 15

# UK health authorities struggle to survive

## Overview

This chapter discusses fundamental changes in provision of health care in the UK since the mid 1980s and how local Health Authorities sought to cope with risks associated with such changes. A case study examines how one Health Authority responded to government directives such as Internal Markets and Resource Management in its Local Community Services Unit.

## Introduction

Health care provision is a major concern of governments and often represents a large proportion of government expenditure. In an ideal world, health care demand would be met in full but there are constraints (largely financial) which make this utopian vision difficult, if not impossible, to achieve. For example, medical science and technology continue to provide newer and better methods of diagnosis and treatment, many of which are expensive. As a result of medical innovations, diseases and medical conditions which were difficult to treat only a few years ago are now controllable or even curable. Increased public awareness of health issues, coupled with a consumer-oriented model at the heart of UK government health policy from 1979 to 1997, has encouraged patient demand. In addition, life expectancy has gradually risen and, as people live longer, diseases of old age, previously relatively uncommon, now place a growing burden on health care resources.

It is self-evident that whereas health care demand is increasing and in principle is limitless, health care resources are finite. It is therefore necessary more than ever before to ensure that such resources are managed as effectively and as efficiently as possible. Prior to the early 1980s, the process of seeking better health care management in the UK had been largely one of periodic structural reorganizations of a hierarchical bureaucracy, with the Department of Health & Social Security (The

DHSS was later split into Department of Health (DoH) and Department of Social Security (DSS).) at the top and local hospitals reporting to District Health Authorities at the bottom. For example, in 1974 Regional Health Authorities were introduced as a new layer of management between District Health Authorities and the DHSS. However, the process started to take a radical turn in the 1980s with a succession of government reports, notably the Griffiths Report (1983), the Körner Reports (1982–84), and the White Papers *Working for Patients* (1989) and *Caring for People* (1989).

## Pressure for health care changes in 1980s

The series of Körner Reports (1982–84) and the Griffiths Report (1983) examined two different but related aspects of health service management. The NHS/DHSS Steering Committee on Health Service Information, chaired by Mrs Edith Körner, focused on deployment of clinical resources and the need to ensure that resources are well targeted. In particular, the DHSS needed a means of measuring efficiency in the use of clinical resources throughout the National Health Service (NHS) and this implied the need for a Health Service information system. The Körner reports recommended 'minimum data sets' which District Health Authorities would be required to collate from different clinical groups and submit to the DHSS on a regular basis. These minimum data sets comprised data such as numbers of clinicians in service, numbers of patients treated and patient waiting lists. For example, the Körner Reports 4 and 5 covered respectively Paramedical Services (e.g. physiotherapy, chiropody, speech therapy) and Community Services (e.g. community nursing, mental health). In the UK, paramedical services denote a wide range of medically related activities and not just ambulance crews.

For paramedical services, the minimum data set was to comprise:

- an annual self-reported sample enquiry;
- numbers of face-to-face contacts; or initial contacts (physiotherapy); or length of treatment (speech therapy).

For community services, the minimum data set was to comprise:

- information about services to the community
  - immunisation
  - health surveillance
  - health promotion and education;
- annual data to be assembled showing
  - local policy and objectives, including target level of coverage
  - estimated target population

- projected expenditure
- level of service provided
- coverage achieved
- estimated actual expenditure.

The Department of Health (DoH, formerly part of the DHSS) set a timetable for Körner implementation which required recommendations of Reports 4 and 5 to be operational as from April 1988.

The Griffiths Report suggested that the long-standing approach to hospital and health care management based on management by clinical professionals was no longer sustainable. Many clinicians were not fully aware of the impact of their clinical decisions on resources and, in some instances, clinicians were carrying out treatments regardless of cost. If limited resources were to be deployed and managed well and with due account of budgets, general managers were required who were not actively engaged in clinical practice. Indeed, some people argued that general managers did not need to be clinically qualified. However, others felt that managers without medical qualifications might more easily absolve themselves of responsibility for damage to patient care.

The 1989 White Papers proposed a radical reorganization of the NHS around an 'internal markets' model. In the new regime, Regional Health Authorities would disappear and District Health Authorities would become relatively small purchasing authorities, responsible for standards, contracts and performance but no longer responsible for delivery of health care. Instead, delivery would be open to competitive tender among numerous contract suppliers across the country, effectively the hospitals and their clinical units and departments who would be allocated annual budgets by the DoH and be responsible for budget holding, marketing, bid costing, operating within costs, etc. Resource management, both as a means of cost control and performance measurement and as a means of influencing clinical purchasers, would be an important part of budget holders' activities.

Under the new regime, hospitals would be allowed to opt out of health authority control by forming NHS Trusts. Trust status would enable, among other things, local flexibility in determining wages. Trusts would be able to enter into business deals with private companies for the building and running of clinical departments or even entire hospitals.

In short, the White Papers sought a culture change from that of an old-style health care system dominated by the medical professions to that of a new-style collection of small clinical businesses run by general managers. The Conservative government had a clear political agenda to introduce market economics into the NHS as a means of demonstrating value for public money to the voting public. A high profile measure of performance would be patient waiting lists which is obviously linked to patient throughput. In order to embed the internal markets model and resource management, it would be imperative (in the government's mind) to wrest control of NHS clinical management from clinical professionals and especially powerful consultants. General management, resource management and internal contracting therefore would also serve a double purpose of breaking the power of the clinical professions. It was publicly reported that the then Prime Minister, Margaret Thatcher, held strong views about powerful professional groups in the civil and public services acting as self-serving stumbling blocks to progress and that she was determined to push through reforms.

## Rapid change 1988–93

The period of 1988–93 saw the overlapping implementation of Griffiths and Körner and finally the two White Papers. It was undoubtedly a period of increasing turbulence, uncertainties and generally adverse reactions among NHS staff. On the one hand, there was widespread agreement among staff that reforms were necessary (Waring 1993b), a fact that has not been generally reported in the public media. On the other hand, clinical staff became increasingly concerned that overall good intentions of the White Papers would be subverted by cynical and self-serving NHS managers and administrators, such that 'value for money' and 'resource management' would become excuses for simplistic cost-cutting of clinical care to the detriment of patients (Reed and Anthony 1991).

One of the first manifest signs of the changing NHS culture was the proliferation of business-school jargon and paraphenalia such as business plans, measures of performance and targets (Parker and Dent 1991). Nevertheless, from confidential interviews with numerous individuals who were participating in the changes, it was clear that the core value of 'patients always come first regardless of economics' remained covert and unchanged (Waring 1993b). Anger against a perceived hidden agenda of resource management was commonly expressed privately by clinical staff, even though they accepted that information management would be critical to survival. Complex power relations which had long existed between different clinical professions, managers and administrators within district authorities provided fertile ground for struggles for 'survival of the fittest' (see Figure 15.1).

The following case study of Körner and White Paper implementation in a large metropolitan health authority (Waring 1993b) exemplifies the tensions, difficulties and risk issues experienced by health authorities as they struggled to cope with the period of rapid change from 1998 to 1993.

*Figure 15.1* Rich picture of a typical UK health authority, June 1990

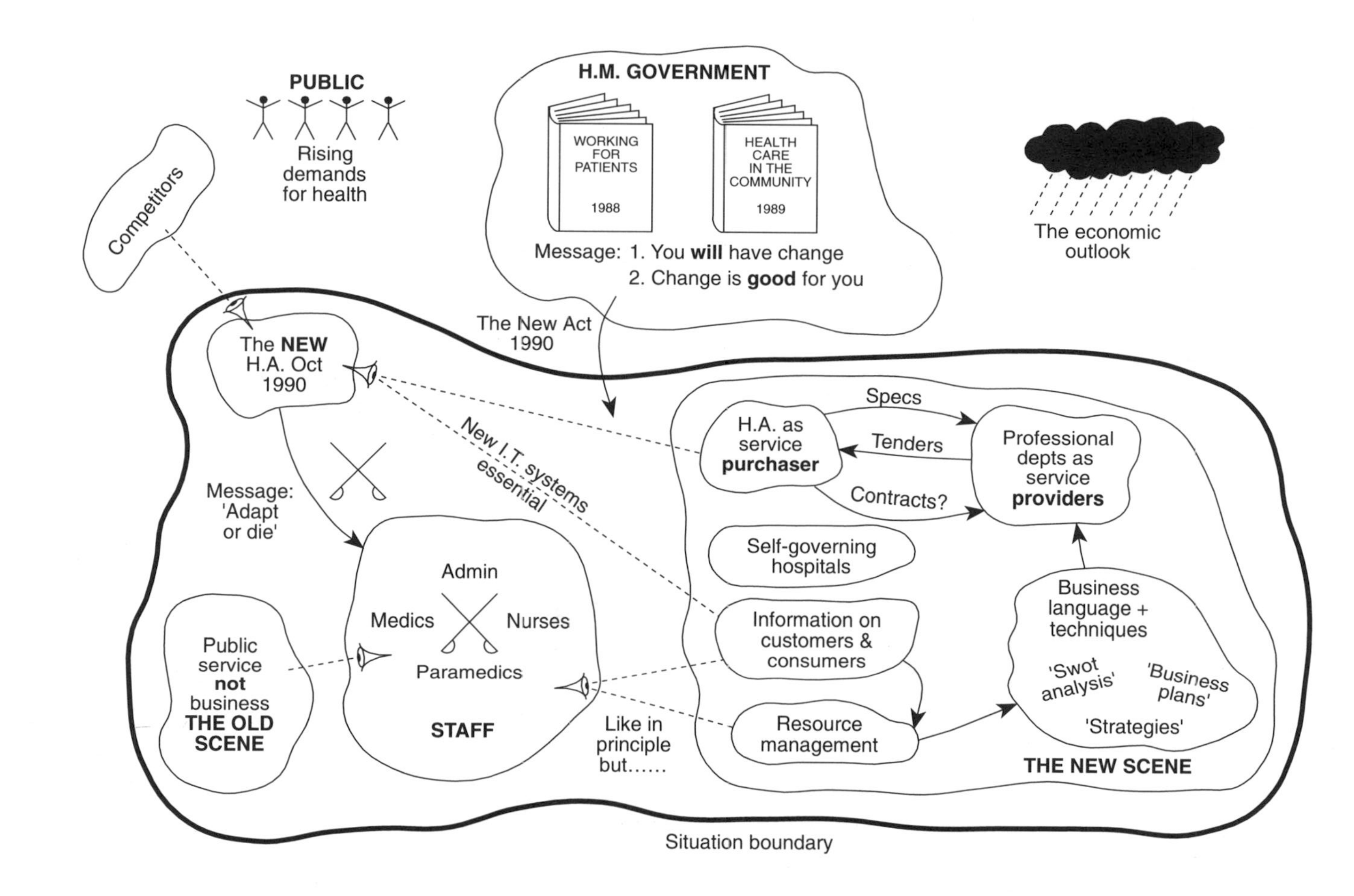

## Metropolitan Health Authority

### *Significant developments 1988–93*

#### *The Community Körner System*

The response of Metropolitan Health Authority (MHA), as far as its Local and Community Services Unit (LCSU) was concerned, was to establish a programme for a computerized Community Körner (CK) system (including paramedical services). It should be noted that Körner did not insist on computerized information systems but, in the climate of technological development, Health Authorities in general judged this to be the most realistic approach.

The LCSU approach in MHA was to set up a Project Steering Group in January 1988 chaired by the Unit General Manager. The Steering Group included representatives from all the service functions within the LCSU. Shortly after, a Project Team was set up under the chairmanship of the Unit General Manager, apparently to make executive decisions about implementation taking into account Steering Group views.

#### *Implementation of Community Körner*

The implementation schedule was set initially for completion by November 1988 but this was judged by the Unit General Manager to be unsuitable as it was out-of-step with financial returns in May each year. There were also delays in getting the equipment installed and the software operating correctly. The Unit General Manager therefore rescheduled the full implementation date to April 1989.

He stated that as far as he was concerned, the objectives were to:

- get the system operating by April 1989;
- give the DoH its minimum data ('feed the beast') which was of little interest to LCSU;
- obtain additional management information to enable analysis, prediction and control of activities by individual managers, with the possibility of further application to Resource Management.

However, further delays occurred in installing the computer hardware (especially terminals and their networking among a number of dispersed sites). It was also discovered that the FIP (Financial Information Package) software was of poor quality (unreliable, software errors, basic functions missing). Considerable time was spent clarifying who had decided on FIP software and who was contractually responsible for its reliability (see Figure 15.2).

As 1988 progressed, there were reports of growing disillusionment among LCSU

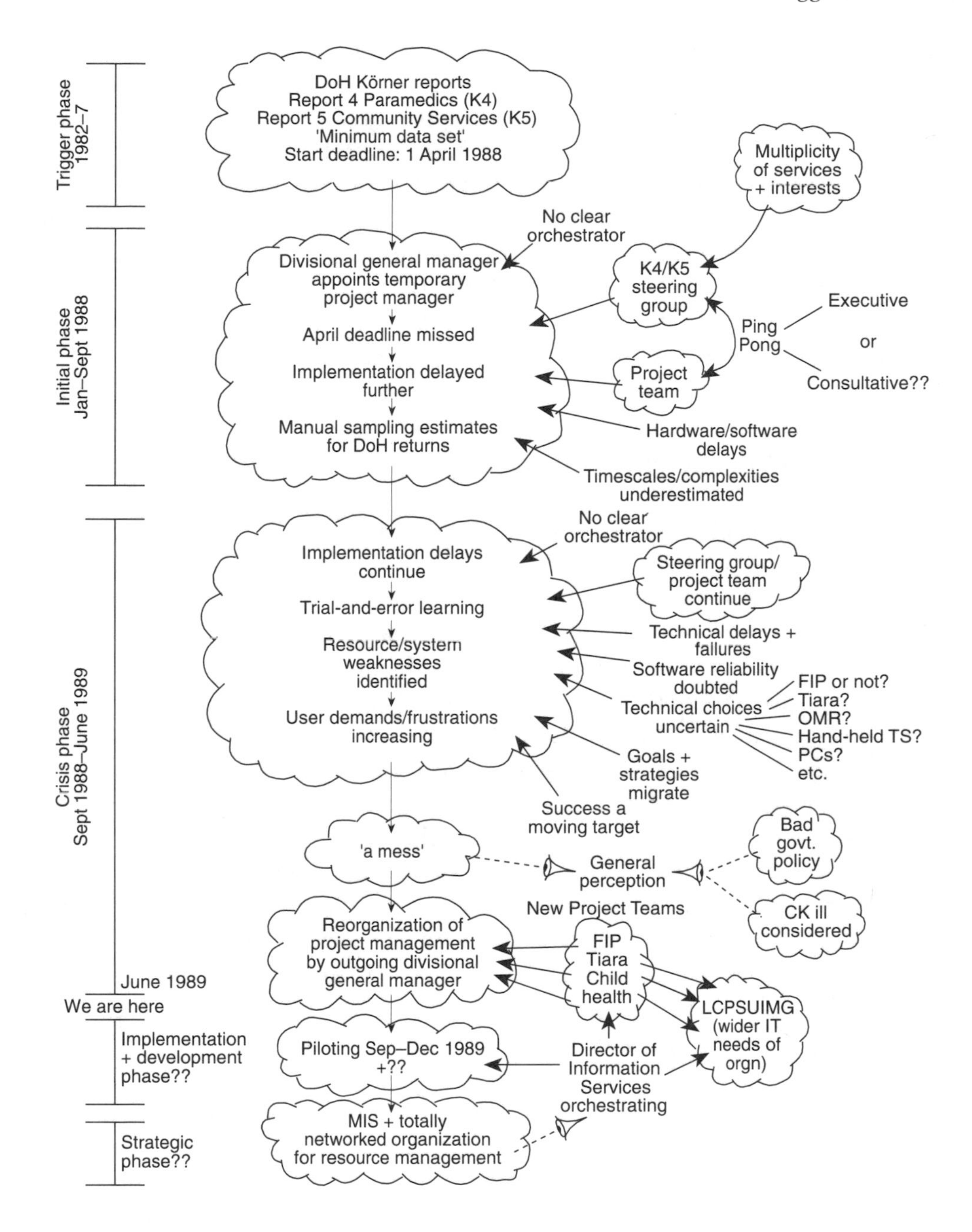


*Figure 15.2* Event flow diagram of Community Körner computerization, 1987–June 1989, in Metropolitan Health Authority

staff whose expectations for Körner implementation had been raised prematurely. Unannounced but none the less perceptible rivalry for control of the project developed between different parties. Political processes became intense. At both Steering Group and Project Team meetings, the competing parties attempted to define and describe the factual reality of the project and its future development in different ways according to their differing valuations. The Unit General Manager as chairman appeared to maintain an independent view of the competing interpretations.

In January 1989, the Government issued its White Paper *Working for Patients* which outlined its plans for reform of the National Health Service in the 1990s. This document only mentioned Community and Paramedical Services obliquely in one sentence, a fact which was widely interpreted within LCSU as an indication that future resources would be concentrated on acute services rather than theirs. Körner data and the advent of Resource Management were widely interpreted as being linked.

### *Community Körner reorganization*

In May 1989, a complete reorganization of the project management was announced. The Körner Steering Group would be replaced by the LCSU Information Management Group (LCSUIMG). With the restructuring came clearer demarcation of roles and responsibilities. In early June 1989, the new FIP Project Manager issued a structured implementation plan based on clear objectives. The Director of Information Services for MHA who had been involved originally in setting up the Steering Group, took charge of the new approach. He was a technical specialist in information systems and this became apparent as he steered both the LCSUIMG and FIP Group through uncertainties. He also introduced a new strategic perspective for the role of FIP in relation to the wider aspects of MHA information strategy. Rather than concentrating on making FIP work for its own sake which had been the main focus, he outlined the main task as using FIP as a test-bed for data networking which was the longer term goal for the District as a whole. See Figure 15.3.

Between June and September 1989, the new implementation plan progressed with piloting. The FIP Project Group was renamed FIP/Information Project Group in recognition of its potentially wider remit and the growing role of LCSUIMG in District information strategy in response to the demands for Resource Management from the DoH. The language of Resource Management such as 'objective criteria', 'evaluation', 'measures of performance' began to appear in FIP Project and LCSUIMG meetings.

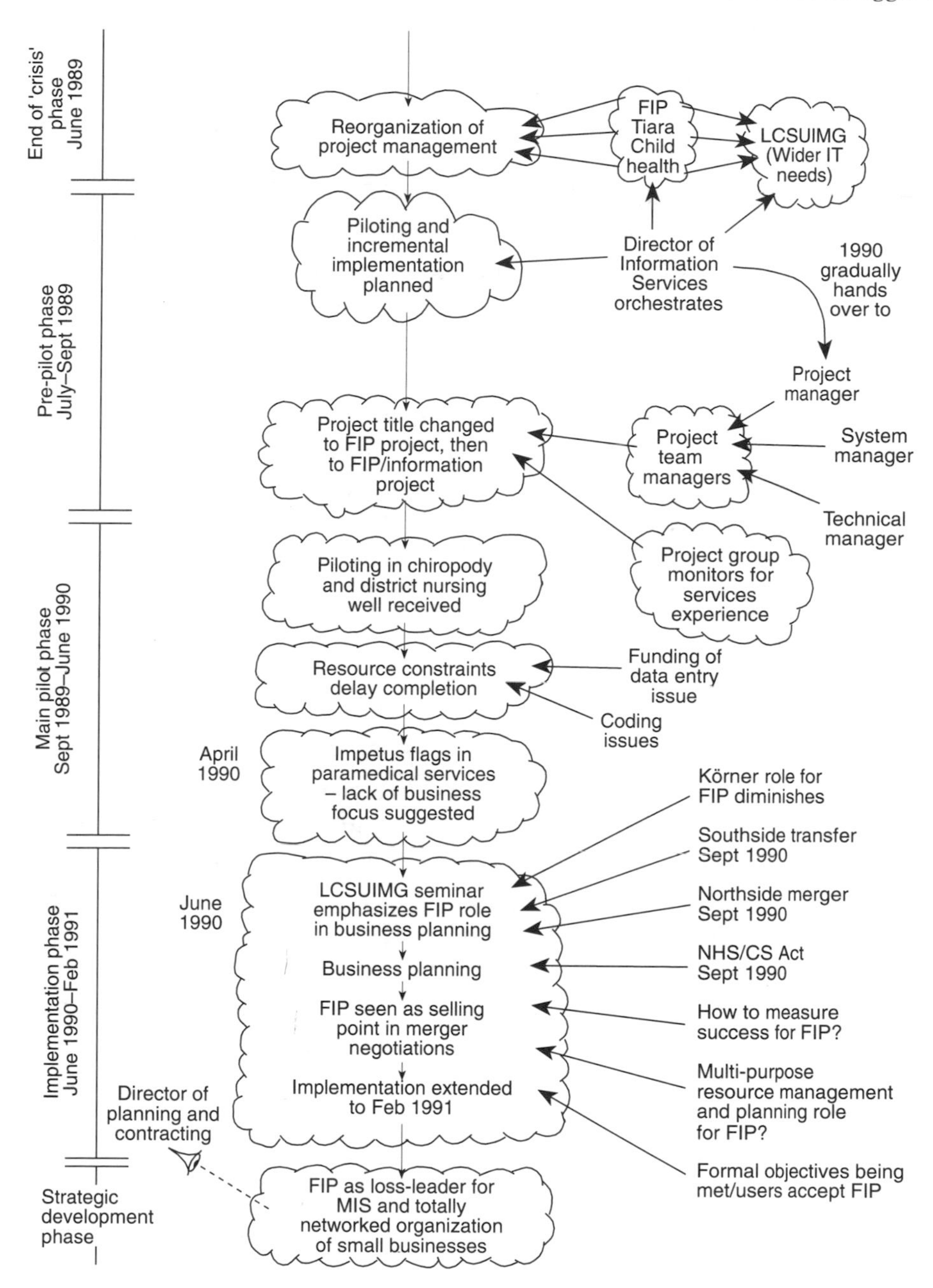


*Figure 15.3* Event flow diagram of FIP introduction, June 1989–February 1991, in Metropolitan Health Authority

### *Health authority reorganization*

In autumn 1989, the Government announced that the Metropolitan Health Authority was to be disaggregated. The southern area would pass to its neighbouring Southside Health Authority. Then, after consultation, a decision would be made about which neighbouring District should take over the northern area and the remainder of MHA. The neighbouring Northside Health Authority was suggested as being the most likely candidate. Subsequently, a decision was made to merge Metropolitan and Northside into a new single authority.

The Director of Information Services informed the LCSUIMG that the disaggregation process could take anywhere from six months to two years. In any event, the FIP project would have to continue for two reasons. First, a working FIP system would be a good trading point with the other Health Authorities, especially if as had been rumoured their own CK systems were not operating properly. Second, the need for detailed information on patient usage in Community and Paramedical Services was vital in any negotiation and transfer process. By December 1989, it was reported that the FIP pilots had been running well and that they were to be extended to other sites.

### *White Paper implementation*

With a start date of 1 April 1990 for implementing the White Paper, at District level much attention and effort throughout 1990 was directed at seeking to meet the major restructuring of the District into a relatively small 'purchasing authority' supplied by 'clinical units' in competition with others in the NHS. The White Paper implementation date also coincided with the merger of Metropolitan and neighbouring Northside Health Authority. The District General Manager set up an Information Strategy Steering Group (ISSG), information on patient trends, clinical demand and clinical resource management being seen as critical to business survival in the new NHS. The NHS Working Paper 11 (Framework for Information Systems) had introduced requirements for:

- Minimum Contract Data Sets;
- Accelerated introduction of individual patient level databases piloted by Resource Management sites;
- Future significance of Case Mix Analysis;
- Merger of Community & Paramedical data sets with Acute Services activity information.

In addition, the ISSG was faced with integrating the information and IT systems of Metropolitan and Northside Health Authorities. In the first round of integration which took place at District Management Board level, the District General Manager post and most of the key Director posts had gone to existing Metropolitan post holders. In the second round, many senior posts in Metropolitan were not assured and post holders had to compete with counterparts in Northside. It was reported that the general feeling among Northside staff was that they were being taken over and that many were avoiding requests for co-operation from Metropolitan counterparts. As the District General Manager commented, 'My problem is taking on board Northside without causing hiatus in the organization and in arrangements such as contracting, resource management, and education and research. I need a clear idea of the shell and framework to inform action over the next two or three months of transition in managerial arrangements.'

Wresting control of patient information and its application from clinical consultants was also a key issue. For example, at one ISSG meeting a clinical consultant argued against medical staff contracts which would specify the time between discharge and summary report, whereas the rest of the group argued against him on the grounds that his approach ignored standards and confounded the revenue process.

The new 'business' approach demanded by the White Paper caused some consternation among the clinical specialists in the Local and Community Services Unit. In particular, ISSG required that each department should draw up a business plan (some 50 were identified by ISSG). In response to concerns expressed by staff, a seminar on Information and Business Planning was held to brief them on the implications of the NHS and Community Care Bill. The new internal contracting arrangements between purchasers and providers of care would necessitate each service producing and operating business plans which in turn would require accurate information about current demand and provision. The Director of Planning and Contracting made a contrast. On the one hand, he said that there was the 'old style culture' of the NHS in which NHS information was seen as a chore and a waste of time and which demanded a large management overhead. On the other hand, there was the 'new style culture' of providers acting as small businesses and requiring investment in information so as to gain competitive edge. FIP had a useful, if temporary, information role.

### *Survival strategy*

At Director level, the organizational, methodological and technological changes which they were now directing were justified by them as imperatives for survival. For example, the Director of Planning and Contracting stated 'We *must* have the information to run the business. It's now *critical*. Such radical steps were unthinkable twelve months ago.' However, six months earlier he also said that the idea that the White Paper had provoked all these changes was false. 'Those of us who had been trying to get strategic planning working for some years are using the White Paper to force the pace.' Thus, in addition to the survival imperative to avert a major crisis, at least one key Director was also using the situation to satisfy ideological motivations. Previously, he had been constrained from so doing and now in his colloquial parlance 'the brakes were off'.

A belief was expressed that there was a cultural dimension to the major changes occurring. The Director of Planning and Contracting stated 'People are the key, they've never been harnessed. It's easier said than done in a large inertia-ridden ship. It used to be the top management team who maintained these values but it was seen as incompetent. . . . Clinicians were seen as the priority. There were internecine struggles but now they've accepted change. The DGM has done it single handedly. . . . It will take two to three years for a cultural change to generate.' However, at other locations in the organization less certainty was expressed about the acceptance of change or its desirability. Generally, respondents expressed resignation about the inevitability of the organizational, technological and related changes and felt that in principle better management of resources was both necessary and welcome. However, nearly every respondent expressed to varying degrees concerns about their own personal or group interests in the context of these changes (cf Watson 1982). Their expressions of concern relate primarily to political, ideological and cultural turbulence within the organization or their part of it and a desire for stability in these dimensions.

## *Analysis and discussion*

### *Strategy*

Until the changes in project management of June 1989, the strategy for Community Körner (CK) in LCSU was unclear and there was a de facto emphasis on emergence. Strategy had been confused with goals and objectives and a number of competing interests had dabbled inconsistently in practical implementation. Not only was the CK strategy unclear among staff but so too were policy decisions made by the District Management Board. Policy decision making at Board level at that time did not appear to interwork with instrumental decision making within LCSU (cf Vickers 1985). Indeed, the Unit General Manager stated that Community Körner was not a priority matter for the Board. Until June 1989, Community Körner did not form part of an integrated IT strategy for MHA as a whole. Then strategy began to be formulated with a much clearer focus under the orchestration of the Director of Information Services. For the eighteen months prior to June 1989, CK strategy in this Authority was an *ad hoc* process operating in isolation (cf Model 0 of Blackler and Brown 1987). There was no national strategy and no software specification from the DoH. Therefore, each Health Authority was obliged to start from scratch. It is clear in hindsight that in this Authority a person was needed with formal authority at Director level, technical expertise in IT, a realistic strategic vision of IT in the long term, and a measure of enthusiasm and political skills.

Then, in mid-1989, the CK strategy was outlined as being a component in the District Information Strategy which in turn was based on Resource Management requirements to monitor and control the operation of the Authority's Business Plan. As the Director of Information Services stated:

> There are several models of Resource Management. It includes buying in services from paramedics. Several IT systems will be needed including the Nurse Management System, and a Patient Administration System feeder system. It goes right the way through to Community Services in relation to post-discharge and budgetting. . . . . There will eventually be a new ISSG with a Core Strategy Group looking at Information Requirements, Organisation of Information Services, and IT. LCSUIMG is effectively formalizing a strategy although it is not written down yet.
>
> With . . . Local & Community Services, the strategy now is to hold back on serious installation until the NHS data model for Community is revealed. We don't want to be committed to FIP for Community Resource Management. . . . . The organization bought an old product in FIP but they bought it because it was readily available off-the-shelf. Management imperatives (of time) determined this decision. But they needed to look ahead. If they had done so they would have seen that FIP led up a blind alley.

### *Outer context*

Prior to the White Paper and merger announcements, the outer context of MHA as a whole was seen as defining the necessary goals of Community Körner. Staff assumed or inferred that 'bottom line' cost control represented the strategic focus of the DoH (via Community Körner) and that qualitative measures were being ignored. Staff did not see themselves as originators and 'owners' of CK but as reluctant custodians for the DoH. Respondents typically referred to CK being imposed on them. Their motivation to cooperate with its implementation stemmed from expectations of other benefits for their own service groups.

Perceptions of government attitudes and intentions towards the Health Service and the possible effects on the Authority and the LCSU provide a contextual backdrop to activity during the study and to fantasies of the future (see also Reed and Anthony 1991). A range of views were expressed by MHA staff. Predominantly they were adverse although a minority felt that processes such as Nurse Regrading and the White Paper would bring some benefits. Typical comments were:

> The White Paper is a concern to our profession. . . . With the future of the NHS in question there is a lot of uncertainty. We have to battle for every item and we get no thanks from higher management for our work and the cuts we have endured. The Authority does not come across as caring about its staff.

> The White Paper has been badly thought out as regards self-governing hospitals. It's not plausible. Major structural changes are bad news. There's never enough time. . . . In the long run it will get worse. . . . The problem with the NHS is that it's a great organization but it's wasted and being deliberately run down. Government policy is that it does not want the NHS, it wants a private sector so the NHS is falling apart.

> Most practitioners remain sceptical about the NHS. They've seen general management arrive but no major changes as a result. They've seen the White Paper, IT and so on. The pace of change is bamboozling people. The agenda is so rapid and lengthy that people switch off or get anxious.

Until September 1989, there was no evidence among MHA staff of perceptions of market conditions in the outer context (Pettigrew 1987). All references were to government policies. However, in the turmoil of disaggregation, the White Paper and Resource Management, the Director of Information Services began to introduce marketing terminology at various meetings. For example: 'We've got away with poor information in the past because of the way Region decides its catchment area. Geographic information will become the *absolute* currency in the near future. We need to have very accurate data on patients, their location, etc., etc. This is no longer a luxury, it really is core business. We need also to look at the *quality* of data – and this is why we're starting data audits. Managers must be well aware of their performance.'

### *Resource management*

Körner itself was seen by staff as a kind of Trojan horse for the ulterior motives of the Government in introducing Resource Management into all areas of Health Service practice. Indeed, senior figures implied that this was the case. For example,

in September 1989 the Director of Information Services told a LCSUIMG meeting: 'The White Paper has had a great impact. By hanging back on IT the Authority has actually gained. Treatment and diagnosis data will be needed as well as location. . . . For the past five weeks we have had a Resource Management Working Party. We've proposed the setting up of four or five pilot Clinical Directorates. There are several models of resource management. . . . It goes right through to Community Services in relation to post-discharge costs and budgeting'.

In October 1989, further confirmation of the Trojan Horse use of FIP was obtained:

**Question**: 'Would it be accurate then to describe FIP as a loss leader for the introduction of Resource Management systems?'

**Director of Information Services**: 'A loss leader, sure. We need the comms lines in anyway. The investment in hardware is safe. The FIP package itself is cheap – only a few thousand pounds. We need to get the infrastructure in and keep the operation low key for the present. But when ready it will tell them what they will need to know to run their businesses.'

Resource Management was seen as an immediate manifestation of the White Paper operating in advance of the latter's official implementation. This resulted in widespread ambivalence towards Resource Management and Körner. On the one hand MHA staff stated that they valued monitoring and control as a necessary function of efficient management and better direction of resources. On the other hand, few expressed any faith in Körner as a credible set of performance measures. They argued that the Körner minimum data set produced such a distorted, reductionist and inaccurate picture of what staff did as necessary and legitimate work that the data were of little use. Further, the fact that these data would be used by managers and others remote from the work raised in staff minds the likelihood of erroneous resource decisions which could adversely affect staffing and patient care.

Overall, concern about the minimum data set as an inaccurate instrument and the potential for its misuse represented the most prominent perception of possible adverse outcomes from the introduction of Community Körner. For example:

> Körner is potentially extremely valuable for us. We could identify patterns of referral, work patterns and make management predictions for resource planning. But Community Körner itself is abysmal. It does not reflect the work done. There's no measurement of quality, of liaison work, clinical processes or outcomes. There are fears of it being used to compare one service with another.

> There is a large measure of discontent regarding the perception of too much focus on quantitative data and not enough on human relations factors. It

> conflicts also with personal aspirations. It's beginning to raise questions about the threat to our professional identity. The concept of patient throughput makes us feel machine-like.

### *Ideology and culture*

The White Paper and merger introduced a new imperative, namely survival as a viable organization in the reconstituted NHS. These developments affected all staff groups in LCSU in a variety of ways. The most obvious common effect was the sudden immersion and participation in the language and rhetoric(s) of business management (cf Parker and Dent 1991). Community Körner as an isolated 'feed the beast' chore aimed at appeasing the DoH was transformed into FIP – the Resource Management tool which, in principle, would enable service provider units in LCSU to cost and tailor their clinical services better. Nevertheless, while this discourse transformation was publicly evident, pre-existing concerns about retaining professional differentiation, control of clinical decisions involving resource allocation, misapplication of performance measures, and so on were expressed as strongly in 1990–91 as they had been previously. For example:

> Our objectives with FIP are to see if we can produce enough information for contracts and planning. . . . Suddenly it's all 'business planning'. . . . We're less fearful and have more confidence over whether Paramedical Heads will go. . . . In Metropolitan we will fight our corner. . . . This is very important. If you have no belief in yourself and the service you will always be a loser. Speech Therapy will fight to the last. People are only concerned with their own service at the end of the day. If you don't then you're a loser. This is the reality as opposed to being paranoid.

> There's a gap between the senior management and the specialisms. There's a lot of self-interest in the individual specialisms in protecting their own empires.

> There's a tradition. . . . Each profession preserves these values. The DGM means little to my staff. Our own professional needs are paramount. . . . The tension will continue between management values and professions' values.

In short, there was a strong, implicit desire to retain as much of the organization's culture as possible. Such retention would serve to moderate potential adverse effects on personal and group interests such as personal and professional identities, power differentials, and indirectly job security. For example, it would be important for a professional provider group to present a strong and united face to a purchaser group.

Overall, political processes and especially conflicts of valuations and sub- and microculture disparities perpetuated in LCSU a lack of unity of purpose which adversely affected CK implementation (viz. failure to implement on time, staff dissatisfaction, loss of staff confidence). The changes in project management and its direction coupled with successful pilots had a unifying effect as far as implementation was concerned. The White Paper and merger implications, i.e. the need for resource management data in order both to negotiate with Northside and to avert a potential major crisis sharpened the focus of staff on the immediate need for FIP. However, despite this fact and the emergence of a business rhetoric (Parker and Dent 1991), the underlying culture of Metropolitan and its sub-cultures appeared to continue largely intact. If anything, the challenge and perceived threat to these cultural characteristics generated a determination that they would be retained.

### *Power and political processes*

Although perceptions of project goals appeared consistent, views about the implementation process and how to proceed were fragmentary up to autumn 1989. Overt political processes dominated decision and action, as is evidenced by competing versions of expert power during 1988 and the first half of 1989.

Conflicts of valuations at different levels and locations fuelled political processes. Although ostensibly all Health Service employees operating in apparently closely allied fields, the various services in LCSU operated autonomously and exhibited their individual sub- and microcultures (see Parker and Dent 1991 for similar comments). Their first allegiance was to their professional group; LCSU was seen as an imposed construction of MHA, which itself was seen as an unwholesome, artificial amalgamation of several pre-existing health authorities. The 'nation states' behaviour is a reflection of a situation which pervaded MHA as a whole. For example, MHA staff commented:

> Nationally, the role of medics in Acute hospitals with whom we liaise is changing. They are no longer the automatic leader in multi-disciplinary teams but in this Authority they're changing very reluctantly. Other professions are still taking opinions of doctors in preference to others. Views are only holistic within each profession. There is still professional jealousy and a lot of professional protectionism.

> There's no sense of corporate image. No sense of being part of a big team. There's in-fighting for money between us and the Acutes. . . . People in power are thinking too much about business matters rather than humanity and patients. . . . It's senior managers versus us.

> There are different outlooks, especially doctors. It's Acute versus Community. Power is seen as being in the Acute services and doctors don't do much in the Community. There's no real in-fighting but disagreements about resource allocation and cuts. They protect their own interests.

### *Decision-making*

Decision-making structures and processes reflected the top-down multi-tiered organization of the NHS: DoH, Region, District, Units, Departments, Sections. Heavy bureaucracy, multiple professional interests, and extended lines of communication tend, in a climate of uncertainty, to deter both the making of incisive, unambiguous decisions and the rapid communication of them to all who need to know them. The Community Körner/FIP project was affected by this more general phenomenon. The general dissatisfaction about decision making as a whole and about Körner in particular was allied to a general dissatisfaction among staff about managerial motivations, intentions and qualities.

For example, various MHA staff commented:

> The Authority is unwieldy and difficult to manage. It's a huge machine to move. The government doesn't understand either. No one will ever take responsibility for a decision. There's so much buck-passing, where does it stop? You've got to keep fighting like a Jack Russell.

> There's a managerial way and there's the nursing way. . . . the managerial way is very different under the UGMs. . . . They make noises about listening to us but actually they've already decided. . . . There's a lack of a holistic or total view and everything is dominated by cost-control and the old hierarchy views. The same people make the decisions about IT and FIP – it always comes down to money.

> There's a whole new management structure. The style has changed and not for the better. They are seeking decisive managers who do *not* always consult. The whole idea of consensus has gone in the last two or three years. Managers are now *selected* for those characteristics. . . . Managers are less risk taking and toe the line. They are quite autocratic whereas they used to fight cuts and shut-downs. It's wrong in the way it's being applied. It's all about numbers, like Körner, and not much about people.

### *Meanings of success*

Success for the CK/FIP project had a variety of meanings depending on the individual concerned, their location in the organizational structure, their vested interests, their allegiances and so on (see Coombs 1992; Glendon and Waring 1996;

Pettigrew *et al.* 1987; Watson 1982). Most staff wished to see the system operational as soon as possible and providing them with information which would help them do their job better. Effective Resource Management *per se* was generally consistent with definitions of success for the project among MHA staff as a whole. However, in view of widespread concern about the validity of the minimum data set, success to many clinical staff meant the avoidance of erroneous conclusions being drawn from Körner data by Health Service managers or the DoH and especially misdirection of resources based on such conclusions. Many also wished to avoid administrative control over clinical work which might adversely affect personal and professional identity or quality of patient care.

The disaggregation of the Authority also had an effect on meanings of success for the project. On the day of the announcement at a LCSUIMG meeting, many of those present appeared nonplussed or worried. One person described her feelings as 'shell-shocked'. It was evident that Paramedical services felt the most threatened since they might find themselves prematurely having to compete to sell their services to other Health Authorities who were already provided for. The Director of Information Services skillfully focused the meeting's attention on the vital need to get FIP operational. He stated that the FIP project had to continue (a) because it was known to work whereas Northside's did not and so it was a good trading point, and (b) it was even more vital to have available detailed information on patient usage in Community and Paramedical Services to inform any negotiation and transfer process.

Thus, meanings of success for the project had expanded to include components to do with bargaining power in which nominally Metropolitan and its neighbouring Authorities were equals but in which some thought that Metropolitan was in a relatively weak position. Detailed information about demand for services and skill resources required became pivotal to forthcoming negotiations for transfer. Individual actors had a personal stake in those negotiations; some stood to lose relative seniority or perhaps even their job. To them, success for the project now meant getting the system operational quickly and getting detailed accurate information from it to support their case for the best possible transfer terms.

As it transpired, the disaggregation was more of a merger between Metropolitan and Northside with Metropolitan in a relatively strong position. For example, the Metropolitan District General Manager who had been previously DGM at Northside became the DGM of the new Metropolitan and Northside Health Authority. The Director of Planning and Contracting at Metropolitan (formerly Director of Information Services) became the Director of Planning and Contracting in the new merged Authority. However, below Board level Metropolitan staff still had to compete for jobs in the new Authority and so to them the ability to demonstrate their track record in resource management was very important.

In tandem with the merger timetable came the White Paper timetable for the purchaser/provider split which required a demonstration of business planning and resource management as a means of securing interim funding and eventually contracts. A potential crisis was thus perceived in a variety of interrelated ways by the social actors involved. Key strategic figures, such as the Director of Planning and Contracting, were able to interpret for the various clinical professions how FIP, despite its drawbacks, was the only viable way of avoiding potential crises in their services. Whereas during 1988 and 1989 there had been competition for resources and long periods of debate, as well as uncertainty and indecision over which computer system to use, in 1990–91 a large measure of co-operation towards a phased introduction of FIP was evident. However, the reduction in intensity of political processes concerned with control of the project itself was not matched by a similar reduction in relation to competition between professional groups for control of resources. FIP data were seen by the various clinical groups as potentially aiding them in such internal competition.

In contrast to perceptions among staff, key management figures anticipated that the new contracting arrangements into which FIP fitted would remove power structures which historically had both strengthened and been strengthened by professional differentiation. A substantive culture change was anticipated whereby professional loyalties would be subordinate to the values of the 'small business' (see Reed and Anthony 1991; Parker and Dent 1991). However, although business planning and resource management, into which FIP fitted, were seen by staff as the only viable means of averting crisis, to many it was certainly not a wholly desirable process. The ideologies, values, identities and other cultural characteristics of the professional groups involved and who interpreted such changes remained firmly anchored in the pre-existing NHS (see Pettigrew *et al.* 1992). Therefore, it was likely that the substantive culture change sought by senior management would take some years to evolve. During this evolution, many outward manifestations of the 'new' culture appeared and some relatively quickly. For example, the language and rhetoric(s) of business planning and resource management were widely evident during 1990–91 whereas previously they were rare. However, the core values of those involved which related to the pre-existing culture of the NHS in general and Metropolitan in particular changed slowly.

## Box 15.1 Concerns and issues expressed by MHA staff

### Effects of White Papers and business planning on professional identity and interests

- Should health care be run as a business?
- Business planning forced by threat of service curtailment.
- Conflict between cost control and quality of care, but FIP seen as essential to both.
- Resource management seen as a good thing provided it is not misapplied.
- Should clinical staff be expected to become managers, which may detract from their primary clinical task?
- Will Local and Community clinical staff be seen as necessary or in such numbers under the new purchaser-provider arrangements?

### Ambiguous role of FIP in relation to protection of professional identity and interests

- FIP data useful to protect and advance own professional group's resource interests in competition with other groups.
- Will FIP data raise awareness among non-clinical managers of the roles of particular professional groups?
- Anticipation by professional groups that FIP data will enhance their own negotiating position with the Health Authority.
- Worry that incomplete FIP data may be misapplied by managers to simplify cost-control decisions against the interests of patients and clinical staff.
- Are assumptions of benign managerial intentions towards the use of FIP data always justified?
- Who does have and who should have control of the use of FIP data?

### General management verus management by professions in the Authority

- Do administrators and UGMs understand all the effects of their decisions?
- Who does have and who should have decision-making power?
- Should non-clinicians be allowed to make decisions which affect adversely clinical practice and patient care?
- Should short-stay administrators be allowed to experiment freely with matters which could affect patient care adversely?

### Diffuse and focused anxieties among staff about changes at work

- Speed, multiplicity and frequency of changes over prolonged period in the Health Service and the Health Authority.
- Uncertainties about the outcomes of the White Papers and the Metropolitan-Northside merger.
- NHS problems of constrained resources versus limitless general need.
- Health Authority finance problems seen as perennial.
- Job insecurity.
- Perceived resource imbalance between 'powerful' Acute Unit and 'weak' Local and Community Services.
- Anticipated power struggle over which services survive.

## UK health care in the mid-1990s

Throughout the early and mid-1990s, many of the concerns and anxieties expressed by health care professionals in the MHA case study of 1988–91 and summarized in Box 15.1 continued to be expressed throughout the NHS. In an increasingly stringent financial climate and the 'internal market', the struggle for survival became a, if not the, major risk issue for NHS hospitals and clinical services. By 1996, the prospect of financial collapse of some hospitals had become imminent. In addition, the 'markets model' had been extended to include local general practitioners or family doctors who had been induced to become practice fundholders and purchasers from hospitals. However, a dramatic shortfall in new GPs, caused partly by disillusionment with the new NHS regime, threatened local health care provision. Not surprisingly, all these developments caused widespread public disquiet and political furore amid sustained media attention.

Recurring controversial topics included:

- the validity and value of hospital performance league tables;
- NHS funding levels;
- ward closures and suspension of operations owing to cash crises midway in financial year;
- suspension of elective surgery owing to cash crises;
- age-limited treatment owing to cash crises;
- patient waiting lists;
- proliferation of managers and administrators;
- large-scale waste through incompetent decisions, e.g. regarding NHS computer systems.

Newspaper headlines throughout 1996 and into 1997 captured the essence of the financial effects of the 'internal markets' regime. For example:

- 'NHS: "Alarm Bells Ring" over Funding of Awards' (*Guardian*, 2 February 1996)
- 'Additional £25m to Ease NHS Crisis' (*Guardian*, 9 May 1996)
- 'GP Exodus Threatens NHS Disaster' (*Guardian*, 26 June 1996)
- 'Hospital Ratings "Give False Picture" ' (*Guardian*, 3 July 1996)
- 'Health Trust Faces Closure over Loss of Contracts' (*Guardian*, 14 September 1996)
- 'Hospitals "On Brink of Collapse" ' (*Guardian*, 11 October 1996)
- 'NHS "Faces Worst Cash Shortage in its History" ' (*Guardian*, 18 October 1996).
- 'Cash Crisis Cripples the NHS' (*Sunday Times*, 3 November 1996)
- 'First NHS Trust to be Forced Out of Business' (*Sunday Times*, 16 February 1997)

From such headlines, it could be construed that government funding had been decreasing. However, by 1996 the annual funding had increased by 74 per cent compared with funding in 1979 and stood at nearly £35 billion. Whereas it is undeniable that NHS funds overall had increased progressively during the 1980s and 1990s, it is less clear whether the funds that were available (a) were meeting rising demand nationally resulting from a combination of increasing health care expectations and an increasingly elderly population, and (b) were being allocated efficiently at local level according to clinical needs and priorities. On the latter point, one of the key premises of the internal market model was that funding would 'follow' patients, i.e.

wherever clinical demand was greatest would determine the distribution of funds. A corollary to this premise was the expectation that Resource Management would determine quality and unit costs and thus induce the flow of both Health Authority and GP purchaser funds to those providers who were most competitive, i.e. relative position in the NHS league tables. However, many Health Authorities make block contracts with acute hospitals in their area, for example for 150 heart bypass operations in a year. The unpredictability of clinical demand in a particular hospital may mean that its full quota of heart patients has to be operated on in the first six months of the year. Since the contract money is defrayed early, the hospital is forced to search for new contract money in order to carry out any new heart bypass operations which may be required during the remaining six months of the year. However, the search for new contracts may result in block contracts with Health Authorities or GPs who are out-of-area, thus denying treatment to local patients. In addition, if new contracts cannot be found, then inevitably wards have to be closed, at least temporarily. In short, instead of 'money following patients', in many cases treatment is obtained preferentially by those Health Authorities and GPs with available money. Such a situation may mean that out-of-area patients who are a lower medical priority may be treated in advance of local patients who require more urgent attention.

In order to promote efficiency, the government imposed an annual requirement for hospitals to make efficiency savings of three per cent. For relatively inefficient hospitals, such savings may be readily achievable. For example, the NHS has been notorious for inefficient and costly purchasing arrangements for its supplies in non-clinical areas such as computer hardware, software, consumables and consultancy. In addition, the number of NHS managers quadrupled between 1989 and 1995 whereas numbers of clinical staff remained static or, in some disciplines and some hospitals, decreased. However, for highly efficient hospitals it may no longer be feasible to find further savings in terms of administrative and logistical overheads and clinical and managerial staffing. Such hospitals become victims of their own success and may be faced with increasing patient throughput as the only remaining option for further efficiency savings.

Increased patient throughput is desirable in order to reduce patient waiting lists but it demands close attention to clinical safety in order to ensure that diagnoses are not skimped and patients are not discharged so early that their recovery is compromised. The government set national targets of 12–month maxima for patient waiting lists, which led to accusations that some health authorities were artificially reducing lists by simply removing patients from lists until the target deadline had passed.

Throughout 1996–97, the existence of a cash crisis in the NHS was dismissed by the government of the day as an exaggeration. However, both the British Medical

Association (BMA) and the National Association of Health Authorities and Trusts (NAHAT) agreed that in the 1996–97 financial year a further £200 million was needed to cover the immediate shortfall of funds. Because of increased clinical demand, BMA and NAHAT estimated that the 1997–98 NHS funding would have to be increased by at least three per cent above inflation in order to provide the same level of health care, compared with the government's proposal of one per cent above inflation.

It is evident from the first few years of the new National Health Service that the consumer-orientated internal markets model, in its simple form, is not a viable way in which to run health care in a modern industrialized society which claims to be civilized. Private health care is an option which the government of the day promoted as part of its consumer choice free-market ideology and the private health care sector has grown popular among those with relatively secure employment and incomes. However, most of the UK population cannot afford to pay for private health care in addition to funding the NHS through taxation and national insurance contributions. Their only realistic option is the state-run NHS.

In November 1996, in recognition of growing public concern about the state of the NHS and its future, the Conservative government issued a White Paper entitled *A Service with Ambitions*. The White Paper reaffirmed the commitment of the government of the day to providing a universal high quality health service on the basis of need rather than ability to pay - i.e. the original principles of the NHS in 1946. The White Paper's rather unremarkable objectives, which include ensuring decision-making based on the latest clinical evidence and providing a highly trained and skilled workforce, may well result in greater efficiency and effectiveness of patient care. However, the unavoidable problem remains, namely that limited resources are never likely to match increasing demand which, in theory, is limitless. In December 1997, a new White Paper was published by the new Labour government which announced, among other things, that the internal market would be abolished. The consequences of this change are as yet unclear.

## Survival risks for UK health authorities

### *Hazards and threats (see chapter 2)*

#### *Demand*

Positive factors include:

- Attempts to inculcate preventive life-style changes among the population.
- Cheaper, more effective treatments for common ailments.
- Encouraging private health care among those who can afford it.

- Devolution of minor surgery and treatments normally performed in hospital to local GP health centres.

Key threats include:

- Demand for new life saving treatments which may be expensive.
- Increasing public expectations of health care provision.
- Increasingly elderly population requiring long-term medical care.
- Competition for bed space among priority cases and from private patients.
- Potential adverse media and political attention.

*Funding and investment*

Positive factors include:

- Year-on-year increases in government funding in real terms (at time of writing).
- Partnerships with private sector to fund capital projects encouraged.

Key threats include:

- Funding not keeping pace with capital requirements and health care demand.
- Reliance on internal market contracts creates feast-famine flow of funds which results in stop-go health care.
- Continued application of efficiency savings to inefficient and highly efficient hospitals alike.
- Incompetent capital investment decisions and/or implementation leading to large scale financial loss, e.g. computer systems.
- Insolvency.
- Potential adverse media and political attention.

*Government policy*

Positive factors include:

- Requirements to manage resources efficiently and effectively.

Key threats include:

- Confusing patient throughput as prime performance measure with cost-effectiveness of clinical treatment.
- Cost accounting taking precedence over clinical needs.
- Using Resource Management performance data as a prextext for clinical staff cuts.
- Potential adverse media and political attention.

*Industrial relations*

Positive factors include:

- Clinicians loath to take industrial action which could damage patient care.
- Industrial relations disputes in the NHS tend to be orderly and well disciplined.

Key threats include:

- NHS managers and administrators not trusted by clinicians and ancillary staff.
- Staff angered by short stay NHS managers and administrators apparently with little idea about clinical realities and effects of their decisions on patient care.
- Nurses remain poorly paid despite pay reviews.
- NHS ancillary staff remain among the poorest paid employees of the UK population whereas managers, UGMs and Directors fare well.
- Salaries and wages not competitive enough in the labour market to attract and retain good staff.
- Potential adverse media and political attention.

*Culture*

Positive factors include:

- Clinical staff collectively put patient care as their first priority.
- Health care tends to attract committed individuals who often work long hours for modest pay.

Key threats include:

- Internal markets ethos will gradually erode the 'patient care first' culture.
- Disillusioned staff opt out of NHS to work privately or abroad.
- Potential adverse media and political attention.

*Power Relations*

Positive factors include:

- Interprofessional relations in relative equilibrium in the clinical area, i.e. long-established pecking order.

Key threats include:

- Central government appointees may influence decisions at the expense of local representation.
- Power of non-clinical UGMs and managers in decision-making which affects clinical resources.
- Rise of computing and IT specialists in determining management and performance information systems.
- Powerful consultants ensure that Acute services gain at expense of Community and Paramedical services.
- Potential adverse media and political attention.

*Change*

Positive factors include:

- General acceptance within the NHS that significant changes in organizational structures and processes and a more business-like approach to efficiency and effectiveness are required.

Key threats include:

- Changes which, directly or indirectly, affect patient care adversely.
- Administrators and managers who enforce changes which interfere with clinical practices to the detriment of patient care.
- Introduction of inappropriate measures of performance.

## *Risk assessment (see chapter 2)*

The following summarizes potential risk levels for the threats discussed above. The attributed risk levels are based on the authors' judgements. Both positive and negative outcomes are possible and may co-exist.

| **Threat** | **Potential risk levels** (as probabilities) | |
|---|---|---|
| | *Negative outcomes* | *Positive outcomes* |
| Demand | Medium–High | Medium–Low |
| Funding and investment | Medium–High | Medium–Low |
| Government policy | Medium–High | Medium |
| Industrial relations | Medium–High | Medium |
| Culture | Medium | Medium |
| Power relations | Medium–High | Medium |
| Change | Medium–High | Medium |

## Comparison with thematic matrix

Table 15.1 indicates the relative salience of each of the risk contexts identified in Part 1, and particularly chapter 9, in relation to this case study. In the table, H = high, M = medium, L = low.

## Conclusions

The original premise of the UK's National Health Service in 1946 was to provide health care for every citizen from cradle to grave free of charge and regardless of ability to pay. Inevitably, the policy shift towards private health care and a tightly resourced NHS which appears unable to meet demand has led to accusations of a 'two-tier' health service in which the affluent minority get the best treatment fast in the private sector while the non-affluent majority get basic treatment slowly via the NHS. The internal market has further complicated the picture as a result of NHS hospitals selling bed space and operations to the private sector and the search for contracts potentially taking precedence over local clinical needs.

*Table 15.1* Thematic matrix applied to the health authorities case study

| *Risk context* | *Salience in case study* |
|---|---|
| *Organizational environment* | |
| Economies and markets | H |
| Public policy, legislation and regulation | H |
| Social and political climate | H |
| Technology | H |
| History, operating territories and conditions | H |
| *Human factors* | |
| Culture | H |
| Power relations, political processes and decision-making | H |
| Perception and cognition | H |
| *Formal coping arrangements* | |
| Risk management | H |
| Risk assessment | H |
| Management systems | H |
| Approaches to change | H |

Difficult questions and dilemmas face any government on health care policy (see also Longley and Warner 1995). For example, how can limited financial resources be best applied so as to ensure fairness? For Health Authorities and hospitals seeking to comply with government policy and legislation while providing the best health care, the dilemma comes down to a stark choice between, on the one hand, putting the clinical needs of all patients first and running the risk of financial crisis and collapse and, on the other hand, putting financial survival first and running the risk of some patients being denied adequate health care. Either way, the risk trade-offs at local level are fraught with potentially adverse consequences, in terms of staff disaffection, 'trial by media' and political controversy.

# Part III
# Conclusions

# Chapter 16
# A management agenda

## Overview

This chapter draws upon some themes from earlier chapters and makes minor excursions along a few trails. It provides neither a definitive list nor an exhaustive review of all topics on the risk management agenda. To produce such a comprehensive document would require a separate book. The topics explored here are for further discussion and debate. A model is provided as a possible framework for considering broad sectors of the world economy. Illustrative risk management topics are subsequently considered.

## Introduction

Risk taking is essential for any organization. Organizations also need to understand the nature of the risks that they face and to manage them appropriately. As noted by Adams (1995: 21), 'Risk comes in many forms'. For most risks probabilities are usually estimates, as are speculations about worst case consequences. However, management monitoring of worst cases and their likelihoods is necessary in any organization. In some instances, it is important for organizations to act in concert with other parties in order to address risks which transcend the capacity of any single organization to assess or to manage effectively. Some risks will be appropriate for an organization to manage on its own.

No organization can remain isolated from its environment and a key aspect of managing risk for any organization will always be its ability to manage the interface between its strategic and operational activities and what is happening in its markets and in broader cultural, financial, political and technological frameworks. This process is becoming more complex because the nature and variety of risks to be faced are increasing. This chapter provides a general framework for considering risks faced by organizations and, by developing topics introduced in earlier chapters, considers some illustrative risks and their management.

## Organizational survival

In a hierarchy of risks, the greatest generic risk facing all organizations is that they will not survive. Senge (1990) records that the average life of an organization is 40 years. Death of an organization might come about through financial collapse or through absorption within a larger structure in the form of a merger or takeover. While such upheavals may result in human costs in respect of shattered careers and emotional distress, they can also represent opportunities for many individuals as well as for organizations. The transformational model of organizational change is represented by a timeline that plateaus after an initial rising growth rate, followed by a cascading period of chaos, to a 'death' which could be succeeded by re-birth.

In the UK, a company called Syspas tracks the financial health of all UK quoted industrial, distribution and service companies (*Health of Corporate UK*, London, Syspas, issues 1–3). Using a model based upon previous company failures, Syspas produces a six-monthly assessment of companies, highlighting those which are deemed to be at risk of corporate failure. The percentage of the 1688 fully-listed and Alternative Investment Market companies at risk on the basis of the Syspas analysis, varies between 11 per cent and 29 per cent, depending upon the state of the national economy and companies' inherent financial strength. The model is rebuilt each year to incorporate up-to-date financial information from the national economy.

In the Syspas model, assessment of the overall financial health of a company is based upon its cashflow and debt ratios – profits relative to liabilities, dependence upon short-term funding and liquidity. Companies within the three broad sectors (industrial, distribution, services) are compared with those within their own sector and are then ranked on the basis of standard scores. Once a company falls through its 'solvency threshold' it is 'at risk', and when its score reaches zero it has the financial characteristics of companies that have previously failed. In 1996, Syspas forecast that around seven per cent (about 100) of UK quoted companies would fail within three years. Sectors with companies particularly at risk of failure included: construction, property, extractive industries, transport and media. Utilities and pharmaceuticals companies tended to be least at risk. Staff employed in vulnerable companies totalled 493,000 – around eight per cent of those employed by the companies surveyed. This represents a potentially large number of people whose jobs are at short-term risk.

The central survival risk that businesses have to manage involves juggling a potential myriad of factors, although in practice this means being able to identify and adequately manage the three or four key survival parameters for that particular business – whether these are: cashflow, long-term R&D investment, appropriate gearing, effective distribution channels, shareholder value, or whatever. However, it is increasingly recognised by many businesses that their capacity to manage the risks faced by their own organization is bounded by factors over which they may have minimal influence – at least in the short term – i.e. uncertainties in their business environment may override their capacity to manage their business. For small organizations, this may take the form of cashflow problems from long credit terms resulting from late payments from large organizations. For large organizations, it may be effective manipulation of their share price through the shifting of investments by institutional shareholders – whose loyalty is not to the companies in which they happen to have their current investment but to their own organizations and their customers.

## Risk management in the 21st century

How will risk management be characterized in the 21st century? While nothing can be known for certain, it is possible to extrapolate from current trends to derive a general picture of change based upon social, cultural, economic, technological and political features of late 20th century developments. Internationally, changes in global relationships have brought about a rich variety of new risks – opportunities, challenges and threats. These may be represented on the one hand in the form of new trading alliances and markets and on the other by the reality or possibility of serious political conflicts and war. As the world economy becomes more tightly coupled, with each component increasingly dependent upon many others, the risk of widespread damage – economic or physical – or even systemic collapse as a result of a dramatic movement somewhere, increases. For example, because of the repercussions upon global financial markets, the scenario of a massive earthquake and tidal wave hitting Tokyo has been considered as a touchstone for plunging the world into deep recession. Political instabilities in many parts of the world which could result in escalating conflict, as well as less credible scenarios, could have similar effects. However, as far as most organizations are concerned, these risks have to be accepted because they cannot be directly managed. Outcomes resulting from such risks generally cannot be insured against and thus most organizations are obliged to consider them as a given in their risk management calculations.

Within nation states, a key feature is increasing diversity of industries accompanying increasing globalization of markets. Increasingly diverse risks follow this pattern, resulting partly from the very different starting points and rates of development of various economies over the past fifty years or so. Several divergent processes may be identified which may be projected to result in a relatively small number of major sectors in the world economy. In this section, three meta-sectors are identified as a basis for characterizing key aspects of risk management for the next generation.

Traditionally a country's economy is divided up according to the nature of products or outputs of different sectors (e.g. using NACE – the international industry classification system). However, traditional ways of dividing up industries are likely to become increasingly inappropriate, irrelevant or even misleading as organizations and industry sectors diversify and change to create sometimes radically new patterns. For example, tourism is now the world's largest industry, yet typically it does not feature in industrial classifications, which tend to be based upon industry patterns of past eras. In the case of tourism, it might be more appropriate to consider it as comprising a range of industry types including, hotel, leisure, catering and transport.

Overall, it might be appropriate to consider revised groupings, perhaps on the basis of the nature and type of risks typically posed by a particular sector type. From the perspective of considering the nature and management of risks from broad types of operation, it may be helpful to consider a small number of meta-sectors within the world economy as a means of improving understanding of the nature of risks which are typically posed and key features of risk management for addressing them. Three broad sector types (meta-sectors) are described – advanced, standard and archaic.

## *Advanced meta-sector*

This sector is characterized by high-tech industries or systems which are complex, information-rich and large scale. Examples include process industries such as petro-chemical, large-scale power transmission and generation – particularly nuclear, and mass transport – including air, rail and marine. Also included in this meta-sector are complex financial markets and institutions comprising them, as well as all national military operations. The high-tech element of organizations or systems comprising this sector may be as much to do with communication, decision-making, guidance or navigation systems required for safe effective operation, as with actual technologies involved – for example, marine navigation systems (see for example, Perrow 1984). The main risks associated with this meta-sector in terms of exposure to typical organizations' operations are to customers, employees, investors, communities and the environment.

Principally, risks associated with operational activities within this meta-sector are those traditionally described as high consequence – low probability events. However, many risks originally thus characterised have turned out to be of higher probability than first estimated – nuclear power generation being an example. Typically, risks in the advanced meta-sector are associated with failures affecting numbers of people – either directly, as for passengers in the Channel Tunnel fire incident (in November 1996) and residents of the Bhopal region during the Union Carbide plant toxic release (in December 1984), or indirectly through environmental impact. For example, communities in the regions of disasters such as the Exxon Valdez oil tanker spillage off Alaska (in 1989) were subsequently found to experience raised levels of a variety of physical and psychological effects, including depression and post-traumatic stress disorder. For failures involving large corporations or systems, such as Lloyds of London, Barings Bank or BCCI, those affected include investors, customers and shareholders, some of whom may subsequently display adverse physical and psychological symptoms, including increased suicide risk and family breakdown.

Key aspects of complex systems in the advanced meta-sector include those described by Perrow (1984). Systems and organizations here are tightly-coupled, meaning that they are vulnerable to small changes or events elsewhere. These may be latent failures (Reason 1990), or human failings – either accidental, as in mismanaging a company or process, or deliberate, as in violations within systems designed to be safe or are acts of fraud, vandalism, sabotage, terrorism or war. Critical aspects of managing the risks of such systems might involve: monitoring human behaviour for signs of severe stress, sophisticated detection technologies for human actions and fail-safe designs for physical hazards. In managing major hazard risks, there is a need for a better balance in respect of technical factors on the one hand and organizational or social factors on the other. While QRA techniques can provide a very useful basis for risk estimation, they need to be incorporated within models which include uncertainties relating to qualitative assessment based upon organizational factors such as culture and individual risk cognitions.

Because of the relatively high intervention costs involved, risk assessment and risk management activities will typically be carried out within long-term strategic frameworks and with political as much as economic factors to the fore. Because of the complexity of systems within this meta-sector and the scale of investments required, formal risk management activity here tends to operate in both pure and speculative risk areas.

## *Standard meta-sector*

This sector is characterized by traditional mainstream manufacturing production and service industries. Factories producing a wide range of consumer goods would be in this meta-sector, as would large public and private sector institutions delivering a range of services, including education, health, individual financial services, emergency service provision, local transport and large-scale retail activities. Much of the detailed operation of activities within this meta-sector might be described as high-tech – for example sophisticated factory production lines which include just-in-time and other features, electronic transfer of funds between customers and providers of a range of products or medical interventions based upon advanced research discoveries. Organizations within this meta-sector are less complex than those in the advanced meta-sector. This has implications for risks characterizing this meta-sector as well as the way in which they are managed.

While risks to customers do exist in this meta-sector – for example as in certain medical inventions, 'unsafe' products or public transport systems, in general people are exposed either individually or in relatively small numbers at any given time. However, in terms of total numbers affected by activities in this meta-sector, the at-risk population is substantial. The main group at risk here are employees of the organizations or systems – which, while they have declined from earlier numbers, are still more labour intensive than organizations and systems in the advanced meta-sector. While organizations in the standard meta-sector have multiple links with other organizations and systems, they are not as tightly-coupled as those in the advanced meta-sector. There are also risks to the environment from activities in this sector, although they tend to be less visible and perhaps generally more insidious than those characterising the advanced meta-sector. For example, activities in the standard meta-sector generate considerable waste, much of it toxic, although its effects are generally dissipated over a wide area and often over considerable periods.

Risks characterising this meta-sector are those identified as traditional management problems such as business survival, cash flow, profitability, competition, potential litigation, human resources and investment. Effectively managing these speculative risks increasingly requires a strategic approach. Risk management in this meta-sector – whether of pure or speculative risks – is primarily based upon economic criteria so that decisions are developed through balancing costs and estimated risks of various courses of action. In the OHS field, where pure risk outcomes result in either traumatic injury or disease development over a longer period, risk assessment and risk management generally follow guidelines proffered in a range of standards and related publications (e.g. HS(G)65, BS 8800, AS/NZS 4360). Safety is primarily addressed through incremental efforts in behavioural or process features, for example training, supervision, procedure developments and design improvements.

## *Archaic meta-sector*

Organizations in this meta-sector are characterised by features mostly at the opposite end of the scale from those in the advanced meta-sector. They are often low-tech and information poor. Some may be small scale, as in many local businesses, although this meta-sector also includes large industries such as agriculture, forestry, fishing, mineral extraction and construction. In this meta-sector, there may be many examples of use of high-tech products – for example in the form of chemicals used in agriculture, sophisticated equipment employed in construction or mining or the technology involved in many small enterprises. However, the origin of these technologies is in more advanced sectors. This meta-sector also includes home-based workers and industries typically employing large numbers of people in developing economies, including labour intensive manufacturing, for example in the clothing industry.

Key features of risk management in much of the archaic meta-sector are often concerned with economic drivers – survival as well as profitability. While the industries represented by organizations in this meta-sector are essential to the success of many modern economies, they tend to be more at the mercy of economic forces than do those in the advanced and standard meta-sectors. With exceptions, workers in this meta-sector tend to be less well remunerated, less skilled – except in very specific ways, and at greater risk of workplace hazards than their counterparts in the other meta-sectors. In addition, industries in this meta-sector in developed economies tend to be in decline or more vulnerable to recession than those in the other meta-sectors. In developing economies, they may experience periods of rapid growth – for example the construction industry throughout most of SE Asia. However, risks and working conditions faced by employees in such instances may be orders of magnitude worse than those of their counterparts in comparable industries in more advanced economies.

Risk assessment and risk management methodologies in general are likely to be at their least well-developed in this meta-sector. While activities in the archaic meta-sector may have dramatic environmental impact – for example upon fish stocks or the world's forests, effective management of such risks often leaves much to be desired. Organizations in this meta-sector are frequently characterized by unregulated (or poorly regulated) exploitation of the environment and of their workforces. Because of their reliance upon apparently plentiful natural or human resources and the lack of internal financial incentives, effective risk management within organizations in this meta-sector, particularly in developing nations, must be driven primarily by regulation and enforcement activities of governments and international bodies. Table 16.1 summarises some of the main features of the three meta-sectors described.

## Risk management in the civil airline industry

This section outlines some features of managing risk in an advanced meta-sector industry with high hazard operations. An airline pilot is quoted as saying: 'The very idea of flying is mad. You fill a tube with hundreds of people and 20,000 litres of highly flammable fuel and ignite it in three or four places. You then accelerate this lethal cocktail to 600 kilometres per hour and lift it to 10,000 metres, where the air is so thin and the temperature is −60 degrees – an environment in which no person can survive'.

Although around 80 per cent of aircraft accidents are attributed to 'human error', many may more accurately be designated as being due to a combination of factors, including design, inadequate training and poorly developed procedures. A good example is the Kegworth air crash in 1989 (Department of Transport 1990). Nevertheless 'poor flight crew judgement' continues to head the list of worldwide aviation safety hazards over a 20–year period (BASI 1996), being identified as a contributory factor in air accidents almost twice as many time as the next hazard – landing gear failure. Of the ascription to 'human error' of many accidents, an article in *Flight Safety Australia* (Summer 1997: 16) notes that: '. . . further analysis based on International Air Transport Association and International Civil Aviation Organization data indicates much of the pilot error is caused by poor operational management'. It might be further ascertained that this in turn is a consequence of inadequate risk management. Potentially conflicting interests mean that civil aviation industry accident statistics may not be neutral. For example, airplane manufacturers' interests might be served by emphasizing human factors in air accidents.

In this industry there has been no significant improvement in the global fatal accident rate over a seven-year period during the late 1980s and 1990s. In 1996, around 1200 passengers worldwide were killed in air crashes, including 350 who lost

*Table 16.1* Summary of risk features in three meta-sectors

| *Meta-sector label* | *Meta-sector characteristics* | *Industry examples* | *Parties mainly exposed to risk* | *Examples of risk factors* | *Critical aspects of risk assessment and risk management* |
|---|---|---|---|---|---|
| *Advanced* | complex systems; information-rich; large-scale; tightly coupled | petro-chemical; nuclear power; mass transport; financial markets | customers; employees; communities; environment; investors | takeovers; business failures; latent failures; violations; fraud; sabotage | goal-setting; high calibre internal standards/systems to meet external risk acceptability criteria; organizational culture; fail-safe design; monitoring safeguards on behaviour; political framework |
| *Standard* | moderately complex systems | factories; mainstream manufacturing; large-scale services | owners; employees; environment; investors | takeovers; business failures; normal work behaviours; standard OHS risks | controls – design; supervision; procedures; training |
| *Archaic* | simple systems; low-tech; information-poor; often small-scale | home-based; small businesses; agriculture; fishing; mining; construction | owners; employees; environment | takeovers; business failures; (poor) regulation; enforcement | management education; statutory regulation |

their lives in the worst-ever mid-air collision near New Delhi in November, making 1996 the year when more civil airline passengers lost their lives than any previous year. That year also witnessed the occasion of over 350 lives lost when a cargo plane crashed into a market in Zaire. The New Delhi accident bore some similarities with the previous worst mid-air collision over Zagreb in 1976, in that military use of air space restricted the availability of civil aircraft corridors and there was alleged linguistic confusion between pilots and air traffic control in carrying out instructions. Communication misunderstanding between pilot and ATC was also a prime feature of the 1977 Tenerife airline disaster in which 583 people died (still the largest number in a single civil airline accident).

An example of how risk management may be applied to reduce accidents in the civil aviation sector is provided in an article in *The Economist* (4 June 1994: 122). The type of accident which results in 53 per cent of passenger fatalities and around one-third of crashes is controlled flight into terrain (CFIT). This occurs when the flight crew has the aircraft under control, all functions are normal and yet the aircraft hits the ground. The article records the efforts of Boeing and other industry experts through an international taskforce to address CFIT crashes, which has: '. . . calculated the chances of cumulative crew errors leading to CFIT. There is one chance in 1000 that the pilot at the controls would be flying at the wrong altitude; one in 100 that the co-pilot could fail to cross-check; air-traffic controllers might fail to spot the wrong altitude one in ten times (it is not really their job); and, based on historical data, there is a one in two chance that the pilot would ignore the ground-proximity warning system (GPWS), an alarm that sounds when an aircraft is too near the ground (early models were prone to false alarms). The probability of this chain of events all happening at once is one in two million flights – about one every two months at current levels of air traffic'. It is argued that making small improvements within the system could result in a five-fold reduction in CFIT accidents. For example, improved training and procedures could halve the chances of a co-pilot failing to cross-check altitude and reduce to one in five the chances of the pilot ignoring the GPWS, thereby reducing the probability of a CFIT accident to one in ten million.

Organizations such as the Flight Safety Foundation, whose staff met with other international air safety experts at the Washington Global Aviation Safety and Security Summit in December 1996, predict an increase in the frequency of air crashes as airline traffic continues to expand dramatically. The Air Transport Action Group, based in Geneva, predicts that by the year 2000, the Asia-Pacific region will account for 41 per cent of the world's scheduled air traffic and 51 per cent by 2010 – representing 400 million passengers annually. Risks associated with the growing congestion, particularly in this region, will be compounded early next century by the new generation of 'super jumbos', capable of carrying more than 500 passengers. While airline safety standards may reasonably be expected to improve in developing nations, the likelihood of major disasters may increase before it falls.

Safety is not the only aspect of risk to be addressed. For example, European countries have incompatible airspace control systems. Fifty-four control centres use 31 different computer systems based on 70 different software programs. According to a study by the European parliament, this diversity results in 116,000 annual hours of 'unnecessary flying' (in the air and on the ground). Additional fuel and other costs compound the safety risk which results from exposure above the minimum necessary.

The US-based summit identified improved instructions to developing countries in respect of running safer aviation systems as a prime short-term goal. For example, the Traffic Alert and Collision Avoidance System is mandatory in the US for planes with more than 30 seats and is likely to be one of the reasons why the US has the safest major aviation system in the world. However, this system, which alerts pilots to approaching or nearby planes within 64 kilometres and can give 40 seconds advance warning before impact, is not a world-wide standard. There are also substantial differences between airports in respect of landing and take-off conditions and the relative sophistication of electronic and other equipment and facilities available for managing risks associated with passenger air travel. Among risk management goals set by the Washington gathering is routine retrieval of information from cockpit data recorders to identify potentially dangerous features prior to an accident occurring, and encouraging problem-sharing between airlines rather than punishing them for errors.

Following a number of air accidents, in 1995 the Australian CAA was separated into Airservices Australia (the air traffic services provider) and CASA (the safety regulator). CASA's prime remit is passenger safety and its principal strategies are regulation and persuading industry to maintain high safety standards. Safety investigation is carried out by the Bureau of Air Safety Investigation (BASI). Noting the difficulties encountered in the US in deriving meaningful safety measures in civil aviation, CASA has determined not to use accidents, incidents or fatalities per hours of operation as safety measures. Instead it is deriving an assessment measure based upon a combination of factors which contribute to safe operations (CASA 1996).

The traditional message to passengers that safety is implicit in a journey by air may change as passengers become increasingly aware of risks associated with air travel and of different carriers' safety records. Large differences exist between airlines' safety records. In Australia, the Civil Aviation Safety Authority (CASA) plans to publish a monthly update on serious breaches of aviation safety. A PlaneSafe report maintained that charter aircraft operations had an accident rate which was three times higher than the low capacity regular passenger transport sector. An industry code of practice means that passengers will be told which carrier is operating each section of their flight.

## Financial risk management

A Touche Ross (1995) interview survey of more than 200 major financial institutions and management consultants in the UK found that 58 per cent of respondents admitted that their systems did not meet then-current market risk requirements for derivative trading. Although most respondent organizations planned to increase their investment in risk management systems, because of falling profit margins, none had on-line risk management systems in place. The report, which predated the Barings collapse, advocates that all banks segregate their dealing and administrative functions. Sophisticated computer systems in themselves cannot prevent rogue trading by a determined employee with the right know-how if adequate monitoring systems are not in place. However, respondents to the Touche Ross survey focused more on 'routine administrative reporting' rather than core risk management systems. The report noted that the emphasis of risk management is changing from credit risk to market risk, reflecting the concern among banks about their potential exposure to large losses, for example in derivative trading. The main deficiencies identified by respondents for all forms of risk were: incomplete information, slow response and difficulty in analysing information.

In the mid-1990s, Deloitte & Touche (*Risk Management Systems for Financial Institutions Benchmark Survey*, London, Deloitte & Touche Consulting Group, undated) surveyed financial risk management systems within 200 financial institutions based in London, including major European, Japanese and North American companies. The narrow definition of risk management used ('. . . deal level to overall risk strategy . . . systems that support the management of credit and market risk . . .') is typical of the concept as practised by financial institutions. This restricted approach to 'risk management' may more accurately be referred to as 'financial risk management'.

The survey found that:

- financial risk management systems were failing to meet requirements;
- main deficiencies were incomplete information, slow response and difficulty in analysing information;

- increasingly sophisticated technologies were being considered;
- financial risk management systems were being increasingly centralised but their development tended to be unstructured;
- both external and in-house financial risk management systems were being developed.

Over half the Deloitte & Touche respondents agreed that their financial risk management systems did not meet requirements and many companies admitted to failed risk management projects. Key reasons for financial companies requiring more sophisticated financial risk management systems include:

- rapid growth in volumes of derivative products;
- increasing competition;
- falling profit margins;
- highly visible operational costs;
- regulators' demands;
- increasing flexibility required to improve customer service.

In respect of important overall business objectives for having a financial risk management system, respondents identified in order of priority:

- quantification of market risk;
- quantification of credit risk;
- protection of capital;
- improving allocation of capital;
- meeting regulatory requirements;
- diversification of business risk.

Respondents' approaches to global financial risk management systems were predominantly strategic, although evolutionary and portfolio approaches, as well as having no global approach, were also found. A generally accepted figure for a consolidated financial risk management system for a medium or large securities business would require at least 100 person-years of effort to develop and cost between £5 million and £25 million.

Technologically sophisticated systems developed by financial services organizations are bounded by a restricted concept of risk management – one applying exclusively to trading and market risks. Other potential risk factors, such as those revealed by analysis of the Barings case in chapter 11, could be included in a more comprehensive risk management framework which could be adopted by companies in this sector.

Evidence that the extent of effective risk management within Australian organizations leaves much to be desired comes from a 1996 Boardroom report *Boards at risk*, in which the Australian Institute of Company Directors (AICD), in combination with KPMG found that 60 per cent of company respondents to a survey admitted to having no formal risk management policy. When asked whether risk management was formally considered as part of the business planning process, 38 per cent of respondents said that it 'always' was while 52 per cent claimed that it 'sometimes' was. Processes used to manage risk included:

- procedures manual (65 per cent of respondents);
- training programs (63 per cent);
- external audit (50 per cent);
- code of conduct/ethics (46 per cent);
- formal monitoring procedures (45 per cent);
- internal audit (45 per cent);
- external advice (43 per cent);
- formal information channels (33 per cent).

Asked about their most critical areas of risk, the following emerged:

- customer satisfaction (65 per cent of respondents mentioned this);
- human resource (HR) management (56 per cent);
- information technology (38 per cent);
- legal/compliance (28 per cent);
- business interruption (28 per cent);
- suppliers (24 per cent);
- public image (23 per cent);
- environment (11 per cent);
- treasury (11 per cent);
- fraud (4 per cent).

Given the findings of a contemporaneous Ernst & Young survey, described below, the relatively low rating of fraud and treasury risks is surprising.

## Security aspects of risk management

An insidious risk to large financial corporations was revealed in a *Sunday Times* 'insight' article (2 June 1996) about 'cyber terrorists' – around four separate gangs, based mainly in the US who had allegedly amassed up to £400m worldwide by threatening to wipe out computer systems. Banks, broking firms and investment houses in the US have apparently secretly paid ransoms to prevent costly deliberately engineered computer breakdowns and subsequent business losses. Most of the victims have chosen to pay the blackmailers' demands rather than inform the police. It was reported that there had been around 40 such attacks over a three-year period, with the attackers loading 'bombs' into target companies' computer systems, which could be triggered if payment was not made. Managing such a risk is hampered by the loss of face which the organizations would experience – reducing the likelihood that the crime will be reported and thereby hampering detection. A further problem is that crime detection and law enforcement agencies are for the most part based within individual countries, whereas this is crime on a global scale. A problem-solving approach involving expertise and gathering research evidence from different countries would seem to be the best initial approach to addressing this issue as a prelude to devising suitable risk management strategies.

The Department of Trade and Industry (1996) has produced guidelines to counter the type of threat described above, as well as others which may be encountered in respect of IT systems security. The guidelines take the form of a checklist for identifying whether IT security measures meet required levels and advice in respect of implementing provision of a higher level of assurance. The main components of information security are shown in Figure 16.1.

Organization assurance is the process of defining and observing that procedures relating to security are implemented. In Figure 16.1, assessment of the risk in each of the four areas precedes decision-making on where to focus activity to protect business assets. For example, different parts of the organization are likely to handle information of differing value; hence segregated security domains may be defined. A basic IT security checklist is provided by BS 7799 and is outlined in Table 16.2 – organizations which can confidently answer 'yes' to all ten questions can claim to have basic information security competence. To achieve higher levels of security, additional measures are necessary, and BS 7799 provides further guidance with respect to these – outlined in Table 16.3.

Threats to IT systems and networks include:

- malicious vandalism;
- system misuse;
- employee subversion;
- industrial espionage;
- sabotage;
- computer fraud;
- intellectual property theft;

*Figure 16.1* Information security and sources of assurance (after DTI (1996))

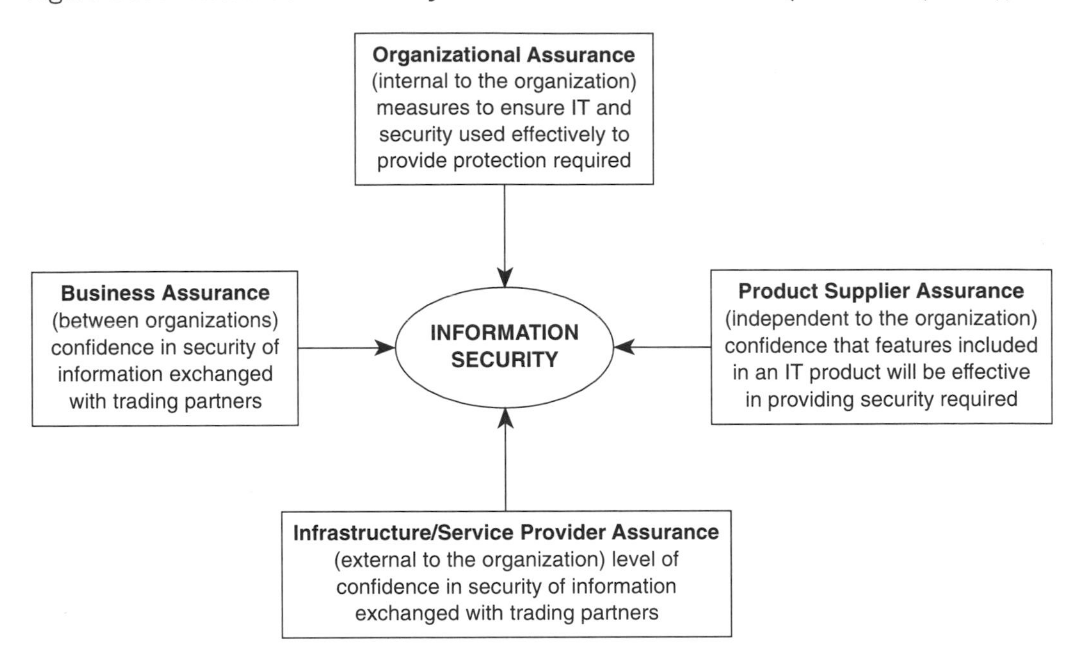


*Table 16.2* BS7799 and AS/NZS 4444 basic information security competence checklist

1. Is there a documented security policy?
2. Are responsibilities for security processes clearly allocated?
3. Are users given adequate security training?
4. Are security incidents always reported?
5. Is there a virus checking policy?
6. Is there a plan for maintaining business continuity?
7. Are legal copyright issues always given due consideration?
8. Are important organizational records protected?
9. Are personal records protected in accordance with the Data Protection Act?
10. Are regular security reviews performed?

*Source*: compiled from BSI (1995); AS/NZS (1996)

*Table 16.3* BS7799 and AS/NZS 4444 advanced information security components

| *Component* | *Outline description* |
|---|---|
| Security policy | Written objectives, education, virus prevention/detection, responsibilities, reporting, review |
| Security organization | Framework for control, management structure, external expert advice, independent review process |
| Asset classification and control | Threats to assets – disclosure, loss, modification; asset ownership and responsibility for protection |
| Personnel security | Minimizing risks associated with human error, theft, fraud, misuse; human resource management – selection and recruitment, job descriptions and contracts, monitoring individuals during employment, incident reporting |
| Physical and environmental security | Cabling security, physical location of equipment, use of equipment off-site |
| Computer and network management | Operational procedures and responsibilities, system planning and acceptance, protection from malicious software, housekeeping, media handling, data software exchange |
| System access control | Business requirements for system use, user access management, user responsibilities, network, computer and application access control, monitoring system access and use |
| Systems development and maintenance | Ensuring that security is built into IT systems from their conception – security requirements of systems, in application systems and files, in development and support |
| Business continuity planning | Plans to counteract interruptions to critical business activities, developing and maintaining plans for speedy restoration of critical business processes and software in the event of serious business interruptions |
| Compliance | Ensuring avoidance of breaches of statutory, criminal or civil obligations or other security requirements – control of proprietary software copying, safeguarding organizational records, data protection, preventing misuse of IT facilities, security reviews of IT systems, system audit |

*Source*: compiled from BSI (1995); AS/NZS (1996)

- intrinsic reliability failure;
- natural disaster.

Threats to IT systems result in either a breach of the confidentiality or integrity of information or else interrupt the availability of information or services. DTI (1996) recommends ranking threats (high, medium, low) in respect of worst case consequences and likelihoods. The impact of a security violation is a measure of the value of the information to the organization or to a third party. The more valuable is information to a third party (e.g. a competitor) the greater is the likelihood of unauthorized use. Another key dimension is vulnerability – which refers to accessibility of an IT system in respect of numbers of both (known) authorized and (potential) unauthorized users. In the risk assessment process, impact levels and the other relevant dimensions – user trust, are also given priority rankings to give an overall (3 × 4 × 4) matrix of values, which are then reduced to six security levels for determining appropriate control measures. BS 7799 and DTI (1996) also provide guidance in respect of managing risks associated with organizations interfacing with other organizations – as outlined in Figure 16.1

## *Crime*

Mirrlees-Black and Ross (1995) carried out a survey for the UK Home Office and found that crime costs retail and manufacturing businesses in England and Wales more than £1bn per annum. The British Retail Consortium maintains that the annual loss through theft in all UK organizations is well over £2bn per year. Theft risk is substantial, with 80 per cent of retailers and around two-thirds of manufacturers reporting theft crimes. Table 16.4 provides some data from this survey to indicate the extent of the risk involved.

Many retail organizations might not relate survey findings to their particular circumstances, being guided by their past experiences rather than future potential for loss – three per cent of all retailers experienced 59 per cent of all reported crimes. Compared with domestic households, retailers are more likely to be burgled, to suffer criminal damage and to have a vehicle stolen (1994 British Crime Survey).

A DTI (1996) report revealed that the number of organizations reporting computer-related thefts had increased by 60 per cent and that the cost of managing the risk of a computer security failure had almost doubled since the previous survey two years before. Of respondents surveyed from both large and small organizations, 90 per cent reported experiencing at least one significant security breach in the

Table 16.4 UK – retail crime (1993)

| *Crime* | *Percentage of retailers reporting* | *Number of offences (000s)* | *Total cost (£m)* |
|---|---|---|---|
| Customer theft | 47 | 5777 | 203 |
| Burglary | 24 | 108 | 205 |
| Theft from vehicles | 23 | 89 | 80 |
| Attempted burglary | 22 | 126 | * |
| Vandalism | 22 | 219 | 83 |
| Fraud | 22 | 319 | 57 |
| Assaults – no injury | 15 | 326 | * |
| Theft of vehicles | 10 | 19 | 16 |
| Employee theft | 8 | 234 | 22 |
| Robbery | 4 | 21 | 28 |
| Bribery & extortion | 2 | 26 | * |
| Assault with injury | 2 | 14 | * |

*Source*: Mirrlees-Black and Ross (1995)
*Figures not available but costs still incurred

previous two years. The average cost of such a breach had increased by 70 per cent over the previous two years.

Managing risk associated with activities such as 'insider dealing' is problematic. Sophisticated monitoring systems exist to detect sharp market price or volume changes which might indicate insider trading. These detection systems can identify 'suspicious' trading patterns within days rather than months as previously. In the US, such systems are reinforced by federal agencies willing to prosecute and bring criminal charges against offenders as well as by civil actions with financial penalties brought by the Securities and Exchange Commission.

Ernst & Young (1996) revealed a high degree of concern about corporate fraud within top Australian companies. However, this concern was not matched by risk management provisions to counter fraud. The report recommends risk management mechanisms such as the adoption of risk control self assessment and regular fraud prevention reviews by organizations. Typically, directors had become detached from the fraud prevention process, delegating this to lower levels of management. The report disclosed that 95 per cent of the responding sample of around 120 companies had experienced a fraud within the previous five years, with over half losing over A$1m in this time, and a mean of A$3m lost through fraud for those companies willing to disclose this information. A general perception was that fraud risk was

h purchasing and computer systems considered to be particularly
ost respondents admitted that their fraud prevention policies were
xistent (Ernst & Young 1996). The findings from this survey were
by the January 1997 issue of DBM Australia *Employment Trend*
which it was reported that corporate fraud is costing Australia over
r and that corporate fraud flourishes when an organization is cha-
lack of internal controls and a high level of employee dissatisfaction.

The Ernst & Young report shows that, within some organizations, all the conditions exist for a collapse similar to that experienced by Barings. Fraud is more likely in businesses where the directors are out of touch with the technicalities of their companies' operations or have lost touch with operations overseas. If a lone desperate individual can bankrupt a large organization, what might a highly motivated, skilled team of people operating across the globe perform in perpetrating large-scale fraud? An organized conspiracy could evade regulators for long enough to clear massive takings.

A useful checklist of factors in respect of auditing fraud risk is provided by Huntington and Davies (1994), who identify a range of fraud risk factors under four risk headings – business, personnel, structural and cultural. Business risks include: inadequate business strategy, atypical profits for the industry, liquidity problems and mismatch between company growth and development of monitoring systems. Personnel risks range from autocratic management style and performance linked compensation through more traditional indices such as poor morale and high staff turnover, to aspects such as expensive lifestyles, untaken holidays and illegal behaviour. Structural risks relate to such features as complex organizational structures, e.g. matrix type structure, and poorly supervised remote locations. Cultural risks include aspects such as: results at any cost, poor control systems, using several auditing firms, lack of an internal code of business ethics and unquestioning obedience of staff.

The risk profile of an organization can alter very quickly as a result of changes in key areas. For example, top personnel changes may affect the culture of a company, which in turn can influence such features as reporting, individual responsibilities, personal competencies and operational controls. Computer systems changes may create gaps in controls. Acquisitions and disposals may result in changed accounting systems and control channels. Huntington and Davies (1994) recommend that whenever any major change in business is considered, then fraud risk should be an agenda item. Prior to its collapse, Barings exhibited many of the fraud risk factors.

Expanding into new markets also carries a variety of risks, the most obvious of which is the potential for failing in a new country and surviving in a culture for which the organization has not prepared itself (see chapter 13). Risks to employees include settling into a new culture and coping with the almost inevitable adjustment stresses such as isolation from family and previous friendship networks. More insidious threats include terrorist attacks, kidnapping, mugging and assault, which might arise at least partly through ignorance of the new terrain and by newcomers being high profile targets within economies which are poorer than those from which the new arrivals originate. Organizations need to develop strategies such as country risk profiling to address territorial trade and other risks associated with opening up new markets in other countries.

For many individuals, crime is a very real risk. Attempts have been made to address issues of risk assessment and risk management in crime and recidivism. An extensive review of practice in the field and relevant literature was produced by Kemshall (1996), who considers the two established methods for assessing risk in this area – clinical and actuarial. The clinical method is based upon a one-to-one case-based professional assessment, which, while it is acknowledged to be subjective, is useful in seeking to understand why certain behaviours occur as a basis for controlling them. Actuarial risk assessment is based upon statistical analysis of data from relevant samples. While actuarial has better predictive validity than clinical assessment, a combination of the two approaches offers the best overall assessment.

Predictive errors associated with both methods can lead to false positives – predictions that a given individual is 'high risk' when they are not, and to false negatives – predicting that someone is 'low risk' who subsequently reoffends. Ethical and resource implications relate to both types of error. In actuarial assessment, errors stem essentially from limits normally associated with statistical prediction. Making individual risk predictions from aggregated data is also problematic.

Adequate risk assessment in the area of crime is important because in addition to recidivism crime risk when offenders are released into the community, there are financial implications. 'Known' costs of keeping a person detained, may be set against contingent costs associated with any crime that they might commit – insurance claims and associated costs, police and other emergency services time, medical treatment costs, litigation and other legal costs, etc. Set against calculable financial costs is the civil liberty issue of retaining low risk individuals in prison.

A number of variables, or risk factors, have been suggested as predictors of recidivism, and these have been postulated as a model of persistent criminal behaviour – shown in Figure 16.2. However, while there is a fairly large number of risk factors for persistent criminal behaviour, a relatively small number of variables is known to account for a large percentage of the variance in recidivism, these being:

*Figure 16.2* Risk factors associated with criminal behaviour

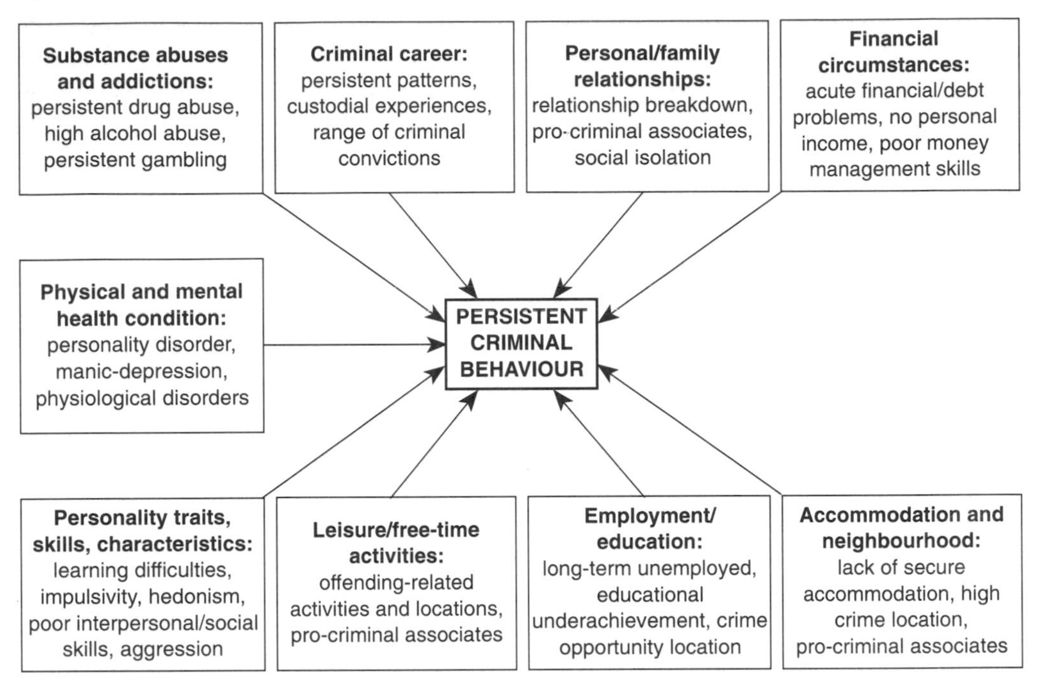


*Source*: after Hampshire Probation Service (1995) and Kemshall (1996)

- age;
- gender;
- number of previous convictions;
- number of previous custodial sentences;
- number of previous court appearances;
- type of offence.

Kemshall (1996: vii) notes that, '. . . interactive factors of gender, marital status, use of disinhibiting agents such as alcohol, the proximity of victims and availability of weapons have been shown to be useful predictors. Male gender, young adulthood and previous violence also have predictive utility'.

## *Clinical risk management*

Clinical risk management originated in the early 1970s US medical malpractice crisis. Risk management programs are now a standard aspect of medical professional practice (e.g. Vincent 1995). Brennan *et al.* (1991) suggest that up to one per cent of patients under treatment suffer injury from medical negligence. Even if only one in ten of these patients sues for negligence, financial costs of litigation are substantial, quite apart from personal and professional costs. Particularly high-risk services include obstetrics, neurosurgery, general surgery and orthopaedics. Risk factors include: inexperience, lack of knowledge, inadequate supervision and inappropriate delegation. Malpractice cases are frequently complex, involving a number of parties.

Given the US claims experience, it is hardly surprising that medicine is an area in which a prime motivator for risk management is litigation avoidance. For example, in the US, and increasingly in the UK and other countries, perinatal outcome analyst (POA) programmes have been designed since the early 1980s as a counter to medical negligence claims and resulting liability losses attributable to obstetric and neonatal care incidents. A prime objective of early assessment and reporting of adverse incidents is to preserve evidence as a defence against possible litigation. However, the POA programme has also benefited neonatal care and early parental counselling in the case of adverse outcomes – irrespective of whether these were related to medical misadventure.

## An approach to risk management through standards

Standards can be generated at national and international level to cover a wide variety of situations involving risk and therefore provide a potentially comprehensive approach to risk management. As well as the possibility of a standard on risk management itself (as in Australia and New Zealand and in Canada), there is the possibility of developing standards on major components, such as occupational health and safety management (as in the UK). Advantages of approaching risk management through standards development include:

- standards are developed through a comprehensive decision-making process involving many parties with a wide range of relevant expertise;
- standards should represent 'best practice' in a particular field;
- each can cover as broad or as narrow a field as desired;
- explicit guidelines may be provided;
- standards provide reassurance to management who follow the guidance;
- they can be produced without the requirement to pass legislation.

However, as with almost any approach, there could also be a downside to using standards as a prime means of managing risks, including:

- standards may be developed prematurely, for example in response to particular incidents or crises;
- they may quickly become outdated – only a problem if there is no effective monitoring system to advise on updates as required;
- there may be a confusion of advice and specifications in some areas;
- developing agreed international standards (e.g. on OHS) can be problematic;
- there may be some inflexibility in respect of taking account of particular circumstances;
- adherence to (lowest common denominator) specifications may engender a false sense of adequacy concerning management of risks.

A specific standard within the field of risk management is BS 7858, concerned with screening security personnel. The main issue addressed here is whether personnel hired to increase the security of premises, personnel, finance or other assets are themselves trustworthy. This BSI code provides guidance, including legal advice, on the recruiting process, including checks that employers can make in respect of employees' past records. When followed, the code reduces the risk that a poor decision will be made in respect of selecting inappropriate candidates for security work. This code of practice is to be followed by BSI codes on related areas, including: cash in transit, secure parcel services, store detective services and door supervision services (bouncers).

## Aspects of risk management likely to receive increasing future attention

Managing risk in the future can be expected to involve an increasingly diverse set of activities compared with traditional areas of risk management. A sample of these is briefly reviewed in the following sub-sections.

### *Managing safety risks associated with change*

For managing OHS, the HSE (1996a) recognizes the synergy between business and OHS management. It advocates a best practice model, which focuses on ensuring that change is an opportunity for improving health and safety, and minimising effects of change upon health and safety. The central component of the model is the interplay between three core features:

1 degree of control – represented by supervision, management, engineered safety, rules and procedures;

2 competence levels;
3 inherent risk.

The empirical component of the study (HSE 1996a) involved the study of ten organizations in sectors with substantial health and safety hazards – with examples from each of the three meta-sectors considered earlier in this chapter. Because of the inadequacy of evidence, the study concluded that effects of change may be either positive or negative upon OHS, but not significantly so. This inability to deliver a definitive conclusion probably reflects, first that 'change' can refer to a wide range of processes and outcomes in different organizational contexts, and second that OHS measures are typically not always adequate for assessing whether a given organizational change has had a positive or negative effect. The possibility remains that a given organizational change could have both positive and negative effects upon OHS – and indeed upon other dimensions of risk (e.g. environment, organizational culture, human resources). Other aspects identified as important to the best practice model include:

- retraining needs analysis for continuing competences;
- supervisory control and team working;
- human resources aspects – e.g. reward, performance management;
- emergency response capability;
- assessment of outsourcing risks – e.g. contractors;
- continuing risk assessment;
- rules and procedures;
- policy;
- OHS management and organization;
- stress and mental health (see below).

The current research base for HSE's proclaimed OHS 'best practice' is slim and a more comprehensive model requires considerable further empirical evidence and analysis.

### *Managing risks associated with employee stress*

It is widely acknowledged throughout developed economies that as organizations reduce numbers of employees and demand greater productivity from those who remain, that increased stress is a major consequence – for both groups. This is particularly true for service-oriented organizations, as the limits of their productive capacity are constrained by the amount of work that individual employees can undertake – hence the phenomenon of burnout found particularly among employees in caring professions. There are considerable individual differences between people's:

- capacity to generate work pressure for themselves;
- capacity to cope with external stressors;
- work efficiency;
- personal effectiveness;
- preferred working hours;
- degree of freedom in selecting their working hours.

As the knowledge-based content of jobs increases in importance, people's ability to process possibly large amounts of information effectively will become an increasing requirement. Managers of knowledge workers need to be able to mobilize organizational support mechanisms to ensure that workers are able to operate close to their optimum effectiveness – a difficult human resource task, particularly at times of radical change.

It is well-known that there are diminishing returns in respect of effectiveness when workers are at their work locations for 'excessive' hours. Lowered capacity, for example in the form of poor productivity and effects of reduced decision-making ability, is among possible risk outcomes for many organizations. However, response to perceived problems associated with poor productivity may take the form of increased supervision or more detailed procedures, rather than greater trust and empowerment to allow individual employees to perform their work in the way that they know best. There are risks for the organization whichever course of action is adopted, for empowerment of individuals and work teams may be perceived as threatening by senior management. A generic risk for organizations is reduced time for strategic and creative thinking required for robust or innovative solutions to a range of problems. A balanced outcome would blend effort and relaxation necessary to health and well-being, both for individuals and for the organizations in which they work.

## *Occupational violence*

Whether violence between individuals or groups is more prevalent than hitherto or whether social attitudes towards it have changed, associated with increased awareness and greater propensities to report violent incidents and considering these as unacceptable aspects of work, is hard to determine. In any case, in principle physical or 'mental' violence between parties – e.g. in the form of bullying or harassment –

can be deemed unacceptable and dealt with accordingly. Although still at a relatively early stage, managing the risk of occupational violence against employees is likely to become an increasing issue for many organizations and in various countries, as evidenced by a growing literature in this area, for example from Australia (e.g. Grainger 1994), the UK (e.g. Cardy 1995) and the US (e.g. Heskett 1996). Grainger (1994) developed the following formula for determining the level of risk for staff:

[A (cash handling) + B (staff working alone) + C (staff working off premises) + D (night work) + E (client aggression)] × F (frequency) = Risk Value

The higher is the risk value, the greater is the likelihood of occupational violence. Factors A–E are scored on a scale of zero to 20 on the basis of exposure to the factor. Frequency is weighted by one point for each worked day in a five-day week. An example of the risk value for a pizza delivery driver (a high risk occupation) might be:

[A (20) + B (20) + C (20) + D (18) + E (2)] × (F) 10 = 800.

## *Driving and commuting*

Although relatively few people are employed specifically for their driving skills, for perhaps 90 per cent of those who use a car or other vehicle to get to work, they will use higher levels of skill in driving than they will need to carry out their jobs. However, despite the much greater likelihood for most of the working population of being killed or suffering traumatic injury on the road than in a traditional workplace, a relatively small number of organizations have addressed the issue of losses in terms of death, injury, damage and lost time which arise from road accidents to their employees. Use of vehicles is an example of a speculative risk, both for individuals and for organizations – because there are benefits and potential costs involved in using road transport. Managing risks associated with road vehicle use involves taking steps to reduce both the amount and the likelihood that costs will be incurred.

In the UK, company cars account for 40 per cent of total annual car mileage and over 50 per cent of new car sales. Largely because of the higher mileages involved, average numbers and costs of insurance claims are considerably higher for company cars than for privately-owned cars. A fleet with an above average claims record is likely to face premium loading. Those responsible for company vehicle fleets and for insuring them have the potential to make considerable improvements in the way in which risks associated with driving are managed. While most fleet operators keep records of accidents, and some undertake analysis of the data, many fail to act on the findings.

Managing risks associated with vehicle fleets is analogous with managing other types of risk in respect of the need to:

- identify the nature and size of the problem – e.g. from accident/claims data;
- analyse factors associated with the problem – e.g. from data analysis and follow-up;
- evaluate consequences in terms of losses – e.g. cost assessment;
- determine and implement appropriate control measures;
- monitor effectiveness of controls.

Control might take the form of avoiding the activity altogether or sub-contracting it – although this is only likely to be an option for a small number of operators. Reducing the risk might involve a combination of financial and physical control measures. Financial controls might involve:

- insurance – e.g. seek best value premiums, ensure quality of repair work;
- contingency fund – for small damage incidents;
- transfer – e.g. to driver, for avoidable accidents;
- self-insurance – particularly for larger fleets.

Physical controls might comprise:

- physical devices – e.g. central third brake lights; collateral safety devices – e.g. airbags;
- safety and security procedures – e.g. maintenance, driver responsibilities, anti-theft devices;
- education and training – e.g. defensive driving, vehicle handling, roadcraft, safe attitudes, stress reduction techniques;
- influencing risk cognition.

Pressures upon company vehicle drivers need to be addressed by organizations that are determined to reduce driving risks. These might include having too large an area to cover, excessive hours of driving required to complete scheduled appointments, too tight a delivery schedule for the time available and lack of control over scheduling. Ensuring that there is a good match between vehicle driven and the driver's ability should also be part of managing driving risks. This could be done on the basis of assessments from a qualified driving assessor. Checking driving licences for convictions or penalty points is a routine procedure which many organizations fail to carry out.

In the US, road traffic accidents (RTAs) are a major cause of lost work time and are the largest single cause of work-related traumatic deaths. This is reflected in substantial compensation costs as well as uninsured costs. Losses accrue through reduced productivity and greater insurance costs. Where organizations have made serious efforts to reduce RTAs among their driving employees, accidents, other losses and insurance premiums have reduced accordingly.

## Corporate reputation

Failure to address adequately any of a wide range of risk issues could adversely affect both corporate reputation and/or financial position. A damaged corporate reputation often results in financial damage. However, such a cause-and-effect relationship is often ignored in boardrooms until the particular organization is already in crisis. Good reputations, which influence an array of behaviours among customers, voters, shareholders, employees and political allies, take a long time to develop but may be destroyed or damaged very quickly.

Reputational risk is speculative – reputations may be enhanced or damaged. As an intangible non-insurable risk it is perhaps one of the most difficult to manage. The risk is not so much to do with what an organization actually does or fails to do but with external perceptions – especially public perceptions – of the organization. Gossip, innuendo and adverse publicity may overwhelm any attempt to portray the organization in a favourable light.

Three cases in the mid-1990s illustrate the fragility of corporate reputations. The so-called 'sleaze factor' badly damaged the UK Conservative Party's image and reputation and was undoubtedly a reason for their administration being voted out of office in 1997 after 18 years. Shell's international reputation was damaged by the Brent Spa offshore installation decommissioning episode and the company's association with the execution of political dissidents in Nigeria – both environmentally based issues. The international reputation of Swiss banks and the Swiss banking system as a whole was devastated by the developing revelations that they had systematically and deliberately lied for 50 years about accounts held for Jews who then became victims of the Nazis.

Corporate reputation, and particularly corporate ethics, has become a key component of risk management in many large organizations and is likely to become a far more prominent issued in the future. No board of directors wants to be associated with the next 'Piper Alpha', 'King's Cross' or 'Barings' for example, although at present they may lack the expertise to prevent such disasters occurring to their own organization.

## *Product liability risks*

Western societies are increasingly litigious as consumers become more knowledgeable and assertive in demanding their rights at law when they believe that duties of care have been broken. This trend is no less so in the area of product safety which transcends all aspects of life; workplaces, medical care, transport, consumer products etc.

Examples of high profile product liability cases include:

- Allegations of benzene contamination of Perrier Water (1990);
- Product formulation defects in Persil Powder detergent (1993);
- Withdrawal of Mercedes-Benz A-Class car owing to instability (1997);
- Compensation claims against Turner & Newall for asbestosis (throughout 1990s).

However, despite these and many more high profile examples, product risks and the liability for them remain relatively unclear and uncertain in the legal arena (Abbot and Tyler 1997). Compliance with legislation, even product specific legislation, and product standards is unlikely to remove all product liabilities and a much broader risk management approach is required.

As with many other areas of risk, such as major hazard installations, capital projects and construction design and management (CDM), a life-cycle approach is required for effective management of product risks, as summarized in Table 16.5. Throughout a product's life-cycle, there is a need to record systematically all risk assessments and decisions based on them. Since such a life-cycle may run to decades, the availability of such records becomes crucial to demonstrating due diligence and to mounting a credible defence to any product liability claims. In the case of asbestos-related diseases and cigarette-smoking related diseases, for example, massive product liability claims may relate to product use and exposure which occurred decades before.

Risk assessment methodologies, and techniques for product safety are well established and relatively stable. However, social expectations continue to shift in the direction of risk aversion. What may be broadly acceptable today may become unacceptable tomorrow, regardless of what risk experts may say. As discussed throughout this book, risk acceptabililty determined solely by risk experts is a recipe for problems, especially in product safety which generally impacts upon a large number of people. A non-holistic dis-integrated approach to product risks, e.g. design risk evaluations remaining remote from evaluations of marketing risks, cultural risks and political risks, is more likely to fall into such a trap (Waring and Tyler 1997).

Globalization of trade and moves towards strict liability for product safety are likely to demand much higher standards of risk reduction, not only through

*Table 16.5* Life-cycle approach to product risk management

| *Life-cycle phase* | *Key activities* | *Key risk management requirements* |
|---|---|---|
| Research | Basic research<br>R&D | Hazards data collection<br>Identifying applicable product regulations |
| Design | Conceptual design<br>Detailed design | Product risk profiling including misuse, application contexts and environments<br>Hazards data analysis<br>Design risk assessments, modifications and reassessments<br>Feedforward to manufacture |
| Testing and approvals | Laboratory tests e.g. NDT, flammability, toxicity<br>Pilot scale trials<br>Field trials | Hazards data analysis, AR&M<br>Design feedback<br>Compliance with standards<br>Feedforward to manufacture<br>Independent certifications |
| Manufacture | Raw materials to formulation<br>Processing<br>Finishing<br>Packaging<br>Batch marking | QA throughout manufacture<br>Compliance with standards<br>Conformity assessments<br>Technical data files |
| Product launch | Labelling and manuals<br>Advertising, marketing<br>Contract terms<br>Insurance | Appropriate instructions, warnings and safety information<br>Ensuring accuracy of claims for product<br>Risk allocation |
| Service life | Monitoring, reviewing, responding to customer complaints, keeping distributors informed | Policy and procedures for maintenance, design mods, recalls, replacements, withdrawals etc<br>Feedback to design |
| Decommission | Surveys<br>Dismantling, demolition, scrapping<br>Disposal | Policy and procedures<br>Risk assessments including environmental effects<br>Ensuring adequacy of risk control measures |

improved design but also by attention to risk management throughout the entire product life-cycle.

## Environmental risks

For the previous generation, the main global political challenge was to manage and control the risk of nuclear war. Although this risk remains, it is now considerably reduced both in absolute terms and relative to other risks, so that political priorities have changed. Current global risk management is primarily concerned with the environment – involving such parameters as human population balance, damage to ecosystems, reduction of bio-diversity, habitat destruction, global warming and long-term pollution effects. Political and scientific arguments may be separable in theory but not necessarily in practice. While the technology probably exists to address most of the world's environmental problems, debate and action on these problems involves a complex web of scientific and technical issues interwoven with political interests. This is likely to remain the single greatest challenge for risk management on a macro scale for the foreseeable future because it involves so many parties with such a variety of deep and differing interests.

At the 1992 Rio de Janeiro UN Earth Summit most states were represented at the highest level. While genuine attempts are being made in some countries to address key issues made in the Rio Declaration: 'States shall cooperate in a spirit of global partnership to conserve, protect and restore the health and integrity of the earth's ecosystem . . . ', many experts consider that too little is being achieved to support this pious declaration. Rio's Agenda 21 ran to 400 pages and gives clear guidance on what ought to be done. However, no nations can be legally bound by it and many governments will not even seriously examine its contents. Action at different levels is required to address this issue because its outcomes affect everyone. While global agreement and action is required to provide a strategic basis, local level solutions to particular problems will emerge. Thus rather than attempting to 'eat the elephant' at one go, governments might deploy resources more effectively by supporting local successes and providing strong incentives for ecologically sound projects and initiatives.

Set against the political will and extensive co-operation between states to achieve outcomes that will benefit the whole planet are powerful lobbies, for example those using non-renewable or non-replenished natural resources (e.g. hard wood timber, water, fossil fuels), often backed implicitly and through incentives by their governments. A key issue is timescale and deferred gratification. As the ability to forgo immediate gratification for a larger reward at some future time is a measure of an individual's emotional maturity, by analogy the same is true for nations and organizations. Outcomes can be positive-sum for all parties, but only in the long term. Managing risks in the political sphere frequently involves finding adequate mechanisms to address short-term deficits in various parties' situations. If this issue is not addressed then in the long term many more parties might be losers.

Corruption and autocracy, bullying and excessive use of political power as well as human rights abuses in many parts of the world, serve to distort decision-making processes on risk issues. These might relate to large-scale water management projects, nuclear power and its negative environmental impact, or large-scale environmental destruction and pollution. Future generations may, with justification, vilify us for not being able to manage these risks adequately. It is desirable that there should be openness in political decision-making involving risk. Secrecy effectively disenfranchises populations. In the short term, a lack of transparency, for example about the nature of known risks of a project or venture, might give powerful parties involved an advantage. However, by artificially restricting participation of less powerful parties with interests in risk outcomes, governments and other agencies fail in their duties to all their constituencies, as well as risking making poor decisions on a range of issues. More open government in respect of treating people as being responsible and capable of understanding risks, providing that the issues are adequately communicated, would benefit risk management decision-making. Cases such as E. Coli outbreaks in various countries and BSE in the UK, indicate that institutions frequently fail to communicate adequately and early enough with the public about the scientific basis of risks which could affect them. Such failures reduce public confidence in institutions of government and big business, hampering subsequent efforts to manage risk controversies effectively.

Since the 1992 Summit in Brazil the gap between rich and poor nations has widened, as has the gap between rich and poor groups within many countries. The serious crises identified then – for example, destruction of forests, freshwater shortages, world overfishing and mass extinction of species – have worsened. Both poverty and wealth act as drivers in the destruction of environments – poor people strip the earth of trees for fuel and to grow food, while the wealthy, generally far removed physically and psychologically from the end point of their demand chains, seek ever greater satisfaction through the consumption of yet more resources. Only by effective communication and action on a global scale can these complex issues be addressed.

## Conclusions

Two global trends are likely to have increasing impact upon risk management, both for nation states and for national institutions and agencies. The first trend is towards increasing diversity and disparity between nations and between different economic sectors and organizations within them. Risks associated with growing differences between structures at all levels need to be continually monitored as part of the risk management feedback loop and re-assessed in respect of their impact upon states, organizations and other groupings. Managing change and diversity is a vital component of managing risk, because risk factors do not remain constant. A second major trend which mirrors the first, is towards a degree of convergence, particularly in respect of economic and political power blocks – e.g. ASEAN, EU, US. Other examples can be found in the growing trend towards strategic global alliances between large companies, which are likely to become increasingly important for the survival and success of organizations in such sectors as civil aviation, financial services and telecommunications. Risks of not being part of a strategic global alliance could include a continual struggle for survival.

Organizations of all types need to manage risk proactively. This could involve development and implementation of risk management policies, but also deliberate learning, both from success (e.g. by benchmarking) and from failures, for example using system failures methodology – Fortune and Peters (1995), Waring (1996c); or learning from disasters – Toft and Reynolds (1994, 1997). Independent expert auditing of risk management systems is important as this can provide valuable feedback on whether risk management systems are adequate for the range of issues which they need to address.

In education and training programmes, rehearsing risk management scenarios is important. This might range from dealing with possible large-scale emergencies to handling angry clients on a one-to-one basis. Design of appropriate training agendas and work sample role plays or case studies will not only help to instil confidence and knowledge into participants but will also involve a range of parties in their development – thereby broadening awareness of threats and risk management issues generally within organizations.

Much greater collaboration between hitherto diverse aspects of risk management, for example in respect of methodologies used, could be advantageous as it can extend the scope as well as increasing integration of risk management. To be robust, risk management decisions need to be based upon as wide a constituency as possible. Ultimately many risk management decisions are political, in that value judgements affecting people's lives impose upon decisions otherwise primarily based upon technical criteria. This is part of the nature of risk and its management.

# Chapter 17
# A research agenda

## Overview

The agenda for risk research is potentially limitless because it involves so many aspects of individual, organizational and social functioning. Because risk-taking is fundamental to much of human activity and endeavour, there are considerable opportunities for multi-disciplinary research. This chapter opens some windows into areas in which research into managing risk at all levels is desirable. The message represents a series of value-judgements and the catalogue of areas for research is not exhaustive. A key theme is that while theoretical advances will always be required, of greater urgency is action research which will impact upon many areas of risk.

## Introduction

A central theme of this book is to seek links between (and within) different, and sometimes disparate areas of risk. Research activity currently exists across many risk domains. For example in the UK, the ESRC's Risk and Human Behaviour Research Programme Initiative, due to run until the year 2000, has sponsored some two dozen projects for an investment of around £3m, much of it multi-disciplinary (ESRC 1997). Multi-disciplinary research can bring benefits in approaches to such topics as risk assessment – which remains a very inexact process in many instances. A number of the ESRC projects reflect issues considered in this book, including railway risk assessment and management, risk management in the health service, risk cognition, cultural bases for risk perception and penal policy risks. The background and range of initial research proposals is considered in the next section. Current research spans both theoretical and applied approaches. Research into managing risk should include action research which is expressly designed to develop, implement and evaluate appropriate and worthwhile interventions. A continuing bias towards applied targeted work is required.

Three levels may be identified as areas for risk management research. The first level is global – represented primarily by threats to the earth's environment through habitat destruction, overpopulation, chemical and other pollution, waste materials and other damaging influences. Also at this level, research is required into international conflicts and associated destruction which frequently accompanies them – of people's lives, homes and communities. Both these large areas present major multi-disciplinary research challenges which require political and social solutions rather than technical ones.

A second level for research activity is that of organizations in the broad sense – including government institutions. The increasing complexity of issues affecting decision-making and the tighter coupling of elements within large-scale systems make for critical risk assessment and risk management. The third level for research activity is the individual. Research into cognitive aspects of decision-making and risk perception has been carried out for some time. However, research is less available into emotional and learning components of risk cognition in the wider sense. As individuals face increasingly complex, stressful and challenging responsibilities, research which can assist their capacity to meet major challenges must be beneficial. Such research should not be tied to the paradigm that risk taking has only a downside (i.e. pure risk), but reflect the potential richness of people's experiences, through acknowledging benefits that can accrue through experiencing and making choices about risk in their lives.

## The Economic and Social Research Council (ESRC) Risk and Human Behaviour Research Programme

In 1993 the ESRC launched a major research initiative on risk, inviting phase one proposals with practical and policy relevance under three broad themes:

- Society and risk, including risk and culture, organizations and risk.
- Personal risk, including risk assessment and reduction, risk-seeking and risk avoiding behaviour and physiological aspects of risk.
- Environmental and technological risk.

With a broad agenda set, it is instructive to consider the 166 proposals (only 14 of which were funded) submitted by almost 300 risk researchers under Phase One of the programme, which were produced in summary form as a booklet by ERSC. While the initial ESRC guidelines clearly had considerable influence upon the substantive content and applications orientation of the proposals, these would also be expected to reflect researchers' particular risk research agendas. A quick analysis was undertaken on the information provided (title and abstract) to determine the range of topics represented.

As would be expected these covered many areas and a wide variety of disciplines was represented. Some proposals were multi-disciplinary while others were based within particular disciplines. The broad categories represented by the proposals are shown in Table 17.1, with the number of proposals in each category submitted and funded. This uni-dimensional categorization ignores the many overlaps as each project is selected to fall into only one category, while meta-categories are also not represented separately – e.g. application-oriented, theoretical-oriented and decision-making. While all the proposals involved one or more of these meta-categories, only a few were specifically oriented towards just one of them.

As will be seen from Table 17.1, the largest category of proposals was labelled 'Social/community/health'. This covered a wide variety of risk topics, although risks affecting groups at particular life-cycle stages were common. Research into risks particularly affecting children and adolescents were much in evidence, as were studies relating to HIV infection, sexual behaviour, drugs and violence. Organizational/business risk was the second largest area, where OHS risks appeared, as well as risks associated with managerial decision-making in a variety of contexts including: TQM,

*Table 17.1* Broad categories of projects submitted and funded under phase one of the ESRC Risk and Human Behaviour Research Programme

| *Broad research area* | *Number of proposals submitted (funded)* |
|---|---|
| Social/community/health | 45 (3) |
| Organizational | 34 (1) |
| Individual | 28 (4) |
| Medical | 12 (2) |
| Communication | 9 (1) |
| Legal | 6 (2) |
| Environmental | 6 (0) |
| Decision-making | 6 (0) |
| Consumer | 5 (0) |
| Statistical | 4 (1) |
| Theoretical | 4 (0) |
| Learning/education | 4 (0) |
| Leisure | 2 (0) |
| Security | 1 (0) |

risk assessment, new technology, small businesses, investment, markets and crises. The third largest area, individual risks, included research advocating study of human behaviour in a variety of settings, driving being foremost among them, but also emphasizing the need to consider everyday risks from the perspective of individuals experiencing them rather than from researchers' pre-existing models or frameworks. The need to build adequate theory in the field of individual risk appraisal – incorporating emotional as well as rational components, which was stressed in the ESRC proposal guidelines – was in evidence in a number of the proposals.

The range of other perspectives from which researchers drew up their phase one proposals was also interesting, with both medical and legal categories featuring – and also experiencing high hit rates for funding compared with other areas. Interestingly, although environmental risk was identified as a major theme component, relatively few proposals were submitted under this heading and none were funded. Phase Two of the programme was initiated in 1994 and potential applicants were urged to consider multidisciplinarity and policy relevance as well as 'the broader context within . . . which human beings navigate an uncertain world' (*ESRC Risk & Human Behaviour Research Programme Specification for Phase 2*) in drawing up their proposals. Seeking to advance the Phase 1 projects, themes identified for Phase 2 were:

- Risk at the Micro Level – individual coherence, the decision-making 'unit'.
- Risk at the Macro Level – government decisions, political, social and policy aspects.
- Risk in Organizational Settings – individual vs. collective attitudes to risk, formal and informal risk analysis, responsibility and blame, change and the status quo.

Out of 170 proposals submitted, ten were funded under Phase Two of the programme. These were primarily in the organizational area with one each in the social/community, individual and medical areas. The complete distribution of categories in Table 17.2 shows a broadly similar pattern to projects submitted under Phase One, with fewer individual (e.g. psychological, driving) proposals submitted and more in the business/employment in Phase Two.

A message from this rather crude analysis of ESRC risk research project funding is that while in theory researchers have freedom to follow their personal preferences in respect of risk, research agendas are established within a broadly political framework which provides key resources, particularly funding. Because risk agendas have a range of defining features it is also inevitable that both temporal and cultural biases will exist in research proposed and funded under such initiatives. For example, while the UK risk research initiative generated a number of proposals in the area of risks faced by young people, none of them dealt specifically with suicide risk. In

*Table 17.2* Broad categories of projects submitted and funded under phase two of the ESRC Risk and Human Behaviour Research Programme

| *Broad research area* | *Number of proposals submitted (funded)* |
|---|---|
| Organizational (including OHS) | 42 (7) |
| Social/community/health/public policy | 41 (1) |
| Business/employment/investment | 18 (0) |
| Individual | 16 (1) |
| Medical | 10 (1) |
| Communication/discourse | 10 (0) |
| Consumer | 9 (0) |
| Decision making | 8 (0) |
| Legal/criminal | 4 (0) |
| Environmental | 4 (0) |
| Information Technology | 3 (0) |
| Government | 1 (0) |
| Insurance | 1 (0) |
| Research | 1 (0) |
| Learning/education | 1 (0) |
| Leisure/sport | 1 (0) |
| Security | 1 (0) |

Australia and New Zealand, where the rate of adolescent – particularly male, suicide is the highest in the world, this is a key risk research area.

## Social context for risk

Bernstein (1996) argues that compared with earlier centuries, risk and uncertainty are more salient and very much at the core of modern society. If this is true, there is a need to research how well equipped humans – and the organizations and institutions that serve them – are for dealing with increasing uncertainty and risk in their lives. A paradox is that the increasing vulnerability of systems to accidental error, deliberate upset or natural disaster is partly founded on increasing levels of technological sophistication which brings decreasing impact tolerances. For manufacturing systems, and the well-documented disasters that they have spawned, this vulnerability has been in evidence for several decades. Social systems have also been affected on a broad scale for some time and are becoming increasingly vulnerable, for example through steadily rising unemployment levels. More recently, through

Barings and other cases, the international financial system has also been revealed as highly vulnerable.

The three levels of risk research are complementary, as interventions within each can have extended benefits. For example, improving organizational environments is likely to enhance the health and well-being of employees and others affected by their activities. Resolving international conflicts and wars alleviates stress and suffering in affected communities. Long-term positive effects upon risk activities in the social sphere should accrue through appropriate interventions at an individual level – if on a large enough scale. At all levels, research designed to determine how best to increase mutual awareness of different world views and perspectives between parties to issues which involve risk could serve as a useful first step towards improved understanding. The case study in chapter 13 represents just one example.

The April 1997 issue of *Risk Management* (from the Geneva Association) editorial points to the role of modern technology in creating more tightly coupled systems which are more vulnerable to 'risk multipliers' – systems which rely on people's behaviour being socially responsible. The editorial explains that opponents of modern society and the socially excluded are discovering the social vulnerability of public systems, giving as examples setting fire to cars, throwing stones from motorway bridges, drive-by shootings as well as various forms of protest and crime. The Swiss Re report *Sigma* 3/1997 identifies major losses in that country during 1996. Just over 64 per cent of all insured losses were caused by 'natural' catastrophes while of the remainder, 20 per cent were due to 'terrorism and social unrest'. The *Risk Management* editorial suggests a number of reasons for the breakdown in 'social ecology':

- An increase in violence within society, exemplified by more bodyguards, increases in private and state security forces and a greater readiness by the general population to arm themselves.
- Increasing disparities of wealth which effectively disenfranchise large portions of the population through unemployment and lack of opportunity, leading many people to feel excluded from the benefits of society and not feeling obliged to contribute to it.
- The random pattern of risk created by those excluded from mainstream society, including poor health and the re-emergence and spread of once eradicated diseases, such as tuberculosis.
- Vulnerability of those dependent upon state benefits to national financial crises and the danger that more people will join the economically disenfranchised group.
- Increasing vulnerability of society to both organized and disorganized forms of

terrorism and violence, for example the ability of the IRA to paralyse transport networks with bomb threats, and the difficulty of identifying rogue individuals who wage vendettas against mainstream society – as in the May 1995 Oklahoma bombing.

It might be argued that loss of social identity and sense of community have been operating over a considerable period of time, particularly in highly individualistic societies typical of Western capitalism. Risks facing people in these societies derive primarily from within, rather than from the machinations of power blocks on the world stage. Risks faced by people in developing nations are likely to be characterized by considerably fewer choices and the prospect of facing an environment which is largely imposed by factors beyond their control. How individuals learn to cope with an increasingly bewildering world will be an area of much needed discovery so that appropriate interventions can be determined. For example, the recently labelled 'road rage' is identified as 'causing' 200 deaths per annum in the US, and has received media attention in the UK, Australia and other countries. More disturbingly, 'rage' has been considered as a defence in other violent crimes (e.g. racial attacks). However, by compartmentalizing rage and anger as relating to specific locations or behaviours we lose sight of the generality of these phenomena. Proven counselling techniques exist for addressing these emotions generically and are likely to be increasingly needed, both as palliative and preventive measures.

The challenges both for risk management and risk research are vast because they reach right to the core of basic social issues and fundamental values, not being problems which relate solely to risk agendas. Solutions at least to some risk issues require bold social changes and real political commitment to roll back vast and increasing wealth disparities without diminishing people's desire for entrepreneurial risk taking and motivation to pursue business goals essential to the health of modern social economies. Tackling endemic unrest produced by personal, social and political dissatisfaction is another major challenge.

Levels of approach to social ills are not mutually exclusive and various disciplines are likely to advocate interventions on different scales. Strategic initiatives at international, national and community level are necessary to address broad-ranging issues which impose unwanted risks upon individuals, institutions and organizations. These parties can also act locally in ways which can provide strong messages of hope as well as indicators of action in the wider sphere. Goleman (1995: 286) highlights some of the risk outcomes of failing to teach emotional competence to individuals in western societies. Of recent increases in the number of juveniles in the US charged with murder, aggravated assault, robbery and forcible rape, he notes:

> These teenagers are the first generation to have not just guns but automatic weaponry easily available to them . . . disagreements that in a former day would have led to fistfights can readily lead to shootings instead . . . these teenagers 'just aren't very good at avoiding disputes'. One reason they are so poor at this basic life skill . . . is that as a society we have not bothered to make sure every child is taught the essentials of handling anger or resolving conflicts positively – nor have we bothered to teach empathy, impulse control, or any of the other fundamentals of emotional competence. By leaving the emotional lessons children learn to chance, we risk largely wasting the window of opportunity presented by the slow maturation of the brain to help children cultivate a healthy emotional repertoire.

Risks which have their roots in emotional incompetence are not confined to acts of overt violence, but permeate our whole society. As another example, Goleman (1995: 240) points to the increasing incidence of depression – which is emerging earlier and earlier in people's lives. Proposed social 'causes' of such depression include: erosion of the nuclear family, greater individual mobility required by increasingly global industrialization, reduction in traditional community support mechanisms and a decline in religious beliefs. Whatever the reasons, outcomes include reduced individual levels of functioning and social competence, and in extreme cases resort to heavy drug use or suicide. When people feel chronically bad about themselves, theories of risk taking as a rational process no longer apply.

Drug use, as an attempted counter to depression or other negative mental states, may be labelled either 'legal' or 'illegal', depending upon the source of the drugs. Galbraith, in *The New Industrial State*, argues that corporations, such as pharmaceutical companies, are not passive in their response to market needs for their products, but actively intervene to create consumer demand. Responsiveness of the total market for addressing individuals' mental health needs is complex and potentially involves many parties, including: government institutions, a range of companies and individuals offering a great variety of goods and services, family and friends, as well as illegal drug agents. How individuals cope with their own changing mental states is central to how they and the wider community manages risks which are a continuous feature of their environment.

There is a need to understand more about human well-being and how to enhance it. Skills and competencies learnt by children at home and in school need to focus upon emotional aspects of intellectual functioning – not to replace current emphasis upon academic intelligence but to complement and enhance it. We should address underlying cognitive emotional issues which fuel many risks – i.e. fundamental aspects of human nature. Factors which pre-dispose to anger, rage, anxiety, depression and other negative states are beginning to be well-documented. The importance of 'social capital' to health is known – both through research and intuitively. For example, smokers report higher levels of stress, distress and malaise than non-smokers do. There are likely to be associations between varieties of risk-taking behaviour and emotional states. Action research programmes, rather than merely 'academic' research, are required to confront these basic issues. For this to happen, social and financial structures need to be politically designed to reward researchers able to develop such interventions.

Goleman (1995) refers to 'toxic emotions' which, if untreated, can increase the risk of heart disease, cancer and other ailments through constant weakening of the body's immune system. Goleman (1995: 169) states that '. . . anger seems to be the one emotion that does most harm to the heart', citing studies which indicate that '. . . being prone to anger was a stronger predictor of dying young than were other risk factors . . .'. The better news is that anger and hostility as habitual responses can be modified by appropriate interventions. Programmes which teach awareness of early signs of a bout of anger, ability to regulate it and empathy – i.e. basic elements of emotional intelligence, can reduce its impact and lead to marked improvements in health and well-being.

To confront workplace violence it is certainly necessary to employ risk management procedures, which if effective, could be expected to reduce incidences – 20 per cent has been suggested as a reasonable target (Blair 1997). However, managing this risk in ways outlined in chapter 16 does not necessarily deal with fundamental issues which generate the violence. It may be that the violence which festers within a person will emerge elsewhere. The legitimate objective of risk management in this case is to protect staff. What is required is a more generic strategy that can address underlying problems.

As a start, we need to understand more about emotional components of risk cognitions and behaviours – particularly fear, anger and anxiety, as these are central to the internal psychological environment within which humans appraise risk and uncertainty. Interventions which help people to manage better their negative feelings – anger, anxiety, depression, pessimism and loneliness, is according to Goleman (1995: 183) a form of disease prevention, as he notes:

> Since the data show that the toxicity of these emotions, when chronic, is on a par with smoking cigarettes, helping people handle them better could potentially have a medical payoff as great as getting heavy smokers to quit. One way to do this that could have broad public-health effects would be to impart most

> basic emotional intelligence skills to children, so that they become lifelong habits. Another high-payoff preventative strategy would be to teach emotion management to people reaching retirement age, since emotional well-being is one factor that determines whether an older person declines rapidly or thrives. A third target group might be so-called at-risk populations – the very poor, single working mothers, residents of high-crime neighborhoods . . . who live under extraordinary pressure . . . and so might do better medically with help in handling the emotional toll of these stresses.

While it might justifiably be argued that removing the causes of such stresses, for example through appropriate social policy interventions, should be a priority, the two approaches are not mutually exclusive in that 'giving a person a fish might keep them from starving for a day but teaching them to fish could enable them to feed themselves for life'.

## *Potential political outlets*

To illustrate the interplay between individual experiences and emotions on the one hand and the wider socio-political arena on the other, numerous political movements and individual politicians in many countries can be identified who have acted as conduits for anger, rage and a range of dissatisfactions among constituents – locally and nationally. When society cannot cater for many of the basic needs of its people and they do not have the personal resources to address their emotions, then extremist politicians – who may themselves be victims of anger, frustration and bitterness in their private lives – can readily channel people's negative emotions against an identifiable target. Frequently such targets are ethnic minorities – which can serve as objects in the 'culture of complaint' which suffuses many societies. Rather than accept personal responsibility for their emotional state, individuals often find it easier to direct their dissatisfactions onto a labelled target which can be conveniently blamed for a variety of ills. Research is political and research which sought to test out this particular thesis would be very evidently so.

Risks associated with not undertaking research into extreme political movements include the perpetuation of destructive social divisions. Social conflict is inevitable and can be functional in respect of testing social norms and acceptable behaviours. However, social divisions based upon hatred and intolerance leave open the possibility that behaviours based upon strongly negative emotions will find legitimized expression – for example through a variety of attacks upon 'out group' members. If research confirms the negative emotions which fuel the corruptness and moral bankruptcy of extreme political movements – and the violence which frequently accompanies them, then people can be confronted with the underlying reasons for their involvement. The next step is to get them to accept personal responsibility for their actions – as it is with the criminal who robs, rapes or otherwise violates others' basic rights. This is a very tall order and represents a major challenge for research. Some might argue that this is not a matter for research but for social and political action. That such action is required is not in dispute. That it should be guided by rigorous research is highly desirable.

The key to harmony could be argued to be successfully addressing the various risks associated with increasing racial, ethnic and religious mixing in many societies, including Cyprus, USA, Balkan states, Israel and her Arab neighbours, and many other places. Given the increasing interdependence of cultures in today's world, negative outcomes associated with not dealing adequately with racial intermixing are also likely to increase. Promotion of harmonious existence between cultures is a major challenge for risk research.

## Individual level risk

Substantial individual differences characterize people's propensities to take risks. However, the increasing variety of inherently hazardous activities that individuals engage in as leisure pursuits suggests that risk taking is an in-built feature of human nature. It has been known for some time that individuals accept higher levels of risk for activities voluntarily engaged in than for risks imposed as a consequence of some other activity (e.g. paid work). To manage risks associated with them, many of these leisure pursuits have strict rules and procedures attached to their participation, but serious injury as a result of accidents remain a possibility for participants in a range of leisure pursuits including: scuba diving, parachuting, bungy jumping, flying (in a variety of machines), caving and racing – again in a variety of vehicles. More exotic pursuits include sky surfing, ballooning across oceans, heli-skiing, sailing single-handed around the world or trekking to the South Pole.

Among the more spectacular of current risk-taking activities is mountaineering, and in particular climbing Mount Everest as the ultimate adventure, which has become a business venture for a number of companies and a romantic goal for many would-be climbers. As with reports of collapsing fairground rides, it seems that disasters on Mount Everest serve to enhance the excitement which leads some people to pay substantial amounts of money to join a group of climbers. Most of the eight people who died on Everest in May 1996 were not mountaineers but amateurs, whose motives might have included a desire to become a minor celebrity, personal mastery, career advancement or ego enhancement. Publication of an account of the 1996 disaster (Krakauer 1997) coincided with a repeat tragedy in May 1997, when nine climbers were again killed in severe storms near the summit. The ingredients for these disasters tend to mirror those in financial and occupational health and safety environments, being a combination of human error, greed, business rivalry, bad luck and misjudgement. The latter is particularly pertinent high up Everest as the thin air renders even experienced climbers' judgements irrational because of hypoxia.

In more everyday pursuits, the increasing complexity of stimuli potentially available to individuals generates a need to investigate and unravel the full range of risks in people's lives. This represents a more holistic approach to risk cognition (perception) than hitherto. A possible starting point would be to test out and refine a theory of individual risk cognition which incorporated emotional components in order to determine the nature of processes that underlie risk judgements and risk behaviours – see chapter 8. In-depth study of cognitive-emotional components through examining a wide variety of risk-related behaviours, would help to build a more adequate theory of individual risk appraisal as well as laying the ground for more effective interventions for when one or more components are dysfunctional.

Cognitive aspects of risk taking are becoming better understood, for example through the fairly large literature on risk perception. However, much of the research on which it is based is method-bound, relates primarily to adults and addresses specific issues – e.g. driving, rating hazards which have little or no direct impact on research participants or using heuristics to make judgements. Many of these studies are interesting and informative in respect of revealing the relatively inadequate intellectual apparatus possessed by humans for assessing risks (e.g. Plous 1992; Bazerman 1993).

When addressing individual risk-taking, it is necessary to examine a much wider spectrum of risk cognitions and behaviours than has hitherto been explored. For example, study of how people behave in response to extreme situations or critical incidents can reveal a great deal about our cognitive and emotional functioning. Use of case studies – in which individuals have performed particularly badly or spectacularly well in response to risk, can also be very illuminating. Developing appropriate psychometric tests to assess individuals' risk-taking preferences, tolerances and competencies, might be useful in some situations.

Although adolescents are an increasingly studied category, a serious gap in the literature is understanding developmental aspects of risk cognition. If more knowledge was available in respect of how children initially acquire concepts of 'risk', 'hazard' and 'danger', then we should be much better placed to influence and nurture their development more appropriately. To advance knowledge in this area, longitudinal studies are required to assess developmental variables as a basis for intervention programmes. For example, it might be possible to intervene with respect to reducing the likelihood of cognitions and behaviours associated with such activities as: heavy drinking, obsessive gambling, drug use, falling prey to extremist political agendas and a whole range of harmful 'adult' behaviours, being activated.

An adequate developmental model in respect of risk could usefully inform a range of interventions for helping people to manage risk in their lives. Understanding better how people balance complex sets of risks and utilities is likely to be one key to unravelling bases of behaviour. This could also help to develop applied models of risk taking, for example the health belief model (Becker 1974) and risk homeostasis theory (RHT) (Wilde 1994). Within RHT there is a need to understand more about cognitions and emotions which predispose individuals to select particular behavioural pathways through which risk compensation effects may be transmitted.

There are considerable opportunities for learning from exchange of research information and experiential knowledge between cultures, for example on socialisation for risk. Compared with many other cultures with more restraining laws and customs, seeking immediate gratification and low impulse control is a feature of western societies' citizens. 'Freedom' to express oneself carries risks, and individuals need to be educated to cope with them. Research which expanded our knowledge of factors which curtailed the extremes of risk taking activities, for example among adolescents in different cultures, would be useful. However, because many aspects of culture are not readily transferable, each culture needs to find its own solutions to problems posed by risk factors – e.g. social norms relating to alcohol, driving and sexual behaviour, and more broadly, obedience to authority and social conformity.

On the benefits side, societies which permit adolescents' freedoms which would be curtailed in other cultures may be more likely to promote original thought, creativity, colour, diversity and excitement in their citizens' everyday experiences. There are various theories about adolescent risk-taking behaviour (e.g. Arnett 1995; Igra and Irwin 1996). Links between adolescent risk-related behaviour and childhood socialization at an individual level are less explored as are links with later adult risk-taking, although enduring individual differences play a part – e.g. in sensation-seeking, self-esteem and risk perception, as well as mood changes (Maule and Hockey 1996). Awareness of both sides of the risk-benefit equation can help in making choices for both individuals and those responsible for social policy. Managing risks effectively is a requirement at both levels.

## Illegal activity

There is a need for more research information on the propensity for individuals to take risks in connection with criminal activity – including relatively recently criminalized activities such as 'insider dealing'. We need to know more about perceived costs and benefits of activities deemed to be illegal, or at least of uncertain legality. Large individual differences will exist, for example between experienced and inexperienced offenders. Illegal activities which involve both costs and benefits might range from speeding to burglary. Benefits would include the thrill or 'buzz' which many offenders derive from criminal behaviour. It would be desirable to know about qualitative differences in criminal risks that individuals are prepared to take, perhaps compared with many legal activities which have associated costs and benefits, for example hazardous leisure pursuits.

Relevant parameters of illegal activity which might be considered could include:

- benefits of successful outcomes;
- perceived likelihood of being detected and caught;
- perceived likelihood of being prosecuted if caught;
- perceived likelihood of being convicted if prosecuted;
- perceived likelihood of a range of punishments if convicted – eg:
  - light
  - moderate
  - severe;
- emotional components – e.g. defiance, thrill-seeking;
- balancing factors which predispose towards offending or not offending;
- personal risk factors – see for example Figure 16.2 in chapter 16.

As with other personal risk equations, benefits are likely to be immediate and readily identifiable, whereas potential disbenefits are likely to be more distant, less readily identifiable and less likely, particularly when a number of stages is involved. Emotional components within the equation are likely to be very important in respect of risk decisions made by individuals.

In the case of illegal stock exchange dealing, the onus of proof under UK and many other legal systems, has hitherto been with the prosecution. Problems of presenting adequate proof in such cases tend to be inversely proportional to the complexity of the case. Thus, substantial costs may be incurred in collecting evidence and taking a case to court. A major downside of this course of action is the possibility that the case may not succeed. As a result of the Barings case, the UK Securities and Futures Authority have a new policy, backed up by a change in the rule book which effectively means that those in charge of such disasters can be considered 'guilty until proven innocent' – reversing traditional UK law. A major difficulty is that all regulatory authorities derive their powers from national legislation whereas the risks that they seek to address are often played across international areas. Research into how state mechanisms might be galvanized to address international risks in all areas of criminal activity would be valuable.

There is a need to understand more about cognitive aspects of risk taking associated with theft of all types, from corporate fraud to theft from a local store. The issue has strong cultural and moral dimensions as it is closely linked with the socialization of individuals within their community and within society more generally. A related issue is the question of 'how much is enough?' (Handy 1995) for individuals in society. How many people are able to self-actualize to the extent that they can decide rationally when they have enough material possessions? Is the observation that 'enough is just one more' a universal imperative or a socially acquired response? Ultimately, risks which people choose to take are intimately bound up with the maturity and collective integrity of the societies in which they live and with that of humankind more generally.

For specifically addressing risks associated with re-offending, application of a number of key variables to predict outcomes could be used. This would be analogous with the Syspas model for predicting company failures (see chapter 16). Multi-variate models (e.g. using multiple regression, ANOVA or path analysis techniques) could be used as decision-making aids in respect of predicting likelihoods of given outcomes. There is considerable scope for developing such models for risk assessment decisions involving several key variables. However, as with any model used in this way, the final decision – for example whether to release a prisoner into the community – will remain a matter for professional judgement. It may be predicted that increasing use will be made of models as aids to decision-making in such decisions in order to provide evidence of the adequacy of the decision-making process in case of the downside of the risk being realized – for example in the form of serious re-offending, and subsequent litigation and vilification through the media of those responsible for the decision to release. The more transparent are the mechanisms for arriving at the such decisions, the better is likely to be the final decision in respect of risk.

## Organizational issues

An important matter to address is the effectiveness of organizational interventions designed to reduce adverse consequence of risk. At one level this appears to be relatively straightforward evaluation research, for example into effects of various forms of: training, risk communications, procedures, design alterations, changes to management and decision-making structures. However, typically it is compounded by the difficulty of demonstrating which particular improvements (or possibly degradations) were produced by the intervention.

As in society, risk in organizations is influenced by culture and may be represented as risk culture or safety culture. Research into dimensions of safety culture and an allied concept, safety climate continues to provide a variety of potential contenders. While it is strongly suspected that risk or safety culture is an important variable in accident antecedents, consensus on key cultural dimensions affecting risk has so far eluded researchers in this field. Hitherto, research has tended to focus upon OHS components or aspects of organizational culture which affect them. Broadening research effort to consider a wider range of organizational risk issues – including financial and environmental, could enrich and render the search for risk culture dimensions more comprehensive. Longer-term objectives might include development of applications to manage risk more effectively through more complete knowledge of its organizational components.

As a further illustration of linkages between individual and organizational levels, greater understanding of individual risk appraisal processes, and in particular how these interact with motivations of individuals in positions of power over others, would add a useful dimension to organizational analyses. This is a challenging area because compared with those in less powerful positions, those in powerful positions are less readily studied. People's desire to maintain some protection against erosion of their power ensures this. This enhances the case for powerful individuals' ability to influence groups, and even whole organizations, to be a legitimate area of study. Notions of groupthink and 'orgthink' could also usefully be extended. By reducing the diversity of perspectives and views available – and hence the robustness of decisions – such phenomena impede the effectiveness of risk management processes.

Research is needed into improved risk management systems and methods for managing risk, bearing in mind different requirements of increasingly diverse sectors and the desirability of benchmarking against best practice to facilitate their further development. Sharing of expertise and designing new mechanisms to promote more effective risk management could be among positive outcomes of such processes. For many organizations, risk management remains an unknown discipline and thus it is particularly important for these bodies to have advice and guidance readily available. For small organizations in particular this is likely to remain a problematic area in respect of ignorance of risk management, for example in the OHS field (Mayhew 1997). Political and organizational mechanisms for communicating relevant information on risk management require further development – again an area for action research.

As well as analysing various types of organizational disasters, more studies are needed of 'normal' operation. While much can be learned from disasters, those which become public through inquiries or other means, are likely to be only the tip of the iceberg in respect of inadequate organizational responses to risk. Understanding better how organizations manage risk effectively, including how they learn – or fail to learn – from mistakes, could provide useful guidance for others to follow. This might be formalized as standards – see the section on an approach to risk management through standards, in chapter 16.

Determining risk management policies, practices and procedures in a range of organizations would provide a baseline from which to assess the present extent and nature of these. Elements provided in chapter 1 – Figure 1.2 – would provide one framework for research on this topic. Cross-national research would provide a valuable further dimension to this research. Examples of useful knowledge in this area include:

- the extent to which espoused risk management policies are implemented;
- whether organizations have or are developing integrated risk management functions;
- extent of integration of risk management decision-making within organizations;
- development of risk management policies – strategic, piecemeal, problem-driven;
- how potential risks and benefits are balanced during decision-making.

As individuals make assessments of risk which are both short term and long term, so do organizations. Study of the factors which respectively influence organizational decisions to be oriented towards short-term at the expense of longer-term decisions could serve as a measure of organizational maturity, analogous with individual maturity represented by deferred gratification. Market and financial pressure might be among the factors which predispose organizations towards making short-term decisions.

Turner (1994) notes that the great majority of disasters are due to managerial factors and proceeds to identify some of them. Systems models (see chapter 3) have general application within organizations and can thus provide a useful framework for the study of decision-making processes and other features of risk management. Flexible models are needed to deal with the wide variety of organizational situations in which behaviour is likely to be a mixture of rational and non-rational decisions and actions. There is a need to be able to assess organizational processes from macro (e.g. strategic) to micro (e.g. error analysis) levels. Waring (1996a) identifies management decisions affecting risk as including those relating to:

- labour saving technology;
- staff reductions;
- labour contracting;
- growth – organic and via acquisitions;
- higher productivity – e.g. increased work rates;
- operations in new territories;
- disaggregation into smaller business units;
- devolvement of decision-making;
- new products.

It remains problematic whether all types of decision-making can be subsumed under one risk model.

There is a need for study into origins and processes involved in organizational learning – about risk and other issues. Models need to be generic and therefore simple enough in terms of the elements used and sufficiently general to be applied across the field of risk management – including: risk identification, assessment, control, implementation and monitoring. Different categories of decision-making might include policy, emergencies and routine activities. Organizations are liable to be particularly vulnerable at times of change, for example when 'downsizing' and when mergers produce culture clashes (see chapter 11 for an example).

The balance between individually 'chosen' risks and utilities probably means that the road environment is likely to remain the largest single target in terms of total numbers of accidents encountered by people in their daily lives. Formulae-driven estimates of 'acceptability', 'tolerability' and 'utility' in respect of individual risk require more thorough investigation, perhaps through developing new methodologies to assess individual cognitive and emotional appraisal of a range of risks. This would be particularly desirable in the case of additional risks, or newly recognised hazards, risks and outcomes – e.g. radiation from portable phones, long-term effects of chemicals upon the human nervous system and fertility, increasing rates of asthma and allergies, acute and chronic stress reactions to a wide range of situations. Technological advancements tend to increase people's exposure to risk and uncertainty.

Continuing national surveys to monitor the extent of risk factors in people's lives could provide a valuable database to supplement other methods. Surveys could also provide a means of tracking individuals who move between occupations, some of which might involve high risk factors, creating problems which motivate those affected to seek other work – e.g. problems with back ache, skin or respiratory ailments. Such movements are one way in which workpeople remain 'healthy' although there are likely to be subsequent costs for the community. Follow-up study of retired samples could usefully supplement the employed persons database.

## Final considerations

Because of the uncertainty inherent in the notion of risk, we have opted not to declare what could be interpreted as definitive 'conclusions' to our treatise – hence the more modest heading for this final section. Researchers are some way from being able to propose a 'general theory of risk'. It is in any case uncertain as to whether such a theory would be helpful. An initial step would be to determine whether risk is a concept which, while it is multi-disciplinary, translates readily between disciplines. A large and growing literature on risk already exists. Building upon current theory, what is needed now are projects that trial interventions to advance applied knowledge on risk taking.

As well as the importance of applications-driven research, there is considerable scope for theory development in managing risk. These are mutually compatible objectives because effective applications require adequate substantive theory, while feedback from interventions usefully informs theory development. However, while there is a need for action research, typically research funding and academic reward structures reinforce publication of research findings rather than their application. Talented and committed researchers as well as resources (albeit always inadequate) exist, but often their prime energies are directed at the production of knowledge rather than its application. Politically, research agendas need to encourage local level interventions to act as pilots. Successful ones can be replicated on a wider scale.

Some of the largest identifiable risks in the foreseeable future are not immediately visible to most people. This makes their assessment and management particularly difficult. The plethora of resultant risks are not amenable to quantitative analysis and require political solutions. Probably the largest single risk factor, which affects many others, is that of over-population. While known food production methods and available resources are capable of supporting a world population much larger than the present six billion or so, production and distribution are subject to massive inequalities resulting from historical, environmental, cultural, social, economic and political variations between societies. Present world population trends are subject to two major influences. The first is the massive projected increases for developing countries – particularly in Africa, Asia and Latin America. The population in these areas has a predominantly young profile. In the developed world in contrast, population growth is very low (e.g. Japan, North America) or static or declining (much of

Europe), and the profile is much older. These contrasting trends will make for increasing imbalances between large sections of the developed and developing world.

A more insidious risk may be to human fertility. While risks exist from many diseases, all these together, including those which are AIDS-related – which are likely to kill millions of people – may have much less overall impact than declining levels of human fertility. Over the past few decades, human sperm count has fallen by 50 per cent (Lincoln 1997) and other species have also been affected by fertility problems. A prime candidate has been identified as the many thousands of environmental pollutants which mimic the action of oestrogen on the male foetus to change the pattern of sexual development. Establishing precise aetiology is extremely difficult because exposure is low level over an extended time period. Of great concern is the 20-year time lag in respect of impact and subsequent effect. This makes for problematic diagnosis and treatment of the underlying problem – which might only be effective on a global scale. An individual or societal counter to this threat – assisted conception – which has been available for some considerable time, raises many ethical and legal issues, particularly if widely used.

Risk and its management is intimately bound up with our increasingly global society, which means that what happens in one location can affect people and institutions on the other side of the world, often very quickly. The rapid development of global electronic networks involves an anonymity which can override many of the normal constraints which apply to human interactions – including sexual ones, as in 'cybersex'! A danger here is that precious parts of our humanity may wither because individuals are no longer obliged to interact face to face. In this scenario, it is imperative that fundamental issues to do with human nature are addressed, particularly adverse effects of human emotions and the converse, their mature development, if we are successfully to manage risks in the 21st century.

The biggest generic risk is that increasingly complex systems – social, technological, financial, etc. will develop at accelerated rates, leaving humans' capacity (particularly emotional) to adapt to them further and further behind. Radically new forms of communication available through the World Wide Web, have the potential for simultaneously considerably enhancing or degrading the quality of human interaction. These developments will require novel solutions for managing risks – for individuals, organizations and society. If we cannot advance our collective wisdom – that complex combination of experiential, emotional, spiritual and intellectual understanding of our increasingly complex world, then its systems, including ourselves, will become increasingly vulnerable to a human nature which evolved to cope with a very different type of environment.

# Abbreviations and acronyms

| | |
|---|---|
| ABI | Association of British Insurers |
| ACAS | Advisory, Conciliation and Arbitration Service (UK) |
| ACSNI | Advisory Committee on the Safety of Nuclear Installations (UK) |
| ADVIR | Association for the Defence of Values of the Islamic Revolution (Iran) |
| AICD | Australian Institute of Company Directors |
| AIDS | Acquired Immuno-Deficiency Syndrome |
| ALARP | As Low As Reasonably Practicable |
| ALCO | Asset and Liability Committee (Barings) |
| ANOVA | Analysis of Variance |
| AR | 'Australia Rail' |
| AR&M | Availability, Reliability and Maintainability |
| AS | Australian Standard |
| ASEAN | Association of South East Asian Nations |
| ATC | Air Traffic Control |
| | |
| BAe | British Aerospace |
| BASI | Bureau of Air Safety Investigation (Australia) |
| BATNEEC | Best Available Technology Not Entailing Excessive Cost |
| BCCI | Bank of Commerce and Credit International |
| BFS | Baring Futures Singapore |
| BIB | Baring Investment Bank |
| BLMC | British Leyland Motor Corporation |
| BMA | British Medical Association |
| BOBS | Board of Banking Supervision |
| BP | British Petroleum |
| BPEO | Best Practical Environmental Option |

| | |
|---|---|
| BPR | Business Process Re-engineering |
| BR | British Rail |
| BS | British Standard |
| BSE | Bovine Spongiform Encephalopathy |
| BSI | British Standards Institution |
| BSL | Baring Securities Limited |
| BSS | Baring Securities Singapore |
| | |
| C&L | Coopers & Lybrand |
| CAA | Civil Aviation Authority |
| CASA | Civil Aviation Safety Authority (Australia) |
| CDM | Construction, Design and Management |
| CEO | Chief Executive Officer |
| CFIT | Controlled Flight Into Terrain |
| CIMAH | Control of Industrial Major Accident Hazards |
| CIS | Confederation of Independent States (in former USSR) |
| CK | Community Körner (UK) |
| COMAH | Control of Major Accident Hazards |
| CRINE | Cost Reduction In The New Era |
| CRT | Cathode Ray Tube |
| CTSA | Channel Tunnel Safety Authority |
| | |
| DGM | District General Manager |
| DoH | Department of Health (UK) |
| DHSS | Department of Health & Social Security (UK) |
| DoT | Department of Transport (UK) |
| DSS | Department of Social Security (UK) |
| DTI | Department of Trade and Industry (UK) |
| | |
| EC | European Community |
| ECGD | Export Credit Gaurantee Department (UK) |
| EER | Escape, Evacuation and Rescue |
| EL | Employer's Liability (insurance) |
| EMS | Environmental Management System |
| ESRC | Economic and Social Research Council |
| ETA | Employment Training Association |
| EU | European Union |

| | |
|---|---|
| FIP | Financial Information Package |
| FMCG | Fast Moving Consumer Goods |
| FMEA | Failure Modes and Effects Analysis |
| FN | Frequency-Number (curve) |
| FSA | Formal Safety Assessment |
| | |
| G6 | G6 Group, Agents of Construction, Iran |
| GP | General Practitioner (UK medical) |
| GPWS | Ground Proximity Warning System |
| | |
| HASAWA | Health and Safety at Work etc Act 1974 (UK) |
| HAZOPS | Hazard and Operability Study |
| HIV | Human Immuno-Deficiency Virus |
| HMSO | Her Majesty's Stationery Office (UK source of government publications, now The Stationery Office) |
| HR | Human Resources |
| HRM | Human Resource Management |
| HRA | Human Reliability Assessment |
| HSC | Health and Safety Commission |
| HSE | Health & Safety Executive (UK safety regulators) |
| HS(G) | Health & Safety Guidance series from the HSE |
| | |
| ICI | Imperial Chemical Industries |
| IMechE | Institution of Mechanical Engineers (UK) |
| IMI | Industrial Management Institute (Iran) |
| IOSH | Institution of Occupational Safety & Health (main UK professional body for health and safety specialists) |
| IRA | Irish Republican Army (Provisional wing) |
| IRI | Islamic Republic of Iran |
| ISO | International Standards Organization |
| ISSG | Information Systems Strategy Group |
| IT | Information Technology |
| | |
| JGB | Japanese Government Bond |
| JRM | Jaame-e Rohaniyat-e Mobarez (Society of Spiritual Fighters, Iran) |
| | |
| Kph | Kilometres per Hour |

| | |
|---|---|
| LCSU | Local & Community Services Unit |
| LCSUIMG | Local & Community Services Unit Information Management Group |
| LOC | Letter of Credit |
| | |
| MHA | Metroplitan Health Authority |
| MHSWR | Management of Health & Safety at Work Regulations 1992 |
| MIS | Management Information System |
| MORT | Management Oversight and Risk Tree |
| MP | Member of Parliament |
| | |
| NACE | International Standard Industrial Classification |
| NAHAT | National Association of Health Authority Trusts (UK) |
| NATO | North Atlantic Treaty Organization |
| NDT | Non-Destructive Testing |
| NHS | National Health Service (UK) |
| NPV | Net Present Value |
| NZS | New Zealand Standard |
| | |
| OHS | Occupational Health and Safety |
| OIM | Offshore Installation Manager |
| OPCL | Occidental Petroleum (Caledonia) Ltd |
| OT | Occupational Therapist |
| | |
| PC | Personal Computer |
| PI | Professional Indemnity (insurance) |
| PL | Public Liability (insurance) |
| POA | Perinatal Outcome Analyst |
| PPE | Personal Protective Equipment |
| PTSD | Post Traumatic Stress Disorder |
| PTW | Permit-To-Work |
| | |
| QA | Quality Assurance |
| QMS | Quality Management System |
| QRA | Quantified Risk Assessment |
| | |
| R&D | Research and Development |
| RHT | Risk Homeostasis Theory |

| | |
|---|---|
| RoSPA | Royal Society for the Prevention of Accidents (a UK safety campaigning body) |
| RTA | Road Traffic Accident |
| SFA | Securities and Futures Authority (UK) |
| SIB | Securities and Investment Board (UK) |
| SIMEX | Singapore International Monetary Exchange Limited |
| SMS | Safety Management System |
| SNCF | Societé Nationale De Chemin de Fer (French railway system) |
| SOR | Stimulus-Organism-Response |
| SPAD | Signal Passed at Danger |
| SQE | Safety, Quality and Environment |
| SR | Stimulus-Response |
| SSM | Soft Systems Methodology |
| SSADM | Structured Systems Analysis and Design Methodology |
| STD | Sexually Transmitted Disease |
| TMI | Three Mile Island |
| TQM | Total Quality Management |
| TSR | Temporary Safe Refuge |
| UAE | United Arab Emirates |
| UGM | Unit General Manager |
| VDU | Visual Display Unit |
| WRULD | Work-Related Upper Limb Disorder |

# Glossary

## A

**abduction** A research process in which an observer samples and seeks to make sense of data from a social setting in which the behaviour of social actors intextricably informs and is informed by their own interpretations.
**actor** A person perceived to play a role in a human activity system; a social 'actor'.
**appreciative system** See world-view.
**ayatollah** Senior muslim religious leader in Iran.

## B

**baseeji** Members of a mobilized volunteer force in Iran ready to defend the Islamic Republic.
**bazargani** Shopkeeper or entrepreneur in Iran.
**bazari** Wholesaler or dealer in the product distribution chain who with others exerts a powerful influence on the Iranian economy.
**behesht** Divine paradise, heaven.
**blue chip company** A top stock-exchange quoted company with consistently high turnover and profitability.
**boundary** A conceptual boundary between the components of a system and the system's environment.
**BS 7850** British Standard guide on total quality management (TQM).
**BS 8800** British Standard guide on occupational health and safety management systems.

## C

**cause-effect** A model which assumes that specified behaviours or effects are caused solely by specified independent variables, leading readily to measurement, prediction and control.

**chador** A black tent-like robe to cover the whole body, worn by women in Iran.
**Checkland methodology** See soft systems methodology.
**closed system** A system which is not perceived to have any interaction with an environment; real-world systems are rarely closed systems.
**cognition** Sense-making processes in the brain.
**component** An identifiable part of a system's structure
**conceptual model** A notional model of a concept.
**control** Action taken by a system to maintain its activity or output at a pre-determined level or rate.
**control paradigm** Model which represents the control concept including the components of control and their relationships
**culture** Unwritten and usually unadmitted attitudes, beliefs, values, rules of behaviour, ideologies, habitual responses, language, rituals, 'quirks' and other characteristics of a particular group of people; cultures may be identified at different levels – e.g. nations, societies, organizations, departments, interest groups.

D

**designed technical system** A notional system of technical components designed and constructed by humans; not necessarily a mechanical system.
**dialectic** A bi-directional informing process.
**discourse** A discussion between two parties in which the exchange of information includes a great deal of unspoken sub-text based on assumptions and understandings.

E

**emergence** A collection of properties which characterize a particular notional system but which could not be attributed to any of the system's components in isolation – e.g. customer satisfaction; the result of synergy between components; see synergy, holism and systemic.
**engineered system** See designed technical system.
**environment** (1) A conceptual area surrounding a system outside its boundary; components in a system's environment affect the system but whereas components in the system may affect those in the environment they have no control over them. (2) The physical and social environments of people.
**environmental management system** (1) A structured systematic means for ensuring that an organization or a defined part of it is capable of achieving and maintaining high standards of environmental performance. (2) The organizational structure, responsibilities, practices, procedures, processes and resources for implementing environmental management (ISO 14001).

**ethnocentrism** Judging other cultures using one's own as a benchmark.
**expressed preference** A preference which is identifiable through what a person says.

F

**fatwa** An edict or statement of punishment issued by a Muslim religious authority against a transgressor of religious law.
**formal system paradigm** A model which provides the essential framework of components and processes needed for a system to exist and function – e.g. decision, control, monitoring, communication; applies especially to human activity systems.
**functionalist world-view** A world-view which suggests that everything has a pre-ordained role and function; the structures of business and industry and how they operate are taken for granted; 'problems' exist to be 'solved'.
**fundamentalism** In religion, an acceptance of a literal interpretation of the founding ideas, beliefs, authoritative documents and codes of behaviour of that religion.

G

**grid-group analysis** An approach to assessment of a culture which seeks to measure social unit characteristics ('group') against structural characteristics ('grid').

H

**hazard** A physical entity, condition, activity, substance, or behaviour which is capable of causing harm.
**hazard identification** The process of identifying a hazard and analysing how it may cause harm as a preliminary step in risk assessment.
**HAZOPS** Hazard and Operability Studies designed to check and challenge assumptions about the operational safety of process plant and equipment.
**hejab** A shawl worn as a head covering by Muslim women.
**heuristic** Assessment using experience or rules-of-thumb.
**hierarchy** The concept of relationships in which sets of items are subordinate to others in some way e.g. a family tree, a set of objectives.
**holism** A concept often expressed as 'the whole is greater than the sum of its parts'; encompasses the concepts of emergence, synergy and systemic properties.
**holon** An alternative term for system proposed by Professor Peter Checkland in order to avoid problems associated with the wide misuse of the term 'system'; crucially, 'what a holon (system) shall contain is determined by the observer'.

**homeostasis** Self-maintaining activity consistent with adaptive, closed-loop control; characteristic of biological systems but may be applied to human activity systems with caution.
**human activity system** One perceived to involve people apparently carrying out some purposeful activity; the system content is conceptual rather than real-world – i.e. it is determined by the observer.
**human factors paradigms** Concepts and models which represent particular aspects of human behaviour – e.g. learning, stress, group dynamics.

## I

**ideational culture** Those aspects of culture which relate to cognitive activity and behaviour rather than tangible artefacts.
**imam** A supreme Muslim leader regarded as a divine messenger.
**information system** A system conceived and designed to provide users with information on prescribed topics.
**inner context** The set of factors within an organization which are likely to be influential on strategy – e.g. organizational culture, organizational structures, power relations, resources, formal systems.
**interpretivc world-view** A world-view which does not regard everything as having a pre-ordained role and function although it does value social order; the structures of business and industry and human activity in general are seen as being socially constructed; many real-world 'problems' require coping and learning strategies rather than 'solutions'.
**ISO 9000** International standard specification for quality management systems.
**issue** A topic about which there is (overt or covert) disagreement among social actors; a bone of contention.
**iteration** The process of repeating actions; a standard activity in systems analysis in order to develop clarity and understanding or improve design.

## K

**key figure** A social actor in a human activity system whom the observer considers to exercise a special or important role.

## L

**liminal learning** Learning on the boundaries between different world-views.

## M

**Majlis** A parliament in Muslim countries.
**management system** (1) A notional system relating to management of an organization or operation. (2) A structured systematic means for ensuring that an organization or a defined part of it is capable of achieving and maintaining high standards of specified performance.
**modernism** A normative, functionalist world-view which emphasizes the legitimacy of existing power structures of business, finance and government to determine social values based on market economics and materialism.
**mujaheddin khalq** Counter-revolutionary Muslim fighters seeking to overthrow the fundamentalist government in Iran.

## N

**natural system** A system which is not made by humans and exists in the natural world – e.g. the weather.
**normative** Relating to a majority, average or standard. Normative assumptions may not be born out in reality.

## O

**objective materialism** A belief in the duality of the spiritual obligations and material aspects of human existence.
**objective risk** A view of a particular risk which is shared by a number of risk experts.
**open system** A system which interacts with an environment; an adaptive system.
**organization** (1) The processes of forming, maintaining and dissolving human relationships. (2) A structure of such relationships as in 'the' organization. (3) A human activity system perceived to relate to 'the' organization. (4) The process of organizing or co-ordinating resources in a systematic way for best efficiency in their application. (5) A company, corporation, firm, enterprise, society or other body.
**organizational learning** A cumulative, reflective, saturating process through which all members of an organization learn to understand and continuously reinterpret the organization. An experiential, cultural activity within the organization.
**outer context** The set of factors outside an organization which are likely to have a great bearing on its strategy and behaviour. The organization's external environment.
**owner** (1) A system owner is the person who has ultimate authority over its existence. (2) A problem owner is the person who has the task of resolving it.

## P

**paradigm** A model of components and their interrelationships which describes a concept.

**pasdar** A revolutionary guard in Iran.

**perception** Processes in the brain whereby sensory stimuli are interpreted. Part of cognition.

**permit-to-work** In operational safety management, an approach which seeks to prevent accidents during hazardous activities by requiring a sequence of documented safety checks and authorizations before, during and on completion of a specified piece of work.

**political processes** Processes in human activity systems by which various power factors (e.g. authority, influence, knowledge, information, world-views) affect the course and outcomes of thinking and action.

**political risk** A risk associated with public policies and decisions made by politicians.

**post-modernism** An interpretive world-view which emphasizes the legitimacy of multiple rationalities and interests in determining social and material values.

**power** An emergent property of social interaction within a particular context; a complex phenomenon (see political processes).

**power relations** Power differentials and political processes between two or more interest groups.

**preconscious** Relating to cognitive processes which occur in advance of conscious thought.

**problem** A source of puzzle, annoyance, frustration or harm to someone; problems may be assumed to exist as cognitive constructs rather than as real-world.

**process** A system component which changes continuously; ‘doing’ of some kind.

**pure risk** An absolute risk or one which relates to harm.

**purposeful** Consciously willed behaviour involving creative choice.

**purposive** Pre-ordained or pre-conscious behaviour resulting from a complex mixture of heredity and previous cultural and other experience.

## Q

**quality management system** The organizational structure, responsibilities, procedures, practices and resources for implementing quality management (ISO 9000).

## R

**real world** The world outside the artificial world of the laboratory.

**reductionism** A process of reducing complexity to simpler and more manageable components; reductionism assumes that all the fine structure that is lost is insignificant to the task.

**reification** Regarding something as an object even if it is intangible e.g. the money supply.

**resource management** Management processes which focus on resource allocation to match need and on resource efficiency as a prime measure of performance.

**revealed preference** A preference which is identifiable through a person's actions and behaviour.

**risk** (1) The probability or likelihood that (for a pure risk) a specified hazard will result in a specified undesired event or (for a speculative risk) a specified event or course of action will result in a specified gain or enhancement and/or specified loss or detriment. (2) For pure risks, the product of the potential severity of hazard consequences and the probability that the undesired event will occur. Other definitions are possible.

**risk acceptability** Use of criteria, usually formally agreed criteria, to determine whether a particular level of risk is acceptable. Often assumes that acceptability determined by risk specialists broadly matches public acceptability.

**risk acceptance** The fact of accepting a particular risk. May not mean that those accepting the risk actually regard the risk as acceptable if their options are constrained or they are under duress.

**risk assessment** The process of estimating and evaluating a risk in order to determine whether current risk strategies are appropriate and adequate.

**risk estimation** Process of calculating the level of risk. For pure risks, the estimate relates to probability of harm associated with a specified hazard. For speculative risks, one estimate relates to probability of benefit or enhancement and a second estimate relates to probability of loss or detriment.

**risk evaluation** Process of interpreting risk estimates and overall results of a risk assessment.

**risk homeostasis** Tendency for risk behaviour patterns and risk levels to remain the same despite actions taken to change them.

**risk management** The overall process of ensuring that risks are managed in the most cost-efficient and cost-effective way.

**risk reduction** A strategy seeking to improve risks by prevention and control techniques.

**risk retention** A strategy seeking to accept specified risks, possibly involving captive insurance.

**risk strategy** An approach to risk seeking the best combination of avoidance, deferment, reduction, retention, transfer, sharing and limiting of risks.

**risk tolerability** Acceptability of a given level of risk on the grounds that significant benefits are derived.
**risk transfer** Seeking through an insurance policy to deflect the financial impact of specified undesired events occurring.

## S

**safety case** A documented statement seeking to demonstrate on safety grounds why a particular installation or organization should be allowed to operate or continue to operate.
**safety culture** Those aspects of an organization's culture which affect health and safety.
**safety management system** A structured systematic means for ensuring that an organization or a defined part of it is capable of achieving and maintaining high standards of health and safety performance.
**socio-technical system** A system conceived as having both engineered or designed components and human activity components e.g. an information system of which computers form a part.
**soft systems methodology** A methodology intended for use where a human activity system exhibits crisis, conflict, uncertainty or unease among the social actors; also called the Checkland methodology; two main forms – basic seven-stage form (Checkland 1981) and developed form (Checkland and Scholes 1990).
**speculative risk** A risk which may have beneficial and/or detrimental outcomes.
**SSADM** Structured Systems Analysis and Design Methodology, an approach to design and development of information technology systems.
**strategy** An overall plan of action to achieve a desired objective.
**strategic risk** A risk which may damage an organization's business or other strategy or damage the organization itself.
**structure** Relatively stable and unchanging components of a system; the 'doers' and the 'done to'.
**sub-system** An identifiable component of a system which itself has the characteristics of a system.
**subjective risk** A personal view of risk. In a sense, all risk is subjective as risk is a perceptual and cognitive phenomenon.
**symbolic system** An abstract system – e.g. safety pictograms, symbols for chemical structures, computer programmimg languages.
**synergy** Interaction between system components to produce an output greater than the sum of component outputs; see emergence and holism.
**system** A concept of a recognisable whole consisting of a number of parts which

interact in an organized way; characterized by inputs, outputs, processes, a boundary, an environment, an owner, emergent properties, control and survival; addition or removal of a component affects both the system and the component.
**systematic** An ordered and organized way of doing something.
**systemic** To do with a system and implying holism and emergence.

**T**
**taghva** A pious approach to management and governance advocated by the authorities in Iran.
**threat** An alternative term for hazard used in some areas of risk such as security.
**Total Quality Management (TQM)** The management philosophy and practices which aim to harness the human and material resources of an organization in the most effective way to achieve the objectives of the organization.

**V**
**value** A belief or set of beliefs which is not testable in a fully objective way – e.g. religious beliefs, political views, moral standpoints.
**value system** A number of values which interact.
**velayat-e faghi** The right of the supreme jurisprudent in Iran to determine matters of state policy.

**W**
**Weltanschauung** See world view.
**world-view** A complex set of perceptions, attitudes, beliefs, values and motivations which characterize how an individual or group of people interpret the world and their existence; characteristic biases; closely allied to ideational culture.

# References

Abbot, H. and Tyler, M. (1997) *Safer by Design*, Gower and Design Council, Gower Publishing, Aldershot.

ABI (1994) *Guidance for Employers on Changes to Employer's Liability Insurance*, Association of British Insurers, London.

ACSNI (1991) *Human Reliability Assessment: a Critical Overview*, second report, Study Group on Human Factors, Advisory Committee on the Safety of Nuclear Installations, Health & Safety Commission, HMSO, London.

Adams, J. (1995) *Risk*, UCL Press, London.

AELR (1993) 853 CA, R v. Board of Trustees of the Science Museum, All-England Law Reports, London.

Apter, M.J. (1989) *Reversal Theory: Motivation, Emotion and Personality*, Routledge, London.

Apter, M.J. (1992) *The Dangerous Edge: The Psychology of Excitement*, The Free Press, New York.

Apter, M.J. (1997) Reversal theory; what is it? *The Psychologist*, **10** (5), pp. 217–20.

Argyris, C. and Schon, D. (1977) *Theory in Practice: Increasing Professional Effectiveness*, Jossey-Bass, San Francisco.

Arnett, J. (1995) The young and reckless: adolescent and reckless behavior, *Current Directions in Psychological Science*, **4** (3), pp. 67–71.

Astley, W.G. and Van de Ven, A.H. (1983) Central perspectives and debates in organization theory, *Administrative Science Quarterly*, **28**, pp. 245–73.

Australian Institute of Company Directors (1996) *Treasury risk management*, AICD, Brisbane.

Bacharach, S.B. and Lawler, E.J. (1980) *Power and Politics in Organisations: the Social Psychology of Conflict, Coalitions and Bargaining*, Jossey-Bass, San Francisco.

Bainbridge, L. (1987) The ironies of automation, in J. Rasmussen, K.D. Duncan and J. Leplat (eds), *New Technology and Human Error*, pp. 271–83, J. Wiley & Sons, Chichester.

Bamberg, J.H. (1994) *The History of the British Petroleum Company: Vol 2*, Cambridge University Press, Cambridge.

Barrett, A. and Zweig, P.L. (1994) Special report: Managing Risk, *Business Week*, 31 October 1994, pp. 50–64.

Barrington, P. (1993) Total business redesign with respect to safety legislation: introduction and implementation of a total quality culture, Deadline 1993 – Will Your Safety Management System be Ready? IBC Conference, 11–12 November 1992, IBC Technical Services, London

Bazerman, M. (1993) *Judgement in Managerial Decision Making* (3rd edn), Wiley, New York.

Becker, M.H. (ed) (1974) The health belief model and personal health behaviour, *Health Education Monographs*, **2**, Winter pp. 324–508, Slack Thorofare, NJ.

Becker, M.H. and Janz, N.K. (1987) Behavioural science perspectives on health hazard/health risk appraisal, *Health Services Research*, **22**, pp. 537–51.

Beer, M., Eisenstat, R.A. and Spector, B. (1990) Why change programs don't produce change, *Harvard Business Review*, **68** (6), pp. 158–66.

Belbin, R.M. (1981) *Management Teams: Why they Succeed or Fail*, Heinemann, London.

Belbin, R.M. (1993) *Team Roles at Work*, Butterworth-Heinemann, Oxford.

Bensman and Gerver (1963) Crime and punishment in the factory: the function of deviancy in maintaining the social system, *American Sociological Review*, **28** (4), pp. 588–98.

Berresford, C. (ed) Kluwer Handbook of Risk Management, Croner Publications, Kingston-upon-Thames, Surrey.

Berstein, P.L. (1996) *Against the Gods: The Remarkable Story of Risk*, Wiley, New York.

Bignell, V. and Fortune, J. (1984) *Understanding System Failures*, Manchester University Press, Manchester.

Binney, G. *et al.* (1992) *Making Quality Work: Lessons from Europe's Leading Companies*, Economist Intelligence Unit, London.

Björgvinsson, T. and Wilde, G.J.S. (1996) Risks of health and safety habits related to perceived value of the future, *Safety Science*, **22**, pp. 27-33.

Blackler, F. (1988) Information technologies and organizations: lessons from the 1980s and issues for the 1990s, *Journal of Occupational Psychology*, **61**, pp. 113–27.

Blackler, F. and Brown, C. (1987) Management, organizations and the new technologies, in F. Blackler and D. Oborne (eds), *Information Technology and People: Designing for the Future*, British Psychological Society, Leicester.

Blair, D. (1997) Violence in the health service, *The Safety and Health Practitioner*, **15** (4), pp. 20–4.

Board of Banking Supervision (1995) Report of the Inquiry into the Circumstances of the Collapse of Barings, chairman E.A.J. George, 18 July 1995, HMSO, London.

Brennan, T.A., Leape, L.L. and Laird, N.M. (1991) Incidence of adverse events and negligence in hospitalised patients, *New England Journal of Medicine*, **324** (6), pp. 370–84.

Briggs Myers, I. and Briggs Myers, P. (1980) *Gifts Differing*, Consulting Psychologists Press, Palo Alto, Ca.

Brown, R.L. and Holmes, H. (1986) The use of a factor-analytic procedure for assessing the validity of an employee safety climate model, *Accident Analysis and Prevention*, **18** (6), pp. 455–70.

BS 7799 (1995) *Code of Practice for Information Security Management*, British Standards, London.

BS 7858 (1996) *Code of Practice for the Security Screening of Personnel Employed in a Security Environment*, British Standards, London.

BSI (1996) BS 8800, *Guide to Occupational Health and Safety Management Systems*, British Standards, London.

Burrell, G. and Morgan, G. (1979) *Sociological Paradigms and Organizational Analysis*, Heinemann.

Byrom, N. (1996) A View from HSE, Putting Health & Safety into Practice – Can Quality Deliver Safety Too? RoSPA Congress, Royal Society for the Prevention of Accidents, Birmingham, England, 21–23 May 1996.

Cadbury, A. (1992) *The Financial Aspects of Corporate Governance and the Code of Best Practice*, Report of the Committee, chairman Adrian Cadbury, Gee Publishing, London.

Canadian Standards Association (1997) *Risk Management: Guideline for Decision-Makers*, CAN/CSA – Q850–97, Canadian Standards Association, Ontario.

Canter, D. (1990) *Fires and Human Behaviour* (2nd edn), David Fulton, London.

Cardy, C. (1995) *Training for Personal Safety at Work*, Gower, Aldershot.

Caring for People – Community Care in the Next Decade and Beyond (1989), Secretaries of State for Health, Social Security, Wales and Scotland, Cm 849, November 1989, HMSO, London.

Carter, P. and Jackson, N. (1991) In defence of paradigm incommensurability, *Organization Studies*, **12** (1), pp. 109–27.

Carter, P. and Jackson, N. (1994) Risk 'analysis' as discourse, Conference on

Changing Perceptions of Risk, Bolton Business School, 27 February-1 March 1994.

Carter, R., Martin, J., Mayblin B. *et al.* (1984) *Systems, Management and Change – a Graphic Guide*, Harper & Row, London.

CASA (1996) *Annual Report 1995–96*, Civil Aviation Safety Authority, Canberra.

Cassidy, K. (1994) Assessment regulation and the public, 27–47, Risks to the Public: The Rules, The Rulers and the Ruled, symposium, 14 December 1994, The Hazards Forum, London.

Caulkin, S. (1995) The new avengers, *Management Today*, November, pp. 48–52.

Caulkin, S. (1996) The road back to recognition, *Management Today*, August, pp. 30–4.

CBI (1990), *Developing a Safety Culture*, Confederation of British Industry, London.

Checkland, P. (1981) *Systems Thinking, Systems Practice*, John Wiley & Sons, Chichester.

Checkland, P. and Scholes, J. (1990) *Soft Systems Methodology in Action*, John Wiley & Sons, Chichester.

Chicken, J. (1994) *Managing Risks and Decisions in Major Projects*, Chapman & Hall/ITBP, London.

Chicken, J. (1996) *Risk Handbook*, International Thomson Business Press, London.

Child, J. (1984) *Organization: a Guide to Problems and Practice* (2nd edn), Harper & Row, London.

Child, J. (1985) Managerial strategies, new technology, and the labour process, in D. Knights *et al.* (eds), *Job Redesign: Critical Perspectives on the Labour Process*, Gower, Aldershot.

Child, J. and Smith, C. (1987) The context and process of organisational transformation: Cadbury Limited in its sector, *Journal of Management Studies*, **24**, pp. 565–93.

Chin, R. and Benne, K.D. (1985) General strategies for effecting changes in human systems, in W.G. Bennis *et al.* (eds), *The Planning of Change in Organisations* (4th edn), Holt, Rinehart and Winston, New York.

Clarke, S.G. (1996) The effect of habit as a behavioural response in risk reduction programmes, *Safety Science*, **22**, pp. 163–75.

Clegg, S. (1980) Power, organization theory, Marx and critique, in S. Clegg and D. Dunkerley (eds), *Critical Issues in Organizations*, Routledge, London.

Consumer Safety Unit (1995) *Report on 1993 Accident Data and Safety Research: Home Accident Surveillance System*, Department of Trade and Industry, London.

Coombs, R. (1992) Organisational Politics and the Strategic Use of Information

Technology, PICT Policy Research Paper No. 20, presented at the Fourth Charles Read Memorial Lecture, Economic and Social Research Council, London.

Cooper, M.D. and Phillips, R.A. (1994) Validation of a safety climate measure, BPS Occupational Psychology Conference, 3–5 January 1994, Birmingham, British Psychological Society, Leicester.

Cox, S. and Cox, T. (1996) *Safety, Systems and People*, Butterworth-Heinemann, Oxford.

Crainer, A. (1996) The rise of guru scepticism, *Management Today*, March, pp. 48–52.

Cullen (1990) *Report of the Official Inquiry into the Piper Alpha Disaster*, chairman Lord Cullen, HMSO. London.

Cutts, G. (1987) *Structured Systems and Design Methodology*, Blackwell Scientific Publications, Oxford.

Davies, A. (1993) Business re-engineering – just another fad? *Strategic Planning Society Newsletter*, December, pp. 2–3.

Davies, L.J. (1988) Understanding organizational culture: a soft systems perspective, *Systems Practice*, **1** (11), p. 30.

Deal, T.E. and Kennedy, A.A. (1986) *Corporate Cultures: Rites and Rituals of Corporate Life*, Addison-Wesley, Reading, Ma.

Denzin, N.K. (1978) *The Research Act*, McGraw-Hill, New York.

Diamond, M.A. (1986) Resistance to change: a psychoanalytic critique of Argyris and Schon's contributions to organization theory and intervention, *Journal of Management Studies*, **23** (5), pp. 543–61.

Dixon, N.F. (1981) *Preconscious Processing*, John Wiley & Sons, Chichester.

Dobson, P. (1988) Changing cultures, *Employment Gazette*, **96** (12), pp. 647–50.

Donaldson, L. (1985) *In Defence of Organization Theory*, Cambridge University Press, Cambridge.

DoT (1990) Report on the Accident to Boeing 737–400 G-OBME near Kegworth, Leicestershire on 8 January 1989, Aircraft Accident Report 4/90, Air Accidents Investigation Branch, Department of Transport, HMSO, London.

DoT (1997) *Inquiry into the fire on heavy goods vehicle shuttle 7539 on 18 November 1996*. Channel Tunnel Safety Authority, HMSO, London.

DoTRD (1996) Proactively Monitoring Airline Safety Performance, Bureau of Air Safety Investigation, Department of Transport and Regional Development, Canberra.

Douglas, M. (1992) *Risk and Blame: Essays in Cultural Theory*, Routledge, London.

Douglas, M. (1994) Who is the public? Risks to the Public: The Rules, The Rulers and The Ruled, pp. 48–66, symposium, The Hazards Forum, 14 December 1994, London.

Dowie, J. and Lefrere, P. (1980) *Risk and Chance: Selected Readings*, Open University Press, Milton Keynes.

Drager, K.H. and Wiklund, J. (1993) Advanced computer modelling for solving practical problems in EER, Human Factors in Emergency Response Offshore – Developments in Evacuation, Escape and Rescue, Aberdeen, 29–30 September 1993, Business Seminars International, London.

DTI (1996) *Computer Assurance Guidelines for the Commercial Sector: Third Information Security Breaches Survey*, Department of Trade and Industry, London.

Duhs, T. (1995) Derivatives – risky but should they be regulated? *QBiz*, February, pp. 3–4, Queensland University of Technology, Brisbane.

Dyer, W.G. and Dyer, W.G. (1986) Organization development: system change or culture change? *Personnel*, **63** (2), pp. 14–22.

E&P Forum (1994) *Guidelines for the Development and Application of Health, Safety and Environmental Management Systems*, The Oil Industry International Exploration & Production Forum, London.

Edwardes, M. (1983) *Back from the Brink: an Apocalyptic Experience*, Collins, London.

Ehteshami, A. (1995) *After Khomeini – the Iranian Second Republic*, Routledge, London.

Ernst & Young (1996) *Fraud: the unmanaged risk: a survey of the views of senior executives in Australia on the effect of fraud on their business*, Ernst & Young, Sydney.

ESRC (1993) *Report of the Commission on Management Research*, Economic and Social Research Council, London.

ESRC (1997) *Risk and Human Behaviour Newsletter*, Issue 1 March, Economic and Social Research Council, Swindon.

Export Times (1997) UK-world trade review, *Export Times*, **324**, November, pp. 16–17.

Fay, S. (1996) *The Collapse of Barings: Panic, Ignorance and Greed*, Richard Cohen, London.

Fennell, D. (1988) Report of the Official Inquiry into the Kings Cross Fire, chairman Desmond Fennell QC, HMSO, London.

Fischhoff, B. (1975) Hindsight does not equal foresight: the effect of outcome knowledge on judgement in uncertainty, *Journal of Experimental Psychology: Human Perception and Performance*, **1**, pp. 288–99.

Fischhoff, B., Slovic, P. and Lichtenstein, S. (1977) Knowing with certainty: the appropriateness of extreme confidence, *Journal of Experimental Psychology, Human Perception and Performance*, **3**, pp. 552–64.

Fitzgerald, B.P., Green, M.D., Pennington, J. and Smith, A.J. (1990) A human factors approach to the effective design of evacuation systems, IChemE Symposium Series No. 122, pp. 167–80, Institution of Chemical Engineers, Rugby.

Flin, R. and Mearns, K. (1993) Decision making in emergencies: a psychological analysis, Human Factors in Emergency Response Offshore – Developments in Evacuation, Escape and Rescue, Aberdeen, 29–30 September 1993, Business Seminars International, London.

Folkman, S. and Lazarus, R.S. (1988) Coping as a mediator of emotion, *Journal of Personality and Social Psychology*, **54**, pp. 466–75.

Fortune, J. and Peters, G. (1995) *Learning from Failures: the Systems Approach*, John Wiley & Sons, Chichester.

Freckelton, S. and Waring, A.E. (1992) Safety management systems: what makes them tick? – a human systems view, Human Factors in Offshore Safety, Aberdeen, 30 September 1992, Business Seminars International, London.

French, J.R.P. and Raven, B.H. (1960) The bases of social power, in D. Cartwright and A. Zander (eds), *Group Dynamics: Research and Theory* (2nd edn), Row, Peterson.

Gapper, J. and Denton, N. (1996) *All that Glitters: The Rise and Fall of Barings*, Hamish Hamilton, London.

Glendon, A.I. (1987) Risk cognition, in W.T. Singleton and J. Hovden (eds), *Risk and Decisions*, pp. 87–107, John Wiley & Sons, Chichester.

Glendon A.I. (1992), Radical change within a British university, in D.M. Hosking and N. Anderson (eds), *Organizational Change and Innovation: Psychological Perspectives and Practices in Europe*, pp. 49–70, Routledge, London.

Glendon, A.I. and Bamber, G. (1996) Organisational culture, added value and the contribution of human resource management, Australia and New Zealand Academy of Management Conference, Wollongong, NSW, December.

Glendon, A.I. and McKenna, E.F. (1995) *Human Safety and Risk Management*, Chapman & Hall/ITBP, London.

Glendon, A.I., O'Loughlin, B. and Booth, R.T. (1998) A case study in risk management: the UK pumped storage business, in Coles E.L., Smith D. and Tombs S. (eds), *Risk Management and Society*, Kluwer Academic Publishers, Lancaster (forthcoming).

Glendon, A.I. and Stanton, N.A. (eds) (1996), Risk homeostasis and risk assessment: Special issue, *Safety Science*, **22**, parts 1–3.

Glendon, A.I. and Waring, A.E. (1996) An exploratory study of strategy, power and meanings of success in organisations, British Academy of Management 10th Annual Conference, Aston University, 16–19 September.

Glendon, A.I. and Waring, A.E. (1997) Risk Management as a framework for occupational health and safety, *Journal of Occupational Health and Safety – Australia and New Zealand*, **13** (6), pp. 525–32.

Goleman, D. (1995) *Emotional Intelligence*, Bantam Books, New York.

Gorman L. (1989) Corporate culture, *Management Decision*, **27** (1), pp. 14–19.

Grainger, C. (1994) *Violence: a Risk Management Handbook Approach for Dealing with Violence at Work!*, Mintinta Press, Everton Park, Queensland.

Green, S. (1988) Strategy, organizational culture and symbolism, *Long Range Planning*, **24** (1), pp. 121–29.

Griffiths (1983) *NHS Management Inquiry (Griffiths Report)*, Department of Health & Social Security, London (out of print).

Gross, J.L. and Rayner, S. (1985) *Measuring Culture: a Paradigm for the Analysis of Social Organisation*, University of Columbia Press, New York.

Guest, D.E., Peccei, R. and Thomas, A. (1994) Safety culture and safety performance: British Rail in the aftermath of the Clapham Junction disaster, Changing Perceptions of Risk – the Implications for Management, Bolton Business School, 27 February-1 March.

Guy, C. (1992) A systematic approach to total quality management through the involvement of people, Deadline 1993 – Will Your Safety Management System be Ready? IBC Conference, 11–12 November 1992, IBC Technical Services, London.

Hale, A.R. and Glendon, A.I. (1987) *Individual Behaviour in the Control of Danger*, Elsevier, Amsterdam.

Handy, C.B. (1981) *Understanding Organizations* (2nd edn), Penguin Education, London.

Handy, C. (1995) *Beyond Certainty*, Arrow, London.

Hardy, C. (1985) The nature of unobtrusive power, *Journal of Management Studies*, **22** (4), pp. 384–99.

Hartley, J. (1984) Industrial relations psychology, in M. Gruneberg and T. Wall (eds), *Social Psychology and Organizational Behaviour*, pp. 149–81, John Wiley and Sons, Chichester.

Hazards Forum (1992) Proposed Syllabus for an Undergraduate Awareness Course on an Engineer's Responsibility for Safety, The Hazards Forum, Thomas Telford Services Ltd, London.

Heino, A., Van der Molen, H.H. and Wilde, G.J.S. (1996) Risk perception, risk taking, accident involvement and the need for stimulation, *Safety Science*, **22**, pp. 35–48.

Hendy, J. and Ford, M. (1993) *Redgrave Fife and Machin on Health and Safety* (2nd edn), Butterworths, London.

Hendy, J. and Ford, M. (1995) *Munkman on Employer's Liability* (12th edn), Butterworths, London.

Heskett, L.S. (1996) *Workplace Violence: Before, During and After*, Butterworth-Heinemann, California.

Hidden, A. (1989) *Investigation into the Clapham Junction Railway Accident*, public inquiry, chairman Anthony Hidden QC, Department of Transport, HMSO, London.

House of Lords (1988) *Visual Display Units – with evidence*, Select Committee on the European Communities, session 1987–88, 22nd Report, House of Lords, HL Paper 110, HMSO, London.

Hoyes, T.W. (1994) Risk homeostasis theory – beyond transportational research, *Safety Science*, **17**, pp. 77–89.

Hoyes, T.W. and Glendon, A.I. (1993) Risk homeostasis: issues for future research, *Safety Science*, **16**, pp. 19–33.

HSC (1991) *Major Hazard Aspects of the Transport of Dangerous Substances*, Advisory Committee on Dangerous Substances, Health & Safety Commission, HMSO, London.

HSC (1992) *Management of Health and Safety at Work Regulations 1992 Approved Code of Practice*, HSE Books, Sudbury.

HSC (1993a) *Ensuring Safety on Britain's Railways*, Health & Safety Commission Report for the Secretary of State for Transport, Department of Transport, London.

HSC (1993b) *Organising for Safety*, Third Report, Human Factors Study Group, Advisory Committee on the Safety of Nuclear Installations, Health & Safety Commission, HMSO, London.

HSE (1988) *The Tolerability of Risks from Nuclear Power Stations*, Health & Safety Executive, HSE Books, Sudbury, Suffolk.

HSE (1989) *The Fires and Explosion at BP Oil (Grangemouth) Refinery Ltd*, report of the investigations by the Health & Safety Executive, HSE Books, Sudbury, Suffolk.

HSE (1991) *Successful Health and Safety Management*, HS(G)65, Health & Safety Executive, HSE Books, Sudbury, Suffolk.

HSE (1992) *Railway Safety*, Report on the safety record of railways in Great Britain 1991/92, Health & Safety Executive, HSE Books, Sudbury, Suffolk.

HSE (1993) *The Cost of Accidents at Work*, HS(G)96, Health & Safety Executive, HSE Books, Sudbury, Suffolk.

HSE (1995a) *Generic Terms and Concepts in the Assessment and Regulation of Industrial Risks*, Discussion Document, Risk Assessment Policy Unit, Health & Safety Executive, London.

HSE (1995b) *Improving Compliance with Safety Procedures: Reducing Industrial Violations*, Health & Safety Executive, HSE Books, Sudbury, Suffolk.

HSE (1996a) *Business Re-engineering and Health and Safety Management: Best Practice Model*, contract research report 123/1996, Health & Safety Executive, HSE Books, Sudbury, Suffolk.

HSE (1996b) *Railway Safety*, HM Chief Inspecting Officer of Railways' Annual Report on the safety record of the railways in Great Britain 1995/96, Health & Safety Executive, HSE Books, Sudbury, Suffolk.

HSE (1996c) *Vehicle Driver Behaviour at Level Crossings*, Transport Research Laboratory, contract research report 98/1996, Health & Safety Executive, HSE Books, Sudbury, Suffolk.

Hunt, R. (1995) A cleaner fight? *Chemistry in Britain*, **31** (11), pp. 874–7.

Huntington, I. and Davies, D. (1994) *Fraud Watch – a Guide for Business*, Accountancy Books, Institute of Chartered Accountants in England and Wales, Milton Keynes.

Hutchinson, C. (1992) Corporate strategy and the environment, *Long Range Planning*, **25** (4), pp. 9–21.

Igra, V. and Irwin, C.E. (1996) Theories of adolescent risk-taking behaviour, pp. 35–51 in R.J. DiClemente, W.B. Hansen and L.E. Ponton (eds), *Handbook of Adolescent Health Risk Behaviour*, Plenum, New York.

IMechE (1995), Emergency Planning and Management, IMechE/Hazards Forum Conference, 21–22 November, *IMechE Conference Transactions* 1995 (7), Institution of Mechanical Engineers, London.

IOSH (1994) *Policy Statement on Safety Culture*, Institution of Occupational Safety & Health, Leicester.

IOSH (1997) *Draft Policy Statement on Integration of Safety Management Systems and Other Management Systems*, Institution of Occupational Safety & Health, Leicester.

Ireland R.D. (1991) Determination by R.D. Ireland QC, Fatal Accident Inquiry into the Death of Timothy John Williams on board the Ocean Odyssey, Sheriff's Court, Aberdeen, 8 November.

IRI-PBO (1996) *General Policies, Strategies and Goals of the Second Five-Year Economic, Social and Cultural Development Plan of the Islamic Republic of Iran (1995–1999)*, translated by Gh. Memarzadeh, IRI Plan and Budget Organisation, Tehran.

ISO 9000 *Specification for Quality Management Systems*, International Standards Organisation, Geneva.

ISO 14000 *Specification for Environmental Management Systems*, International Standards Organisation, Geneva.

*Janes Sentinel* (1995) Regional Security Assessment, the Gulf States, Janes Information Group, Coulsdon, Surrey.

Janis, I.L. (1972) *Victims of Group Think: a Psychological Study of Foreign Policy Decisions and Fiascos*, Houghton and Mifflin, Boston, Ma.

Jeffcutt, P. (1991) From Interpretation to Representation in Organisational Analysis: Post-Modernism, Ethnography and Organisational Culture, paper presented at the New Theory of Organisations Conference, Keele, April.

Johnson, G. (1987) *Strategic Change and the Management Process*, Basil Blackwell, Oxford.

Johnson, G. (1992) Managing strategic change – strategy, culture and action, *Long Range Planning*, **25** (1), pp. 28–36.

Joing, M.M. (1992) Risk Management at the SNCF: the example of speed control to improve traffic safety, Risk Assessment International Conference, October 1992, pp. 364–73, Health & Safety Executive, London.

Jose, P.D. (1996) Corporate strategy and the environment: a portfolio approach, *Long Range Planning*, **29** (4), pp. 462–72.

Kahneman, D., Slovic, P. and Tversky, A. (eds) (1982) *Judgement Under Uncertainty: Heuristics and Biases*, CUP, Cambridge.

Kayhan International daily, passim, Kayhan Newspaper Group, PO Box 11365/9631, Martyr Shah Cheraghi Street, Feardowsi Avenue, Tehran.

Kemshall, H. (1996) *Reviewing Risk – a Review of Research on the Assessment and Management of Risk and Dangerousness: Implications for Policy and Practice in the Probation Service*, Home Office, London.

Kennedy, C. (1994) Re-engineering: the human costs and benefits, *Long Range Planning*, **27** (5), pp. 64–72.

Kennedy, J. (1995) The UK approach to safety management – cost or benefit? Paper presented at the Offshore Mediterranean Conference 95, Ravenna, 15–17 March.

Khameini, A.H. (1996) The message of the Leader of the Muslim Ummah on the auspicious occasion of Hajj 1996, 23 April 1996, published in *The Guardian*, 14 May 1996, London.

Kirwan, B. (1987) Human reliability analysis of an offshore emergency blowdown system, *Applied Ergonomics*, **18**, pp. 23–33.

Knights, D. and Morgan, G. (1991) Strategic discourse and subjectivity, *Organization Studies*, **12** (2), pp. 251–73.

Kogan, N. and Wallach, M.A. (1967) Group risk taking as a function of members' anxiety and defensiveness, *Journal of Personality*, **35**, pp. 50–63.

Kono, T. (1990) Corporate culture and long-range planning, *Long Range Planning*, **23** (4), pp. 9–19.

Körner, E. (1984) Fourth Report to the Secretary of State, Steering Group on Health Service Information, chairman Mrs E. Körner, HMSO, London.

Krakauer, J. (1997) *Into Thin Air: A Personal Account of the Mount Everest Disaster*, Pan Macmillian, London.

Lasserre, P. and Probert, J. (1994) Competing on the Pacific Rim: high risks and high returns, *Long Range Planning*, **27** (2), pp. 12–35.

Laszlo, P. and Petrakis, L. (1995) A risky business? *Chemistry in Britain*, **31**, pp. 555–6, Royal Society of Chemistry, London.

Lawrenson, R. (1990) The application of safety management techniques offshore, The Introduction of Formal Safety Assessments after Piper Alpha, IBC Seminar, 5–6 December, IBC Technical Services, London.

Lazarus, R.S. and Folkman, S. (1984) *Stress, Appraisal and Coping*, Springer, New York.

Leeson, N. (1996) *Rogue Trader*, Little Brown, London.

Legge, K. (1984) *Evaluating Planned Organisational Change*, Academic Press.

Legge, K., Clegg, C. and Kemp, N. (1991) *Case Studies in Information Technology, People and Organisations*, NCC Blackwell, Oxford.

Lex Service (1994) Lex Report on Motoring, Lex Service, London

Lex Service (1995) *Lex Report on Motoring: What Drives the Motorist?*, Lex Service, London.

Lex Service (1996) Lex Report on Motoring Lex Service, London.

Lichtenstein, S., Slovic, P., Fischhoff, B., Layman, M. and Combs, B. (1978) Judged frequency of lethal events, *Journal of Experimental Psychology: Human Learning and Memory*, **4**, pp. 551–78.

Lincoln, D.W. (1997) *Human Reproduction 1960–2000: Ten Developments that Changed the Future of Mankind*, Inaugural Professorial Lecture, Griffith University, Queensland.

Longley, M. and Warner, M. (1995) Future health scenarios – strategic issues for the British Health Service, *Long Range Planning*, **28** (4), pp. 22–32.

Lovegrove, M. (1990) The economic implications of safety, Offshore Safety – the Way Ahead, conference, November, Institute of Petroleum, London.

Lundberg, C.C. (1990) Surfacing organizational culture, *Journal of Managerial Psychology*, **5** (4), pp. 19–26.

Lyles, M.A. and Schwenk, C.R. (1992) Top management strategy and organizational knowledge structures, *Journal of Management Studies*, **29** (2), pp. 155–74.

Mangham, I. (1979) *The Politics of Organisational Change*, Associated Business Press, London.

Mara'shi, J. (1995) *Conceptual Challenges in the Islamic System*, Industrial Management Institute, Tehran.

Mara'shi, J. (1996) personal interviews 9 March 1996, IMI, Tehran and 10 October 1996, London.

Mara'shi, J. (1997) *Conceptual Challenges in the Islamic System* (expanded edition), Industrial Management Institute, Tehran, February 1997.

Maule, A.J. and Hockey G.R.J. (1996) The effects of mood on risk-taking behaviour, *The Psychologist*, October, pp. 464–7.

Mayhew, C. (1997) *Barriers to Implementation of Known Occupational Health and Safety Solutions in Small Business*, Worksafe Australia, Sydney.

McClelland, D.C., Atkinson, J.W., Clark, R.A. and Lowell, E.L. (1953) *The Achievement Motive*, Appleton Century Crofts, New York.

McDonald, R. (1993) Review of SI 971 – What next? Human Factors in Emergency Response Offshore – Developments in Evacuation, Escape and Rescue, Aberdeen, 29–30 September, Business Seminars International, London.

McLachlan, K. (1994) Hydrocarbons and Iranian policies towards the Gulf States, pp. 223–8, in R. Schofield (ed), *Territorial Foundations of the Gulf States*, UCL Press, London.

McLoughlin, I., Rose, H. and Clark, J. (1985) Managing the introduction of new technology, *Omega*, **13** (4), pp. 251–62.

Mehdizadeh, H. (1995) Revaluation of companies' assets as a means of evaluating management performance, Tadbir, **5** (50) (Bahman 1373), pp. 17–21, Industrial Management Institute, Tehran.

Meredith, S. (1992) Water privatisation: the dangers and benefits, *Long Range Planning*, **25** (4), pp. 72–81.

Miller, G.A. (1956) The magical number seven, plus or minus two: some limits on our capcity for processing information, *Psychological Review*, **63**, pp. 81–97.

Mintzberg, H. (1989) Strategy Formation, Strategic Planning Society Conference, London, 2 February.

Mintzberg, H. (1992) Mintzberg on the rise and fall of strategic planning, interview with Bruce Lloyd, *Long Range Planning*, **25** (4), pp. 99–104.

Mintzberg, H. (1994) Rethinking strategic planning, Part 1: Pitfalls and fallacies, *Long Range Planning*, **27** (3), pp. 12–21.

Mirrlees-Black, C. and Ross, A. (1995) *Crime Against Retail and Manufacturing Premises*, Findings from the 1994 Commercial Victimisation Survey, Home Office, London.

Mojtahed-Zadeh, P. (1995) The Islands of Tunb and Abu Musa, Occasional Paper 15, Centre of Near and Middle Eastern Studies, School of Oriental and African Studies, University of London, July 1995.

Morgan, G. (1986) *Images of Organization*, Sage, London.

Morley I.E. and Hosking D.M. (1984) Decision-making and negotiation, in M. Gruneberg and T. Wall (eds), *Social Psychology and Organizational Behaviour*, pp. 71–92, John Wiley & Sons, Chichester.

Morton, A., Noulton, J. and Morris, R. (1995) The Channel Tunnel: Planning for Safety – an Example to be Followed?, Emergency Planning and Management, IMechE Conference Transactions 1995, pp. 49–55 Institution of Mechanical Engineers, London.

Mumford, E. (1981) *Values, Technology and Work*, Martinus Nijhof, Amsterdam.

Mumford, E. (1983) Successful systems design, pp. 68–85 in H.J. Otway and M. Peltu (eds), *New Office Technology: Human and Organizational Aspects*, Frances Pinter, London.

NCC (1996) The Information Security Breaches Survey 1996, National Computing Centre, Manchester.

Nichols, T. and Armstrong, P. (1973) *Safety or Profit?* Falling Wall Press, Bristol.

NRC (1983) *Video Displays, Work and Vision*, National Research Council, National Academy Press, Washington.

Open University (1984) T301 Complexity, Management and Change – a Systems Approach, course texts (revised 1993), Open University, Milton Keynes.

Owen, D. (1992) The Amerada Hess SMS as part of a QA system for production and drilling operations, Deadline 1993 – Will Your Safety Management System be Ready? IBC Conference, 11–12 November, IBC Technical Services, London.

Parker, R.J. (1975) *The Flixborough Disaster*, Report of the Court of Inquiry, chairman R.J. Parker QC, Department of Employment, HMSO, London.

Parker, M. and Dent, M. (1991) The Changing Culture and Language of the NHS, paper presented at BSA Annual Conference, Manchester, 25–28 March.

Patel, J. (1994) personal communication.

Pedersen, O.M. (1986) Human performance improvement by job design and post-incident analysis, pp. 245–52 in C. Kuo, A.J. Thunem and N.P. Sundby (eds), *Automation for Shipping and Offshore Petroleum Operations*, IFIP, Elsevier.

Perrod, M. (1992) Safety Case of the Channel Tunnel, Risk Assessment International Conference, October, pp. 391–6, Health & Safety Executive, London.

Perrow, C. (1984) *Normal Accidents: Living with High Risk Technologies*, Basic Books, New York.

Perry, R. (1979) Taking risks with children, *Community Care*, January, **4**, pp. 23–4.

Pettigrew, A. (1973) *The Politics of Organizational Decision Making*, Tavistock, London.

Pettigrew, A. (1985) *The Awakening Giant: Continuity and Change in ICI*, Blackwell, Oxford.

Pettigrew, A. (1987) Context and action in the transformation of the firm, *Journal of Management Studies*, **24** (6), pp. 649–70.

Pettigrew, A. (1994) personal communication.

Pettigrew, A., McKee, L. and Ferlie, E. (1987) *Understanding change in the NHS: a review and research agenda*, Centre for Corporate Strategy and Change, University of Warwick.

Pettigrew, A., McKee, L. and Ferlie, E. (1992) *Shaping Strategic Change*, Sage, London.

Peyvandi, M.H. (1996) Management views on operational units, Safety & The Petroleum Industry Seminar, NIORDC, Tehran, 8–10 January.

Pfeffer, J. (1981) *Power in Organizations*, Pitman, London.

Pfeffer, J. (1982) *Organizations and Organization Theory*, Pitman, London.

Pidgeon, N., Hood, C., Jones, D. *et al.* (1992) Chapter 5, Risk perception, in *Risk: Analysis, Perception and Management*, Report of a Royal Society Study Group, pp. 89–134, The Royal Society, London.

Plous, S. (1992) *The Psychology of Judgement and Decision Making*, McGraw-Hill, New York.

Proulx, G. and Sime, J.D. (1991) To prevent 'panic' in an underground emergency: why not tell people the truth? in G. Cox and B. Langford (eds) *Proceedings of the Third International Symposium*, International Association for Fire Safety Science, pp. 843–52, Elsevier Applied Science, London & New York.

Quinn, J.B. (1980) *Strategies for Change: Logical Incrementalism*, Richard D. Irwin, New York.

Rasmusen, J., Duncan, K. and Leplat, J. (eds) (1987) *New Technology and Human Error*, John Wiley & Sons, Chichester.

Rawnsley, J. (1995) *Going for Broke: Nick Leeson and the Collapse of Barings Bank*, Harper Collins, London.

Reason, J.T. (1990) *Human Error*, CUP, Cambridge.

Reed, M. (1991a) From paradigms to images: the paradigm warrior turns post-modernist guru, *Personnel Review*, **19** (3), pp. 35–40.

Reed, M. (1991b) Organizations and modernity: continuity and discontinuity in organization theory, paper presented at The New Theory of Orgnizations Conference, Keele, April.

Reed, M. and Anthony, P. (1991) Between an ideological rock and an organizational hard place: NHS Management in the 1980s and 1990s, paper presented at Conference on Internal Privatisation: Strategies and Practices, St Andrews, 12–14 September.

Reid, R. (1992) Risk Assessment as an Aid to Decision-Making, Risk Assessment International Conference, pp. 404–9, Health & Safety Executive, London.

Rimington, J.D. (1993) Coping with Technological Risk: a 21st Century Problem, Engineers and Society – The CSE Lecture, Royal Academy of Engineering, London.

Ritchie, R. and Marshall, D.V. (1993) *Business Risk Management*, Chapman & Hall/ITBP, London.

Robens (1972), *Safety and Health at Work*, Report of the Committee 1970–72, chairman Lord Robens, Cmnd 5034, HMSO, London.

Rowe, C.J. (1985) Identifying causes of failure: a case study in computerised stock control, *Behaviour and Information Technology*, **4** (1), pp. 63–72.

Royal Society (1983) *Risk Assessment: Report of a Royal Society Study Group*, Royal Society, London.

Royal Society (1992) *Risk: Analysis, Perception, Management, Report of a Royal Society Study Group*, Royal Society, London.

Rousseau D.M. (1990) Assessing organizational culture: the case for multiple methods, in B. Schneider (ed), *Organizational Climate and Culture*, Jossey Bass, San Francisco.

Ryan T.G. (1991) Organizational Factors Regulatory Research, briefing to the ACSNI Study Group on Human Factors and Safety, July, London.

San, M.L.C. and Kuang, N.T.N. (1995) Barings Futures (Singapore PTE) Ltd, Investigation Pursuant to Section 231 of the Companies Act (Chapter 50), The Report of the Inspectors Appointed by the Minister for Finance, Michael Lim Choo San and Nicky Tan Ng Kuang, High Commission of Singapore.

Schein, E.H. (1985) *Organizational Culture and Leadership*, Jossey-Bass Inc., San Francisco.

Segars, A.H. and Grover, V. (1996) Designing company-wide information systems: risk factors and coping strategies, *Long Range Planning*, **29** (3), pp. 381–92.

Semin, G.R. and Glendon, A.I. (1973) Polarisation and the established group, *British Journal of Social and Clinical Psychology*, **12**, pp. 113–21.

Senge, P.M. (1990) *The Fifth Discipline: the Art and Practice of the Learning Organisation*, Century Press, London.

Sheaffer Z., Richardson W. and Rosenblatt Z. (1998) Early warning signals management: a lesson from the Barings crisis, *Journal of Contingencies and Crisis Management*, **6** (forthcoming).

Sime, J. (1980) The concept of panic, pp. 63–81, in D. Canter (ed), *Fires and Human Behaviour*, John Wiley & Sons, 2nd edition 1990, David Fulton, London.

Sime, J.D. (1993) Crowd psychology and engineering: designing for people or ballbearings? in R.A. Smith & J.F. Dickie (eds), *Engineering for Crowd Safety*, Elsevier, Amsterdam.

Smircich, L. (1983) Concepts of culture and organizational analysis, *Administrative Science Quarterly*, **28** (3), pp. 339–58.

Spouge, J.R. (1990) Recent developments in offshore risk assessment, The Introduction of Formal Risk Assessments after Piper Alpha, IBC Seminar, 5–6 December, IBC Technical Services, London

AS/NZ 4360 (1995) Risk Management, joint standard, Standards Australia, Homebush, New South Wales and Standards New Zealand, Wellington.

Stanton, N.A. and Glendon, A.I. (1996) Risk homeostasis and risk assessment, editorial, *Safety Science*, **22**, pp. 1–13.

Stellman, J.M. and Daum, S.M. (1973) *Work is Dangerous to Your Health: a Handbook of Health Hazards in the Workplace and What You Can Do About Them*, Vintage Books, New York.

Stephens, P. and Lucas, D. (1993) Modelling the human response in emergency escape, Human Factors in Emergency Response Offshore – Developments in Evacuation, Escape and Rescue, Aberdeen, 29–30 September, Business Seminars International, London.

Storey, J. (1987) The management of new office technology: choice, control and social structure in the insurance industry, *Journal of Management Studies*, **24** (1), pp. 43–62.

Svebak, S. and Apter, M.J. (eds) (1997) *Stress and Health: A Reversal Theory Perspective*, Taylor & Francis, Washinton, DC.

SYSPAS, passim, The Health of Corporate UK, six-monthly reports, G.B. Steinitz (ed), SYSPAS Ltd, London.

Talwar, R. (1993) Business re-engineering – a strategy driven approach, *Long Range Planning*, **26** (6), pp. 22–40.

Taylor, R.K. and Lucas, D.A. (1991) Signals passed at danger: near-miss reporting from a railway perspective, in T.W. van der Schaaf, D.A. Lucas and A.R. Hale (eds), *Near-Miss Reporting as a Safety Tool*, pp. 79–92, Butterworth-Heinemann, Oxford.

Tehran Times daily, passim, Tehran Times News Service, Tehran.

Thomas, M. (1997) An Analysis of Fatal Accidents in Agriculture in Great Britain, PhD Thesis, Aston University, Birmingham.

Thomas, M., Booth, R.T. and Glendon, A.I. (1998) An analysis of causal factors leading to fatal accidents in agriculture in Great Britain, *Journal of Health and Safety* (in press).

Thomson, J.R. (1987) *Engineering Safety Assessment*, Addison Wesley Longman, Harlow.

Toft, B. (1990) The failure of hindsight, PhD Thesis, Department of Sociology, University of Exeter, Exeter.

Toft, B. (1992) Changing a Safety Culture: a Holistic Approach, British Academy of Management 6th Annual Conference, 14–16 September, Bradford University.

Toft, B. (1993) Behavioural aspects of risk management, Association of Risk Managers in Industry and Commerce Annual Conference, University of Warwick, 1–4 April, AIRMIC Conference Proceedings, London.

Toft, B. (1996) Limits to the Mathematical Modelling of Disasters, in C. Hood and D. Jones (eds), pp. 99–110, *Accident and Design: Contemporary Debates in Risk Management*, UCL Press, London.

Toft, B. and Reynolds, S. (1994) *Learning from Disasters: a Management Approach* (1st edn), Butterworth-Heinemann, London.

Toft, B. and Reynolds, S. (1997) *Learning from Disasters: a Management Approach* (2nd edn), Perpetuity Press, Leicester.

Torhaug, M. (1992) Where is QRA today?, Proceedings of conference on Risk Analysis and Crisis Management, 22–23 September, BPP Technical Services, London.

Touche-Ross (1995) *Risk Management Systems for Financial Institutions Benchmark Survey*, Touche-Ross, London.

Treasury Committee (1996) First Report – Barings Bank and International Regulation Vol 1: Report together with the Proceedings of the Committee, HC65–1, The Stationery Office, London.

Tudor, O. (1996) letter to the editor, *Safety & Health Practitioner*, **14** (4), p. 14.

Turner, B.A. (1988) Connoisseurship in the study of organizational cultures, in A. Bryman (ed) *Doing Research in Organizations*, pp. 108–22, Routledge, London.

Turner, B.A. (1992) Organizational learning and the management of risk, British Academy of Management 6th Annual Conference, Bradford University, 14–16 September.

Turner, B.A. (1994) Causes of disaster: sloppy management, *British Journal of Management*, **5**, pp. 215–19.

Van der Schaaf, T.W., Lucas, D.A. and Hale, A.R. (eds) (1991) *Near-Miss Reporting as a Safety Tool*, Butterworth-Heinemann, Oxford.

Vickers, G. (1983) *The Art of Judgement: a Study of Policy Making*, Harper & Row, London.

Vickers, G. (1984) *The Vickers Papers*, OU Open Systems Group, Harper & Row, London.

Vincent, C.A. (ed) (1995) *Clinical Risk Management*, BMJ Publications, London.

Waring, A.E. (1987) New technology, *Occupational Safety & Health*, **17** (9), pp. 16–19.

Waring, A.E. (1989) *Systems Methods for Managers – a Practical Guide*, Blackwell Scientific Publishing (out of print).

Waring, A.E. (1992a) Organizational culture, management, and safety, British Academy of Management 6th Annual Conference, Bradford University, 14–16 September.

Waring, A.E. (1992b) Organizations respond characteristically, not ideally, Proceedings of Risk Analysis and Crisis Management Conference, London, 22–23 September, BPP Technical Services.

Waring, A.E. (1993a) Power and culture – their implications for safety cases and EER, Human Factors in Emergency Response Offshore, Aberdeen, 29–30 September, Business Seminars International, London.

Waring, A.E. (1993b) Management of Change and Information Technology: Three Case Studies, PhD Thesis, November, London Management Centre, University of Westminster.

Waring, A.E. (1994) Power and culture in organisations and their implications for management of risk, Conference on Changing Perceptions of Risk, Bolton Business School, 27 February-1 March.

Waring, A.E. (1995) Management systems, behaviour and emergencies, Emergency Planning and Management, IMechE Conference Transactions 1995(7), pp. 1–8, Institution of Mechanical Engineers, London.

Waring, A.E. (1996a) *Safety Management Systems*, Chapman & Hall/ITBP, London.

Waring, A.E. (1996b) Safety management systems in the oil, gas and related industries, Safety & the Petroleum Industry Seminar, National Iranian Oil Refineries and Distribution Company, 8–10 January, Tehran.

Waring, A.E. (1996c) *Practical Systems Thinking*, International Thomson Business Press, London.

Waring, A.E. (1996d) Breaking into new markets: strategic risk assessment, paper presented at Innocom Seminar, Participating and Competing in the Global Automotive Industry, Warwick Business School, 30 May.

Waring, A.E. and Glendon, A.I. (1997) Strategic issues in risk management, *Journal of the Institution of Occupational Safety & Health*, **1** (1), pp. 8–16.

Waring, A.E. and Mehdizadeh, H. (1996) Strategic risk management, *Tadbir*, **6** (59), Jan 1996 (Dei 1374), pp. 26–8, Industrial Management Institute, Tehran.

Waring, A.E. and Tyler, M. (1997) Managing product risks, *Risk Management Bulletin*, **2** (5), 4–8 December.

Watson, T.J. (1982) Group ideologies and organisational change, *Journal of Management Studies*, **19** (3), pp. 259–75.

Webb, A. (1994) *Managing Innovative Projects*, Chapman & Hall/ITBP, London.

Weber, M. (1947) *The Theory of Social and Economic Organisation*, Free Press, Glencoe, Ill.

Westley, F.R. (1990) The eye of the needle: cultural and personal transformation in a traditional organization, *Human Relations*, **43** (3), pp. 273–93.

Weyndling, C. and Sandham, J. (1992) 1993 – some alternative ideas, Deadline 1993 – Will Your Safety Management System be Ready? IBC Conference, 11–12 November, IBC Technical Services, London.

Which? (1995) Swimming Pool Safety, *Holiday Which*? March, pp. 91–3, Consumers Association Ltd, London.

WHO (1987) *Visual Display Terminals and Workers' Health*, WHO Offset Publication No 99, World Health Organisation, Geneva.

WHO (1996), private communication from World Health Organisation, Copenhagen.

Wilde, G.J.S. (1982) The theory of risk homeostasis: implications for safety and health, *Risk Analysis*, **2**, pp. 209–25.

Wilde, G.J.S. (1994) *Target Risk*, PDE Publications, Toronto.

Wilkins, A.L. and Dyer, W.G. (1988) Towards culturally sensitive theories of culture change, *Academy of Management Review*, **13** (4), pp. 522–33.

Wilkins, L. and Patterson, P. (1990) The political amplification of risk: media coverage of disasters and hazards, pp. 79–94 in J. Handmer and E. Penning-Rosell (eds), *Hazards and the Communication of Risk*, Gower, Aldershot.

Wilkinson, A., Redman, T. and Snape, E. (1994) The problems with quality management – the view of managers in findings from an Institute of Management survey, *Total Quality Management*, **15** (6), pp. 397–404.

Williams, A. (1992) A study of the major hazard aspects of the transport of dangerous substances, Risk Assessment International Conference, October 1992, pp. 328–52, Health & Safety Executive, London.

Woodhouse, J. (1993) *Managing Industrial Risk*, Chapman & Hall/ITBP, London.

Woolfson, C., Foster, J. and Beck, M. (1996) *Paying for the Piper – Capital and Labour in Britain's Offshore Oil Industry*, Mansell, London.

Working for Patients (1989) Secretaries of State for Health, Wales, Northern Ireland and Scotland, Cm 555, January 1989, HMSO, London.

Zajonc, R.B. (1980) Compresence, in P.B. Paulus (ed), *Psychology of Group Influence*, Erlbaum, Hillsdale, NJ.

Zarif, M.J. (1996) Address to the 26th Session of the World Forum, Davos, Switzerland, 5 February.

Zohar, D. (1980) Safety climate in industrial organizations: theoretical and applied implications, *Journal of Applied Psychology*, **65** (1), pp. 96–101.

# Author Index

# Subject index